THE PASSING-ON PROBLEM IN DAMAGES AND RESTITUTION UNDER EU LAW

ELGAR EUROPEAN LAW AND PRACTICE

The *Elgar European Law and Practice* series is a library of reference works by leading practitioners, agency officials and scholars covering discrete areas of substantive law and procedure in the field of European Law. Rigorous in their analysis, each title is extensively referenced and shines a spotlight on the legal issues that are most relevant to practice. Designed to be detailed yet focused works, the books in this series offer an in-depth treatment and an authoritative statement on the law, and illuminate key aspects of practice and procedure, relating to topics ranging from Judicial Review to Private Enforcement, from Transport Law to Private International Law and from Public Procurement to Value Added Tax.

Presented in a format that allows for ease of navigation to a particular point of law, each title in the series is written by specialists in their respective fields, often with insight either from private practice or from an enforcement perspective.

Titles in the series include:

Private Enforcement of EU Law Before National Courts
The EU Legislative Framework
Folkert Wilman

The Passing-On Problem in Damages and Restitution under EU Law
Magnus Strand

THE PASSING-ON PROBLEM IN DAMAGES AND RESTITUTION UNDER EU LAW

MAGNUS STRAND

Senior Lecturer in Commercial Law, Uppsala University, Sweden

ELGAR EUROPEAN LAW AND PRACTICE

Edward Elgar
PUBLISHING

Cheltenham, UK • Northampton, MA, USA

Published by
Edward Elgar Publishing Limited
The Lypiatts
15 Lansdown Road
Cheltenham
Glos GL50 2JA
UK

Edward Elgar Publishing, Inc.
William Pratt House
9 Dewey Court
Northampton
Massachusetts 01060
USA

A catalogue record for this book
is available from the British Library

Library of Congress Control Number: 2016949980

This book is available electronically in the **Elgar**online
Law subject collection
DOI 10.4337/9781786430182

ISBN 978 1 78643 017 5 (cased)
ISBN 978 1 78643 018 2 (eBook)

Typeset by Columns Design XML Ltd, Reading

Printed on FSC-certified paper

Printed and bound in Great Britain by Marston Book Services Ltd, Oxfordshire

Till min högt och djupt älskade hustru och bästa vän Hedvig

och till våra Gudagåvor: Hilda, Eskil, Irma, Sixten och Greta

Kram! Jag älskar er!

CONTENTS

EXTENDED TABLE OF CONTENTS

PREFACE

It has been my great privilege to carry out the research resulting in this book under the generous and very stimulating conditions offered by Uppsala University and in particular its Faculty of Law. Thanks for many interesting discussions on aspects of this research are due to all my friends in the departments of European Legal Studies and private law. Among my Uppsala colleagues, very special thanks to Professors Torbjörn Andersson and Håkan Andersson. Special thanks also to Professors Jane Reichel, Carl Fredrik Bergström and Bertil Bengtsson, Professor and Judge Jonas Malmberg (now at the Swedish Labour Court), Dr Marios C Iacovides, Dr Erik Sjödin, and doctoral candidate Magnus Gulliksson. Warm thanks are due also to the staff of the Uppsala Law Library and to the administrative staff of the Faculty of Law.

Outside Uppsala, special thanks to Professors Alison Jones (King's College, London) and Andreas Heinemann (Zürich), and to Advocate General Nils Wahl (Luxembourg).

For particular contributions thanks are due to Professor Mikael Möller (Uppsala), Professor Ulf Bernitz and Associate Professor Judge Ingeborg Simonsson (Stockholm), Professor Christian Dahlman (Lund), and, again, Professor Alison Jones.

For their kind and patient assistance in matters great and small, my warmest thanks to the staff of Edward Elgar Publishing.

My love, my life, my wife Hedvig: for your love, for your everlasting encouragements and understanding, my very warmest thanks are not remotely enough. Let's spend our lives together!

It has been endeavoured to state the law as it stood at the end of May 2016. Materials that I have unfortunately not been able to consider include RBB Economics and Cuatrecasas, Gonçalves Pereira, 'Study on the Passing-on of Overcharges. Final report' (European Commission 2016) and *Sainsbury's Supermarkets Ltd v MasterCard Incorporated and Others* [2016] CAT 11.

ABBREVIATIONS

EC	European Community
ECHR	European Convention on the Protection of Human Rights and Fundamental Freedoms
ECSC	European Coal and Steel Community
EEC	European Economic Community
EU	European Union
TEU	Treaty on European Union
TFEU	Treaty on the Functioning of the European Union

TABLE OF CASES AND OPINIONS

EUROPEAN COURTS

Court of Justice of the European Union

Court of Justice

General Court

NATIONAL COURTS

Canada

Denmark

Sweden

USA

OPINIONS OF ADVOCATES GENERAL

TABLE OF LEGISLATION AND OFFICIAL DOCUMENTS

TREATIES AND CONVENTIONS

LEGISLATION

European Union Legislation

Regulations

Regulation (EU) No 1215/2012 of the European Parliament and of the Council of 12 December 2012 on jurisdiction and the recognition and enforcement of judgments in civil and commercial matters (recast) [2102] OJ L351/1
Art. 30 .... 7.200

Directives

Council Directive 64/433/EEC of 26 June 1964 on health problems affecting intra-Community trade in fresh meat [1964] OJ 121/2012 .... 6.031
Council Directive 76/207/EEC of 9 February 1976 on the implementation of the principle of equal treatment for men and women as regards access to employment, vocational training and promotion, and working conditions 2.025
Council Directive (Sixth) 77/388/EEC of 17 May 1977 on the harmonization of the laws of the Member States relating to turnover taxes [1977] OJ L145/1 .... 2.124
Council Directive 79/7/EEC of 19 December 1978 on the progressive implementation of the principle of equal treatment for men and women in matters of social security [1979] OJ L6/24 .... 2.035, 2.036, 5.026
Council Directive (Second) 79/32/EEC of 18 December 1978 on taxes other than turnover taxes which affect the consumption of manufactured tobacco [1979] OJ L10/8 .... 6.055
Council Directive 80/987/EEC of 20 October 1980 on the approximation of the laws of the Member States relating to the protection of employees in the event of the insolvency of their employer [1980] OJ L283/23 .... 6.037
Council Directive 85/337/EEC of 27 June 1985 on the assessment of the effects of certain public and private projects on the environment [1985] OJ L175/40, as amended by Council Directive 97/11/EC of 3 March 1997 [1997] OJ L73/5 and by Directive 2003/35/EC of the European Parliament and of the Council of 26 May 2003 [2003] OJ L156/17 .... 6.065, 6.066
Art. 3 .... 6.067
Council Directive 90/314/EEC of 13 June 1990 on package travel, package holidays and package tours [1990] OJ L158/59 .... 6.060, 6.061, 6.031
Art. 7 .... 6.017
Directive 96/71/EC of the European Parliament and of the Council of 16 December 1996 concerning the posting of workers in the framework of the provision of services [1997] OJ L18/1
Art. 3 .... 8.017
Council Directive 2000/43/EC of 29 June 2000 implementing the principle of equal treatment between persons irrespective of racial or ethnic origin [2000] OJ L180/22
Art. 15 .... 2.023
Council Directive 2000/78/EC of 27 November 2000 establishing a general framework for equal treatment in employment and occupation [2000] OJ L303/16
Art. 17 .... 2.203
Directive 2004/48/EC of the European Parliament and of the Council of 29 April 2004 on the enforcement of intellectual property rights [2004] OJ L157/45
Art. 13 .... 8.001
Directive 2006/54/EC of the European Parliament and of the Council of 5 July 2006 on the implementation of the principle of equal opportunities and equal treatment of men and women in matters of employment and occupation (recast) [2006] OJ L204/23
Art. 25 .... 2.023

Other

National Legislation

OFFICIAL DOCUMENTS

European Union Documents

USA Documents

Other Documents

Part I

INTRODUCTION AND BACKGROUND

1

INTRODUCTION

A. WHAT IS PASSING-ON?

I. A short story

If you were a baker, your business would be very sensitive to wheat flour prices. **1.001** Imagine a 5 per cent increase in wheat flour prices. How would you respond? Well, if you wanted to maintain your profit margin, you would consider increasing your own prices by 5 per cent. But what if your local competitor didn't increase her prices that way? Maybe then it would be better to maintain your prices intact, in order to avoid losing market shares. But then again, if you know your bread is so much better than hers, and that your customers are not likely to buy her bread instead of yours just because of the increased prices, maybe it would be safe to make the 5 per cent increase? Actually, maybe you just might consider a 6 or 7 per cent increase, as it could still be blamed on the wheat flour prices?

Now if instead you ran a famous sandwich parlour, and the bakery from which **1.002** you bought your bread increased its prices by 5 (or even 7) per cent, what would you do? Well, as above, your answer would depend on your need of a maintained profit margin, local competition, and your experience of customer behavior. You might keep current prices, absorbing the loss, or you might increase your prices, passing the loss on to your customers – perhaps even with an extra increase of profit margin if you felt confident in doing so.

1.003 Now, imagine that the increased wheat flour prices were caused by a new system for grain quality declarations introduced by your Member State, which included a charge to cover costs for examining the declarations submitted. Wholesalers on the grain markets had decided to respond to the new costs incurred by reason of this system by incorporating them, or rather an estimate of the incurred costs, in their selling prices. Some of them had even indicated this cost as a specific item on their invoices. However, after a few years, the grain quality assurance system was struck down by the European Court of Justice.

1.004 Following the judgment of the Court, the wholesalers bring an action against the national administration responsible for the grain quality declarations, claiming damages at the amount of costs illegally incurred. The national administration however will pay no damages, as the costs at issue were compensated for by increased selling prices. In some instances, the costs were even specified in invoices. Under such circumstances, the national administration argues, an award of damages would be pure profit – indeed, an unjust profit.

1.005 Contemplating these arguments as they are presented in the media, you – the baker or sandwich maker – will begin to wonder: if the economic burden of the grain quality declarations was passed on to me, should I perhaps try to bring an action for damages against the national administration? Or should I try to recover from the wholesalers? Meanwhile, the neighbouring café owner starts thinking along the same lines …

II. The passing-on problem: A set of factual circumstances …

1.006 Situations such as the one in the above example are not easily solved in law, as they involve at least three – but usually many more – parties, general interests (such as compensation, justice and deterrence from illegal conduct) and, more often than not, severe problems with regard to establishing what harm has been suffered by whom and to what extent losses, that seem to have spread through the markets like ripples on water, can be traced for the purposes of reparation. The presupposition is that an economic burden can sometimes be passed on, in whole or in part, down the supply chain. The act of letting harm incurred pass through a business and move on to burden your own customers, at the next level of the supply chain, is known as passing-on. Consequently, the 'passing-on problem' is not a distinct legal problem but a set of factual circumstances that triggers various legal problems. Those legal problems will be referred to collectively as the passing-on problem.

In the above example the context of the EU internal market was used in order to give a brief illustration of the passing-on problem, but the problem as such can occur in a variety of legal contexts. In EU law, the passing-on problem belongs to the context of private enforcement, i.e., claims brought by individuals or undertakings enforcing their rights under EU law. More precisely it can arise in the context of claims for damages or restitution for a breach of EU law. More generally however, the passing-on problem can arise in the context of any action where the relevant injury has been incurred in the form of increased production costs in a business.[1] Notwithstanding whether passing-on is recognized explicitly, implicitly[2] or not at all, the problem may arise in restitution as well as in damages, and in contractual as well as in non-contractual liability. In the context of competition law damages, the Commission has stated that the passing-on problem is 'at the heart of the way in which a system for damages for breach of antitrust law … functions.[3] **1.007**

An analysis of the passing-on problem is not concerned with whether the party who allegedly gave rise to the initial incidence of economic disadvantage for its counterpart (be it the EU, a Member State or a private individual) has committed a tort or been unjustly enriched, as the case may be. Argumentation with regard to passing-on may in other words presuppose a certain position concerning the tort or unjust enrichment, either in the positive or in the negative. Assuming it was the Council, the Council's legal representative in the proceedings might use a phrase like: 'Even if the decision of the Council was illegally discriminatory, the Council cannot be held liable in damages because any injury suffered by the claimant will have been passed on to its customers … '. At this point in the argumentation, i.e., the point in which we proceed to discuss the passing-on problem, the issue of tort or unjust enrichment *per se* can in other words be put in parenthesis, because the passing-on problem arises only in certain problems having to do with how the tort or unjust enrichment can be legally remedied. **1.008**

The passing-on problem has many aspects. The legal problems entailed include who among the parties involved should be able to sue whom, how far down the supply chain it is reasonable to trace the passing-on of an economic burden, whether or not to take passing-on into account in the quantification of **1.009**

1 This was first brought to my attention by Richard A Miller, 'Federal Antitrust Law: Price Discrimination: Proof and Measurement of Damages in Treble Damages Actions' (1962) 60 *Michigan L Review* 1104, 1124 n 66. See Section 1.A.IV for an endeavour to find a more precise understanding of what circumstances will relevantly trigger the passing-on problem.

2 Recognition of the defence of passing-on can follow implicitly from the method used by courts to estimate damages, especially in damages law, without it being considered as an issue at all.

3 Commission, 'Staff Working Paper Annex to the Green Paper Damages action for breach of the EC antitrust rules' SEC(2005) 1732 para. 158.

awards, and of how to prove the existence and extent of passing-on. It is common to give structure to these problems by distinguishing the use of passing-on by defendants as a defence or 'shield' against an action, from the use of passing-on by claimants positioned down the supply chain as a 'sword'. Passing-on as a 'shield' means arguing that a claimant cannot recover as the alleged harm has been passed on and any award would therefore constitute a windfall. This is also called 'the defence of passing-on' and will largely be referred to as such in this book. Passing-on as a 'sword' means arguing that the economic burden at issue has been passed on to the claimant, and that the competent court must therefore allow the action brought before it although there may not have been any direct nexus between the claimant and the defendant. This image of the sword and shield is quite helpful, but it fails to identify the specific legal issues triggered by the passing-on problem and, therefore, also fails to distinguish different legal issues pertaining to 'sword' use of passing-on: court access issues and substantive proximity issues (e.g., causation).

1.010 The major legal issues triggered by the passing-on problem are accordingly three, and these three will now be introduced with more detail.

III. ... Triggering a set of legal problems

Legal Problem 1

1.011 Who should have access to court for the purposes of bringing an action for damages or restitution, as the case may be, in a passing-on situation?

1.012 It follows from case law such as *Danfoss*[4] and *Kone*[5] that the Court of Justice is inclined to strike down national rules that automatically exclude certain classes of claimants from the possibility of bringing an action before the competent national courts. It furthermore follows from Directive 2014/104/EU on competition law damages that Gamma claimants must be granted access to bring an action for damages for a breach of EU competition law.[6] As illustrated by Milutinovic however, it does not follow that EU law requires for anyone, no matter how remote from the initial tort or transaction, to have

4 Case C-94/10 *Danfoss A/S and Sauer-Danfoss ApS v Skatteministeriet* [2011] ECR I-9963. A summary of relevant facts and first holdings is available in para. 5.030, with further holdings summarized in para. 6.042.

5 Case C-557/12 *Kone AG and Others v ÖBB-Infrastruktur AG* EU:C:2014:1317. A summary of relevant facts and holdings is available in para. 7.035.

6 Directive 2014/104/EU of the European Parliament and of the Council of 26 November 2014 on certain rules governing actions for damages under national law for infringements of the competition law provisions of the Member States and of the European Union [2014] OJ L349/1 Art 12(1).

unfettered access to bring an action.[7] Moreover rules hindering access need not be as blunt as an automatic bar. The Court itself has laid down certain limitations of access to court to bring an action under Article 340(2) TFEU that are of interest here, e.g., the requirement to show that the alleged harm pertains to the claimant's own assets.[8] The Court has also accepted national rules that bar a claimant from bringing an action for competition law damages where it is established that that party bears significant responsibility for the distortion of competition.[9]

This book includes an in-depth analysis of EU law on access to court and assesses the possibilities for Gamma claimants to bring proceedings within the various contexts listed above. **1.013**

Legal Problem 2

To what extent is a causal or other nexus required for the purposes of establishing causation or, in restitution, that the enrichment of the defendant is attributable to the disadvantage of the claimant? **1.014**

Although access to court may very well be a problem for many claimants who were not directly involved in the initial tort or transaction, the highest hurdle to jump may yet be the substantive assessment of whether there is a causal link between a breach of law and the injury sustained by such a party or, in the context of restitution, that the disadvantage corresponding to the alleged enrichment is attributable to such a party. As noticed by Toth the proving of such points can be difficult for claimants 'in the field of economic and commercial relations where the cause of an event can usually be traced back to a number of factors ... operating simultaneously or successively and producing direct as well as indirect effects'.[10] This applies *a fortiori* to claimants downstream, who need to prove not only that harm or loss was suffered by its supplier (or supplier's supplier ...) but also that the same harm or loss was subsequently passed on to them, and that the connection is still strong enough for an award of damages or restitution to be payable. Downstream claimants **1.015**

---

7 Veljko Milutinovic, *The 'Right to Damages' under EU Competition Law: From* Courage v. Crehan *to the White Paper and Beyond* (Wolters Kluwer 2010) 242.

8 Case 72/74 *Union syndicale-Service public européen and others v Council of the European Communities* [1975] ECR 401 para. 21; case 114/83 *Société d'Initiatives et de Coopération Agricole et al v Commission of the European Communities* [1984] ECR 2598 paras 3–5; and parallel case 289/83 *GAARM v Commission of the European Communities* [1984] ECR 4295 paras 3–5.

9 Case C-453/99 *Courage Ltd v Bernard Crehan and Bernard Crehan v Courage Ltd and Others* [2001] ECR I-6297 Operative part para. 3.

10 Akos George Toth, 'The Concepts of Damage and Causality as Elements of Non-Contractual Liability' in Ton Heukels and Alison McDonnell (eds), *The Action for Damages in Community Law* (Kluwer Law 1997) 192.

are thus vulnerable to arguments of being too remote from the transaction at issue to bring a successful action. This set of problems has been bundled together here as problems of substantive proximity.

1.016 It has been endeavoured to distinguish these proximity problems from procedural bars, but it should immediately be admitted that this distinction is not always easily upheld, as a procedural bar may be legitimized by proximity reasons, as in *Danfoss* and *Kone*. There is therefore some overlapping. Nevertheless the grey zone is surrounded by more clear-cut cases, and the grey zone itself can be accepted and managed as such.

Legal Problem 3

1.017 How should awards be estimated – e.g., what heads of damages are available and to what extent should passing-on have an impact on the calculation of the award?

1.018 Access to court issues and proximity problems usually face downstream claimants rather than claimants who were directly involved in the initial tort or transaction. By contrast the issue of how awards are estimated constitutes a problem for both types of claimants, although most case law has concerned actions brought by the latter category. This is the specific context in which we are concerned with the classic defence of passing-on, which is perhaps the most often discussed aspect of the passing-on problem.

1.019 The underlying issue in this regard is whether the passing-on of the harm or disadvantage should be considered in the estimation of an award of damages or restitution, as the case may be. In damages the ideology of reparation arguably speaks in favour of considering passing-on, and to disregard passing-on it is necessary to let reparation yield to deterrence.[11] In order to eliminate any lingering incentives to act in breach of EU law, the estimation of damages could thus be designed to ensure the disgorgement of Alpha's profit from the breach. In restitution the ideology of reversal of an illegitimate transaction speaks against considering passing-on. These differing tendencies will be discussed and compared in this book.

1.020 Each of these themes 1–3 will be discussed separately in the chapters below. For every theme there will be issues concerning evidence. These will not be discussed separately but in connection to the discussion of each theme

11 The respective roles of these two interests in the passing-on problem will be the subject of Section 9.E.

identified above. Anyone interested in evidence issues is also strongly recommended to see section 9.E.I where such issues are discussed in detail.

The above subdivision of the legal issues triggered by the passing-on problem may entail that a number of issues that should perhaps be distinguished in national jurisdictions will be discussed indiscriminately. These include the distinctions between causation issues and remoteness issues, between the right to take legal action and the occurrence of procedural hindrances, and between quantification of harm and estimation of the award. Too much attention to national distinctions would however have burdened the structure of this presentation, and it is hoped that readers who need to make such distinctions can identify which line of reasoning in this book is relevant to each specific class in the national context. **1.021**

What of other EU law problems triggered by the passing-on problem that are not covered at all? A few should be mentioned. One is that parties who were directly burdened by the initial tort or transaction need not necessarily respond to the costs thus incurred by trying to raise customer prices: they might also try to do so by cutting other costs. In this way the burden of the illegitimate cost originating from the tort or transaction may 'pass back' rather than pass on. In other words it would be pushed back up the supply chain instead of continuing down. Accordingly suppliers might suffer. Although their situation will not be analysed as such in this book, it should be pointed out that such claimants will find themselves in a situation reminiscent of that of downstream claimants, and much of the discussions below that concerns downstream claimants will be relevant to supplier claimants as well.[12] Another legal problem that has already been mentioned is that potential claimants at any level of the supply chain might be held back from bringing an action by business reasons. This is not a legal problem but better analysed in economics. A final issue to be mentioned in the context of passing-on is the availability of class actions. Although the availability of a class action may promote private enforcement of EU law, such considerations fall outside the chosen scope of this book. Therefore it will not be discussed in depth but only be touched upon where immediately relevant.[13] **1.022**

12 This 'passing-back' problem is acknowledged in Directive 2014/104/EU (n 6) Art. 12(4). See also rec. 38 and Art. 11(4)–(6).

13 E.g., in paras 7.205–7.206.

IV. What situations are passing-on situations?

1.023 It is difficult to define precisely what situations are passing-on situations and what situations are not, but for the purposes of a legal approach to passing-on it is necessary to find a working definition of the concept. This section is intended to bring some stability to the discussion by indicating what economic events can plausibly trigger a passing-on situation, and what economic events cannot.[14] It is not intended here however to conduct any review of the case law of the European Court of Justice and the existing legislation to delineate passing-on instances.[15] Nor should the model suggested here be mistaken as being anything but a proposed working model. Nevertheless the suggestions submitted are based on the case law and legislation that will be presented and analysed in the following chapters. Interested readers are therefore encouraged to re-read this section in light of those chapters.

1.024 Passing-on argumentation is commonly used in EU law when a cost can be connected to the production, purchase or import of a specific commodity and that commodity is subsequently sold – as it was or following its incorporation into another commodity – to the next party in the supply chain. The most typical example of a cost that is passed on in this manner is VAT, which is explicitly designed to follow the commodity at issue down the supply chain. Other examples are less obvious, making it difficult to decide precisely what situations will be legally relevant passing-on situations. Is passing-on legally relevant only when products are resold unaltered (e.g., shoes)? Whenever the overcharged product is included in the final product (e.g., leather for shoes)? What about overcharges in other factors of production (e.g., shoe-making machinery)? The further away from the reselling of unaltered products the situation at hand is, the more remote it seems that an overcharge will have been passed on within the meaning of Directive 2014/104/EU.[16] Volume effects (i.e., losses due to a drop in sales that follows an increase in prices) are perhaps the most remote, seemingly impossible to 'pass on' as such. Nevertheless, any business will arguably wish to cover all costs, and make a profit, through revenue. If so, they will not only take steps to manage costs, but also ensure that all losses are covered by pricing (at least in the long run, as price

14 For a similar overview of 'likely pass-on scenarios' see Milutinovic (n 7) 183–6. Cf. also the examples provided in Elisabeth Eklund, 'Indirect Purchasers – Is there Anything New in the Directive? An Introductory Overview of the Current and Future Status of Indirect Purchasers in the EU' in Maria Bergström, Marios C Iacovides and Magnus Strand (eds), *Harmonising EU Competition Litigation: The New Directive and Beyond* (Swedish Studies in European Law vol. 8, Hart Publishing 2016) 271–4.

15 It should be mentioned however that the EU Courts have not in their case law delineated the use of passing-on reasoning but have rather been reluctant to make clear demarcations with regard to the circumstances within which passing-on might be considered.

16 Directive 2014/104/EU (n 6).

elasticity of demand may require adjustments of pricing from time to time). This would indicate a wide substantive scope for passing-on argumentation, with no lines drawn that could exclude economic burdens such as loss of profit from the burdens which could be 'passed on'. Time is also a problem. Assume that a purchaser of products from a cartel company absorbs the loss incurred by reason of having paid an overcharge one year, as fierce competition on its selling market makes passing-on impossible. At the end of the year the overcharge is revealed and the cartel dissolved. The purchaser nevertheless raises its prices the next year, when there is less competition, to compensate for loss sustained the year before. Is this passing-on?

It is indeed difficult to pinpoint in general terms the character of the event **1.025**
giving rise to an economic disadvantage for the party or parties directly burdened by the initial tort or unlawful transaction. In American passing-on discourse Miller has submitted, as mentioned, that the passing-on problem can arise in the context of any action where the relevant injury has been incurred in the form of increased production costs in a business.[17] Pursuing this line of thought, the harmful event may have taken the form of a direct product-related cost,[18] the cost object of which was the specific commodity to which an infringement of EU law was distinctly related and which was subsequently sold to the next link in the supply chain (unaltered or as part or raw material for goods or services sold). This would typically be the case if the purchase price of the commodity had been raised and the raising of the price was somehow illegal. A related example which would not, I believe, qualify as a production cost in economic terms is the levying of a charge, duty, tax or other fee on the production, import, selling or the like of specific goods or services. In the gritz and quellmehl cases however the relevant event took the form of unpaid subsidies for the production of certain commodities, i.e., a loss of product-related income, which was subsequently sold to the next link in the supply chain.[19] The economic disadvantage suffered and allegedly passed on

17 Miller (n 1).

18 I admit I am no economist and I am sure this could be stated with more economic elegance. If the cost at issue has been challenged for being contrary to EU law, it would probably be economically more accurate to speak of deferred costs (becoming direct costs only if the challenge is unsuccessful). I wish to thank my mother-in-law Charlotte Byström, Head of Finance at Linneaus University, for input on economic terminology. Any misunderstandings are my own – and evidence that I should have listened better to my mother-in-law.

19 Case 238/78 *Ireks-Arkady GmbH v Council and Commission of the European Communities* [1979] ECR 2955; joined cases 261 and 262/78 *Interquell Stärke-Chemie GmbH and Diamalt AG v Council and Commission of the European Communities* [1979] ECR 3045; joined cases 64 and 113/76, 167 and 239/78, 27, 28 and 45/79 *P Dumortier frères SA and others v Council of the European Communities* [1979] ECR 3091; and joined cases 241, 242, 245 to 250/78 *DGV, Deutsche Getreideverwertung und Rheinische Kraftfutterwerke GmbH and others v Council and Commission of the European Communities* [1979] ECR 3017. These cases are extensively discussed in Section 3.E.

cannot therefore be pinpointed in terms of whether it was a cost or a loss of income. We must accordingly proceed from Miller's definition and find a better option for the EU law context.

1.026 A common denominator for the different economic events that have been at issue in EU case law is that they have all constituted an economic disadvantage (instant or deferred) for the party or parties directly burdened by the initial tort or unlawful transaction. All economic events have also been very closely related to a specific commodity: unpaid subsidies for their production, charges on their import, turnover taxes and the like. A similar connection furthermore appears from Directive 2014/104/EU on competition law damages, where the infringement of competition law is understood as having occurred with regard to specific goods or services. In Article 14 of the Directive it is thus expressed that passing-on occurs where 'goods or services [have been] the object of [an] infringement of competition law' and the downstream party 'has purchased goods or services derived from or containing them'.[20] A preliminary demarcation of what situations are passing-on situations would therefore be to reserve the possibility of passing-on to economic burdens that are sufficiently closely linked to the commercial handling (production, purchase, transport or the like) of services or goods that are subsequently transferred to the next link in the supply chain (unaltered or as part or raw material for goods or services sold). Such a demarcation would make it legally irrelevant to the passing-on problem that indirect costs and fixed costs can also be said to be included, albeit less directly, in selling prices. It could, e.g., not be argued that an illegal overcharge on concrete had been passed on in the prices for products manufactured in a factory built with concrete that had been subject to the overcharge, or that an increase in insurance costs due to new and unlawful statutory requirements on insurance for the production in the factory concrete had been passed on in the prices for products. There are however more difficult examples. A charge on the import of machinery used for the production at issue would be more closely related to the production costs. Could such a charge be passed on in prices for the products? What if collective action in breach of EU law led to increased labour costs – could they be passed on?

1.027 It is submitted that a definition drawing on the wording used in Article 14 of Directive 2014/104/EU could be useful and would probably yield the most reasonable results. The Directive speaks of economic events connected to

20 Possibly an elaborated working definition for the purposes of competition law will be supplied by the Commission in its upcoming Guidelines for national courts on the passing-on of overcharges, expected in 2017. See also Directive 2014/104/EU (n 6) Art. 14 which includes rules on the burden of proof.

'goods or services [that have been] the object of [an] infringement' and the subsequent distribution, to the next level in the supply chain, of 'goods or services derived from or containing them'. It would follow from these requirements that a sufficiently close link must first be established between an infringement of EU law and an increase in costs for the commercial handling of specific goods or services. Of course, the existence of the infringement of EU law and the increase in costs must also be established. It would then need to be established that goods or services subsequently distributed to the next level of the supply chain were 'derived from or [contained]' the aforementioned goods or services. If such a solution were adopted then as a consequence volume effects, such as decreased sales following an increase in selling prices, could not reasonably be argued to have been passed on in the relevant manner. Such a requirement would also, arguably, make charges related to the machinery used in production legally irrelevant to the passing-on problem.[21] The potential passing-on of labour costs would however remain open, as labour might be seen as being contained in products. It would ultimately be for the courts and the Court of Justice to determine issues such as these. It is nonetheless submitted that a demarcation of this kind would be sound and useful for courts, and that it would be for the parties to present evidence on the character of the economic event at issue and its relationship to the alleged infringement of EU law.

By contrast it is submitted that the lapse of time should be of little consequence to the possibility of passing-on an economic burden. Consider the production of matured whisky. If a producer pays a charge on malt which is levied contrary to EU law, and the relevant units of produced whisky are sold ten years later, it is submitted that passing-on should not be excluded by reason of the lapse of time. The relevant criterion should be whether the whisky 'derived from or [contained]' the malt. **1.028**

This is not however the end of the story – only its point of departure, as the issue of whether or not the cost has in fact been passed on remains. Suffice it here to mention that the crucial points of this next step include the pricing policy of the party or parties who allegedly passed on an economic burden as well as the price elasticity of demand on the relevant market. Was the burden passed on? Could it have been? If the party passed on a burden by increasing its selling prices, did that party consequently suffer a decrease in sales? These are questions to address through evidence. It is for the EU legislature and the EU courts to set the burdens and standards of proof necessary for the purposes **1.029**

21 A situation of this kind was brought before the United States Supreme Court in *Hanover Shoe Inc v United Shoe Machinery Corp* 392 US 481 (1968).

of identifying whether passing-on has occurred in the individual case. They have indeed been called upon to do so, and to scrutinize national rules on standards and the burden of proof. The resulting EU law on evidence of passing-on will be examined in the chapters below. This section has served to bring some stability to the discussion by indicating what economic events can plausibly trigger passing-on, and what costs cannot.

B. THE PARTIES

1. Introducing the acronyms

1.030 The purpose of this section is to get acquainted with the parties involved in the passing-on problem and to introduce the acronyms I have chosen in order to refer to them without needing to use lengthy descriptions every time. This section also serves to illustrate the interests of the parties involved in the passing-on problem before making the plunge into legal detail. A number of arguments and possible positions will be mentioned, but for the purposes of this section, they will only be introduced, and accordingly they will not be elaborated upon in detail.

1.031 This book thus uses a simplified model of three persons: Alpha, Beta, and Gamma. Alpha can be the EU, a Member State, or a commercial enterprise. Beta is always a commercial enterprise – otherwise the passing-on problem would not apply. Gamma can be a commercial enterprise too, but can also be a consumer or a Member State – it is of little or no consequence to the analysis.

1.032 A legal dispute in which the passing-on problem arises has usually originated in a money transaction between Alpha and Beta. This transaction may have been the payment of a tax by Beta to Alpha or payment for goods or services sold by Alpha. In some cases the dispute originated instead in the omission of a money transaction from Alpha to Beta.[22] Gamma, finally, is the heterogeneous class of natural and legal persons who can be found down the supply chain from Beta (i.e., they are Beta's customers, customers of Beta's customers, and so on down to final consumers). It follows that Gamma, as a common denominator for all these, may include both commercial enterprises and individual consumers. Beta and Gamma will both be claimants, while Alpha will be the defendant.[23]

22 See e.g. the so-called gritz and quellmehl cases (n 19).

23 Actions brought by Gamma against Beta are possible e.g. in Germany (see Anne Howard and Anneliese Blackwood, 'Litigating Infringements in the National Courts' in Vivien Rose and David Bailey (eds) *Bellamy*

II. Alpha

Alpha obviously would not wish to pay damages or restitution, neither to Beta nor to Gamma.[24] Alpha would use all available arguments to prove that no awards were payable at all, to any of the claimants. In relation to Beta, Alpha might argue that any and all injury suffered had been passed on to Gamma and that the passing-on of a loss meant that the loss no longer existed with Beta as an award can be payable only if the loss has been sustained more permanently. If the loss had not been sustained in this sense by Beta, Alpha would contend that it followed that no award was payable to Beta. Indeed, Alpha would submit, an award of damages or restitution to Beta (or Gamma) under circumstances where no loss has been sustained would be a windfall award constituting an unjust enrichment of Beta.[25] **1.033**

In relation to Gamma however, Alpha might instead assert that the entire injury was absorbed by Beta and that no amount whatsoever was passed on to Gamma. Furthermore, if the 'Gamma' claimant at issue was not a final consumer, Alpha would also shamelessly argue that even if some part of the injury had been passed on to Gamma, Gamma would continue to pass it further on down the chain of distribution. And so on. **1.034**

Under its assertive surface, however, Alpha would fear being held liable to pay multiple awards. Consider the possibility of one court holding that Beta did not pass on any loss, and that an award was therefore payable to Beta corresponding to the entire amount initially paid (but not due) by Beta to Alpha, and another court holding in parallel proceedings that Beta did pass on all its loss to Gamma, and that an award was payable to Gamma claimants corresponding to the entire amount initially paid (but not due) by Beta. Under such circumstances Alpha would be held liable to pay the same amount twice. If the Gamma claimants at issue here were moreover only the first tier of a long supply chain of potential claimants, there might be a risk of even further multiplication of the amount payable in parallel proceedings. **1.035**

& Child: European Union Law of Competition (7th edn, Oxford University Press 2013) 1257), but have not been addressed by the European Court of Justice as such. The Court has nevertheless made reference to this possibility in joined cases C-192/95 to 218/95 *Société Comateb and others v Directeur Général des Douanes et Droits Indirects* [1997] ECR I-165 para. 24; and in case C-94/10 *Danfoss A/S and Sauer-Danfoss ApS v Skatteministeriet* [2011] ECR I-9963 para. 26.

24 Knowing that Alpha may be facing substantial penal sanctions due to its violation of law, especially in the competition law context, this is understandable.

25 These are all arguments on how to estimate the award (Alpha is arguing, along pragmatic lines, that it should be estimated to zero).

III. Beta

1.036 Beta would have either: (1) paid money to Alpha that was not due; (2) paid an overcharge to Alpha, i.e., an amount of excess over and above the sum properly due to Alpha; or (3) have been denied a sum that was due from Alpha to Beta. Under any of these circumstances, it would not be likely for Beta to find it relevant whether this economic burden might have been compensated for through prices set by Beta vis-à-vis Gamma. In the first two instances Beta's lawyer might argue that the situation should be settled by plain restitution of the nominal amount unduly paid to Alpha by Beta, as it was simply a *solutio indebiti* and should be treated as such. Whatever steps Beta may have taken to adjust to the loss constituted by that payment, the lawyer will argue, are business decisions of Beta of no concern to Alpha.[26] In the third instance the argument would be similar although the point of departure would be that Alpha owes Beta money and should stop beating around the bush about it.

1.037 If pushed to scrutinize the passing-on defence in further detail, Beta would disagree with the notion that prices are set by summing up costs and adding a fixed profit margin. Beta would argue that prices are instead set with regard to market prices and Beta's position on that market – admittedly with a view to making a profit, but profits are never guaranteed in business. There would be times when profits were high, thanks to low costs and high market prices, and times when profits were low (and even at times a loss) due to high costs and low market prices. Thus Beta would challenge the existence of a direct nexus between costs and prices. Beta would accordingly submit that if Beta had not incurred extra costs because of Alpha's illegal conduct Beta would have enjoyed higher profits, which would serve to demonstrate that the pricing policy of Beta was not cost-based. Under such circumstances, Beta would conclude, Alpha must be made liable to pay a full award to Beta.

1.038 Beta might also challenge Alpha's line of argument by following it through to its final consequence. Beta might then argue that if it were true that businesses used a fixed profit margin and that the injury had thus been passed on to Gamma, the payment of an award to Beta would consequentially also lead to compensation for Gamma as well as Beta. This would be so because, under the passing-on logic asserted by Alpha, a full award of compensation from Alpha to Beta would enable Beta to lower its prices while nevertheless maintaining its profits – passing-on the award, if you will, and thereby restoring balance to the supply chain.

---

26 For an argument of this kind see e.g. Peter Birks, *Unjust Enrichment* (2nd edn, Clarendon Law Series, Oxford University Press 2005) 221: 'Everyone takes steps to adjust to a minus.'

Beta might also reject the notion that the payment of a compensatory award by Alpha to Beta in excess of loss actually absorbed by Beta would lead to an unjust enrichment. If anyone had been unjustly enriched in this situation, Beta would argue, it was Alpha. Alpha had profited from violating the law. That profit should rightly be disgorged and transferred to Beta, from whom it was exacted.[27] **1.039**

Finally, however, and notwithstanding these possibilities of legal argumentation, Beta might still be reluctant to bring an action against Alpha for practical business reasons. Suing a business partner might be detrimental to business, especially if Alpha were a very important or even essential partner. Even if Alpha were an exchangeable partner, suing partners does not look good. For such reasons Beta might hesitate to pursue its claim in court.[28] **1.040**

IV. Gamma

From the point of view of Gamma, it would be clear that any award to be paid by Alpha must be payable to Gamma first and foremost. It was Gamma who ultimately suffered injury due to Alpha's violation of law, while the injury simply passed through the assets of Beta. Alpha has been enriched, Beta is left at *status quo* – the actual loss would remain with Gamma, and that loss would be unfair and should be remedied by holding Alpha liable to pay an award to Gamma directly. **1.041**

Gamma would, however, face great legal difficulties. Gamma would risk being legally defined as a third party with no direct nexus with Alpha. This could lead to a denial of access to court, leaving Gamma cut off from the possibility of bringing an action against Alpha. Even if Gamma were granted access to court the lack of a direct nexus would still be a problem in view of substantive proximity. In damages it would be difficult to prove causation. In restitution it would probably be even more difficult to leapfrog Beta and prove sufficient proximity between the breach of law by Alpha and the loss incurred by Gamma. To overcome these difficulties it would be crucial that Gamma was able to prove that the injury had indeed passed on from Beta to Gamma. Gamma might find such a burden of evidence difficult: should not such evidence instead be requested from Beta, whose assets this issue concerns and **1.042**

27 See e.g. Francis Hubeau, 'La répétition de l'indu en droit communautaire' (1981) 17 Revue Trimestrielle de Droit Européen 442, 451.

28 This is a business concern to be weighed against the possible benefits from pursuing the claim. As it is a business concern it will not be analysed as such in this book. Nonetheless, this aspect is occasionally mentioned in legal debate and will be mentioned again below.

whose pricing policy gave rise to passing-on in the first place?[29] By itself Gamma would at best be able to produce general evidence on price elasticity of demand on the relevant market. Such evidence would however be inconclusive with regard to the actual pricing policy applied by Beta in the individual case. And even if passing-on was proved it would remain uncertain whether the court would accept Gamma's passing-on argument at law.

1.043 Gamma would have little sympathy concerning the issue of Alpha risking multiple liabilities. Gamma would almost certainly argue that whether or not Alpha has paid an award of compensation to Beta, and notwithstanding how that award was determined, Gamma's prospects of bringing a successful direct action against Alpha should be undiminished. If Alpha violated the law, Alpha will suffer. After all, US antitrust violators pay treble damages. Why should European law violators be better off?

V. The need for coordination

1.044 It has been demonstrated above that passing-on is not a single legal problem but a specific set of factual circumstances that triggers a number of distinct legal problems: access to court issues, substantive proximity problems, and problems of how to estimate awards. Although solutions could, in theory, be found for each of these problems individually, it is evident from the above that those solutions must somehow be coordinated or the parties will risk severe adverse consequences – e.g., multiple liabilities for Alpha.

1.045 There are a number of suggestions on how to approach these coordination problems, e.g., on how to remove the risk for multiple liabilities and stop Alpha from using contradictory arguments in parallel proceedings. One suggestion is to join the actions at issue for the purposes of establishing that an award is payable *per se*.[30] Another suggestion is to let Beta claim for all harm initially incurred and then let Gamma claimants sue Beta in turn.[31] Suggestions such as these will be discussed in the chapters below and in particular in section 9.E.

---

29 In this kind of situation, Beta and Gamma would have little incentive to give mutual aid in litigation against Alpha. It will be discussed below how to design an approach to the passing-on problem where such conflicts of interest among the potentially injured parties may be avoided.

30 See e.g. Antitrust Modernization Commission, 'Report and Recommendations' (2007) <http://govinfo.library.unt.edu/amc/report_recommendation/toc.htm> (last accessed 31 May 2016) 277, for a litigation model that would have such an effect.

31 See Howard & Blackwood (n 23) 1256–7.

C. PURPOSE AND APPROACH OF THE BOOK

I. Purpose

The purpose of this book is to analyse and to discuss the approach to the passing-on problem that has been chosen in EU law. It must however be immediately stressed that there is not one single and coherent approach in EU law, but a number of approaches with a varying degree of legal detail. It will be discussed in this book if, how and to what extent these approaches are interrelated and compatible with each other. The merit of the approaches chosen will also be discussed. Reasoned suggestions on how to fill gaps will be submitted, and, on occasion, there will be suggestions for revision of the choices made. **1.046**

II. Contexts and perspectives

The heterogeneity of EU law on passing-on is due not only to the aforementioned range of legal issues triggered by passing-on itself, but also to the variety of legal courses of action in which it may arise. In EU law the passing-on problem has been explicitly addressed in three different courses of action: (1) in actions for damages brought against the EU under Article 340(2) TFEU; (2) in actions against Member States for the repayment of charges levied by Member States in breach of EU law; and (3) in damages actions brought against private individuals[32] for a breach of EU competition law.[33] In actions 1 and 2 an approach has been chosen by the Court of Justice and, in action 3, by the EU legislature. The discussion will also cover other EU law courses of action in which the problem may need to be addressed in the future. **1.047**

As the perspective here employed is the EU law perspective, the legal issues addressed will also be embedded in the EU law context. This means inter alia that the law governing the respective actions for damages or restitution will not always be EU law only. Actions brought against the EU are governed by **1.048**

---

32 The term 'private individual' will be used throughout this text (with the exception of quotes using different terminology). It is intended to serve as shorthand for any kind of natural or legal person capable of carrying rights and/or obligations pursuant to EU law, who is not an emanation of the Member State within the meaning of EU law. The criteria used for identifying legal bodies as emanations of the Member State within the meaning of EU law were laid down by the European Court of Justice in case C-188/89 *A Foster and others v British Gas plc* [1990] ECR I-3313 para. 20.

33 It deserves to be pointed out that an action for damages or restitution for a breach of competition law may also be brought against an institution, agency or other emanation of a Member State; see e.g. case C-242/95 *GT-Link A/S v De Danske Statsbaner (DSB)* [1997] ECR I-4449 which was for restitution by reason of a breach of competition law.

EU law exclusively, and the EU (in particular its courts) has full jurisdiction and responsibility to develop the conditions and criteria that apply to such actions. By contrast, actions for damages or restitution brought against Member States or against a private individual for a breach of EU law are governed by a complex combination of EU law and national law. Although the right or interest infringed will be protected by EU law, such actions must be brought before the national courts.[34] With regard to damages actions for a breach of competition law, there is an instrument of EU law harmonizing aspects of such actions before national courts.[35] With regard to actions for restitution of charges levied by a Member State in breach of EU law there is no EU law harmonization. Where there is no harmonizing instrument, EU law has traditionally relied on the national courts to provide appropriate remedies and conditions for private enforcement of EU law. This reliance on national law has been subject to an increasingly intricate web of EU law requirements, however, developed to secure the effective judicial protection of rights and interests protected by EU law. It is in this context that much of EU case law on the passing-on problem is found. It importantly follows that the passing-on problem is not only a concern for the EU courts and legislature, but also for their national counterparts. It also follows that the EU law requirements of effective judicial protection are crucial to this inquiry. Furthermore, there is an interesting extra dimension of tension, for in every discussion of the integration of EU law and national law it must be assessed how far the Court of Justice has been inclined to push the impact of EU law on national private law.

1.049 The passing-on problem will consequently be contextualized in three ways. First, in order to assess with full precision the policy options available to the courts seized with a passing-on situation, the three main legal aspects of passing-on (access to court, substantive proximity (e.g., causation in damages), and the estimation of awards) will be distinguished and examined in the context of general observations on those three aspects. Second, as EU law, just as any other legal system, has created specific rules and principles for specific courses of action, it is necessary to carry out the examination in the context of the different courses of action individually. Accordingly, there will be separate examination of the legal aspects triggered by passing-on in the context of damages actions against the EU under Article 340(2) TFEU, repayment actions against Member States, and competition damages actions. Third, all these discussions will remain within the paradigm of EU law. As a result of the

34 It is another matter that the national courts have the opportunity, and at last instance the duty, to refer questions on EU law that may arise in such proceedings to the European Court of Justice for a preliminary ruling; see Art. 267 TFEU.

35 Directive 2014/104/EU (n 6).

contextual approach chosen for this book, many central topics in EU law damages and restitution will be covered.

The EU law discussed in this book must be distinguished from the compara- **1.050**
tive law field called European private law. Discussions in the latter field of research have in recent years revolved very much around the grand Draft Common Frame of Reference (DCFR) project,[36] which was funded by the European Commission.[37] As European private law is comparative law, its findings are academic, providing perspectives on national private law. By contrast, EU law is binding. It forms part of the law of all national jurisdictions of the EU Member States, providing a more or less detailed framework of rules and principles whenever the legal situation at hand comes within the scope of EU law. It has not however been intended to cover the particular problems that may arise in specific national jurisdictions in connection with the operation of integrating EU law and national law. Although problems particular to a certain jurisdiction may be discussed in connection to specific case law, such examinations are only intended to aid the abstract assessment of the interface between EU law and national law, to be carried out from the EU law perspective. This limitation has been chosen from consideration of the heterogeneous reading audience. On the one hand, this approach has the advantage of rendering this book interesting to lawyers of any EU jurisdiction who find themselves preoccupied by the passing-on problem. On the other hand, however, it also has the disadvantage of being unhelpful to all these lawyers in their efforts to understand how particular rules of their national jurisdiction, which may come into play in a passing-on situation, will fit with the EU law framework. This problem however underlies much of the presentation, and it is hoped that some of the case law and hypothetical situations discussed in this book will provide a good start for considerations of problems particular to the national jurisdiction at issue.

There are three courses of action in which the passing-on problem has arisen, **1.051**
namely:

1. Damages from the EU under Article 340(2) TFEU,
2. Restitution from a Member State, and
3. Damages for a breach of EU competition law.

36 The very physical result of which is Christian von Bar and Eric Clive (eds), *Principles, Definitions and Model Rules of European Private Law: Draft Common Frame of Reference (DCFR) Full Edition* (6 vols, Sellier European Law Publishers 2009).

37 The Commission called for such endeavours in 'Communication from the Commission to the European Parliament and the Council: A More Coherent European Contract Law: An Action Plan' COM(2003) 68 final section 4.1.1.

1.052 There are also some alternative courses of action in which the problem might occur:[38] namely

4. Restitution from the EU,
5. Damages from a Member State,
6. Restitution pursuant to a breach of EU competition law, and
7. Damages and restitutionary actions brought against private individuals for a breach of EU law other than competition law.

1.053 Among these alternative courses of action, 4 and 5 exist in EU case law, 6 also exists in case law but in very particular circumstances, and those in 7 are only being discussed hypothetically. Nonetheless potential passing-on approaches will be discussed, albeit more briefly.

III. Structure of the presentation

1.054 Part I of this book includes two chapters. In this first chapter the passing-on problem and its characteristics in EU law have been introduced, in a nutshell, alongside the approach chosen for the purposes of this inquiry into the legal issues triggered by passing-on. Chapter 2 will be devoted to introducing the EU law requirements developed to secure the effective judicial protection of rights and interests protected by EU law. These requirements are crucial to the passing-on problem, irrespective of which specific legal aspect of the problem is discussed. Nonetheless there are differences in their scope of application, depending on whether the action is under the exclusive jurisdiction of the EU Courts or should be brought before the competent national court.

1.055 Parts II, III and IV include the main three Chapters 3, 5 and 7 of the book, in which existing EU law on passing-on is discussed in relation to each of the relevant courses of action. Parts II, III and IV also include Chapters 4, 6 and 8 in which alternative courses of action are discussed. These are courses of action where the passing-on problem has not, as yet, arisen. Each chapter begins with an introduction to the action, tracing its most salient features. With regard to the alternative courses of action their interrelationship with the main action will be addressed. Focus then turns to the three major legal issues connected with the passing-on problem, as already mentioned above: access to court;

38 Apart from the actions listed here one might also discuss the importance of passing-on in the context of the duty to repay illegal state aid. However, in that context the circumstances are quite different from the circumstances of the actions discussed in this book, as the defendant is not arguing disimpoverishment of the claimant, but arguing disenrichment of itself. The term 'disimpoverishment' as an option to 'passing-on' has been suggested for the purposes of restitution law by Birks (n 26) 219–21; and Michael Rush, *The Defence of Passing On* (Hart Publishing 2006) 11–17.

substantive proximity; and estimation of awards.[39] Each assessment begins with general observations on the area (e.g., on causation under Article 340(2) TFEU) before proceeding to discuss the existing case law or legislation on passing-on in that particular context.[40] The character and length of the respective presentations and discussions will vary considerably, as some have not been touched upon at all by the EU Courts or legislature, while others have been the subject of extensive case law developments. Notwithstanding these differences, it will be consistently endeavoured to find the decisive problems, to address them with attention to case law and legal debate in the context at issue, and to submit reasoned opinions and suggestions where appropriate.

Comparisons, analysis across contexts, a few conclusions and overall sugges- **1.056**
tions will follow in the final Part V which comprises only Chapter 9.

39 The choice of approaching each EU law theme in the context of the specific courses of action inevitably causes some repetition. However, every other sequence considered for this presentation either resulted in even more repetition or risked rendering the discussion unintelligible.

40 In Chs 4, 6 and 8 the discussion will be speculative as there is no case law and no legislation.

2

EFFECTIVE JUDICIAL PROTECTION IN EU LAW

A. A COAT OF MANY COLOURS

2.001 The massive *Judicial Protection in the European Union* by Schermers and Waelbroeck does not define the concept of judicial protection for the purposes of EU law.[1] Perhaps it is considered self-evident that the subject matter of the book is the protection – or enforcement, if you will – of rights conferred on the subjects of EU law (private individuals, other private entities such as undertakings and organizations, Member States, and indeed the EU itself) by the judiciary, which includes both national courts and tribunals and the EU Courts. In this sense any kind of judicial application or interpretation of EU law, whatever the form of review, reference, direct or indirect action involved, will be covered by the concept of judicial protection. To understand effective judicial protection in the EU law context and more specifically to understand EU law discourse on that subject, it is necessary however to distinguish judicial protection in a broad sense from more narrowly defined principles. Judicial protection in a broad sense designates the general interest of ensuring that this judicial protection is effective. This interest is safeguarded in EU case law by a number of legal principles, doctrines and mechanisms, e.g., the principles of

1 Henry G Schermers and Denis F Waelbroeck, *Judicial Protection in the European Union* (6th edn, Kluwer Law International 2001).

equivalence and effectiveness, the primacy of EU law, direct effect of EU law, consistent interpretation, and of course the more specific EU law principle of effective judicial protection which was developed by the European Court of Justice and is now enshrined in Article 47 of the Charter of Fundamental Rights of the European Union (hereinafter the Charter). There is moreover some confusion of terminology with regard to effective judicial protection as such. Other tags used as alternatives to 'effective judicial protection' include 'the effectiveness requirement'[2] and '*effet utile*'.[3] Some commentators also trace the interest of effective judicial protection further back to the principle of sincere cooperation expressed in Article 4(3) TEU.[4]

Former Advocate General van Gerven has created a useful structure for how to make the confounding multiplicity of EU law (in particular case law) on judicial protection intelligible. His mind-map is based on a distinction between the concepts of rights, remedies[5] and procedures, respectively.[6] To van Gerven a 'right' is a legal position which can be general to all (such as the right to life or the freedom of expression) or specific to an individual (such as ownership of a specific object). The holder of a right should normally be able to enforce that right before a competent court through one or other adequate 'remedy' or 'classes of action'. Finally these remedies will be governed by 'procedures' laid down by applicable law – which may or may not be easily distinguishable from the remedies as such.[7] In the research presented in this book, various legal concepts that serve the interest of effective judicial **2.002**

2 Paul Craig and Gráinne de Búrca, *EU Law: Text, Cases, and Materials* (6th edn, Oxford University Press 2015) 231.

3 Koen Lenaerts and Piet van Nuffel (Robert Bray and Nathan Cambien (eds)), *European Union Law* (3rd edn, Sweet and Maxwell 2011) 151, who distinguish legal protection of EU law rights conferred by provisions with direct effect from *effet utile* of EU law provisions with no direct effect.

4 E.g., Magnus Gulliksson, '*Ne Bis in Idem* and Effective Sanctions in EU Law' in Joakim Nergelius and Eleonor Kristoffersson (eds) *Human Rights in Contemporary European Law* (Swedish Studies in European Law vol. 6, Hart Publishing 2015) 158–9. On this and many other aspects of the principle of sincere cooperation in Art. 4(3) TEU see Lenaerts and van Nuffel (n 3) 147–55.

5 The concept of 'remedies' can be understood in various ways; see Sacha Prechal, *Directives in EC Law* (2nd edn, Oxford EC Law Library, Oxford University Press 2006) 145 n 99. In this presentation the concept of remedies signifies legal actions brought before a court or administrative body with a view to enforce a right. One way of doing so is to bring an action the purpose of which is to secure a certain form of redress; e.g., an injunction or the award of damages or restitution.

6 Walter van Gerven, 'Of Rights, Remedies and Procedures' (2000) 37 *Common Market Law Review* 501, 502–4. For a recent contribution building on the van Gerven model see Nina Półtorak, *European Union Rights in National Courts* (Wolters Kluwer 2015) 7–15.

7 The compatibility of this 'classic' presentation with more recent case law is discussed in Pieter van Cleynenbruegel, 'Case C-69/10, *Brahim Samba Diouf v Ministre du Travail, de l'Emploi et de l'Immigration*, Judgment of the Court of Justice (Second Chamber) of 28 July 2011, nyr' (2012) 49 *Common Market Law Review* 327, 337–47. The model suggested by van Gerven is discussed also by Rebecca Williams, *Unjust Enrichment and Public Law: A Comparative Study of England, France and the UK* (Hart Publishing, 2011) 242–7; in that discussion, Williams juxtaposes van Gerven's model with a similar model suggested by Peter Birks, 'Rights, Wrongs and Remedies' (2000) 20 *Oxford Journal of Legal Studies* 1.

protection are of essence to the analysis. These legal concepts have been construed narrowly in order to examine the precise role of each in the various issues included in the passing-on problem. To that end the distinctions made by van Gerven offer a pattern which can serve to clarify the respective roles played by the models and principles developed by the Court of Justice. By reason of its usefulness as an explanatory model in EU law, it has consequently been adopted for the purposes of this book. There is also ample evidence that the EU Courts use this model, e.g., in the recent *E.ON*.[8]

2.003 Under the van Gerven model it must first be established that a right is conferred on the claimant by EU law. In the alternative the claimant may have a certain particular interest which is protected by EU law.[9] Unless a right or particular interest protected by EU law can be identified by the claimant none of the arguments or principles employed by the Court of Justice will be triggered.[10] This may seem self-evident but a reminder is warranted in order to avoid short-circuiting our discussion of effective judicial protection. Effective judicial protection, even in the broadest of senses, thus presupposes the conferral on the claimant of a substantive right or interest protected by EU law which it is possible to identify. This is highlighted in the case law of the EU Courts on access to claim damages from the EU pursuant to Article 340(2) TFEU, as the General Court has held that such an action is admissible only if the claimant 'is able to assert in law either a particular interest of his own or a right to compensation which has been assigned to him by others'.[11] Similarly the Court of Justice has consistently identified the existence of a right under EU law as one of the conditions for liability in damages for Member States.[12] In other words it is not possible to bring any kind of claim before the courts of the EU or the Member States and invoke the fundamental right of access to court as a *carte blanche* to litigate.

8 Case C-510/13 *E.ON Földgáz Trade Zrt v Magyar Energetikai és Közmű-szabályozási Hivatal* EU:C:2015:189 paras 48–50.

9 Joined cases C-87/90, C-88/90 and C-89/90 *A Verholen and others v Sociale Verzekeringsbank Amsterdam* [1991] ECR I-3757 para. 23.

10 On this prerequisite for the applicability of Art. 47 of the Charter, see Pekka Aalto et al, 'Article 47' in Steve Peers, Tamara Hervey, Jeff Kenner and Angela Ward (eds), *The EU Charter of Fundamental Rights: A Commentary* (Verlag CH Beck/Hart Publishing/Nomos 2014) 1199 and 1215.

11 Case T-219/08 *İşçi Partisi (Turkish Labour Party) v Commission of the European Communities* EU:T:2008:538 para. 7; and case T-223/09 *İşçi Partisi (Turkish Labour Party) v Commission of the European Communities* EU:T:2009:524 para. 11. See also Koen Lenaerts, Ignace Maselis and Kathleen Gutman (Janek Tomasz Nowak (ed.)), *EU Procedural Law* (Oxford EU Law Library, Oxford University Press 2014) 493–5. On this case law see further Ch. 3.

12 See further Ch. 6.

Where there is a right, there must also be a remedy (*ubi ius, ibi remedium*).[13] This right to an effective remedy is now enshrined in Article 47(1) of the Charter. Where, e.g., the action is brought against the EU before the EU Courts, it follows from Article 340(2) TFEU that the remedy of damages is available. Where the action is brought against a Member State or a private individual before national courts, it follows from the case law of the Court of Justice that the point of departure is that the remedies available under national law should suffice. By contrast, in situations where the holder of a right conferred on that individual by EU law does not under national law (or indeed under EU law, where the action is against the EU) have any adequate remedy by means of which to enforce that right, the introduction of such a remedy may be required by the Court of Justice. Examples of such a requirement can be seen in case law such as *Factortame I*,[14] *Francovich*[15] and *Courage*.[16] In the context of actions brought against the EU a parallel situation arose in *Masdar*.[17] **2.004**

The proceedings brought by means of the applicable remedy will be governed by applicable substantive and procedural conditions. Before the EU Courts, the Statute of the Court of Justice and the Rules of Procedure of the respective EU Courts will apply. Before national courts, in the absence of EU law rules and conditions harmonizing the action at issue, national law will apply but will also be subject to review against standards laid down in EU law. Those standards are the principle of effective judicial protection (in the narrow sense, now enshrined in Article 47 of the Charter) and the dual test of the principles of equivalence and effectiveness. The scope, the elements and the interrelationship of these standards are the subject of controversy and need further examination. The respective scope and elements of the principles will be analysed in sections 2.C and 2.D. With regard to their interrelationship some treat them as distinct principles of law that apply in parallel[18] while others **2.005**

13 Aalto et al (n 10) 1214.

14 Case C-213/89 *The Queen v Secretary of State for Transport, ex parte: Factortame Ltd and others* [1990] ECR I-2433.

15 Joined cases C-6/90 and 9/90 *Andrea Francovich and Daniela Bonifaci and others v Italian Republic* [1991] ECR I-5357.

16 Case C-453/99 *Courage Ltd v Bernard Crehan and Bernard Crehan v Courage Ltd and Others* [2001] ECR I-6297.

17 Case C-47/07 P *Masdar (UK) Ltd v Commission of the European Communities* [2008] ECR I-9761.

18 E.g., Alan Dashwood *et al*, *Wyatt and Dashwood's European Union Law* (6th edn, Hart Publishing 2011) 289–302; Michael Dougan, 'The Vicissitudes of Life at the Coalface: Remedies and Procedures for Enforcing Union Law before the National Courts' in Paul Craig and Gráinne de Búrca (eds), *The Evolution of EU Law* (2nd edn, Oxford University Press 2011) 431–433; Sacha Prechal and Rob Widdershoven, 'Effectiveness or Effective Judicial Protection: A Poorly Articulated Relationship' in Tristan Baumé et al (eds), *Today's Multi-layered Legal Order: Current Issues and Perspectives. Liber amicorum in honour of Arjen W.H. MEIJ* (Paris Legal Publishers, Zutphen 2011) 296.

claim they are one and the same,[19] related,[20] overlap,[21] or will imply that equivalence and effectiveness are the EU law version of a universally acknowledged principle of effective judicial protection[22] – or, vice versa, that effective judicial protection is a component of the EU law principle of effectiveness.[23]

2.006 The confusion pertains in particular to the interrelationship of the principle of effective judicial protection and the principle of effectiveness.[24] Admittedly the Court of Justice itself has been nothing short of inconsistent on this matter.[25] Some of the confusion may have originated from inconsistent terminology.[26] To some extent the confusion is attributable to the distinction between (effective) judicial protection in a broad sense and the narrower principle of effective judicial protection, as explained above. In *DEB* the Court of Justice made some remarks that are of interest in this context. The claim was for damages from Germany for a breach of EU law, but German law required an advance payment in respect of litigation costs and precluded legal persons from legal aid even though the claimant was unable to make the required advance payment. Under those circumstances the national court had

19 Peter Oliver, 'Case C-279/09, *DEB* v. *Germany*, Judgment of the European Court of Justice (Second Chamber) of 22 December 2010, nyr' (2011) 48 *Common Market Law Review* 2023, 2038–2039. Gulliksson (n 4) has submitted that the different effectiveness notions may come into conflict. Gulliksson has thus noticed that if those notions were all part of a single EU law principle of effectiveness, such an EU law principle would be capable of coming into conflict with itself.

20 E.g., Koen Lenaerts, 'National remedies for private individuals in the light of the EU law principles of equivalence and effectiveness' (2011) 46 *Irish Jurist* 13, 25; and, as mentioned, Lenaerts, Maselis and Gutman (n 11) 110.

21 E.g., Folkert Wilman, *Private Enforcement of EU Law before National Courts: The EU Legislative Framework* (Elgar European Law and Practice, Edward Elgar Publishing 2015) 39; and Torbjörn Andersson, *Rättsskyddsprincipen: EG-rätt och nationell sanktions- och processrätt ur ett svenskt civilprocessuellt perspektiv* (Iustus förlag 1997) 135.

22 E.g., Craig and de Búrca (n 2) 239; Johanna Engström, *The Europeanisation of Remedies and Procedures Through Judge-made Law – Can a Trojan Horse Achieve Effectiveness?* (EUI Department of Law 2009) 45.

23 Półtorak (n 6) 46.

24 Irrespective of the interrelationship of the principles of effectiveness and effective judicial protection, it is quite clear that the principle of equivalence is a legal construction based on the concept of discrimination which is entirely different from both these principles. See further Section 2.D.II.

25 Compare the holdings in case C-432/05 *Unibet (London) Ltd and Unibet (International) Ltd v Justitiekanslern* [2007] ECR I-2271 paras 42–43; case C-268/06 *Impact v Minister for Agriculture and Food and Others* [2008] ECR I-2483 para. 47; case C-63/08 *Virginie Pontin v T-Comalux SA* [2009] ECR I-10467 para. 44; joined cases C-317/08, C-318/08, C-319/08 and C-320/08 *Rosalba Alassini v Telecom Italia SpA* (C-317/08), *Filomena Califano v Wind SpA* (C-318/08), *Lucia Anna Giorgia Iacono v Telecom Italia SpA* (C-319/08) and *Multiservice Srl v Telecom Italia SpA* (C-320/08) [2010] ECR I-2213 paras 49 and 61–66 and the Opinion of AG Kokott para. 42.

26 See Sara Drake, 'Scope of *Courage* and the principle of 'individual liability' for damages: further development of the principle of effective judicial protection by the Court of Justice' (2006) 31 *European Law Review* 841, 843–4. Oliver (n 19) 2038–9 seems to have agreed that the distinction between the principle of effective judicial protection and the principle of effectiveness is only one of inconsistent terminology, concluding that it should therefore be abandoned. This author would not agree that such a conclusion follows from the confusion.

asked whether such national rules were compatible with the EU principle of effectiveness.[27] The Court of Justice began its reasoning with this observation:

> The question referred thus concerns the right of a legal person to effective access to justice and, accordingly, in the context of EU law, it concerns the principle of effective judicial protection. That principle is a general principle of EU law stemming from the constitutional traditions common to the Member States, which has been enshrined in Articles 6 and 13 [ECHR] … .[28] **2.007**
>
> According to the explanations relating to that article, which, in accordance with the third subparagraph of Article 6(1) TEU and Article 52(7) of the Charter, have to be taken into consideration for the interpretation of the Charter, the second paragraph of Article 47 of the Charter corresponds to Article 6(1) of the ECHR.
>
> In the light of the above, it is necessary to recast the question referred so that it relates to the interpretation of the principle of effective judicial protection as enshrined in Article 47 of the Charter … .[29]

Thereafter the Court neither returned to the principle of effectiveness nor to **2.008**
the phrases commonly associated with it (i.e., national rules making it virtually impossible or excessively difficult to pursue a claim). Instead its reasoning built almost exclusively on case law of the Strasbourg Court. In the Operative part of the judgment, the Court furthermore explicitly relied on the principle of effective judicial protection 'as enshrined in Article 47 of the Charter'. This view has been endorsed in this book. In other words, the narrowly defined principle of effective judicial protection will be seen as a specific principle of EU law to be distinguished from the principle of effectiveness, and Article 47 of the Charter will be seen as the expression of the principle of effective judicial protection in present EU law. The right of access to court, which is immediately relevant to this inquiry, is included in Article 47. The principle of effectiveness, on the other hand, will be identified exclusively with the well-established requirement that actions based on EU law must not be subject to national rules liable to make their exercise virtually impossible or excessively difficult. To distinguish the two principles in this way finds support not only in *DEB* but also in their different origins. The principle of effectiveness was originally derived from the principle of sincere cooperation now enshrined in Article 4(3) TEU.[30] The principle of effective judicial protection,

27 Case 279/09 *DEB Deutsche Energiehandels- und Beratungsgesellschaft mbH v Bundesrepublik Deutschland* [2010] ECR I-13849 para. 27.

28 Ibid., para. 29.

29 Ibid., paras 32–33.

30 Case 33/76 *Rewe-Zentralfinanz eG and Rewe-Zentral AG v Landwirtschaftskammer für das Saarland* [1976] ECR 1989 para. 5; case 45/76 *Comet BV v Produktschap voor Siergewassen* [1976] ECR 2043 paras 12–16. References to the principle of sincere cooperation in connection to the principle of effectiveness have since become scarce. See also Lenaerts, Maselis and Gutman (n 11) 109.

however, has quite consistently been derived from the constitutional traditions common to the Member States and expressed in Articles 6 and 13 ECHR.[31]

2.009 For these reasons distinctions between the different rules and principles have been upheld below and the structure of the discussion of different aspects of effective judicial protection will be as follows. From the existence of an EU law right follows the right to an effective remedy for the protection of that right – hence the right to an effective remedy will be discussed first. This general discussion of the right to an effective remedy will be followed by a discussion of relevant aspects of Article 47 of the Charter, in particular the EU law right of access to court. To assist readers in the avoidance of confusion it has also been attempted to refer consistently to Article 47 of the Charter rather than to the principle of effective judicial protection. Finally the principles of equivalence and effectiveness will be addressed. The approach of distinguishing these different aspects of judicial protection has the advantage of expecting no more from any tool in the toolbox of EU law than the performance of the precise task it has been designed for. It may to some readers have the disadvantage of a certain lack of overview. Hopefully this introductory presentation will to some extent have overcome that disadvantage. It is also hoped that this section has helped explain that the discussion below must be read with awareness that the concepts involved have been interpreted narrowly, and that alternative interpretations are available in the contributions cited above for those readers who prefer them.

B. THE RIGHT TO AN EFFECTIVE REMEDY

1. Effective remedies in EU law and national law

2.010 Rights conferred on individuals by EU law can be enforced against the EU itself before the EU Courts. In such cases the remedies and procedures available are those provided for in the EU Treaties, as complemented e.g. by the Statute of the EU Courts.[32] They can also be enforced against Member States and against other private individuals. In these categories of cases the

31 E.g. in case 222/84 *Marguerite Johnston v Chief Constable of the Royal Ulster Constabulary* [1986] ECR 1651 para. 18; there called the general principle of 'judicial control'. However, the term 'effective judicial protection' had previously occurred in case 14/83 *Sabine von Colson and Elisabeth Kamann v Land Nordrhein-Westfalen* [1984] ECR 1891 para. 23, as an EU law requirement on national sanctions to be imposed for discrimination on grounds of sex.

32 Protocol (No 3) on the Statute of the Court of Justice of the European Union, annexed to the EU Treaties. See also e.g. Rules of procedure of the General Court, consolidated version of the Rules of procedure of the Court of First Instance of the European Communities [1991] OJ L136/1.

action should be brought before the competent national court or administration. The remedies and procedures applicable may have been subject to full or partial harmonization, but in the absence of EU rules the remedies and procedures of national law will apply. The applicable remedies and procedures of national law will however be subject to a number of EU law requirements, including Article 47 of the EU Charter and the principles of equivalence and effectiveness.

In this section the impact of EU law requirements with regard to the remedies available for the private enforcement of rights conferred on individuals by EU law will be explored. Where a right or interest protected by EU law is vested in a claimant, EU law presupposes that EU or national law, as the case may be, will provide such claimants with sufficient remedies for the enforcement of their right. In circumstances where the remedies available do not suffice for the effective judicial protection of a right or interest however, special requirements developed in EU law will come into play. **2.011**

The general right to an effective remedy is now enshrined in Article 19(1) TEU. Its first sub-paragraph introduces the Court of Justice of the European Union (i.e., the EU Courts collectively) and its task to 'ensure that in the interpretation and application of the Treaties the law is observed'. The second sub-paragraph of Article 19(1) TEU applies where rights conferred on individuals are enforced before national courts and administrative bodies. It reads: **2.012**

> Member States shall provide remedies sufficient to ensure effective legal protection in the fields covered by Union law. **2.013**

The same right is also expressed in Article 47(1) of the Charter, which was based on Article 13 ECHR.[33] Article 47(1) of the Charter reads: **2.014**

> Everyone whose rights and freedoms guaranteed by the law of the Union are violated has the right to an effective remedy before a tribunal in compliance with the conditions laid down in this Article. **2.015**

This EU law right to an effective remedy does not only apply where EU law rights are enforced before national courts and administrative bodies, but also when they are enforced before the EU Courts. This is illustrated by *Masdar* where the European Court of Justice recognized that an action of unjust **2.016**

33 'Explanations relating to the Charter of fundamental rights' [2007] OJ C303/17, 29. See also case C-239/14 *Abdoulaye Amadou Tall v Centre public d'action sociale de Huy* EU:C:2015:824 paras 50–54.

enrichment must be available against the EU in circumstances where the action for non-contractual damages in Article 340(2) TFEU will not suffice to safeguard the effective judicial protection of rights conferred on an individual by EU law.[34]

2.017 The same right to an effective remedy applies before national courts and administrations.[35] Accordingly where no effective remedy is available under the national legal system, EU law may require the national court to make an effective remedy available to the claimant.[36] This does not however automatically mean that any particular remedy, e.g., the remedy of damages, should necessarily be made available by the national courts of the Member States.[37] The Court of Justice held in the *Butter Buying Cruises* case that:

2.018 > … although the Treaty has made it possible in a number of instances for private persons to bring a direct action, where appropriate, before the Court of Justice, it was not intended to create new remedies in the national courts to ensure the observance of Community law other than those already laid down by national law. On the other hand the system of legal protection established by the Treaty, as set out in Article 177 in particular, implies that it must be possible for every type of action provided for by national law to be available for the purpose of ensuring observance of Community provisions having direct effect, on the same conditions concerning the admissibility and procedure as would apply were it a question of ensuring observance of national law.[38]

2.019 The first element of this holding stressed the reliance of EU law on the remedies available in the Member States. As is well known this holding has since been qualified in the wake of cases such as *Factortame I*,[39] *Francovich*[40] and *Courage*.[41] The Court thus held in *Inuit* that EU law will not usually require for particular remedies to be made available by the national courts, but would have to do so:

2.020 > … if the structure of the domestic legal system concerned were such that there was no remedy making it possible, even indirectly, to ensure respect for the rights which

34 *Masdar* (n 17) para. 50. See further Ch. 4.

35 See e.g. *Unibet* (n 25) para. 42.

36 Aalto et al (n 10) 1217.

37 Cf. Norbert Reich, *General Principles of EU Civil Law* (Intersentia 2014) Ch. 4, in particular 120–23.

38 Case 158/80 *Rewe-Handelsgesellschaft Nord mbH and Rewe-Markt Steffen v Hauptzollamt Kiel (Butter Buying Cruises)* [1981] ECR 1805 para. 44 (cf Operative part para. 7). Art. 177 of the Rome Treaty is now Art. 267 TFEU.

39 *Factortame I* (n 14).

40 *Francovich* (n 15).

41 *Courage* (n 16).

> individuals derive from European Union law, or again if the sole means of access to a court was available to parties who were compelled to act unlawfully … .[42]

In situations where the holder of a right conferred on that individual by EU law does not under national law have any adequate and effective remedy by means of which to enforce that right, the introduction of such a remedy may consequently be required by the Court of Justice. As remarked by Craig and de Búrca the infamous 'no new remedies' *dictum* in *Butter Buying Cruises*, quoted above, was in fact preceded by case law requiring the remedy of repayment of charges levied in breach of (now) EU law to be available before national courts.[43] In *Pigs and Bacon* the Court thus held that any trader who had been required to pay such a charge had the right to claim repayment.[44] Consequently there seems to be a tension between the EU law right to an effective remedy and national autonomy on remedies. To this author it seems that the Court of Justice endeavours as far as possible to entrust national courts and administrations to provide claimants with the remedies necessary for the enforcement of their rights. Only where the remedies available do not suffice for the effective judicial protection of a right or interest will the EU law right to an effective remedy come into play. **2.021**

Finally, reference is made to section 2.C.II in which Article 52(1) of the EU Charter is discussed. Article 52(1) sets the standard for permissible limitations to fundamental rights in the Charter, such as the right to an effective remedy in Article 47(1). However, it is not clear whether an assessment of limitations of the right to an effective remedy under the Article 52(1) standard would result in any significant changes to the case law here described. This will be for the EU Courts to determine in future case law. **2.022**

II. What qualities make remedies 'effective'?

Not every remedy can reasonably be an effective remedy. In other words the remedy must have certain qualities that make it effective as such. The Court of Justice has not however explained what qualities or criteria indicate that a national remedy should be considered effective within the meaning of the EU law right to an effective remedy. There is however some case law and indeed some EU legislation on the adjacent matter of EU law requirements, in the event of a breach of certain specific EU law rules, for effective national sanctions to be put in place by the Member States. There are two parallel **2.023**

42 Case C-583/11 P *Inuit Tapiriit Kanatami and Others v European Parliament and Council of the European Union* EU:C:2013:625 para. 104; cf. also *Unibet* (n 25) paras 40–41.

43 Craig and de Búrca (n 2) 228.

44 Case 177/78 *Pigs and Bacon Commission v McCarren and Co Ltd* [1979] ECR 2161 para. 25.

threads of EU case law on the qualities that make such national sanctions effective. The first thread concerns national sanctions in the event of illegal discrimination. The Court of Justice held in *von Colson* that sanctions for a breach of EU law rules on equal treatment of men and women must be such as to guarantee real and effective judicial protection and have a deterrent effect,[45] and this phrase has since been included in some EU Directives on non-discrimination.[46] The other thread concerns national penal law sanctions in the event of a breach of certain EU law rules (e.g., a rule in an EU Regulation or a national rule implementing norms in a Directive) by individuals and is less relevant to this inquiry.[47]

2.024 In the non-discrimination thread the Court has indicated that national sanctions for a breach of the EU law rules on equal treatment must 'guarantee real and effective judicial protection and have a real deterrent effect on the employer'.[48] Under this case law merely symbolic sanctions, such as the award of compensation for direct costs only, are not compatible with the EU law right to an effective remedy.[49] Furthermore compensation in damages must not be limited to any specific amount or the like but must be payable to the full extent of proved loss due to a breach of EU law.[50] And, importantly, the Court held in *Draehmpaehl* that it is not compatible with the EU law right to an effective remedy to limit the total amount of damages payable by a defendant to a multitude of claimants bringing parallel actions by reason of the same breach of EU law.[51] If applicable *mutatis mutandis* to situations where the passing-on problem might occur (an issue which will be discussed shortly), this statement would be immediately relevant to the multiple and parallel actions arising from different levels of the supply chain in the passing-on

---

45 *von Colson* (n 31) para. 23. Subsequent case law includes case C-271/91 *M Helen Marshall v Southampton and South-West Hampshire Area Health Authority (Marshall II)* [1993] ECR I-4367; case C-180/95 *Nils Draehmpaehl v Urania Immobilienservice OHG* [1997] ECR I-2195 and case C-81/12 *Asociația Accept v CNCD* EU:C:2013:275.

46 Council Directive 2000/43/EC of 29 June 2000 implementing the principle of equal treatment between persons irrespective of racial or ethnic origin [2000] OJ L180/22 Art. 15; Council Directive 2000/78/EC of 27 November 2000 establishing a general framework for equal treatment in employment and occupation [2000] OJ L303/16 Art. 17; and Directive 2006/54/EC of the European Parliament and of the Council of 5 July 2006 on the implementation of the principle of equal opportunities and equal treatment of men and women in matters of employment and occupation (recast) [2006] OJ L204/23 Art. 25.

47 Beginning with case 68/88 *Commission of the European Communities v Hellenic Republic* [1989] ECR 2965 paras 22–24. Subsequent case law of significance in this thread is cited by the Court in case C-617/10 *Åklagaren v Hans Åkerberg Fransson* EU:C:2013:105 para. 36.

48 In the non-discrimination thread see *von Colson* (n 31) para. 23; *Marshall II* (n 45) para. 24; *Draehmpaehl* (n 45) para. 25; and case C-460/06 *Nadine Paquay v Société d'architects Hoet + Minne SPRL* [2007] ECR I-8511 para. 45.

49 *von Colson* (n 31) para. 28; *Accept* (n 45) para. 64.

50 *Marshall II* (n 45) para. 30.

51 *Draehmpaehl* (n 45) para. 40.

context. There is of course a difference, as parties in the passing-on context may quarrel over who suffered which portion of the initial harm caused while there would have been no such disagreement among the various claimants referred to by the Court in *Draehmpaehl*. Nonetheless, in the passing-on context, parties at various levels of the supply chain may have suffered decreased sales. It would follow from this statement in *Draehmpaehl* that liability to compensate for such losses must not be limited.

However it is not clear that case law on compensation for a breach of EU non-discrimination law is applicable *mutatis mutandis* to situations where the passing-on problem might occur, e.g., competition law damages. The Court of Justice reached its conclusions in *Draehmpaehl* through a line of reasoning which was explicitly based on the relevant provisions of Directive 76/207/EEC and case law on that Directive. This suggests for *Draehmpaehl* to be read narrowly, as applicable to that Directive only, or at least with great caution with regard to situations outside non-discrimination law. **2.025**

The inclusion of the right to an effective remedy in Article 47(1) of the EU Charter of Fundamental Rights, read in conjunction with its Article 52(3), does by contrast offer an opportunity to find more general guidance. These Articles jointly stipulate that the qualities that will make a remedy effective within the meaning of the EU law right to an effective remedy must be at least those that follow from the ECHR, and more precisely Article 13 ECHR and the case law of the Strasbourg Court in connection with that Article.[52] Under Strasbourg case law 'an individual [who] has an arguable claim to be the victim of a violation of the rights set forth in the Convention ... should have a remedy before a national authority in order both to have his claim decided and, if appropriate, to obtain redress'.[53] The remedy must not necessarily be judicial in order to be effective, but the remedy at issue must be effective both in law and in practice.[54] The more precise qualities of an effective remedy have been assessed by the Strasbourg Court in the individual case and in particular in light of the nature of the right at stake.[55] The Strasbourg Court has ruled for instance that a remedy is not effective unless the order resulting from use of that remedy will also be implemented by the competent authorities,[56] that a remedy is not effective if its purpose has been lost before the remedy can be **2.026**

52 See the Explanations (n 33) 29 and 33.

53 *Silver and others v the United Kingdom* Apps nos 5947/72; 6205/73; 7052/75; 7061/75; 7107/75; 7113/75; 7136/75 (ECtHR 25 March 1983) para. 113.

54 Bernadette Rainey, Elizabeth Wicks and Clare Ovey, *Jacobs, White and Ovey: The European Convention on Human Rights* (6th edn, Oxford University Press 2014) 133 with references to case law.

55 Ibid., 140 (with references).

56 *Iatridis v Greece* App no 31107/96 (ECtHR 25 March 1999) para. 66.

used or becomes enforceable,[57] and that a remedy is not effective if its existence has been kept from potential applicants or if applicants have been kept back from using it.[58] For clarity however it must be stressed that a remedy can be effective within the meaning of Article 13 ECHR notwithstanding that an application can be dismissed for procedural reasons and/or for lack of merit.[59]

2.027 By virtue of Article 52(3) of the EU Charter, protection of the EU law right to an effective remedy must be at least as extensive as that which follows from Strasbourg case law on Article 13 ECHR. In that regard the Explanations to the EU Charter highlight that the European Court of Justice stresses access to judicial review more than the Strasbourg Court does.[60] Where the latter is contented with effective administrative remedies, EU law seems to require court remedies to be available where an alleged infringement of rights conferred on individuals by EU law are at stake. This EU case law on access to court will be examined in section 2.C. Another main difference is that the Strasbourg approach is to allow Contracting States discretion to decide on the particular form of the remedy[61] while the European Court of Justice has on occasion required for specific remedies to be made available.[62] This was discussed in section 2.B. Otherwise the qualitative criteria 'real and effective judicial protection and a deterrent effect' have been reserved by the Court of Justice for the specific sanctions discussed in paragraphs 2.023 and 2.024 above. In other contexts the Court has, to the best of this author's knowledge, instead used the principles of equivalence and effectiveness to enhance the quality of remedies. These principles will be discussed in section 2.D.

III. Equal remedies before national courts

2.028 Returning to *Butter Buying Cruises*, it follows from the second element of the holding quoted in section 2.B.I that there is also a 'right to equal remedies'

57 E.g., *Camenzind v Switzerland* App no 21353/93 (ECtHR 16 December 1997) para. 54, *Messina v Italy (No 2)* App no 25498/94 (ECtHR 28 September 2000) paras 95–97, *Bączkowski and others v Poland* App no 1543/06 (ECtHR 3 May 2007) paras 82–84.

58 *Shamayev and others v Georgia and Russia* App no 36378/02 (ECtHR 12 April 2005) paras 455–466, *Al-Sadoon and Mufdhi v the United Kingdom* App no 61498/08 (ECtHR 2 March 2010) paras 162–166.

59 *Swedish Engine Drivers' Union v Sweden* App no 5614/72 (ECtHR 6 February 1976) para. 50, *Soering v the United Kingdom* App no 14038/88 (ECtHR 7 July 1989) para. 122. Under EU law, procedural rules can also be tested against the principles of equivalence and effectiveness rather than against the right to an effective remedy; see Section 2.D.

60 Explanations (n 33) 33 with references to relevant EU case law.

61 See e.g. *Shamayev* (n 58) para. 446; and *Iovchev v Bulgaria* App no 41211/98 (ECtHR 2 February 2006) para. 142.

62 See e.g. *Factortame I* (n 14, injunction); *Francovich* (n 15, damages from a Member State for a breach of EU law); and *Courage* (n 16, damages for a breach of Art. (now) 101 TFEU).

where the right at issue is protected by an EU law rule with direct effect. It is not quite certain whether this element of *Butter Buying Cruises* should be regarded as an aspect of the EU law principle of equivalence or as an independent right to equal remedies to be distinguished from the former,[63] but such distinctions are arguably of less interest to this inquiry. Suffice it to notice that such a right to equal access to remedies was settled in the Operative part of the judgment in *Butter Buying Cruises* and is still generally acknowledged.[64] It was not touched upon in *Butter Buying Cruises* whether the duty of national courts was to extend all remedies known to the national jurisdiction to claims based on EU law. Plausibly the limitations settled with regard to the principle of equivalence might apply *mutatis mutandis* in this context, so that it would not be required of the national courts to extend any remedies known to their jurisdiction to all claims based on EU law,[65] but only those applying in relevantly similar circumstances. If this interpretation is correct claimants bringing an action based on EU law have a right to equal treatment in access to remedies as compared to claimants bringing a similar action based on national law.[66]

Where the action is brought before a national court or administration EU law thus requires equal remedies to be available for actions based on an EU law provision with direct effect as are available for similar actions based on national law. Finally, where no adequate remedy is available even by virtue of this right to equal treatment, EU law may intervene to require specific remedies to be made available to the claimant – as it did for example in *Pigs and Bacon* and in *Factortame I*.[67] **2.029**

C. ARTICLE 47 OF THE EU CHARTER

With the entry into force of the Lisbon Treaty the EU Charter was awarded the same legal status as the Treaties.[68] The EU law principle of effective **2.030**

63 Stringent application of the three-fold distinction inherited from van Gerven (n 6) would imply the latter (see further Section 2.A with more references). However, the case law does not clearly confirm either this view or the former view.

64 See e.g. Lenaerts, Maselis and Gutman (n 11) 118; Prechal (n 5) 146; and Andersson (n 21) 79. See also *Draehmpaehl* (n 45) para. 26 for what is also arguably an instance of this EU law requirement for equal treatment in remedies.

65 Cf. case C-231/96 *Edilizia Industriale Siderurgica Srl (Edis) v Ministero delle Finanze* [1998] ECR I-4951 para. 36; and joined cases C-279/96, C-280/96 and C-281/96 *Ansaldo Energia SpA v Amministrazione delle Finanze dello Stato, Amministrazione delle Finanze dello Stato v Marine Insurance Consultants Srl* and *GMB Srl and Others v Amministrazione delle Finanze dello Stato* [1998] ECR I-5025 para. 29.

66 Cf. *Edis* (n 65) para. 37; *Ansaldo Energia* (n 65) para. 29.

67 *Pigs and Bacon* (n 44); *Factortame I* (n 14).

68 Art. 6(1) TEU.

judicial protection in a narrow sense, i.e., as developed by the European Court of Justice since *Johnston*,[69] is since then primarily enshrined in Article 47 of the Charter[70] which will apply whenever EU or Member State bodies are implementing EU law.[71] Article 47 encompasses any action based on rights or interests protected by EU law, including actions for compensation and restitution, and is therefore immediately relevant to this inquiry on the passing-on problem in damages and restitution. The Article reads:

2.031 Everyone whose rights and freedoms guaranteed by the law of the Union are violated has the right to an effective remedy before a tribunal in compliance with the conditions laid down in this Article.

> Everyone is entitled to a fair and public hearing within a reasonable time by an independent and impartial tribunal previously established by law. Everyone shall have the possibility of being advised, defended and represented.

> Legal aid shall be made available to those who lack sufficient resources in so far as such aid is necessary to ensure effective access to justice.

2.032 Article 47(1) expresses the right to an effective remedy (based on Article 13 ECHR),[72] and Article 47(2) represents the right to a fair court procedure (corresponding to Article 6(1) ECHR).[73] Article 47(3) concerns legal aid. In the context of passing-on, Gamma claimants may be barred from bringing an action against Alpha by reason of the lack of a direct nexus between Gamma and Alpha.[74] For the purposes of this inquiry the immediately relevant elements of this broad Charter Article are accordingly those governing access to court.

---

69 *Johnston* (n 31). On this case law see Section 2.A.

70 But also notably in Art. 19(1) TEU.

71 Art. 51(1) of the Charter. The debate on whether the scope of 'implementing EU law' was narrower than the scope of EU law as such has been settled in *Åkerberg Fransson* (n 47) para. 21. It is not narrower. The Court clarified in that case that the Charter applies whenever EU law applies.

72 See further Section 2.B.

73 For further details see the Explanations (n 33) 29–30. My choice of the words 'based on' and 'corresponds to', respectively, follows the wording in the Explanations. They reflect a real difference, as Art. 47(1) stays closer to the wording of Art. 13 ECHR than Art. 47(2) does to that of Art. 6(1) ECHR.

74 In this book, Alpha signifies a tortfeasor or enriched party, Beta a party first burdened by loss arising from Alpha's breach of EU law, and Gamma any party downstream from Beta (including all from the party dealing directly with Beta to the final consumer) to whom the burden of that loss may have been passed on; see Section 1.B.

I. Introducing the EU law right of access to court

The EU law right of access to court can be derived from Article 47(1) and 47(2) of the Charter.[75] The European Court of Human Rights in Strasbourg has similarly held that Article 13 ECHR, which requires access to an effective remedy, can in certain cases be 'absorbed by' Article 6(1) ECHR, from which a right of access to court has been derived.[76] Ward has accordingly demonstrated that the European Court of Justice has not made a consistent distinction between the right to an effective remedy and the right to access to a fair court procedure, now embodied in Article 47(1) and 47(2) respectively.[77] Although legal distinctions are generally clarifying, it would under such circumstances be misleading to attempt an artificial distinction between access to court aspects under Article 47(1) and 47(2) of the Charter respectively. Instead the EU law right of access to court will discussed as one specific right following from Article 47 of the Charter. **2.033**

The European Court of Justice has not yet developed any distinct approach to access to court with explicit reference to Article 47 of the Charter (or, alternatively, is still developing its approach under the Charter). The issue of access to court has nonetheless been recognized by the Court of Justice before the Charter gained the same legal value as the Treaties, beginning in *Johnston* where the Court ruled that a principle of effective judicial protection underlies the constitutional traditions common to the Member States and is also laid down in Articles 6(1) and 13 ECHR.[78] This EU case law, albeit preceding the Lisbon Treaty, is relevant for the interpretation of Article 47 of the Charter. Accordingly the following analysis of the right of access to court in Article 47 of the Charter will take into account earlier EU case law on effective judicial protection. Strasbourg case law on the right of access to court under the ECHR will also be used to shed light on the EU law principle. **2.034**

But even with such a broad view of relevant case law on the EU right of access to court only fragments of the implications of the principle are available. This is largely due to the fact that the positive legal meaning of the right has been **2.035**

75 For an extensive presentation of the right of access to court in EU law see Półtorak (n 6) Chs 5 and, in respect of standing and time-limits, 11–12.

76 The 'absorption' holding is found in *Kamasinski v Austria* App no 9783/82 (ECtHR 19 December 1989) para. 110. On the right of access to court pursuant to Art. 6(1) ECHR see further Rainey, Wicks and Ovey (n 54) 257–62.

77 Ward (n 138) 173–8. Cf *Unibet* (n 25) para. 41; case C-199/11 *Europese Gemeenschap v Otis NV and Others* EU:C:2012:684 para. 48. From Strasbourg cf *Stubbings and others v the United Kingdom* Apps nos 22083/93 and 22095/93 (ECtHR, 22 October 1996) paras 50–57; and *Golder v the United Kingdom* App no 4451/70 (ECtHR, 21 February 1975) para. 36. On the right to an effective remedy in general see Section 2.B.

78 *Johnston* (n 31) para. 18; but cf *von Colson* (n 45) para. 23.

developed through negative rulings on what national rules or doctrines are not compatible with the right. Nevertheless an important point of a general nature was addressed by the Court of Justice in *Verholen*,[79] where the Court invoked the principle of effective judicial protection to extend the category of persons that should be granted access to bring a claim relying on Directive 79/7/EEC[80] before the competent national court. It was argued in section 2.A that the applicability of the rights and principles of EU law, e.g., the right of access to court, presuppose the existence of a right or particular interest conferred on the individual claimant by EU law or otherwise protected by EU law. The problem in *Verholen* was to determine the personal scope of the relevant substantive EU law rules. In other words the issue was to identify the class of persons who were in a position to invoke the substantive EU law right at issue, thereby enjoying also the right of access to court. The Court recalled that it was, 'in principle, for national law to determine an individual's standing and legal interest in bringing proceedings'.[81] Having cited case law on the principle of effective judicial protection and the principle of effectiveness however, the Court continued to hold that not only those who came within the *ratione personae* of the Directive would have standing but also individuals who bore 'the effects of a discriminatory national provision regarding [a] spouse, who is not a party to the proceedings, provided that [the] spouse ... comes within the scope of the directive'.[82]

2.036 *Verholen* was ambiguous as to whether it should be read narrowly, i.e., as relevant for claimants relying on Directive 79/7 only (as indicated by the many references made in *Verholen* to that Directive),[83] or whether it could be interpreted broadly.[84] A broad interpretation would suggest that any person who had 'a direct interest' in securing compliance with EU law could rely on the principle of effective judicial protection to secure access to pursue that

79 *Verholen* (n 9).

80 Council Directive 79/7/EEC of 19 December 1978 on the progressive implementation of the principle of equal treatment for men and women in matters of social security [1979] OJ L6/24.

81 *Verholen* (n 9) para. 24. The issue of having a legal interest in bringing proceedings is here distinguished from the issue of standing, but both issues are left within the procedural autonomy of the Member States, subject to the relevant principles of EU law here discussed. Whereas the legal interest in bringing proceedings is not an issue where the claim is for monetary restitution or compensation, it does not constitute a relevant problem in the context of passing-on. For a case where the principle of effective judicial protection became relevant to national law on legal interest in bringing proceedings see case C-174/02 *Streekgewest Westelijk Noord-Brabant v Staatssecretaris van Financiën* [2005] ECR I-85.

82 *Verholen* (n 9) para. 26.

83 E.g., *Verholen* (n 9) Operative part para. 3.

84 Peter Oliver, 'State Liability in Damages following *Factortame III*: A Remedy Seen in Context' in Jack Beatson and Takis Tridimas (eds), *New Directions in European Public Law* (Hart Publishing 1998) 54–6 argued in favour of a far-reaching interpretation of the effect of the principle of effective judicial protection in access to court. Swedish readers see Andersson (n 21) 108–16 and 135–9.

interest before the competent national court.[85] This broader interpretation was subsequently confirmed in *Metallgesellschaft* where two companies resident in the UK had paid advance corporation tax in respect of dividends paid to parent companies resident in Germany. The advance corporation tax was later offset by the subsidiaries against payable mainstream corporation tax. Had the parent companies also been resident in the UK the group would have been able to opt for 'group income election', an alternative tax payment scheme under which no advance sums were payable. The companies took the view that they had suffered competitive disadvantage due to less cash flow following payment of the advance sums, and claimed repayment or damages from the UK. Interestingly the European Court of Justice not only held that the subsidiaries having paid the advance sums had a right to an effective remedy in order to obtain repayment or damages, but also their parent companies.[86] *Metallgesellschaft* thereby confirmed a broader rule of access to court, as previously suggested by a broad interpretation of *Verholen*. This broader interpretation was recently confirmed again in *E.ON* where the Court of Justice explicitly relied on Article 47 of the Charter in order to preclude national legislation that deprived the applicant from the possibility to seek judicial review of a decision taken by a national authority.[87]

The more specific requirements following from Article 47 Charter must be assessed in context. Such assessments will be made in the chapters below. In the carrying out of such assessments a crucial element – paradoxically as it may perhaps seem – is the application of another Charter provision, namely Article 52(1). Unlike the rights included in Title I of the Charter, the right of access to court is not absolute: certain limitations of access to court are warranted by the general interest of judicial effectiveness. The positive meaning of the right of access to court in Article 47 must consequently be explored through its negative impact, i.e., by findings of the Court of Justice on what national limitations of access to court are not compatible with that right.[88] The general standards for limitations of such qualified rights of the Charter are set in Article 52(1).[89] **2.037**

85 Cf. Lenaerts, Maselis and Gutman (n 11) 119.

86 Joined cases C-397/98 and C-410/98 *Metallgesellschaft Ltd and Others* (C-397/98), *Hoechst AG and Hoechst (UK) Ltd* (C-410/98) *v Commissioners of Inland Revenue and HM Attorney General* [2001] ECR I-1727 Operative part para. 2.

87 *E.ON* (n 8) paras 50–51.

88 Even the aforementioned positive finding in *DEB* (n 27) para. 59 is framed in negative terms; that 'it is not impossible for legal persons' to rely on Art. 47 of the Charter.

89 By contrast, in the ECHR the criteria for permissible limitations to qualified rights are included in each Convention Article. As is well known, some of the rights in the ECHR allow for no derogations, e.g., Arts 3 and 4 ECHR. It follows from Art. 52(3) of the EU Charter that corresponding rights in the Charter cannot allow for any derogations not allowed under the ECHR; hence there can be no derogations from Arts 4 and 5 of the Charter notwithstanding the open-ended wording of Art. 52(1).

II. Permissible limitations under Article 52(1) of the Charter

2.038 The operation of scrutinizing EU rules or national rules limiting the right of access to court against the standard specified in Article 52(1) of the Charter will result in a decision on whether they are permissible or non-permissible limitations of the right. It is not intended here to examine the details of this multipartite test,[90] but a few comments are warranted in order to provide some background to the assessments made below. Article 52(1) of the Charter reads:

2.039

> Any limitation on the exercise of the rights and freedoms recognised by this Charter must be provided for by law and respect the essence of those rights and freedoms. Subject to the principle of proportionality, limitations may be made only if they are necessary and genuinely meet objectives of general interest recognised by the Union or the need to protect the rights and freedoms of others.

2.040 The first element of the Article requires for limitations to be 'provided for by law'. The official Explanations to the Charter do not explain this element.[91] In recent EU case law some answers have been provided.[92] In this recent case law, which will be presented shortly, the Court of Justice has interestingly made reference to Strasbourg case law on the same criterion.[93] Articles of the ECHR including a reference to limitations 'prescribed by law' include Articles 9, 10 and 11. In the case law of the Strasbourg Court such limitations do not need to be statutory. Unwritten law will suffice as long as it meets certain criteria. These criteria have been summarized by Rainey, Wicks and Ovey as 'identifiability, accessibility, and foreseeability', the latter two being referred to 'as the "quality of law" requirements'.[94] The criterion of identifiability requires the interference with the Convention right to have some basis in national law. The criterion of accessibility indicates that citizens must be able to have an adequate indication of the legal rules applicable to their case. The final criterion of foreseeability requires norms to be formulated with sufficient precision to enable citizens to foresee the consequences of a given action well enough, if necessary with legal advice, to regulate their conduct in accordance with the norm.[95]

---

90 A detailed analysis was presented by this author in Magnus Strand, *The Passing-On Problem in EU Law Damages and Restitution* (Uppsala University (diss) 2015) 69–82.

91 Explanations (n 33).

92 It has been submitted that earlier EU case law was inconsistent with regard to the meaning of 'provided for by law', see Steve Peers and Sacha Prechal, 'Article 52' in Steve Peers, Tamara Hervey, Jeff Kenner and Angela Ward (eds), *The EU Charter of Fundamental Rights: A Commentary* (Verlag CH Beck/Hart Publishing/Nomos 2014) 1470.

93 Case C-419/14 *WebMindLicenses Kft. v Nemzeti Adó-és Vámhivatal Kiemelt Adó és Vám Főigazgatóság* EU:C:2015:832 para. 81.

94 Rainey, Wicks and Ovey (n 54) 312.

95 Ibid., 310–11. The authors cite *Sunday Times v United Kingdom* App no 6538/74 (ECtHR, 26 April 1976).

With regard to limitations provided for by EU law norms the Court of Justice seemed to take a stringent view in *Knauf Gips*,[96] endorsing only limitations provided for in the Treaties and Protocols or in legislative acts within the meaning of Article 289(3) TFEU.[97] Triantafyllou has argued that, ideally, only legislative acts adopted under the (now) ordinary legislative procedure in Article 289 TFEU should be capable of carrying the democratic legitimacy necessary to be accepted as 'provided for by law'.[98] Peers and Prechal have argued against this view, submitting that in various EU law contexts this would not be feasible.[99] Recent case law developments seem to support the latter view. As observed by Lenaerts it follows from *Volker und Markus Schecke*[100] that the criterion is met if the limitation is based on a Commission Regulation.[101] It therefore seems that it may be sufficient to meet the criterion of 'provided for by law' if the legal provision upon which the limitation is based appears in a delegated act.[102] Whether general principles of EU law are 'provided for by law' is open to discussion.[103] Peers and Prechal have added that the assessment of whether the interference with a fundamental right has been provided for by law should also take into account the character and gravity of the interference with the right.[104] **2.041**

With regard to limitations in national law it has been suggested by Triantafyllou that 'by law' should be interpreted as meaning by statute passed by the **2.042**

96 Case C-407/08 P *Knauf Gips KG v European Commission* [2010] ECR I-6375 paras 89–91.

97 That legislative acts are 'provided for by law' within the meaning of Art. 52(1) of the Charter has been confirmed in case C-157/14 *Neptune Distribution SNC v Ministre de l'Économie et des Finances* EU:C:2015:823 para. 69; case C-601/15 PPU *J N v Staatssecretaris van Veiligheid en Justitie* EU:C:2016:84 para. 51 (mentioning explicitly that the rule at issue was provided for in a legislative act); case C-547/14 *Philip Morris Brands SARL and Others v Secretary of State for Health* EU:C:2016:325 para. 150 (referring to "a provision adopted by the EU legislature"); and case C-477/14 *Pillbox 38 (UK) Ltd, trading as Totally Wicked v Secretary of State for Health* EU:C:2016:324 para. 161.

98 Dimitris Triantafyllou, 'The European Charter of Fundamental Rights and the "Rule of Law": Restricting Fundamental Rights by Reference' (2002) 39 *Common Market Law Review* 53, 61.

99 Peers and Prechal (n 92) 1471–2.

100 Joined cases C-92/09 and C-93/09 *Volker und Markus Schecke GbR* (C-92/09) and *Hartmut Eifert* (C-93/09) *v Land Hessen* [2010] ECR I-11063.

101 Lenaerts (n 20) 390 writes 'Council Regulation', but quotes the Court (*Volker und Markus Schecke* (n 100) para. 66) referring to Commission Regulation (EC) No 259/2008 of 18 March 2008 laying down detailed rules for the application of Council Regulation (EC) No 1290/2005 as regards the publication of information on the beneficiaries of funds deriving from the European Agricultural Guarantee Fund (EAGF) and the European Agricultural Fund for Rural Development (EAFRD) [2008] OJ L76/28. The correct observation is therefore that a Commission Regulation will suffice.

102 I.e., a non-legislative act of general application within the meaning of Art. 290 TFEU.

103 Support for an argument that general principles are provided for by law within the meaning of Art. 52(1) of the Charter can be found in *Knauf Gips* (n 96) para. 89, where the Court of Justice referred only to the lack of a rule 'under the law of the European Union'. General principles do follow from the law of the European Union.

104 Peers and Prechal (n 92) 1472–1473, quoting case C-355/10 *European Parliament v Council of the European Union* EU:C:2012:516 para. 77. A similar flexibility seems to be available under Strasbourg case law; Rainey, Wicks and Ovey (n 54) 311–12.

national parliament.[105] By contrast Lebeck has argued that 'by law' should be read in light of Strasbourg case law with a view to maintain the latitude enjoyed by Member States with regard to the constitutional form of legal rules implementing EU law.[106] Similarly it has been submitted by Peers and Prechal that an approach close to that chosen by the Strasbourg Court should be adopted for the purposes of the Charter in order to avoid the existence of parallel but different fundamental rights standards within and outside the scope of the Charter from vexing the legislative efforts of the Member States.[107] The Court of Justice has now clarified that the legal basis of national limitations of fundamental rights must be 'sufficiently clear and precise' and must afford 'a measure of legal protection against any arbitrary interferences' by 'defining by itself the scope of the limitation on the exercise of the right guaranteed'.[108] This test, which is interestingly focused on the qualities of the provision at issue rather than its legal character as such, seems to echo the Strasbourg case law summarized in paragraph 2.040, and the Court of Justice did indeed cite Strasbourg case law in support of its holding. In respect of limitations in national law intended to implement EU law, perhaps a more complex matter, Peers and Prechal argue for a context-based approach taking into account 'the subject-matter of the measure concerned, and in particular the degree of harmonization or uniformity which the EU legislature seeks to achieve', but do also submit that it is a 'joint and several responsibility' of the EU and the Member State to satisfy the requirements of the Charter.[109] EU case law is scarce, limited to the knowledge of this author to two cases. In *Liivimaa Lihaveis* the Court of Justice unsurprisingly held that instructions in a programme manual drawn up by a national agency were not provided for by law and could not limit fundamental rights.[110] In *Léger*, by contrast, a rule in a ministerial decree implementing an EU Directive was regarded as being provided for by law within the meaning of Article 52(1) of the Charter.[111] *Léger* arguably also supports the broader view of what types of national rules, more generally, can be 'provided for by law' that has been advocated by Lebeck and by Peers and Prechal.

---

105 Triantafyllou (n 98) 59. That statutory national law meets the criterion of being 'provided for by law' has been confirmed in case C-650/13 *Thierry Delvigne v Commune de Lesparre-Médoc and Préfet de la Gironde* EU:C:2015:648 para. 47.

106 Carl Lebeck, *EU-stadgan om grundläggande rättigheter* (Studentlitteratur 2013) 68.

107 Peers and Prechal (n 92) 1471.

108 *WebMindLicenses* (n 93) para. 81.

109 Peers and Prechal (n 92) 1473.

110 Case C-562/12 *Liivimaa Lihaveis MTÜ v Eesti-Läti programmi 2007–2013 Seirekomitee* EU:C:2014:2229 paras 72–74.

111 Case C-528/13 *Geoffrey Léger v Ministre des Affaires sociales, de la Santé et des Droits des femmes and Etablissement français du sang* EU:C:2015:288 para. 53.

The second element of Article 52(1) requires that any limitation must 'respect the essence of the right', here the essence of the right of access to court. This second element has been recognized by the Court of Justice in pre-Lisbon case law.[112] In Strasbourg case law, which is abundant, the very essence of the right of access to court is impaired where the applicant has not had 'even a theoretical opportunity to be heard', or 'has had a theoretical opportunity but had no practical opportunity due to the application of a particularly stringent rule'.[113] In *Cavanilles* for example the Strasbourg Court struck down a time-limit for impairing the very essence of the right of access to court.[114] The applicant was engaged in a dispute with one of her neighbours and wished to lodge a so-called *reposición* application with the competent court, in essence appealing a specific decision of that court in the course of proceedings. Such an application was however due in the competent court within three days of service of the decision to be appealed. The applicant, who lived some 400 kilometres from the seat of the competent court, tried to comply with the time-limit but failed. Consequently her appeal to the next court of instance, the *Audiencia Provincial*, was barred. The Strasbourg Court held that under the circumstances the particularly strict application of the procedural rule at issue deprived the applicant of her right of access to court.[115] Pursuant to Article 52(3) of the Charter the right of access to court enshrined in Article 47 should be no less protected. The case law of the Court of Justice indicates that the essence of a right is respected as long as the scope of the limitation at issue is adequately restricted.[116] This was perhaps stretched rather far in *Delvigne* where the Court held that a limitation of the right to vote, excluding certain persons convicted of serious criminal offences from the right to vote, respected the essence of that right if it applied 'under specific conditions and on account of their conduct' and only as long as those conditions were fulfilled.[117] **2.043**

The third element of Article 52(1) is a proportionality test, which in turn consists of a necessity test, a test to assess whether the limitation is genuinely **2.044**

112 E.g., in case 44/79 *Liselotte Hauer v Land Rheinland-Pfalz* [1979] ECR 3727 paras 23 and 30; case C-293/97 *The Queen v Secretary of State for the Environment and Ministry of Agriculture, Fisheries and Food, ex parte HA Standley and Others and DGD Metson and Others* [1999] ECR I-2603 paras 54 and 56; joined cases C-20/00 and C-64/00 *Booker Aquacultur Ltd* (C-20/00) and *Hydro Seafood GSP Ltd* (C-64/00) *v The Scottish Ministers* [2003] ECR I-7411 paras 88–93. See further Peers and Prechal (n 92) 1480.

113 Shirley Shipman, 'Compulsory Mediation: The Elephant in the Room' (2011) 30 *Civil Justice Quarterly* 163, 177–178. See e.g. *Winterwerp v the Netherlands* App no 6301/73 (ECtHR, 24 October 1979); *Philis v Greece* Apps nos 12750/87, 13780/88, and 14003/88 (ECtHR, 27 August 1991); and *Stubbings and others v the United Kingdom* Apps nos 22083/93 and 22095/93 (ECtHR, 22 October 1996).

114 *Perez de Rada Cavanilles v Spain* App No 28090/95 (ECtHR, 28 October 1998).

115 Ibid., para. 49.

116 See in recent case law *Léger* (n 111) para. 54; *Neptune Distribution* (n 97) paras 70–71; *J N* (n 97) para. 52; *Philip Morris* (n 97) para. 151; and *Pillbox 38* (n 97) para. 161.

117 *Delvigne* (n 105) para. 48.

suitable to meet either (a) objectives of general interest of the EU or (b) the need to protect the rights and freedoms of others, and a proportionality test *sensu stricto*. The European Court of Justice does not however always distinguish these elements very clearly.[118] For instance the proportionality test is repeatedly summarized as an assessment of whether the limitation of the right at issue was 'appropriate and necessary in order to attain the objectives legitimately pursued'.[119] Nevertheless these elements will be distinguished for this presentation, and it is submitted that they should be distinguished in the interest of improving the clarity and transparency of the proportionality assessment.

2.045 The necessity test prohibits measures entailing a limitation of rights that go beyond what is necessary for achieving the aim pursued through those measures. On closer examination, this assessment is not uniform. It is often carried out by searching for an alternative measure which would be less restrictive than the measure chosen.[120] Another way of approaching the same problem is to examine whether the measure chosen has undesired side effects. The pattern emerging from the case law is that measures that are categorical and generalized, failing to take into consideration the particularities of the individual case, or are liable to have an adverse impact on the rights of individuals over and above the limitations explicitly intended, may be disproportionate within the meaning of the necessity test.[121] The case law also suggests that the necessity test should be applied more or less stringently depending on the importance of the fundamental right concerned.[122]

2.046 The assessment of suitability (or appropriateness) entails an assessment of whether the limitation of a right protected by the Charter is genuinely suitable to meet its alleged aim. The Court will strike down limitations where it considers that the alleged aim is not the real aim of the contested measure, or where the defendant institution or agency has not been able to establish that the limiting measure is capable of attaining the alleged aim.[123] It is further presupposed that (a) an objective of general interest of the EU or (b) a need to

---

118 See e.g. the very brief assessments in *Delvigne* (n 105) para. 49 and in *Pillbox 38* (n 97) para. 162.

119 See e.g. *Léger* (n 111) para. 58; and *J N* (n 97) para. 54.

120 See e.g. *Léger* (n 111) para. 59 where the Court held that the principle of proportionality was 'respected only where [the aim pursued] cannot be ensured by [means] that are less onerous'. See also Takis Tridimas, *The General Principles of EU Law* (2nd edn, Oxford EC Law Library, Oxford University Press 2006) 139; and Paul Craig, *EU Administrative Law* (2nd edn, Oxford University Press 2012) 591.

121 See e.g. *Scarlet Extended* (n 128) paras 47–48; and *ASNEF* (n 128) para. 48, and case C-291/12 *Michael Schwarz v Stadt Bochum* EU:C:2013:670 para. 46. See also *Volker und Markus Schecke* (n 100) paras 76–89.

122 Cf. *J N* (n 97) para. 56.

123 With regard to both see case C-390/12 *Proceedings brought by Robert Pfleger and Others* EU:C:2014:281 paras 48–56.

protect the rights and freedoms of others has first been identified as the underlying reason for the limitation under review. Beginning with (a), objectives of general interest, the Explanations lists 'the objectives mentioned in Article 3 [TEU] … and other interests protected by specific provisions of the Treaties', and offers a non-exhaustive list for guidance. As noted by Peers and Prechal this list of grounds is 'extremely broad' and even 'potentially limitless' and encompasses interests both of the EU and of the Member States.[124] Legitimate aims identified in recent case law include the protection of national security and public order,[125] protection of human health,[126] and consumer protection.[127] As regards (b), the protection of rights and freedoms of others, the Court of Justice has consistently held that a fair balance must be struck in conflicts between rights protected by EU law.[128] The case law suggests that any right conferred on an individual should be protected in this sense, i.e., not only a fundamental right or freedom but also internal market freedoms and other rights and interests recognized by EU law.[129]

Finally there is 'proportionality *sensu stricto*', the final balancing of the aims **2.047** pursued by a contested measure against the limitations of rights caused by it. Craig has observed that there is some discussion on whether this element forms part of EU law proportionality at all, or whether the tests of suitability and of necessity are exhaustive.[130] Craig has nonetheless presented evidence of an independent proportionality *sensu stricto* test in the case law submitting that this final test is relevant where a contested measure may have passed the suitability and necessity tests 'but the applicant argues that the burden placed on it by the measure should nonetheless be regarded as disproportionate to the benefits secured'.[131]

---

124 Peers and Prechal (n 92) 1475–6. See also Lenaerts (n 20) 391. Strasbourg case law, similarly, has been described by Shipman (n 113) 184 as containing 'little or no analysis of the underlying reasons or needs' for the aims invoked. Shipman concluded that focus was instead on examining the proportionality of the measure taken to pursue the aim.

125 *J N* (n 97) para. 53.

126 *Léger* (n 111) para. 55; *Neptune Distribution* (n 97) para. 72; and *Philip Morris* (n 97) para. 152.

127 *Neptune Distribution* (n 97) para. 72.

128 E.g., in case C-275/06 *Productores de Música de España (Promusicae) v Telefónica de España SAU* [2008] ECR I-271 para. 68; and case C-70/10 *Scarlet Extended SA v Société belge des auteurs, compositeurs et éditeurs SCRL (SABAM)* [2011] ECR I-11959 paras 45–46.

129 Lenaerts (n 20) 392. For examples of balancing against other rights than fundamental rights see e.g. case C-271/08 *European Commission v Federal Republic of Germany* [2010] ECR I-7091 para. 52; or joined cases C-468/10 and C-469/10 *Asociación Nacional de Establecimientos Financieros de Crédito (ASNEF)* (C-468/10) and *Federación de Comercio Electrónico y Marketing Directo (FECEMD)* (C-469/10) *v Administración del Estado* [2011] ECR I-12181 paras 43–49. Peers and Prechal (n 92) 1477 criticize the latter case as, in their view, the relevant right is not properly identified by the Court.

130 Craig (n 120) 591–2. Nicholas Emiliou, *The Principle of Proportionality in European Law: A Comparative Study* (Kluwer Law International 1996) 193 seems to use the term 'proportionality *sensu stricto*' to signify the assessment of whether a limitation infringes the essence of a right.

131 Craig (n 120) 602.

2.048 The intensity of review varies depending on a number of factors, which it is not intended here to list exhaustively (if that is possible). The Court of Justice generally tends to apply proportionality tests more leniently where the EU legislature exercises a certain discretionary power involving economic policy choices[132] and more stringently in review of national measures liable to restrict fundamental freedoms protected by the Treaties.[133] In *Digital Rights Ireland* the Court of Justice was called upon to interpret the proportionality test in Article 52(1) for the purposes of limitations to the right to protection of personal data in Article 8 of the Charter. The Court held:

2.049

> … where interferences with fundamental rights are at issue, the extent of the EU legislature's discretion may prove to be limited, depending on a number of factors, including, in particular, the area concerned, the nature of the right at issue guaranteed by the Charter, the nature and seriousness of the interference and the object pursued by the interference … .[134]

2.050 The Court of Justice thus recognized that the discretion of the EU legislature may be limited but was open to the possibility of more lenient review.[135] In *Philip Morris* a balance had been struck between the freedom to conduct a business and the general interest of protection for human health. The Court held that 'the discretion enjoyed by the EU legislature, in determining the balance to be struck, varies for each of the goals justifying restrictions on that freedom and depends on the nature of the activities in question'.[136] It follows that the scope of discretion, and consequently the intensity of review, is difficult – if at all possible – to pinpoint in the abstract. It rather seems that the proportionality test to be applied under Article 52(1) of the Charter to limitations of access to court should be a flexible and context-based assessment.[137]

2.051 It is consequently still rather unclear how precisely to apply the test in Article 52(1) of the Charter to limitations of the right of access to court. It is nonetheless submitted that the inclusion of the right of access to court in

---

132 See e.g. *Neptune Distribution* (n 97) para. 76.

133 Tridimas (n 120) 209 but see also 146 on EU measures not involving policy measures.

134 Joined cases C-293/12 and C-594/12 *Digital Rights Ireland Ltd* (C-293/12) *v Minister for Communications, Marine and Natural Resources and Others and Kärntner Landesregierung* (C-594/12) *and Others* EU:C:2014:238 para. 47.

135 For an example of lenient proportionality review under Art. 52(1) of the Charter see case C-101/12 *Herbert Schaible v Land Baden-Württemberg* EU:C:2013:661 paras 47–49.

136 *Philip Morris* (n 97) para. 155.

137 This would reflect the flexibility of Strasbourg case law well; see e.g. *The National & Provincial Building Society, the Leeds Permanent Building Society and the Yorkshire Building Society v the United Kingdom* Apps nos 21319/93, 21449/93, and 21675/93 (ECtHR, 23 October 1997) paras 112–113, and *Stran Greek Refineries and Stratis Andreadis v Greece*, App no 13427/87 (ECtHR, 9 December 1994) paras 49–50.

Article 47 and the introduction of the Article 52(1) test must be seen as advances in the protection of the right of access to court. The elements of the Article 52(1) test must be taken seriously and must accordingly be met for a limitation of the right of access to court to be permissible. It will be interesting to follow EU case law on the new test and access to court.

D. THE PRINCIPLES OF EQUIVALENCE AND EFFECTIVENESS

The EU law principles of equivalence and effectiveness have been developed as a dual test for the framework of national rules and conditions within which actions based on EU law are brought before national courts.[138] As mentioned this inquiry focuses on three problems that arise in connection with the passing-on problem. One of these – access to court – is generally held to be a procedural law issue, while the other two are commonly seen as belonging to substantive law – namely, substantive proximity (e.g., causation in damages) and the estimation of awards. Do the principles of equivalence and effectiveness apply only to the first of these, or to all? This preliminary question needs to be answered for the purposes of this book. A few remarks on the scope of application of the principles are therefore offered in this section before proceeding to an analysis of the principles as such. The European Court of Justice has consistently invoked these principles together, as complements to each other. In the absence of any indication to the contrary this consistency will here be accepted as evidence that the two principles have the same scope of application.[139] **2.052**

I. Scope of application of the principles of equivalence and effectiveness

As private enforcement of EU law before national courts grew pursuant to case law such as *van Gend en Loos*,[140] *Costa v ENEL*[141] and *van Duyn*,[142] the Court of Justice was confronted with the problem of balancing rights conferred on **2.053**

138 Writing on the principles includes Anthony Arnull, *The European Union and its Court of Justice* (2nd edn, Oxford EC Law Library, Oxford University Press 2006) Ch. 9; Michael Dougan, *National Remedies before the Court of Justice: Issues of Harmonisation and Differentiation* (Modern Studies in European Law, Hart Publishing 2004) Ch. 5; Engström (n 22); Tridimas, (n 120) Ch. 9; and Angela Ward, *Judicial Review and the Rights of Private Parties in EU Law* (2nd edn, Oxford University Press 2007) Ch. 4.

139 However, a very particular use of the principle of effectiveness in cases where its application borders on circumstances of fact rather than law – a problem that could not arise with regard to the principle of equivalence – will be discussed at the end of this section.

140 Case 26/62 *NV Algemene Transport en Expeditie Onderneming van Gend & Loos v Netherlands Inland Revenue Administration* [1963] ECR 1.

141 Case 6/64 *Flaminio Costa v ENEL* [1964] ECR 585.

142 Case 41/74 *Yvonne van Duyn v Home Office* [1974] ECR 1337.

individuals by EU law with national rules and conditions governing actions for the enforcement of those rights. In *Rewe* and *Comet*, delivered simultaneously, the Court held that national courts were required to protect the rights conferred on individuals by EU law and specified:

2.054 Applying the principle of sincere cooperation laid down in Article 5 of the Treaty,[143] it is the national courts which are entrusted with ensuring the legal protection which citizens derive from the direct effect of the provisions of Community law.

> Accordingly, in the absence of Community rules on this subject, it is for the domestic legal system of each Member State to designate the courts having jurisdiction and to determine the procedural conditions governing actions at law intended to ensure the protection of the rights which citizens have from the direct effect of Community law, it being understood that such conditions cannot be less favourable than those relating to similar actions of a domestic nature.
>
> … In the absence of such measures of harmonization the right conferred by Community law must be exercised before the national courts in accordance with the conditions laid down by national rules.
>
> The position would be different only if the conditions and time-limits made it impossible in practice to exercise the rights which the national courts are obliged to protect.[144]

2.055 The wording of the judgment illustrates that the Court of Justice was prepared to rely on and give mandate to the national courts to protect EU law rights in the framework of national actions brought before them. To that end such actions were to be governed by national procedural conditions, albeit (as the Court twice emphasizes) only in the absence of EU rules harmonizing the applicable procedural conditions. This national procedural autonomy is sometimes referred to as a principle of national procedural autonomy to which the principles of equivalence and effectiveness stand in a relation of suspended tension.[145] The EU law principle of national procedural autonomy has been explicitly acknowledged by the Court of Justice in more recent case law.[146]

---

143 Now Art. 4(3) TFEU.

144 *Rewe* (n 30) para. 5. Cf *Comet* (n 30) paras 12–16.

145 Cf. e.g. Arnull (n 138) 268–78 with references.

146 The Court of Justice mentioned the procedural autonomy of the Member States for the first time in case C-201/02 *The Queen, on the application of Delena Wells v Secretary of State for Transport, Local Government and the Regions* [2004] ECR I-723 paras 67 and 70 and Operative part para. 3. Other examples include case C-232/05 *Commission of the European Communities v French Republic* [2006] ECR I-10071, in the keywords; joined cases C-378/07 to C-380/07 *Kiriaki Angelidaki and Others v Organismos Nomarchiakis Autodioikisis Rethymnis and Others* [2009] ECR I-3071 paras 159, 174 and 176; and case C-550/07 P *Akzo Nobel Chemicals Ltd and Akcros Chemicals Ltd v European Commission* [2010] ECR I-8301 paras 113 and 120.

It also follows from *Rewe* that national procedural autonomy is subject to the dual test of equivalence and effectiveness. But do they apply only to *procedural* conditions? And, if so, should the legal character of national rules – i.e., whether they are procedural or other – be determined by national law or by EU law? **2.056**

It falls outside the scope of this book to present any extensive survey of the case law aiming to answer those questions.[147] Suffice it to say that the Court of Justice has not been consistent on the phrasing of the scope of application of the principles in its case law. Ward has consequently submitted that the case law is so open-ended that it becomes difficult to delineate the scope of application of the principles.[148] It would certainly add clarity if the scope of application of the EU law principles of equivalence and effectiveness was to be phrased consistently by the European Court of Justice. Lenaerts, Marselis and Gutman argue that the case law includes 'several expressions of the principle of effectiveness which are intertwined'. Within an overall 'principle of effectiveness' concept, they distinguish: (1) the principle of effective judicial protection (now Article 47 of the EU Charter); (2) full effectiveness of EU law as a corollary to its primacy; and (3) the principle of effectiveness as the dual test of equivalence and effectiveness with which national law on procedure and sanctions must comply.[149] The discussion in this section is preoccupied with the third expression, which Lenaerts et al name 'the principle of effectiveness *sensu stricto*'. The principles of equivalence and effectiveness would thus, in the view of Lenaerts et al, apply to 'national law relating to procedure and sanctions'.[150] Such a view of the scope of the principles does seem compatible with the case law, if 'law relating to sanctions' is understood in a broad sense, encompassing not only penal sanctions (as discussed in paragraph 2.023) but any national conditions circumscribing the availability and exercise of sanctions and any kind of sanctions (e.g., administrative or private law sanctions). **2.057**

For the purposes of this book suffice it accordingly to endorse that the principles apply to sanctions, including the private enforcement sanctions sought through the actions for damages or restitution concerned here and notwithstanding whether elements of such private enforcement sanctions are perceived as substantive law elements in the national jurisdiction at issue. If **2.058**

147 For such a survey see my doctoral thesis *The Passing-On Problem in EU Law Damages and Restitution* (Uppsala University (diss) 2015) 49–56.

148 Ward (n 138) 193 and 197. Notice however that Ward refers to the principle of *effet utile*, which she does not distinguish from the principle of effectiveness as here discussed. This author would argue that the two should be carefully distinguished, and if Ward had distinguished them, she might have taken a different view.

149 Lenaerts, Maselis and Gutman (n 11) 110. For an analysis of the interrelationship between the principle of effectiveness (in the 'strict' sense) and the principle of effective judicial protection, see Section 2.A.

150 Ibid., 109.

this does not follow clearly from the abstract analysis above, it nevertheless follows from the fact that the Court of Justice has interpreted them in the context of estimation of damages in actions for damages from a Member State,[151] and in actions for damages for a breach of EU competition law.[152] That context qualifies as a substantive law context in e.g. Sweden.

2.059 Before leaving the subject of the scope of the principles of equivalence and effectiveness, it will be mentioned that there are two cases in which the principle of effectiveness has been used in a way that borders on application to factual circumstances. The general problem – which cannot arise on application of the principle of equivalence – is whether EU law requires special measures to be taken by the national court in order to overcome a hindrance to the exercise of rights conferred on individuals by EU law, where that hindrance originates from circumstances of fact rendering the common national law action for the enforcement of those rights ineffective. The Court of Justice opted for a very pragmatic approach to this problem in *Reemtsma* and *Danfoss*,[153] where it was suggested by the Court that the principle of effectiveness would apply also where circumstances like the insolvency of a third party would make it virtually impossible or excessively difficult to exercise rights conferred on individuals by EU law.[154]

2.060 *Reemtsma* and *Danfoss* can be interpreted as implying that the Court of Justice has now extended the scope of application of the principle of effectiveness beyond 'national law relating to procedure and sanctions'.[155] Expanding the field of application of the principle of effectiveness in this way arguably blurs the borders between legal rules and factual circumstances.[156] It seems however

151 See joined cases C-46/93 and C-48/93 *Brasserie du Pêcheur SA v Bundesrepublik Deutschland* and *The Queen v Secretary of State for Transport, ex parte: Factortame Ltd and others* [1996] ECR I-1029 Operative part para. 4 (principles of equivalence and effectiveness).

152 See joined cases C-295/04 to 298/04 *Vincenzo Manfredi v Lloyd Adriatico Assicurazioni SpA* (C-295/04), *Antonio Cannito v Fondiaria Sai SpA* (C-296/04) and *Nicolò Tricarico* (C-297/04) and *Pasqualina Murgolo* (C-298/04) *v Assitalia SpA* [2006] ECR I-6619 Operative part para. 5 (principles of equivalence and effectiveness).

153 Case C-35/05 *Reemtsma Cigarettenfabriken GmbH v Ministero delle Finanze* [2007] ECR I-2425; case C-94/10 *Danfoss A/S and Sauer-Danfoss ApS v Skatteministeriet* [2011] ECR I-9963.

154 *Danfoss* (n 153) para. 28.

155 Lenaerts, Maselis and Gutman (n 11).

156 The example of insolvency, provided by the Court itself, opens a new space where factual circumstances liable to impede the enforcement of rights conferred on individuals by EU law may create a duty for national courts to find new forms of action where there would otherwise be none; cf. also case C-191/12 *Alakor Gabonatermelő és Forgalmazó Kft v Nemzeti Adó- és Vámhivatal Észak-alföldi Regionális Adó Főigazgatósága* EU:C:2013:315 paras 22–35, where the reasoning of the Court, which is based on the principle of effectiveness, is very clearly focused on the consequences in fact of its ruling. The Court could alternatively have used an *effet utile* line of reasoning, as it did in cases like *Factortame I* (n 14) para. 22, *Francovich* (n 15) para. 34 and *Courage* (n 16) para. 26, thereby staying consistent with its tradition of using such reasoning when introducing new and important judicial constructs.

from the facts and reasoning in *Reemtsma* and *Danfoss* that this new field of application of the principle of effectiveness has its limits: the innovation is designed to allow actions against those who have breached EU law (as in *Danfoss*) or have benefitted from such a breach (as in *Reemtsma*) under circumstances where it is virtually impossible or excessively difficult for the individual who bears the financial burden of the breach to remedy the loss through the common course of action. Only then must the national court find an alternative judicial route that can be opened – which is still a significant expansion of the scope of application of the EU principle of effectiveness.

II. The principle of equivalence

According to the EU law principle of equivalence national rules and conditions governing actions based on EU law must not be less favourable than those governing similar domestic actions. From its humble beginnings in *Rewe* and *Comet* it took some time for the Court of Justice to develop this principle of equivalence. Finally, in 1998, the Court seized some opportunities to provide further guidance on its application. It is of particular interest here to notice that some of the cases delivered in 1998, notably *Edis* and *Ansaldo Energia*, revolved around the repayment of charges levied in breach of EU law. **2.061**

The Court of Justice had held in a line of cases that time-limits, barring claims for the repayment of charges levied in breach of EU law, were not themselves incompatible with EU law unless they infringed the principles of equivalence and/or effectiveness.[157] In *Edis* and *Ansaldo Energia* the Court examined Italian law under which repayment claims between private individuals were treated more favourably than repayment claims against the State. The Court importantly accepted such a distinction and ruled that the principle of equivalence did not require for the procedural rules applicable in litigation between private individuals to be extended to claims against the State even if based on EU law. The Court also importantly ruled that the principle of equivalence does not require Member States to extend their most favourable procedural rules to all actions based on EU law.[158] However, the Court added, Member States must not give adverse treatment to actions for repayment of unlawfully levied charges based on EU law compared to actions for repayment **2.062**

157 E.g., case C-90/94 *Haahr Petroleum Ltd v Åbenrå Havn, Ålborg Havn, Horsens Havn, Kastrup Havn NKE A/S, Næstved Havn, Odense Havn, Struer Havn and Vejle Havn, and Trafikministeriet* [1997] ECR I-4085; and case C-188/95 *Fantask A/S ea v Industriministeriet (Erhvervministeriet)* [1997] ECR I-6783.

158 *Edis* (n 65) para. 36; *Ansaldo Energia* (n 65) para. 29. In case C-69/14 *Dragoş Constantin Târşia v Statul român, Serviciul public comunitar regim permise de conducere şi înmatriculare a autovehiculelor* EU:C:2015:662 para. 34 the Court accordingly held that the principle of equivalence did not require 'equivalence of national procedural rules applicable to different types of proceedings such as – as in the dispute in the main proceedings – civil proceedings on the one hand and administrative proceedings on the other'.

of unlawfully levied charges based on national law.[159] Therefore, the relevant *comparator* when applying the principle of equivalence was not procedural rules applicable to any unspecified restitutionary actions, but those applicable to restitutionary actions against the state. This was confirmed in *Weber's Wine World* where the principle of equivalence was held to preclude national procedural rules that treated restitutionary actions more preferably if they were based on a declaratory judgment by a national court holding that the contested payment was unconstitutional, than if they were based on a judgment of the Court of Justice holding that the payment was contrary to EU law.[160]

2.063 The first step of this analysis will be to find a relevant national action for the comparison, a so-called *comparator*. Where, as in *Edis* and *Ansaldo Energia*, there is an easily identifiable domestic action this will be quite straightforward. In respect of claims for repayment of charges levied in breach of EU law, 'similar domestic actions' will thus mean domestic actions brought against the state for the repayment of sums. If there are no such similar actions under national law however, the principle of equivalence will most probably be of little use (but perhaps the right to an effective remedy and/or the principle of effectiveness will be). There is also a third possibility: in respect of claims for damages for a breach of EU competition law, 'similar domestic actions' will mean domestic actions for damages. Obviously there may be several such actions. It is of course also possible that the identification of a similar domestic action is difficult because the eligible domestic actions overlap or because there is some uncertainty on what domestic actions might apply. Under such circumstances the choice of *comparator* action may be more delicate.

2.064 In *Levez* the Court stressed that it was for the national court to ascertain whether domestic procedural rules intended to safeguard the rights derived by individuals from EU law comply with the principle of equivalence,[161] but continued to provide some further guidance on what was to be understood as 'similar actions'. The Court held that the national rule at issue (in *Levez* the 'rule at issue' was a contested time bar) must be applied without distinction to actions based on national law and EU law where the purpose, cause of action, and essential characteristics of the respective actions were similar.[162]

---

159 *Edis* (n 65) para. 37; *Ansaldo Energia* (n 65) para. 29.

160 Case C-147/01 *Weber's Wine World Handels-GmbH and others v Abgabenberufungskommission Wien* [2003] ECR I-11365 para. 107.

161 Case C-326/96 *BS Levez v TH Jennings (Harlow Pools) Ltd* [1998] ECR I-7835 para. 39.

162 *Levez* (n 161) paras 41 and 43.

In *Transportes Urbanos*[163] the Court of Justice gave quite detailed and systematic directions to the national court on how to compare the purpose and essential characteristics of the respective actions in order to ascertain whether they were 'similar'. Comparing a specific national action to the action based on EU law that had been brought before the national court, the Court held that the purposes of the actions were identical, namely to be compensated for harm caused by the state.[164] The Court then examined the essential characteristics of the respective actions, concluding that the only relevant difference between them was that one was based on a judgment by the Court of Justice while the other was based on a judgment by the national constitutional court.[165] Such a distinction, the Court held, could not 'suffice to establish a distinction between those two actions in the light of the principle of equivalence'.[166] It followed that the national limitation at issue in *Transportes Urbanos* was precluded from application by the principle of equivalence.[167] **2.065**

The second stage in the equivalence assessment described by the Court of Justice in *Levez* was to examine whether the application of a specific national rule to actions based on EU law (which, it was implied, did not apply to the *comparator* action) was liable to make it less favourable to pursue such an action rather than the *comparator* action. In this second stage it was necessary to take into account the role played by that provision in the procedure as a whole, as well as the operation and any special features of that procedure before the different national courts.[168] In implementing these findings the Court of Justice advised the national court to examine whether a claimant, compelled to bring an action relying on a right conferred by EU law before the County Court, was liable e.g. to incur additional costs and delay compared to a claimant bringing a similar action based on domestic law before the Industrial Tribunal.[169] If so, the Court of Justice held, the application of such less favourable rules would be contrary to the principle of equivalence.[170] In *Preston*, it was further clarified that this examination 'may not be carried out subjectively by reference to circumstances of fact but must involve an objective comparison, in the abstract, of the procedural rules at issue'.[171] In *Transportes* **2.066**

163 Case C-118/08 *Transportes Urbanos y Servicios Generales SAL v Administración del Estado* [2010] ECR I-635.

164 Ibid., paras 35–36. The Court of Justice did not, however, consider the 'cause of action' element in earlier case law.

165 Ibid., paras 37–43.

166 Ibid., para. 44. This holding arguably pushes even further than to finding that the two actions are 'similar', which is the requirement of the principle of equivalence.

167 Ibid., Operative part.

168 *Levez* (n 161) para. 44.

169 Ibid., para. 51.

170 Ibid., Operative part para. 2.

171 Case C-78/98 *Shirley Preston and Others v Wolverhampton Healthcare NHS Trust and Others* and *Dorothy Fletcher and Others v Midland Bank plc* [2000] ECR I-3201 para. 62.

Urbanos a condition of prior exhaustion of remedies was applicable to the action based on EU law, but not to the *comparator* action. The Court did not seem to find it necessary to engage in a detailed analysis in the second stage of the equivalence assessment described in *Levez*, but only implied that such a difference between the two actions was contrary to the principle of equivalence.

2.067 The reasoning of the Court of Justice in *Transportes Urbanos* reflects the influence of the principle of non-discrimination on how to apply the principle of equivalence. Anti-discrimination law identifies certain grounds on the basis of which one must not make distinctions, e.g., sex and nationality.[172] The principle of equivalence likewise prohibits differentiation between claims based on EU law and claims based on national law, provided of course that the overall context is similar. In *Transportes Urbanos* the Court found that there was such a differentiation. Hence (in order to ascertain whether the differentiation was prohibited) it asked for the reason for that differentiation. Having found that the reason was simply that one action was based on EU law and the other on domestic law, the Court concluded that the differentiation was prohibited and had to be abolished.[173]

III. The principle of effectiveness

2.068 In this section attention is on the EU law principle of effectiveness, which is distinguished in this presentation from the principle of effective judicial protection now enshrined in Article 47 of the EU Charter.[174] Originally the wording of the principle of effectiveness allowed a wide margin of discretion for Member States. This is apparent in the quote from *Rewe* above[175] prohibiting only the use of national conditions making it 'impossible in practice' to exercise rights conferred by EU law. That formula was however soon changed into the classic formula used to express the principle of effectiveness, that national rules governing actions based on EU law must not render the exercise of rights conferred on individuals by EU law virtually impossible or excessively difficult. The latter formula, which has served to

---

172 Cf. Art. 21 of the Charter. This is simplified, of course (especially, it applies better to direct than to indirect discrimination), but it is submitted that this captures the basic structure of anti-discrimination law, the limits of which are also the limits of the possible use of anti-discrimination law to promote equality.

173 Arguably, this was an *application* of EU law to the facts, rather than an *interpretation* of EU law for the national court to apply. As there may have been alternative explanations for the differentiation, a stricter interpretation of Art. 267 TFEU might have left the final decision on compatibility with the principle of equivalence to the national court.

174 See Section 2.A on the interrelationship of the principles.

175 *Rewe* (n 30) para. 5.

limit substantially the margin of discretion enjoyed by Member States, first appeared in *San Giorgio*.[176]

The principle of effectiveness has been invoked by the Court of Justice in a range of situations, making it virtually impossible or at least excessively difficult to capture the principle in abstract description. Most commentators will indeed examine the impact of the principle by grouping case law into categories based on the character of the national rule against which it was invoked.[177] Such an approach will predominantly be used here too. However, it should be noted that in *Peterbroeck* and *van Schijndel* the Court of Justice did offer some general guidance on the application of the EU principle of effectiveness. The Court held that for the purposes of applying the principle: **2.069**

> … each case which raises the question whether a national procedural provision renders application of Community law impossible or excessively difficult must be analysed by reference to the role of that provision in the procedure, its progress and its special features, viewed as a whole, before the various national instances. In the light of that analysis the basic principles of the domestic judicial system, such as protection of the rights of the defence, the principle of legal certainty and the proper conduct of procedure, must, where appropriate, be taken into consideration.[178] **2.070**

The usefulness of this guidance has been questioned by Heukels, in whose view this is simply an *ad hoc* approach.[179] The holdings of the Court could certainly be boiled down to saying that the national rule at issue must be viewed in context. It is nevertheless submitted that the *Peterbroeck* and *van Schijndel* holdings serve to illustrate that the principle of effectiveness does still entail a certain margin of appreciation for Member States that does not come across as clearly in the 'virtually impossible or excessively difficult' formula. The holdings clarified that the assessment is not as blunt as simply examining whether EU law is denied its effectiveness. Rather, the characteristics of the rule hindering EU law effectiveness must be taken into consideration. It has **2.071**

176 Case 199/82 *Amministrazione delle Finanze dello Stato v SpA San Giorgio* [1983] ECR 3595 para. 14.

177 E.g., Tridimas (n 120) Ch. 9; Ward (n 138) Ch. 4. Some authors opt for a historical approach, e.g., Craig and de Búrca (n 2) Ch. 8.

178 Case C-312/93 *Peterbroeck, Van Campenhout and Cie SCS v Belgian State* [1995] ECR I-4599 para. 14; and joined cases C-430/93 and C-431/93 *Jeroen van Schijndel* and *Johannes Nicolaas Cornelis van Veen v Stichting Pensioenfonds voor Fysiotherapeuten* [1995] ECR I-4705 para. 19. These identical holdings were cited by the Court in *Levez* (n 161) para. 44, indicating that it was a source of inspiration for the Court's elaboration of how to compare rules for the purposes of the principle of equivalence, cf. Section 2.D.II.

179 Ton Heukels, 'Joined Cases C-430/93 and C-431/93, *Van Schijndel* and *Van Veen* v. *Stichting Pensioenfonds voor Fysiotherapeuten*; and Case C-312/93, *Peterbroeck, Van Campenhout and Cie SCS* v. *Belgian State*, both judgments of the Court of 14 December 1995 (full Court), not yet reported' (1996) 33 *Common Market Law Review* 337, 349. Lenaerts, Maselis and Gutman (n 11) 119 agree that the principle of effectiveness (as well as the principle of equivalence) is applied on a case-by-case basis, but do not seem to view this trait of the principle to be a problem.

also, and interestingly, been submitted by Wallerman that the extent of court discretion in the application of national rules is significant to the intensity of review used by the Court of Justice.[180]

2.072 In *Alassini* the Court of Justice added further flesh to the bones of the principle of effectiveness. *Alassini* was admittedly another instance of *in casu* interpretation of the principle of effectiveness by the Court of Justice, but the problems identified by the Court were telling. The background of the case was that national law permitted certain disputes to be brought before courts only if there had been an attempt to achieve an out-of-court settlement. First, the Court observed that the outcome of such a settlement procedure did not prejudice the right of the parties to bring subsequent proceedings before a court. Second, the Court observed that the settlement procedure was not liable to result in a substantial delay for the purposes of bringing proceedings. Third, the Court noted that the time period to be observed for the purposes of bringing proceedings was suspended during the settlement procedure. Fourth, it did not seem that the settlement procedure would entail significant costs. Fifth, the Court further held that if the settlement procedure could be accessed only by electronic means, it could be contrary to the principle of effectiveness to uphold the condition of mandatory attempt at settlement in respect of individuals without access to the Internet. Sixth, and finally, the Court also explained that in exceptional cases it could be contrary to the principle of effectiveness to uphold the condition of mandatory attempt at settlement if interim measures were necessary but unavailable during the settlement procedure.[181]

2.073 The Court did not in *Alassini* make use of its *Peterbroeck* and *van Schijndel* holdings. Instead of proceeding to any detailed analysis it dismissed the first four possible consequences of the national rule as obviously compatible with the principle of effectiveness and left it to the national court to rule on the compatibility of the final two. Nevertheless it follows from *Alassini* that all six types of consequences may, depending on the circumstances in individual cases, be such as to make the exercise of rights conferred on individuals by EU law practically impossible or excessively difficult. Thereby the national rule at issue would be incompatible with EU law. The *Alassini* list is clearly not intended to be exhaustive, but one may infer from that list a few typical adverse consequences that are of special interest for the purposes of an

180 Anna Wallerman, 'Towards an EU Law Doctrine on the Exercise of Discretion in National Courts? The Member States' Self-Imposed Limits on National Procedural Autonomy' (2016) 53 *Common Market Law Review* 339.

181 *Alassini* (n 25) paras 54–59.

effectiveness assessment: bars, impracticalities, delays, and costs. Notwithstanding the pragmatic approach chosen in *Alassini* it is submitted that the proper systematic method for making an effectiveness assessment of such, and other, limitations is by using the *Peterbroeck/van Schijndel* test. To conclude, this effectiveness assessment is applicable to any national rules on procedure and sanctions which may come into play in actions enforcing rights conferred on individuals by EU law, including rules triggered by the passing-on problem in the context of private enforcement.

Part II

PASSING-ON IN ACTIONS AGAINST THE EU

3

PASSING-ON IN DAMAGES FROM THE EU

A. CHAPTER OUTLINE

Most actions that are discussed in this book have been established through case law of the European Court of Justice – an indication as strong as any of the much-debated 'activism' of the Court.[1] In fact only one is explicitly provided for in the TFEU: the action for non-contractual damages under Article 340(2) TFEU.[2] **3.001**

Non-contractual damages under Article 340(2) TFEU are distinguished from contractual damages under Article 340(1) TFEU. The latter action is not covered in this book because, in principle, it is not governed by EU law but by the national law applicable to the contract at issue. Further, the European **3.002**

1 See, e.g., Hjalte Rasmussen, *On Law and Policy in the European Court of Justice: A Comparative Study In Judicial Policymaking* (Nijhoff 1986); Mauro Cappelletti, *The Judicial Process in Comparative Perspective* (Clarendon Law Series, Oxford University Press 1989); Patrick Neill, *The European Court of Justice: A Case Study in Judicial Activism* (European Policy Forum 1995); Trevor Hartley, 'The European Court, Judicial Objectivity and the Constitution of the European Union' (1996) 112 *Law Quarterly Review* 95; Anthony Arnull, 'The European Court and Judicial Objectivity: A Reply to Professor Hartley' (1996) 112 *Law Quarterly Review* 411; and Constantinos Kombos, *The ECJ and Judicial Activism: Myth or Reality?* (Sakkoulas 2010).

2 Literature on this action includes Göran Lysén, *The Non-Contractual and Contractual Liability of the European Communities* (Acta Universitatis Upsaliensis 1976); Andrea Biondi and Martin Farley, *The Right to Damages in European Law* (Kluwer European Law Collection, Kluwer Law International 2009); and Pekka Aalto, *Public Liability in EU Law:* Brasserie, Bergaderm *and Beyond* (Hart Publishing 2011).

Court of Justice has jurisdiction to give judgment in contractual disputes only if awarded such jurisdiction by an arbitration clause in a contract to which the EU is a contracting party.[3] With regard to the choice of law, Article 340(1) TFEU states that '[t]he contractual liability of the Union shall be governed by the law applicable to the contract in question'. The Article does not further specify how to identify the applicable law, which falls to be determined by the rules of private international law.[4] It follows that if the passing-on problem should arise in the context of an action against the EU for contractual damages, the approach to be chosen would have to be decided on the basis of applicable national law. It therefore falls outside the scope of this inquiry.

3.003 With regard to damages under Article 340(2) TFEU the Court of Justice has been seized with the problem of passing-on. The relevant case law has related to the defence of passing-on, i.e., the fact of real or possible passing-on of an economic burden was invoked as a 'shield'. More precisely the argument was that the amount of harm passed on should reduce the award of damages payable. The other main aspects of the passing-on problem (access to court and substantive proximity) have not been addressed under Article 340(2) TFEU.

3.004 In this chapter, Section 3.B has been devoted to an introduction to the action for damages under Article 340(2) TFEU. The relevant case law developments are discussed, focusing on the general conditions for liability. In Section 3.C the applicable conditions for admissibility are examined in light of Article 47 of the EU Charter of fundamental rights. In particular, the impact of those conditions for admissibility in actions brought by Beta or Gamma parties will

3 Arts 268 and 270 TFEU. See also case C-377/09 *Françoise-Eléonor Hanssens-Ensch v European Community* [2010] ECR I-7751 paras 18–19, and the case law there cited. Of course, such a dispute may also come before the Court of Justice in the context of a reference for a preliminary ruling, but the Court does not then have jurisdiction to give judgment but only to rule on the interpretation of the EU Treaties and the validity and interpretation of acts of the EU, as specified in Art. 267(1) TFEU. With regard to the term 'arbitration clause', Hartley argues that, as it is inconceivable that an arbitral award of the Court of Justice would be challenged before a national court, the term is misleading and that 'jurisdiction clause' would have been preferable; see Trevor C Hartley, *The Foundations of European Union Law* (8th edn, Oxford University Press 2014) 443.

4 In EU jurisdictions with the exception of Denmark and the UK, this means the choice will be determined by the rules of Regulation (EC) No 593/2008 of the European Parliament and of the Council of 17 June 2008 on the law applicable to contractual obligations (Rome I) [2008] OJ L177/6. The Rome I Regulation would most likely be applied also by the Court of Justice as arbitrator, see Hartley, ibid., 446. In Denmark and the UK, and for contracts entered into before 17 December 2009, the Convention 80/934/ECC on the law applicable to contractual obligations opened for signature in Rome on 19 June 1980 (Rome Convention) will apply.

be discussed.[5] Section 3.D is devoted to the problem of substantive proximity. In the context of damages, this problem is addressed through the assessment of causation. General observations on causation under Article 340(2) TFEU are made, followed by a specific discussion of the implications of those findings to actions brought by Gamma. Section 3.E concerns the estimation of damages. In the general observations, available heads of damages are identified and discussed. Thereafter the aforementioned case law on the defence of passing-on will be presented in detail. The presentation of the case law will be followed by an in-depth analysis in light of legal debate on that case law.

Chapter 4 will examine whether passing-on situations could occur in the context of restitutionary actions brought against the EU. It will be concluded that this is unlikely. Nonetheless the problems triggered by alleged passing-on and their specific characteristics in a restitutionary context will be outlined in brief. Consequently restitution from the EU will not be discussed in this chapter. **3.005**

B. INTRODUCTION TO ARTICLE 340(2) TFEU

The wording of the Article has remained virtually unchanged since it was included as Article 215(2) EEC in the original 1957 Rome Treaty. The only change has been made in order to extend its scope: as the Treaty of Lisbon entered into force on 1 December 2009, it was no longer only the (therefrom abolished) Community that could be held liable in damages, but the Union. Article 340(2) TFEU now reads: **3.006**

> In the case of non-contractual liability, the Union shall, in accordance with the general principles common to the laws of the Member States, make good any damage caused by its institutions or by its servants in the performance of their duties. **3.007**

The Court of Justice of the European Union has jurisdiction to hear actions brought pursuant to Article 340(2) TFEU.[6] It is settled case law that this jurisdiction is exclusive.[7] Under Article 256 TFEU actions for damages **3.008**

5 In this book, Alpha signifies a tortfeasor or enriched party, Beta a party first burdened by loss arising from Alpha's breach of EU law, and Gamma any party downstream from Beta (including all from the party dealing directly with Beta to the final consumer) to whom the burden of that loss may have been passed on; see Section 1.B.

6 Art. 268 TFEU.

7 See e.g. case 281/84 *Zuckerfabrik Bedburg AG and others v Council and Commission of the European Communities* [1987] ECR 49 para. 12; and joined cases 106 to 120/87 *Asteris AE and others v Hellenic Republic and European Economic Community* [1988] ECR 5515 Operative part para. 1. On jurisdiction in the event of joint liability of the EU and a Member State see Biondi and Farley (n 2) 165–77; Paul Craig, *EU*

brought against the EU shall be heard and determined by the General Court at first instance.[8] Its decisions are subject to a right of appeal to the European Court of Justice on points of law only. As a consequence the EU Courts enjoy full discretion to develop the substantive criteria applicable to such actions, unless otherwise instructed by the EU legislature – which has not, so far, intervened.

3.009 In early case law the Court of Justice recognized that liability under Article (now) 340(2) TFEU 'presupposes the existence of a set of circumstances comprising actual damage, a causal link between the damage claimed and the conduct alleged against the institution, and the illegality of such conduct'.[9] These three elements, in the opposite order, can be described as representing: (1) the liability element (i.e., illegal conduct in the quote); (2) causation; and (3) damage. The onus of proving that all three elements are satisfied is on the claimant.[10] As shown in Section 1.A the passing-on problem triggers issues pertaining to elements (2) and (3). The case law on Article 340(2) TFEU nevertheless concentrates on element (1), on which a few remarks will follow here. With regard to elements (2) and (3) an overview of the case law is available in Sections 3.D and 3.E respectively.

3.010 With regard to the first element, i.e., liability as such, it is of special interest to notice the endeavour of the Court of Justice to align actions under Article 340(2) and actions for damages from a Member State.[11] This development began with *Brasserie*[12] but for the purposes of actions under Article 340(2) TEU it began with *Bergaderm*.[13] In case law preceding *Bergaderm* however, the Court distinguished two different tests for liability.

Administrative Law (2nd edn, Oxford University Press 2012) 698–701; and Peter Oliver, 'Joint Liability of the Community and the Member States' in Ton Heukels and Alison McDonnell (eds), *The Action for Damages in Community Law* (Kluwer Law 1997).

8 The exception is staff disputes entailing damages claims, which are brought before the Civil Service Tribunal at first instance; see Art. 270 TFEU.

9 Case 4/69 *Alfons Lütticke GmbH v Commission of the European Communities* [1971] ECR 325 para. 10.

10 Case C-100/07 P *ÉR, OO, JR and Others v Council of the European Union and Commission of the European Communities* [2007] ECR I-136* (summary publication, the full text of the order is available in French only) paras 27 and 37.

11 See joined cases C-6/90 and C-9/90 *Andrea Francovich and Danila Bonifaci and others v Italian Republic* [1991] ECR I-5357.

12 Joined cases C-46/93 and C-48/93 *Brasserie du Pêcheur SA v Bundesrepublik Deutschland* and *The Queen v Secretary of State for Transport, ex parte: Factortame Ltd and others* [1996] ECR I-1029.

13 Case C-352/98 P *Laboratoires pharmaceutiques Bergaderm SA and Jean-Jacques Goupil v Commission of the European Communities* [2000] ECR I-5291.

The original *Lütticke* formula, under which liability under Article (now) 340(2) TFEU arose in case of 'illegal conduct', was generally applicable to administrative acts of the EU institutions. Under this case law any infringement of law constituted illegality which might give rise to liability on the part of the EU.[14] It has been less clear in case law whether an administrative act which is in breach of a rule of EU law was sufficient in itself to satisfy the criterion of illegality, or whether subjective fault was also necessary,[15] but since *Bergaderm* the legal content of the element of unlawfulness should be clarified. Before continuing to examine *Bergaderm* however, it is appropriate to trace some more early developments of the action for damages pursuant to Article 340(2) TFEU. **3.011**

The *Schöppenstedt* test, which was applicable to legislative action by the EU 'involving measures of economic policy', prescribed that the EU could be liable in damages for such legislative actions only in case of 'a sufficiently flagrant violation of a superior rule of law for the protection of the individual'.[16] The test thus involved a standard for the unlawfulness of the act constituting liability, and a requirement that the superior rule at issue be intended to protect interests of individuals, i.e., that it was a protective norm (German: *Schutzgesetz*).[17] Subsequent case law arguably extended the scope of the *Schöppenstedt* test to encompass legislative acts wherever the EU legislature enjoyed wide discretion.[18] In *Bayerische HNL* the Court specified for the purposes of the unlawfulness standard that the EU would incur liability 'in a legislative field such as the one in question, in which one of the chief features **3.012**

14 Case T-390/94 *Aloys Schröder, Jan and Karl-Julius Thamann v Commission of the European Communities* [1997] ECR II-501 para. 51. A systematic overview over EU liability for illegal administrative acts (and civil wrongs), with references to case law, is available in Henry G Schermers and Denis F Waelbroeck, *Judicial Protection in the European Union* (6th edn, Kluwer Law International 2001) 541–5.

15 See Koen Lenaerts, Ignace Maselis and Kathleen Gutman (Janek Tomasz Nowak (ed.)), *EU Procedural Law* (Oxford EU Law Library, Oxford University Press 2014) 512, and the case law there cited.

16 Case 5/71 *Aktien-Zuckerfabrik Schöppenstedt v Council of the European Communities* [1971] ECR 975 para. 11. For a list of rules and principles identified by the EU Courts as 'superior rules of law' for the purposes of the *Schöppenstedt* test see Lenaerts, Maselis and Gutman (n 15) 518–19.

17 This concept is used here without prejudice to the precise meaning given to that concept in German law. On the notion of *Schutzgesetz* in German law see Walter van Gerven, Jeremy Lever and Pierre Larouche (eds), *The Common Law of Europe Casebooks: Tort Law* (Hart Publishing 2000) 306. On the application of this element in EU Courts see Biondi and Farley (n 2) 109–10; and Lenaerts, Maselis and Gutman (n 15) 516–17.

18 See joined cases T-481/93 and T-484/93 *Vereniging van Exporteurs in Levende Varkens and others* and *Nederlandse Bond van Waaghouders van Levend Vee and others v Commission of the European Communities* [1995] ECR II-2941 paras 80–82 and 89–96; and Schermers and Waelbroeck (n 14) 547. Indeed, it is debatable whether this test (or at least a similar one) was not extended to any act – legislative or other – by the EU institutions, in which they enjoyed a wide discretion; see case T-108/94 *Elena Candiotte v Council of the European Union* [1996] ECR II-87 para. 32.

is the exercise of a wide discretion' only if the institution concerned had 'manifestly and gravely disregarded the limits on the exercise of its powers'.[19]

3.013 The quite stringent test formulated in *Schöppenstedt* and subsequent case law and its restrictive application by the EU Courts, as well as the difficulty of managing the distinction between those acts which would fall under the *Schöppenstedt* test and those which would not, became the target of some criticism.[20] Following the introduction of liability for Member States for a breach of EU law in *Francovich*[21] critics also pointed at the imbalance between the two damages regimes.[22] The Court of Justice itself picked up on this issue in *Brasserie*, as it held that the conditions under which a Member State might incur liability could not, in the absence of particular justification, differ from those governing the liability of the EU in like circumstances.[23] The Court did not however intend in *Brasserie* to herald the abolition of the *Schöppenstedt* test for the purposes of Article (now) 340(2) TFEU. Instead the Court was introducing a distinction into Member State liability case law parallel to that created for the purposes of EU liability through *Schöppenstedt*. To that end the Court's reasoning continued to focus on the extent of discretion enjoyed by the Member States in the circumstances of the case before it.[24] The purpose therefore seemed to be to make the law of liability for Member States more similar to the law of liability for the EU, rather than the opposite.

3.014 For the purposes of Article 340(2) TFEU the *dictum* on non-differentiation of conditions was picked up by the Court of Justice in *Bergaderm*,[25] where an action for damages had been brought against the Commission. From that point of departure the Court continued to recall the criteria established for the purposes of actions for damages from a Member State:

3.015 As regards Member State liability for damage caused to individuals, the Court has held that Community law confers a right to reparation where three conditions are met:

---

19 Joined cases 83 and 94/76, 4, 15 and 40/77 *Bayerische HNL Vermehrungsbetriebe GmbH & Co KG and others v Council and Commission of the European Communities* [1978] ECR 1209 para. 6.

20 For a summary with references see Aalto (n 2) 86–7. See also Biondi and Farley (n 2) 101–3; and Angela Ward, *Judicial Review and the Rights of Private Parties in EU Law* (2nd edn, Oxford University Press 2007) 393–9.

21 Joined cases C-6/90 and 9/90 *Andrea Francovich and Daniela Bonifaci and others v Italian Republic* [1991] ECR I-5357.

22 See Ward (n 20) 398–9.

23 *Brasserie* (n 12) para. 42.

24 See *Brasserie* (n 12) paras 43–53, and Operative part para. 2. The uniform criteria for Member State liability were introduced later, by the full Court, in joined cases C-178/94, C-179/94, C-188/94, C-189/94 and C-190/94 *Erich Dillenkofer, Christian Erdmann, Hans-Jürgen Schulte, Anke Heuer, Werner, Ursula and Torsten Knor v Bundesrepublik Deutschland* [1996] ECR I-4845 paras 19–28. See further Section 6.B.

25 *Bergaderm* (n 13) para. 41.

> the rule of law infringed must be intended to confer rights on individuals; the breach must be sufficiently serious; and there must be a direct causal link between the breach of the obligation resting on the State and the damage sustained by the injured parties … .
>
> As to the second condition, as regards both Community liability under Article 215 of the Treaty and Member State liability for breaches of Community law, the decisive test for finding that a breach of Community law is sufficiently serious is whether the Member State or the Community institution concerned manifestly and gravely disregarded the limits on its discretion … .
>
> Where the Member State or the institution in question has only considerably reduced, or even no, discretion, the mere infringement of Community law may be sufficient to establish the existence of a sufficiently serious breach … .
>
> In that regard, the Court finds that the general or individual nature of a measure taken by an institution is not a decisive criterion for identifying the limits of the discretion enjoyed by the institution in question.[26]

Thereby the Court of Justice introduced a new and general test for the purposes of actions pursuant to Article 340(2) TFEU, which was – on the whole – the same as that which applied to liability in damages for Member States. As in such actions for damages from a Member State, different standards would still apply depending on how to apply the 'sufficiently serious breach' element in different contexts.[27] The Court explained in *Camar and Tico* that the decisive factor in pinpointing the standard to apply was 'not the individual nature of the act in question, but the discretion available to the institution when it was adopted'.[28] **3.016**

Even though the *Schöppenstedt* test as such must be regarded as legal history in the aftermath of *Bergaderm*,[29] fragments of the *Schöppenstedt* case law linger in the details of the new test.[30] In the new test the liability element is captured in the criteria that the rule of law infringed must be intended to confer rights on individuals and that the breach must be sufficiently serious. **3.017**

With regard to the first of these criteria, Lenaerts, Maselis and Gutman submit that there is no difference in substance between the new phrase and the *Schöppenstedt* requirement that the rule at issue be intended to protect interests **3.018**

26 *Bergaderm* (n 13) paras 42–44 and 46.

27 See *Dillenkofer* (n 24) paras 24–25; and case C-224/01 *Gerhard Köbler v Republik Österreich* [2003] ECR I-10239 para. 53.

28 Case C-312/00 P *Commission of the European Communities v Camar Srl and Tico Srl* [2002] ECR I-11355 para. 55.

29 See Aalto (n 2) 90–91.

30 Cf. Takis Tridimas, *The General Principles of EU Law* (2nd edn, Oxford EC Law Library, Oxford University Press 2006) 488–92.

of individuals, as both phrases indicate that the rule at issue must be intended to confer rights on individuals, i.e., be a *Schutzgesetz*.[31] Following *Bergaderm* however it is no longer of essence whether the rule infringed is a 'superior' rule of law or not. Thus any rule of primary or secondary EU law, or general principle of EU law, will do – provided that it is intended to protect the interests of individuals.[32]

3.019 With regard to the second criterion, i.e., that the breach must be sufficiently serious, alleged inconsistencies in the approaches chosen by the General Court and the Court of Justice, respectively, have given rise to some debate among scholars.[33] Suffice it here to notice that the Court of Justice seems to have settled the issue in *CEVA and Pfizer* (delivered in Grand Chamber), where it stressed again that the decisive factor governing the standard to apply within the 'sufficiently serious breach' element was the discretion enjoyed by the EU institution.[34]

3.020 Alongside liability for administrative and legislative acts the EU has also been held liable for civil wrongs.[35] In *Grifoni*, for example, the manager of a sheet-metal shop fell from a roof on the premises of a research centre run by the European Atomic Energy Community at Ispra, Italy.[36] The Court of Justice found that the Commission had failed to show due diligence with regard to safety measures, by omitting to take the safety measures prescribed by applicable Italian law in order to prevent those working on the Centre's flat roof from falling. Therefore the Court concluded that the Commission had acted unlawfully within the meaning of EU law.[37] In this kind of context there may be more room for a subjective fault assessment than there is under the *Bergaderm* test.

---

31 See Lenaerts, Maselis and Gutman (n 15) 515–17, citing e.g. case C-221/10 P *Artegodan GmbH v European Commission and Federal Republic of Germany* EU:C:2012:216 paras 81–82. Lenaerts, Maselis and Gutman also emphasize that the interest harmed must fall within the protective scope (German: *Schutzzweck der Gesetz*) of the rule at issue.

32 For an overview of rules and principles invoked and the response of the EU Courts see Lenaerts, Maselis and Gutman (n 15) 517–21.

33 See Tridimas (n 30) 489–92; and Ward (n 20) 399–402; but cf. Biondi and Farley (n 2) 128–34.

34 Case C-198/03 P *Commission of the European Communities v CEVA Santé Animale SA and Pfizer Enterprises Sàrl* [2005] ECR I-6357 paras 67–69. Biondi and Farley (n 2) 135–8, maintain that the case law of the General Court has continued to stray from that of the Court of Justice after *CEVA and Pfizer*. A comprehensive analysis of the case law of both courts with a view to achieve reconciliation is found in Aalto (n 2) 134–48. A systematic analysis can also be found in Lenaerts, Maselis and Gutman (n 15) 522–8.

35 See Schermers and Waelbroeck (n 14) 541–5.

36 Case C-308/87 *Alfredo Grifoni v European Atomic Energy Community* [1990] ECR I-1203. The case was decided under Art. 188(2) of the Euratom Treaty (still in force), which is identical to Art. 340(2) TFEU. There is no reason to distinguish case law under the respective articles for the purposes of their substantive content. See also Art. 106a(1) of the Euratom Treaty and Lenaerts, Maselis and Gutman (n 15) 482.

37 *Grifoni* (n 36) paras 13–14.

It has been debated whether the EU may under any circumstances be held liable in damages for lawful acts – i.e., whether there is any room for strict liability under Article 340(2) TFEU.[38] Such liability has been hinted at in the case law,[39] but was dismissed by the Court of Justice 'as Community law now stands' in *FIAMM*.[40] Subsequent case law has nonetheless been open to such liability in the event that the claimant has suffered 'unusual and special' harm caused by a lawful act of the EU.[41] **3.021**

For an action for damages under Article 340(2) TFEU to be successful the claimant must also show that there is a direct causal link between the unlawful act or conduct and the alleged harm, and that the claimant has suffered harm eligible for compensation. These preconditions are directly relevant to the passing-on problem and they will therefore be examined in detail in Sections 3.D and 3.E. First, however, the equally relevant conditions for admissibility will be discussed. **3.022**

C. ACCESS TO CLAIM DAMAGES UNDER ARTICLE 340(2) TFEU

I. General observations on access

Compared to the vast amount of writing on access to court under Article 263(4) TFEU,[42] not a great deal has been written on the issue of access under Article 340(2) TFEU. For clarity, actions under Article 340(2) TFEU fall under the exclusive jurisdiction of the EU Courts pursuant to Article 268 TFEU. Such actions are to be brought before the General Court at first instance, and to the Court of Justice on appeal.[43] Hence the problem of **3.023**

38 On the concept of strict liability see e.g., Konrad Zweigert and Hein Kötz, *An Introduction to Comparative Law* (3rd edn, Oxford University Press 1998) Ch. 42. Strict liability in tort law should not be confused with liability to make restitution of an unjust enrichment, e.g., in actions of unjust enrichment of the EU, which is governed by other criteria and considerations. On restitutionary actions against the EU see Ch. 4.

39 For a discussion with references to case law see Tridimas (n 30) 492–5.

40 Joined cases C-120/06 P and C-121/06 P *Fabbrica italiana accumulatori motocarri Montecchio SpA (FIAMM) and Fabbrica italiana accumulatori motocarri Montecchio Technologies LLC* (C-120/06 P), *Giorgio Fedon and Figli SpA and Fedon America, Inc.* (C-121/06 P) *v Council of the European Union and Commission of the European Communities* [2008] ECR I-6513 paras 175–176.

41 Case C-414/08 P *Sviluppo Italia Basilicata v Commission* [2010] ECR I-2559 para. 141; case C-556/14 P *Holcim (Romania) SA v European Commission* EU:C:2016:207 para. 105. The meaning of the terms 'unusual and special harm' are explained in case T-184/95 *Dorsch Consult v Council and Commission* [1998] ECR II-667 paras 80–85.

42 Updated and insightful overviews are available in Craig (n 7) 305–19; and Arjen Meij, 'Access to the European Union Courts: Standing in Direct Actions after Lisbon' in Marjolein van Roosmalen et al (eds), *Fundamental Rights and Principles: Liber Amicorum Pieter van Dijk* (Intersentia 2013).

43 Arts 268 and 256(1) TFEU and Art. 51 of Protocol (No 3) on the Statute of the Court of Justice of the European Union, annexed to the EU Treaties.

balancing national procedural autonomy against the principles of equivalence and effectiveness will not apply. The EU fundamental right of access to court in Article 47 of the EU Charter nevertheless does apply.[44] Therefore this right must be taken into consideration as the issue of access to court under Article 340(2) TFEU is approached.

3.024 The text of Article 340(2) TFEU does not itself set any limits on who can claim damages from the EU institutions. Instead general requirements for admissibility are laid down in Article 21 of the Statute of the Court of Justice of the European Union,[45] with further details in the Rules of Procedure of the General Court (which adjudicates at first instance).[46] These requirements have been elaborated in case law. The aim of this section is accordingly to assess those requirements and the case law in light of Article 47 of the Charter.

3.025 It was pointed out in the discussion in paragraph 2.003, and further developed in Section 2.C, that Article 47 is no *carte blanche* to bring any action before the courts of the EU or of its Member States. It will become applicable only where the claimant is the holder of a right or interest protected by EU law. It has been submitted by Lenaerts, Maselis and Gutman that it is sufficient in that regard for a claimant to 'claim to have been injured by acts or conduct of a Union institution or its officials'.[47] The General Court has further specified that to have access to claim damages under Article 340(2) TFEU, the claimant must be 'able to assert in law either a particular interest of his own or a right to compensation which has been assigned to him by others'.[48] To show a particular interest or right to compensation, it is necessary that the alleged injury affected the claimant's own assets. A mere interest (of e.g., a trade union vis-à-vis a member of the trade union) in seeing that the person who suffered damage obtains compensation is not sufficient to establish a particular interest.[49] As mentioned, an action is also admissible where the injured right has been validly assigned to the claimant and the interest to bring proceedings has

---

44 For a general presentation of the right of access to court in EU law see Section 2.C. For the full text of Art. 47 of the EU Charter see para. 2.031.

45 Protocol (No 3) on the Statute of the Court of Justice of the European Union, annexed to the Treaties [2010] OJ C83/210.

46 Rules of procedure of the General Court, consolidated version of the Rules of procedure of the Court of First Instance of the European Communities [1991] OJ L136/1.

47 Lenaerts, Maselis and Gutman (n 15) 493.

48 Case T-219/08 *İşçi Partisi (Turkish Labour Party) v Commission of the European Communities* EU:T:2008:538 para. 7; case T-223/09 *İşçi Partisi (Turkish Labour Party) v Commission of the European Communities* EU:T:2009:524 para. 11. In this and the following see also Lenaerts, Maselis and Gutman (n 15) 493–5.

49 Case 72/74 *Union syndicale-Service public européen and others v Council of the European Communities* [1975] ECR 401 para. 21; case 114/83 *Société d'Initiatives et de Coopération Agricole et al v Commission of the European Communities* [1984] ECR 2598 paras 3–5; and parallel case 289/83 *GAARM v Commission of the European Communities* [1984] ECR 4295 paras 3–5; case T-223/09 *İşçi Partisi* (n 48) para. 12.

therefore passed over to the claimant by subrogation. This alternative possibility is available if the claimant can produce evidence of 'a specific legal act of assignment between the person having suffered the alleged damage and the claimant (meaning that the former has transferred its right to the latter) or an express legal mandate to bring proceedings that has been explicitly extended by the person having suffered the damage'.[50]

However, the identification of a particular interest or assigned right does not suffice in itself. The details of the claim must also be specified with some detail and in correspondence to the conditions for liability under Article 340(2) TFEU. The general requirements on how to specify follow from Article 21 of the Statute of the EU Courts, and further details follow from the Rules of Procedure of the General Court. These requirements serve several interests, e.g., good administration and the interests of the defendant, but function also as limitations on the right of access to court of the claimant. Pursuant to Article 21 of the Statute, a written application for a case to be brought before the EU Courts shall, inter alia, state the subject matter of the dispute and include a brief statement of the pleas in law on which the application is based. Under the Rules of Procedure the application must also state 'the nature of any evidence offered in support'.[51] The EU Courts have elaborated on these requirements for the purposes of actions for damages pursuant to Article 340(2) TFEU. The point of departure was *Schöppenstedt*, where the Court of Justice held that 'a claim for any unspecified form of damages is not sufficiently concrete and must therefore be regarded as inadmissible'.[52] From that holding the General Court has developed a set of consistent holdings appearing in many cases,[53] here quoted from *Guérin Automobiles*: **3.026**

> In order to ensure legal certainty and the sound administration of justice, if an action is to be admissible the essential facts and law on which it is based must be apparent from the text of the application itself, even if only stated briefly, provided the statement is coherent and comprehensible. **3.027**

---

50 Case T-223/09 *İşçi Partisi* (n 48) para. 13; citing case 238/78 *Ireks-Arkady GmbH v Council and Commission of the European Communities* [1979] ECR 2955 para. 5; and case T-149/96 *Confederazione Nazionale Coltivatori Diretti (Coldiretti) and 110 farmers v Council of the European Union and Commission of the European Communities* [1998] ECR II-3841 para. 59.

51 Rules of procedure of the General Court, consolidated version of the Rules of procedure of the Court of First Instance of the European Communities [1991] OJ L136/1 Art. 44(1)(e). A handbook presentation of the requirements in Art. 44 is available in Bertrand Wägenbaur, *Court of Justice of the EU: Commentary on Statute and Rules of Procedure* (Verlag CH Beck/Hart Publishing/Nomos 2013) 584–607.

52 *Schöppenstedt* (n 16) para. 9.

53 The earliest example known to this author is case T-64/89 *Automec Srl v Commission of the European Communities* [1990] ECR II-367 paras 73–74, which in turn cites *Schöppenstedt*. For a recent example see case T-187/11 *Mohamed Trabelsi and Others v Council of the European Union* EU:T:2013:273 paras 46–48.

> In order to satisfy those requirements, an application seeking compensation for damage caused by a Community institution must state the evidence from which the conduct alleged against the institution can be identified, the reasons for which the applicant considers that there is a causal link between the conduct and the damage it claims to have suffered, and the nature and extent of that damage.
>
> It also appears from the case-law that an application which lacks the necessary precision must be declared inadmissible and that an infringement of Article 19 of the Statute of the Court of Justice and of Article 44(1)(c) of the Rules of Procedure of the Court of First Instance is a bar to proceeding which the Court may raise of its own motion at any time in accordance with Article 113 of the Rules of Procedure.[54]

3.028 In practice the General Court has stressed the necessity for applications to be detailed enough to enable the Court and the defendant to understand how the alleged breach of EU law has led to harm for the claimant. In sum the application in itself must state the circumstances corresponding to the conditions for liability for the EU, and must do so with clarity and precision.[55] If the claimant fails to do so the application may be declared inadmissible. Nevertheless, the case law suggests that the intensity of review at this stage is not strict. What is required is that the application makes it plausible, provided that the assertions made by the claimant can be proved, that the claim has merit. For example the requirement with regard to the suffering of damage is that the claimant demonstrates with sufficient certainty the existence of actual damage, not the precise quantum of damage.[56] The grounds for damages must however be set out in a manner which makes it possible to foresee how the claimant intends to quantify damages in the proceedings.[57]

3.029 It was explained in Section 2.C.II that the proper test for any limitation to that right is the test laid down in Article 52(1) of the Charter.[58] Testing this case law against the standard of Article 52(1) it has been mentioned already that the admissibility test applied by the EU Courts is an interpretation of Article 21 of the Statute of the EU Courts. If the interpretation of the 'provided for by law' criterion adopted in paragraph 2.041 is accepted, it follows that the EU admissibility test is provided for by law.

---

54 Case T-195/95 *Guérin Automobiles v Commission of the European Communities* [1997] ECR II-679 paras 20–22 (citations omitted). The Court of First Instance is now the General Court.

55 Ibid., para. 24.

56 See Biondi and Farley (n 2) 156–7 with references; and Lenaerts, Maselis and Gutman (n 15) 535 with references.

57 See Schermers and Waelbroeck (n 14) 558–9. On damages for future losses see ibid., 559–60; and Lenaerts, Maselis and Gutman (n 15) 530.

58 For the text of Art. 52(1) of the EU Charter see para. 2.039.

The general interests protected by the admissibility test are, as stated by the General Court, 'to ensure legal certainty and the sound administration of justice'. It was explained in Section 2.C.II that the proportionality test in Article 52(1) of the Charter includes three tiers.[59] The first tier is a test of suitability whereby it is assessed whether the measure at issue is suitable for the achievement of its aim. Reasonable limitations of access to court can, it is submitted, make a suitable contribution to the aims identified by the General Court. The second tier is a 'necessity test', or in essence a 'less restrictive means test'.[60] In this context a less restrictive alternative should be a less restrictive limitation of access to court. It is difficult however to envisage a less restrictive alternative to the current rules, as Article 113 of the Rules of Procedure of the General Court instructs the General Court to hear the parties before it decides to declare the application inadmissible. Finally, the third tier is designed to ensure that the limitation at issue is not excessively restrictive in view of the claimant's interests. Tridimas seems to imply that this third tier comprises a final balancing operation taking into account circumstances particular to the claimant. Such a balancing operation cannot be carried out in the abstract. Suffice it to conclude that these limitations of access to court seem compatible with Article 52(1) of the Charter when examined in the abstract, but that we should remain open to particular circumstances making it impossible in the individual case to uphold the limitations developed by the EU Courts. **3.030**

It merits mentioning also that access has been restricted in cases where claimants have tried to use Article 340(2) TFEU in order to circumvent time-limits for other actions.[61] Thus where the action for damages seeks to obtain the same benefit as would have been obtained through an action of annulment or is too closely connected to a failure by the claimant to seek annulment in time, the action will be declared inadmissible. Lenaerts, Maselis and Gutman observe in this regard that the General Court has endeavoured to maintain the autonomy of the action for damages under Article 340(2) TFEU by limiting the applicability of this case law on abuse of process to applications where the claimant is indeed trying to accomplish the withdrawal of a decision by bringing an action for damages.[62] Such case law limitations should equally meet the standard of Article 52(1) of the Charter, as interpreted here. **3.031**

59 In the following see Tridimas (n 30) 139–41.

60 Tridimas (n 30) 139.

61 E.g., case 4/67 *Anne Muller (née Collignon) v Commission of the European Communities* [1967] ECR 469. For a discussion of this case law see Biondi and Farley (n 2) 95–9; and Philip Mead, 'The Relationship Between an Action for Damages and an Action for Annulment: The Return of *Plaumann*' in Ton Heukels and Alison McDonnell (eds), *The Action for Damages in Community Law* (Kluwer Law 1997).

62 Lenaerts, Maselis and Gutman (n 15) 490–92 with references.

II. Access and passing-on

3.032 It would seem far-fetched to suggest for the passing-on context as such to cause admissibility problems in proceedings brought by Beta claimants. By contrast however, it might very well cause such problems in proceedings brought by Gamma claimants.[63] Indeed it has, in the context of an action brought against a Member State.[64] The underlying policy argument might be, e.g., that Gamma claimants are too remote from Alpha to have a reasonable possibility of proving a causal relationship between the breach of EU law and the harm incurred[65] or that the effective enforcement of EU law is better served if courts are allowed to focus on actions brought by Beta.[66]

3.033 As mentioned there is no case law on access to court and the passing-on problem under Article 340(2) TFEU. Interesting comparisons can nonetheless be made with the related problem of losses caused to third parties, i.e., parties who have not been the direct addressees of the harmful measure. With regard to claims brought by such third parties, the Court of Justice has held in *CMC* that:

3.034

> … it would be wrong to dismiss the possibility that acts or conduct of the [EU institutions or their] agents or officials … might cause damage to third parties. Any person who claims to have been injured by such acts or conduct must therefore have the possibility of bringing an action, if he is able to establish liability, that is, the existence of damage caused by an illegal act or by illegal conduct on the part of the [Union].[67]

3.035 The final part of this holding should not be read as an indication that a claimant must show the illegality of the act, causation, and injury sustained in order to have access to court. It rather seems to be an example of the case law discussed in Section 3.C.I under which an application submitted to the General Court must state the circumstances corresponding to the conditions for liability for the EU, and must do so with clarity and precision in order to make it plausible to the Court that the claim might have merit. If this interpretation is correct then the relevant content of the holding is that third

---

63 In this book, Alpha signifies a tortfeasor or enriched party, Beta a party first burdened by loss arising from Alpha's breach of EU law, and Gamma any party downstream from Beta (including all from the party dealing directly with Beta to the final consumer) to whom the burden of that loss may have been passed on; see Section 1.B.

64 Case C-94/10 *Danfoss A/S and Sauer-Danfoss ApS v Skatteministeriet* [2011] ECR I-9963.

65 Cf. ibid., para. 30.

66 Cf. *Illinois Brick Co et al v Illinois et al* 431 US 720 (1977) 746–7.

67 Case 118/83 *CMC Cooperativa muratori e cementisti and others v Commission of the European Communities* [1985] ECR 2325 para. 31. Recalled in case 267/82 *Développement SA and Clemessy v Commission of the European Communities* [1986] ECR 1907 para. 16.

parties suffering consequential loss cannot be automatically barred from bringing a claim for damages pursuant to Article 340(2) TFEU before the EU Courts, but that the general requirements for the application to be admissible apply equally to such third parties.

If the holding quoted above is read as a statement on claims brought by Gamma claimants, it would follow that Gamma claimants cannot be automatically excluded from enjoying a right to damages under Article 340(2) TFEU either. Indeed, the nexus between the initial harm caused to Beta and the subsequent passing-on of that harm to Gamma is arguably closer than that between harm incurred by the direct addressee of an illegal act or of illegal conduct on the part of the EU and consequential harm incurred by third parties. Therefore *CMC* provides a strong indication that Gamma claimants should not be automatically barred from bringing a claim for damages pursuant to Article 340(2) TFEU before the EU Courts by reference to the lack of proximity between Alpha and Gamma. In the words used by the General Court, Gamma claimants should be regarded as being able to assert in law a particular interest of their own, as the harm at issue would pertain to their own assets.[68] It also follows that Gamma is able to invoke the EU fundamental right of access to court. **3.036**

It is furthermore submitted that it follows from a comparison with *Danfoss* that the EU Courts cannot reasonably deny court access for Gamma by automatically ruling out the possibility of a direct causal link between EU measures and harm allegedly inflicted by Gamma claimants.[69] *Danfoss* partly concerned an action for damages from a Member State, brought by Gamma (Danfoss and Sauer-Danfoss) directly against Alpha (the Danish State). The Court of Justice was asked whether such an action could be rejected (Danish: *afvist*, i.e. not admitted) 'on the ground that a direct causal link between the levying of [a] duty by the State and the damage suffered by [the claimants] is automatically ruled out'. The Court of Justice, bearing in mind that it was not for the Court to rule on the legal classification of actions brought before national courts, took the view that the question asked must pertain to the condition of causation in an action for damages from the Member State.[70] The **3.037**

68 Case T-219/08 *İşçi Partisi* (n 48) para. 7; case T-223/09 *İşçi Partisi* (n 48) para. 11. The second of the two options, i.e., that the right has been assigned, does not apply in this context as it presupposes the valid transfer of an injured right, through which the right to compensation is also transferred by subrogation. The passing-on of loss is not commonly understood to entail subrogation of rights; but for a Norwegian argument in that direction see Erik Monsen, 'Fradrag for overvelting ved utmåling av erstatnings- og tilbakesøkingskrav?' (2007) *Tidsskrift for Erstatningsrett* 195, 204 *et passim*.

69 This aspect of *Danfoss* (n 64) is analysed in further detail in sub-section 6.C.I.b; cf. also para. 5.030 for a summary of the relevant facts.

70 *Danfoss* (n 64) paras 30–34.

question was therefore whether the national court could rely on a national rule which automatically ruled out the possibility of a direct causal link between the levy of a charge by Alpha and harm incurred by Gamma, in order to refuse Gamma access to court. The Court ruled that such a bar could be upheld only if Gamma was able to bring a claim against Beta and provided that it would not be virtually impossible or excessively difficult to obtain compensation from Beta.[71]

3.038 These findings are arguably transferrable to the context of Article 340(2) TFEU. In the absence of particular justification, damages actions against the EU should not be treated differently under EU law from damages actions against the Member States.[72] There would need to be some kind of particular justification in the individual case to allow the EU institutions to be better off than the Member States in the event of a breach of EU law giving rise to liability in damages.

3.039 However, the ruling in *Danfoss* was reached by interpretation of the EU principle of effectiveness, which is not as such applicable under Article 340(2) TFEU. If the holdings of the Court of Justice in *Danfoss* are to be transferrable to the context of Article 340(2) TFEU, another legal basis must therefore be found. To this author it seems the same result could be reached by application of Article 47 of the Charter. This is so because the national rule under review in *Danfoss* was such as to make it impossible for Gamma to get access to court. Such a rule is not only contrary to the EU law principle of effectiveness, as in *Danfoss*, but is also contrary to the fundamental right of access to court now included in Article 47 of the Charter. Such an absolute bar could not pass the Article 52(1) test, as it would not be necessary for the objectives of legal certainty and sound administration of justice – the pursuit of those objectives would already be satisfied by the general requirements for admissibility.[73] An absolute bar would indeed be liable to impair the very essence of the right.[74] It follows that such a rule would have to be set aside in the context of Article 340(2) TFEU as well. For these reasons it is concluded that just as a direct causal link between a breach of EU law by Alpha and harm incurred by Gamma cannot be automatically ruled out in the context of damages actions against a Member State, it cannot either be automatically ruled out in the context of damages actions brought against the EU pursuant to Article 340(2) TFEU.

71 Ibid., Operative part para. 2; see also paras 36–38.
72 See *Brasserie* (n 12) para. 42.
73 See Section 3.C.I.
74 Cf. para. 2.043.

It thus seems that harm allegedly caused to Gamma claimants does pertain to their own assets within the meaning of the case law under Article 340(2) TFEU, and that Gamma should not therefore be automatically barred from bringing proceedings under that Treaty Article. Moreover it cannot be automatically ruled out that there is a direct causal link between a breach of EU law by Alpha and harm incurred by Gamma. However, Gamma must still meet the general requirements for an application to be admissible under the Statute of the EU Courts. As pointed out above Gamma must state the circumstances corresponding to the conditions for liability for the EU, and must do so with clarity and precision.[75] If Gamma fails to do so the application may be declared inadmissible. This is not an easy task for Gamma, but at this stage, it is only necessary to make it plausible to the General Court that the claim may have merit. The real burden is to prove causation in the main substantive examination of the merits of the action – to which we will revert in Section 3.D. **3.040**

D. SUBSTANTIVE PROXIMITY UNDER ARTICLE 340(2) TFEU

In the context of damages actions pursuant to Article 340(2) TFEU the issue of substantive proximity between the breach of EU law and the alleged harm incurred is addressed through the requirement of a causal link between the act or conduct of an EU institution, agent or official and the alleged harm incurred by the claimant. The requirement of causation will therefore be discussed in this section, as it appears from the case law of the Court of Justice. The causation requirement under Article 340(2) TFEU has been inferred from the general principles of non-contractual liability for public authorities common to the Member States. This requirement will first be examined from a general point of view. The possible implications of the case law for Gamma claimants in the passing-on problem will be discussed thereafter. The situation of Beta claimants will receive scarce attention in this context, as the problems brought by the requirement of causation for Beta will not be particular to the passing-on problem, but will be of a general nature and is thus covered by the general observations.[76] **3.041**

Before proceeding it should also be noted that as actions under Article 340(2) TFEU fall under the exclusive jurisdiction of the EU Courts pursuant to **3.042**

75 *Guérin Automobiles* (n 54) para. 24. See further Section 3.C.I.

76 In this book, Alpha signifies a tortfeasor or enriched party, Beta a party first burdened by loss arising from Alpha's breach of EU law, and Gamma any party downstream from Beta (including all from the party dealing directly with Beta to the final consumer) to whom the burden of that loss may have been passed on; see Section 1.B.

Article 268 TFEU, the problem of balancing national procedural autonomy against the principles of equivalence and effectiveness will not apply. Under Article 340(2) TFEU the EU Courts have full power to design the details of EU damages law (in the absence of EU legislative efforts to that effect), including rules on causation. It will be discussed in this section whether the EU Courts have seized this power.

I. General observations on causation

3.043 It is well settled that the EU incurs liability 'where three conditions are met: the rule of law infringed must be intended to confer rights on individuals; the breach must be sufficiently serious; and there must be a direct causal link between the breach of the obligation resting on the State and the damage sustained by the injured parties'.[77] However, the approach of the EU Courts to causation under Article 340(2) TFEU does not easily lend itself to abstract description. The case law implies – albeit not unambiguously – that the EU will assume liability in damages under Article 340(2) TFEU where tortious conduct by EU institutions or agents is the direct and determining cause of harm. The EU Courts have not been clear on the systematic details of this causation assessment.[78] Rather than engaging in the development of such a systematic approach, the case law suggests an eclectic approach where the Courts have sought, in each case, to find a factor that will break the chain of causation from the tortious act to the alleged harm. Instead of developing an abstract formula of causation, the EU Courts have concentrated on *in casu* factual circumstances. In particular the EU Courts have emphasized that the onus of proving causation for the purposes of an action under Article 340(2) TFEU is on the claimant.[79]

3.044 To illustrate it is appropriate to begin where EU law first faced the passing-on problem. *Dumortier frères*[80] was one of the maize gritz cases. Here, as in the quellmehl cases, the action was for damages under Article (now) 340(2) TFEU in compensation for refunds due but not paid. The EU legislature had

---

77 *Bergaderm* (n 13) para. 42. In para. 62, it was clarified that these conditions were to be applied generally under Art. 340(2) TFEU.

78 Noticed e.g. by Tridimas (n 30) 495. For a critique see Fiona Smith and Lorna Woods, 'Causation in *Francovich*: The Neglected Problem' (1997) 46 *The International and Comparative Law Quarterly* 925, 937–41.

79 This has been maintained in consistent case law, see e.g. joined cases C-363/88 and C-364/88 *Finanziaria Siderurgica Finsider SpA (in liquidation), Italsider SpA (in liquidation) and Societa Acciaierie e Ferriere Lombarde Falck SpA v Commission of the European Communities* [1992] ECR I-359 para. 25. For further case law see references in case T-168/94 *Blackspur DIY Ltd, Steven Kellar, JMA Glancy and Ronald Cohen v Council of the European Union and Commission of the European Communities* [1995] ECR II-2627 para. 40.

80 Joined cases 64 and 113/76, 167 and 239/78, 27, 28 and 45/79 *P Dumortier frères SA and others v Council of the European Communities* [1979] ECR 3091.

abolished refunds for the production of maize gritz, while retaining them for maize starch. It had been settled by the European Court of Justice in *SA Moulins* that this was incompatible with the principle of equality.[81] Here as in the other gritz and quellmehl cases, the defence of passing-on was raised and acknowledged but dismissed on the facts.[82] Some of the claimants in *Dumortier frères* however claimed compensation with respect to other costs, over and above damages calculated on the basis of refunds due but no paid. Two of them had been compelled to close factories and a third had entered into insolvency proceedings. The Court of Justice did not find that costs incurred through these commercial difficulties were such as to make the EU liable in damages:

> The data supplied by the parties on that question in the course of proceedings are not such as to establish the true causes of the further damage alleged. However, it is sufficient to state that even if it were assumed that the abolition of the refunds exacerbated the difficulties encountered by those applicants, those difficulties would not be a sufficiently direct consequence of the unlawful conduct of the Council to render the Community liable to make good the damage. In the field of non-contractual liability of public authorities for legislative measures, the principles common to the Member States to which the second paragraph of Article 215 of the EEC Treaty[83] refers cannot be relied on to deduce an obligation to make good every harmful consequence, even a remote one, of unlawful legislation. **3.045**
>
> It follows that the claims for compensation for the further damage cannot be upheld.[84]

It follows from *Dumortier frères* that the onus of proving causation is, as mentioned, on the claimant,[85] and that the claimants at issue in these paragraphs had not been able to prove that the discriminatory abolition of refunds had been the 'true cause' of the costs incurred through their difficulties. It also follows that the causation requirement under Article 340(2) TFEU can be specified as a requirement that the harm incurred be 'a sufficiently direct consequence' of the tortious act. The Court of Justice did not however elaborate on how to apply that formula. Furthermore, it is far from clear to what facts the Court applied the formula developed in *Dumortier frères*. Lenaerts, Maselis and Gutman argue that 'there is not one standard or uniform formulation' of the causation requirement under Article 340(2) TFEU, but that the requirement is expressed in a number of varying ways.[86] **3.046**

81 Joined cases 124/76 and 20/77 *SA Moulins & Huileries de Pont-à-Mousson and Société coopérative Providence agricole de la Champagne v Office national interprofessionnel des céréales* [1977] ECR 1795.

82 *Dumortier frères* (n 80) paras 14–18. See further Section 3.E.II.

83 Now Art. 340(2) TFEU.

84 *Dumortier frères* (n 80) paras 21–22.

85 See also Lenaerts, Maselis and Gutman (n 15) 537 and the (vast) case law there cited.

86 Ibid., 536.

3.047 It is plausibly due to this pragmatism that, insofar as we are concerned with finding an identifiable EU law on causation under Article 340(2) TFEU, the most revealing cases (including *Dumortier frères*) revolve around EU liability where several plausibly contributing causes for the harm incurred can be identified. In the event of contributing or competing causes, under what circumstances will the EU assume liability, and to what extent? *Dumortier frères* is far from clear on this point. Although the Court of Justice clearly finds that the claimants have not established the 'true causes' of the harm incurred, it is not clear what is meant by a 'true cause'. For example, does it refer to a *conditio sine qua non*[87] or to a *causa causans*,[88] or some other legal construction of causation? Further, the Court seems to imply that where commercial difficulties exist before and independently of the tortious act, the exacerbation of those difficulties through a tortious act does not in itself render the EU liable in damages. The Court would thus be saying that the tortious conduct of the EU institution or agent must be the determining cause of the difficulties as such for there to be causation within the meaning of Article 340(2) TFEU. *Dumortier frères* could – in the extreme – be interpreted as implying that in the event of competing causes of commercial difficulties, the existence of a prior cause for which the EU is not responsible will automatically rule out causation, within the meaning of Article 340(2) TFEU, between the tortious conduct of the EU institution or agent and the harm incurred.[89] Conclusions on these matters cannot however be drawn from *Dumortier frères*.

3.048 Since the creation of the General Court (then the Court of First Instance), details of the causation test and the task of applying it have for the most part been entrusted to the General Court. On appeal the Court of Justice has generally been reluctant to review the findings of the General Court with regard to causation, albeit for slightly differing reasons. Although the Court of Justice has acknowledged that 'the question as to whether there is a causal link between the wrongful act and the damage, a condition for that liability to be incurred, is a question of law which, as a consequence, is subject to review by the Court of Justice',[90] the Court has nevertheless declined to undertake such

87 Also known as 'necessary cause' or as the 'but for test': '[I]n order for an event or circumstance to be considered at all as a cause of the injury to the victim, it must be demonstrated that the injury would not have occurred *but for* that event'; van Gerven et al (n 87) 452. Italics in original.

88 Also known as 'sufficient cause'; an event which is sufficient to cause the harm. Swedish readers see on this point Mia Carlsson, *Arbetsskada: Samspelet mellan skadestånd och andra ersättningsordningar* (Jure Förlag 2008) 285.

89 Cf. also the ambiguous holding of the Court of Justice in joined cases 241, 242, 245 to 250/78 *DGV, Deutsche Getreideverwertung und Rheinische Kraftfutterwerke GmbH and others v Council and Commission of the European Communities* [1979] ECR 3017 para. 19.

90 Case C-440/07 P *Commission of the European Communities v Schneider Electric SA* [2009] ECR I-6413 para. 192.

a review in circumstances where it would only amount to a reassessment of the facts of the case.[91] In *TEAM Srl* for example, the Court of Justice held that the appellant had failed to put forward a specific plea in law under which such a review would be possible, whereas the General Court had exclusive jurisdiction to establish and to assess the facts.[92] The Court similarly held in *Blackspur* that a review of the General Court's assessment of the facts would be possible only if the appellant established that the General Court had distorted the sense of the evidence presented.[93] In *T Port* the Court of Justice held that review was not possible because the outcome of the review could not lead to the setting aside of the General Court's judgment.[94]

In *Trubowest Handel*[95] the Court of Justice however did find reason to return to the legal issue. The Court held that the condition of causality in Article 340(2) TFEU concerned 'a sufficiently direct causal nexus between the conduct of the institutions and the damage'.[96] Further: **3.049**

> It is necessary that such damage was actually caused by the conduct alleged against the institutions. ... [E]ven in the case of a possible contribution by the institutions to the damage for which compensation is sought, that contribution might be too remote because of some responsibility resting on others, possibly the appellants.[97] **3.050**

It follows from this holding that the Court of Justice does not uphold a strict criterion of exclusivity for the purposes of establishing a causal link. The Court was seemingly indicating that it was open to an alternative interpretation of its case law, under which it would not even be necessary to establish that the contribution by an EU institution was the predominant contribution to the damage suffered. Instead, where there are several contributing causes, and the conduct of the institution is one of them, that contribution 'might' be too remote on a closer examination of the circumstances. An *in casu* assessment would thus be necessary to estimate the degree of contribution attributable to the EU. The case law of the Court of Justice thus implies – not unambiguously – that the EU will assume liability under Article 340(2) TFEU insofar as it **3.051**

91 The exclusive jurisdiction of the General Court to establish and to assess the facts follows from Art 256(1)(2) TFEU.

92 Case C-13/99 P *TEAM Srl v Commission of the European Communities* [2000] ECR I-4671 paras 63–66.

93 C-362/95 P *Blackspur DIY Ltd, Steven Kellar, JMA Glancy and Ronald Cohen v Council of the European Union and Commission of the European Communities* [1997] ECR I-4775 paras 29–33.

94 Case C-122/01 P *T Port GmbH & Co KG v Commission of the European Communities* [2003] ECR I-4261 paras 15–18.

95 Case C-419/08 P *Trubowest Handel GmbH and Viktor Makarov v Council of the European Union and European Commission* [2010] ECR I-2259.

96 Ibid., para. 53.

97 Ibid., para. 59.

can be proved that its conduct is the direct and determining cause of a certain contribution to the total harm incurred.[98]

3.052 Any further hints on the approach of the EU Courts must be sought in the case law of the General Court. The case law does not suggest any systematic approach, but a pragmatic one under which the General Court has sought to examine whether or not the claimant has established a chain of causation from the tortious act to the alleged harm. For the most part claimants have failed to do so. In some cases the claimant has failed to establish that the act or omission of the EU could reasonably have caused the harm.[99] In other cases causation has been ruled out by reason of other plausibly direct and determining causes of harm for which the EU cannot be held responsible, and which would hence take the place of the targeted EU act as the cause of harm.[100] The claimant has failed to establish in the latter cases that another (competing) event was *not* the direct and determining cause of the harm incurred. Under such circumstances the General Court has also ruled that the claimant has failed to establish a causal link between the targeted EU act and the harm. In particular, the General Court has found on several occasions that the claimant should have foreseen the risk of incurring harm under the circumstances at hand, and that the applicant's failure to take action to avoid injury excludes any causal link between the acts or omissions of the EU and the harm incurred.[101] It was further explained by the Court of Justice in *Trubowest Handel* that the causal link 'may be broken by negligence on the part of the person adversely affected, where that negligence proves to be the determinant cause of the damage'.[102]

3.053 With regard to the problem of several contributing causes, it has been submitted by Toth that the causal link under Article 340(2) TFEU 'must be

98 Possibly, this also implies that damages will be payable to an amount which is proportionate to the EU contribution.

99 E.g., *Blackspur DIY* (n 79); case T-1/99 *T Port GmbH & Co KG v Commission of the European Communities* [2001] ECR II-415. In case T-193/04 *Hans-Martin Tillack v Commission of the European Communities* [2006] ECR II-3995, this assessment is not clearly distinguished from the assessment of whether actual harm has been incurred.

100 E.g., case T-220/96 *Elliniki Viomichania Oplon AE (EVO) v Council of the European Union and Commission of the European Communities* [2002] ECR II-2265; case T-146/01 *DLD Trading Co v Council of the European Union* [2003] ECR II-6005; but most notably, perhaps, the BSE cases, including case T-149/96 *Coldiretti and 110 farmers v Council of the European Union and Commission of the European Communities* [1998] ECR II 3841.

101 E.g., case T-572/93 *Odigitria AAE v Council of the European Union and Commission of the European Communities* [1995] ECR II-2025; joined cases T-3/00 and T-337/04 *Athanasios Pitsiorlas v Council of the European Union and European Central Bank* [2007] ECR II-4779. See also Lenaerts, Maselis and Gutman (n 15) 542–4. To a Swedish lawyer, such a line of argument would fall closer to considerations of contributory negligence or mitigation of loss than to issues of causation.

102 *Trubowest Handel* (n 95) para. 61. See also Craig (n 7) 692.

direct, immediate and exclusive'. Therefore, Toth argued, sufficiently direct causality could be established only if damage had arisen 'directly from the conduct of the institutions' and did not depend on 'the intervention of other causes, positive or negative'.[103] Toth consequently anticipated problems for claimants 'in the field of economic and commercial relations where the cause of an event can usually be traced back to a number of factors ... operating simultaneously or successively and producing direct as well as indirect effects'.[104] Toth concluded:

> ... where a contributory (intervening) cause can also be shown to exist, it must always be examined whether it is not of such a nature as to break the chain of causation between the institution's conduct and the damage.[105] **3.054**

The view submitted by Toth is not fully consistent. On the one hand Toth indicates that, in the event of contributing causes, it must be 'examined whether' the contributing causes are such as to break the causal link. On the other hand the word 'exclusive' in the phrase 'direct, immediate and exclusive' indicates that the existence of any contributing factor, however small the contribution may be, would as such break the chain of causality and rule out the possibility of a causal link between the conduct and the damage. Most probably this latter interpretation was not intended. Toth rather seems to intend that the conduct of the EU institution must be the determining cause for the harm incurred, which is not the same as saying that the mere existence of contributing causes will rule out causation within the meaning of Article 340(2) TFEU between the tortious conduct of the EU institution or agent and the harm incurred. In context therefore, the word 'exclusive' in Toth's text should be interpreted as pointing to the determining role of EU conduct in the complex totality of events resulting in harm for the claimant. With such an interpretation the arguments of Toth are consistent with the case law. **3.055**

Besides these issues of factual causation it has been argued by Biondi and Farley that the causation test applied by the Courts also includes the notion of legal causation.[106] The factual causation test would consist in an evaluation of the evidence in order to decide whether the damage seems to have been caused directly by an EU institution. By contrast, the legal causation test would consist in deciding whether or not it was relevantly foreseeable that the actions **3.056**

103 Akos George Toth, 'The Concepts of Damage and Causality as Elements of Non-Contractual Liability' in Ton Heukels and Alison McDonnell (eds) *The Action for Damages in Community Law* (Kluwer Law 1997); cf. case 169/73 *Compagnie Continentale France v Council of the European Communities* [1975] ECR 117 Opinion of AG Trabucchi para. 4.

104 Toth, ibid., 192.

105 Ibid., 193.

106 Biondi and Farley (n 2) 147–54.

at issue could cause the type of harm incurred. The latter test thus comprises a legal evaluation (not to be confused with the evaluation of evidence in the factual causation test) of whether the connection between the targeted EU act or omission and the damage at issue is close enough to legitimize liability in damages.[107] Such a distinction between factual and legal causation tests might serve to illustrate two different approaches to the concept of causation. This distinction is moreover common to major European legal traditions.[108] As we are instructed by Article 340(2) TFEU to construe the non-contractual liability of the EU in accordance with general principles of law common to the laws of the Member States, there are good reasons to take notice of this distinction and to contemplate its possible importance for causation assessments in EU law.

3.057 The EU Courts have not, however, explicitly structured their causation assessment in this manner. The case law rather suggests, it is submitted, that the EU Courts have opted for a minimum of rigour when defining causation under Article 340(2) TFEU, retaining a margin of discretion to make an assessment based on the facts of the individual case. Notwithstanding this relative eclecticism of the EU Courts, the case law does include assessments that would be perceived in national law as part of an assessment of legal causation, e.g., reasoning on the protective scope of the EU law provision breached. In early case law such reasoning appears to be triggered by the defendant, invoking that the alleged harm incurred does not fall within the protective scope of the EU rule at issue.[109] Since *Bergaderm* it is settled for the purposes of Article 340(2) TFEU that the EU law provision must confer a 'right' on the claimant.[110] The issue of the protective character of a rule, i.e., whether the rule is a *Schutzgesetz*, is distinguished in German law from the precise determination of the protective scope of the rule, i.e., the *Schutzzweck der Gesetz*.[111] In more recent case law of the EU Courts the distinction is less clear, and reasoning on the protective scope of an EU law provision will usually appear in the context of reasoning on whether that provision confers a right on

107 See Cees van Dam, *European Tort Law* (2nd edn, Oxford University Press 2013) 310–11, stressing also that the distinction between factual and legal causation is not unproblematic, as the identification of plausible factual causes will inevitably entail pre-judgments based on legal evaluations. Swedish readers, cf. Håkan Andersson, *Gränsproblem i skadeståndsrätten: Skadeståndsrättsliga utvecklingslinjer bok II* (Iustus förlag 2013) 23–56, distinguishing a variety of legal problems in 'causation'.

108 The division into a factual and a legal test corresponds to the understanding of causation in both German and English law, and, albeit to a lesser extent, in French law. See van Gerven et al (n 87) 452–4.

109 E.g., joined cases 5, 7 and 13 to 24/66 *Firma E Kampffmeyer and others v Commission of the EEC* [1967] ECR 245, 260 and 262.

110 *Bergaderm* (n 13). See further paras 3.015 and 3.018.

111 van Gerven et al (n 87) 403–7.

the claimant.[112] The criterion of the existence of a right may therefore include this element, which might be classified as pertaining to legal causation in national law.

The ambiguity of the case law with regard to legal causation elements can be criticized for being contrary to the interest of legal certainty. It is submitted that Biondi and Farley are right, insofar as any causation assessment must necessarily entail an evaluation of substantive proximity which is not an assessment of proven facts but a normative assessment of substantive proximity.[113] The elements of this normative assessment do however differ between European jurisdictions.[114] Litigants should therefore welcome further clarity on the approach to be chosen for the purposes of Article 340(2) TFEU. **3.058**

The overall impression of the case law is that the requirement of causation under Article 340(2) TFEU is stringent indeed. The General Court has nevertheless found, on occasion, that there is a sufficient causal link between an EU act and harm incurred for the EU to be liable in damages under Article 340(2) TFEU.[115] It remains for the EU Courts to find a coherent approach to the problem of causation under Article 340(2) TFEU – if they wish to do so. The EU Courts have not been inclined to develop any abstract legal definition of the concept of causation under Article 340(2) TFEU, save for the formula ultimately derived from *Dumortier frères* according to which the alleged harm must be a sufficiently direct consequence of the conduct complained of, which must be the determinant cause of the harm, whereas there is no obligation to make good every harmful consequence, even a remote one, of an unlawful situation.[116] **3.059**

The case law does still lend itself to some cautious interpretation. First, it has been noted above that the General Court applies a preliminary test of causal **3.060**

112 See case T-341/07 *Jose Maria Sison v Council of the European Union* [2011] ECR II-7915 para. 47; case T-429/05 *Artegodan GmbH v European Commission* [2010] ECR II-491 paras 88–89; but less clearly part of the 'right' assessment in case T-209/00 *Frank Lamberts v European Ombudsman* [2002] ECR II-2203 para. 87, where it seems rather to be approached from the perspective of legal causation classified as such.

113 van Gerven et al (n 87) 466; Andersson (n 107) 28–9.

114 See van Dam (n 107) 412–21.

115 E.g., case T-246/93 *Günther Bühring v Council of the European Union and Commission of the European Communities* [1998] ECR II-171; case T-178/98 *Fresh Marine Company A/S v Commission of the European Communities* [2000] ECR II-3331 (upheld in case C-472/00 P *Commission of the European Communities v Fresh Marine Company A/S* [2003] ECR I-7541); joined cases T-344/00 and T-345/00 *CEVA Santé Animale SA and Pharmacia Entreprises SA v Commission of the European Communities* [2003] ECR II-229; case T-48/05 *Yves Franchet and Daniel Byk v Commission of the European Communities* [2008] ECR II-1585; and the WTO banana import cases, including case T-69/00 *FIAMM and FIAMM Technologies v Council of the European Union and Commission of the European Communities* [2005] ECR II-5393.

116 Succinctly put by the General Court in case T-429/04 *Trubowest Handel GmbH and Viktor Makarov v Council of the European Union and Commission of the European Communities* EU:T:2008:263 para. 99.

capacity, i.e., that the tortious act or omission at issue is capable of harming the claimant in the alleged way.[117] Second, neither the Court of Justice nor the General Court has explicitly referred to *conditio sine qua non*, i.e., the 'but for test', as basis for its causation assessment although it could of course be argued that a test of causal capacity is in fact a *conditio sine qua non* test.[118] Third, no clear distinction between factual causation and legal causation is traceable in the case law. Fourth, it appears from *Trubowest Handel* that the Court of Justice will not *a priori* exclude the possibility of liability for the EU under Article 340(2) TFEU where harm has been incurred through a combination of factors.[119] Finally however, the General Court has excluded liability where there were other plausibly direct and determining causes of harm for which the EU could not be held responsible, and the claimant has failed to establish that those other events were *not* the direct and determining cause of the harm incurred.[120] This implies a very cumbersome burden of proof, reminiscent of criminal law rather than of actions for damages from public bodies. It is also difficult to reconcile with *Trubowest Handel* where the Court of Justice sought a '*sufficiently* direct causal nexus'.[121] As pointed out by Toth complexity is inherent in both directions of a causal chain: the causes of an event are manifold, and the consequences of an event are equally manifold.[122] It follows that the directness and determinative relationship between a specific event and the harm incurred is a matter of degree and of legal interpretation. The quote from *Trubowest Handel* illustrates this, as it speaks of a *sufficiently* direct causal nexus. The approach chosen by the General Court by contrast implies, or at least risks implying, that there is always one and only one direct and determining cause for harm.

II. Causation and passing-on

3.061 Moving on to the passing-on problem, it can be noticed first of all that Beta will not be facing any particular obstacles with regard to establishing causation. It will be for Beta to establish a direct causal link between the targeted act or omission of Alpha (the EU) and harm incurred by Beta. For Beta the discussion in the previous section is thus likely to have exhausted the relevant

---

117 See n 99.

118 Lenaerts, Maselis and Gutman (n 15) 538 submit that the *conditio sine qua non* test was rejected by the General Court in case T-113/04 *Atlantic Container Line AB and Others v Commission of the European Communities* EU:T:2007:377 para. 40. The precise point made by the General Court was, however, that the *sine qua non* criterion would not suffice in itself to establish causation within the meaning of Art. 340(2) TFEU.

119 *Trubowest Handel* (n 95) para. 59.

120 See the case law cited in n 100.

121 *Trubowest Handel* (n 95) para. 53. Italics added.

122 See Toth (n 103) 192, quoted in para. 3.054.

problems.[123] By contrast, Gamma will have the onus of establishing a direct causal link not only between the targeted act or omission of Alpha and harm incurred by Beta but between the act or omission and the subsequent suffering of harm by Gamma, at the next level of the supply chain. In this section focus will therefore be on discussing how Gamma can overcome the difficulties of establishing such a direct causal link.

It seems from the previous section that the requirement of causation under Article 340(2) TFEU is approached on a case-by-case basis. There is no case law on the main substantive assessment of causation in the context of passing-on under Article 340(2) TFEU (or, for that matter, in any other context). Nevertheless it should be kept in mind that the Court of Justice has held in *CMC* that it could not be ruled out that EU institutions (or their agents or officials) might cause damage to 'third persons' and that it should therefore be open to such persons to bring an action for damages under Article 340(2).[124] It should consequently be regarded as settled that causation must not be *a priori* ruled out in the context of Gamma actions under Article 340(2) TFEU. And yet, it was evident in the previous section that it will be quite difficult to prove that remote consequences were caused by the harmful act or conduct on behalf of the EU.[125] The burden of demonstrating causation is on the claimant. **3.062**

There are however a few hints in the case law that may give an indication for Gamma. In *Schneider II*[126] the claimant had brought an action for damages against the Commission in compensation for costs incurred following a decision in which the merger of Schneider Electric SA and Legrand SA had, unlawfully, been declared incompatible with the common market. The General Court took the view that it could not be assumed that, had the Commission not acted unlawfully, the merger would have been authorized. Such a conclusion, the General Court held, could be drawn only if it were established that the incompatibility was declared by the Commission as a direct and certain consequence of an established failure to fulfil its legal obligations. The General Court nevertheless held that, Schneider 'might admittedly have had a meaningful chance of securing a favourable decision, **3.063**

123 It is another matter that Alpha may invoke a defence of passing-on against Beta. This will be discussed in connection to the estimation of damages, in Section 3.E.II.

124 *CMC* (n 67) para. 16. See also Lenaerts, Maselis and Gutman (n 15) 531–2.

125 With regard to third-party losses, such a claim was dismissed by the Court of Justice with reference to the damage being too remote from the carelessness of the EU in an action for damages brought for a civil wrong attributable to the Commission; see joined cases 169/83 and 136/84 *Gerhardus Leussink and others v Commission of the European Communities* [1986] ECR 2801 para. 22.

126 Case T-351/03 *Schneider Electric SA v Commission of the European Communities* [2007] ECR II-2237.

and the forfeiture of that chance would amount to certain and compensatable loss'.[127] However:

3.064 ... an assessment of the changes to the economic parameters which would necessarily have accompanied any decision of compatibility is too uncertain to be a basis for a useful comparison with the situation resulting from the incompatibility decision. Even if it is accepted that Schneider may have lost a real opportunity to secure a decision of compatibility, the materialisation of that opportunity is linked to parameters that are too uncertain to be the subject of any convincing quantification. ...

> Consequently, compensation for the loss suffered by Schneider through forfeiture of a real opportunity to be able to retain the assets in Legrand cannot be envisaged.

> It must therefore be concluded that there is no sufficiently close causal link between the unlawful act committed and the loss of any opportunity of obtaining a decision that the transaction was compatible for the Community to incur liability ... .[128]

3.065 The General Court thus stressed that the economic complexity of the situation made it too difficult to carry out an analysis of causation. The question was whether Schneider would have had an opportunity of securing a favourable decision but for the unlawful act.[129] It was the materialization of that opportunity that was fraught with uncertainty. Therefore, it was too uncertain whether that opportunity would have presented itself in the absence of unlawful conduct by the Commission. Hence, the General Court concluded that no causal link had been established.

3.066 With regard to the passing-on problem it is of special interest to notice that the General Court emphasized the uncertainty of relevant economic parameters.[130] The essence of the above quotes from *Schneider II* seems to be that where it is not practically possible to carry out a causation analysis, it must be held that there is no causation. This would follow from the placing of the burden of proof on the claimant. One of the instances where such practical impossibility will occur is where the economic parameters involved in the hypothetical 'but-for'-assessment are 'too uncertain to be a basis for a useful comparison' with the actual situation. Could the same line of argumentation be applied to a Gamma claim? That is not inconceivable. It could thus be argued that the passing-on of a loss to Gamma involves a great number of economic parameters, and that the assessment of those parameters involved a

127 Ibid., paras 267, 269, 280.

128 Ibid., paras 283, 285–286.

129 For clarity, it should be pointed out that the General Court did not use the concept of 'but for' itself.

130 In this context, such reasoning inevitably summons the ghost of US Supreme Court case law on passing-on, where the Supreme Court refused to engage in theoretical economic reasoning for the purposes of tracing the burden of an overcharge; see Section 7.C.II.a and in particular para. 7–075.

high level of uncertainty. The alleged harm incurred by Gamma might not, therefore, be a sufficiently direct consequence of an EU measure striking primarily at Beta for there to be causation within the meaning of Article 340(2) TFEU.

Toth anticipated problems for claimants 'in the field of economic and commercial relations where the cause of an event can usually be traced back to a number of factors ... operating simultaneously or successively and producing direct as well as indirect effects'.[131] For instance, was the pricing policy of Beta really such that the price paid by Gamma would have been lower but for the targeted EU measure? The burden of proving this would rest upon Gamma – and Gamma might (depending on the circumstances) need the cooperation of Beta to meet that burden.[132] Further, was it not a business decision, for which only Gamma itself is responsible, to purchase from Beta at the price offered? If the price was too high Gamma could (again, depending on the circumstances) have chosen another seller.[133] The burden of proving due diligence in this regard would rest on Gamma. **3.067**

On certain markets it might nevertheless be that market conditions or other circumstances would allow for it to be established that loss had been passed on to Gamma.[134] Gamma might equally be able to establish that it had no real option but to purchase from Beta. With regard to a breach of the causal link by the conduct of Gamma itself, the stringency of the due diligence requirement may also vary depending on circumstances. Case law suggests that, where the claimant is fully informed of the conditions on the market, and thus able to appreciate the effects of the contested EU measure to its own business, the chain of causation will be broken if the claimant does not establish that it has taken appropriate action to avoid harm.[135] Where the claimant is not in such a position, however, a less strict test has been applied. In *Trubowest Handel* the Court of Justice thus held that the causal link might be broken where the determinant cause of harm is negligence on the part of the person adversely **3.068**

131 Toth (n 103) 192.

132 By comparison, Directive 2014/104/EU of the European Parliament and of the Council of 26 November 2014 on certain rules governing actions for damages under national law for infringements of the competition law provisions of the Member States and of the European Union [2014] OJ L349/1 Art. 14 allows Gamma to reasonably require disclosure from Beta in order to establish passing-on.

133 Cf. *Trubowest Handel* (n 95) para. 61.

134 See for instance the Gamma-friendly submissions in *Danfoss* (n 64) Opinion of AG Kokott paras 80–81. However, indirect charges are perhaps an extreme example with no parallel in actions pursuant to Art. 340(2) TFEU. It is a separate problem to establish the extent to which loss was passed on, in order to estimate the actual harm incurred for the purposes of calculating damages. See Sections 3.E.II and 3.E.III.

135 *Compagnie Continentale* (n 103) paras 28–32.

affected.[136] The hurdle for Gamma to jump would vary accordingly, depending on its capability to foresee and to avoid harm from the EU measure.

3.069 To conclude, prospects for Gamma seem rather dark, but not altogether black – it boils down to context. It is evident that the further from the harmful act or omission Gamma is, the more difficult it will be to prove a direct causal link. It is difficult enough to establish causation for Gamma claimants to whom Beta has passed on harm, but what about Gamma claimants of the next level down the supply chain? And the next? And so on? The further away, the more difficult it will be for Gamma. Gamma may exceptionally be able to point out a specific item on invoices that corresponds to the harm passed on. Under such circumstances, or where the relevant market somehow allows for the identification of harm passed on with equivalent certainty, the direct causal link might plausibly persist down several levels of the supply chain.

E. ESTIMATION OF DAMAGES UNDER ARTICLE 340(2) TFEU

3.070 The third subject area of law in damages which is triggered by the circumstances of passing-on is the estimation of damages. This is perhaps the area most commonly associated with passing-on, as this is the context in which the defence of passing-on, whether raised against Beta or Gamma, can be invoked.[137] The defence of passing-on is an argument according to which the damages payable for a breach of law should be reduced to the extent that the claimant has been able to pass on the harm incurred to the next level in the supply chain. In this section case law of the Court of Justice with regard to this defence will be examined and discussed. First, however, it is appropriate to make some general observations on the estimation of damages under Article 340(2) TFEU.

I. General observations on the estimation of damages

3.071 There is consensus that '[t]he object of compensation is to restore the assets of the victim to the condition in which they would have been apart from the unlawful act, or at least to the condition closest to that which would have been

136 *Trubowest Handel* (n 95) para. 61.

137 In this book, Alpha signifies a tortfeasor or enriched party, Beta a party first burdened by loss arising from Alpha's breach of EU law, and Gamma any party downstream from Beta (including all from the party dealing directly with Beta to the final consumer) to whom the burden of that loss may have been passed on; see Section 1.B.

produced if the unlawful act had not taken place'.[138] This view encapsulates the so-called *restitutio in integrum*, or endeavour to achieve full reparation as far as possible.[139] In respect of pecuniary losses the yardstick for *restitutio in integrum* is the amount of diminution of the assets of the claimant. In other words it is the difference between the assets as they are and the hypothetical state of those assets if the harmful event had not occurred.[140]

In *Société Anonyme des Laminoirs* the Court of Justice indicated that the assessment of damage consisted in 'imagining the position which would have arisen' if the unlawful act had not taken place.[141] Advocate General Capotorti opined in *Ireks-Arkady* that in order for the harm incurred to be eligible for compensation in damages, the harm must be direct (directly caused by the harmful act, i.e., that there is causation), certain (the existence of harm must not be questionable), specific (the assets of the claimant were harmed), and serious (*de minimis non curat lex*).[142] Toth has compiled a number of similar *dicta* from the case law, adding importantly that the alleged harm must be quantifiable and proved by the claimant.[143] Those criteria serve to highlight the interrelationship between the causation assessment and the estimation of damages. **3.072**

It is settled case law that the onus of proving harm is on the claimant.[144] It will however become apparent in Section 3.E.II that the defendant institution may have the onus of proving special circumstances invoked by that institution in defence to the claim for damages, e.g., that the harm incurred has been passed on.[145] Where certain, specific and serious damages are claimed, the General **3.073**

138 *Ireks-Arkady* (n 50) Opinion of AG Capotorti para. 9. See also joined cases C-104/89 and C-37/90 *JM Mulder, WH Brinkhoff, JMM Muskens, T Twijnstra and Otto Heinemann v Council of the European Union and Commission of the European Communities* [2000] ECR I-203 para. 63. Cf. Lenaerts, Maselis and Gutman (n 15) 530; Craig (n 7) 693; and Biondi and Farley (n 2) 158. Schermers and Waelbroeck (n 14) 560 use a slightly different phrase: '[T]he reparation must be "commensurate with the loss or damage so as to ensure [effective protection of the applicants'] rights"', quoting *Brasserie* (n 12) para. 42.

139 See e.g. van Gerven et al (n 87) 770.

140 Cf. Draft Common Frame of Reference (Christian von Bar and Eric Clive (eds), *Principles, Definitions and Model Rules of European Private Law: Draft Common Frame of Reference (DCFR) Full Edition* (6 vols, Sellier European Law Publishers 2009)) Art VI. – 6:101(1) and the accompanying Comments. See also European Group on Tort Law, *Principles of European Tort Law: Text and Commentary* (Springer 2005) 161–3. Swedish readers can see Ulf Persson, *Skada och värde* (CWK Gleerup 1953) Ch. 2 on damage as difference and its interrelationship with causation.

141 Joined cases 29, 31, 36, 39 to 47, 50 and 51–63 *Société Anonyme des Laminoirs, Hauts Fourneaux, Forges, Fonderies et Usines de la Providence and others v High Authority of the ECSC* [1965] ECR 911, 939.

142 *Ireks-Arkady* (n 50) Opinion of AG Capotorti para. 9.

143 Toth (n 103) 180–81.

144 E.g., case 26/74 *Société Roquette frères v Commission of the European Communities* [1976] ECR 677 para. 24; *Blackspur* (n 93) para. 31; *Mulder* (n 138) para. 82.

145 Most clearly so in joined cases 256, 257, 265, 267/80, 5 and 51/81 and 282/82 *Birra Wührer SpA and others v Council and Commission of the European Communities* [1984] ECR 3693 para. 28. See further Section 3.E.II.

Court has taken quite a strict view on the necessity of precise quantification by the claimant while the Court of Justice seems to be more lenient in its assessment.[146] In *Société Anonyme des Laminoirs* the Court of Justice thus recognized that circumstances may be such that 'it is not possible to arrive at an exact assessment of the damage', but nevertheless it may well be possible 'to reach acceptable approximations'.[147]

3.074 Notwithstanding the requirement for harm to be specified in the application,[148] the EU Courts will usually give interlocutory judgments on liability of the EU[149] instructing the parties to negotiate the quantum of damages payable and report back to the Courts who will rule on the quantum only if the parties have not been able to agree.[150] In e.g. the gritz and quellmehl cases the Court of Justice provided guidelines for the determination of the quantum to be observed by the parties in their negotiations.[151] The more recent *Sanders* can be used to illustrate: in 2004 the General Court gave quite detailed guidelines on the estimation of damages in that case and awarded the parties a six-month time-limit within which to reach an agreement on the quantum payable in damages.[152] The parties failed to agree however, and therefore they each submitted their respective assessments to the General Court for a ruling on the quantum. Having requested some clarifications from the parties in December 2006, the General Court gathered the information requested in 2007 and heard the oral arguments of the parties at a hearing in March 2007. The General Court delivered its ruling on the quantum of damages payable in July 2007.[153] The parties nonetheless disagreed further, now on the amount of costs recoverable by the claimants. The General Court was therefore compelled to rule again on that specific issue.[154]

---

146 See e.g. case C-243/05 P *Agraz, SA and Others v Commission of the European Communities* [2006] ECR I-10833, where the Court of Justice quashed a judgment of the General Court in which the latter had found that the alleged damage was too uncertain to be compensated.

147 *Société Anonyme des Laminoirs* (n 141) 939. Cf also *Ireks-Arkady* (n 50) Opinion of AG Capotorti para. 9.

148 See para. 3.027.

149 Joined cases 56 to 60/74 *Kurt Kampffmeyer Mühlenvereinigung KG and others v Commission and Council of the European Communities* [1976] ECR 711 para. 6.

150 *Société Anonyme des Laminoirs* (n 141) 940, and Operative part.

151 *Ireks-Arkady* (n 50) para. 18 and Operative part; joined cases 261 and 262/78 *Interquell Stärke-Chemie GmbH and Diamalt AG v Council and Commission of the European Communities* [1979] ECR 3045 para. 21 and Operative part; *Dumortier frères* (n 80) para. 23 and Operative part; *DGV* (n 89) para. 20 and Operative part; case 256/81 *Pauls Agriculture Ltd v Council and Commission of the European Communities* [1983] ECR 1707 para. 15 and Operative part; *Birra Wührer* (n 145) para. 35 and Operative part. For a recent example of this solution see case T-299/11 *European Dynamics Luxembourg SA and others v OHIM* EU:T:2015:757 paras 147–157.

152 Case T-45/01 *Stephen Sanders and Others v Commission of the European Communities* [2004] ECR II-3315 paras 170–177 and Order.

153 Case T-45/01 *Stephen Sanders and Others v Commission of the European Communities* [2007] ECR II-2665.

154 Case T-45/01 DEP *Stephen Sanders and Others v Commission of the European Communities* [2009] ECR II-4093.

The details of the estimation of damages are contingent on the type of harm suffered. An example of estimation by the Court of Justice of damages payable in compensation for personal injury caused by negligence attributable to the European Atomic Energy Community is available in *Grifoni*.[155] The claimant had been injured by falling from a roof. Damages were payable for expenditure resulting from the accident, for loss of earnings caused by the accident due to temporary incapacity and permanent invalidity, and for physical and mental suffering (non-material loss)[156] plus interest. For the purposes of this research, however, the relevant type of harm is pecuniary in nature: e.g., the non-payment of funds due, the illegal levying of charges, lost business opportunities, and the like. The EU Courts have recognized a number of heads of damages that are available to claimants who have suffered such economic harm. Lenaerts, Maselis and Gutman have summarized these heads of damages: actual loss (*damnum emergens*), loss of profit (*lucrum cessans*), and interest.[157] These heads of damages will be discussed below. **3.075**

In certain circumstances, damages have also been payable for non-material loss suffered in business.[158] Lenaerts, Maselis and Gutman also list future damage[159] although future damage is not a head of damage as such. In early case law, claims for future damage were rejected as inadmissible.[160] However, in *Kurt Kampffmeyer*, the Court denied to declare inadmissible an action for damages that were 'foreseeable with sufficient certainty even if the damage cannot yet be precisely assessed'. The Court admitted the application in the interest of preventing even greater damage.[161] **3.076**

As mentioned, the general approach under Article 340(2) TFEU is to restore, as closely as possible, the assets of the claimant to the position they would have been in if it had not been for the harmful act. To that end damages for material loss are available for actual loss, loss of profit and interest. The analysis of 'actual loss' (*damnum emergens*) in EU law writing scarcely moves beyond **3.077**

---

155 Case C-308/87 *Alfredo Grifoni v European Atomic Energy Community* [1994] ECR I-341. Cf n 36 and accompanying text.

156 See Toth (n 103) 190 for further case law with regard to non-material loss, in particular in staff cases.

157 Lenaerts, Maselis and Gutman (n 15) 528–9, 533.

158 See e.g. case T-88/09 *Idromacchine Srl, Alessandro Capuzzo and Roberto Capuzzo v European Commission* [2011] ECR II-7833 and case T-384/11 *Safa Nicu Sepahan Co v Council of the European Union* EU:T:2014:986 paras 78–92.

159 Lenaerts, Maselis and Gutman (n 15) 529–30.

160 See joined cases 9 and 25/64 *Acciaieria Ferriera di Roma (FERAM) and others v High Authority of the ECSC* [1965] ECR 311, 320.

161 *Kurt Kampffmeyer* (n 149) para. 6. A judgment in favour of the claimant in an action with regard to future damage will be an interlocutory judgment; see e.g. joined cases T-79/96, T-260/97 and T-117/98 *Camar Srl and Tico Srl v Commission of the European Communities and Council of the European Union* [2000] ECR II-2193 paras 207–208, 211.

statements such as that reparation must be 'adequate' or 'commensurate with the loss'.[162] The analysis is inclined to focus on more particular issues, such as loss of profit or passing-on. Toth however does elaborate somewhat, explaining that the concept of actual loss includes direct losses resulting from the harmful act and expenses by reason of the harmful act. Toth further takes the view that loss of earnings for private individuals (a concern in staff cases mostly) should be regarded as a form of actual loss rather than as a loss of profit, the latter concept being reserved for business profit.[163]

3.078 The case law confirms that compensation for actual loss should be payable to an amount which is, e.g., equal to the amount of a levy which has been unduly charged,[164] equal to the amount of a subsidy which should have been paid but was not paid[165] or equal to the amount of earnings lost by private individuals (including lost remuneration, related benefits and pension rights – all calculated so as to take into account probable promotions and tax treatment).[166] Hartley cites further illustrative examples:[167] expenses incurred by an undertaking for a breach of contract to which the undertaking was compelled by an illegal act by an EU institution;[168] and losses incurred due to currency fluctuations to which the claimant was exposed due to acts or omissions of an EU institution.[169]

3.079 It thus seems, in sum, that where the parties fail to agree on the quantum of damages payable for actual loss, the EU Courts seem open to assess the alleged harm without special limitations except those that follow from the general requirements, i.e., that the harm must be certain, specific and serious.[170]

3.080 With regard to loss of profit (*lucrum cessans*), the case law is apprehensive, the Court showing a reluctance to award damages unless it is established that the loss of profit is real and certain.[171] In *E Kampffmeyer* the Court went so far as

162 Schermers and Waelbroeck (n 14) 560.

163 Toth (n 103) 187.

164 *E Kampffmeyer* (n 109) 263.

165 That is, an amount of damages equal to the amount of the subsidy at the time at which it should have been paid; case 261/78 *Interquell Stärke-Chemie GmbH and Co KG v European Economic Community* [1982] ECR 3271 paras 10–11.

166 Case T-45/01 *Sanders* (n 153). See also case 79/71 *Alo Heinemann v Commission of the European Communities* [1972] ECR 579.

167 Hartley (n 3) 457.

168 *E Kampffmeyer* (n 109) 265.

169 Case 74/74 *Comptoir national technique agricole (CNTA) SA v Commission of the European Communities* [1976] ECR 797 para. 6.

170 *Ireks-Arkady* (n 50) Opinion of AG Capotorti para. 9. See also e.g. *Agraz* (n 146) para. 27 with references.

171 See e.g. case 74/74 *Comptoir national technique agricole (CNTA) SA v Commission of the European Communities* [1975] ECR 533 paras 45–46; case T-231/97 *New Europe Consulting and Michael P Brown v Commission of the European Communities* [1999] ECR II-2403 paras 50–52.

to estimate the profit lost at 10 per cent of the amount estimated by the claimants, holding that '[t]he alleged injury in respect to the loss of profit is based on facts of an essentially speculative nature'.[172] This *dictum* must however not be read as a policy statement with regard to damages for loss of profit[173] but rather in context of the facts of the case: the Court identified unusual activities on the relevant market at the time and seemed to suspect that the claimants were trying to use administrative mistakes to make an easy profit. Similar outcomes can be noted in other cases where the loss of profit has been contingent on the occurrence of uncertain factors such as currency fluctuations[174] or the award of a contract in a tender.[175]

By contrast, successful claims for loss of profit were brought in *Mulder* notwithstanding that the circumstances were such that the assessment of the amount of profits lost was of an 'essentially hypothetical nature'.[176] The Court of Justice had held in interlocutory judgment that the assessment of damages should take into account 'the loss of earnings consisting in the difference between, on the one hand, the income which the applicants would have obtained in the normal course of events ... and, on the other hand, the income which they actually obtained'.[177] Interestingly, especially in light of the passing-on problem, the Court also held that it was relevant whether the claimant had been able to mitigate the loss suffered through alternative business activities. Such income was to be deducted from the damages payable, taking into account 'not only that which the applicants actually obtained from replacement activities, but also that income which they could have obtained had they reasonably engaged in such activities'.[178] The overall assessment was carried out in detail by the Court in its final ruling, on the basis of a calculation method agreed by the parties and guided by expert evidence and statistics.[179] In *Camar* too, the loss of profit could not be precisely quantified, but the General Court nevertheless held that the figures submitted by the claimant were 'sufficiently conclusive and provide a sound basis' for proceeding on the basis of 'reasonable and acceptable' estimates.[180] **3.081**

---

172 *E Kampffmeyer* (n 109) 266, criticized by Hartley (n 3) 458.

173 See Toth (n 103) 187.

174 See *CNTA* (n 171) paras 45–46.

175 See *New Europe Consulting* (n 171) para. 52. Similar in case T-39/08 *Evropaïki Dynamiki – Proigmena Systimata Tilepikoinonion Pliroforikis kai Tilematikis AE v European Commission* [2011] ECR II-437 (summary publication) paras 47–49.

176 *Mulder* (n 138) para. 84, and cf. paras 64–66.

177 Joined cases C-104/89 and C-37/90 *J M Mulder and others and Otto Heinemann v Council of the European Communities and Commission of the European Communities* [1992] ECR I-3061 para. 26.

178 Ibid., para. 33.

179 On that agreed method see *Mulder* (n 138) paras 67–72 *et passim*.

180 Case T-260/97 *Camar Srl v Council of the European Union and Commission of the European Communities* [2005] ECR II-2741 para. 126.

3.082 Damages are accordingly available for loss of profit in principle, but the onus of proving such harm is on the claimant and unless the parties can agree on the quantum the EU Courts apply that requirement strictly. Where certain, specific and serious loss of profit is proved to have been incurred the precise quantum may nonetheless be approximated on the basis of reasonable estimates.

3.083 A few final remarks on interest.[181] Default interest may be awarded 'from the date of delivery of the judgment declaring a party liable to make good the damage claimed' until full payment of that compensation.[182] Compensatory interest may be payable from an earlier point, usually the date on which the harm first arose, and until the date of delivery of judgment.[183] The purpose of compensatory interest is to compensate for 'the adverse consequences of a lapse of time between the occurrence of the actionable event and the date of payment of compensation ... inasmuch as the effects of inflation must be taken into account'.[184] To provide full coverage for adverse consequences until the date of payment of compensation, compensatory interest must thus be combined with default interest.[185]

II. The defence of passing-on in case law

3.084 The European Court of Justice began its passing-on odyssey on 4 October 1979 by the simultaneous delivery of its judgments in *Ireks-Arkady*; *Interquell Stärke-Chemie*; *Dumortier frères*; and *DGV*.[186] These cases all concerned actions for damages under Article (now) 340(2) TFEU. The circumstances were similar and the respective judgments are almost identical in the respects relevant to the passing-on problem.

3.085 The claimants in *Ireks-Arkady* and *Interquell Stärke-Chemie* produced quellmehl, a maize- or wheat-based product used as starch in baking. As a result of Regulation

181 An informative but now partly dated discussion of this issue is available in A van Casteren, 'Article 215(2) EC and the Question of Interest' in Ton Heukels and Alison McDonnell (eds), *The Action for Damages in Community Law* (Kluwer Law 1997).

182 *Idromacchine* (n 158) para. 79; see also the references there. On the date of commencement in staff cases see Lenaerts, Maselis and Gutman (n 15) 533. In early case law, the rate of default interest was at the discretion of the Court of Justice (see van Casteren (n 181) 202–5 and also Lenaerts, Maselis and Gutman (n 15) 533), but in more recent case law it has been established that 'the interest rate to be applied is calculated on the basis of the rate set by the ECB for main refinancing operations, applicable during the period in question, increased by two percentage points' (*Idromacchine* (n 158) para. 79).

183 *Idromacchine* (n 158) para. 78.

184 Ibid., para. 77; see also the references there. In *Mulder*, the rate of compensatory interest was set at a percentage calculated to compensate particularly for inflation. In more recent case law the rate has been the same as the rate of default interest (*Idromacchine* (n 158) para. 78).

185 *Mulder* (n 138) paras 214–221.

186 *Ireks-Arkady* (n 50); *Interquell Stärke-Chemie* (n 151); *Dumortier frères* (n 80); and *DGV* (n 89).

No 1125/74 amending Regulation No 120/67 on the Common Organisation of the Market in cereals, applied as from 1 August 1974, the thereunto payable refunds for quellmehl production were abolished. The Court of Justice however held in *Ruckdeschel* that it was incompatible with the principle of equal treatment to abolish production refunds for quellmehl while the refund was maintained for maize-based starch.[187] Following that judgment production refunds for quellmehl were re-introduced by Regulation No 1125/78 amending Regulation No 2727/75 on the Common Organisation of the Market in cereals, with retroactive effect from the date of the *Ruckdeschel* judgment.

The claimants in *Dumortier frères* and *DGV* were producers of maize groats and meal ('gritz') used for the brewing of beer. As a result of Regulation No 665/75 of the Council of 4 March 1975 amending Regulation No 120/67 on the common organization of the market in cereals, production refunds on such maize gritz were abolished, even though refunds on the competitor maize starch product were retained. In *SA Moulins*[188] it was settled by the European Court of Justice that the abolition of refunds for maize gritz while maintaining refunds for maize starch was contrary to the principle of equality of treatment. Pursuant to that judgment production refunds for maize gritz used by the brewing industry were reintroduced by Council Regulation No 1125/78 of 22 May 1978.

The claimants brought actions for damages against the Council and the Commission claiming compensation for damage suffered as a result of the period of absence of refunds. They claimed damages equal to the amount of production refunds that would have been payable if quellmehl and maize gritz production had benefited from the same refunds as starch. In *Dumortier frères*, some of the claimants also claimed compensation for additional losses caused by a fall in sales and operating deficits.[189]

On the issue of liability as such the Court of Justice recalled settled case law stating that the Community did not incur liability on account of a legislative measure which involves choices of economic policy unless a sufficiently serious breach of a superior rule of law for the protection of the individual has occurred, and unless the institution concerned had manifestly and gravely disregarded the limits on the exercise of its powers. In the circumstances of the cases at hand, the Court held that these prerequisites were met and that the Community did incur liability for the abolition of production refunds for quellmehl and maize gritz.[190]

On the issue of the amount of damage to be compensated the Council and the Commission argued that under Article (now) 340(2) TFEU, compensation was not payable for the loss of income in the form of unpaid aids, but only for commercial profit yielded by the activity pursued by an undertaking which did not accrue as a

---

187 Joined cases 117/76 and 16/77 *Ruckdeschel & Co v Hauptzollamt Hamburg – St Annen* and *Diamalt AG v Hauptzollamt Itzehoe* [1977] ECR 1753 para. 10.

188 *Moulins & Huileries* (n 81).

189 Regarding the claims brought with regard to additional losses in *Dumortier frères* (n 80) see the discussion on causation in Section 3.D.I.

190 *Ireks-Arkady* (n 50) paras 9–12; *Interquell Stärke-Chemie* (n 151) paras 12–15; *Dumortier frères* (n 80) paras 9–13; *DGV* (n 89) paras 9–13.

result of an unlawful act by the institutions.[191] The Council and the Commission further submitted that the claimants had eliminated any loss resulting from the abolition of the production refunds, or could have eliminated it, by passing the loss on in their selling prices.[192] To that end, the Council indicated a series of figures concerning price increases in the applications brought.[193] The claimants disputed the possibility of passing-on the loss in that way,[194] stating that in the face of competition from starch producers benefiting from refunds they had chosen as a matter of commercial policy to sell quellmehl at a loss in order to retain market shares rather than to increase prices at the risk of losing market shares. The claimants submitted that the price increases referred to by the Council and the Commission were due to a rise in the threshold price for maize and increased production costs.[195]

3.086 Advocate General Capotorti delivered an Opinion covering all four cases.[196] The Opinion has been quite influential with regard to passing-on in EU law and it is therefore appropriate to cite it extensively. Beginning with a general analysis of the concept of damage, the Advocate General opined that 'the damage suffered by the applicants must be assessed in relation to the right infringed, namely the right to equality of treatment', and that therefore 'the correct solution seems to be to measure the damage with reference to the inequality. In financial terms the inequality lies in the amount of the refunds not having been paid.' In that regard, the Advocate General continued, 'the damage for which the applicants are asking to be compensated coincides with the loss of income from the refunds, and the lost income constitutes damage in itself ... without its being necessary to prove material losses of a different nature'.[197] With regard to the passing-on problem in particular, the Advocate General distinguished two arguments used for the justification of the objections made by the defendant institutions. The first argument was that any benefit flowing from an unlawful act must be set off against damage flowing from the same unlawful act, and that it would follow that the damage recoverable would be reduced by the amount passed on. This, the Advocate General submitted, was a misinterpretation of the *compensatio lucri cum damno* rule.[198] On proper application the damage and benefit must both be the direct and automatic consequences of the same unlawful act. In this case, the Advocate General continued, 'the benefit which is presumed to be connected

191 *Ireks-Arkady* (n 50) Opinion of AG Capotorti para. 10.

192 *Ireks-Arkady* (n 50) para. 14; *Interquell Stärke-Chemie* (n 151) para. 17; *Dumortier frères* (n 80) para. 15; *DGV* (n 89) para. 15.

193 *Ireks-Arkady* (n 50) Opinion of AG Capotorti para. 11.

194 With the exception of a brief period in the circumstances of *Dumortier frères* (n 80), see para. 15.

195 *Ireks-Arkady* (n 50) para. 15; *Interquell Stärke-Chemie* (n 151) para. 18; *Dumortier frères* (n 80) para. 16; *DGV* (n 89) para. 16.

196 The Opinion was published in the ECR in connection to *Ireks-Arkady*. Hence, footnotes will refer to that case.

197 *Ireks-Arkady* (n 50) Opinion of AG Capotorti para. 9.

198 On *compensatio lucri cum damno* see DCFR (n 140) Art. VI. – 6:103 with Comments and Notes.

with the increase in prices could never be said to have been *caused* by the abolition of the production refunds: it is in truth the result of an independent decision of the producers'.[199]

The second argument was that compensation was not recoverable for damage which the victim could have avoided by means of due diligence.[200] It would follow that the payment of damages would be precluded to the extent it was possible to pass on the effect of the harm incurred to customers. The Advocate General dismissed this argument, opining that 'although it is true that by increasing their earnings from other sources the victims could to some extent compensate for the adverse effect of that damage to their assets, they were certainly not in a position to prevent the loss of the income by their diligence'. On the contrary, the Advocate General argued, 'we must leave out of consideration any achievements due to the management of the applicant undertakings during the period in which Community financial aid was not available'.[201] The Advocate General also opined that was impossible to establish how the claimants would have used the refunds if they had been paid: '... perhaps they would have used them to renew their plant ... or to fix their selling prices at more competitive levels ... However, one thing is clear: the financial resources of the producers of gritz and quellmehl were smaller than those at the disposal of the producers of starch ...'[202] **3.087**

The Advocate General moreover questioned the idea that prices are generally set through the passing-on of costs plus a profit margin. Rather, he argued, 'undertakings act according to the logic inspired by the profit motive and on the basis of the market conditions'. Therefore 'where the market does not permit of price increases, they must refrain from making such increases ... when a public financial aid ceases to be paid' as to do otherwise 'might constitute a grave commercial error'.[203] The Advocate General then turned to the issue of the burden of proof, opining that 'to counter the claim for damages with one of the arguments in question [i.e., a defence of passing-on] involves raising a special plea; therefore, the burden of proof falls on the party raising that plea', and concluded: **3.088**

> In sum, therefore: there is no valid justification in principle for considering compensation precluded, or reduced, on the ground that the damage lying in the producers' **3.089**

199 *Ireks-Arkady* (n 50) Opinion of AG Capotorti para. 11. Italics in original.

200 On such mitigation of loss see DCFR (n 140) Art. VI. – 5:102(1) with Comments 3628–3629; and Notes 3642–3646.

201 *Ireks-Arkady* (n 50) Opinion of AG Capotorti para. 11.

202 Ibid., para. 9.

203 Ibid., para. 11.

loss of receipts was, or could have been, passed on in the selling prices; in each of the cases with which we are dealing the party which would have had to prove such circumstances has not adduced convincing evidence.[204]

3.090 The Court of Justice held in all four cases that as the damage complained of by the claimants lay in the abolition by the Council of the refunds which would have been paid if equality of treatment had been observed, the amount of the unpaid refunds must provide a yardstick for the assessment of the damage suffered. The Court nonetheless held that in the context of an action for damages, the passing-on objection of the Council could not be dismissed as unfounded. If the loss had or could have been passed on in prices the damage should not, the Court held, be measured by reference to the refunds not paid. The price increase would take the place of the refunds, compensating the claimants.[205]

3.091 On the basis of available evidence the Court of Justice held that it could not be established that the refunds not paid had or could have been passed on in the prices set by the claimants.[206] In *Dumortier frères* and *DGV*, with the exception of a brief period recognized in *Dumortier frères*, the Court similarly found that the evidence supported the argument of the claimants that prices on gritz and competitor starch did not during the relevant period reflect the absence of refunds for gritz. The claimants in *Dumortier frères* had moreover shown that during the brief period within which prices for gritz did reflect the absence of refunds those price increases had been accepted by breweries only on the inclusion of a contract clause guaranteeing the buyer the retroactive benefit of any new refund granted.[207] The Court therefore held that damage consisting in the loss of receipts equal to the amounts of the refunds not paid must be calculated on the basis of its being equivalent to the refunds not paid.[208]

3.092 The gritz and quellmehl saga continued with new cases. Circumstances were quite similar again in the subsequent *Pauls Agriculture*,[209] and the judgment of the Court of Justice added no news to the first gritz and quellmehl cases. Interestingly, however, the Council and the Commission still contended that it

204 Ibid. This summary by the Advocate General somewhat blurs the impression otherwise given by his Opinion that he would dismiss the defence of passing-on at law. Most probably, however, it was intended to show that he would dismiss it both at law and, if upheld by the Court of Justice, on the facts.

205 *Ireks-Arkady* (n 50) paras 13–14; *Interquell Stärke-Chemie* (n 151) paras 16–17; *Dumortier frères* (n 80) paras 14–15; *DGV* (n 89) paras 14–15.

206 *Ireks-Arkady* (n 50) para. 15; *Interquell Stärke-Chemie* (n 151) para. 19: *Dumortier frères* (n 80) para. 17; *DGV* (n 89) para. 17.

207 *Dumortier frères* (n 80) para. 17; *DGV* (n 89) para. 17.

208 *Ireks-Arkady* (n 50) para. 16; *Interquell Stärke-Chemie* (n 151) para. 20; *Dumortier frères* (n 80) para. 18; *DGV* (n 89) para. 18.

209 *Pauls Agriculture* (n 151).

was for the claimant to prove that damage had not been, and could not have been, eliminated by passing on the loss resulting from the abolition of the refunds in its selling prices.[210] In *Birra Wührer*[211] matters were slightly more complicated.

The claimants were Italian producers of maize gritz or broken rice, or both, intended for the brewing industry. Production refunds for such broken rice had been abolished by Regulation No 668/75 of the Council of 4 March 1975 amending Regulation No 120/67 on the common organization of the market in cereals. Following the judgment of the Court of Justice in *Moulins & Huileries*[212] production refunds for broken rice were reintroduced by Council Regulation No 1127/78 of 22 May 1978. **3.093**

The claimants brought actions against the Council and the Commission of the European Communities, seeking compensation for harm they claimed to have incurred as a result of the period of absence of production refunds. The alleged damage consisted in the loss of receipts equal to the amounts of the refunds which would have been paid to them if the production of maize gritz and broken rice had benefited from the same refunds as the production of starch.

One of the claimants, Riseria Modenese, had assigned its rights to the refunds at issue to another applicant, Birra Peroni. Consequently the action brought by Riseria Modenese was dismissed. Another claimant, Birra Wührer, was also an assignee of rights to the refunds at issue.[213] Both assignees purchased the products at issue from their respective assignors. With regard to the actions brought by assignees the Commission argued first, that their actions would not have been admissible under Italian law, secondly, that the assignments pertained to payment of refunds and not to payment of compensation for unpaid refunds, and thirdly, that the assignments could not be effective as the assignors were not, at the time of assignment, entitled to refunds. Contrary to the arguments submitted by the Commission, the actions of the assignees were admitted by the Court of Justice.[214]

With regard to the estimation of harm incurred the Council and the Commission argued that the producers had or could have eliminated the damage by passing-on in their selling prices the loss caused by the abolition of the refunds and (still) contended that it was for the claimants to prove the contrary.[215] The Council and the Commission insisted that it might be assumed that the producers had passed on the damage in their selling prices because the rights to the refunds were assigned, and that the assignment must surely have been effected in return for an increase in prices. The

210 Ibid., para. 8. Drawing on many points made by AG Capotorti in his Opinion in *Ireks-Arkady* (n 50) Advocate General Mancini seemed in *Pauls Agriculture* to wish for the Court to reconsider its acceptance of the defence of passing-on. AG Mancini went so far as to opine that '[t]he idea that losses may be passed on and the principles which govern non-contractual liability are as a general rule irreconcilable'; *Pauls Agriculture* (n 151) Opinion of AG Mancini para. 5.

211 *Birra Wührer* (n 145).

212 *Moulins & Huileries* (n 81).

213 *Birra Wührer* (n 145) paras 7–8.

214 Ibid., paras 8–14.

215 Ibid., para. 26.

Council and Commission moreover argued that since the prices of all producers were on the same level, the presumption resulting from the instances of assignment indicated that the damage had been passed on by all producers.[216] With regard to assignee claimants, however, the Council and Commission instead contended that they must prove that they paid to the assignor producers a supplementary price corresponding to the unpaid refunds.[217]

3.094 Advocate General verLoren van Themaat maintained that the defendant institutions should bear the burden of proving that the loss was passed on, and submitted three arguments in favour of that proposition. First, the Advocate General stressed that 'the production refunds in question were introduced in order to make it possible for maize gritz and broken rice to find a competitive use'. It might therefore be 'assumed that the loss arising from the abolition of the refunds was in principle not incorporated in the selling price, since otherwise the products would have lost their competitiveness' and, consequently, 'the Council should be required to rebut that presumption'. Second, the Advocate General continued, 'there is an economic but not a legal connection between the amounts of the refunds and the selling prices', as the right to receive refunds 'does not depend on the prices that were actually charged but solely on the use of broken rice for the manufacture of beer and the production of maize gritz … . The starting point must therefore be that the loss is equal to the refunds that were abolished, *unless* it can be proven that the loss was passed on'. Third, the Advocate General opined that as the Court of Justice had held for the purposes of the repayment of charges levied in breach of EU law that 'the incidence of the burden of proof … may not be such as to make it impossible in practice to secure repayment' and 'that that would be so, in particular, where the person concerned had the burden of establishing that the charges had *not* been passed on to other persons', such a principle 'also applies *mutatis mutandis* where, contrary to Community law, subsidies have not been paid'.[218]

3.095 The Court of Justice settled the burden of proof issue by dismissing the arguments submitted by the Council and the Commission, holding that as they had not produced any evidence which could cast doubt on the figures presented by the claimants and the conclusions which the claimants had drawn from them, their objection could not be upheld. The Court hence did not only refuse to adopt the presumptions of passing-on suggested by the Council and the Commission but effectively placed the burden of proving passing-on on them. The Court did not on the basis of presented evidence

216 Ibid., para. 29.

217 Ibid., para. 31.

218 Ibid., Opinion of AG verLoren van Themaat para. 4. Italics in original.

consider it proved that the assignments were effected in return for an increase in selling prices and even less that there had been a general price increase.[219]

With regard to the assignee claimants the Court held that they had not based their claim on the assignors' having passed on to them the damage at issue, but because of not having received refunds on the basis of the rights assigned to them. The Court therefore concluded that the argument put forth by the Council and the Commission in this regard was not relevant.[220] **3.096**

The Court of Justice held for those reasons that the damage incurred must be calculated on the basis of its being equivalent to the amounts of the refunds which would have been paid to the claimants if the production of maize gritz and broken rice had benefited from the same refunds as the production of starch.[221] **3.097**

No subsequent case law on the defence of passing-on exists within the context of Article 340(2) TFEU. **3.098**

III. Analysis of the case law

Summarizing the case law it is evident that the defence of passing-on has been accepted by the Court of Justice for the purposes of Article 340(2) TFEU. If the loss had or could have been passed on in prices the damage should not, the Court has held, be measured by reference to the refunds not paid. The price increase would take the place of the refunds, compensating the claimants.[222] In the context of Article 340(2) TFEU, the defence of passing-on thus functions as an argument on the extent of actual loss (*damnum emergens*). It was seen in Section 3.E.I that the burden of proof with regard to harm incurred is on the claimant. With regard to the defence of passing-on, however, the burden has been reversed by the Court. In *Birra Wührer* the Court of Justice thus unequivocally placed the burden of proving passing-on on the Council and the Commission.[223] The defendants were not able to meet that burden of proof in any of the cases presented above, and there was consequently no reduction of the damages payable for actual loss by reason of real or possible passing-on. *Birra Wührer* also introduced Gamma claimants, i.e., the assignees. Due to the **3.099**

219 Ibid., paras 28 and 30.
220 Ibid., para. 32.
221 Ibid., para. 33.
222 *Ireks-Arkady* (n 50) para. 14; *Interquell Stärke-Chemie* (n 151) para. 17; *Dumortier frères* (n 80) para. 15; *DGV* (n 89) para. 15.
223 *Birra Wührer* (n 145) para. 28.

facts explained above however, their actions were treated as subrogated Beta actions by the Court of Justice.

3.100 The gritz and quellmehl cases do not discuss loss of profit (*lucrum cessans*) in the form of reduced sales caused by the need to increase prices. The claimants do not seem from the reports for the hearings to have argued that their sales decreased – and indeed, such an argument would have been in contradiction with their assertions that the harm incurred could not be passed on in the manner suggested by the defendants. It was interestingly submitted by the Commission in *Ireks-Arkady* that the turnover of the claimants had remained unaffected by the abolition of refunds and that they could not therefore have suffered harm. The claimants counter-argued that they had had to sell at a loss to maintain market shares.[224] The Court apparently remained unconvinced by the argument of the Commission.

3.101 Toth has criticized the Court's acceptance of the defence of passing-on in the gritz and quellmehl cases, submitting two distinct arguments. The first argument was that 'there is no legal or economic nexus whatsoever between the abolition of the refunds and the applicants' pricing policies'. Toth submitted that prices were set by 'factors entirely independent of' the abolition of refunds, e.g., market prices and profit motives. Therefore, Toth argued, even if the claimants had been able to raise prices, the benefit of such increases and the harm incurred through the abolition of refunds would have been 'of an entirely different origin and legal nature' – thus the former should not have been set off against the latter.[225] This author agrees that pricing policies will typically have competitiveness on the relevant market as their first priority, but does not agree that pricing is entirely independent of production costs.[226] Pricing policies do not lend themselves to simplistic or uniform descriptions, they differ too much. The price can be set quite independently from production costs, e.g., as part of the marketing of a service or product as belonging to the premium quality segment of the market. But market conditions may also be such that producers must keep very close to production costs in their pricing in order to avoid bankruptcy on a market with fierce competition over a long period of time. Accordingly, if the analysis of Toth is taken one step back, it gains more merit.

---

224 *Ireks-Arkady* (n 50) 2966–2967.

225 Toth (n 103) 189.

226 The abolished refunds were intended to subsidize production, i.e., to reduce production costs; *Birra Wührer* (n 145) Opinion of AG verLoren van Themaat para. 4. In this discussion, the broader term 'production costs' is used, as the passing-on situation in the gritz and quellmehl cases is applicable to any category of harm causing an increase of production costs.

The opposite presumption, i.e., that selling prices are determined by production costs, cannot apply either. This latter point is stressed by Toth but to a point at which the argument, it is submitted, goes too far. It is sufficient to notice that pricing is not necessarily dependent on production costs in order for the basis of a general acceptance of a passing-on defence under Article 340(2) TFEU to be questioned. As opined by Advocate General Capotorti in the 1979 cases, 'undertakings act according to the logic inspired by the profit motive and on the basis of the market conditions'. Therefore 'where the market does not permit of price increases, they must refrain from making such increases ... when a public financial aid ceases to be paid' as to do otherwise 'might constitute a grave commercial error'.[227] This does not however as such mean that the defence of passing-on could not apply in special circumstances, it only means that it does not apply in every circumstance. Such a view on passing-on acknowledges that the passing-on of loss may be possible in special circumstances, namely to the extent that pricing can be shown to be dependent on production costs. Two policy options are available if this is accepted. The first is to reject the defence of passing-on, in the interest of deterrence and in order to avoid excessive litigation costs in connection with evidence on market structures and pricing strategies.[228] In a critique of the gritz and quellmehl judgments, Rudden and Bishop have argued along those lines that the defence of passing-on should have been rejected, inter alia in order to save the costs necessary to determine the extent of passing-on.[229] The other policy option is to accept the defence of passing-on for the sake of circumstances where passing-on is possible, but to put the onus of proving those circumstances in the individual case on the defendant. In the gritz and quellmehl cases, the Court of Justice chose the second policy option. This choice serves the interest of reparatory compensation – no more, no less – but can be criticized for not serving the interest of deterrence and for being liable to give rise to excessive litigation costs. 3.102

Toth also submitted that it was wrong for the Court of Justice to allow defendants to invoke mere possibilities to pass on as a defence. To recall, the Court held that if the loss had *or could have been* passed on in prices the damage should not be measured by reference to the refunds not paid as the 3.103

227 *Ireks-Arkady* (n 50) Opinion of AG Capotorti para. 11.

228 The US Supreme Court has been inclined to choose this policy option for the purposes of federal law; see e.g. *Southern Pac Co v Darnell-Taenzer Lumber Co* 245 US 531 (1918) on damages for excessive interstate railway charges and *Hanover Shoe Inc v United Shoe Machinery Corp*, 392 US 481 (1968) on harm incurred through overcharges contrary to antitrust law. The interest of deterrence and its role in the passing-on problem is addressed in Section 9.E.II.

229 Bernard Rudden and William Bishop, 'Gritz and Quellmehl: Pass It On' (1981) 6 *European Law Review* 243, 254.

price increase would take the place of the refunds, compensating the claimants.[230] Toth accepted that victims of torts have a general duty to mitigate loss, but strongly opposed the notion that the mitigation of loss would include a duty to pass on to customers harm incurred through the unlawful actions of EU institutions:

3.104 Such an obligation would ultimately mean that damage caused by the Community institutions in clear infringement of Community law should be borne by the customers of the injured party, and through them by society at large, rather than by those responsible for it.[231]

3.105 Again the argument was partly sound. The economic consequences of an infringement of EU law would spread likes waves on water irrespective of whether a Beta claimant is able to obtain reparation. The outcome of litigation could not stop this from happening, it could only bring some relief to the individual claimant, if successful. Therefore the implicit expectation of Toth that an award of damages would save society at large from bearing the burdens of law infringements would not have been met even if the Court had rejected the defence of passing-on.[232]

3.106 A different and arguably more rewarding analysis of this diluent effect of passing-on has been submitted by Rudden and Bishop, who discussed at some length the coordination of claims from different levels of the supply chain in the context of the defence of passing-on. If, they submitted, the defence of passing-on is accepted at law (as it was in the gritz and quellmehl cases), 'it is very difficult, as a matter of abstract justice, to deny [Gamma] an action'. However, they continued, this gives rise to further vexations where there are a multitude of 'Gamma levels' down the supply chain. At each level from Beta and down to the final consumer it would become necessary to analyse the relevant market conditions in order to ascertain whether the initial harm has been passed further on. Rudden and Bishop also recognized that other factors, e.g., the pricing policy at each level of the supply chain, will need to be accounted for in such an analysis. If 'all cases could be litigated costlessly', Rudden and Bishop recognized that all those harmed might bring an action with respect to the loss sustained by them. But, they argued, 'in the real world, they would not find a lawsuit worthwhile even if the fact of loss could be

---

230 *Ireks-Arkady* (n 50) para. 14; *Interquell Stärke-Chemie* (n 151) para. 17; *Dumortier frères* (n 80) para. 15; *DGV* (n 89) para. 15. Italics added. In *Mulder* (n 177) para. 33 the Court similarly held that a claimant who had been hindered in its business had to mitigate loss by trying alternative business opportunities, see para. 3.081.

231 Toth (n 103) 189.

232 See Rudden and Bishop (n 229) 253. Danish readers can enjoy the still illuminating discussion of the function of tort and damages law in society by Henry Ussing, *Skyld og Skade* (GEC Gad 1914) 24–9.

proved'. By contrast, if claimants were permitted to recover in full, with no reduction for passing-on, Rudden and Bishop expected that they would have more incentive to bring an action pursuant to Article 340(2) TFEU, thereby contributing to the effective supervision of the EU legal order. In conclusion Rudden and Bishop advocated that the defence of passing-on should have been rejected in order to engage Beta as 'watchdog' over Alpha, notwithstanding the possibility of Beta's enrichment. In that regard Rudden and Bishop explicitly preferred Beta's enrichment over Alpha's enrichment.[233]

The last point made by Rudden and Bishop is implicit also in Toth's second argument, and highlights that the policy option chosen by the Court of Justice risks leaving the EU with a gain earned through an infringement of EU law, an unjust enrichment if you will, in cases where the defendant institution successfully invokes the defence of passing-on against a Beta claimant and is not subsequently held liable to compensate Gamma. A parallel critique was voiced by Hubeau in the context of repayment actions against a Member State.[234] This risk is manifest and should not be ignored. One way of procuring the disgorgement of such gains is to design a system of liability to that end. Such a system could include actions of unjust enrichment,[235] it could be open to gain-based damages,[236] and it would reject the defence of passing-on. The acknowledgement of the defence of passing-on however works in the opposite direction. **3.107**

At the end of the day a choice of policy is a political choice, not a legal issue. Neither precedent nor EU law provisions compelled the Court of Justice to choose strictly reparative compensation in the gritz and quellmehl cases. It can be speculated that such a policy seemed a balanced middle way, avoiding the seeming pitfalls of damages awards in excess of harm or a too stringent burden of proof on claimants (including the burden of proving that harm was *not* and could not have been passed on). Perhaps the Court felt that the need to deter (now) EU institutions from acting in breach of EU law was relatively low, that costs for establishing passing-on should not be overestimated, and that the occasional occurrence of unlawful gains of the EU could be tolerated. Of course it is open for anyone to disagree and to argue that it is discomforting to see the EU Courts protect the interests of the EU in this manner. It is **3.108**

233 Rudden and Bishop (n 229) 254–6.

234 Francis Hubeau, 'La répétition de l'indu en droit communautaire' (1981) 17 Revue Trimestrielle de Droit Européen 442, 451. See also case 199/82 *Amministrazione delle Finanze dello Stato v SpA San Giorgio* [1983] ECR 3595 Opinion of AG Mancini para. 7.

235 See Ch. 4 for a discussion of restitutionary actions against the EU.

236 On gain-based damages see James Edelman, *Gain-Based Damages: Contract, Tort, Equity and Intellectual Property* (Hart Publishing, 2002) in particular Ch. 3.

similarly evident that Rudden and Bishop favoured effective enforcement of EU law over reparatory compensation, and took the view that the acknowledgement of the defence of passing-on amounted to a missed opportunity in that regard.

3.109 The arguments in favour of the defence of passing-on do however presuppose that there is a legally viable nexus between Beta's suffering of harm and the prices set by Beta. The Opinion of Advocate General verLoren van Themaat in *Birra Wührer* includes a point which potentially undermines that presupposition, at least for the purposes of the gritz and quellmehl cases. The Advocate General noted that the right to receive refunds 'does not depend on the prices that were actually charged but solely on the use of broken rice for the manufacture of beer and the production of maize gritz'.[237] With such a view the legal nexus between the illegal abolition of refunds and the pricing policy of the recipients is strained to the point of disruption. Advocate General Capotorti too opined in the 1979 cases that even if Beta was able to pass on the loss incurred 'the benefit which is presumed to be connected with the increase in prices could never be said to have been *caused* by the abolition of the production refunds: it is in truth the result of an independent decision of the producers'.[238] It would indeed be more likely that successful passing-on would be attributable to factors such as successful marketing or other factors. In that regard this author agrees with Advocate General Capotorti that 'we must leave out of consideration any achievements due to the management of the applicant undertakings during the period in which Community financial aid was not available'.[239]

3.110 If these arguments are accepted there is no legal nexus between Beta's suffering of harm and the prices set by Beta in the gritz and quellmehl cases, and the defence of passing-on should consequently have been rejected. The observations of the Advocates General moreover give little room for a defence of passing-on in other circumstances – the circumstances would need to be quite particular for the business achievements of the claimant to be irrelevant to the assessment. The onus of proving that circumstances were such should, of course, rest with the defendant.

3.111 Finally it should be duly noticed that, in all four 1979 judgments, the Court of Justice stressed that the defence should not be dismissed as unfounded 'in the

237 *Birra Wührer* (n 145) Opinion of AG verLoren van Themaat para. 4.

238 *Ireks-Arkady* (n 50) Opinion of AG Capotorti para. 11. Italics in original.

239 Ibid.

context of an action for damages'.[240] As noticed by Lenaerts, Maselis and Gutman, the Court has taken a more restrictive view in the context of an action for repayment of charges levied by Member States in breach of EU law.[241] This could be taken as an indication that the defence of passing-on is more easily acceptable to the Court in the context of damages than in the context of restitution. Indeed, the EU legislature has endorsed the defence of passing-on for the purposes of competition law damages.[242] Therefore, even though the case law here analysed dates back 30 years or more and notwithstanding the valid criticism just discussed, it seems consistent with the contemporary EU law approach to the defence of passing-on in damages.

F. CONCLUSIONS AND SUGGESTIONS

This section concerns the coordination of litigation where the passing-on problem arises in the context of an action for damages pursuant to Article 340(2) TFEU. In other words, how should the risk of multiple liability for Alpha, the interests of reparation to Beta and Gamma, and the more general interests of consistency in law and deterrence from illegal conduct be reconciled? This is discussed in depth in the concluding Chapter 9, in which it is attempted to draw from all the various contexts discussed throughout the book. Here the conclusions and suggestions will be brief. **3.112**

In the context of damages actions against the EU the issues of access and substantive proximity in relation to Gamma claimants have not been addressed as such by the EU Courts. The defence of passing-on by contrast has, and the Court of Justice has recognized the defence at law. Under this case law Alpha must prove the existence and extent of real or possible passing-on. It remains to be seen whether consequential losses of profit must be compensated by Alpha in that context.[243] Therefore any predictions on the coordination of multiple and parallel litigation arising from a passing-on situation under Article 340(2) TFEU are speculative. **3.113**

In order to offer a few suggestions on how to fill the gaps, it is submitted that consequential losses of profit suffered by Beta and Gamma claimants should be compensated by Alpha. Loss of profit can be compensated under Article 340(2) TFEU, but the onus of proving such harm will be on the Beta or **3.114**

240 Ibid., para. 14; *Interquell Stärke-Chemie* (n 151) para. 17; and *Dumortier frères* (n 80) para. 15.
241 Lenaerts, Maselis and Gutman (n 15) 532. See para. 5.137 and sub-section 5.E.II.d generally.
242 Directive 2014/104/EU (n 132), Arts 12–16.
243 But see *Ireks-Arkady* (n 50) 2166–2167.

Gamma claimant.[244] It is further submitted that Gamma claimants should not be automatically barred from bringing proceedings under Article 340(2) TFEU, but be allowed to attempt to state the circumstances corresponding to the conditions for liability for the EU with the clarity and precision required for the action to be admitted.[245] Their success in doing so should depend on the circumstances, not any bar. With regard to substantive proximity, problems will increase the further away from Alpha the Gamma claimant is positioned. Gamma may exceptionally be able to point out a specific item on invoices that corresponds to the harm passed on. Under such circumstances, or where the relevant market somehow allows for the identification of harm passed on with equivalent certainty, the direct causal link might plausibly persist down several levels of the supply chain.

3.115 The main problem with regard to coordination of multiple actions is to find and to assemble all the necessary evidence in all the parallel proceedings, so that Alpha is able to invoke passing-on as a shield to the same extent that Gamma claimants are able to invoke it as a sword. This problem cannot, it is submitted, be solved to the full satisfaction of justice perfectionists. At best a class action mechanism could approximate a fair distribution of damages among those who have suffered harm.

3.116 Alternatively the EU Courts could overrule its case law and reject the defence of passing-on, allowing Beta claimants to recover the full amount of harm initially suffered. If Beta successfully recovers that amount from Alpha, the interests of Gamma claimants to whom Beta may have passed on harm might nevertheless be fairly contented by introducing a right for them to bring a subsequent action against Beta for the portion of harm passed on. Such a solution has been used by the Berlin Kammergericht for the purposes of competition damages claims.[246] This solution has three great benefits. First, Alpha need not worry about multiple liability but will be able to foresee the amount of damages claimed with a high degree of certainty. Second, Alpha and Beta need not concern themselves with evidence on passing-on. Third, Gamma claimants will not need to concern themselves with anything but the availability of convincing evidence of passing-on to them from Beta. Only if Beta choses not to bring an action against Alpha will Gamma claimants need

---

244 See paras 3.080–3.082.

245 Cf. *Guérin Automobiles* (n 54) para. 24; and para. 3.040.

246 Anne Howard and Anneliese Blackwood, 'Litigating Infringements in the National Courts' in Vivien Rose and David Bailey (eds) *Bellamy & Child: European Union Law of Competition* (7th edn, Oxford University Press 2013) 1257. See also Assimakis P Komninos, 'Private Enforcement in the EU with Emphasis on Damages Actions' in Ioannis Lianos and Damien Geradin (eds), *Handbook on European Competition Law: Enforcement and Procedure* (Edward Elgar Publishing 2013) 249.

to pursue a direct action against Alpha – a possibility that should remain unrestricted. In sum this solution would amount to a departure from previous case law but does seem able to reconcile all involved interests in a fair, effective and cost-efficient manner.[247]

247 Admittedly however it would be open for discussion whether the EU Courts or national courts should have jurisdiction to hear actions brought by Gamma claimants against Beta. For further discussion see Ch. 9.

4

PASSING-ON IN OTHER ACTIONS AGAINST THE EU?

A. CHAPTER OUTLINE

4.001 In the previous chapter the problem of passing-on was discussed with regard to damages actions brought against the EU. In this chapter it will be (comparatively briefly) considered whether there is any room for passing-on arguments in other money actions brought against the EU.

4.002 The action at issue would be a restitutionary action of some kind. In an action of unjust enrichment against the EU the claimant seeks recovery from the EU in circumstances where the EU has allegedly been unjustly enriched to the detriment of the claimant.[1] The action thus aims at recovering the enrichment of the EU rather than at compensating the loss of the claimant. The legal basis of unjust enrichment should be distinguished from its legal consequence, i.e., the form of recovery, which will usually be a repayment or other restitution. Most importantly an order for restitution may find its legal basis in doctrines other than that of unjust enrichment.

1 Case C-47/07 P *Masdar (UK) Ltd v Commission of the European Communities* [2008] ECR I-9761 para. 47.

Actions for restitution have very rarely been brought against the EU.[2] The opposite, i.e., the EU claiming restitution from others, has been more common and has occurred particularly in staff cases.[3] Such case law is less relevant to this research, as the EU as such is not in a position to 'pass on' financial burdens in the manner that a commercial undertaking would be. Consequently the restitutionary actions relevant to this presentation are those brought against the EU. As mentioned however such case law is scarce. Legal scholars have therefore been uncertain whether the EU Courts have jurisdiction to hear an action of unjust enrichment brought against the EU. The argument was that, as contractual liability of the EU is under the jurisdiction of national courts, perhaps quasi-contractual liability should be too? It was at least evident that no express Treaty provision gave jurisdiction to the EU Courts over such liability.[4] Although by now it seems safe to say that these reservations have been dispersed, the doubts might perhaps account for some of the past hesitation on the part of the Courts. **4.003**

The most common form of restitution in private law is simple repayment of sums not due (*condictio indebiti*). Such an action against the EU has been made available by the EU Courts where the claimant has paid a fine to the EU for an alleged breach of EU competition law and that fine has subsequently been reduced or altogether quashed by an EU Court.[5] The EU Courts have also acknowledged that it is possible pursuant to Article 340(2) TFEU to bring an action of unjust enrichment against the EU even though that provision was designed for liability in damages.[6] **4.004**

In these scraps of case law on restitution from the EU the passing-on problem has not been addressed. It will indeed be discussed below whether there is at all any room for arguing that passing-on may have occurred in these restitutionary contexts. In the event of passing-on argumentation in this context it will be examined in Section 4.D how such argumentation might be shaped in connection to the main EU law issues triggered by the passing-on problem **4.005**

2 On the unwillingness of the EU Courts in earlier case law to open the field for restitution from the EU see Rebecca Williams, *Unjust Enrichment and Public Law: A Comparative Study of England, France and the EU* (Hart Publishing, 2011) 214.

3 See joined cases 4/59 to 13/59 *Mannesmann AG and others v High Authority of the European Coal and Steel Community* [1960] ECR 113 for an early example of the EU claiming restitution. On the staff case law see Williams (n 2) 212–14.

4 See Francette Fines, 'A General Analytical Perspective on Community Liability' in Ton Heukels and Alison McDonnell (eds), *The Action for Damages in Community Law* (Kluwer Law 1997) 12, with references. On jurisdiction in contractual liability of the EU see para. 3.002.

5 Case T-171/99 *Corus UK Ltd v Commission of the European Communities* [2001] ECR II-2967. See further Section 4.B.I.

6 *Masdar* (n 1). See further Section 4.C.

(i.e., access to court, substantive proximity and the estimation of awards). Conclusions and suggestions are summarized in Section 4.E.

B. THE ACTION FOR RESTITUTION OF SUMS UNDULY LEVIED

I. General observations on the action

4.006 It has been mentioned above that a *condictio indebiti* action against the EU has been allowed where the claimant has paid a fine to the EU for an alleged breach of EU competition law and that fine has subsequently been reduced by an EU Court.[7] Before examining that case law however, another claim will be discussed.

4.007 It is well known – and this will be explored in detail in Chapter 5 – that there is EU case law outlining the action for restitution against Member States where sums have been levied by them in breach of EU law. In situations where the charges at issue have been collected by national authorities on behalf of the EU, or pursuant to an EU law instrument or provision which is subsequently declared invalid, the issue arises whether there is a parallel action for restitution against the EU for the repayment of such charges. In early case law an action for the recovery of such charges brought against the EU was admissible before the Court of Justice, but it was held by the Court that claimants must first exhaust the remedies available under national law against the collecting national authority.[8] The Court however then held in *Pigs and Bacon* that traders who had paid charges levied in breach of EU law to a national authority had a right to be reimbursed by the national authority.[9] That judgment all but extinguished the possibility of EU liability. In more recent case law it has moreover been established that claims belonging to this category fall under the exclusive jurisdiction of national courts, irrespective of the fact that the underlying unlawfulness of the levy is attributable in whole or in part to the EU.[10] In sum therefore the EU has been able to safeguard its own purse from restitutionary actions arising from the levying of charges by

---

7 *Corus UK Ltd* (n 5).

8 Joined cases 5, 7 and 13 to 24/66 *Firma E Kampffmeyer and others v Commission of the EEC* [1967] ECR 245, 264 and 266.

9 Case 177/78 *Pigs and Bacon Commission v McCarren and Co Ltd* [1979] ECR 2161 para. 25.

10 Case C-282/90 *Industrie- en Handelsonderneming Vreugdenhil BV v Commission of the European Communities* [1992] ECR I-1937 para. 12; case C-351/04 *Ikea Wholesale Ltd v Commissioners of Customs and Excise* [2007] ECR I-7723 paras 67–68; case C-419/08 P *Trubowest Handel GmbH and Viktor Makarov v Council of the European Union and European Commission* [2010] ECR I-2259 paras 23–26. For a critical discussion see Andrea Biondi and Martin Farley, *The Right to Damages in European Law* (Kluwer European Law Collection, Kluwer Law International 2009) 178–80.

national authorities on behalf of the EU, leaving it to the Member States to pay for any and all reimbursements. Although a Member State could in theory be expected to bring an action of recourse against the EU by reason of having reimbursed claimants, this does not seem to have occurred.[11]

Consequently we return to the repayment of fines charged by the EU Commission. The obligation for the Commission to pay restitution with regard to fines subsequently reduced or annulled by an EU Court follows from Article 266 TFEU. Such an action (albeit based on Articles 34 and 40 of the ECSC Treaty) came before the General Court in *Corus UK*. **4.008**

> The claimant, Corus UK Ltd, had paid a fine of EUR 32 000 000 to the Commission on 2 June 1994. On appeal the amount of the fine payable was reduced by the General Court to EUR 20 000 000. The excess of EUR 12 000 000 was consequently repaid by the Commission on 23 April 1999. The Commission however refused to pay interest on the amount of the excess, even though the sum in excess had yielded a return calculated at EUR 3 016 608. The claimant therefore brought an action against the Commission before the General Court pursuant to Article 40 of the ECSC Treaty (or in the alternative Article 34 of the ECSC Treaty) seeking compensation for harm incurred by the non-payment of interest. **4.009**

The General Court first held that the Commission was obliged to repay the sums paid in excess of the final amount of the fine and that full restoration included the payment of interest.[12] Moreover, the General Court continued, the circumstances of the case were such that 'a failure to reimburse interest could result … in the unjust enrichment of the Community, which would be contrary to the general principles of Community law'. The Court therefore concluded that 'not only the principal amount of the fine unduly paid, but also the amount of any enrichment or benefit it has obtained as a result of such payment' was to be reimbursed by the Commission.[13] **4.010**

The General Court further ruled that interest was payable on the amounts of such repayments in order to avoid the unjust enrichment of the Community.[14] With regard to the amount of interest to be paid the General Court also interestingly held that even though the most common solution would be to order payment of interest on the principal amount of the excessive fine at a **4.011**

---

11 Biondi and Farley ibid., 88, consider it unlikely 'in view of the overall judicial scheme provided' by the EU Treaties for Member States to bring a claim against the EU. See also Koen Lenaerts, Ignace Maselis and Kathleen Gutman (Janek Tomasz Nowak (ed)), *EU Procedural Law* (Oxford EU Law Library, Oxford University Press 2014) 495.

12 *Corus UK* (n 5) paras 50–54.

13 Ibid., para. 55.

14 Ibid.

rate decided by the Court and for the period from the payment of the excess until final payment is made, it was 'fair in the circumstances' to award to the claimant the enrichment calculated by the Commission plus interest on that sum from the date of repayment of the principal amount until the date of the judgment, and interest on the total from the date of judgment until final and full payment was made, both at a fixed rate of 5.75 per cent.[15] In *Corus UK* the General Court thus ordered the restitution not only of the amount of reduction of the fine, but also of an unjust enrichment of the EU (or more precisely the ECSC) disguised as an individualized calculation of interest.[16]

4.012 Subsequent case law has clarified that claimants have an option to pursue an action for damages under Article 340(2) TFEU as an alternative to restitution,[17] and that although the Commission decision to impose a fine has been annulled restitution is not thereby automatically due to parties who have not brought an action for annulment.[18]

II. Passing-on in restitution pursuant to fine reductions?

4.013 The scope of the sound use of passing-on argumentation was outlined in Section 1.A.IV. It was acknowledged that it is difficult to define precisely what situations are passing-on situations and that the EU Courts have not made any clear demarcations with regard to the circumstances within which passing-on might be considered. Nevertheless it was argued that the wording used in Article 14 of Directive 2014/104/EU could be useful and would probably yield the most reasonable results. It was accordingly argued that passing-on could occur if an infringement of EU law by Alpha had caused an increase in costs for Beta's commercial handling of specific goods or services and Beta had then distributed those goods or services (or goods or services derived from or containing them) to Gamma. Under such circumstances, it was argued, could it be relevant to examine whether the increased costs at issue had in fact been passed on in selling prices and whether the claimant had suffered other loss, e.g., decreased sales, as a result of its passing-on of increased costs in its selling prices. An ideal passing-on situation is VAT, or other circumstances where the cost at issue can be identified as a specific item on invoices which follows the

---

15 Ibid., paras 61–65.

16 If, by chance, the General Court had instead ordered the payment of interest at a fixed rate of 5.57 per cent on the EUR 12 000 000 excess from 2 June 1994 to 23 April 1999, the total amount of interest payable would have exceeded the EUR 3 016 608 enrichment. My rough calculation of the amount payable under such circumstances renders a total of EUR 3 353 400.

17 Case T-86/03 *Holcim (France) SA v Commission of the European Communities* [2005] ECR II-1539.

18 Case C-310/97 P *Commission of the European Communities v AssiDomän Kraft Products AB, Iggesunds Bruk AB, Korsnäs AB, MoDo Paper AB, Södra Cell AB, Stora Kopparbergs Bergslags AB and Svenska Cellulosa AB* [1999] ECR I-5363. For further details see Lenaerts, Maselis and Gutman (n 11) 417–18.

commodity at issue down the supply chain. Nonetheless other less clear situations must also be acknowledged as being capable on the facts to include legally relevant passing-on of costs.

Fines are designed to impact the finances of the undertaking fined and not those of others up or down the supply chain. Consequently fines seem to be an extreme opposite to the range of costs that an undertaking could credibly argue to have passed on. Although the scope of the passing-on problem has not been authoritatively defined but is open to discussion in light of the circumstances of each individual case, it does not follow from this that any theoretic passing-on must be considered by courts. The circumstances would have to be particular indeed for passing-on argumentation to be plausible in the context of restitution of fine reductions. To present an example it is necessary to include a good portion of storytelling. Consider a monopolist undertaking that has been fined by the Commission for an alleged abuse of its dominant position. The undertaking publicly condemns the decision and declares that the fine will have to be passed on to its customers, in order for it to survive commercially. Under such circumstances, passing-on argumentation might succeed if the decision to fine is quashed on appeal – but the scenario is, as indicated, far-fetched. **4.014**

It is accordingly concluded that it would be unlikely for a party to argue passing-on in this context. In the event the unlikely should come to pass however, the discussion in Section 4.D can serve to illustrate the focal points of the passing-on problem in this context. **4.015**

C. THE ACTION OF UNJUST ENRICHMENT

I. General observations on the action

Besides the restitution of money paid but not due there are restitutionary actions based on other forms of allegedly unjust enrichment of the defendant. Exactly what kind of enrichment qualify as unjust has not been defined for the purposes of EU law, and approaches differ among the Member States.[19] In **4.016**

19 See in general Draft Common Frame of Reference (Christian von Bar and Eric Clive (eds), *Principles, Definitions and Model Rules of European Private Law: Draft Common Frame of Reference (DCFR) Full Edition* (6 vols, Sellier European Law Publishers 2009)) VII-2:101 with Comments and Notes; Jack Beatson and Eltjo Schrage (eds), *Cases, Materials and Texts on Unjustified Enrichment* (Hart Publishing, 2003) Ch. 6; Sonja Meier, 'Unjust factors and legal grounds' and Thomas Krebs, 'In defence of unjust factors', both in David Johnston and Reinhard Zimmermann (eds), *Unjustified Enrichment: Key Issues in Comparative Perspective* (Cambridge University Press 2002).

1990 the Court of Justice was seized with a dispute between Greece and the Commission pertaining to the calculation of funds due from the European Agricultural Guidance and Guarantee Fund. In that regard the Court held that the Commission could not disregard relevant information submitted by Greece 'without unjustly enriching the Community contrary to the general principles of Community law'.[20] The wording used revealed that the Court took the view that prevention of unjust enrichment was a general principle of EU law,[21] but the legal content of that principle was not elaborated by the Court.

4.017 It was not until *Masdar* that the Court of Justice was more specific about unjust enrichment of the EU. In that case the Court recognized that an action of unjust enrichment could be brought against the EU pursuant to Article (now) 340(2) TFEU.[22]

4.018 Masdar (UK) Ltd was a subcontractor to Hellenic Management Investment Consultants SA (Helmico), who had been contracted by the Commission to carry out certain aid projects in Moldova and Russia. Helmico did not properly pay Masdar for work carried out. Subsequently the Commission found Helmico guilty of fraud in the context of the aforementioned projects. The Commission consequently suspended payments to Helmico and claimed the repayment of funds totalling over EUR 2 000 000 from Helmico. Neither Helmico nor its directors could however be reached. Under these circumstances Masdar brought an action against the Commission under Article 288(2) EC[23] for (inter alia) unjust enrichment.

The Court of First Instance recognized that such an action could be brought but dismissed the action on the facts.[24] Masdar appealed to the Court of Justice. Masdar's first plea alleged errors in law and failure to state reasons in relation to the treatment of the issue of unjust enrichment.

---

20 Case C-259/87 *Hellenic Republic v Commission of the European Communities* [1990] ECR I-2845 (summary publication) para. 2 of the summary. Williams (n 2) 212 also cites *Corus UK Ltd* (n 5) para. 55; and joined cases T-44/01, T-119/01 and T-126/01 *Eduardo Vieira, SA, Vieira Argentina, SA and Pescanova, SA v Commission of the European Communities* [2003] ECR II-1209 para. 86. See further case T-7/99 *Medici Grimm KG v Council of the European Union* [2000] ECR II-2671 para. 89; and case T-166/98 *Cantina sociale di Dolianova Soc coop rl and Others v Commission of the European Communities* [2004] ECR II-3991 paras 158–162, commented by Williams ibid., at 219–20 and 222–4, respectively.

21 Noted by Williams (n 2) 211; and Paul Craig, *EU Administrative Law* (2nd edn, Oxford University Press 2012) 698.

22 *Masdar* (n 1) para. 47. The General Court, however, had held before *Masdar* that such an action was available under EU law; see *Cantina sociale* (n 20) para. 160 and case law there cited. This case law was based on the *dictum* on unjustified enrichment in case C-259/87 *Hellenic Republic* (n 20).

23 Now Art. 340(2) TFEU.

24 Case T-333/03 *Masdar (UK) Ltd v Commission of the European Communities* [2006] ECR II-4377. The Court of First Instance is now the General Court.

Even though the wording of Article 340(2) TFEU does not expressly provide for an action of unjust enrichment, the Court held that an exclusion of such actions against the EU would be contrary to the principle of effective judicial protection laid down in the Court's case law and confirmed in Article 47 of the Charter.[25] With regard to criteria the Court held that an action of unjust enrichment pursuant to Article 340(2) TFEU requires 'proof of enrichment on the part of the defendant for which there is no valid legal basis and of impoverishment on the part of the applicant which is linked to that enrichment'.[26] Four criteria are discernible from this holding: (1) proof of enrichment on the part of the EU; (2) no valid basis for that enrichment; (3) proof of impoverishment on the part of the claimant; and (4) a link between enrichment and impoverishment. **4.019**

The Court came to focus its assessment of the merits of the plea on the second of these criteria, holding that an enrichment that derives from contractual obligations cannot be categorized as 'unjust'.[27] In that regard the Court clarified that 'where contracts under which services are provided prove to be invalid and cease to exist, the enrichment of the beneficiary of those services must, in accordance with the principles developed in the legal systems of the Member States, give rise, in certain circumstances, to restitution'.[28] The Court thus seemed to adopt the systematic approach that an action of unjust enrichment cannot be brought against a co-contractor but only in non-contractual relationships, and further that situations where a contract has become invalid or otherwise ceases to exist belong to the latter category.[29] In *Masdar* the circumstances were such that the contractual relationships at issue (i.e., those between the Commission and Helmico, on the one hand, and between Helmico and Masdar, on the other hand) had not ceased to exist. Rather, Helmico was in breach of its contractual obligations.[30] In that regard the Court held that 'in all contractual relationships there is a certain risk that a party will not perform the contract satisfactorily or that it will become **4.020**

25 *Masdar* (n 1) para. 50. To be more specific, this reference must reasonably be intended to pertain to Art. 47(1) of the Charter, i.e., the right to an effective legal remedy, corresponding to Art. 13 ECHR. Trevor C Hartley, *The Foundations of European Union Law* (8th edn, Oxford University Press 2014) 450, has submitted that this is a 'strained interpretation of the Treaties' but would endorse it in the interest of ensuring a legal remedy for claimants such as Masdar.

26 *Masdar* (n 1) para. 49.

27 Ibid., para. 54.

28 Ibid., para. 55.

29 Cf. DCFR (n 19) II.-7:212 and II.-7:303, under which restitution due to the invalidity of a contract are governed by Book VII on unjustified enrichment. By contrast, restitution pursuant to termination of a contract is governed by contractual rules (III.-3:510–514). For comparative information see the accompanying Notes. In the common law, there are some unjust enrichment actions within contract law; see Tarich A Baloq, *Unjust Enrichment and Contract* (Hart Publishing 2009).

30 *Masdar* (n 1) paras 57–58.

insolvent. That is a commercial risk inherent in the activities of economic operators.'[31] The Court continued:

4.021 In such a context, each economic operator involved in the project must accept the risk that its co-contractor may become insolvent or that it may commit irregularities leading the Community to suspend payments or even to issue recovery orders. In those circumstances, it cannot easily be accepted that the losses flowing from the materialisation of such risks must give rise to ad hoc payments on the part of the Community.[32]

On those grounds, the Court of Justice rejected the plea.

4.022 It follows from the ruling of the Court of Justice in *Masdar* that non-contractual liability in unjust enrichment will not be possible unless at least one of the contracts in such a two-contract situation is invalid or has ceased to exist.[33] This issue was crucial not only to the Court of Justice but also to the General Court and to the Advocate General.[34] As explained above, the Court thus upheld the distinction between contractual and non-contractual liability.[35] The Court also noticed that Masdar pursued a contractual claim against Helmico before the competent national court. The Court's subsequent *dictum* on commercial risk should be interpreted in that context, explaining that recourse to unjust enrichment will not expedite everyone who suffers loss due to the insolvency or wrongdoing of third parties.[36]

4.023 In subsequent case law the EU Courts have applied the findings in *Masdar*, but the criteria have not been elaborated upon.[37] To summarize the case law, the EU Courts have assumed jurisdiction over actions of unjust enrichment brought against the EU. The four criteria identified above for such an action (i.e.: (1) proof of enrichment on the part of the EU; (2) no valid basis for that enrichment; (3) proof of impoverishment on the part of the claimant; and (4) a

---

31 Ibid., para. 59.

32 Ibid., para. 60.

33 Ibid., paras 54–57.

34 Cf. *Masdar* (n 24) paras 97–99; *Masdar* (n 1) Opinion of AG Mazák paras 46–56.

35 See n 29 and accompanying text. Of course, such a position may be vulnerable to criticism for being 'formalistic'.

36 For a different and critical reading of *Masdar* see Williams (n 2) 225–7. The critique is discussed by this author in Magnus Strand, *The Passing-On Problem in EU Law Damages and Restitution* (Uppsala University (diss) 2015) 153–4.

37 See case C-309/10 *Agrana Zucker GmbH v Bundesminister für Land- und Forstwirtschaft, Umwelt und Wasserwirtschaft* [2011] ECR I-7333 paras 52–54; case T-116/11 *Association médicale européenne (EMA) v European Commission* EU:T:2013:634 (appealed as case C-100/14 P but the issue of unjust enrichment was not discussed by the Court of Justice); *Israel Institute of Technology and Technion Research & Development Foundation Ltd v European Commission* EU:T:2015:746 paras 103–105; and case F-55/09 *Allan Maxwell v European Commission* EU:F:2010:44 paras 95–99.

link between enrichment and impoverishment)[38] seem to fit well with the general principles common to the laws of the Member States[39] even though they will need to be fleshed out in forthcoming case law. With regard to the second criterion it follows from *Masdar* that the EU Courts will uphold the distinction between contractual liabilities and non-contractual liabilities and reject actions of unjust enrichment where the enrichment has accrued pursuant to a contract.

II. Passing-on in unjust enrichment actions?

The scope of the sound use of passing-on argumentation was outlined in Section 1.A.IV and was recalled in brief in Section 4.B.II. Neither *Masdar* nor any of the subsequent cases on unjust enrichment of the EU triggered the passing-on problem. It is indeed difficult to envisage circumstances under which passing-on would be triggered in the context of an unjust enrichment action which is not an action for restitution of money paid but not due. The attempts of this author to construe such circumstances fall back into general covering of costs and loss of expected income through pricing. Even though it deserves to be repeated that the scope of the passing-on problem has not been defined but is open to discussion in light of the circumstances of each individual case, a general endeavour to cover costs will not credibly suffice. It is therefore concluded that the passing-on problem will not likely arise in unjust enrichment actions brought against the EU other than actions for restitution of sums unduly levied (and even then, as stated in Section 4.B.II, the room for passing-on arguments is small indeed). **4.024**

D. PASSING-ON ISSUES IN RESTITUTION FROM THE EU

It follows from the discussion above that the following outlines of relevant points for the passing-on problem in a restitutionary action brought against the EU are likely to apply only to a very limited range of actions for the repayment of fines paid for an alleged breach of competition law where the decision to impose the fine has subsequently been quashed, or where the amount of the fine has been reduced, by the EU Courts. Perhaps this section may therefore be, as they say, mainly of academic interest. **4.025**

---

38 *Masdar* (n 1) para. 49.

39 Cf. Art. 340(2) TFEU. The elements match those in the main rule on unjustified enrichment in the DCFR (n 19); VII. – 1:101(1).

I. Access issues for Gamma claimants

4.026 The general requirements for an action of unjust enrichment pursuant to Article 340(2) TFEU to be admissible and the impact of Article 47 of the Charter were discussed in Section 3.C.I. Most of what was said there is directly applicable to an action of unjust enrichment and need not be repeated at any length. In brief, pursuant to Article 21 of the Statute of the EU Courts, a written application for a case to be brought before the EU Courts shall, inter alia, state the subject matter of the dispute and include a brief statement of the pleas in law on which the application is based. The application must also state 'the nature of any evidence offered in support'.[40] The application must accordingly state the circumstances corresponding to the conditions for liability for the EU in unjust enrichment and must do so with clarity and precision.[41] A claim for unspecified restitution will be regarded as inadmissible.[42] Case law on abuse of process will apply.[43]

4.027 Gamma claimants bringing a restitutionary action against the EU would be struggling to state with clarity and precision the circumstances constituting a sufficient link between its alleged impoverishment and an enrichment of the EU. It is not commonly accepted in European jurisdictions that Gamma should be able to leapfrog Beta and bring a direct restitutionary action against Alpha.[44] Applications submitted by Gamma therefore risk being declared inadmissible. An argument to the contrary could be inspired by *Danfoss*, where it was established for the purposes of restitutionary actions brought against a Member State that a claim brought by Gamma could not be opposed on the ground that it was not the Gamma claimant who had paid the duty at issue. The Court of Justice would accept only one exception to this rule, namely where Gamma was able to bring a civil action against Beta for recovery of the sum unduly paid and provided that it was not virtually impossible or excessively difficult for Gamma to obtain reimbursement from Beta.[45] Otherwise the right conferred on the individual by EU law would have no *effet utile*. It could consequently be argued that the issue of access to court should not be left to be decided on grounds of automatic bars. Any claimant who is capable

40 Rules of procedure of the General Court, consolidated version of the Rules of procedure of the Court of First Instance of the European Communities [1991] OJ L 136/1 Art. 44(1)(e). The Court of First Instance is now the General Court.

41 Cf. case T-195/95 *Guérin Automobiles v Commission of the European Communities* [1997] ECR II-679 para. 24.

42 Cf. case 5/71 *Aktien-Zuckerfabrik Schöppenstedt v Council of the European Communities* [1971] ECR 975 para. 9.

43 See Lenaerts, Maselis and Gutman (n 11) 490–91 with references.

44 See Section 4.D.II.

45 Case C-94/10 *Danfoss A/S and Sauer-Danfoss ApS v Skatteministeriet* [2011] ECR I-9963 paras 25–28, and Operative part para. 1.

of demonstrating in an application a particular interest or entitlement in unjust enrichment will trigger the package of effective judicial protection, and should therefore be heard by the EU Courts.[46] As will be illustrated in the next section however, a declaration of admissibility may prove to be a pyrrhic victory.

II. Substantive proximity issues for Gamma claimants

The fourth criterion identified for the purposes of restitutionary liability pursuant to Article 340(2) TFEU in *Masdar* was that a link was established between the enrichment of the EU and an impoverishment of the claimant.[47] It will be demonstrated in this section that it is problematic for Gamma claimants to establish the necessary link between the enrichment of the EU and their own impoverishment. The criterion might hypothetically be met if it were possible for a Gamma claimant to produce conclusive evidence that the impoverishment corresponding to the enrichment of the EU has been passed on to that Gamma claimant. As already concluded such hypothetical situations can however be expected to be quite scarce. **4.028**

Furthermore the applicable rule in the DCFR would prevent Gamma claimants, as a consequence of legal definition, from being able to establish a link. For an enrichment accrued through the transfer of assets to be attributable to an impoverishment the DCFR requires that the assets were transferred to the enriched person by the impoverished person.[48] This view was reflected also in the Opinion of Advocate General Mancini in *San Giorgio* (which concerned the repayment of charges levied by Member States in breach of EU law). The Advocate General there opined that there was no basis for an action of unjust enrichment brought by Gamma against Alpha in passing-on situations, and further that it was 'difficult to imagine a proposition which is more implausible in practice and more venturesome in theory'. The Advocate General went so far as to call the notion of such an action 'absurd'.[49] If the fourth criterion applicable to actions of unjust enrichment of the EU were to be interpreted in accordance with the DCFR rule, Gamma claimants might therefore be legally incapable of satisfying that criterion. **4.029**

Should it consequently be accepted that substantive proximity for Gamma is *a priori* excluded, or have other policy options been presented? A brief survey of **4.030**

46 Cf. Section 3.C.I.

47 See n 26 and accompanying text.

48 DCFR (n 19) Art. VII. – 4:101(a).

49 Case 199/82 *Amministrazione delle Finanze dello Stato v SpA San Giorgio* [1983] ECR 3595 Opinion of AG Mancini para. 7.

European scholarship on unjust enrichment reveals that very little attention, if any, is devoted to the possibility for Gamma claimants to bring an action of unjust enrichment against Alpha. Either (as in the DCFR rule) the claimant must have performed towards the defendant, thus causing the latter to be enriched,[50] or the concern is whether Beta could bring an action against a third party to whom Alpha has transferred the enrichment, not the mirror image at issue here.[51] The exception is Rush, who has observed that Gamma would not be able to bring an action against Alpha in English common or statutory law, but who has also submitted that it is unclear why this is so.[52] Rush suggested two reasons. First, in the context of overpaid taxes, that the government would likely bar Gamma actions.[53] Second, because of the lack of a nexus between Alpha and Gamma.[54] The solution advocated by Rush was to allow Beta to claim the entire enrichment from Alpha, rejecting any defence of passing-on tried by Alpha, and to allow Gamma to bring a subsequent action against Beta.[55] Burrows has found support for the solution suggested by Rush in Commonwealth case law and has consequently submitted that it is open for English courts to adopt that solution.[56] In the absence of EU case law it is submitted that this option is likewise open to the EU Courts. Nevertheless the Rush model does not help Gamma to leapfrog Beta to bring an action against Alpha directly, for instance if Beta omits to bring an action against Alpha. The door to leapfrogging thus seems to be shut in European private law.

4.031 Should EU law follow European private law and bar Gamma from bringing a restitutionary action directly against the EU for lack of substantive proximity? As Article 340(2) TFEU cites the 'general principles common to the laws of the Member States' it is plausible that such a view would be adopted by the EU Courts unless circumstances were very particular.[57] It would still remain open to the EU Courts to adopt the solution suggested by Rush. Gamma might accordingly have the option of bringing a restitutionary action against Beta, provided that Beta had first brought a successful action against Alpha.

---

50 Gerhard Dannemann, *The German Law of Unjustified Enrichment and Restitution* (Oxford University Press 2009) 34; see also DCFR (n 19) vol. 4, 4036–7 and the accompanying Notes.

51 See Williams (n 2) 173 (on French law); Peter Birks, *Unjust Enrichment* (2nd edn, Clarendon Law Series, Oxford University Press 2005) 93–8 (on English law).

52 Michael Rush, *The Defence of Passing On* (Hart Publishing 2006) 209–10.

53 As the Danish Government tried to in *Danfoss* (n 45).

54 Rush (n 52) 210–11.

55 Ibid., 218, with an extensive discussion of different constructions to this end at 211–17. A similar solution has reportedly been adopted by the Berlin Kammergericht for the purposes of competition law damages actions, see Anne Howard and Anneliese Blackwood, 'Litigating Infringements in the National Courts' in Vivien Rose and David Bailey (eds) *Bellamy & Child: European Union Law of Competition* (7th edn, Oxford University Press 2013) 1257. This model will be compared to the Rush model in Ch. 9.

56 Andrew Burrows, *The Law of Restitution* (3rd edn, Oxford University Press 2011) 617–18.

57 See para. 4.014 for a scenario that might serve.

And in the event that Beta does not bring an action against Alpha or is not successful with such an action, Gamma might still be able to bring an action for damages pursuant to Article 340(2) TFEU against the EU instead of the restitutionary action.

III. The defence of passing-on

It has been stressed above that the situations where passing-on could be successfully invoked by Gamma claimants in support of a direct action against the EU (passing-on as a 'sword' against Alpha) are very few – if any. It should be equally difficult for the EU to invoke the defence of passing-on (passing-on as a 'shield' against Beta). With this said, a few observations will be submitted. **4.032**

With regard to the defence of passing-on it is relevant to make a comparison with case law on restitution from a Member State. For the purposes of this section the findings of the Court of Justice in that context can be briefly summarized as follows. The Court has tolerated national rules allowing Alpha to invoke the defence of passing-on to the extent that the impoverishment of Beta has been passed on by Beta. The Court has nonetheless required Beta to be able to counter-argue that it has suffered from decreased sales caused by the passing-on of the charge levied in breach of EU law.[58] It has further been observed by the Court that actual passing-on, either in whole or in part, will be dependent on various factors in each commercial transaction which distinguish it from other transactions in other contexts.[59] Therefore the Court has required national law to ensure that Alpha can resist restitution only to the extent that it has been established that the impoverishment has been borne by someone other than Beta.[60] As in actions for damages brought pursuant to Article 340(2) TFEU,[61] the onus of proving the extent of passing-on has been on the defendant in actions for restitution from a Member State.[62] **4.033**

It would arguably be possible for the EU Courts to adopt this view for the purposes of restitutionary actions brought against the agents and institutions **4.034**

58 Joined cases C-192/95 to 218/95 *Société Comateb and others v Directeur Général des Douanes et Droits Indirects* [1997] ECR I-165 paras 28, 32. In this book, Alpha signifies a tortfeasor or enriched party, Beta a party first burdened by loss arising from Alpha's breach of EU law, and Gamma any party downstream from Beta (including all from the party dealing directly with Beta to the final consumer) to whom the burden of that loss may have been passed on; see Section 1.B.

59 Joined cases 331/85, 376/85 and 378/85 *SA Les Fils de Jules Bianco and J Girard Fils SA v Directeur Général des Douanes et Droits Indirects* [1988] ECR 1099 para. 17.

60 *Comateb* (n 58) para. 27.

61 Joined cases 256, 257, 265, 267/80, 5 and 51/81 and 282/82 *Birra Wührer SpA and others v Council and Commission of the European Communities* [1984] ECR 3693 para. 28.

62 *Comateb* (n 58) para. 28.

of the EU with only a few refinements. In the absence of precedent however, it would also be open for the EU Court seized with such a dispute to reject the defence of passing-on for the purposes of actions for restitution brought against the EU. Indeed it is submitted that the EU Courts would be wise to do so. It is one thing that the Court of Justice has allowed the defence some leeway in the national courts. EU law tolerates such national rules, subject to a number of conditions, but it does not embrace them. It must consequently be stressed that the defence of passing-on must first be available in the national law governing the action for restitution in order for the issue of its compatibility with EU law to arise. The limitations thus developed by the Court of Justice have been designed to balance the national procedural autonomy of the Member States against the effective protection of rights conferred on individuals by EU law, and should be read against that background. Actions falling to be governed exclusively by EU law, such as the action for restitution pursuant to Article 340(2) TFEU, do not trigger such considerations. It will therefore be open to the EU Courts to rule simply that any amounts obtained by the EU without legal basis are to be reversed – end of story.

4.035 There would moreover be no need for the EU Courts to follow the case law of the Court of Justice on passing-on in the context of damages actions brought under Article 340(2) TFEU.[63] The two actions are different and different criteria for liability apply.[64]

4.036 Indeed, a rejection of the defence would work better with the all-but-impossibility for Gamma claimants to bring an action, and would furthermore enhance possibilities to use the Rush model solution described in Section 4.D.II. It is accordingly submitted that the better option, in view of the general principles common to the laws of the Member States,[65] is to follow the example of those Member States who have rejected the defence of passing-on for the purposes of restitution.[66] If the EU Courts chose not to follow this recommendation, it would be crucial for the policy chosen to consider the coordination of a defence of passing-on with the possibilities for Gamma to bring an action.

---

63 On this case law see Section 3.E.II.

64 *Masdar* (n 1) paras 44–50.

65 Cf. Art. 340(2) TFEU.

66 See Dannemann (n 50) 103 (on German disinterest in passing-on); Burrows (n 56) 615–17 and of course Rush (n 52) on the rejection (with some deviations) of the defence at common law but endorsement in some English statutory law; and the unequivocal rejection in DCFR (n 19) Art. VII. – 3:102(2). In French law, the defence is unavailable in *répétition de l'indu* while the situation in *enrichissement sans cause* seems less clear; Williams (n 2) 173–6.

E. CONCLUSIONS AND SUGGESTIONS

It has been submitted in this chapter that the passing-on problem is not likely to arise in the context of a restitutionary action brought against the EU. A very slim possibility for such a situation has nevertheless been found where an action for the repayment of fines paid for an alleged breach of competition law, presuming that the decision to impose the fine has subsequently been quashed (or the amount of the fine has been reduced) by the EU Courts.[67] **4.037**

If by chance a passing-on situation did occur in restitution from the EU, it has been submitted that Gamma claimants will have great difficulty to leapfrog Beta and claim from Alpha directly. It has instead been suggested for the EU Courts to reject all passing-on argumentation for the purposes of actions brought against Alpha, and to encourage Gamma instead to bring a subsequent action against Beta if the latter has brought a successful action (for the entire amount paid but not due) against Alpha.[68] This would be without consequence to the availability of damages under Article 340(2) TFEU for harm incurred by any Beta or Gamma party in the form of, e.g., decreased sales. **4.038**

67 In Section 4.B.II it was suggested that a monopolist undertaking that has been fined by the Commission for an alleged abuse of its dominant position, but publicly condemns the decision and declares that the fine will have to be passed on to its customers in order for it to survive commercially, could possibly trigger a passing-on situation – but the scenario is admittedly far-fetched.

68 See Section 4.D.II.

Part III

PASSING-ON IN ACTIONS AGAINST A MEMBER STATE

5

PASSING-ON IN RESTITUTION FROM A MEMBER STATE

A. CHAPTER OUTLINE

Most of the case law of the European Court of Justice on the passing-on problem has been developed by reason of claims for repayment of charges levied in breach of EU law. In fact, in the context of actions brought against a Member State, the passing-on problem has hardly been a concern in actions for damages – it has been addressed by the Court of Justice in only one single (and comparatively recent) case. It has therefore been chosen to shift the sequence between damages and restitution in this presentation in respect of actions against Member States, in order to address the action for restitution first. 5.001

5.002 The case law discussed in this chapter deals exclusively with the repayment of charges.[1] The more general term of 'restitution' has nevertheless been maintained in headings for clarity in the distinction between these actions and damages actions brought against a Member State, the latter remaining to be discussed in Chapter 6. The more precise term 'repayment of charges' will mostly be used in the text. Notwithstanding the distinction between restitution in general and repayment specifically, the findings in this chapter should generally be applicable *mutatis mutandis* in other instances of restitution from a Member State when based on an infringement of EU law by that Member State.

5.003 A brief introduction to the repayment of charges levied in breach of EU law will follow in Section 5.B, the purpose of which is mainly to trace its origins in EU case law. In Section 5.C the impact of EU law requirements of effective judicial protection on national limitations of access to court will be addressed, in light of both Article 47 of the EU Charter of Fundamental Rights and of the dual EU law test of equivalence and effectiveness. Focus will be on case law concerning national limitations of access barring Gamma parties from bringing an action by invoking passing-on as a 'sword' (i.e., invoking the fact that a charge has been passed on to them by Beta).[2] In Section 5.D the problem of substantive proximity will be addressed. This problem has received scarce attention from the Court of Justice. It will nevertheless be endeavoured to trace the impact of the principles of equivalence and effectiveness to national rules on substantive proximity, drawing inspiration from adjacent concerns that have been addressed by the Court.

5.004 The extensive Section 5.E concerns the estimation of restitutionary awards from a Member State. Following a presentation of some general EU law requirements, Section 5.E.II sets out to present the case law of the Court of Justice on the defence of passing-on in this context. Through this defence Alpha seeks to argue that the amount of repayment should be reduced to the extent that the claimant has or could have passed on the burden of the charge levied in breach of EU law. In other words the fact that a charge has been passed on is used as a 'shield'.

---

1 I.e., restitution of money paid but not due, which is one type of restitutionary action. An overview of possibilities for restitution in kind from public authorities in Germany, France and England is available in Robert Rebhahn, 'Public Liability in Comparison: England, France, Germany' in Helmut Koziol and Barbara C Steininger (eds), *Tort and Insurance Law Yearbook: European Tort Law 2005* (Springer 2006) 89–90.

2 In this book, Alpha signifies a tortfeasor or enriched party, Beta a party first burdened by loss arising from Alpha's breach of EU law, and Gamma any party downstream from Beta (including all from the party dealing directly with Beta to the final consumer) to whom the burden of that loss may have been passed on; see Section 1.B.

5.005 Due to the number of cases, the presentation has been subdivided into three sub-sections roughly corresponding to time periods. It has also been chosen to begin sub-section 5.E.II.d with a summary of the case law. That sub-section further encompasses an in-depth discussion of the case law in light of the main arguments presented in legal debate. In the next Section 5.E.III it is discussed whether there are other defences of 'unjust enrichment' that a Member State may use as a shield against a claim for repayment of charges levied in breach of EU law or whether the defence of passing-on is the one and only defence of unjust enrichment. In Section 5.E.IV a few remarks are gathered on the estimation of restitution if the action were brought by a Gamma claimant.

5.006 Conclusions and suggestions are summarized in Section 5.F.

B. INTRODUCTION TO RESTITUTION FROM A MEMBER STATE

5.007 Since *Francovich*,[3] or at least since *Brasserie*,[4] the main money action available to individuals against Member States for a breach of EU law has been the action for damages. The action for damages, which will be examined in more detail in Chapter 6, is a broad action that applies whenever the conditions developed for its purposes by the European Court of Justice are met. The action for restitution is comparatively narrow in its scope, and it is accordingly less often available to claimants. In the context of passing-on it is interesting to notice that the two actions are generally both available as alternative or complementary courses of action where an amount has been levied by a Member State in breach of EU law.[5] It moreover seems the comparative straightforwardness of the restitutionary action has produced a tendency for claimants to use it rather than the damages action. A case law has consequently developed where claimants have tried to push the scope of application of the restitutionary action. Without going into detail on this case law and the scholarly debate over it,[6] it seems the Court of Justice has traditionally left it for the claimants, under the supervision of the national court, to specify

3 Joined cases C-6/90 and 9/90 *Andrea Francovich and Daniela Bonifaci and others v Italian Republic* [1991] ECR I-5357.

4 Joined cases C-46/93 and C-48/93 *Brasserie du Pêcheur SA v Bundesrepublik Deutschland* and *The Queen v Secretary of State for Transport, ex parte: Factortame Ltd and others* [1996] ECR I-1029.

5 This was acknowledged by the Court of Justice in joined cases C-192/95 to 218/95 *Société Comateb and others v Directeur Général des Douanes et Droits Indirects* [1997] ECR I-165 para. 34.

6 Commentators include Michael Dougan, 'Cutting Your Losses in the Enforcement Deficit: A Community Right to the Recovery of Unlawfully Levied Charges?' (1998) 1 *Cambridge Yearbook of European Legal Studies* 233, 262; Alison Jones, *Restitution and European Community Law* (Mansfield Press 2000) 75; Veljko Milutinovic, *The 'Right to Damages' under EU Competition Law: From* Courage v. Crehan *to the White Paper and Beyond* (Wolters Kluwer 2010) 165–170; and Rebecca Williams, *Unjust Enrichment and Public Law: A Comparative Study of England, France and the UK* (Hart Publishing 2011) 113–18. For a longer discussion of

the nature and basis for their actions in circumstances where the scope of different actions overlap.[7] An action for repayment of charges levied in breach of EU law will however only apply where the enrichment of the state and the corresponding impoverishment of the claimant have flown from the same event.[8] In the words used by the Court of Justice the action for repayment will apply if the event from which impoverishment of the claimant arose is an inevitable consequence of the event from which enrichment of the Member State arose.[9] Otherwise the claimant will need to bring an action for damages in accordance with the case law discussed in Chapter 6.

5.008 With regard now to the right to restitution from a Member State, the Court of Justice has long held that there is a right to repayment of charges levied in breach of EU law.[10] It arguably followed from *Rewe*[11] and *Comet*[12] that such levies should be repaid in accordance with applicable national laws and procedures. *Pigs and Bacon*[13] nonetheless represents the origin of this case law insofar as the Court there made it explicit for the first time that, in principle, Community law confers a right on individuals to claim repayment of charges levied in breach of EU law.[14] *Pigs and Bacon* further made it clear that a

---

the case law, and the comments submitted, by this author see Magnus Strand, *The Problem of Passing-On in EU Law Damages and Restitution* (Uppsala University (diss) 2015) section 3.3.3.

7 Joined cases C-397/98 and C-410/98 *Metallgesellschaft Ltd and Others* (C-397/98), *Hoechst AG and Hoechst (UK) Ltd* (C-410/98) *v Commissioners of Inland Revenue and HM Attorney General* [2001] ECR I-1727 para. 81; case C-446/04 *Test Claimants in the FII Group Litigation v Commissioners of Inland Revenue* [2006] ECR I-11753 para. 201; case C-524/04 *Test Claimants in the Thin Cap Group Litigation v Commissioners of Inland Revenue* [2007] ECR I-2107 para. 109; and case C-94/10 *Danfoss A/S and Sauer-Danfoss ApS v Skatteministeriet* [2011] ECR I-9963 para. 32.

8 This doctrine of restitution or unjust enrichment law is explained in Jack Beatson and Eltjo Schrage (eds), *Cases, Materials and Texts on Unjustified Enrichment* (Hart Publishing, 2003) 207. Indivisibility of origin is linked to the degree of 'directness' with which the impoverishment and enrichment have flown from the transaction. It is not always easy to pinpoint this 'directness'. For an overview of European approaches to this problem in the context of private unjust enrichment law see Draft Common Frame of Reference (Christian von Bar and Eric Clive (eds), *Principles, Definitions and Model Rules of European Private Law: Draft Common Frame of Reference (DCFR) Full Edition* (6 vols, Sellier European Law Publishers 2009)) Art. VII. – 4:101.

9 See *FII* (n 7) paras 207–208; *Danfoss* (n 7) Opinion of AG Kokott para. 43; and case C-310/09 *Ministre du Budget, des Comptes publics et de la Fonction publique v Accor SA* [2011] ECR I-8115 Opinion of AG Mengozzi paras 72–78. The inevitable consequence test has been criticized by Williams (n 6) 113–18. For a discussion of the test by this author see Strand (n 6) section 3.3.3. It can finally be added, as will be seen in Section 5.E, that loss due to a decline in sales caused by the passing-on of a charge levied in breach of EU law – a loss usually remedied through damages only – has been taken into consideration in the estimation of restitutionary awards.

10 Very long, see e.g. case 6/60 *Jean-E Humblet v Belgian State* [1960] ECR 559, 569, on reimbursement following a breach of the ECSC Treaty.

11 Case 33/76 *Rewe-Zentralfinanz eG et Rewe-Zentral AG v Landwirtschaftskammer für das Saarland* [1976] ECR 1989.

12 Case 45/76 *Comet BV v Produktschap voor Siergewassen* [1976] ECR 2043.

13 Case 177/78 *Pigs and Bacon Commission v McCarren and Co Ltd* [1979] ECR 2161.

14 Jones (n 6) 57.

remedy of reimbursement from the Member State must be available, as a matter of Community (now EU) law, when charges have been levied in breach of that law.

> The claimant, the Pigs and Bacon Commission (the PBC), was a public body holding statutory right to charge a levy on pig carcasses intended for the manufacture of bacon. The levy was used, inter alia, for the payment of a bonus for the export of bacon through the intermediary of the PBC acting as a central marketing agency. The defendant, McCarren and Co Ltd (McCarren), withdrew from the export scheme of the PBC as from 30 April 1975, and refused to pay the levy to the PBC from that date. As from the same date, the PBC had refused to pay export bonuses to McCarren for bacon exported by McCarren independently. **5.009**
>
> The PBC brought an action against McCarren claiming levies due as from 30 April 1975. McCarren counterclaimed for reimbursement of levies paid from 1 February 1973, at which date Ireland began to apply the Common Organisation of the Market in pigmeat, until 30 April 1975. McCarren claimed that the charging of the levy and the use of proceeds for payment of export bonuses as carried out by the PBC were contrary to the EEC Treaty and the Regulations relating to the Common Organisation of the Market in pig meat.
>
> The European Court of Justice referred to settled case law stating that once the Community had legislated for the common organization of the market in a given sector, Member States were under an obligation to refrain from taking any measure which might undermine or make exceptions to it. Hence, the Court held, the marketing system established by Regulation No 2759/75 precluded any intervention by Member States otherwise than expressly laid down by the Regulation itself. Therefore, the Court concluded, the payment of a bonus for the marketing of bacon was in itself incompatible with the rules of the Common Market under the provisions of the Treaty and more particularly under the provisions of Regulation No 2759/75. Moreover, the Court held, the system of the PBC was incompatible with the provisions of Regulation No 2759/75 by reason of the difference in treatment of producers according to whether or not they made use of the intermediary of the PBC.[15]
>
> The Court therefore held that the levy demanded by the PBC was not due to the extent to which it was employed for purposes incompatible with the requirements of the Treaty and with the Common Organisation of the Market.[16]

With regard to the levies paid but not due, the Court held that any trader who had paid the levy therefore had the right to claim reimbursement of that part of the levy which was devoted to purposes incompatible with Community law. The Court however also held that it was for the national court to assess, according to its national law and in each individual case, whether and to what **5.010**

15 *Pigs and Bacon* (n 13) paras 14, 17–18.

16 Ibid., para. 20.

extent the levy paid may be recovered and whether the sums paid to an exporter by way of export bonus may be offset against such a debt.[17]

5.011 The result of *Pigs and Bacon* was that sums paid but not due under EU law were, in principle, recoverable as a matter of EU law.[18] This was the crucial starting point for the abundance of case law elaborating the details of such repayment, including case law on the passing-on problem. Immediately after *Pigs and Bacon* however, the content of this right and its relationship to substantive and procedural rules governing its enforcement were still very much in the dark. There was a 'right to reimbursement' but in light of the Court's holding that the right existed 'in principle', the interrelationship between that right and national procedural rules capable of limiting access to that remedy was uncertain.

5.012 It was clarified in subsequent case law that the meaning of a right 'in principle', as declared by the Court of Justice in *Pigs and Bacon*, did not exclude the possibility of national substantive and procedural rules legitimately limiting the exercise of such a right. Such national limitations were of course subject to the dual test of the EU principles of equivalence and effectiveness,[19] but the EU law right to reimbursement was nonetheless to be enforced within the legal framework of national law, using national actions. The Court itself interestingly declared in *Express Dairy Foods* that it was 'regrettable' that there were no EU rules harmonizing procedure and time-limits that might bar claims, but held that it was outside the scope of its competence to give a ruling that would amount to such harmonization.[20] This call went unheard however, and it remains a fact that the details of the action for repayment of charges

17 Ibid., para. 25.

18 Interestingly however, it was for the national court to decide whether and to what extent there could be recovery and whether bonus payments received could be set off against the recoverable amount. The decision to allow national courts to decide on the extent of recovery anticipates the position later adopted by the Court in case 68/79 *Hans Just I/S v Danish Ministry for Fiscal Affairs* [1980] ECR 501, discussed in some detail below.

19 The applicability of the EU law principles of equivalence and effectiveness in this context has been verified by the Court of Justice in e.g., *Just* (n 18) para. 25; case 199/82 *Amministrazione delle Finanze dello Stato v SpA San Giorgio* [1983] ECR 3595 para. 12; joined cases 331/85, 376/85 and 378/85 *SA Les Fils de Jules Bianco and J Girard Fils SA v Directeur Général des Douanes et Droits Indirects* [1988] ECR 1099 para 10; joined cases C-441/98 and C-442/98 *Kapniki Michaïlidis AE v Idryma Koinonikon Asfaliseon (IKA)* [2000] ECR I-7145 para. 36; case C-147/01 *Weber's Wine World Handels-GmbH and others v Abgabenberufungs-kommission Wien* [2003] ECR I-11365 para. 103; *Accor* (n 9) para. 79; *Danfoss* (n 7) para. 24; and case C-191/12 *Alakor Gabonatermelő és Forgalmazó Kft v Nemzeti Adó- és Vámhivatal Észak-alföldi Regionális Adó Főigazgatósága* EU:C:2013:315 para. 26.

20 Case 130/79, *Express Dairy Foods Ltd v Intervention Board for Agricultural Produce* [1980] ECR 1887 para. 12. See further paras 5.173–5.175.

levied in breach of EU law have never been subject to harmonization through EU legislation.[21]

In *Just* the Court consequently explained that in the absence of EU rules concerning the refunding of national charges which had been unlawfully levied it was for the domestic legal system to designate the courts having jurisdiction and to determine the procedural conditions governing actions at law intended to ensure the protection of the rights which subjects derive from the direct effect of EU law, it being understood that such conditions could not be less favourable than those relating to similar actions of a domestic nature and that under no circumstances might they be so adapted as to make it impossible in practice to exercise the rights which the national courts were bound to protect.[22] In sum, the action for repayment of charges levied in breach of EU law must be brought before the competent national courts and be governed by the applicable national procedural rules, subject to the principles of equivalence and effectiveness.[23] Today it can be added that the national conditions at issue are also subject to Article 47 of the EU Charter.[24] **5.013**

There has been little further guidance on the general character of the action in the case law of the Court of Justice. A few points will still be mentioned. In *San Giorgio* the Court of Justice put further emphasis on the need to respect the right to repayment by introducing the formula, thereafter reoccurring in many cases, that entitlement to the repayment of charges levied by a Member State contrary to the rules of EU law is a consequence of, and an adjunct to, the rights conferred on individuals by the Community provisions prohibiting such charges.[25] There is moreover a well-known strand of case law on the impact of the principles of equivalence and effectiveness on national time-limits applicable to repayment actions.[26] This case law will be discussed further in Section 5.C.I. In brief, the Court of Justice has ruled that the laying down of reasonable limitation periods was not contrary to the principles of equivalence and effectiveness, 'even if the expiry of those periods necessarily **5.014**

21 Such harmonization was suggested in Andrea Biondi and Lindsay Johnson, 'The Right to Recovery of Charges levied in Breach of Community Law: No Small Matter' (1998) 4 *European Public Law* 313.

22 *Just* (n 18) para. 25.

23 On these principles see Section 2.D.

24 See Section 2.C.

25 *San Giorgio* (n 19) para. 12. The formula reappears in, e.g., joined cases C-192/95 to 218/95 *Société Comateb and others v Directeur Général des Douanes et Droits Indirects* [1997] ECR I-165 para. 20; joined cases C-114/95 and C-115/95 *Texaco A/S v Middelfart Havn et al* [1997] ECR I-4263 paras 40 and 45; case C-242/95 *GT-Link A/S* v *De Danske Statsbaner (DSB)* [1997] ECR I-4449 para. 58; and case C-188/95 *Fantask A/S ea v Industriministeriet (Erhvervministeriet)* [1997] ECR I-6783 para. 38.

26 The first of these cases were *Rewe* (n 11) and *Comet* (n 12).

entails the dismissal, in whole or in part, of the action brought'.[27] Finally, it deserves mentioning that the Court of Justice would not in *Târşia* preclude, by reference to the principles of equivalence and effectiveness, a situation where there was no possibility for a national court to revise a final decision of a court or tribunal made in the course of civil proceedings even though that decision was incompatible with EU law.[28]

C. ACCESS TO CLAIM RESTITUTION FROM A MEMBER STATE

I. General observations on access

5.015 Case law on access to bring an action for the repayment of charges levied in breach of EU law is somewhat one-dimensional. With the exception of *Danfoss*[29] (a case which is immediately relevant to the passing-on problem and will hence be discussed in Section 5.C.II) the case law mostly revolves around the particular issue of time-limits. That case law will be touched upon below. Otherwise discussions on effective judicial protection in this section will need to be rather abstract, recalling findings in Chapter 2 in order to discuss more generally the impact of the EU law principles of equivalence and effectiveness and of Article 47 of the Charter on national limitations of access to bring a claim for restitution against a Member State.

5.016 It is necessary to keep in mind that none of those rules and principles on effective judicial protection in EU law will apply unless the claimant can first demonstrate that she or he is the holder of a substantive right or particular interest protected by EU law. The claimant must further choose a remedy available under national law for the enforcement of that right. If no effective remedy is available under the national legal system, EU law may require the national court to make an effective remedy available to the claimant,[30] as in case law such as *Factortame I*[31] or *Francovich*.[32] With regard to the repayment

27 Case C-90/94 *Haahr Petroleum Ltd v Åbenrå Havn, Ålborg Havn, Horsens Havn, Kastrup Havn NKE A/S, Næstved Havn, Odense Havn, Struer Havn and Vejle Havn, and Trafikministeriet* [1997] ECR I-4085 para. 48. See also case C-231/96 *Edilizia Industriale Siderurgica Srl (Edis) v Ministero delle Finanze* [1998] ECR I-4951 para. 20 and the case law there cited. For an extensive overview and discussion see Angela Ward, *Judicial Review and the Rights of Private Parties in EU Law* (2nd edn, Oxford University Press 2007) Ch. 4B.

28 Case C-69/14 *Dragoş Constantin Târşia v Statul român, Serviciul public comunitar regim permise de conducere şi înmatriculare a autovehiculelor* EU:C:2015:662. The Court however pointed out in para. 40 that the taxpayer might under such circumstances be able to bring an action for damages against the Member State concerned if the final decision at issue constituted a sufficiently serious breach of EU law. Cf. para. 6.022.

29 *Danfoss* (n 7).

30 On this EU law right to an effective remedy see further Section 2.B.

31 Case C-213/89 *The Queen v Secretary of State for Transport, ex parte: Factortame Ltd and others* [1990] ECR I-2433.

of charges it was demonstrated in Section 5.B that EU law confers a right to reimbursement on the individuals who have paid them and that the Court has held that those entitled must be able to bring an action for the repayment of such charges. There is consequently a right and a remedy, at least with regard to Beta claimants.[33]

Under such circumstances Article 47 of the Charter requires national courts to grant access to court to claimants who wish to enforce the right. Nonetheless, national limitations of the right of access to court will be compatible with the Charter insofar as they meet the conditions laid down in its Article 52(1). Such national limitations must hence be provided for by law, respect the essence of the right, and meet the proportionality test prescribed by that Article. The proportionality test at issue permits only limitations which are necessary and genuinely meet objectives of a general interest recognized by the EU or the need to protect the rights and freedoms of others. The details of these requirements were presented in Section 2.C.II and need not be repeated here. However, the Article 52(1) test has not yet been discussed by the Court in the context of repayment of charges levied in breach of EU law. Focus has been instead on the principles of equivalence and effectiveness, which we will soon continue to examine. With regard to Article 47 and the Article 52(1) test, suffice it to notice that they are applicable and that it is open for claimants to use them as part of their argumentation in proceedings before the national courts. **5.017**

The EU law principles of equivalence and effectiveness comprise a dual test under which the national rules and conditions within which actions based on EU law are brought before national courts must neither be treated less favourably than 'similar domestic actions' (equivalence) nor render the enforcement of EU law impossible or excessively difficult (effectiveness). **5.018**

With regard to the principle of equivalence, the relevant *comparator* is actions where the purpose, cause of action, and essential characteristics of the action based on national law are similar to those of the action based on EU law.[34] It must further be examined whether the application of a specific rule to actions based on EU law is liable to make it less favourable to pursue such an action rather than the *comparator* action, taking into account the role played by that provision in the procedure as a whole, as well as the operation and any special **5.019**

32 *Francovich* (n 3).

33 In anticipation of Section 5.C.II it can be submitted already for the purposes of passing-on that it follows from *Danfoss* (n 7) Operative part para. 1 that such a right is conferred on Gamma claimants as well as on Beta claimants, although *Danfoss* is without prejudice to the existence of alternative remedies.

34 Case C-326/96 *BS Levez v TH Jennings (Harlow Pools) Ltd* [1998] ECR I-7835 paras 41 and 43.

features of that procedure before the different national courts.[35] In actions for repayment of charges levied in breach of EU law the relevant *comparator* will typically be domestic actions against the state for the repayment of sums illegally levied. If there are several such actions, a choice of *comparator* must be made. If there are no such actions in domestic law, the relevant *comparator* will probably be the *condictio indebiti* or similar private law remedy. It is however settled case law that the principle of equivalence does not require Member States to extend their most favourable rules to all actions brought in a certain field of law.[36] Thus, the choice of *comparator* is not to be mistaken for a choice of the *comparator* most favourable for the claimant.

5.020 The Court of Justice has used the principle of equivalence to examine national conditions limiting access to bring a claim against a Member State in a few cases. In *Q-Beef* the Court examined a time-limit applicable to claims against the Belgian state. The Court held that the principle of equivalence was not infringed as long as the time-limit under scrutiny applied to all debts owed by the state, and as long as its applicability did not depend on whether those debts had arisen from a breach of national or EU law.[37] The findings of fact were left to the national court to determine. In light of *Levez* it could be added that even if the time-limit had not applied to all debts owed, and even if it had not been applicable to claims where the debt had arisen from a breach of EU law, it would still be necessary to examine the role played by that provision in the procedure as a whole, as well as the operation and any special features of that procedure before the different national courts, before it could be concluded if there was a breach of the principle of equivalence.[38] A ruling along those lines was indeed delivered in *Dilexport* where a certain time-limit in Italian law applied only to actions based on EU law. The Court nevertheless held that the national rules at issue were not less favourable within the meaning of the principle of equivalence, since the time-limit for similar domestic actions was the same.[39] To summarize, it does not amount to a breach of the principle of equivalence that different sets of rules and/or conditions apply to actions based on national and EU law respectively. For

---

35 Ibid., para. 44.

36 E.g., case C-231/96 *Edilizia Industriale Siderurgica Srl (Edis) v Ministero delle Finanze* [1998] ECR I-4951 para. 36; case C-343/96 *Dilexport Srl v Amministrazione delle Finanzo dello Stato* [1999] ECR I-579 para. 27; case C-118/08 *Transportes Urbanos y Servicios Generales SAL v Administración del Estado* [2010] ECR I-635 para. 34.

37 Joined cases C-89/10 and C-96/10 *Q-Beef NV* (C-89/10) *v Belgische Staat* and *Frans Bosschaert* (C-96/10) *v Belgische Staat, Vleesgroothandel Georges Goossens en Zonen NV and Slachthuizen Goossens NV* [2011] ECR I-7819 para. 35. A similar ruling is found in case C-88/99 *Roquette Frères SA v Direction des services fiscaux du Pas-de-Calais* [2000] ECR I-10465 paras 29–32.

38 Cf. *Levez* (n 34) para. 44.

39 *Dilexport* (n 36) paras 30–31.

there to be a breach of the principle of equivalence it is furthermore necessary that the practical application of these different rules or conditions result in actual adverse treatment of actions for the exercise of rights conferred by EU law.

Before leaving the principle of equivalence it must be remarked also that this principle may give rise to different treatment of claims based on EU law depending on the national jurisdiction hearing the action. If, e.g., Polish rules were to prove more favourable than Greek rules, claimants seeking restitution for a breach of EU law in Poland would be better off than their Greek counterparts. This is a problem which supports the plea for harmonization voiced by Biondi and Johnson.[40] **5.021**

As regards the principle of effectiveness, the Court of Justice has held that: **5.022**

> ... whether a national procedural provision renders application of Community law impossible or excessively difficult must be analysed by reference to the role of that provision in the procedure, its progress and its special features, viewed as a whole, before the various national instances. In the light of that analysis the basic principles of the domestic judicial system, such as protection of the rights of the defence, the principle of legal certainty and the proper conduct of procedure, must, where appropriate, be taken into consideration.[41]

Case law on the principle of effectiveness with regard to actions for the repayment of charges levied in breach of EU law is abundant. It is in fact difficult to find a case in this case law that does not include a discussion on the interpretation of the principle of effectiveness.[42] However, none of them deals specifically with the issue of access to court in the context of passing-on. Not even in *Comateb*, where one could have expected French law to have limited access for Beta[43] by reference to the legal obligation for traders to pass on the **5.023**

---

40 Biondi and Johnson (n 21) 321. See also Peter Oliver, 'Enforcing Community Rights in the English Courts' (1987) 50 *Modern Law Review* 881, 894–5, including further references. For a sceptical view on harmonization see Lesley Jane Smith, 'A European Concept of Condictio Indebiti?' (1982) 19 *Common Market Law Review* 269, 274–6; or (aiming more generally) Cees van Dam, 'European tort law: features of a diverse landscape' in Christian Twigg-Fleisner (ed.), *European Union Private Law* (Cambridge University Press 2010) 171–2.

41 Case C-312/93 *Peterbroeck, Van Campenhout & Cie SCS v Belgian State* [1995] ECR I-4599 para. 14; joined cases C-430/93 and C-431/93 *Jeroen van Schijndel* and *Johannes Nicolaas Cornelis van Veen v Stichting Pensioenfonds voor Fysiotherapeuten* [1995] ECR I-4705 para. 19.

42 Notable exceptions are *Comateb* (n 25) and case C-398/09 *Lady & Kid A/S and Others v Skatteministeriet* [2011] ECR I-7375.

43 In this book, Alpha signifies a tortfeasor or enriched party, Beta a party first burdened by loss arising from Alpha's breach of EU law, and Gamma any party downstream from Beta (including all from the party dealing directly with Beta to the final consumer) to whom the burden of that loss may have been passed on; see Section 1.B.

dock dues levied, does it seem from the judgment or the Opinion of Advocate General Tesauro that there were any limitations of access to court as such.[44] The bulk of the case law is instead concerned with the aforementioned issue of time-limits in national law.

5.024 It is settled case law in that regard that the setting of reasonable limitation periods for bringing proceedings cannot be regarded as rendering virtually impossible or excessively difficult the exercise of rights conferred by EU law, even if the expiry of those periods necessarily entails the dismissal in whole or in part of the action brought.[45] In *Recheio* the Court held that a period of 90 days for bringing proceedings for the recovery of charges paid but not due was reasonable, under the circumstances.[46] In *Banca Antoniana* however, the Court held that even though a two-year time-limit had applied, the principle of effectiveness had been infringed if it was impossible or excessively difficult for the claimant to obtain repayment even during that period.[47]

5.025 In Banca Antoniana the claimant had collected contributions on behalf of certain public bodies, Consorzi, that carried out public infrastructure work. In accordance with instructions from the competent tax authority, VAT was payable on the contributions. Banca Antoniana had charged and paid the VAT from 1984 to 1994. In 1999 the tax authority announced that it had changed its interpretation of the relevant VAT regulations, and that under its new interpretation the contributions collected by Banca Antoniana were exempt from VAT.[48] The Consorzi therefore brought an action against Banca Antoniana for the repayment of sums paid but not due. As a consequence Banca Antoniana came to bear the burden of the VAT paid but not due, but was time-barred from claiming the VAT back from the tax authority.[49]

5.026 Under the circumstances in *Banca Antoniana* the applicable time period had lapsed before the claimant had had any reason to anticipate that the VAT had been levied in breach of EU law, and before it had come to bear the burden of the VAT. Therefore the Court of Justice held that even though it did not preclude reasonable time-limits being applicable to claims for the recovery of sums paid but not due, the principle of effectiveness required for that taxable person to be effectively able to claim reimbursement of the VAT from the tax authority. That condition, the Court continued, was not satisfied:

---

44 *Comateb* (n 25).

45 E.g., *Haahr* (n 27) para. 50; *Texaco* (n 25) para. 46; *Fantask* (n 25) para. 48.

46 Case C-30/02 *Recheio – Cash & Carry SA v Fazenda Pública/Registo Nacional de Pessoas Colectivas, and Ministério Público* [2004] ECR I-6051 paras 20–25.

47 Case C-427/10 *Banca Antoniana Popolare Veneta SpA v Ministero dell'Economia e delle Finanze and Agenzia delle Entrate* [2011] ECR I-13377 para. 32.

48 Ibid., paras 12–13.

49 Ibid., paras 35–36.

> … where the application of such rules has the effect of totally depriving the taxable person of the right to obtain from the tax authority a refund of the VAT paid but not due, which the taxable person has himself had to pay back to the recipient of his services.[50]

However, it follows from the analysis of *Alassini*[51] in paragraphs 2.072 and 2.073 that the principle of effectiveness may be even more stringent in the individual case than follows from *Banca Antoniana*. It has been submitted that it follows from *Alassini* that the question whether the principle of effectiveness will preclude the application of a national limitation of access to court cannot be answered in the abstract, but must be decided on a case-by-case basis. In *Alassini* a few typical adverse consequences of national substantive and procedural conditions were nonetheless identified, all of which were liable to make the exercise of rights conferred by EU law virtually impossible or excessively difficult: bars, impracticalities, delays, and costs. The last two are parallel to the examples of adverse consequences named in *Levez* in respect of the principle of equivalence: costs and delays.[52] It consequently seems that where national conditions for access to court have the effect of making it virtually impossible or excessively difficult to gain access to national courts in order to bring an action for the repayment of charges levied in breach of EU law, e.g., by barring such actions under circumstances where the burden of the charge is presumed to have been passed on or by making it excessively time-consuming, costly, or otherwise impractical to gain access to justice for such actions, the principle of effectiveness might preclude such conditions of national law. In the next section we will examine *Danfoss*,[53] a case which provides an example of such an exclusionary effect pursuant to the principle of effectiveness. **5.027**

50 Ibid., para. 42. The reasoning of the Court of Justice in *Banca Antoniana* is reminiscent of the approach taken by the Strasbourg Court in *Perez de Rada Cavanilles v Spain* App No 28090/95 (ECtHR, 28 October 1998) paras 45–49, reported in Section 2.C.II, where the essence of the right of access to court under Art. 6(1) ECHR was considered to have been infringed. This highlights that the practical impact of the principle of effectiveness may often overlap with that of Art. 47 of the Charter (s. 2 of which corresponds to Art. 6(1) ECHR; 'Explanations relating to the Charter of fundamental rights' [2007] OJ C303/02, 30). In case C-640/13 *European Commission v United Kingdom of Great Britain and Northern Ireland* EU:C:2014:2457 Operative part, the Court of Justice similarly held that the adoption of national provisions 'which curtailed, retroactively and without notice or transitional arrangements, the right of taxpayers to recover taxes levied in breach of EU law' was contrary to Art. 4(3) TEU.

51 Joined cases C-317/08, C-318/08, C-319/08 and C-320/08 *Rosalba Alassini v Telecom Italia SpA* (C-317/08), *Filomena Califano v Wind SpA* (C-318/08), *Lucia Anna Giorgia Iacono v Telecom Italia SpA* (C-319/08) and *Multiservice Srl v Telecom Italia SpA* (C-320/08) [2010] ECR I-2213.

52 *Levez* (n 34) para. 51.

53 *Danfoss* (n 7).

II. Access and passing-on

5.028 Effective judicial protection under EU law is contingent on the existence of a substantive right or particular interest held by the claimant which is protected by EU law.[54] With regard to Beta claimants it follows from the case law discussed in Section 5.B that Beta holds such a right and is therefore covered by the rules and principles of EU law ensuring the effective judicial protection of that right. Gamma claimants have by contrast made no payments to Alpha, and it may therefore seem odd to discuss the possibilities for Gamma claimants bringing an action for repayment. It would seem to follow that Gamma can have no right to repayment from Alpha, and if so, the issue of effective judicial protection would not arise. It will however be demonstrated below that the European Court of Justice has not been inclined to allow *a priori* rejections of Gamma claims for that reason. In this regard it can be recalled that the Court of Justice similarly extended the category of persons that should be granted access to bring a claim relying on Directive 79/7/EEC[55] before the competent national court in *Verholen*, holding that not only those who came within the *ratione personae* of the Directive would have access to court but also individuals who bore 'the effects of a discriminatory national provision regarding [a] spouse, who is not a party to the proceedings, provided that [the] spouse ... comes within the scope of the directive'.[56] The Court has consequently been no stranger to broadening the personal scope of an EU law right in order to avoid inequitable consequences of a stricter interpretation.

5.029 In the more recent *Danfoss*[57] the Court of Justice delivered a far-reaching interpretation of the principle of effectiveness. The issue was, in essence, whether a Gamma claimant could bring a direct action for repayment against the Member State (Alpha), leapfrogging Beta. In *San Giorgio* Advocate General Mancini had dismissed such Gamma actions, opining that there was no basis for an action of unjust enrichment brought by Gamma in passing-on situations.[58] In *Danfoss* the Court was to prove him wrong – albeit within the specific circumstances of the case.

54 See Section 2.A.

55 Council Directive 79/7/EEC of 19 December 1978 on the progressive implementation of the principle of equal treatment for men and women in matters of social security [1979] OJ L6/24.

56 Joined cases C-87/90, C-88/90 and C-89/90 *A Verholen and others v Sociale Verzekeringsbank Amsterdam* [1991] ECR I-3757 para. 26.

57 *Danfoss* (n 7).

58 *San Giorgio* (n 19) Opinion of AG Mancini para. 7.

Danfoss A/S had purchased mineral oils from a number of oil companies. The oil companies had imported the mineral oils into Denmark. Under Danish law an excise duty was payable on the mineral oils. The oil companies had paid these duties and it was common ground that the duties had been passed on to Danfoss A/S. Danfoss A/S had in turn sold some of the mineral oils to Sauer-Danfoss ApS, including the duty in its selling price. **5.030**

Pursuant to *Braathens*[59] and *Commission v Italy*[60] it was clear that the excise duty on mineral oils had been levied in breach of EU law. The oil companies did not however claim repayment. Instead, Danfoss A/S and Sauer-Danfoss ApS (the claimants) brought proceedings against the Danish tax authority (Skatteministeriet) arguing that they, who had borne the financial burden of the excise duties levied in breach of EU law, had a right to recover the sums paid but not due from the Skatteministeriet, and compensation from damage suffered as a consequence of the levying of the excise duties.[61]

The claims were rejected (Danish: *afvist*). The Danish tax authorities held that the right to repayment of charges levied in breach of EU law accrued only to the persons directly taxable, and not to persons further down the chain of distribution since such persons had not paid any amount to the tax authority.[62] The Danish tax authorities also rejected any claims for compensation, holding that there was no direct causal link between the levying of the excise duties and the alleged harm suffered.[63] The claimants appealed the decisions to the Vestre Landsret (Western Regional Court) which decided to stay proceedings and to refer the case to the European Court of Justice for a preliminary ruling.

Advocate General Kokott was somewhat ambivalent with regard to the action for repayment, opining that the case law could be interpreted in two conflicting ways depending on the precise meaning of the so-called 'inevitable consequence test'. The Advocate General explained that an action for restitution from a Member State is available under this test only if the alleged loss suffered is an inevitable consequence of a breach of EU law involving the illegal levying of a charge.[64] In the first interpretation not only Beta's loss consisting in payment of an unlawful charge was to be regarded as an inevitable consequence of the levy of that charge, but also loss or damage incurred by Beta in the form of a decline in sales linked to the levy. If such an interpretation was adopted the business decision to pass on the charge was of **5.031**

59 Case C-346/97 *Braathens Sverige AB v Riksskatteverket* [1999] ECR I-3419.

60 Case C-437/01 *Commission of the European Communities v Italian Republic* [2003] ECR I-9861.

61 *Danfoss* (n 7) para. 15. Danfoss thus brought a subsidiary action for damages. The national court indicated that this action would not be admitted as, under Danish law, the existence of the necessary direct causal link would automatically be ruled out where the action was brought by a Gamma party. This second part of the judgment did not concern repayment as such but an action for damages from the Member State. Therefore the holdings of the Court with regard to this second issue will be summarized and analyzed in Ch. 6.

62 Ibid., para. 16.

63 Ibid., para. 17.

64 See *FII* (n 7) para. 207; and para. 5.007.

no consequence to the concept of 'inevitable consequence'. Under such circumstances the Advocate General argued that 'the diminution of the final consumer's assets associated with the passing on of the charge is no less inevitable'.[65] If on the other hand 'the real meaning of the criterion of inevitable consequence' was applied, it would not be fulfilled with respect to Gamma claimants. This was so, the Advocate General submitted, because the charge was not passed on automatically but through an entrepreneurial decision taken by Beta.[66]

5.032 Finding that the case law was not decisive on this point, the Advocate General proceeded to consider the impact of the EU law principles of equivalence and effectiveness. On the principle of equivalence the Advocate General opined that if a Gamma claimant could bring an action directly against the state when a charge had been levied in breach of Danish law, an action of such kind had to be granted also where the charge had been levied in breach of EU law.[67] On the principle of effectiveness the Advocate General cited *Reemtsma*, in which the Court of Justice held that where it became impossible or excessively difficult to seek repayment, in particular in the case of the insolvency of a Beta party, the principle of effectiveness might require that a Gamma claimant be able to address an action for repayment to the tax authorities directly.[68] The Advocate General opined that '[t]hat must most certainly apply where the mistake has been made … by the State itself'.[69] The Advocate General moreover submitted that the claim should:

5.033

> … be, by its very nature, a restitutionary claim, since it would be made excessively difficult for the final consumer to exercise his rights if he had, for example, to satisfy the more stringent conditions which apply … to claims for damages based on European Union law. Nor is it possible to see why, in such a case, the State should be able to seek refuge behind those more stringent claim conditions. After all, it has still been enriched by the amount of the charge levied contrary to European union law, and it is solely a question of repaying that amount to the person who was last to bear it economically.[70]

---

65 *Danfoss* (n 7) Opinion of AG Kokott para. 53.

66 Ibid., para. 54.

67 Ibid., para. 59.

68 Case C-35/05 *Reemtsma Cigarettenfabriken GmbH v Ministero delle Finanze* [2007] ECR I-2425 para. 41. On this interpretation of the EU principle of effectiveness see paras 2.059–2.060.

69 *Danfoss* (n 7) Opinion of AG Kokott para. 60.

70 Ibid., para. 61. To this author, it is not convincing to argue, as AG Kokott does in the beginning of this paragraph, that a certain action must be made available because the conditions of another, which is available, are stringent. Such a line of argument presupposes a primacy of the interests of claimants, and disregards the necessity to balance those interests against those of defendants in order to find a working legal solution. The second argument submitted by AG Kokott is of course not targeted by this remark.

Also: **5.034**

> If national law grants to the economically burdened final consumer a claim for restitution against neither the State nor the taxable person, it still follows from the principle of effectiveness that at least one of those two claims for repayment must be created … .[71]

The Advocate General nonetheless argued that EU law did 'not necessarily require a uniform rule' governing such actions for repayment, but should tolerate a certain variance among Member States.[72] Therefore the Advocate General finally submitted that the Court should answer the national court as follows: **5.035**

> It is a matter for national law and, if appropriate, the national courts, to determine whether the party to whom the taxable person has passed on a national charge levied by a Member State in breach of European Union law can claim the repayment of the charge directly from the State or, in principle, only from the taxable person, or whether he may choose in that regard, provided however that the principles of equivalence and effectiveness are observed.[73] **5.036**

The European Court of Justice first examined whether a Member State might oppose a claim for repayment brought by a party to whom the duty unduly paid had been passed on, on the ground that that party was not the person liable for payment of the duty and had therefore not paid the duty to the tax authorities. The Court recalled in that regard, citing *Comateb*,[74] that if the final consumer was able on the basis of national law to obtain reimbursement through the taxable person of the amount of the charge passed on to him, that taxable person must in turn be able to obtain reimbursement from the national authorities. The Court also cited *Reemtsma* in which it had held that a national legal system which allowed the supplier who had paid VAT to the tax authorities in error to seek reimbursement, and which allowed the recipient of the services to bring a civil law action against that supplier for recovery of the sums paid but not due, observed the principle of effectiveness as that system enabled the recipient who bore the tax invoiced in error to obtain reimbursement of the sums unduly paid.[75] **5.037**

71 Ibid., para. 62. This argument refers to the EU law requirement for the existence of an effective remedy; see Section 2.B.

72 Ibid., paras 65–67. For an opposite view see Biondi and Johnson (n 21).

73 Ibid., para. 70, but cf. para. 69. It should be remembered that AG Kokott took a stringent view on what was required under the principle of effectiveness, and that therefore this suggested answer to the national court was probably not intended to be very lenient towards the Member State.

74 *Comateb* (n 25).

75 *Danfoss* (n 7) para. 26.

5.038 Therefore, the Court of Justice held, a Member State might in principle oppose a claim for the repayment of a duty unduly paid pursued by the final consumer to whom that duty had been passed on, on the ground that it was not that consumer who had paid the duty to the tax authorities, provided that the consumer – who in the final analysis bears the burden of that duty – was able on the basis of national law to bring a civil action against the taxable person for recovery of the sums unduly paid.[76] However, the Court continued, if such reimbursement by the taxable person were to prove impossible or excessively difficult – in particular in the case of the insolvency of that person – the principle of effectiveness required that the purchaser was able to bring the claim for reimbursement against the tax authorities directly. The Member State must furthermore provide the necessary instruments and detailed procedural rules to that end.[77]

5.039 The Court of Justice consequently ruled that a Member State may oppose a claim for repayment of a duty unduly paid, brought by the purchaser to whom that duty has been passed on, on the ground that it is not the purchaser who has paid the duty to the tax authorities, provided that the purchaser is able on the basis of national law to bring a civil action against the taxable person for recovery of the sum unduly paid, and provided that it is not virtually impossible or excessively difficult to obtain reimbursement from that taxable person of the duty unduly paid.[78]

5.040 *Danfoss* is the only ruling of the Court of Justice which has directly concerned an action brought by Gamma. It is therefore of particular interest in this inquiry. Proceeding to analysis of this judgment, it deserves to be pointed out first and foremost that it follows from *Danfoss* that Gamma claimants do indeed share the right, in principle, to repayment of charges levied in breach of EU law.[79] This is crucial as it follows that the EU law rules and principles ensuring effective judicial protection of rights, the impact of which was outlined in the general observations, will therefore apply to Gamma claims as well as to Beta claims.

5.041 A preliminary question mark on the scope of *Danfoss* may however arise by reason of the term 'final consumer' appearing in paragraphs 26 and 27 of the judgment, and the term 'final purchaser' in the summary keywords. Should

---

76 Ibid., para. 27. The use of the term 'final consumer' in this paragraph is confusing, as it signals a limitation of the scope of the judgment. However, such an interpretation cannot be upheld in light of the Operative Part of the judgment. See further below.

77 Ibid., para. 28.

78 Ibid., Operative part para. 1.

79 Ibid., paras 20–23.

this be an indication that the group of Gamma litigants who could benefit from *Danfoss* was limited to those who were at the final end of the supply chain? It is submitted that such an interpretation does not hold water. In the judgment 'final consumers' are first mentioned in paragraph 26, citing *Comateb*. In the relevant paragraph of the latter case the Court of Justice spoke precisely of 'final consumers'.[80] This therefore seems to be a quote from *Comateb*. The term 'final consumer' reappearing in the following paragraph 27 would then arguably be due to the fact that the Court in that paragraph is drawing conclusions from paragraph 26. Furthermore, the Court does not use these terms consistently. The judgment more often speaks of 'the operator/purchaser to whom the amount of the duty has been passed on'.[81] And, most importantly, this other phrase is the one used in the Operative part of the judgment.[82] It is accordingly submitted that the use of the term 'final consumer' in paragraphs 26 and 27 should not be interpreted as constituting any limitation of the scope of Gamma claimants who can benefit from *Danfoss*.

It is interesting to notice that *Danfoss* was the first case in which the Court of **5.042** Justice voiced an explicit policy for its case law on the repayment of charges levied in breach of EU law, namely, to offset the consequences of the charge by neutralizing the economic burden which it has unduly imposed on those who, in the final analysis, have actually borne it.[83] The reasoning of the Court in *Danfoss* suggested that this was a logical consequence of *Comateb* and *Reemtsma*. It is submitted however that it would still have been compatible with earlier case law to stress disgorgement of those enriched by the charge (i.e., the Member State) as the main aim, in parallel with the aim of compensating for harm incurred. The cited holding in *Comateb* does point in the direction of *Danfoss*, but does not as such exclude a disgorgement policy. *Reemtsma* could have been distinguished as a VAT case. The Court instead explicitly opted for a policy of compensation to those burdened by the charge, giving priority to this objective over the disgorgement of those enriched by the charge. This policy choice has been confirmed in *Alakor*.[84] In essence the Court has thus given priority to the interest of individual reimbursement over the interest of effective enforcement of EU law. Although these interests may often support the same legal solution, they may nevertheless support differing solutions in the individual case. This is illustrated by the defence of passing-on, which risks providing an opportunity for Alpha to avoid liability under

80 *Comateb* (n 25) para. 24.
81 *Danfoss* (n 7) paras 19, 22, 28 and 29.
82 Ibid., Operative part para. 1.
83 Ibid., para. 23.
84 *Alakor* (n 19) para. 24.

circumstances where the burden of a charge or loss has been passed on down an intricate supply chain to persons 'who, in the final analysis, have actually borne it', but who may have little or no incentive to bring an action for the repayment of petty sums.[85] This problem, which is linked to the interrelationship of the concepts of reparation and deterrence in the passing-on problem, will be discussed further in Section 9.E.

5.043 It has been mentioned that the judgment in *Danfoss* makes it quite clear that the right to reimbursement for loss incurred by reason of the levying of charges in breach of EU law does indeed extend to Gamma claimants. It did not follow however that EU law would require for that right to be enforceable against Alpha. The Court of Justice was in fact neutral to the form of redress available to Gamma and against whom such redress was available, accepting a possibility of obtaining reimbursement from Beta rather than from Alpha.[86] Moreover, in the second part of the judgment, which will be analysed further in Chapter 6, the Court held that:

5.044

> ... it is not for the Court to assign a legal classification to the actions brought by the plaintiffs before the national court claiming reimbursement of a duty unduly paid or claiming compensation for damage suffered.[87]

5.045 It is instead (as follows from settled case law) for the parties to do so, subject to the supervision of the national court.[88] The Court of Justice was accordingly neutral also to the classification of the remedy under national law, as long as some form of redress was available to Gamma.

5.046 Where an action was in fact brought by Gamma against Alpha, the Court did however clarify that such an action could only be opposed if two requirements were met. First, Gamma must be able on the basis of national law to bring a civil action against Beta for recovery of the sum unduly paid. Second, it must not be virtually impossible or excessively difficult for Gamma to obtain

---

85 Daniel Beard and Alison Jones, 'Co-Contractors, Damages and Article 81: The ECJ Finally Speaks' (2002) 23 *European Competition Law Review* 246, 255.

86 Such a solution was recently chosen in Swedish law; see Swedish Supreme Court judgment 22 December 2015, NJA 2015 s 1072, where the *condictio indebiti* action was declared available to a Gamma claimant against Beta. The facts were that Beta had charged Gamma 25 per cent VAT for printing services and paid the VAT to the Swedish Tax Agency. It was later discovered (in light of case C-88/09 *Graphic Procédé v Ministère du Budget, des Comptes publics et de la Fonction publique* [2010] ECR I-1049) that only 6 per cent VAT was payable. The Tax Agency repaid the excess to Beta but charged Gamma for additional tax in respect of the erroneous input VAT deduction by Gamma. Under such circumstances the Supreme Court held that Beta was liable to repay to Gamma the VAT charged but not due. Beta argued disenrichment but that argument was dismissed by the Supreme Court.

87 *Danfoss* (n 7) para. 32.

88 *Metallgesellschaft Ltd* (n 7) para. 81; *FII* (n 7) para. 201. See further para. 5.007.

reimbursement from Beta, e.g., due to Beta being insolvent.[89] As noted in paragraphs 2.059–2.060 this interpretation of the principle of effectiveness, previously appearing only in *Reemtsma*,[90] was indeed far-reaching.

By contrast the Court did not clarify whether the Gamma claimant had the onus of proving that it had exhausted its possibilities to obtain such reimbursement from Beta. Such a precondition of 'exhaustion of domestic remedies'[91] is compatible with *Unibet* and *Inuit*, where the existence of a specific remedy was not required if an alternative remedy existed in national law which made it possible to ensure the protection of the right conferred on the individual by EU law.[92] This logic comes across more clearly in the Opinion of Advocate General Kokott who pointed out that there must be a remedy, but also that if there is a remedy there is no requirement under EU law for national law to have further remedies at the disposal of the claimant.[93] **5.047**

Contemplating these holdings on the principle of effectiveness in *Danfoss*, it becomes apparent that they are very close to – or do indeed overlap into – the EU law right to an effective remedy. As the requirements of the principle of effectiveness were not met, the remedy offered was not adequately effective. Consequently the requirements of the right to an effective remedy were not met either. It will be interesting to see in forthcoming case law if this stringent interpretation of the principle of effectiveness in *Danfoss* is upheld or whether *Danfoss* should be read on its facts. An alternative way to achieve the same result was, it is submitted, open to the Court of Justice: the Court could have held instead, in the interest of effective enforcement of EU law by way of disgorgement of enrichments earned by Alpha through the levying of charges in breach of EU law, that Alpha was liable to compensate Gamma notwithstanding a possible alternative of seeking redress from Beta. **5.048**

It is interesting (or perhaps puzzling) in that regard to contemplate the choice of the word 'oppose' in the Operative part of the judgment.[94] The corresponding words in the Danish language version are *modsætte sig*: in the French language version it is *s'opposer*. This seems to be a broader term than to 'reject' (Danish: *afvise*, French: *rejeter*) which was used in both questions asked by the national court and in the ruling of the Court on question 2. A prohibition **5.049**

---

89 Cf. *Danfoss* (n 7) Operative part para. 1; and para. 28.

90 *Reemtsma* (n 68) para. 41.

91 Cf. Art. 35(1) ECHR.

92 Case C-432/05 *Unibet (London) Ltd and Unibet (International) Ltd v Justitiekanslern* [2007] ECR I-2271 paras 40–41; case C-583/11 P *Inuit Tapiriit Kanatami and Others v European Parliament and Council of the European Union* EU:C:2013:625 paras 103–104.

93 *Danfoss* (n 7) Opinion of AG Kokott paras 62–67.

94 Ibid., Operative part para. 1.

against 'opposition' to a claim even seems to carry some kind of indication that the action should be successful. The word 'oppose' is introduced by the Court in its rephrasing of question 1, with no further explanation.[95] It does not seem likely that this was done by accident. The only reasonable explanation to this author is that the word 'oppose' was chosen in order to broaden the scope of the ruling of the Court on question 1. The question asked pertained to a national rule under which the action was to be rejected, i.e., (if this author correctly understands the Danish original term *afvise*) it was not admitted. In other words the question asked concerned the issue of access to court. If the answer is intended to have a broader scope than access to court, the Court must logically have wished to cover yet another issue.

5.050 The identity of this 'other' issue is vexing. In the extreme this ruling in *Danfoss* can be interpreted as meaning that the Danish authorities must comply with the restitutionary claim brought by the applicant. A more limited interpretation is that the Court wished to broaden the scope of its ruling so as to prevent national laws of the Member States from dismissing claims such as the ones brought in *Danfoss* on their merits, but nonetheless generally, by reference to national substantive concepts of proximity or attribution. It could very well be argued that since there is no nexus between Alpha and Gamma, the loss passed on cannot legally be attributed to Gamma in the context of an action for repayment. In even simpler terms: as Gamma did not make the original payment to Alpha, it is not logical for Gamma to claim repayment from Alpha.[96] Perhaps by choosing the word 'oppose' the Court of Justice intended to clear the way for future case law – to open up a discursive space, if you will – in which it will be able to dispense with substantive concepts in national law barring Gamma claimants just as effectively as any procedural bar would. This seems a plausible interpretation that fits well with the facts of *Danfoss*, where it was reported that Beta did not claim repayment (and seems to have had no incentive to do so).[97] It is hoped that a clarification will come in future case law on the action for repayment of charges levied in breach of EU law.

D. SUBSTANTIVE PROXIMITY IN RESTITUTION FROM A MEMBER STATE

5.051 In this section substantive proximity problems in restitution from a Member State are examined with a view in particular to assessing the situation of

---

95 Ibid., para. 19.

96 Cf. further Section 5.D.II.

97 *Danfoss* (n 7) para. 14.

Gamma claimants seeking restitution.[98] More specifically it is examined how the general requirements of EU law such as the EU law principles of equivalence and effectiveness will influence national rules and doctrines concerning the nexus between claimant and defendant in an action for restitution brought against the state.

I. General observations on substantive proximity

Substantive proximity problems have received scarce attention in materials on restitution from a Member State, and relevant case law is limited to *FII*[99] and *Danfoss*. The Court of Justice did not however examine the issue in detail in any of those two cases. Therefore the general observations made here will need to make use of European private law on the issue of substantive proximity in restitution, and attempt to interpret the scarce EU law materials in the light of such comparative materials. It is admittedly only with great caution, if at all, that conclusions can be drawn from the comparative efforts of European private law writing, and private unjust enrichment law does not necessarily apply to repayment actions brought against the state.[100] The speculative nature of the discussion in this section must consequently be underlined. Nevertheless I will attempt to use EU law materials and European private law materials combined to trace the discursively legitimate possibilities available to EU law. **5.052**

In actions for repayment the issue of proximity will not typically arise. It will generally suffice to establish that a payment was made and that it was not due.[101] If this is established it follows that the person who made the payment was impoverished by the transaction without need for further analysis of causation or the like.[102] Such is for instance the case in the French *répétition de l'indu* action. In the subsidiary action of *enrichissement sans cause* however, French law does require evidence of a causal nexus between the enrichment of the defendant and the impoverishment of the claimant.[103] The Draft Common Frame of Reference (DCFR) states that this requirement of a causal **5.053**

98 In this book, Alpha signifies a tortfeasor or enriched party, Beta a party first burdened by loss arising from Alpha's breach of EU law, and Gamma any party downstream from Beta (including all from the party dealing directly with Beta to the final consumer) to whom the burden of that loss may have been passed on; see Section 1.B.

99 *FII* (n 7).

100 In many jurisdictions public law provisions with varying content will apply to such actions; see the DCFR (n 8) Art. VII. – 7:103.

101 DCFR (n 8) 3860–65; cf 4032 on German law where 'a performance always occurs "at the expense" of the person rendering the performance' under the *Leistungskondiktion* (see also Gerhard Dannemann, *The German Law of Unjustified Enrichment and Restitution* (Oxford University Press 2009) 34); or of the person whose 'domain … of rights' is interfered with under the *Eingriffskondiktion*.

102 The consequences of subsequent passing-on of the impoverishment will be touched upon in Section 5.D.II.

103 DCFR (n 8) 3850–51.

nexus in French restitution law will be met in circumstances where 'one and the same intervening event caused the enrichment as well as the impoverishment'.[104] This is sometimes called the doctrine of 'indivisibility of origin', under which an action for restitution is available only if both the enrichment and the corresponding impoverishment have flown from the same event and the one would not exist without the other.[105]

5.054 A similar position on substantive proximity has been hinted at in EU case law. The Court of Justice held in *FII* that an action against a Member State would qualify as an action for repayment only if the loss of the claimant was an 'inevitable consequence' of the breach of EU law on behalf of the Member State.[106] In *Danfoss* Advocate General Kokott reasoned on the precise meaning of the inevitable consequence test. The Advocate General observed that if the 'real meaning' of the criterion of inevitable consequence was applied, it would not be fulfilled with respect to claimants downstream from Beta since the charge was not passed on automatically but through an entrepreneurial decision taken by Beta.[107] Read this way the inevitable consequence test would amount to an EU law condition of substantive proximity which could plausibly apply just as well in restitutionary actions brought against private individuals. The Advocate General however stressed that the case law was not clear on this point.[108]

5.055 To conclude this brief overview the materials examined indicate a stringent substantive law requirement for the existence of a direct nexus between the impoverished claimant and the enriched defendant, although it is possible in some jurisdictions to bring a successful action against a defendant to whom an enrichment has passed through the patrimony of others. This possibility does not however lend itself to conclusions relevant to the situation of Gamma, which is to be considered next.

---

104 Ibid., 3851; see also Williams (n 6) 173. The DCFR and Williams both report lax interpretations of this requirement for a nexus in French and Belgian law that would accept claims for the restitution of enrichments that have passed through patrimonies to the enriched defendant. The DCFR 3851–2 further reports very similar positions in Spanish and Italian law. The 'passing-on' of enrichments must however be distinguished from the passing-on of impoverishment which will be discussed in Section 5.D.II.

105 See Beatson and Schrage (n 8) 207.

106 *FII* (n 7) para. 207. See further para. 5.007.

107 *Danfoss* (n 7) Opinion of AG Kokott para. 54.

108 Ibid., paras 53, 55. The Court of Justice did not pick up on this point, but held that the principle of effectiveness would require that Gamma claimants were allowed to bring a restitutionary action against the Member State under certain conditions; see further Section 5.D.II.

II. Substantive proximity and passing-on

It follows from the general observations submitted above that Beta parties will not under typical circumstances face any particular substantive proximity problems when bringing an action for restitution. As Beta will have made the initial transaction to Alpha, Beta will also be the typical reclaimant. If Beta claims also to have incurred harm over and above the amount claimed in repayment, e.g., because of a drop in sales, Beta will by contrast need to establish that such alleged harm was caused by the transaction. Such a claim would be for damages, and causation in damages claims against a Member State as discussed in Chapter 6. **5.056**

The situation is more problematic where an action for repayment of charges levied in breach of EU law is brought by Gamma against Alpha, as it was in *Danfoss*.[109] Gamma was not the party making the initial transaction to Alpha, but Beta had passed on all or part of the disadvantage suffered through the initial transaction to Gamma. Under such circumstances it may nonetheless follow from the applicable substantive conditions of national law that Gamma is too remote from the transaction to bring a successful claim for repayment of charges against Alpha. In consideration of such difficulties it may be preferable to Gamma claimants to bring a claim for damages instead of a claim for restitution. In *Danfoss* the claimant did indeed bring a subsidiary claim for damages. Proximity problems facing Gamma in the context of damages actions will be discussed in Chapter 6. The concern in this section is proximity problems in restitution, i.e., whether Gamma can leapfrog Beta in order to bring a direct action for repayment of charges levied in breach of EU law against Alpha. **5.057**

The proper approach to three-party situations seems to be a universal problem of unjust enrichment law.[110] In the European private law materials considered there is no mention of the possibility of impoverishments passing-on through the patrimony of Beta and into the patrimony of a Gamma claimant. It is therefore unclear whether, e.g., the requirement of causation in *enrichissement sans cause* could be met within such a scenario. The idea of an action for restitution brought by someone other than the person who made the payment which was not due generally seems alien to the materials examined. There is no mentioning of this possibility in neither the DCFR, nor by Beatson and Schrage,[111] nor by any of the commentators of national substantive restitution **5.058**

109 Ibid.

110 Beatson and Schrage (n 8) 207.

111 Ibid.

law consulted with the exception of Rush[112] and Burrows (citing Rush).[113] As discussed in Section 4.D.II Rush has observed that Gamma would not be able to bring an action against Alpha in English common or statutory law, submitting that the reasons for this were unclear. Rush suggested two reasons: first, in the context of overpaid taxes, that the government would likely bar Gamma actions;[114] and secondly because of the lack of a nexus between Alpha and Gamma.[115] The solution advocated by Rush was to allow Beta to claim the entire enrichment from Alpha, rejecting any defence of passing-on attempted by Alpha, and to allow Gamma to bring a subsequent action against Beta.[116] Neither Rush nor Burrows suggest however for Gamma to be considered proximate enough to be able to claim restitution from Alpha. The austerity of European private law towards the possibility of Gamma claims is further apparent in DCFR Article VII.–4:101, which provides a non-exhaustive list of instances of attribution. In all instances the impoverishment (or 'disadvantage' in the terminology of the DCFR) pertains to the person who has transferred wealth directly to the enriched person.[117] Consequently the possibility for a claimant to whom an impoverishment has passed through the patrimony of others to bring an action for restitution against the enriched defendant finds no support in the European private law materials considered.

5.059 It thus seems that Gamma claimants attempting to bring an action for restitution from a Member State are likely to encounter severe legal problems in the context of the substantive assessment of proximity. The question is thus whether EU law will accept such strict national conditions for the enforcement of a right which, pursuant to *Danfoss*,[118] is conferred on Gamma claimants by EU law. More precisely the question is whether these stringent conditions are compatible with the EU law principle of effectiveness.[119] Unfortunately the Court of Justice has not explicitly ruled on this issue.

5.060 With regard to access to court it follows from *Danfoss* that Gamma claimants can be barred from claiming repayment of charges levied in breach of EU law from Alpha only if Gamma is able to bring an action for reimbursement

112 Michael Rush, *The Defence of Passing On* (Hart Publishing 2006) 209–10.

113 Andrew Burrows, *The Law of Restitution* (3rd edn, Oxford University Press 2011) 617–18.

114 As the Danish Government tried to in *Danfoss* (n 7).

115 Rush (n 112) 210–11.

116 Ibid., 218, with an extensive discussion of different constructions to this end at 211–17. See n 86 on such a solution in Swedish law. A similar solution has reportedly been adopted by the Berlin Kammergericht for the purposes of competition law damages actions, see Ch. 4 n 55.

117 See DCFR (n 8) 4035 and the accompanying Comments and Notes.

118 *Danfoss* (n 7) para. 27.

119 On the scope and meaning of this principle see Section 2.D. The principle of equivalence (Section 2.D.II) is less relevant in this context.

against Beta and it is not virtually impossible or excessively difficult for Gamma to obtain reimbursement from Beta.[120] It was noticed in paragraph 5.055 that the Court of Justice plausibly extended this point beyond the issue of access to court by holding that the Member State (Alpha) could not 'oppose' a claim brought by Gamma unless those requirements with regard to a possible action against Beta were met. The corresponding words in the Danish language version are *modsætte sig*: in the French language version *s'opposer*. This is a broader term than to 'reject' (Danish: *afvise* (to declare inadmissible), French: *rejeter*) which was used by the national court. A prohibition against 'opposition' to a claim even seems to carry some kind of indication that the action should be successful. It is submitted however that such an interpretation is going a bridge too far. A more limited interpretation is that national laws of the Member States will thus be hindered from dismissing claims such as the ones brought in *Danfoss* on their merits, but nonetheless generally, by reference to national substantive concepts of proximity or attribution such as those described above. In *Danfoss* Beta did not claim repayment and seems to have had no incentive to do so.[121] There was therefore a risk that Alpha, i.e., the Member State, would not be held liable to make restitution to anyone. Although the national rule scrutinized seems to have belonged to the realm of administrative procedure, the outline of European private law above suggests that it is likely that the substantive assessment of the action brought would likewise be prejudiced by the lack of a direct nexus between Gamma and Alpha. This likelihood persists and is perhaps even accentuated by the fact that a claim for repayment of publicly levied charges will be of a public law nature rather than a private law nature.[122] Against this background, the choice of the word 'oppose' in *Danfoss* can be read as indicating that the substantive assessment must not be so prejudiced as to deprive Gamma of a fair hearing and full examination of the evidence produced by Gamma in support of its claim. National courts seized with an action for restitution brought by Gamma against a Member State (Alpha) must, on this reading, be prepared to disregard the possible abnormality of a Gamma action under national law and consider its merits. It should however be noticed that such an EU law requirement for a full assessment in the individual case is without prejudice to the possibility that the national court may conclude on the facts that the claim must be dismissed for lack of proximity between the claimant and defendant.

To summarize, the European Court of Justice has not explicitly ruled on whether it is necessary for a successful claim for repayment of charges levied in **5.061**

120 See Section 5.D.II.

121 *Danfoss* (n 7) para. 14.

122 See paras 5.188–5.189 for a discussion of Member State tendencies towards protection of public revenue.

breach of EU law that the charge was levied from the claimant or whether it is sufficient that the levy of the charge has impoverished the claimant (i.e., following the passing-on of the impoverishment). There is considerable uncertainty, and where this issue arises the national court should refer the case to the Court of Justice for a preliminary ruling. Uncertainties notwithstanding, it has been submitted that it follows from the EU principle of effectiveness as interpreted by the Court in *Danfoss* that national courts should not be able to reject *a priori* an action for repayment brought by Gamma with reference to the lack of a nexus between Alpha and Gamma, even where such an *a priori* conclusion formally follows from substantive proximity concepts rather than from a procedural law bar.

E. ESTIMATING RESTITUTION FROM A MEMBER STATE

5.062 Restitutionary actions are manifold and the measure of restitution is contingent on the type of enrichment transferred to the enriched defendant. For example, restitution of an enrichment which consists of specified or generic goods which are retained unspoilt and unaltered by the enriched defendant is made by restoring the goods to the claimant.[123] If the goods are lost, destroyed or altered, restitution can alternatively be made by paying the monetary value to the claimant. Where the enrichment is not a transferable asset, e.g., if it consists of the receipt of services, restitution is also made by paying the monetary value of those non-transferrable enrichments to the claimant. If the defendant has been further enriched through its possession of the enrichment, the measure of restitution may include the value of such fruits or use of the principal enrichment.[124] In this section a comparatively simple form of restitution is concerned, namely, the repayment of money paid but not due.

5.063 In actions for repayment of money paid but not due, courts will use the amount unduly paid as a yardstick for the measure of repayment. This basic measure can however be both increased and decreased for various reasons. In case law concerning actions for repayment of charges levied in breach of EU law, the European Court of Justice has indicated a number of circumstances

123 On restitution in kind from public authorities see the texts cited in n 1.

124 These examples are simplified illustrations of the rules and principles on the estimation of restitutionary awards in the DCFR (n 8) Arts VII. – 5:101 to 5:104. E.g., the defence of disenrichment (also known as 'change of position') included in DCFR Art. VII. – 6:101 has not been mentioned. Cf. also DCFR Arts III. – 3:510–3:514 on restitution pursuant to the termination of a contract; and Commission, 'Proposal for a Regulation of the European Parliament and of the Council on a Common European Sales Law' COM(2011) 635 final, Ch. 17 of the proposed contract rules, also on restitution pursuant to the termination of a contract.

capable of increasing or decreasing the amount of the award. This case law will be examined in this section. Emphasis will be on the defence of passing-on, the purpose of which is to decrease the amount payable by reference to the passing-on of impoverishment. In the context of repayment of charges levied in breach of EU law the defence of passing-on is sometimes referred to as the defence of unjust enrichment, or as an instance of a defence of unjust enrichment which would also encompass other circumstances over and above passing-on. These issues have been devoted a separate Section 5.E.III. Issues concerning the estimation of restitution in actions brought against the Member State by a Gamma claimant specifically will be outlined in Section 5.E.IV. First, there will be some general observations on the estimation of awards in actions for restitution brought against a Member State.

I. General observations on the estimation of restitution

5.064 In an action for repayment of charges levied in breach of EU law the basic measure of repayment will be at an amount equivalent to the amount paid but not due. This follows from the consistent holdings of the Court of Justice that anyone who has paid such charges has a right to claim repayment.[125] The defence of passing-on which is used by defendants to argue for a decrease of this basic measure of repayment will be discussed in Section 5.E.II. This section will briefly outline other adjustments to the basic measure of repayment.

5.065 The DCFR allows the reduction of a restitutionary award to the extent that the enriched defendant has been 'disenriched', i.e., to the extent that the defendant has already disposed of the enrichment in good faith and without obtaining a substitute for the enrichment.[126] This model rule was designed to apply in legal relationships between private individuals but it may nevertheless be available to the public authorities in some Member States. In respect of English law for instance, Jones and Williams have both found that the case law leans towards acceptance of a defence of disenrichment (change of position) for public authorities.[127] Although the Court of Justice has not been given an opportunity to rule on this matter, it can be pointed out that in the context of repayment actions brought against a Member State such national conditions for repayment would be subject to the dual test of equivalence and effectiveness.

125 E.g., *Pigs and Bacon* (n 13) para. 25; *San Giorgio* (n 19) para. 12; *Lady & Kid* (n 42) para. 17.
126 DCFR (n 8) Art. VII. – 6:101, with more details.
127 Jones (n 6) 45–7; Williams (n 6) 136–7.

5.066 Under the principle of equivalence such a defence of disenrichment could not be upheld if it applied to repayment actions brought for a breach of EU law but did not apply for similar actions brought for a breach of domestic law.[128] Under the principle of effectiveness such a defence of disenrichment could not be upheld if it made it virtually impossible or excessively difficult for the claimant to obtain reimbursement. As noticed in paragraph 2.071 however, the principle of effectiveness also allows Member States a certain margin of appreciation. Even if the availability of a defence of disenrichment to public authorities under national law would be liable to impede the successful recovery of charges levied in breach of EU law, it would therefore not necessarily follow that national rules allowing such a defence must be set aside. The outcome of the effectiveness assessment would, it is submitted, rather depend on the detailed features of the national rule or practice at issue. A national rule or practice which amounted to a presumption that the public authority had been disenriched, or required for the claimant to prove that the public authority had not been disenriched,[129] would probably need to be set aside pursuant to the principle of effectiveness. By contrast the mere availability of such a defence of disenrichment in circumstances where it was for the public authority to establish that it had been disenriched would be less vulnerable.

5.067 Circumstances can also be such as to allow for increases of a restitutionary award. In *Corus UK* – a case concerning an action for restitution from the EU – the General Court held that the award should include 'not only the principal amount ... but also the amount of any enrichment or benefit [the EU] has obtained as a result of such payment'.[130] It will be recalled that the Commission had been able to invest the money paid by the claimant, and made considerable profit from that investment. The General Court found it fair that restitution to the claimant should under such circumstances include an amount equivalent to the returns yielded by investment of the principal amount.[131] This result matches the approach of the DCFR in which restitution 'extends to the fruits and use of the enrichment'.[132] In the context of restitutionary claims brought against the Member States however, the proper question in EU law is whether the Court of Justice should require for the restitutionary award to include sums of this kind? There is no case law dealing

128 For details on the equivalence assessment see Section 2.D.II.

129 Cf. *San Giorgio* (n 19) para. 14.

130 *Corus UK Ltd* (n 5) para. 55.

131 Ibid., para. 63.

132 DCFR (n 8) Art. VII. – 5:104(1). However, in situations where the enrichment has been held in good faith and has enabled the defendant to make some savings that are as such lesser than the value of the aforementioned fruits and use, only an amount equivalent to those savings are to be repaid; Art. VII. – 5:104(1)–(2).

explicitly with this matter, but it can be noticed that in several cases the Court has held that the restitution to which individuals are entitled of a charge levied in breach of EU law includes not only the charge or tax levied:

> ... but also of the amounts paid to that State or retained by it which relate directly to that tax. That also includes losses constituted by the unavailability of sums of money as a result of a tax being levied prematurely ... .[133] **5.068**

5.069 This holding can be traced back to *Metallgesellschaft* in which the right to restitution with interest was first acknowledged by the Court of Justice.[134] The wording quoted above however, which first appeared in *FII*,[135] can be read as indicating that not only the payment of interest is required. The availability of interest is 'included' among losses 'constituted by the unavailability of sums of money' which in turn has occurred as the amounts paid have been 'retained by' the Member State. Such a close reading reveals that this holding opens up the possibility of reaching results similar to that in *Corus UK* also in the context of repayment actions brought against Member States.

5.070 Notwithstanding the availability of special increases due to the fruits and use of money retained, it has been effectively settled by the Court of Justice that interest is payable as part of an award of repayment from a Member State of charges levied in breach of EU law but the details remain within the discretion of the Member States. The Court of Justice held in early case law that where a national court heard an action for reimbursement of charges (albeit in that case charges levied by national authorities on behalf of the Community), 'ancillary questions' such as the payment of interest were to be settled by national authorities in accordance with national law.[136] In the more recent advance corporation tax (ACT) cases, which partly concerned situations where taxes had been levied prematurely, the Court of Justice maintained that the rate of interest and the date from which it must be calculated were ancillary issues to be settled by national law.[137] In *Metallgesellschaft* the Court nonetheless held that a payment of interest was of essence where the breach of EU law arose not from the levy of the tax as such, but from it being levied prematurely. Under

---

133 Case C-591/10 *Littlewoods Retail Ltd and Others v Her Majesty's Commissioners of Revenue and Customs* EU:C:2012:478 para. 25; joined cases C-113/10, C-147/10 and C-234/10 *Zuckerfabrik Jülich AG* (C-113/10) *v Hauptzollamt Aachen, British Sugar plc* (C-147/10) *v Rural Payments Agency, an Executive Agency of the Department for Environment, Food & Rural Affairs* and *Tereos – Union de coopératives agricoles à capital variable* (C-234/10) *v Directeur Général des douanes et droits indirects* and *Receveur principal des douanes et droits indirects de Gennevilliers* EU:C:2012:591 para. 65; case C-565/11 *Mariana Irimie v Administraţia Finanţelor Publice Sibiu et Administraţia Fondului pentru Mediu* EU:C:2013:250 para. 21.

134 *Metallgesellschaft* (n 88) paras 86–89.

135 *FII* (n 7) para. 205.

136 Case 26/74 *Société Roquette frères v Commission of the European Communities* [1976] ECR 677 paras 11–12.

137 *Metallgesellschaft* (n 88) para. 86, and Operative part para. 2.

such circumstances, the Court observed, the claim for interest was not an ancillary claim but the very objective of the action. The Court therefore held that the claimant in *Metallgesellschaft* was entitled to a payment of interest as a matter of EU law.[138]

5.071 *Metallgesellschaft* thus implied that interest was payable as a matter of EU law only within a set of circumstances where a tax or other charge had been levied prematurely, and the loss of the claimant predominantly pertained to the unavailability of an amount of money during a certain period of time. The scope of this EU law requirement for interest was however broadened to encompass any action for the repayment of charges levied in breach of EU law in the subsequent *Littlewoods Retail*. In that case the Court cited *Metallgesellschaft* and *FII*, but continued to hold that '[i]t follows from that case-law that the principle of the obligation of Member States to repay with interest amounts of tax levied in breach of EU law follows from that law'.[139] Still, '[i]n the absence of EU legislation, it is for the internal legal order of each Member State to lay down the conditions in which such interest must be paid, particularly the rate of that interest and its method of calculation', subject to the EU law principles of equivalence and effectiveness.[140] With regard to the principle of equivalence the Court of Justice left it for the national court to determine within its discretion which rate of interest was the relevant *comparator* to a claim based on EU law.[141] With regard to the principle of effectiveness the Court held that 'the national rules referring in particular to the calculation of interest which may be due should not lead to depriving the taxpayer of an adequate indemnity for the loss' incurred through an undue payment to the Member State, but left it to the national court to make the final assessment.[142] In *Irimie* Romanian law, under which interest was payable only for time which had passed from the day following the day on which the claim for repayment of the tax unduly levied was filed, was however explicitly held to be incompatible with the principle of effectiveness.[143]

5.072 A specific issue in the determination of the restitutionary award arises in the context of passing-on. The general idea in passing-on is that the award to be repaid should be decreased to the extent that impoverishment has been passed on. If an impoverishment has indeed been passed on in increased selling

138 Ibid., paras 87–89.

139 *Littlewoods Retail* (n 133) para. 26.

140 Ibid., para. 27 and Operative part.

141 Ibid., paras 3–33; on the equivalence assessment see also Section 2.D.II. The author wishes to add a slight disclaimer: These paragraphs in *Littlewoods Retail* are somewhat obscure.

142 Ibid., para. 29.

143 *Irimie* (n 133) paras 26–28.

prices, the raised prices may however lead to decreased sales. Should the award therefore be re-increased to compensate for the corresponding loss, or should such loss be distinguished as harm eligible for compensation in damages only? The Court of Justice has considered decreases in sales volumes suffered by the claimant which have been connected to the payment of charges levied in breach of EU law.[144] The case law of the Court of Justice on this matter will be discussed in the next section.

In conclusion the measure of repayment amounts not only to the amount unduly paid, but will also include an award of interest on that principal amount calculated in accordance with national law. The measure of restitution might also, under certain circumstances, include other benefits earned by the Member State from retaining the undue payment. In the event that national law will allow public authorities to argue disenrichment, such a defence – as well as other conditions in national law including details on the calculation of interest – will be subject to scrutiny under the EU law principles of equivalence and effectiveness. **5.073**

II. The defence of passing-on

Most case law of the European Court of Justice on the defence of passing-on has been delivered in the context of repayment of charges levied in breach of EU law. The questions asked by national courts in the preliminary reference procedure have revolved around the extent to which a national defence of passing-on is compatible with the EU law principle of effectiveness.[145] The most important of those cases will be presented in some detail in this section. Due to the amount of case law presented this section has been divided into sub-sections roughly based on three time periods. For the sake of clarity it is not intended that these time periods are necessarily representative of distinct approaches,[146] although it will be evident that each period has been more concerned with particular aspects of the defence of passing-on. The presentation of the case law will be followed by a special sub-section devoted to analysis of the approach emerging from the case law. Accordingly the first **5.074**

144 Cf. e.g. *Comateb* (n 25) para. 34. On the action for damages against Member States see Ch. 6.

145 On the principle of effectiveness see Section 2.D.III. The principle of equivalence (see Section 2.D.II) is less relevant in this context, although it must be remembered that it follows from the latter principle that national conditions governing the estimation of an award, such as the availability of a defence of passing-on, cannot be less favourable than those relating to similar actions of a domestic nature.

146 On three phases in the case law on the principle of effectiveness see Anthony Arnull, *The European Union and its Court of Justice* (2nd edn, Oxford EC Law Library, Oxford University Press 2006) Ch. 9; and Takis Tridimas, *The General Principles of EU Law* (2nd edn, Oxford University Press 2006) 420–22. A fourth neo-interventionist phase would be added by Katri Havu, 'Horizontal Liability for Damages in EU Law – the Changing Relationship of EU and National Law' (2012) 18 *European Law Journal* 407, 410.

three sub-sections will mostly report facts and holdings which are crucial to the subsequent analysis, but they do also serve the purpose of informing the reader of relevant historic developments and trends in the case law.

5.075 In the context of repayment of charges levied in breach of EU law the defence of passing-on is sometimes referred to as the defence of unjust enrichment, or as an instance of the latter. In the light of recent case law it is debatable whether there are defences of unjust enrichment other than the defence of passing-on. This particular discussion has been devoted a separate Section 5.E.III.

a. *From* Just *to* Bianco*: Case law of the 1980s*

5.076 On 27 February 1980 the Court delivered its ruling in *Just*.[147] In this case the Court of Justice was for the first time confronted with a defence of passing-on in the context of charges levied in breach of EU law. *Just* was also the starting point of a development of case law on the passing-on problem in the context of repayment of charges levied in breach of EU law that still continues today.

5.077 The claimant, Hans Just I/S (Just), imported wine and spirits into Denmark. By statute applied as from 7 September 1977 Denmark introduced an increase in taxes on spirits. Aquavit was taxed at DKR 167.50 per litre of pure ethyl alcohol, and other spirits at DKR 257.15 per litre of pure ethyl alcohol. In June 1978 Just declared a consignment of imported alcoholic beverages. The consignment consisted of a small proportion of aquavit and a large proportion of other spirits.

Just brought an action against the Danish Ministry of Fiscal Affairs (the Ministry) claiming repayment of the sums it had been compelled to pay at a rate higher than that for aquavit. Just argued that the higher tax levied on imported spirits other than aquavit were contrary to Article 95 of the EEC Treaty (now 110 TFEU).

Before the delivery of judgment in *Just* the European Court of Justice ruled in separate proceedings that the contested tax rate distinction between aquavit and other spirits in Denmark discriminated against an indeterminate number of products which had been or could be imported into Denmark and that it was moreover of such a nature as to afford protection to domestic production of aquavit. Therefore, the Court held, the Danish system was contrary to Article 95 of the Treaty.

In *Just* focus consequently turned to the issue of loss suffered by Just. Just submitted in that regard that Danish courts were unlikely to allow a recovery of taxes paid but not due if it could be presumed to have been passed on to consumers. Just asserted that sales of spirits other than aquavit had dropped all over Denmark, not only causing a serious reduction of profits but also forcing Just to reduce its staff. The Danish Government objected that Just had sold its products at normal prices; covering cost

147 *Just* (n 18).

> prices, the disputed charges and a normal profit margin. Thus, the government argued, the charges had in fact been paid by the consumers and Just had suffered no damage. Refunding the charges would therefore, the government concluded, amount to an unjust enrichment of Just. The government further argued that the Ministry might face claims from those who had ultimately borne the burden of the tax. If repayment was made to Just there was therefore a risk that the Ministry would be held liable to repay the same amount twice.

In his Opinion Advocate General Reischl used *Rewe* and *Comet* as the point of departure for his argumentation. The Advocate General thus noted that Article 95 of the Treaty had direct effect and created individual rights which the national courts must protect. Therefore, the Advocate General continued, charges could not be levied in breach of Article 95 of the EEC Treaty. In instances where they had already been paid, they should be repaid. However, the Advocate General continued, insofar as Community law (now EU law) did not itself provide rules governing matters such as admissibility, the prerequisites for bringing an action and the periods within which actions must be brought, the national courts were permitted to uphold such actions only in accordance with their own procedural law, subject to the principles of equivalence and effectiveness.[148] The Advocate General moreover opined: **5.078**

> In my opinion these references to domestic law apply not only to procedural rules, but also to conditions for entitlement to the rights afforded by Community law ... in so far as Community law contains no rules applicable in the matter. ... Proof of damage or impoverishment as a precondition for bringing proceedings is known in the legal systems of all the Member States and in the Community legal system itself as an expression of the general principle of natural justice.[149] **5.079**

For those reasons Advocate General Reischl would leave it to the national court to decide whether and to what extent the taxes at issue were to be repaid, albeit subject to the EU law principles of equivalence and effectiveness.[150] **5.080**

The Court of Justice began its assessment in *Just* by noting that when assessing claims for the repayment of charges levied but not due, Danish law would take into account the fact that such charges were incorporated in the price of the goods and passed on to subsequent stages in the economic chain. The Court also noted that Danish courts seemed to take into consideration any damage which may have been suffered by the taxpayer as a result of the incidence of the tax on his turnover. Like the Advocate General the Court then referred to **5.081**

148 Ibid., Opinion of AG Reischl, 530–31.
149 Ibid., 532.
150 Ibid., 533.

its judgments in *Rewe* and *Comet*, explaining that in the absence of Community rules concerning the refunding of national charges which have been unlawfully levied, it was for the domestic legal system to designate the courts having jurisdiction and to determine the procedural conditions governing actions at law intended to ensure the protection of the rights which subjects derive from the direct effect of Community law, it being understood that such conditions cannot be less favourable than those relating to similar actions of a domestic nature and that under no circumstances may they be so adapted as to make it impossible in practice to exercise the rights which the national courts were bound to protect.[151]

5.082 The Court specified that the protection of rights guaranteed in the matter by Community law did not require an order for the recovery of charges improperly made to be granted in conditions which would involve the unjust enrichment of those entitled. Therefore, the Court held, Community law did not prevent national courts from taking account of, in accordance with their national law, the fact that the burden of the charges which had been unlawfully levied might have been passed on to other traders or to consumers. The Court however also held that it was compatible with the principles of Community law to take into consideration, if appropriate, in accordance with the laws of the Member State concerned, the damage suffered by the restrictive effect of the charges on the volume of imports by the taxpayer from other Member States.[152]

5.083 It has been submitted that the approach chosen in *Just* resulted in the opening of Pandora's box, as Denmark was at that time the only EEC Member State allowing the defence of passing-on, and even then did so only in limited circumstances.[153] After *Just* other Member States came to argue and even legislate following the Danish example, as illustrated by subsequent case law to which we will now continue. One month after delivering the *Just* judgment the Court of Justice returned to the issue of passing-on in *Denkavit*.[154]

5.084 The claimant, Denkavit Italiana Srl (Denkavit), had paid public health inspection charges to a total amount of LIT 2 783 140 between 1971 and 1974. It was settled for the purposes of this case that the charges in question had been levied in breach of Community law. Denkavit claimed repayment of the charges.

151 Ibid., paras 24–25.

152 Ibid., paras 26–27.

153 See *San Giorgio* (n 19) Opinion of AG Mancini paras 8–9; Oliver (n 40) 890; *Comateb* (n 25) Opinion of AG Tesauro para. 14; and Jones (n 6) 89; the last two both with references. Cf. also n 275.

154 Case 61/79 *Amministrazione delle Finanze dello Stato v Denkavit Italiana Srl* [1980] ECR 1205. This case also discusses the temporal scope, as regards the availability of an action for repayment of unlawfully levied charges, of a judgment declaring the levying of charges to be contrary to Community law.

> The Italian Government submitted that repayment should not be made as the repayment of charges unlawfully levied could cause serious financial difficulties for the Member States.[155] The government furthermore argued that the charges which were improperly levied had, by their very nature, been passed on by the traders who paid them so that they had ultimately been borne by the final consumer. To repay them, the government concluded, would constitute an unjust enrichment and would in fact constitute an aid.[156]

Advocate General Reischl (submitting an Opinion in *Denkavit* as well as in *Just*) maintained that in the absence of Community rules it should be 'for the courts of the Member States alone to decide according to their own rules of law whether, and if so to what extent, charges ... which were wrongly levied are to be repaid', but also recognized the difficulties of establishing pass-on and the possibility of suffering loss in the form of decreased sales.[157] **5.085**

The Court also, as in *Just*, held that the protection of rights guaranteed in the matter by the Community legal order did not require the grant of an order for the recovery of charges improperly levied in conditions such as would involve an unjustified enrichment of those entitled. Therefore, the Court held, Community law did not prevent national courts from taking into account, in accordance with their national law, the fact that the burden of the charges which had been unlawfully levied may have been passed on to other traders or to consumers.[158] **5.086**

With regard to the argument that repayment could constitute an aid however, the Court distinguished decisions by which Member States, in pursuit of their own economic and social objectives, gave undertakings or other persons resources or procured for them advantages intended to encourage the attainment of the economic or social objective sought, from a duty to pay or repay sums caused by the fact that those sums had not been payable by the person **5.087**

155 Ibid., para. 5.

156 Ibid., para. 8.

157 Ibid., Opinion of AG Reischl, 1234.

158 Ibid., para. 26. This is one of very few occasions where the Court has referred to *unjustified* enrichment rather than *unjust* enrichment. In comparative law, the two are carefully distinguished, as 'unjustified enrichment' signals the use of a civil law approach where the enrichment is unjustified if there is no legal basis for it (e.g., German *ohne Rechtlichen Grund*, § 812 BGB), while 'unjust enrichment' signals the use of the traditional (but debated) common law approach under which an unjust factor for the enrichment must be identified (see further Francesco Giglio, 'A Systematic Approach to "Unjust" and "Unjustified" Enrichment' (2003) 23 *Oxford Journal of Legal Studies* 455, who argues that these are two separate actions). In this book, the term unjust enrichment is used, not for the sake of arguing that the Court of Justice applies the traditional common law approach – on the contrary, it rather applies the civil law approach, see case C-47/07 P *Masdar (UK) Ltd v Commission of the European Communities* [2008] ECR I-9761 paras 44–47, 49 – but because it is the term most commonly used by the Court itself in the English language versions of its judgments (e.g., in *Masdar*).

who had paid them. The latter, the Court held, did not constitute an aid within the meaning of Article 92 of the Treaty.[159]

5.088 It was consequently settled by *Just* and *Denkavit* combined that the Court had left the issue of passing-on to the discretion of the Member States to be settled within their jurisdictions. In the peculiar *International Chemical Corporation* however,[160] the Court took a very different approach and searched for a solution to the passing-on issue in Community law. It should be stressed at the outset that this case has been severely criticized and that this author too subscribes to the view that it is legal history. Nevertheless, as such, it must be reported in this context.

5.089 The claimant, SpA International Chemical Corporation (ICC), manufactured compound feedingstuffs. Under Council Regulation No 563/76[161] the release of certain imported feedingstuffs to circulation in the Community was made subject to the purchasing of prescribed amounts of skimmed-milk powder. To ensure compliance importers had to prove that they had purchased the prescribed amounts of skimmed-milk powder or have provided a security which was forfeited if the purchasing obligation was not complied with. ICC had provided securities to the Italian administration in accordance with the regulation. As ICC had not purchased the prescribed amounts of skimmed-milk powder however, the securities had been forfeited.

Council Regulation No 563/76 was declared void by the European Court of Justice in *Bela-Mühle*.[162] ICC subsequently brought an action for the recovery of the securities which had been provided to the Italian administration.

5.090 The Court of Justice recalled that disputes relating to the refund of amounts collected on behalf of the Community fell within the jurisdiction of national courts and should be settled by those courts applying their own national law, both procedural and substantive, to the extent to which Community law had not provided otherwise. Under the circumstances however, the Court held that Council Regulation No 563/76 should be examined in order to ascertain whether it contained provisions affecting the recovery of sums received by the Community authorities or by national authorities acting on their behalf pursuant to that Regulation.[163]

---

159 *Denkavit* (n 154) para. 31. Art. 92 of the EEC Treaty is now Art. 107 TFEU.

160 Case 66/80 *SpA International Chemical Corporation v Amministrazione delle finanze dello Stato* [1981] ECR 1191.

161 Council Regulation (EEC) No 563/76 of 15 March 1976 on the compulsory purchase of skimmed-milk powder held by intervention agencies for use in feedingstuffs [1976] OJ L67/18.

162 Case 114/76 *Bela-Mühle Josef Bergmann KG v Grows-Farm GmbH & CO KG* [1977] ECR 1211.

163 *International Chemical Corporation* (n 160) paras 21–22.

In that regard, the Court observed that under Council Regulation No 563/76 the burden of costs for the compulsory purchase of skimmed-milk powder was to be shared among all operators on the relevant market. The Court stressed that Article 5 of the Regulation implied that commercial contracts were if necessary to be amended unilaterally in order to ensure that the burden of costs was shared equitably. Accordingly, the Court continued, operators subject to the obligation to purchase skimmed-milk powder and for that reason exposed to the risk of losing their security should not suffer any loss owing to the charge imposed, because the charge was automatically passed on to successive buyers. The Court consequently held that a scheme specially designed with a view to spreading the effects of a measure of economic policy would destroy the basis of an action for the recovery of securities which had been provided and declared forfeit. It did not matter, the Court further held, whether the operator had actually passed on the charge.[164] **5.091**

International Chemical Corporation has been criticized by Oliver who submitted in 1987 that it was 'open to question' and 'most difficult to reconcile' with other case law,[165] and by Dougan who was able to conclude in 1998 that it could 'no longer be regarded as good either in law or in spirit'.[166] In light of subsequent case law which will be presented below, this author agrees that *International Chemical Corporation* (or at least this aspect of the case) has been overruled or must in the very least be distinguished on its facts. Therefore it will not be discussed further. **5.092**

The subsequent *San Giorgio*,[167] delivered 9 November 1983, remains by contrast of the utmost importance. **5.093**

> The claimant, SpA San Giorgio (San Giorgio), imported dairy products from other Member States. Between 1974 and 1977 San Giorgio paid health inspection charges which were levied contrary to Community law. San Giorgio brought an action before the Tribunale di Trento claiming repayment of the charges. The Tribunale ordered repayment of LIT 65 160 585 after summary proceedings. **5.094**
>
> The Amministrazione delle Finanze dello Stato (AFS) appealed the order. AFS relied on Article 10 of Decree-Law No 430 of 10 July 1982 which provided:
>
> A person who has paid import duties … which have been unduly levied … is not entitled to the repayment of the sums paid when the charge in question has been passed on in any way whatsoever to other persons, except in cases of substantive error. The charge is presumed to have been passed on whenever the goods in respect of

164 Ibid., paras 23–24.
165 Oliver (n 40) 890.
166 Dougan (n 6) 247.
167 *San Giorgio* (n 19).

> which the payment was effected have been transferred, even after processing, transformation, erection, assembly or adaptation, in the absence of documentary proof to the contrary.
>
> These provisions were an exception to the general provisions concerning the recovery of undue payments and applied specifically to charges levied in breach of Community law. San Giorgio questioned the compatibility of those provisions with Community law.

5.095 With regard to the defence of passing-on (here raised by the Italian Government) Advocate General Mancini opined:

> I concede that that argument is ingenious: however, it is not convincing. In the first place, it does not defeat the criticism levelled by those who consider it impossible to prove the link between tax and price. … There is an instance of unjust enrichment – the only one in this case which may be mentioned without fear of denial – which the rule [of national law prohibiting repayment by reference to passing-on] not only tolerates, but actually promotes: namely the unjust enrichment of the State which unlawfully levies a tax and does not reimburse the person who paid it.[168]

5.096 Moreover:

> … the passing on of charges is not generally relevant because of the innumerable variables which affect price formation in a free market and because of the consequent impossibility of definitively relating any part of the price exclusively to any certain cost.[169]

5.097 The Advocate General nevertheless continued to identify a few cases where, in his view, a defence of passing-on would be warranted. The Advocate General cited *Just* and argued that the Danish view originated from the particular circumstances of a specific case before the Danish Højesteret where a milling enterprise claimed repayment of a charge even though the price of their produce was fixed by Danish authorities and had been increased to include the charge.[170] While the Advocate General sympathized with the conclusion of the Danish Højesteret in that case he was dissatisfied with its generalization in

---

168 *San Giorgio* (n 19) Opinion of AG Mancini para. 7. It is no wild guess that AG Mancini had been inspired by Francis Hubeau, 'La répétition de l'indu en droit communautaire' (1981) 17 Revue Trimestrielle de Droit Européen 442, 451: 'S'il y a enrichissement sans cause, c'est plutôt au benefice de l'autorité publique (*accipiens*) qui a perçu la taxe illicite, puisque la base légale sur laquelle la perception a été effectué est mise postérieurement à néant, ce qui lui fait perdre toute cause.'

169 *San Giorgio* (n 19) Opinion of AG Mancini para. 8.

170 U 1952.974 H. The earliest US case law on passing-on is very similar to this case, as it concerns charges on the market for interstate railway carriage, where prices were controlled by federal authorities. In this case law, contrary to the findings of the Danish Højesteret, the defence of passing-on was rejected by the Supreme Court of the US; see *Southern Pac Co v Darnell-Taenzer Lumber Co* 245 US 531 (1918) 533–4; and *Adams v Mills* 286 US 397 (1932) 406–8.

Just and with the approach chosen by the Court of Justice, arguing that with the exception of Denmark the defence accepted in *Just* had, until then, been 'alien to the legal experience of the Member States'. The Advocate General thus argued that the defence of passing-on could be accepted in some cases, 'but they must be looked upon with caution and their limits must be precisely defined'.[171]

Notwithstanding the severe criticism of previous case law submitted by the Advocate General, the primary importance of *San Giorgio* came to pertain to the holdings of the Court of Justice on national requirements of proof in relation to the passing-on problem. The Court first held that entitlement to the repayment of charges levied by a Member State contrary to the rules of Community law was a consequence of, and an adjunct to, the rights conferred on individuals by the Community provisions prohibiting charges having an effect equivalent to customs duties or, as the case may be, the discriminatory application of internal taxes.[172] The Court secondly recalled that although repayment might be sought only within the framework of the conditions as to both substance and form, laid down by the various national laws applicable thereto, the fact nevertheless remained that that those conditions must not be less favourable than those relating to similar claims regarding national charges and might not be so framed as to render virtually impossible the exercise of rights conferred by Community law. The Court thirdly pointed out that Community law did not prevent a national legal system from disallowing the repayment of charges which had been unduly levied where to do so would entail unjust enrichment of the recipients. The Court therefore held that Community law did not prevent courts from taking account, under their national law, of the fact that the unduly levied charges had been incorporated into the price of the goods and thus passed on to the purchasers. Consequently, the Court summarized, national legislative provisions which prevent the reimbursement of charges levied in breach of Community law could not be regarded as contrary to Community law where it was established that the person required to pay such charges had actually passed them on to other persons.[173] **5.098**

The Court however also held that any requirement of proof which had the effect of making it virtually impossible or excessively difficult to secure the repayment of charges levied contrary to Community law would be incompatible with Community law. That was so particularly in the case of presumptions **5.099**

171 *San Giorgio* (n 19) Opinion of AG Mancini paras 8–9.

172 Ibid., para. 12. *San Giorgio* thus developed the 'right, in principle' in *Pigs and Bacon* (n 13) para. 25.

173 *San Giorgio* (n 19) paras 12–13.

or rules of evidence intended to place upon the taxpayer the burden of establishing that the charges unduly paid had not been passed on to other persons or of special limitations concerning the form of the evidence to be adduced, such as the exclusion of evidence other than documentary evidence. In a market economy based on freedom of competition the question whether, and if so to what extent, a fiscal charge imposed on an importer had actually been passed on in subsequent transactions involved a degree of uncertainty for which the person obliged to pay a charge contrary to Community law could not in the view of the Court be systematically held responsible.[174]

5.100 The Court hence concluded that once it had established that the levying of the charge was incompatible with Community law, the national court must be free to decide whether or not the burden of the charge had been passed on, wholly or in part, to other persons. Furthermore, if the same treatment was extended to taxpayers who had similar claims arising from an infringement of national tax law, such non-discrimination was no reason for withholding the repayment of charges levied contrary to Community law.[175]

5.101 The issues of presumptions concerning the passing-on of charges and of who should have the burden of proving any such passing-on remained in focus in *Bianco*,[176] the judgment of which was delivered on 25 February 1988. In *Bianco* the Court of Justice examined indirect taxes, levied contrary to Community law, that were designed in national law specifically to be passed on to the final consumer. The Court also developed the meaning of the somewhat obscure words 'free to decide' used in *San Giorgio*.[177]

5.102 The claimants, SA Les Fils de Jules Bianco and J. Girard Fils SA (the claimants), pursued commercial activities involving the purchase, importation and distribution of petroleum products. The claimants had paid parafiscal charges on the consumption of high-grade fuel, petrol and domestic fuel oil. The claimants brought three separate actions for repayment of the charges, arguing that the charges levied were unlawful, in particular under Community law.

> The claimants argued that the statutory admissibility requirement of proof of a negative fact, namely that the charges had not been passed on to the buyers of their products, established a condition with which it was practically impossible to comply.[178]

---

174 Ibid., paras 14–15.
175 Ibid., paras 14, 17.
176 *Bianco* (n 19).
177 *San Giorgio* (n 19) para. 14.
178 *Bianco* (n 19) para. 9.

> The defendant, the Directeur Général des Douanes et Droits Indirects (the French Government), argued that the requirement was for proof of a positive fact, i.e., that the charge had in fact been borne by the claimants, and did not make the exercise of the rights conferred by Community law virtually impossible or extremely difficult.[179]
>
> In the national court of first instance the actions were declared inadmissible. On appeal the judgments at first instance were upheld. The claimants appealed in cassation in all three cases. The Cour de cassation referred the case to the European Court of Justice for a preliminary ruling.

The Court of Justice held it to be irrelevant whether the requirement at issue could have been framed in positive terms as long as it placed the burden of proof upon the taxpayers. The Court cited *San Giorgio* and held that a Member State was not entitled to adopt provisions which made the repayment of charges levied contrary to Community law conditional upon the production of proof that those charges had not been passed on to the purchasers of the products that were subject to the charges and to place the burden of adducing such negative proof entirely on the natural or legal persons claiming repayment.[180] **5.103**

The Court of Justice further held that even though indirect taxes were designed in national law to be passed on to the final consumer and in commerce were normally passed on in whole or in part, it could not be generally assumed that the charge was actually passed on in every case. The actual passing-on of such taxes, either in whole or in part, depended on various factors in each commercial transaction which distinguished it from other transactions in other contexts. Consequently, the Court concluded, the question whether an indirect tax had or had not been passed on in each case was a question of fact to be determined by the national court, which might freely assess the evidence. The Court of Justice however warned that in the case of indirect taxes it could not be assumed that there was a presumption that they had been passed on and that it was for the taxpayer to prove the contrary.[181] **5.104**

Although the Court of Justice observed that it was quite probable, depending on the nature of the market, that the charge had been passed on, it also acknowledged that the numerous factors which determine commercial strategy varied from one case to another so that it was virtually impossible to determine how they each affected the passing-on of the charge. The Court therefore held that the nature of the charge or the market could not affect the **5.105**

179 Ibid., para. 10.
180 Ibid., paras 11, 13.
181 Ibid., para. 17.

requirements of Community law on national provisions concerning the repayment of charges levied contrary to Community law.[182]

b. From Comateb *to* Weber's Wine World: *The second phase*

5.106 On 14 January 1997, following more than ten years of relative silence on the defence of passing-on after the delivery of *Bianco*, the Court of Justice delivered its landmark judgment in *Comateb*.[183] This judgment has since served as the paramount illustration of the approach taken by the Court of Justice to the defence of passing-on.

5.107 The claimants Société Comateb and 27 other companies (the claimants) imported goods into France from Guadeloupe. The French Service des Douanes et Droits Indirects levied dock dues from the claimants. Those dock dues were however held by the European Court of Justice, in *Legros*,[184] to have an effect equivalent to a customs duty, notwithstanding the fact that the charge was levied also on imports from other parts of the same Member State.

The claimants brought an action against the defendant, the Directeur Général des Douanes et Droits Indirects (the Directeur), for the repayment of the dock dues. The Directeur refused repayment with reference to statutory provisions excluding repayment of duties and charges where they had been passed on to the purchaser. French law moreover stipulated that traders must sell their products at a price covering costs for purchases, transport and applicable taxes, constituting a statutory requirement to pass on any and all charges levied.

5.108 By this time the non-interventionist approach of the Court of Justice to national defences of passing-on had attracted critique from legal scholars.[185] This critique, and to some extent the critique voiced by Advocate General Mancini in *San Giorgio*, echoed in the Opinion submitted in *Comateb* by Advocate General Tesauro:

5.109 In point of fact, it is plain, indeed abundantly plain in my view, that it can be positively established that the sum has been passed on to a third party only if supply is elastic and demand rigid, something that does not happen in the real economy. Those involved in administering the law have also to take account of this fundamental reality and draw the rational consequences.

---

182 Ibid., paras 20–21.

183 *Comateb* (n 25).

184 Case C-163/90 *Administration des Douanes et Droits Indirects v Legros and Others* [1992] ECR I-4625.

185 The commentators most often cited are perhaps Hubeau (n 168); Denis Waelbroeck, 'La garantie du respect du droit communautaire par les États Membres. Les actions au niveau national' (1985) Cahiers de droit européen 37; and Oliver (n 40). Another example is Francis Hubeau, 'Case 199/82, *Amministrazione delle Finanze dello Stato* v. *San Giorgio S.p.A.*, (1984) E.C.R. 3595' (1985) 22 *Common Market Law Review* 87. See sub-section 5.E.II.d for a discussion of the arguments submitted.

> More generally ... : I do not in fact believe it can be right to describe as unjust enrichment the profit derived by an individual from the reimbursement of a charge unduly required and levied by the authorities. More especially, I do not believe that the state, which itself has actually obtained unjust enrichment by levying – for years, even – an unlawful charge, may then specifically rely on a principle of that kind to refuse to repay the sums unduly paid.[186]

The Advocate General submitted therefore that the Court should reverse its earlier case law and reject the defence of passing-on: **5.110**

> In those circumstances, I can only propose to the Court of Justice the most obvious solution: that it rule explicitly that passing on the charge to third parties that have purchased the goods in no way affects the right of the individual to reimbursement of the sums unduly paid. Not only does that solution cause less uncertainty between traders and those who interpret the law, it better reflects economic reality.[187]

The Court did not however go so far as to reverse its previous case law. **5.111** Nonetheless it is possible to trace some sensitivity to the Opinion of the Advocate General in the judgment. The Court of Justice stressed that the rights of individuals so guaranteed by the Community legal order did not require repayment of charges where it was established that the person required to pay such charges had actually passed them on to other persons. In such circumstances, the Court held, the burden of the charge levied but not due had been borne not by the trader but by the purchaser to whom the cost had been passed on. To repay the trader the amount of the charge already received from the purchaser would therefore be tantamount to paying him twice over, which might be described as unjust enrichment, while in no way remedying the consequences for the purchaser of the illegality of the charge. The Court concluded that it was for the national court to determine, in the light of the facts in each case, whether the burden of the charge had been transferred in whole or in part by the trader to other persons and, if so, whether reimbursement to the trader would amount to unjust enrichment.[188]

The Court of Justice thus held that if the final consumer was able to obtain **5.112** reimbursement through the trader of the amount of the charge passed on to him, that trader must in turn be able to obtain reimbursement from the national authorities. On the other hand, the Court further held, if the final consumer could obtain repayment directly from the national authorities of the

186 *Comateb* (n 25) Opinion of AG Tesauro paras 20–21.
187 Ibid., para. 24.
188 Ibid., paras 21–23. Paragraph 22 seems a direct reply to AG Tesauro.

amount of the charge which he had paid but which was not due, the question of reimbursing the trader did not as such arise.[189]

5.113 The Court of Justice however also observed that even though indirect taxes were designed in national law to be passed on to the final consumer and even if in commerce they were normally passed on in whole or in part, it could not be generally assumed that the charge was actually passed on in every case. The actual passing-on of such taxes either in whole or in part depended on various factors in each commercial transaction which distinguished it from other transactions in other contexts. The Court consequently concluded that the question whether an indirect tax had or had not been passed on in each case was a question of fact to be determined by the national court which might freely assess the evidence. With regard to indirect taxes the Court moreover held that it could not be assumed that there was a presumption that they had been passed on and that it was for the taxpayer to prove the contrary. The same applied where taxpayers had been obliged by the relevant legislation to incorporate the charge in the cost price of the product concerned. The fact that such a legal obligation existed, the Court continued, did not mean that there was a presumption that the entire charge had been passed on, even when failure to comply with the obligation carried a penalty. Accordingly, the Court of Justice held, a Member State could resist repayment to the trader of a charge levied in breach of Community law only where it was established that the charge had been borne in its entirety by someone other than the trader and that reimbursement of the latter would constitute unjust enrichment. Furthermore, if the burden of the charge had been passed on only in part, it was for the national authorities to repay the trader the amount not passed on.[190]

5.114 These holdings notwithstanding, the Court also clarified that even where it was established that the burden of the charge had been passed on in whole or in part to the purchaser, repayment to the trader of the amount thus passed on did not necessarily entail his unjust enrichment. The trader could have suffered damage as a result of the very fact that he had passed on the charge levied by the administration in breach of Community law, because the increase in the price of the product brought about by passing-on the charge had led to a decrease in sales. In such circumstances the trader could justly claim that, although the charge had been passed on to the purchaser, the inclusion of that charge in the cost price had, by increasing the price of the goods and reducing sales, caused him damage which excluded in whole or in part any unjust enrichment which would otherwise have been caused by reimbursement. It

189 Ibid., para. 24.
190 Ibid., paras 25–28.

followed, the Court of Justice concluded, that where domestic law permitted the trader to plead such damage in the main proceedings, it was for the national court to give such effect to the claim as was appropriate.[191]

The Court of Justice further pointed out that traders could not be prevented from applying to the courts having jurisdiction, in accordance with the appropriate procedures of national law and subject to the conditions laid down in *Brasserie*,[192] for reparation of loss caused by the levying of charges not due irrespective of whether those charges have been passed on.[193] **5.115**

The defence of passing-on was at issue also in *Dilexport* which was delivered on 9 February 1999. *Dilexport* added little to previous case law. The main concern was that the presumption of passing-on in national law did not follow from specific legislation, but from administrative and judicial practice.[194] The Court addressed this by clarifying again that the Member State had the onus of proving pass-on, as the Court of Justice explicitly held that it should be for the administration to show by any form of evidence generally accepted by national law that the charge was passed on to other persons.[195] The subsequent *Michaïlidis*, delivered on 21 September 2000, also generally served to confirm settled case law on several points. A novel point on evidence was made in *Michaïlidis* however: if it were for the taxpayer to show that the disputed charge caused an increase in the price of products causing, in turn, a reduction in the volume of trade, the provisions in question would have to be considered contrary to Community law.[196] The Court of Justice thus extended its settled rule that the taxpayer must not bear the onus of proving that the burden of the charge has not been passed on into a rule encompassing also the burden of proving reduced trade volumes caused by the imposition of the charge. It thus importantly followed from *Michaïlidis* that the burden of proof rests with the administration on both points. **5.116**

The Court of Justice did not however go so far in *Michaïlidis* as to explicitly rule that the onus of proving that repayment would lead to an unjust enrichment of the claimant (i.e., to produce comprehensive evidence to that end, including evidence that the burden of the charge had been passed on and evidence that the taxable person had not suffered harm in the form of **5.117**

---

191 Ibid., paras 29–33.

192 *Brasserie* (n 4).

193 *Comateb* (n 25) para. 34. Cf. para. 5.007.

194 *Dilexport* (n 36) paras 13, 17 (question 4). The Italian Government however contested the submission of the national court on this point, see para. 46.

195 Ibid., para. 53.

196 Joined cases C-441/98 and C-442/98 *Kapniki Michaïlidis AE v Idryma Koinonikon Asfaliseon (IKA)* [2000] ECR I-7145 para. 38.

decreased sales, but plausibly also other evidence depending on circumstances) was placed upon the administration, although such a conclusion could arguably be drawn from the wording of the case. This issue was explicitly addressed by the Court of Justice in its judgment in *Weber's Wine World*,[197] delivered on 2 October 2003. The reasoning of the Court in this case was extensive and quite detailed. *Weber's Wine World* also includes a striking example of legislation specifically intended to obstruct the repayment of charges.

5.118 The claimants in the main proceedings, Weber's Wine World Handels-GmbH, Ernestine Rathgeber, Karl Schlosser, and Beta-Leasing GmbH (the claimants), had paid duties on beverages pursuant to Austrian law. Weber's Wine World Handels-GmbH was a wine dealer operating in Austria, whereas the remaining claimants all operated restaurants in Austria.

In 1998 the claimants applied to the Abgabenbehörde erster Instanz (the authority competent at first instance for collection of duties) for repayment of duties paid for beverages during certain periods between 1995 and 1998. The claimants argued that the duties had been collected in breach of Community law. The Abgabenbehörde erster Instanz dismissed the claim. The claimants appealed to the tax authority.

On 9 March 2000 the European Court of Justice delivered its judgment in case C-437/97 *EKW*[198] in which the Court of Justice held that Article 3(2) of Directive 92/12 precluded the maintenance of the Austrian duties at issue insofar as they concerned alcoholic beverages. Only one week earlier, on 2 March 2000, the Wiener Abgabenordnung (Vienna Tax Code) had been amended in order to make claims for repayment of duties subject to the precondition that the economic burden of such duties was not borne by someone other than the taxable person. This amendment was also made applicable to tax liabilities which had arisen before the promulgation of the act.

Pursuant to the judgment of the Court of Justice in *EKW* the tax authority recognized that duties were only payable in respect of non-alcoholic beverages. The tax authority however also took the view that the inquiry revealed that the duties paid by the claimants had been passed on by the claimants to the final consumer. Therefore the tax authority dismissed the claim with regard to duties paid in respect of alcoholic beverages as well as non-alcoholic beverages.

The claimants appealed the decision of the tax authority to the Verwaltungsgerichthof insofar as it concerned duties paid in respect of alcoholic beverages. The claimants argued that the legal provision under which repayment was denied had been adopted specifically to reduce the possibilities for taxable persons to bring proceedings for recovery of taxes which were levied though not due. Such rules, the claimants argued, constituted a breach of the prohibition on frustrating Community law, deriving from Article 5 EC (now 4(3) TEU). The claimants moreover argued that the

197 *Weber's Wine World* (n 19).

198 Case C-437/97 *Evangelischer Krankenhausverein Wien v Abgabenberufungskommission Wien and Wein & Co HandelsgesmbH v Oberösterreichische Landesregierung* [2000] ECR I-1157.

retroactive effect of this legal provision constituted a breach of the principle of protection for legitimate expectations. The claimants also asserted that the taxes at issue had not been passed on.

The Verwaltungsgerichthof chose to stay proceedings and to refer the case to the European Court of Justice for a preliminary ruling.

The Court of Justice first examined the issue of whether the adoption of the amendment to the Wiener Abgabenordnung constituted a breach of Article 5 EC (now 4(3) TEU). The Court of Justice recalled settled case law, notably *Dilexport*, according to which Member States were not allowed, subsequent to a judgment of the Court from which it followed that certain legislation was incompatible with the Treaty, to adopt a procedural rule which specifically reduced the possibilities of bringing proceedings for recovery of taxes which were levied though not due under that legislation.[199]

The Court of Justice further held that it had been established that the purpose of the amendment made to the Wiener Abgabenordnung was to preclude the effects of the judgment of the Court in *EKW*, should the Court in that case find that that the duty on alcoholic beverages was contrary to Community law. The Court however recognized that the amendment did not refer solely to repayment of duties which were levied in breach of Community law. Therefore the Court held that the amendment was contrary to Community law only insofar as the amendment sought specifically to restrict the right to repayment of a sum levied but not due, in order to forestall the possible effects of a judgment of the Court holding that Community law precludes the maintenance of that duty. The Court left it to the national court to determine this point.[200]

With regard to the relationship between the passing-on of a duty and the concept of unjust enrichment the Court of Justice pointed out that individuals were entitled to obtain repayment of charges levied in breach of Community law and that Member States were, in principle, required to repay such charges. The Court of Justice held that repayment could be resisted only where it was established by the national authorities that the charge had been borne in its entirety by someone other than the taxable person and that reimbursement of the charge would constitute unjust enrichment of the latter. If the burden of the charge had been passed on only in part, national authorities were required to repay the amount not passed on. As that restriction was a restriction on a subjective right derived from the Community legal order, the Court further held that it must be interpreted restrictively, taking into account in particular the fact that passing-on a charge does not necessarily neutralize the economic effects of the tax on the taxable person.[201] **5.119**

199 *Weber's Wine World* (n 19) para. 86. These holdings are presented in a small font, as they do not concern the passing-on problem as such but may still be of interest to the reader.

200 Ibid., paras 90–92.

201 Ibid., paras 93–95.

5.120 On the issue of evidence the Court of Justice observed that the actual passing-on of charges, either in whole or in part, depended on various factors in each commercial transaction which distinguished it from other transactions in other contexts. Consequently the Court reiterated that questions concerning these facts were to be determined by the national court, which was free to assess the evidence adduced before it. The Court of Justice further stressed that even where it was established that the burden of the charge levied though not due had been passed on in whole or in part, repayment of the amount passed on to the trader did not necessarily entail unjust enrichment of the trader. The taxable person might also suffer as a result of a fall in the volume of sales. The existence and the degree of unjust enrichment could accordingly be established only following economic analysis in which all the relevant circumstances were taken into account. Moreover, the Court continued, the rules of Community law on the recovery of sums paid but not due precluded national rules which refused repayment on the sole ground that the charge was passed on to third parties without requiring that the degree of unjust enrichment that repayment would entail for the trader be established.[202]

5.121 The Court of Justice then turned to examine the impact of the principles of equivalence and effectiveness. On the principle of equivalence the Court of Justice held that it followed from the wording of the national provisions at issue that there was a derogation for certain claims for recovery of sums levied but not due based on national law, as the amendment at issue would not apply to persons who could rely on the effects of the so-called *Anlaßfallwirkung*. The *Anlaßfallwirkung* was applicable, inter alia, following a judgment of the Verfassungsgerichtshof declaring a law unconstitutional and had the effect of annulling the law, albeit without retroactive effect, allowing the law to remain applicable to facts that arose before the declaration of unconstitutionality. In this regard the Court called on the national court to ascertain whether it was actually the case that only claimants who brought proceedings based on domestic constitutional law could rely on the *Anlaßfallwirkung* and whether the rules governing repayment of charges held to be incompatible with domestic constitutional law were more favourable than those applicable to actions relating to taxes held to be contrary to Community law.[203]

5.122 On the principle of effectiveness the Court of Justice held that it was apparent from the order for reference that the tax authority had concluded that the economic burden of the duty on alcoholic beverages had not been borne by the claimants simply because the price invoiced to consumers of those beverages

---

202 Ibid., paras 98–102.
203 Ibid., paras 105–108.

included that duty. The Court further held that such an approach might constitute a presumption that the duty had been passed on, and also of unjust enrichment of the taxable persons such as would render repayment of the duty levied though not due impossible or at least excessively difficult. Such a presumption was contrary to Community law. The Court called on the national court to determine whether the tax authority's practice had the effect of establishing such a presumption of unjust enrichment, and to what extent the cooperation required on the part of taxable persons in supplying the tax authority with access to documents relevant to the tax authority's assessment of whether or not the duty had been passed on amounted to a presumption that the duty had been passed on unless evidence to the contrary was adduced.[204]

c. *From* Lady & Kid *to* Alakor: *Recent recasts*

5.123 It still remained debatable after these cases whether EU law allowed a defence of unjust enrichment, the defence of passing-on being one of several examples of such a defence, or whether there was a defence of passing-on which was sometimes referred to as the defence of unjust enrichment.[205] This issue was addressed by the Court of Justice in *Lady & Kid*,[206] delivered in Grand Chamber on 6 September 2011.

5.124 The claimants, Lady & Kid A/S and three others (the claimants), were all active in the retail trade in Denmark. In 1987 Denmark abolished a number of social charges payable by employers. In order to maintain neutrality with regard to public finances however, Denmark simultaneously introduced a business tax known as the employment market contribution (*arbejdsmarkedbidrag*, aka the Ambi). In this way Denmark also hoped to eliminate the link between the number of employees in a business and the amount of social contributions payable by it, thereby stimulating growth and developing employment. The Ambi had a fixed rate of 2.5 per cent calculated on the same basis as VAT. It was not payable upon import of goods into the territory of Denmark but was charged on the full sale price of imported goods upon first sale in Denmark.

204 Ibid., paras 113–116.

205 A discussion of that issue by this author is available in Magnus Strand, 'Case C-398/09, Lady & Kid A/S and others v. Skatteministeriet, Judgment of the Court of Justice (Grand Chamber) of 6 September 2011, nyr.' (2012) 49 *Common Market Law Review* 381, 387–396. See also *Lady & Kid* (n 42) Opinion of AG Cruz Villalón paras 36–76; Jones (n 6) 92–3; and Takis Tridimas, *The General Principles of EU Law* (2nd edn, Oxford EC Law Library, Oxford University Press 2006) 438–43.

206 *Lady & Kid* (n 42).

In *Dansk Denkavit*[207] the European Court of Justice held that Article 33 of Directive 77/388/EEC[208] precluded a tax such as the Ambi. By that time the Ambi had however been repealed with effect from 1 January 1992.

The Claimants applied for reimbursement of the amounts wrongly levied from them under the Ambi scheme. The Skatteministeriet (the Danish Ministry for Fiscal Affairs) rejected their applications on the grounds that the expenses of the Claimants under the Ambi scheme had been covered. The Skatteministeriet conceded that the amount of social charges that would have been payable unless they had been abolished under the Ambi scheme exceeded the amount of Ambi paid. Therefore, the Skatteministeriet argued, there could be no reimbursement. In 1997 and 1998 the claimants lodged complaints before the Københavns Byret (Copenhagen District Court) maintaining that the excise of the Ambi was contrary to EU law. In its judgment the Københavns Byret found in favour of the Skatteministeriet in all four cases. The claimants appealed to the Østre Landsret. In 2009 the Østre Landsret decided to stay proceedings and to refer the cases to the European Court of Justice for a preliminary ruling.

5.125 Advocate General Cruz Villalón argued in his Opinion that the EU law defence of unjust enrichment had several possible manifestations, of which the defence of passing-on was the most typical but which could also include other circumstances where unjust enrichment could arise if the Member State was to repay a tax even though the taxpayer had benefitted from parallel savings. The Advocate General argued that circumstances in *Lady & Kid* were of the latter character.[209] The Advocate General nonetheless opined that an exception for unjust enrichment under such circumstances could only be allowed under strict conditions. Thus, he submitted, EU law should not preclude a Member State from refusing to repay a tax unduly levied when it was in a position to prove that the amounts unduly levied could be regarded as offset by a simultaneous and corresponding reduction in other charges from which the same taxable persons actually benefitted, provided that there was a direct relationship of cause and effect between the creation of one charge and the removal of the other.[210]

5.126 In its ruling the Court of Justice first recalled that the right to a refund of charges levied in breach of Union law was the consequence and complement of the rights conferred on individuals by provisions of Union law prohibiting such charges and that therefore the Member State was required, in principle,

207 Case C-200/90 *Dansk Denkavit ApS and P Poulsen Trading ApS, supported by Monsanto-Searle A/S v Skatteministeriet* [1992] ECR I-2217.

208 Sixth Council Directive 77/388/EEC of 17 May 1977 on the harmonization of the laws of the Member States relating to turnover taxes [1977] OJ L145/1.

209 *Lady & Kid* (n 42) Opinion of AG Cruz Villalón paras 38–42 and 56–67.

210 Ibid., paras 68–76.

to repay such charges. By way of exception however, repayment could be refused where it would entail unjust enrichment of the persons concerned. The protection of rights so guaranteed by EU law did not according to the Court require repayment where it was established that the person who was required to pay such charges had actually passed them on to others.[211] The Court moreover cited previous case law in which the Court had not ruled out a possibility for national courts, when applying national law, to take into consideration other methods of refusing reimbursement of an unlawful tax than passing-on.[212]

Notwithstanding that case law the Court held that since such a refusal of reimbursement was a limitation of a subjective right derived from EU law, it must be interpreted narrowly. The Court therefore concluded that the direct passing-on to a purchaser of the tax wrongly levied constituted the sole exception to the right to reimbursement of taxes levied in breach of EU law. The Court further observed that even where it was established that the burden of a charge levied had been passed on to third parties, repayment to the trader of the amount thus passed did not necessarily entail his unjust enrichment. Even when the charge was wholly incorporated in the price the taxable person might suffer as a result of a fall in the volume of his sales. The Court also held that Member States could not reject an application for reimbursement of an unlawful tax on the ground that the tax had been set off by the abolition of a lawful levy of an equivalent amount. Such an abolition, the Court argued, fell within the ambit of choices made by the state in the field of taxation and could have the most diverse consequences which precluded the possibility of regarding reimbursement of an unlawful tax as giving rise to unjust enrichment, even when disregarding the potential difficulties of ascertaining whether and, if so, to what extent one tax had in reality replaced another.[213] **5.127**

The Court of Justice thus held that the rules of EU law on recovery of sums wrongly paid must be interpreted to the effect that recovery of sums wrongly paid could give rise to unjust enrichment only when the amounts wrongly paid by a taxpayer under a tax levied in a Member State in breach of EU law had been passed on directly to the purchaser. Consequently EU law precluded a Member State from refusing reimbursement of a tax wrongfully levied on the ground that the amounts wrongly paid by the taxpayer had been set off by a saving made as a result of the concomitant abolition of other levies. Such a **5.128**

211 Ibid., paras 17–18.

212 Ibid., para. 25. The case law cited was *Pigs and Bacon* (n 13) and case 222/82 *Apple and Pear Development Council v KJ Lewis Ltd and others* [1983] ECR 4083. Both were cited by AG Cruz Villalón in his Opinion.

213 Ibid., paras 20–21, 24.

set-off could not be regarded as an unjust enrichment as regards that tax from the point of view of EU law.[214]

5.129 The strict findings of the Court in *Lady & Kid* were confirmed shortly afterwards in *Accor*,[215] delivered on 15 September 2011. Some ambiguity however followed from the subsequent *Alakor*,[216] delivered on 16 May 2013.

5.130 Alakor Gabonatermelő és Forgalmazó Kft ('Alakor') administered financing of an agricultural and rural development programme in Hungary. Funds for the programme were provided by the Nemzeti Adó- és Vámhivatal Észak-alföldi Regionális Adó Főigazgatósága (Hungarian Ministry of Agriculture and Rural Development, 'the Ministry'). Alakor paid VAT on costs relating to the project. The VAT amounts paid were considered non-deductible under Hungarian law, but were covered by the Ministry as part of the costs for the programme.

Following the judgment of the Court of Justice in *PARAT*[217] Alakor considered that it could deduct the amount of input VAT paid in its entirety and that VAT could hence no longer be covered by the Ministry as part of the costs for the programme. Therefore Alakor repaid to the Ministry amounts paid to cover VAT and requested an amendment to its contract with the Ministry. The Ministry declined and returned the repayment to Alakor.

Alakor further applied to the tax authority for repayment of VAT which had thereto been considered non-deductible. The first-instance tax authority found that the VAT was deductible but determined the amounts to be repaid at a lower amount than that applied for by Alakor. The Ministry upheld the decision of the tax authority with reference to the amounts already obtained by Alakor. On appeal the national court of first instance annulled the decisions and sent the case back to the tax authority. The Ministry appealed to the Court of Cassation, which decided to stay proceedings and to refer the case to the European Court of Justice for a preliminary ruling.

5.131 The Court observed that, by way of exception, repayment of charges levied in breach of EU law could be refused where it entailed unjust enrichment of the persons concerned. Therefore, the Court continued, the protection of the rights guaranteed by the legal order of the EU did not require repayment of taxes, charges and duties levied in breach of EU law where it was established that the person required to pay such charges had actually passed them on to other persons.[218] The Court held, citing *Danfoss*,[219] that on condition that the

214 Ibid., Operative part. Cf. however *Alakor* (n 19) and case C-331/13 *Ilie Nicolae Nicula v Administrația Finanțelor Publice a Municipiului Sibiu and Administrația Fondului pentru Mediu* EU:C:2014:2285; discussed in Section 5.E.III.

215 *Accor* (n 9) paras 72–74.

216 Ibid.

217 Case C-74/08 *PARAT Automotive Cabrio Textiltetőket Gyártó Kft v Adó- és Pénzügyi Ellenőrzési Hivatal, Hatósági Főosztály, Észak-magyarországi Kihelyezett Hatósági Osztály* [2009] ECR I-3459.

218 *Alakor* (n 19) para. 25.

economic burden that the tax unduly paid imposed on the taxable person had been completely neutralized, a Member State might refuse to repay part of that tax on the ground that such repayment would give rise to unjust enrichment for the benefit of the taxable person.[220]

In the form of guidance to the national court the Court of Justice recommended the national court examine whether the amount of funds paid to Alakor would have been less than the amount actually granted if Alakor had been able to deduct VAT. If that were that the case, the excess resulting from the higher amount of the aid which Alakor accordingly was able to benefit from would be the consequence of the fact that part of the non-deductible VAT had been covered by that aid. The economic burden relating to the part of the tax corresponding to that excess would, on that basis, be subsidized by the Ministry and not by Alakor. Therefore, the Court advised, the amount of repayment which Alakor could claim must correspond to the difference between the amount of VAT which was wrongly considered non-deductible and the amount of funds granted to Alakor in excess of funds that would have been granted if Alakor had been able to deduct the VAT at issue.[221] **5.132**

The Court of Justice concluded that EU law did not preclude a Member State from refusing to repay part of VAT, the deduction of which had been precluded by a national measure contrary to EU law, on the ground that that part of the tax had been subsidized by aid granted to the taxable person and financed by the EU and by that state. This was however subject to the proviso that the economic burden relating to the refusal to deduct VAT has been completely neutralized, which was for the national court to determine.[222] **5.133**

Alakor was problematic as it seemed to blur again the sharp holdings of the Court of Justice in *Lady & Kid* and *Accor* with regard to the scope of defences to an action for repayment of charges levied in breach of EU law.[223] This will be discussed in Section 5.E.III. In the next sub-section there will be an analysis of the case law of the Court of Justice with regard to the defence of passing-on as such. **5.134**

---

219 *Danfoss* (n 7) which concerned access to court for Gamma claimants and is therefore discussed in Section 5.C.II. In this book, Alpha signifies a tortfeasor or enriched party, Beta a party first burdened by loss arising from Alpha's breach of EU law, and Gamma any party downstream from Beta (including all from the party dealing directly with Beta to the final consumer) to whom the burden of that loss may have been passed on; see Section 1.B.

220 *Alakor* (n 19) para. 28.

221 Ibid., paras 31–33.

222 Ibid., Operative part.

223 Cf. also *Nicula* (n 214).

d. Summary and analysis of the case law

5.135 It has been mentioned already that the vast majority of EU case law on the passing-on problem pertains to repayment actions brought against a Member State. In this context Beta is the direct payer of a charge or tax to Alpha, i.e., the Member State. Beta may have been able to pass on the burden of the charge or tax, in whole or in part, to parties further down the supply chain, here collectively referred to as Gamma. Alpha will rely on this possibility and argue the defence of passing-on, according to which repayment of the charge should not be available to the extent that such passing-on of the burden of the charge or tax to Gamma was possible for Beta. Such a defence of passing-on could also be raised against a claim brought by Gamma, as long as Gamma is not a final consumer. This has not yet occurred in the case law of the Court of Justice.[224] In this sub-section, the approach of the Court of Justice in respect of claims brought by Beta against Alpha will first be summarized and then discussed.

5.136 In its case law reported above the Court of Justice has consistently held that EU law neither prevents nor requires national courts to take into account, in accordance with their national law, the fact that the burden of charges unlawfully levied may have been passed on.[225] The isolated issue of whether or not, in principle, a defence of passing-on should be available to Alpha consequently remains within the discretion of the national legal system. This must be stressed. Nevertheless the case law has significantly circumscribed this national discretion in order to safeguard the rights conferred on individuals by EU law.

5.137 The Court of Justice has thus allowed Alpha to resist repayment only where two criteria are met, namely:

1. The charge must have been borne, in whole or in part, by someone other than the claimant; and
2. reimbursement must constitute unjust enrichment of the claimant.[226]

The Court of Justice has furthermore introduced a number of requirements concerning evidence and the burden of proof in relation to the two criteria identified above. These will be examined below in conjunction with the criteria themselves.

224 For a discussion of the defence of passing-on in actions brought by Gamma see Section 5.E.IV.

225 *Just* (n 18) para. 26; *Denkavit* (n 154) para. 31.

226 See e.g. *Comateb* (n 25) paras 27–29; *Michaïlidis* (n 196) paras 33–35; *Weber's Wine World* (n 19) paras 94–102.

Beginning with the first criterion, it is recalled that the actual passing-on of charges levied contrary to EU law, either in whole or in part, was held by the Court of Justice to depend on various factors in each commercial transaction which distinguished it from other transactions in other contexts.[227] This problem can be referred to as the passing-on problem *sensu stricto*, as it is asked specifically whether the charge has been passed on and, if so, to what extent. Although the case law expands on exceptions and limitations to the defence of passing-on, it is clear that the defence is accepted at law for the purposes of actions for repayment against Member States. The amount repayable with respect to a charge levied in breach of EU law can consequently, albeit subject to the subsequent test under the second criterion above, be reduced to the extent that the charge has been passed on. Where only a portion of the charge has been passed on the reduction will be equivalent to the portion passed on.[228] It follows that no repayment will be due where the entire amount of the unlawful charge has been passed on (again, subject to the subsequent test under the second criterion above). It also follows that if no portion of the charge has been passed on a defence of passing-on cannot be upheld. Accordingly the Court of Justice has held that repayment can be resisted only to the extent that it is established that the charge has been borne in its entirety by someone other than the claimant.[229] **5.138**

It should be noticed that there is a difference between this case law and the case law examined in Chapter 3, where a defence of passing-on was also available where loss could have been passed on by the claimant.[230] This use of the defence by reason of the mere possibility of passing-on is not mentioned in the case law on repayment of charges levied in breach of EU law. Instead it follows from the case law here cited that real and proven passing-on is necessary in order for a defence of passing-on to be accepted in the context of restitution from a Member State. **5.139**

On the burden of proving passing-on the Court has held that presumptions or rules of evidence intended to place upon the taxpayer the burden of establishing that the charges unduly paid have not been passed on to other persons are incompatible with EU law, irrespective of whether such special limitations are special to claims brought pursuant to a breach of EU law or apply to any claims for repayment of charges levied illegally.[231] Such presumptions cannot even be upheld where national law obliges Beta to pass on the burden of a **5.140**

227 *Bianco* (n 19) para. 17.

228 *Comateb* (n 25) para. 28.

229 Ibid., para. 27.

230 See paras 3.090–3.091 and 3.103–3.105.

231 *San Giorgio* (n 19) paras 14, 17. Cf. *Weber's Wine World* (n 19) paras 111–114.

charge.[232] Furthermore, if it is only proven that a certain part the burden of the charge has been passed on, it is for the national authorities to repay the claimant the amount not passed on.[233] Although the Court has not explicitly held that the burden of proving that a charge levied in breach of EU law has been passed on is on Alpha, the consequence of these holdings is that it will be for Alpha to prove the existence and extent of passing-on in order to be successful with a defence of passing-on.

5.141 The Court of Justice has also reviewed a number of specific national limitations on evidence that were liable to impede actions for repayment. With respect to limitations of admissible evidence, any requirement of proof which has the effect of making it virtually impossible or excessively difficult to secure the repayment of charges levied contrary to Community law has been held to be incompatible with EU law. Therefore the Court has held that to establish whether taxes have been passed on is a question of fact to be determined by the national court which must be able to freely assess the evidence.[234] Beta and Alpha alike are free to present any form of evidence generally accepted by national law.[235] Accordingly no special limitations concerning the form of the evidence to be adduced are allowed, irrespective of whether such special limitations are special to claims brought pursuant to a breach of EU law or apply to any claims for repayment of charges levied illegally.[236] National courts thus have a duty under EU law to make a free assessment of the evidence, notwithstanding any limitations in that respect that may follow from national law.

5.142 In addition to proving passing-on *sensu stricto*, a successful defence of passing-on must equally satisfy the second criterion identified above. In other words Alpha must demonstrate that reimbursement would constitute an unjust enrichment of the claimant. This criterion concerns the impact of so-called turnover losses which the Court considered as early as in *Just*.[237] In *Comateb* the Court of Justice established that proven passing-on of the burden of a charge levied contrary to Community law, in whole or in part, is not sufficient to allow Alpha to resist repayment of the charge. It must also be proved that reimbursement of the passed on portion of the charge would constitute an unjust enrichment of the claimant.[238] To establish that a

232 *Comateb* (n 25) para. 26.
233 Ibid., para. 28.
234 *Bianco* (n 19) para. 17.
235 *Dilexport* (n 36) para. 53.
236 *San Giorgio* (n 19) paras 14, 17.
237 *Just* (n 18) para. 26.
238 *Comateb* (n 25) para. 27.

repayment would constitute unjust enrichment of the claimant it is necessary to take into account harm incurred through loss of turnover. This typically occurs because the inclusion of a charge in the prices set by Beta – i.e., an increase of Beta's prices – will make Beta's produce less competitive on the market, causing Beta's sales to drop. Such reduced sales might exclude, in whole or in part, any unjust enrichment which would otherwise have been caused by reimbursement.[239] The Court of Justice has further held that to reach the conclusion that repayment would lead to unjust enrichment it is necessary to carry out an economic analysis in which all the relevant circumstances are taken into account.[240] It should be well noticed that this wording leaves it open as to what such relevant circumstances may be, possibly opting to leave the assessment to be resolved on a case-to-case basis. Higher prices may typically lead to lower turnover on markets with price elasticity of demand, but other circumstances are equally eligible to be taken into account. It seems therefore that the particularities of the market at issue in each case must be carefully examined in order to assess, e.g., whether the claimant has suffered any kind of loss of profit (including but not limited to turnover losses) that may exclude unjust enrichment. There may of course also be other relevant circumstances to take into account. In *Comateb* the Court seemed happy to leave these considerations to the national court, as it held that where domestic law permits a claimant to argue that the illegal levying of the charge has caused him damage which excludes, in whole or in part, any unjust enrichment, it is for the national court to give such effect to that argument 'as may be appropriate'.[241]

On the issue of evidence the general findings of the Court of Justice with **5.143**
regard to passing-on *sensu stricto* will apply also to the second criterion. In other words requirements of proof and/or forms of evidence must be compatible with the EU law principles of equivalence and effectiveness.[242] The more pressing issue is the burden of proof with regard to turnover losses and other reasons for lost profit (or other circumstances excluding unjust enrichment). In this regard the Court of Justice has held that even when it is settled that the burden of a charge has been passed on, it must not be presumed on this sole ground that reimbursement will lead to unjust enrichment of the claimant.[243]

239 Ibid., para. 32. Of course, a reduction in sales does not by any means follow automatically from an increase in prices. Such an effect is dependent on the price elasticity of demand on the market at issue; see e.g., case C-129/00 *Commission of the European Communities v Italian Republic* [2003] ECR I-14637 Opinion of AG Geelhoed paras 73–78.

240 *Weber's Wine World* (n 19) para. 100.

241 *Comateb* (n 25) Operative part, para. 3.

242 E.g., *Bianco* (n 19) para. 17; *Dilexport* (n 36) para. 53. On the principles of equivalence and effectiveness see Section 2.D.

243 *Weber's Wine World* (n 19) para. 117 and Operative Part, para. 4.

Furthermore, in *Michaïlidis*, national rules under which it was for the taxpayer to show that the disputed charge caused an increase in the price of the products, causing in turn a reduction in the volume of trade, were considered contrary to Community law.[244] It seems therefore that the national administration will have the onus of proving these points in order to support its defence of passing-on. Nevertheless it may still be for the claimant to prove less typical circumstances and that they exclude unjust enrichment. As noted above, the existence and the degree of unjust enrichment can be established only following economic analysis in which all the relevant circumstances are taken into account.[245] The Court of Justice has not explicitly ruled that the entire burden of proof with regard to the second criterion of unjust enrichment rests with the national administration.

5.144 It has been mentioned already that the approach chosen by the Court of Justice to these issues has attracted some critique in legal writing. The principal views put forth in that critique are arguably the following:

1. The availability of a defence of passing-on is in itself contrary to EU law;
2. The availability of a defence of passing-on in some Member States but not in others gives rise to unwarranted differential treatment of claimants;
3. The availability of a defence of passing-on impedes the effective sanctioning of breaches of EU law by Member States;
4. The existence and extent of passing-on is in most cases virtually impossible to ascertain, and therefore it is better to disregard the issue;
5. The availability of a defence of passing-on deprives claimants who have paid charges levied in breach of EU law of effective judicial protection;
6. The availability of a defence of passing-on is liable to lead to unjust enrichment of Member States profiting from breaches of EU law; and
7. There was little or no support in the jurisdictions of the Member States for a defence of passing-on prior to *Just*.

5.145 The first argument above has been raised by Hubeau who submitted in 1981, and again in 1985, that the availability of a defence of passing-on under national law is in fact a measure having an effect equivalent to quantitative restrictions.[246] Hubeau argued that the passing-on of charges would lead to artificially raised prices which would constitute a direct and actual hindrance to trade. If charges were not passed on, there would at least be an indirect and

244 *Michaïlidis* (n 196) para. 38.

245 *Weber's Wine World* (n 19) para. 100.

246 Hubeau (n 168) 455–6; Hubeau (n 185) 104–5.

potential hindrance to trade. It is respectfully submitted that this argument confuses two different aspects. In the context of repayment of charges it is already settled that those charges were levied in breach of EU law. That issue need not be discussed further. What we are now discussing is how to remedy the losses caused to traders by that breach. In another reading, the argument of Hubeau might be interpreted as meaning that it is undesirable for limitations of the remedy to result in the perpetuation of negative effects caused by the breach of EU law. A similar point has been made by Dougan, arguing that to allow the defence of passing-on 'risks the *de facto* persistence of barriers to trade'.[247] This alternative reading of Hubeau seems rather to express the third argument listed above and it will therefore be discussed further in the context of that argument.

With regard to the second argument it has been pointed out by Arnull (among **5.146** others) that in the absence of harmonizing rules the availability of a defence of passing-on in some Member States may cause repayment actions in those Member States to be unsuccessful, while repayment actions under like circumstances will be successful in Member States that do not allow the defence of passing-on.[248] It was mentioned in paragraph 5.012 that in *Express Dairy Foods* the Court of Justice itself called for harmonization so as to create a level playing field for claimants of charges levied in breach of EU law. The relevant holdings deserve to be quoted in their entirety. The Court held:

> In the regrettable absence of Community provisions harmonizing procedure … the **5.147** Court finds that this situation entails differences in treatment on a Community scale. It is not for the Court to issue general rules of substance or procedural provisions which only the competent institutions may adopt. The rules to be adopted should involve equal treatment as regards conditions of form and substance in which traders may contest Community charges imposed upon them and claim their recovery in the event of undue payment together with a similar harmonization of the conditions in which the administrative authorities of the Member States, acting on behalf of the Community, impose the said charges and, where appropriate, recover financial benefits which have been irregularly granted. In the absence of Community rules however, the necessary reference to national laws is nevertheless subject to limits the need for which has been acknowledged inasmuch as the application of national legislation must be effected in a non-discriminatory manner having regard to the procedural rules relating to disputes of the same type, but purely national, and in so far as procedural rules

247 Dougan (n 6) 253.

248 Arnull (n 146) 277. See also Biondi and Johnson (n 21) 321. For instance Swedish law does not recognize a defence of passing-on in the context of repayment of charges levied in breach of EU law unless the defence has been explicitly provided for in applicable statutory law, see Administrative Supreme Court judgment RÅ 2002 ref 108; commented on by Johanna Engström, 'RÅ 2002 ref 108 och rätten till ett effektivt rättsmedel' 2005 *Europarättslig tidskrift* 340.

> cannot have the result of making impossible in practice the exercise of rights conferred by Community law.
>
> The essential point submitted to the Court concerns the amount of the sums to be reimbursed, which includes the question whether or not the sums paid but not owed are to be recovered in their entirety in the event of the charge having been passed on to subsequent purchasers by the aggrieved trader.
>
> The Court has already ruled that the protection of rights guaranteed in the matter by the Community legal order does not require the grant of an order for the recovery of charges improperly levied in conditions such as would involve an unjustified enrichment of assigns and that from the point of view of Community law there is therefore nothing to prevent national courts from taking account in accordance with their national law of the fact that it has been possible for charges unduly levied to be incorporated in the prices of the undertaking liable for the charge and to be passed on to the purchasers of the products in question … .[249]

5.148 In these holdings the Court seemed almost to be crying out for the legislature to intervene. The cry for harmonized standards was not heard however, and the case law of which *Express Dairy Foods* forms part remains the only source of EU law in this context. That is not to say that the development of case law has not proved a fruitful way to at least partially levelling the playing field. In the absence of the legislative intervention called for the Court has, since *Express Dairy Foods*, substantially limited the scope of reference to national law, thereby answering its own call where the EU legislature did not.

5.149 The third argument was that the availability of a defence of passing-on impedes the effective sanctioning of breaches of EU law by Member States. In *San Giorgio* Advocate General Mancini opined that Member States could not be prevented from 'continuing to levy charges having an effect equivalent to customs duties … if entrepreneurs were deprived of any judicial means of stopping such a practice'.[250] In *Comateb* Advocate General Tesauro likewise feared that the acceptance of a defence of passing-on would lead to non-compliance among the Member States, as charges levied in breach of EU law would not need to be repaid.[251] It is respectfully submitted that Advocate General Mancini had more reason to present this argument in 1983 than Advocate General Tesauro had in 1996. Since the entry into force of the Treaty of Maastricht this argument has arguably become less convincing, as the enforcement action under Article 258 TFEU can be used by the Commission to push Member States into compliance with EU law. The Commission has twice brought infringement proceedings against Italy by reason of Italy

249 *Express Dairy Foods* (n 20) paras 12–13.

250 *San Giorgio* (n 19) Opinion of AG Mancini para. 10.

251 *Comateb* (n 25) Opinion of AG Tesauro para. 21.

maintaining legal rules or principles that were not compliant with EU case law on the defence of passing-on, first in 1986 and again in 2000.[252] Italy lost both cases. The Commission did not enforce the Court's ruling in the latter case by bringing a second proceeding pursuant to Article (now) 260(2) TFEU, so presumably Italy complied with the ruling.

It is infamously difficult to establish the existence and extent of passing-on in most cases, as was pointed out by Oliver in 1987. In light of these difficulties it has been discussed whether the defence of passing-on should be disregarded – listed above as argument number four. For the purposes of repayment of charges levied in breach of EU law, Oliver criticized the findings of the Court of Justice in *Just* and submitted that 'it is impossible or virtually impossible to establish whether a charge has indeed been passed on, since the importer's price will be determined by a number of factors other than the charge'.[253] This view echoes the submissions of Toth and of Rudden and Bishop discussed in Section 3.E.III. Similarly, in *San Giorgio*, Advocate General Mancini reported that the Commission's representative had submitted at the hearing that '[i]n order to be certain that charges were passed on, supply would have to be elastic and demand would have to be ... rigid, but I believe the only product for which both those conditions are fulfilled is salt'.[254] This issue was not discussed as such in that case but it is likely to have influenced the Court of Justice in ruling that the onus of proving passing-on could not be on the claimant.[255] The connected problem of where to place the burden of proof with regard to the existence and extent of passing-on has indeed dominated subsequent case law. **5.150**

In *Bianco* the Court of Justice picked up on the issue more clearly, holding that even though indirect taxes were designed in national law to be passed on to the final consumer, and even if the nature of the market was such that they were normally passed on in whole or in part, there could be no general assumption or presumption that the charge was actually passed on in every case. The Court further held that actual passing-on of such taxes, either in whole or in part, depended on various factors in each commercial transaction which distinguished it from other transactions in other contexts. The Court of Justice moreover observed that, depending on the nature of the market, it was quite **5.151**

252 Case 104/86 *Commission of the European Communities v Italian Republic* [1988] ECR 1799; *Commission v Italian Republic* (n 239). See also Oliver (n 40) 890–91. On the interrelationship of Member State liability to repay charges levied in breach of EU law and Art. 258 TFEU see also paras 9.046–9.049.

253 Oliver (n 40) 889–90. See also *Comateb* (n 25) Opinion of AG Tesauro para. 20; and Biondi and Johnson (n 21) 317.

254 Reported in *San Giorgio* (n 19) Opinion of AG Mancini para. 6.

255 Ibid., para. 14.

probable that the charge had been passed on. Nevertheless it also acknowledged that the numerous factors which determine commercial strategy varied from one case to another so that it was virtually impossible to determine how they each affected the passing-on of the charge. Therefore the Court held that the nature of the charge or the market could not affect the requirements of Community law on national provisions concerning the repayment of charges levied contrary to Community law.[256]

5.152 The Court of Justice finished the job in *Comateb* by imposing strict requirements of evidence of actual passing-on of the burden of the charge. The Court held in *Comateb* that a Member State has the onus of proving its claim that a trader has passed on the burden of a charge levied in breach of Community law even when national law makes it an obligation – failure of which being subject to a penalty – of the trader to pass it on. Repayment to the trader could thus be resisted only to the extent that it was established that the charge had been borne in whole or in part by someone other than the trader. The Court of Justice added as a separate criterion that it must also be proved that reimbursement of the passed-on portion of the charge would constitute unjust enrichment.[257] It therefore followed from the reasoning of the Court in *Comateb* that a Member State could resist repayment to the trader of a charge levied in breach of Community law only to the extent that it was established that such repayment would cause the trader to be unjustly enriched, as stated in the summary above.

5.153 In *Weber's Wine World* it was confirmed that the onus of proving that the economic burden of charges levied but not due had been borne in its entirety by someone other than the claimant was placed upon the national authorities and that it had to be established that reimbursement of the charge would constitute unjust enrichment of the claimant. To that end the Court held that it was necessary to carry out 'an economic analysis in which all the relevant circumstances are taken into account'.[258]

5.154 To summarize, the critique voiced by Oliver has arguably been heard and followed by the Court of Justice. Through its case law the cumbersome task of bringing evidence of the existence and extent of passing-on has been placed firmly on the national authorities. Hence, if it was correct to argue that 'it is impossible or virtually impossible to establish whether a charge has indeed

256 *Bianco* (n 19) paras 17, 20–21.

257 *Comateb* (n 25) paras 27–28. See also *Weber's Wine World* (n 19) paras 98, 110.

258 *Weber's Wine World* (n 19) para. 100. The similar points in *Bianco* and in *Weber's Wine World*, respectively, relate to different stages in the assessment; the former to the determination of whether or not the charge had been passed on, and the latter to the extent of unjust enrichment in the event of repayment.

been passed on', those difficulties will now be facing the national authorities rather than the claimant, thereby perhaps making the issue less of a problem than it appeared to Oliver.[259]

The fifth argument has been expressed by, e.g., Advocate General Mancini who opined in *San Giorgio* that 'a State which exercises its residual and temporary power to regulate actions for the recovery of undue payments which ... in reality are likely to defeat negates a subjective right founded on Community law; ... [this] is manifestly unacceptable'.[260] Advocate General Tesauro took the same view in *Comateb*, opining that the defence of passing-on was liable to 'render nugatory a legal position guaranteed to the individual by Community law'.[261] It has similarly been submitted by Biondi and Johnson that the right to recover money unduly paid is 'in our view, a fundamental individual right' and that there should be no possibility for national legislation to introduce any kind of exception to that right.[262] These views can be contrasted against those submitted by Advocate General Reischl in *Just*. Advocate General Reischl recognized that charges levied in breach of EU law should be repaid, but was content to give national courts discretion to decide whether and to what extent the taxes at issue were to be repaid under applicable national rules of procedural rules and 'conditions for entitlement', albeit subject to the EU law principles of equivalence and effectiveness.[263] In *Denkavit* Advocate General Reischl was somewhat more cautious, suggesting instead that charges levied in breach of EU law should always be repaid. The Advocate General further suggested that it would be proper if Gamma parties to whom the burden of such charges had been passed on could have recourse under national law against Beta in cases where the latter had successfully recovered from Alpha.[264] Advocate General Reischl nonetheless preferred leaving the issue to be decided by the national courts, pointing both to the absence of Community rules governing the matter and to the practical difficulties of ascertaining whether and to what extent charges had been passed on.[265] **5.155**

Contemplating these contrasting views it becomes apparent that the difference lies in the division of powers preferred by the respective Advocates General **5.156**

259 Hubeau (n 185) 100 submitted even after the much less far-reaching *San Giorgio* that it would probably be impossible for national administrations to prove passing-on. However, cf. the more doubtful views of Dougan (n 6) 245–6.

260 *San Giorgio* (n 19) Opinion of AG Mancini para. 6.

261 *Comateb* (n 25) Opinion of AG Tesauro para. 22.

262 Biondi and Johnson (n 21) 319.

263 *Just* (n 18) Opinion of AG Reischl, 530–33.

264 See n 86 for a Swedish example along those lines. Cf. also para. 5.058.

265 *Denkavit* (n 154) Opinion of AG Reischl, 1234.

and commentators. Those preferring intervention by the Court of Justice would necessarily support EU jurisdiction on passing-on in the context of charges levied in breach of EU law, while submissions supporting non-intervention made reference to the absence of Community rules and the autonomy of national law. In the reasoning of the Court of Justice it is therefore interesting to notice the structure of its reasoning in *Just*. The Court first held that the protection of rights guaranteed in the matter by Community law did not require an order for the recovery of charges improperly made to be granted in conditions which would involve the unjust enrichment of those entitled. *Therefore*, the Court continued, Community law did not prevent national courts from *taking account* in accordance with their national law of the fact that the burden of the charges which had been unlawfully levied might have been passed on to other traders or to consumers.[266] It follows that established passing-on could be taken into consideration, as one factor, when deciding whether or not repayment would lead to unjust enrichment of those entitled.

5.157 It did not follow however that established passing-on would, in the Court's view, automatically mean that it was established that repayment would lead to unjust enrichment. This illustrates that the approach chosen in *Just* was non-interventionist, awarding the Member States latitude to find a proper solution themselves where the passing-on problem would arise in an action for repayment of charges levied in breach of Community law.[267] Consequently 'the ball was, so to speak, lobbed back from the Luxemburg centre court to the local playing ground'.[268] Subsequent case law has moved further and further away from that non-interventionism, but has not abandoned it completely in spite of pleas from Advocate General Tesauro[269] and Dougan.[270] The merits of the critique submitted by Advocates General Mancini and Tesauro was perhaps implicitly recognized by the Court of Justice in *Weber's Wine World* as it held that the possibility of resisting repayment where it was established by the national authorities that the charge had been borne by someone other than the claimant and that reimbursement would constitute unjust enrichment of the claimant was a restriction on a subjective right derived from the Community legal order and must therefore be interpreted restrictively.[271]

---

266 *Just* (n 18) para. 26. Italics added.
267 Tridimas (n 205) 439.
268 Smith (n 40) 272.
269 *Comateb* (n 25) Opinion of AG Tesauro para. 24.
270 Dougan (n 6) 251–2.
271 *Weber's Wine World* (n 19) paras 93–95.

Many commentators have still found it 'peculiar to regard the principle of unjust enrichment only as a reason for denying recovery to the applicant'.[272] As famously stated by Hubeau, '[s]'il y a enrichissement sans cause, c'est plutôt au benefice de l'autorité publique (*accipiens*) qui a perçu la taxe illicite, puisque la base légale sur laquelle la perception a été effectué est mise postérieurement à néant, ce qui lui fait perdre toute cause'.[273] This sixth argument above has echoed in the Opinions of Advocates General Mancini and Tesauro both.[274] The argument can in fact be subdivided into two arguments: one formal and one substantive. The formal argument is that considerations of unjust enrichment of the claimant by reason of passing-on are alien to the concept of repayment. The substantive argument doubts the moral wisdom of allowing Member States to retain benefits earned from illegal actions instead of requiring repayment notwithstanding the possibility of passing-on. Both critiques are strong and both are related to an issue which will be discussed below, namely that the Danish rule permitted by the Court of Justice in *Just* may have been unique (at the time).[275] **5.158**

Still, to this author, the formal argument appears now to have been undermined by the case law of the Court of Justice. It may very well be that considerations of unjust enrichment of the claimant by reason of passing-on are alien to national concepts of repayment.[276] The Court of Justice also held in the gritz and quellmehl cases that the defence of passing-on should not be dismissed as unfounded 'in the context of an action for damages',[277] which could be read as a hint on the strangeness of the defence in restitution, at least before the case law developments summarized above. However, even if it once was alien to every Member State jurisdiction, and even if it was still so today, it would nevertheless follow from the case law of the European Court of Justice that a national defence of passing-on will be tolerated within the boundaries **5.159**

272 Jones (n 6) 88. See also Hubeau (n 185) 101, 104; Oliver (n 40) 889; Biondi and Johnson (n 21) 317; and Dougan (n 6) 252.

273 Hubeau (n 168) 451.

274 *San Giorgio* (n 19) Opinion of AG Mancini para. 7, quoted in sub-section 5.E.II.a; *Comateb* (n 25) Opinion of AG Tesauro para. 21, quoted in sub-section 5.E.II.b.

275 Even in Danish law it has been reported that the legal basis for the rule at issue was not entirely stable; Karen Dykjær-Hansen, 'Restitution af beløb opkrævet med urette' (1994) *Ugeskrift for Retsvæsen* B 407, 408, has observed that the notorious U.1952.974:H was the only Danish Supreme Court judgment in the 20th century in which the defence of passing-on had been explicitly embraced in order to rule out liability to repay an amount levied in breach of law, and that the legal reasoning of the Supreme Court in that judgment was not easily compatible with traditional views on such repayment in Danish law. Danish readers can see also the frank dismissal of the defence of passing-on for the purposes of contractual damages liability in Danish law by Torsten Iversen, *Erstatningsberegning i kontraktsforhold* (Thomson 2000) 719 (the assessment beginning at 712).

276 Argued in *San Giorgio* (n 19) Opinion of AG Mancini paras 8–9.

277 See para. 3.111; cf. Koen Lenaerts, Ignace Maselis and Kathleen Gutman (Janek Tomasz Nowak (ed.)), *EU Procedural Law* (Oxford EU Law Library, Oxford University Press 2014) 532.

set by the Court for the purposes of EU law. This latitude in EU law must be distinguished from the actual existence of the defence in national law. Therefore formal legal reasoning referring to national concepts does not suffice.

5.160 If by contrast this argument is read as a substantive moral critique, it is quite reasonable to concede that considerations of the strategies adopted by claimants by reason of having paid charges levied in breach of EU law – including the strategy of passing-on the burden of such charges to the extent possible – should in principle be regarded as '*res inter alios acta* (something done between other parties) and as such irrelevant to the legal relations between the present litigants',[278] i.e., irrelevant to the relations between Beta and Alpha. The possibility that the claimant may under some circumstances gain a windfall should not, in this view, prejudice the necessity of disgorging the defendant Member State of enrichments gained through a breach of EU law.[279] It is submitted, notwithstanding the strength of this argument, that it should not either be excluded that a defence of passing-on may have merit in the individual case. Where for example a Member State has unlawfully exacted VAT on products made or bought by Beta, and that product is resold substantially unaltered to Gamma, and the passing-on of the amount of VAT can be traced down the supply chain in invoices, it would not appear unfair to uphold a defence of passing-on against claims for repayment brought by Beta. The same would apply to Gamma claimants if they have equally obviously passed on the VAT.[280] There may furthermore be situations where passing-on can be ascertained with similar certainty. It is consequently submitted that the defence of passing-on should perhaps not be dismissed for all situations even though its value may be dubious in many situations. Notwithstanding the view preferred, the power to decide ultimately to endorse or reject the defence of passing-on remains with the Member States – which leads us on to the final argument.

5.161 The seventh and final argument listed above points out that the defence of passing-on was not commonly known in European jurisdictions prior to *Just*. This view must immediately be qualified, as it was known from the case law of the Court of Justice under Article (now) 340(2) TFEU[281] and from American

278 Peter Birks, *Unjust Enrichment* (2nd edn, Clarendon Law Series, Oxford University Press 2005) 221.

279 A similar view was expressed by Rudden and Bishop with regard to damages actions pursuant to Art. 340(2) TFEU; Bernard Rudden and William Bishop, 'Gritz and Quellmehl: Pass It On' (1981) 6 *European Law Review* 243, 255–6, discussed in Section 3.E.III.

280 See Section 5.E.IV.

281 See Section 3.E.II.

antitrust case law.[282] In both these well-known contexts however, the defence of passing-on has been raised against an action for damages rather than for repayment. This was arguably a new and less familiar use of the defence.[283] The findings of the Court in *Just* were therefore criticized by Advocate General Mancini in *San Giorgio*. To the Advocate General it seemed the Court had opened Pandora's box by allowing a dubious interpretation of Danish law.[284] *San Giorgio* was indeed a striking example of the Pandora's box effect of *Just*: Italy had seized the opportunity to use the Danish legislation as a blueprint for a piece of legislation aimed directly and exclusively at the repayment of charges levied in breach of Community law – it did not apply if the levy was illegal on other grounds – and had furthermore included a presumption of passing-on in it. Moreover the Court of Justice seemed in *San Giorgio* to disregard the problem of decreased sales, which it did, by contrast, make reference to in *Just*.[285] The wording of the relevant paragraph in *San Giorgio* would rather imply that if passing-on has been established, then it has also been established that traders would be unjustly enriched by a repayment of charges unduly levied.[286] In *Just* and *Denkavit* the Court stressed more clearly that passing-on was one of many factors to be taken into consideration when assessing whether traders would be unjustly enriched by a repayment of charges unduly levied.[287]

The most extreme example of the 'Pandora's box effect' of *Just* may be that French law in *Comateb* in fact required traders to pass on the dock dues at issue, at the risk of being penalized if they did not do so. The UK has also enacted a statutory defence of passing-on in the wake of *Just*, notwithstanding the rejection of the defence at common law by the national courts.[288] Notwithstanding these attempts to profit from *Just* it follows from the subsequent case law of the Court of Justice summarized above that the scope for doing so has become very narrow. One might of course regret the findings of the Court in *Just*, but here we are, and it is submitted that the result of the case law taken as a whole is to confine the defence of passing-on to circumstances that are limited enough to satisfy the strive for fairness on those who have paid charges levied in breach of EU law. **5.162**

282 *Hanover Shoe Inc v United Shoe Machinery Corp*, 392 US 481 (1968).

283 In fact the earliest American case law on the defence of passing-on concerned excessive freight or loading charges, and the actions could arguably be categorized as repayment actions. See *Southern Pac Co* (n 170) and *Adams v Mills* (n 170).

284 *San Giorgio* (n 19) Opinion of AG Mancini paras 8–9. See also sub-section 5.E.II.a and n 275.

285 Cf. *Just* (n 18) para. 27, and Operative part para. 3.

286 *San Giorgio* (n 19) para. 13.

287 Cf. *Just* (n 18) para. 26, and *Denkavit* (n 154) para. 26.

288 Birks (n 278) 220 and 230–32.

5.163 To conclude, it should first be observed that the main thrust of the critique against the findings of the Court of Justice in this case law seems to aim at the relevance of the defence of passing-on within actions for restitution, or more precisely for repayment. Other strong criticism aims at the difficulty of ascertaining passing-on in the everyday dealings of trade, in similarity with the submissions discussed in Section 3.E.III. It deserves to be repeated that it remains within the power of each and every Member State to uphold or reject the defence of passing-on within the confines of the residual normative power left to them by the Court of Justice under this case law. If fingers are pointed they should therefore be pointed in the direction of the Member States at least as much as in the direction of the Court.

III. A defence of unjust enrichment?

5.164 In the context of repayment of charges levied in breach of EU law the defence of passing-on is occasionally referred to as the 'defence of unjust enrichment'.[289] It was noticed in section 5.E.II.d that some commentators have considered it peculiar to refer to 'unjust enrichment' in a discussion of possible windfall benefits earned by repayment claimants who have been able to pass on the whole or part of a charge levied in breach of EU law.[290] Critics have preferred to save that label for the enrichment gained by the Member State through the levying of the charge.[291] Against this background it is to be noticed that the concept of unjust enrichment has not been referred to by the European Court of Justice in case law on the defence of passing-on under Article 340(2) TFEU. Repayment cases aside, the only other instances in the case law of the Court of Justice in which the concept of unjust enrichment has been referred to in a context which could be related to passing-on was in *Courage* and *Manfredi*,[292] both of which were cases on damages for an infringement of EU competition law. It will however be submitted below that the *dicta* in *Courage* and *Manfredi* did not necessarily concern the defence of passing-on.[293] In EU legislative materials the most relevant mentioning of unjust enrichment is in the 2008 White Paper on competition law damages actions.[294] In the recently adopted Directive 2014/104/EU on competition law

289 E.g., Tridimas (n 205) 438. For further references see para. 5.165.

290 See ns 272–274 and the accompanying text.

291 E.g., Hubeau (n 168) 451.

292 Case C-453/99 *Courage Ltd v Bernard Crehan and Bernard Crehan v Courage Ltd and Others* [2001] ECR I-6297 para. 30; joined cases C-295/04 to 298/04 *Vincenzo Manfredi v Lloyd Adriatico Assicurazioni SpA* (C-295/04), *Antonio Cannito v Fondiaria Sai SpA* (C-296/04) and *Nicolò Tricarico* (C-297/04) and *Pasqualina Murgolo* (C-298/04) *v Assitalia SpA* [2006] ECR I-6619 para. 94.

293 See sub-section 7.E.II.a.

294 Commission, 'White Paper on Damages actions for breach of the EC antitrust rules' COM(2008) 165 final. See also Commission, 'Staff Working Paper accompanying the White Paper on Damages actions for breach

damages there is by contrast no mentioning of unjust enrichment in the context of passing-on.[295] The only EU law context where it has been authoritatively referred to as 'unjust enrichment' for a claimant to receive an award, in circumstances where that claimant might have passed on the whole or part of the corresponding loss, is consequently the repayment of charges. This is noteworthy as it is also in this particular context that the unjust enrichment terminology in passing-on has been so severely criticized.

It has also been asked whether Alpha's defence of passing-on is an instance of a more general defence of unjust enrichment, or whether unjust enrichment is an element to consider in the assessment of a defence of passing-on? In the case law of the Court of Justice it is not easy to assess the interrelationship of the concepts of 'passing-on' and 'unjust enrichment'. The summary in Section 5.E.II.d implied that unjust enrichment is an element to consider in the assessment of a defence of passing-on. This interpretation, which is based on a close reading of the case law, does not as such exclude the possibility that this pattern in fact indicates that the defence of passing-on is one of several instances of a general defence of unjust enrichment. Commentators writing on passing-on in the context of repayment of charges levied in breach of EU law interestingly tend to discuss it as the 'defence of unjust enrichment',[296] while those who write on damages actions tend to discuss the 'defence of passing-on' with little or no reference to unjust enrichment.[297] The exception is Komninos, who discusses the 'defence of unjust enrichment' in the context of damages for a breach of competition law,[298] and Nebbia, who explicitly favours the term 'defence of unjust enrichment' for competition damages actions so as to avoid too much focus on the first of the two tiers of the passing-on test identified for the purposes of repayment of charges levied in breach of EU law **5.165**

of the EC antitrust rules' SEC(2008) 404, ch 6B; and Commission, 'Staff Working Paper Annex to the Green Paper Damages action for breach of the EC antitrust rules' SEC(2005) 1732 paras 164–175.

295 Directive 2014/104/EU of the European Parliament and of the Council of 26 November 2014 on certain rules governing actions for damages under national law for infringements of the competition law provisions of the Member States and of the European Union [2014] OJ L349/1.

296 The defence of passing-on is considered an instance of a heterogeneous defence of unjust enrichment by Jones (n 6) 87–94; see further paras 5.193 and 5.209. Similarly in Dougan (n 6) 242–54; Tridimas (n 205) 438–43; and Ward (n 27) 154–60.

297 A defence of passing-on in its own right, with little or no reference to unjust enrichment, is discussed in David Ashton and David Henry, *Competition Damages Actions in the EU: Law and Practice* (Edward Elgar Publishing 2013) 43–55 (who are critical of the use of the term 'unjust enrichment' in this context); Beard and Jones (n 85) 254–5; Andrea Biondi and Martin Farley, *The Right to Damages in European Law* (Kluwer European Law Collection, Kluwer Law International 2009) 159; Friedrich Wenzel Bulst, 'Passing-on' in Jürgen Basedow, Jörg Philipp Terhechte and Luboš Tichý (eds), *Private Enforcement of Competition Law* (Nomos Verlagsgesellschaft 2011); and Milutinovic (n 6) Chs 9 and 10.

298 Assimakis P Komninos, *EC Private Antitrust Enforcement*, (Hart Publishing, 2008) 199–202.

in Section 5.E.II.d.[299] To complicate things further English restitution lawyers have submitted that the defence of passing-on should be called the 'defence of disimpoverishment'.[300]

5.166 Is there any practical significance of terminology in this context? Insofar as we are discussing the defence of passing-on it may be of little consequence what we call it, as long as we understand each other well enough to communicate. The real issue connects to situations that are not passing-on situations. In that regard the issue is not what to call the defence of passing-on, but whether there are other defences of unjust enrichment outside the passing-on problem. Jones has answered that question in the affirmative, and has listed three instances of the defence of unjust enrichment: (1) passing-on; (2) the right of Alpha to set off sums owed by the claimant to the national administration; and (3) counter-restitution of benefits received by Beta in return for payments to Alpha.[301] This section is therefore devoted to an updated examination of the basis for identifying other defences of unjust enrichment besides the defence of passing-on.

5.167 Some early case law on the repayment of charges levied in breach of EU law did suggest that the defence of unjust enrichment is a broad concept encompassing more than one situation. In *Pigs and Bacon* a public body charged a levy on pig carcasses intended for the manufacture of bacon. The levies paid were subsequently redistributed, inter alia, as bonus for the export of bacon. With regard to reimbursement of levies charged, the Court of Justice held that it was for the national court to assess, according to its national law, whether and to what extent the sums paid by way of export bonus could be set off against the amount to be reimbursed.[302] In *Jensen* amounts of agricultural aid were payable to the claimant pursuant to Council Regulation (EEC) No 1765/92.[303] The national administration however set off sums owed by the claimant against the amount of aid payable to him. Holding that such set-off did not have the effect of reducing the amount of the aid the Court of Justice concluded that such set-off was not contrary to the Regulation.[304] In *Apple and Pear* three growers of apples and pears similarly claimed restitution of annual charges levied by a national development organization for their

299 Paolisa Nebbia, 'Damages Actions for the Infringement of EC Competition Law: Compensation or Deterrence' (2008) 33 *European Law Review* 23, 41–2.

300 Birks (n 278) 219–21; and Rush (n 112) 11–17.

301 Jones (n 6) 87–94.

302 *Pigs and Bacon* (n 13) para. 25. A summary of relevant facts and holdings is available in paras 5.009–5.010.

303 Council Regulation (EEC) No 1765/92 of 30 June 1992 establishing a support system for producers of certain arable crops [1992] OJ L181/12.

304 Case C-132/95 *Bent Jensen and Korn- og Foderstofkompagniet A/S v Landbrugsministeriet – EF-Direktoratet* [1998] ECR I-2975 paras 61–62 and Operative part para. 2.

industry, which had been established by ministerial order. With regard to the refund of such charges the Court held that it was for the national court to determine, according to its national law, whether and to what extent an entitlement to refund was offset by the advantages accruing directly to the claimants as a result of the activities of the national development organization.[305] These cases implied that the possibilities to resist repayment of charges levied in breach of EU law extend beyond the defence of passing-on, and were possible to interpret as other instances of a general defence of unjust enrichment.[306] In *Cotter and McDermott* the tendency was nevertheless the opposite.[307] The circumstances of *Cotter and McDermott* should be explained in some detail.

Under the Irish Social Welfare (Consolidation) Act 1981 a married man was automatically entitled to increases in his social security benefits in respect of a spouse and children, without having to prove that they were actually dependent on him. A married woman was required to fulfil additional conditions. Moreover a lower rate of unemployment benefit was payable to a married woman than to a married man, and for a shorter period. **5.168**

By Social Welfare (No 2) Act 1985 (Commencement) Order 1986 equality of treatment for men and women was established by extending the requirement of showing actual dependency to all claimants, irrespective of sex. However, the Social Welfare (Preservation of Rights) (No 2) Regulations 1986 provided (albeit on a transitional basis) for married men who, because of the new Act establishing equal treatment, ceased to be entitled to an increase in respect of a spouse to be eligible for a compensatory allowance.

The applicants, Mrs Cotter and Mrs McDermott (the applicants), applied to the High Court for a declaration that they were entitled under Article 4(1) of Directive 79/7/EEC on the progressive implementation of the principle of equal treatment for men and women in matters of social security (the Directive) to the same increases in their social security benefits as married men in their circumstances received before the entry into force of the Social Welfare (No 2) Act 1985, and to the transitional compensatory payments which such men received after that date.

The High Court rejected the application considering that it would be unfair and inequitable to pay the sums claimed to the applicants when their spouses were not financially dependent on them. The applicants appealed to the Supreme Court of Ireland which stayed proceedings and referred the case to the European Court of Justice.

---

305 *Apple and Pear* (n 212) para. 41.

306 Jones (n 6) 92–94, lists the first two cases under the heading 'set-off', and the third under the heading 'counter-restitution'.

307 Case C-377/89 *Ann Cotter and Norah McDermott v Minister for Social Welfare and Attorney General* [1991] ECR I-1155.

5.169 The Irish Government submitted before the Court of Justice that to grant a right to the payment of increases to married women as well as married men could in certain circumstances result in double payment of the same increases to the same families. The Irish Government argued that such payments would be manifestly absurd and would infringe the prohibition on unjust enrichment laid down in national law.[308]

5.170 The Court of Justice however rejected that argument and held that to permit reliance on such a prohibition would enable the national authorities to use their own unlawful conduct as a ground for depriving Article 4(1) of its full effect. Therefore, the Court of Justice ruled, married women were entitled to the same increases in social security benefits in respect of spouses and children as married men, without having to prove actual dependency, even if in some circumstances that would result in double payment of such increases, and even if that would infringe the prohibition on unjust enrichment laid down in national law.[309] In *Cotter and McDermott* the Court thus rejected a defence of unjust enrichment at law.

5.171 In light of this divergent case law it had become uncertain whether the defence of passing-on was one of several instances of a general defence of unjust enrichment or if it was the only defence against a claim for repayment of charges levied in breach of EU law.[310] The problem seemed finally to have been solved by *Lady & Kid*.[311] It was explained above that Denmark had enacted a scheme under which certain social contributions payable by employers were abolished. To neutralize the effects on fiscal income, a special turnover-based tax (the Ambi) was introduced. Unfortunately however the Ambi was contrary to the Sixth VAT Directive.[312] The claimants hence applied for reimbursement of the amounts wrongly levied from them under the Ambi scheme. The Danish Ministry for Fiscal Affairs objected that the amount of social charges that would have been payable unless they had been abolished exceeded the amount of Ambi paid. Therefore, the Ministry argued, there could be no reimbursement. Advocate General Cruz Villalón found support for the arguments thus submitted by the Danish Ministry for Fiscal Affairs in case law such as *Pigs and Bacon* and *Apple and Pear* and opined that amounts unduly levied could be regarded as offset by a simultaneous and

308 Ibid., para. 20.

309 Ibid., paras 21–22, 27.

310 The interrelationship between the *Just* case law, on the one hand, and *Cotter and McDermott*, on the other hand, seems to have been the subject of some debate among English scholars. See Jones (n 6) 87–88; Dougan (n 6) 252–3; and Williams (n 6) 256–7.

311 *Lady & Kid* (n 42). A summary of relevant facts and holdings is available in sub-section 5.E.II.c.

312 Directive 77/388/EEC (n 208) Art. 33.

corresponding reduction in other charges from which a taxable person actually benefited, provided that there was a direct relationship of cause and effect between the creation of one charge and the removal of the other.[313]

The European Court of Justice took the opposite view, holding that the possibility to refuse repayment where it would entail unjust enrichment of the persons concerned was a limitation of a subjective right derived from EU law, and as such must be interpreted narrowly. Accordingly the direct passing-on to a purchaser of the tax wrongly levied constituted the sole exception, the Court held, to the right to reimbursement of taxes levied in breach of EU law.[314] With regard to the case law cited by the Advocate General the Court recognized that the relevant paragraphs of those judgments indicated another view, but dismissed that contrary view by holding – very frankly – that it had now ruled otherwise.[315] Thus, the Court of Justice concluded, the rules of EU law on recovery of sums wrongly paid must be interpreted to the effect that recovery of sums wrongly paid could give rise to unjust enrichment only when the amounts wrongly paid by a taxpayer under a tax levied in a Member State in breach of EU law had been passed on directly to the purchaser. *Lady & Kid* thus seemed to have swept away early case law such as *Pigs and Bacon*, *Jensen*, and *Apple and Pear*, to establish that the direct passing-on to a purchaser of the tax wrongly levied constituted the sole exception to the right to reimbursement of taxes levied in breach of EU law – or rather the sole exception which it was relevant to classify as a defence of unjust enrichment.[316] If passing-on was thus the sole exception, it also appeared less precise to speak of a defence of unjust enrichment for the purposes of the repayment of charges levied in breach of EU law than to speak of a defence of passing-on. The findings of the Court in *Lady & Kid* were confirmed shortly afterwards in *Accor*.[317] 5.172

Nonetheless the possibility of other defences of unjust enrichment was soon revived in *Alakor*.[318] Circumstances in *Alakor* seemed similar to *Lady & Kid* as the basic problem was that Alakor had been burdened by non-deductible VAT (as Lady & Kid was burdened by the Ambi) but compensated through Ministry funding covering those costs (as Lady & Kid was compensated by the abolition of employer social security contributions). There are however two important reasons to distinguish *Alakor*. First, *Alakor* was not considered to be 5.173

313 *Lady & Kid* (n 42) Opinion of AG Cruz Villalón para. 76.
314 Ibid., para. 20.
315 Ibid., para. 25.
316 Member States may still invoke other types of defences, e.g., reasonable time-limits for the bringing of proceedings for repayment. See e.g. *Haahr* (n 27); and *Fantask* (n 25).
317 *Accor* (n 9) paras 72–74.
318 *Alakor* (n 19). A summary of relevant facts and holdings is available in sub-section 5.E.II.c.

a very important case – it was delivered by a Chamber of three Judges who proceeded to judgment without an Opinion of the Advocate General.[319] By contrast *Lady & Kid* was delivered by a Grand Chamber. It follows that findings in *Alakor* should be read and compared to *Lady & Kid* with some caution. Second, in *Alakor* the nexus between the cost incurred in the form of non-deductible VAT and its compensation in the form of increased funding was much closer than that between the Ambi and employer social security contributions was in *Lady & Kid*. In the latter case the Court held that the abolition of employer social security contributions had the most diverse consequences which precluded Denmark from regarding the repayment of an unlawful tax as giving rise to unjust enrichment on behalf of the recipient.[320] In *Alakor* the increase in funding was by contrast targeted precisely at compensating Alakor for the amounts of non-deductible VAT paid. It follows that, in practice, repayment had already occurred in *Alakor*. It is therefore submitted that *Alakor* should be distinguished from *Lady & Kid* and *Accor*, and that the scope of *Alakor* should be considered narrow.

5.174 It is interesting to compare *Alakor* to the paragraph in the Opinion of Advocate General Cruz Villalón in *Lady & Kid* cited above. The Advocate General suggested that amounts unduly levied could be regarded as offset by a simultaneous and corresponding reduction in other charges from which a taxable person actually benefited, provided that there was a direct relationship of cause and effect between the creation of one charge and the removal of the other.[321] The findings of the Court in *Alakor* were very close to the submission of the Advocate General, with one important difference: the offset was not against a simultaneous and corresponding reduction in other charges from which a taxable person actually benefited, but against a simultaneous and corresponding increase in the funding from which Alakor benefited. The circumstances of *Alakor* were therefore more similar to those in *Apple and Pear* than to those in *Lady & Kid*.

5.175 The issue of setting off sums payable by a Member State against sums owed to it was considered again in *Nicula*.[322]

5.176 The claimant, Mr Nicula, had bought a second-hand vehicle in Germany and wanted to register it in Romania, his home country. In order to register the vehicle in Romania he was required to pay pollution tax to an amount of RON 5 153. Mr Nicula

319 See Art. 20(5) of Protocol (No 3) on the Statute of the Court of Justice of the European Union.

320 *Lady & Kid* (n 42) para. 24.

321 Ibid., Opinion of AG Cruz Villalón para. 76.

322 *Nicula* (n 214).

subsequently reclaimed that amount as the pollution tax paid had been introduced contrary to Article 110 TFEU.[323]

In the course of proceedings however, Romania introduced a new environmental stamp duty. The amount of such stamp duty payable for Mr Nicula's vehicle was RON 8 126.44. Furthermore, pollution taxes repayable by virtue of having been levied in breach of EU law would be repaid only if the amount repayable exceeded the amount of the stamp duty payable. As the amount of stamp duty payable for Mr Nicula's vehicle exceeded the amount of pollution tax repayable, the latter amount was withheld by the national authorities.

The Court of Justice examined this system of repayment by offsetting and found that it had the effect of restricting or completely eliminating the requirement to repay the pollution tax levied in breach of EU law, thereby perpetuating the tax discrimination which was the very reason that the tax scheme at issue had initially been held to be contrary to EU law. In addition, the Court continued, the effect of that system was to exempt the national authorities from the requirement to take account of the interest payable to the taxpayer on charges unduly levied. Therefore the Court concluded that the system at issue did not make it possible for individuals effectively to exercise their right under EU law to seek repayment of a tax levied in breach of EU law, and that it was precluded by EU law for those reasons. It must nevertheless be carefully noted that the Court of Justice would not rule out the possibility that a national system of repayment by offsetting could be capable of meeting those requirements of EU law.[324] It follows from *Nicula* that such a theoretical system would need to be non-discriminatory and would need to take into account any interest accrued on sums repayable. **5.177**

To summarize, it seems the defence of passing-on is not necessarily the one and only defence accepted by the Court of Justice which could be described as a defence of unjust enrichment. Even though *Lady & Kid* and *Accor* seemed to have established that the defence of passing-on (category no 1 in the Jones taxonomy presented in the beginning of this section) was the only defence of this kind, it now seems from *Nicula* (offsetting, category no 2) and *Alakor* (counter-restitution, category no 3) that the other adjacent defences are still alive and may coexist with the defence of passing-on. In other words there may still be room for a broader concept covering several defences that are similar in character. There are however two important reasons not to use the defence of unjust enrichment as an umbrella concept for these defences. The first reason **5.178**

323 The Court of Justice held that Art. 110 TFEU precluded the introduction of a pollution tax such as that at issue in case C-402/09 *Ioan Tatu v Statul român prin Ministerul Finanţelor şi Economiei and Others* [2011] ECR I-2711.

324 *Nicula* (n 214) paras 34–38 and Operative part.

is that it may obscure the distinctions between these related but not identical defences. The second reason is that the term 'unjust enrichment', in this context, is ambiguous in itself. It has been stressed that any unjust enrichment in this situation will be the enrichment of Alpha, not of Beta or, as the case may be, Gamma claimants who are not final consumers.[325] Suffice it here to submit that in light of the case law and these considerations it serves precision to call each defence by its own name, e.g., the defence of passing-on, rather than the defence of unjust enrichment jointly.[326] The defences of offsetting and counter-restitution identified by Jones thus remain open but should be distinguished from passing-on. Their scope of application does also seem narrower than the scope of the defence of passing-on.

IV. Estimating restitution in Gamma actions

5.179 With regard to actions brought against the Member State (Alpha) by a Gamma claimant, the European Court of Justice has been seized with a repayment action brought by Gamma against Alpha in one case only, *Danfoss*.[327] The defence of passing-on was not discussed in *Danfoss* as the question asked by the national court was whether a Member State could bar Gamma from bringing the action by reason of it not being Gamma who had been liable to pay the charge levied in breach of EU law. The findings of the Court on that issue were discussed in Section 5.C.II. With regard to the assessments relevant to the estimation of a restitutionary award in such cases, it would however need to be established in the context of such an action whether and to what extent the burden of the charge had been passed on to Gamma. Further, where Gamma was not a final consumer, the same issues would arise here as between Beta and Alpha, i.e., Alpha might again try invoking a passing-on defence. It is as yet unknown how the Court of Justice would allocate the burden of proof in these issues, but it is to be expected that many of the general points made in case law on Beta claims would apply. National requirements of proof and/or forms of evidence must thus be compatible with the EU law principles of equivalence and effectiveness. Moreover, if Alpha argued that Gamma had passed the burden of the charge further on, Alpha might have to prove passing-on *sensu stricto* and that reimbursement would lead to unjust enrichment of the claimant. Reference can be made to Section 5.E.II.d and discussions there which will apply *mutatis mutandis*. The more difficult issue is who should have to prove that the burden of the charge had been passed on

325 *Comateb* (n 25) Opinion of AG Tesauro para. 21; Hubeau (n 168) 451; Hubeau (n 185) 100–104.

326 The merits of using the term 'defence of disimpoverishment' as suggested by Birks (n 278) 219–21; and Rush (n 112) 11–17 are overlooked here.

327 *Danfoss* (n 7). A summary of facts and holdings in respect of the action for repayment is available in Section 5.C.II.

from Beta to Gamma. This remains uncertain, but the breach of EU law committed by Alpha speaks in favour of allowing Gamma some latitude in that regard.[328]

There is also the possibility that Gamma would bring an action for restitution against Beta.[329] In *Comateb* the Court of Justice was open to that possibility, holding that if Gamma was able to obtain reimbursement through Beta of the amount of the charge passed on to Gamma then Beta must be able to obtain reimbursement from the national authorities ('Alpha'). On the other hand, the Court continued, if Gamma could obtain repayment directly from Alpha of the amount of the charge which Gamma had paid but which was not due, the question of reimbursing Beta did not as such arise.[330] The reasoning of the Court in this context is however obviously focusing on preconditions for repayment to Beta of charges unduly levied. It does not aim at giving any directions for the treatment of claims raised by Gamma, although it does acknowledge the possibility of such claims and discusses their consequences for the claims raised by Beta. The Court of Justice further held in *Danfoss* that the existence of a real possibility for Gamma to obtain reimbursement through an action brought against Beta is a prerequisite for the possibility of barring Gamma from bringing an action against Alpha.[331] The Court nonetheless declined to require for such an action against Beta to be available to Gamma. It arguably follows that the Court does not require for every remedy to be available to Gamma but will be satisfied if there is an effective remedy available to Gamma under national law – be it against Alpha or against Beta – that will ensure Gamma is compensated.[332] **5.180**

There are unfortunately no details in the case law of the Court of Justice on repayment actions brought by Gamma against Beta following the levying, by a Member State, of a charge in breach of EU law. It can only be speculated that where Gamma is not a final consumer the same issues would arise here as in litigation between Gamma and Alpha. The burden of proof may however be allocated differently, as Beta does not bear responsibility for the losses that have allegedly burdened Gamma in the same manner as Alpha does. It remains to be seen whether the Court of Justice will be called upon to make clarifications on these issues. **5.181**

328 Cf. Directive 2014/104 (n 295) Art. 14.

329 Cf. ns 86 and 116 and accompanying text.

330 *Comateb* (n 25) para. 24. These holdings may be the starting point of the focus on reparative justice in EU law on the passing-on problem, which contrasts with the US solutions in which effectiveness and practicality seem to have been the priority; cf. e.g. *Southern Pac Co* (n 170) 534; and *Hanover Shoe* (n 282) 492–4.

331 *Danfoss* (n 7) Operative part para. 1.

332 Cf. the discussion in Section 2.B.I.

F. CONCLUSIONS AND SUGGESTIONS

5.182 With regard to the issue of whether Gamma claimants should have access to bring an action for repayment of charges levied in breach of EU law before the competent national court, *Danfoss* made it quite clear that the right to reimbursement for loss incurred by reason of the levying of charges in breach of EU law does indeed extend to Gamma claimants. It did not follow however that EU law would require for that right to be enforceable against Alpha. The Court of Justice was in fact neutral to the form of redress available to Gamma and against whom such redress was available, accepting a possibility of obtaining reimbursement from Beta rather than from Alpha.[333] Wishing to safeguard the possibility for individuals to offset the consequences of the charge,[334] the Court stipulated two requirements to be met in order for it to be possible to oppose a Gamma claim. First, Gamma must be able on the basis of national law to bring a civil action against Beta for recovery of the sum unduly paid. Second, it must not be virtually impossible or excessively difficult for Gamma to obtain reimbursement from Beta, e.g., due to Beta being insolvent.[335] By contrast the Court did not clarify whether the Gamma claimant had the onus of proving that it had exhausted its possibilities to obtain such reimbursement from Beta.

5.183 With regard to substantive proximity problems in restitution, i.e., whether Gamma can leapfrog Beta in order to bring a direct action for repayment of charges levied in breach of EU law against Alpha, European private law has been found to be unfavourable to the possibility of such Gamma claims.[336] The question examined was whether these stringent conditions were compatible with the EU law principle of effectiveness.[337] Unfortunately the Court of Justice has not explicitly ruled on this issue. Uncertainties notwithstanding, it has been submitted that it follows from the EU principle of effectiveness as interpreted by the Court in *Danfoss* that national courts should not be able to reject *a priori* an action for repayment brought by Gamma with reference to the lack of a nexus between Alpha and Gamma, even where such an *a priori* conclusion formally follows from substantive proximity concepts rather than from a procedural law bar.

---

333 Such a solution was recently chosen in Swedish law, see n 86.

334 *Danfoss* (n 7) para. 23.

335 Cf *Danfoss* (n 7) Operative part para. 1; and para. 28.

336 See DCFR (n 8) 4035 and the accompanying Comments and Notes.

337 On the scope and meaning of this principle see Section 2.D. The principle of equivalence (Section 2.D.II) is less relevant in this context.

Turning to the defence of passing-on, the Court of Justice has allowed Alpha **5.184**
to resist repayment only where two criteria are met, namely:

1. The charge must have been borne, in whole or in part, by someone other than the claimant; and
2. Reimbursement must constitute unjust enrichment of the claimant.[338]

The amount repayable with respect to a charge levied in breach of EU law can consequently, albeit subject to the subsequent test under the second criterion above, be reduced to the extent that the charge has been passed on. Accordingly the Court of Justice has held that repayment can be resisted only to the extent that it is established that the charge has been borne in its entirety by someone other than the claimant.[339] In *Comateb* the Court of Justice further established that proven passing-on of the burden of a charge levied contrary to EU law, in whole or in part, is not sufficient to allow Alpha to resist repayment of the charge. It must also be proven that reimbursement of the passed on portion of the charge would constitute an unjust enrichment of the claimant.[340] The Court of Justice has also held that to reach the conclusion that repayment would lead to unjust enrichment it is necessary to carry out an economic analysis in which all the relevant circumstances are taken into account.[341]

The Court of Justice has introduced a number of requirements concerning **5.185**
evidence and the burden of proof in relation to the two criteria identified above. On the burden of proving passing-on the Court has held that presumptions or rules of evidence intended to place upon the taxpayer the burden of establishing that the charges unduly paid have not been passed on to other persons are incompatible with EU law, irrespective of whether such special limitations are special to claims brought pursuant to a breach of EU law or apply to any claims for repayment of charges levied illegally.[342] The more pressing issue is the burden of proof with regard to turnover losses and other reasons for lost profit (or other circumstances excluding unjust enrichment). In this regard the Court of Justice has held that even when it is settled that the burden of a charge has been passed on, it must not be presumed on this sole ground that reimbursement will lead to unjust enrichment of the claimant.[343]

338 See e.g., *Comateb* (n 25) paras 27–29; *Michaïlidis* (n 196) paras 33–35; *Weber's Wine World* (n 19) paras 94–102.

339 *Comateb* (n 25) para. 27.

340 Ibid.

341 *Weber's Wine World* (n 19) para. 100.

342 *San Giorgio* (n 19) paras 14, 17. Cf *Weber's Wine World* (n 19) paras 111–114.

343 *Weber's Wine World* (n 19) para. 117 and Operative Part, para. 4.

Furthermore, in *Michaïlidis*, national rules under which it was for the taxpayer to show that the disputed charge caused an increase in the price of the products, causing in turn a reduction in the volume of trade, were considered contrary to EU law.[344] It seems therefore that the national administration will have the onus of proving these points in order to support its defence of passing-on. Nevertheless it may still be for the claimant to prove less typical circumstances and that they exclude unjust enrichment.

5.186 It has been observed that the main thrust of the critique against the findings of the Court of Justice in this case law seems to aim at the relevance of the defence of passing-on within actions for restitution. Other strong criticism aims at the difficulty of ascertaining passing-on in the everyday dealings of trade, in similarity with the submissions discussed in Section 3.E.III. It was submitted, notwithstanding the strength of these arguments, that it should not either be excluded that a defence of passing-on may have merit in the individual case. Where for example a Member State has unlawfully exacted VAT on products made or bought by Beta, and that product is resold substantially unaltered to Gamma, and the passing-on of the amount of VAT can be traced down the supply chain in invoices, it would not appear unfair to uphold a defence of passing-on against claims for repayment brought by Beta. The same would apply to Gamma claimants if they have equally obviously passed on the VAT.[345] There may furthermore be situations where passing-on can be ascertained with similar certainty. It was consequently submitted that the defence of passing-on should perhaps not be dismissed for all situations even though its value may be dubious in many situations. It was furthermore stressed that it remains within the power of each and every Member State to uphold or reject the defence of passing-on within the confines of the residual normative power left to them by the Court of Justice under this case law. If fingers are pointed they should therefore, it was submitted, be pointed in the direction of the Member States at least as much as in the direction of the Court.

344 *Michaïlidis* (n 196) para. 38.

345 See Section 5.E.IV.

6

PASSING-ON IN DAMAGES FROM A MEMBER STATE?

A. CHAPTER OUTLINE

The European Court of Justice indicated in *Comateb* that an action for damages can be brought against a Member State alongside or instead of an action for repayment of charges levied in breach of EU law.[1] Claimants thus have an option to bring an action for damages against the Member State instead of the restitutionary action under circumstances where the former action might be preferable, but also as an alternative or complementary cause of action within the same proceedings. It follows that the action for damages from a Member State is relevant in this inquiry. **6.001**

There is nevertheless very little case law which could serve to indicate how the Court would approach the passing-on problem in the context of an action for damages from the Member State. It has been addressed only in the second part of *Danfoss*[2] which concerned access to court for Gamma claimants.[3] **6.002**

1 Joined cases C-192/95 to 218/95 *Société Comateb and others v Directeur Général des Douanes et Droits Indirects* [1997] ECR I-165 para. 34. Cf. paras 5.007 and 5.132.

2 Case C-94/10 *Danfoss A/S and Sauer-Danfoss ApS v Skatteministeriet* [2011] ECR I-9963.

3 In this book, Alpha signifies a tortfeasor or enriched party, Beta a party first burdened by loss arising from Alpha's breach of EU law, and Gamma any party downstream from Beta (including all from the party dealing directly with Beta to the final consumer) to whom the burden of that loss may have been passed on; see Section 1.B.

Notwithstanding the scarcity of relevant case law it will be endeavoured below to address all three main issues of EU law triggered by the passing-on problem, i.e., not only access to court but also substantive proximity (here causation) and the estimation of damages.

6.003 In this chapter Section 6.B will provide an introduction to the EU law action for damages against a Member State, tracing its origins in case law and the subsequent development of applicable conditions for such liability. Section 6.C is devoted to the particular issues identified as inherent in the passing-on problem.[4] Accordingly access to court, causation and the estimation of damages will be examined in turn. In each of these three sub-sections the particularities of the specific context of damages from a Member State for a breach of EU law must be kept in mind. Therefore, as in previous chapters, general observations on the respective themes will be presented from that specific contextual perspective before continuing to the more detailed discussions of how passing-on issues will likely be managed by the Court of Justice. In sub-section 6.C.I on access to court the impact of EU law requirements of effective judicial protection on national limitations of access will be addressed, i.e., the impact of both Article 47 of the EU Charter of Fundamental Rights and of the dual EU law test of equivalence and effectiveness. Focus will be on national limitations of access barring Gamma parties from bringing an action based on the fact that harm has been passed on to them by Beta (i.e., passing-on as a 'sword') and especially on the holdings of the Court in *Danfoss*. Sub-section 6.C.II will be devoted to the problem of substantive proximity, which in the context of damages is addressed through the assessment of causation. In Chapter 3 on Article 340(2) TFEU it was stressed that the causation assessment was governed by EU law exclusively. In this chapter the point of departure is, by contrast, that the causation assessment is not primarily governed by EU law but by national law, albeit subject to the EU law principles of equivalence and effectiveness. The presentation here will therefore focus on the impact of those principles on national causation tests, discussing in particular difficulties pertaining to actions brought by Gamma claimants. The final sub-section 6.C.III will cover the estimation of damages. The Court of Justice has identified some heads of damages that should be available in the context of an action for damages against a Member State. This case law will be presented and discussed. In the absence of EU case law the possible response of the Court to a defence of passing-on in this context will be considered in light of the general observations and case law on other actions. Finally conclusions and suggestions will be summarized in Section 6.D.

4 See Section 1.A.III.

B. INTRODUCTION TO DAMAGES FROM A MEMBER STATE

Considering the crucial role of the action for damages from a Member State in contemporary EU law it can seem remote that there was a time before *Francovich*,[5] when uniform conditions for liability in damages for Member States for a breach of EU law was only a possibility being discussed.[6] However, it should be clarified that liability in damages for Member States was not unknown before *Francovich*. Indications of Member State liability as a form of redress that should be available for a breach of Community law for which the Member State was responsible was indicated and perhaps presupposed by the Court of Justice as early as in 1960.[7] There was arguably consensus before *Francovich* that Member States should be held liable in damages for a breach of EU law, but there were differences over the conditions for such liability and whether they should be governed by EU law or by 'the provisions of national law on the liability of the State'.[8] **6.004**

The current era of harmonized conditions for Member State liability in damages began on 19 November 1991, with the delivery of judgment in *Francovich*. As the facts are well-known they will not be repeated here.[9] Suffice it to recall that the Court of Justice found a legal basis for introducing the **6.005**

5 Joined cases C-6/90 and 9/90 *Andrea Francovich and Daniela Bonifaci and others v Italian Republic* [1991] ECR I-5357.

6 For an account of discussions and case law leading up to *Francovich* see e.g. Anthony Arnull, *The European Union and its Court of Justice* (2nd edn, Oxford EC Law Library, Oxford University Press 2006) 274–6; Andrea Biondi and Martin Farley, *The Right to Damages in European Law* (Kluwer European Law Collection, Kluwer Law International 2009) 11–12; Damaso Ruiz-Jarabo Colomer, 'Once Upon a Time – *Francovich*: From Fairy Tale to Cruel Reality?' in Miguel Poiares-Maduro and Loïc Azoulai (eds), *The Past and Future of EU Law: The Classics of EU Law Revisited on the 50th Anniversary of the Rome Treaty* (Hart Publishing, Oxford 2010); and Sacha Prechal, *Directives in EC Law* (2nd edn, Oxford EC Law Library, Oxford University Press, Oxford 2006) 271–5. On the 'lack of effective remedies to ensure the execution of Community obligations' before *Francovich* see Gerhard Bebr, 'Joined Cases C-6/90 and 9/90, Francovich v. Italy, Bonifaci v. Italy Judgment of the Court of Justice of 19 November 1991, not yet reported' (1992) 29 *Common Market Law Review* 557, 558–559 and 582–4. At the time, the sanction in Art. (now) 260(2) TFEU had not been introduced either. A telling example of discussions 'before' and 'after' *Francovich* is available by comparing Ami Barav, 'Damages in the Domestic Courts for Breach of Community Law by National Public Authorities' in Henry G Schermers, Ton Heukels and Philip Mead (eds), *Non-Contractual Liability of the European Communities* (Martinus Nijhoff Publishers 1988) with the revised version of the same contribution; Ami Barav, 'State Liability in Damages for Breach of Community Law in the National Courts' in Ton Heukels and Alison McDonnell (eds), *The Action for Damages in Community Law* (Kluwer Law 1997).

7 See case 6/60 *Jean-E Humblet v Belgian State* [1960] ECR 559, 569; where the Court mentioned reparation for a breach of the ECSC Treaty. Significant Court of Justice *dicta* up until *Francovich* include case 60/75 *Carmine Antonio Russo v Azienda di Stato per gli interventi sul mercato agricolo (AIMA)* [1976] ECR 45 para. 9; and case 158/80 *Rewe-Handelsgesellschaft Nord mbH and Rewe-Markt Steffen v Hauptzollamt Kiel (Butter Buying Cruises)* [1981] ECR 1805 para. 44 and Operative part para. 7.

8 *Russo* (n 7) para. 9.

9 For a narrative summary see e.g. Biondi and Farley (n 6) 13–17.

action for damages from a Member State by holding that the 'full effectiveness of Community rules would be impaired and the protection of the rights which they grant would be weakened if individuals were unable to obtain redress when their rights are infringed by a breach of Community law for which a Member State can be held responsible', and that it followed that 'the principle whereby a State must be liable for loss and damage caused to individuals as a result of breaches of Community law for which the State can be held responsible is inherent in the system of the Treaty' and in particular followed from Article 5 EEC (now Article 4(3) TEU), which included an 'obligation to nullify the unlawful consequences of a breach of Community law'.[10]

6.006 With regard to the applicable conditions for liability the Court of Justice indicated that 'the conditions under which that liability gives rise to a right to reparation depend on the nature of the breach of Community law giving rise to the loss and damage'.[11] This holding already hinted that the context-based distinctions present in case law on the action for damages under Article (now) 340(2) TFEU, or similar distinctions, might have a role to play in actions for damages from a Member State also.[12] For the purposes of cases such as *Francovich*, where damage had allegedly been caused by reason of a Member State's failure to take all the measures necessary to achieve the result prescribed by a directive, the Court of Justice held that three conditions would apply:

6.007

> The first of those conditions is that the result prescribed by the directive should entail the grant of rights to individuals. The second condition is that it should be possible to identify the content of those rights on the basis of the provisions of the directive. Finally, the third condition is the existence of a causal link between the breach of the State's obligation and the loss and damage suffered by the injured parties.[13]
>
> Those conditions are sufficient to give rise to a right on the part of individuals to obtain reparation, a right founded directly on Community law.
>
> Subject to that reservation, it is on the basis of the rules of national law on liability that the State must make reparation for the consequences of the loss and damage caused. …
>
> Further, the substantive and procedural conditions for reparation of loss and damage laid down by the national law of the Member States must not be less favourable than

10 *Francovich* (n 5) paras 33 and 35–36.

11 Ibid., para. 38.

12 On the distinctions developed for the purposes of Art. 340(2) TFEU see Section 3.B.

13 *Francovich* (n 5) para. 40. For a critique of the 'rights' criterion see Ruiz-Jarabo Colomer (n 6) 409. For a detailed analysis of the heterogeneous legal phenomena capable of being identified as a 'right' in this context see Pekka Aalto, *Public Liability in EU Law:* Brasserie, Bergaderm *and Beyond* (Hart Publishing 2011) 162–75.

those relating to similar domestic claims and must not be so framed as to make it virtually impossible or excessively difficult to obtain reparation[14]

The Court of Justice thus identified three core conditions, prescribed by Community law. If these were met the right to reparation would arise. Nevertheless the three conditions would have to be filled out with national law on liability, subject to the principles of equivalence and effectiveness. E.g., the Court did not in *Francovich* provide details on how to estimate the alleged harm for the purposes of calculating payable damages. This assessment would need to be governed by national rules as indicated. The findings of the Court in *Francovich* were repeated in *Dori*,[15] which also concerned a Member State's failure to transpose a directive. **6.008**

In the subsequent *Brasserie* however,[16] the situation and the Court's wording of the applicable criteria were both different. In *Brasserie* the legal basis for the action for damages was not a failure to implement a directive but breaches by the Member States of provisions of the EEC Treaty.[17] The Court clarified that an action for damages from the Member State was not only available where an individual was unable to rely on the provisions of a non-transposed directive, but also where a Member State had infringed Treaty provisions, even when these had direct effect.[18] Citing *Francovich* and referring to the analogy between the action for damages from a Member State and the action for damages under Article (now) 340(2) TFEU, the Court concluded that the principle of Member State liability established in *Francovich* held good 'for any case in which a Member State breaches Community law, whatever be the organ of the State whose act or omission was responsible for the breach', including the national legislature.[19] These clarifications were crucial as they established beyond doubt that an action for damages from the Member State was available irrespective of the nature of the breach of EU law for which the Member State could be held responsible. **6.009**

As mentioned in paragraph 3.013 the Court of Justice also held in *Brasserie* that the conditions under which a Member State might incur liability could not, in the absence of particular justification, differ from those governing the **6.010**

14 *Francovich* (n 5) paras 41–43.

15 Case C-91/92 *Paola Faccini Dori v Recreb Srl* [1994] ECR I-3325 para. 27.

16 Joined cases C-46/93 and C-48/93 *Brasserie du Pêcheur SA v Bundesrepublik Deutschland* and *The Queen v Secretary of State for Transport, ex parte: Factortame Ltd and others* [1996] ECR I-1029.

17 In case 46/93 *Brasserie du Pêcheur SA v Bundesrepublik Deutschland* it was Art. 30 EEC (now Art. 34 TFEU); in case 48/93 *The Queen v Secretary of State for Transport, ex parte: Factortame Ltd and others* it was Art. 52 EEC (now Art. 49 TFEU).

18 *Brasserie* (n 16) para. 22.

19 Ibid., paras 32, 35.

liability of the Community in like circumstances.[20] The Court also stressed (as in *Francovich*) that the applicable conditions did depend on the nature of the breach.[21] In that regard the Court continued to draw parallels to its case law on Article (now) 340(2) TFEU and the importance of taking into account, inter alia, 'the margin of discretion available to the author of the act in question'.[22] In circumstances such as those in *Francovich*, the Court held, the Member State did not have a wide discretion but was under an obligation to achieve the result required by a directive.[23] By contrast, in circumstances such as those in the joined cases in *Brasserie*, the Court held that:

6.011 ... the German and United Kingdom legislatures were faced with situations involving choices comparable to those made by the Community institutions when they adopt legislative measures pursuant to a Community policy.

6.012 In such circumstances the Court explained that Community law conferred a right to reparation where three conditions are met: the rule of law infringed must be intended to confer rights on individuals; the breach must be sufficiently serious; and there must be a direct causal link between the breach of the obligation resting on the state and the damage sustained by the injured parties.[24] The Court further recognized that those conditions corresponded to those developed for the purposes of Article (now) 340(2) TFEU.[25] It was evident however that they differed from those laid down in *Francovich* insofar as the second condition in that case, that it should be possible to identify the content of the infringed right on the basis of the provisions of the directive, had been replaced in *Brasserie* by the requirement for a sufficiently serious breach. The question consequently arose whether the Court had now introduced two separate sets of criteria, each applicable in the different contexts illustrated by this case law.[26]

6.013 That question was answered in *Dillenkofer*. The underlying breach was again non-transposition of a directive provision. The Court of Justice seized the opportunity to reinterpret its own case law with regard especially to the different sets of conditions laid down in *Francovich* and *Brasserie* respectively:

---

20 Ibid., para. 42. Interestingly, AG Mischo suggested for the Court to draw from its case law on Art. (now) 340(2) TFEU in his Opinion in *Francovich*, but to no avail – then. See *Francovich* (n 5) Opinion of AG Mischo paras 71–81.

21 Ibid., para. 38.

22 Ibid., para. 43. For details on the conditions applicable under Art. 340(2) TFEU see Section 3.B.

23 Ibid., para. 46.

24 Ibid., paras 50–51.

25 Ibid., para. 53.

26 For a contemporary discussion see David Edward and William Robinson, 'Is There a Place for Private Law Principles in Community Law?' in Ton Heukels and Alison McDonnell (eds), *The Action for Damages in Community Law* (Kluwer Law 1997) 342–5.

> In substance, the conditions ... are the same, since the condition that there should be a sufficiently serious breach, although not expressly mentioned in Francovich, was nevertheless evident from the circumstances of that case. **6.014**
>
> When the Court held that the conditions under which State liability gives rise to a right to reparation depended on the nature of the breach of Community law causing the damage, that meant that those conditions are to be applied according to each type of situation.[27]

6.015 In *Dillenkofer* the Court found that the better condition was the requirement of a sufficiently serious breach:

> On the one hand, a breach of Community law is sufficiently serious if a Community institution or a Member State, in the exercise of its rule-making powers, manifestly and gravely disregards the limits on those powers ... On the other hand, if, at the time when it committed the infringement, the Member State in question was not called upon to make any legislative choices and had only considerably reduced, or even no, discretion, the mere infringement of Community law may be sufficient to establish the existence of a sufficiently serious breach ... .[28]

6.016 For those reasons, the Court concluded:

> ... that failure to take any measure to transpose a directive in order to achieve the result it prescribes within the period laid down for that purpose constitutes per se a serious breach of Community law and consequently gives rise to a right of reparation for individuals suffering injury if the result prescribed by the directive entails the grant to individuals of rights whose content is identifiable and a causal link exists between the breach of the State' s obligation and the loss and damage suffered.[29]

6.017 Apart from the apparently teleological interpretive method employed by the Court of Justice, the most striking feature of these holdings is the eagerness of the Court to complete the alignment of the criteria applicable to an action for damages from the Member State to those developed under Article (now) 340(2) TFEU. In paragraph 25 (quoted above) the Court cited *Bayerische HNL*,[30] a well-known case on the latter action. Nevertheless the Court

27 Joined cases C-178/94, C-179/94, C-188/94, C-189/94 and C-190/94 *Erich Dillenkofer, Christian Erdmann, Hans-Jürgen Schulte, Anke Heuer, Werner, Ursula and Torsten Knor v Bundesrepublik Deutschland* [1996] ECR I-4845 para. 23.

28 *Dillenkofer* (n 27) para. 25. For an example of liability where a Member State had no discretion; see e.g., case 5/94 *The Queen v Ministry of Agriculture, Fisheries and Food, ex parte: Hedley Lomas (Ireland) Ltd* [1996] ECR I-2553.

29 *Dillenkofer* (n 27) para. 29.

30 Joined cases 83 and 94/76, 4, 15 and 40/77 *Bayerische HNL Vermehrungsbetriebe GmbH & Co KG and others v Council and Commission of the European Communities* [1978] ECR 1209.

maintained a role to play for the second condition in *Francovich* as it would still be necessary in the context of non-transposed directive provisions that those provisions granted individual rights whose content was identifiable.[31]

6.018 The Court thus settled the three uniformly applicable conditions for an action for damages from the Member State: the rule of law breached must be intended to confer rights on individuals; the breach must be sufficiently serious; and there must be a direct causal link between the breach and the damage sustained. The conditions identified by the Court of Justice in this case law are necessary and sufficient to give rise to a right for individuals to obtain compensation in damages,[32] and Member States are precluded from applying additional conditions.[33] The Court of Justice has accordingly ordered national courts to set aside national rules to the extent that such rules would add further criteria for the right to compensation to arise. For instance, the German law requirement that a breach of official duty for which the state can be liable in damages must be of individual concern to a third party, i.e., to the claimant or to a class of protected persons to which the claimant belongs (German: *Drittbezogenheit*),[34] was declared to be contrary to the EU law principle of effectiveness in *Brasserie* and the Court of Justice therefore ordered for it to be set aside.[35]

6.019 The first condition settled by the Court of Justice requires that the rule of law breached must be intended to confer rights on individuals. As pointed out in

31 The Court continued in *Dillenkofer* (n 27) paras 44–45 to assess whether the content of the right conferred by Art. 7 of Council Directive 90/314/EEC was sufficiently identifiable. It was.

32 *Brasserie* (n 16) para. 66.

33 Case C-429/09 *Günter Fuß v Stadt Halle* [2010] ECR I-12167 paras 65–66. The additional conditions in mind are typically national concepts of fault. However, an assessment of whether the harm incurred is eligible for compensation must be carried out on the basis of national law, subject to the principles of equivalence and effectiveness; see Koen Lenaerts and Piet van Nuffel (Robert Bray and Nathan Cambien (eds)), *European Union Law* (3rd edn, Sweet and Maxwell 2011) 769–70.

34 This requirement functions as a general qualification of the scope of public liability under § 839 BGB (German Civil Code).

35 *Brasserie* (n 16) paras 6–7 and 71–72. Cf. the Opinion of AG Tesauro paras 4–5; Cees van Dam, *European Tort Law* (2nd edn, Oxford University Press 2013) 541–2; Raymond Youngs, *English, French and German Comparative Law* (3rd edn, Routledge 2014) 465–6. By contrast, in case C-222/02 *Peter Paul, Cornelia Sonnen-Lütte and Christel Mörkens v Bundesrepublik Deutschland* [2004] ECR I-9425 paras 50–51, the practical implications of the same requirement coincided with the EU law requirement of the identification of a right, and it was consequently compatible with EU law under the circumstances of that case. See further van Dam (n 34) 290–93, 542. For an overview of national criteria for public liability that have been set aside by the European Court of Justice in order to maintain the primacy of the criteria developed in its case law see Biondi and Farley (n 6) 78.

paragraph 3.021, this seems in essence to be an EU law criterion by which the rule at issue must have a protective purpose (or, if you will, be a *Schutzgesetz*).[36]

The second condition, that the breach must be sufficiently serious, is perhaps the most flexible one. Its application differs depending on a number of circumstances identified by the Court of Justice. As seen above the type of rule breached is of no consequence to the condition as such, but the precise application of the condition may vary accordingly. The same is true with regard to other factors, e.g., which State body is responsible for the breach.[37] In *Brasserie* the Court held: **6.020**

> The factors which the competent court may take into consideration include the clarity and precision of the rule breached, the measure of discretion left by that rule to the national or Community authorities, whether the infringement and the damage caused was intentional or involuntary, whether any error of law was excusable or inexcusable, the fact that the position taken by a Community institution may have contributed towards the omission, and the adoption or retention of national measures or practices contrary to Community law. **6.021**
>
> On any view, a breach of Community law will clearly be sufficiently serious if it has persisted despite a judgment finding the infringement in question to be established, or a preliminary ruling or settled case-law of the Court on the matter from which it is clear that the conduct in question constituted an infringement.[38]

The precise application of these factors is not quite clear although examples are available in the case law.[39] For the purposes of this inquiry suffice it to offer the illustrative example of a breach committed by a national court adjudicating at last instance. The Court of Justice indicated in *Köbler* that such national courts must have a wide margin of discretion, as 'regard must be had to the specific nature of the judicial function and to the legitimate requirements of legal certainty'.[40] Therefore the application of the 'sufficiently serious' test was different in *Köbler*. The Court held that to determine whether an infringement committed by a national court adjudicating at last instance is sufficiently serious within the meaning of the action for damages from a Member State, **6.022**

36 This concept is used here without prejudice to the precise meaning given to that concept in German law. See further Prechal (n 6) 284–5 and cf. paras 3.012 and 3.018. For a detailed analysis of the types of rules capable of being identified as a 'right' in this context see Aalto (n 13) 162–75.

37 The EU law concept of 'State body' was developed in case C-188/89 *A Foster and others v British Gas plc* [1990] ECR I-3313. See further Prechal (n 6) 58–61.

38 *Brasserie* (n 16) paras 56–57.

39 For a detailed analysis and systematic overview see Aalto (n 13) Ch. 6.III. The Court of Justice will often leave the final assessment to be made by the national court, e.g., in case C-318/13 *X* EU:C:2014:2133 paras 40–43 where the Court did nonetheless point out a number of circumstances for the national court to take into account in its assessment.

40 Case C-224/01 *Gerhard Köbler v Republik Österreich* [2003] ECR I-10239 para. 53.

'the competent national court, taking into account the specific nature of the judicial function, must determine whether that infringement is manifest'.[41]

6.023 For an action for damages from the Member State to be successful, the claimant must also show that there is a direct causal link between the breach of EU law and the alleged harm, and that the claimant has suffered harm eligible for compensation. These preconditions are directly relevant to the passing-on problem and will therefore be examined in Sections 6.C.II and 6.C.III.

6.024 It must finally be added that it follows from the EU principle of equivalence that if more lenient criteria apply to an action for damages from the state under national law, the national courts of that jurisdiction must apply such more lenient criteria to an action for damages from the Member State based on EU law.[42]

C. PASSING-ON ISSUES IN DAMAGES FROM A MEMBER STATE

6.025 In the general system of EU law, as it has been (and continues to be) developed over the years, actions for damages from a Member State have very much in common with actions for repayment of charges levied in breach of EU law. They are essentially governed by national law subject to the EU law principles of equivalence and effectiveness and (now) to Article 47 of the Charter.[43] In this section the discussion will focus on passing-on issues in damages from a Member State. The section is divided into sub-sections on each of the three legal issues identified within the passing-on problem:[44] access to court (especially for Gamma claimants);[45] substantive proximity issues (in this context causation problems for Gamma claimants); and the estimation of damages awards. As mentioned however case law on passing-on in the context of Member State liability in damages is limited to one case only, *Danfoss*,[46] and to only one legal issue triggered by the passing-on problem, namely access to court (although the holdings of the Court of Justice are relevant also to

---

41 Ibid., Operative part para. 1.

42 *Brasserie* (n 16) para. 66. On the principle of equivalence see Section 2.D.II.

43 The details of this balance of powers between the EU and the Member States in private enforcement of EU law rights before the national courts was the theme of Ch. 2.

44 See Section 1.A.III.

45 In this book, Alpha signifies a tortfeasor or enriched party, Beta a party first burdened by loss arising from Alpha's breach of EU law, and Gamma any party downstream from Beta (including all from the party dealing directly with Beta to the final consumer) to whom the burden of that loss may have been passed on; see Section 1.B.

46 *Danfoss* (n 2).

causation).[47] By reason of the scarcity of case law much of the discussion will need to be carried out in the abstract. To help identify the relevant considerations in each of the legal issues discussed, the general observations will be comparatively extensive.

I. Access issues for Gamma claimants

a. *General observations on access*

6.026 As explained in Section 2.A the aforementioned rules and principles of EU law will apply in cases where the claimant can demonstrate that she or he is the holder of a substantive right or particular interest protected by EU law. The claimant must further choose a remedy available under national law for the enforcement of that right.[48] If no effective remedy is available under the national legal system then EU law may require the national court to make an effective remedy available to the claimant,[49] as in case law such as *Factortame I*[50] or *Francovich*.[51] With regard to the action for damages from a Member State it was demonstrated in Section 6.B that the Court of Justice requires the national courts to hold the Member State liable in damages where the conditions for such liability, as developed by the Court of Justice, are met. The action for damages from a Member State is consequently a specific remedy which EU law requires to be available before the national courts of the Member States. It further follows from *Comateb* that this remedy must be available even if a parallel action for restitution from the Member State applies to the circumstances of the individual case.[52] Notwithstanding the uniformity of the three conditions developed by the Court of Justice for the purposes of this remedy of Member State liability, the procedural and other details governing the action have not been harmonized. In the absence of such harmonizing EU rules certain details, e.g., restrictions on access to bring the action before the national court, remain governed by national law.[53] This section will consequently focus on the impact of Article 47 of the Charter and of the EU law principles of equivalence and effectiveness on such national

47 See further sub-sections 6.C.I.b and 6.C.II.b, respectively.

48 See Section 2.B.I.

49 Pekka Aalto et al, 'Article 47' in Steve Peers, Tamara Hervey, Jeff Kenner and Angela Ward (eds), *The EU Charter of Fundamental Rights: A Commentary* (Verlag CH Beck/Hart Publishing/Nomos 2014) 1217. It has been pointed out that Member States have an incentive to have generous rules on access to simpler administrative review actions so as to avoid being held liable in damages; see Peter Oliver, 'State Liability in Damages following *Factortame III*: A Remedy Seen in Context' in Jack Beatson and Takis Tridimas (eds), *New Directions in European Public Law* (Hart Publishing 1998) 57.

50 Case C-213/89 *The Queen v Secretary of State for Transport, ex parte: Factortame Ltd and others* [1990] ECR I-2433.

51 *Francovich* (n 5).

52 *Comateb* (n 1) para. 34.

53 See e.g. case C-445/06 *Danske Slagterier v Bundesrepublik Deutschland* [2009] ECR I-2119 para. 31.

restrictions on bringing an action for damages against a Member State for a breach of EU law. Unfortunately there is no case law (yet) from the Court of Justice on the impact of Article 47 of the Charter on national limitations of access to the action for damages from a Member State for a breach of EU law. By contrast the impact of the EU law principles of equivalence and effectiveness to such limitations has been examined many times. These general observations will therefore primarily shed some light on the application of the dual test. It will be endeavoured also to provide some hints on how Article 47 might come into play.

6.027 Beginning with the EU law principles of equivalence and effectiveness, these comprise a dual test under which the national rules and conditions within which actions based on EU law are brought before national courts must neither be treated less favourably than 'similar domestic actions' (equivalence) nor render the enforcement of EU law virtually impossible or excessively difficult (effectiveness).[54] The majority of the case law on the impact of those principles on national limitations of access to court concerns time-limits. Such limitations will be discussed in paragraphs 6.036–6.039 below. Before proceeding to that discussion however, a few comments are warranted with regard to another national limitation of access to the action for damages from a Member State and to the case law of the Court of Justice on that limitation.

6.028 In several Member States the failure of a claimant to avert loss will restrict, in whole or in part, the claimant's possibilities to bring a successful action for damages against the Member State. This is a particular kind of restriction which is not easily categorized as belonging to the context of access to court, causation, or the estimation of damages, as its classification differs between jurisdictions. It is therefore capable of occurring in any of these contexts. In *Brasserie* Advocate General Tesauro discerned three distinct approaches in the domestic legal systems of Member States. Under the first approach, common e.g. in France, actions available to claimants who wished to contest an administrative or other measure for which the state was responsible were 'completely autonomous', giving claimants full discretion to choose the most appropriate action for the protection of their interests. The second approach, found e.g. in Italy and the UK, classified the action for damages from the state as being ancillary to an action for annulment of the measure and it could consequently be brought only in supplement to the latter action. Third, in Germany, public liability under § 839 BGB would not arise if the claimant had wilfully or negligently failed to avert the damage by using a legal remedy

54 For a detailed assessment of the dual test see Section 2.D.

such as an action for annulment.[55] This third approach is closely related to concepts of causation and it might therefore have been proper to discuss it in Section 6.C.II. However, the available materials do not allow for a discussion of the main issue without integrating rulings on all three approaches. Case law on the third approach will therefore be included in the discussion in this section. It is finally possible also to discuss a fourth or at least related aspect of the main issue, not recognized by Advocate General Tesauro: the duty to mitigate loss. In its judgment in *Brasserie* the Court of Justice discussed the duty of claimants to avert loss in the context of estimating the extent of reparation.[56] This fourth aspect is more easily distinguished and will therefore be covered in Section 6.C.III.a.

In his Opinion in *Brasserie* Advocate General Tesauro found support for limitations of the kind here discussed in EU case law on the action for damages pursuant to Article 340(2) TFEU. The Advocate General therefore submitted that such national restrictions should be allowed insofar as they were applied in accordance with the principle of equivalence.[57] By contrast Advocate General Jacobs opined in *Fantask* that the action for damages from a Member State should be regarded as being 'wholly independent' from restitutionary actions and that the failure of claimants to bring a restitutionary action within the applicable time-limit should not be allowed to prejudice their possibilities to bring an action for damages instead.[58] The Court of Justice did not discuss the issue in any of these two cases, but it did in the more recent *Danske Slagterier*.[59] **6.029**

> The claimant, Danske Slagterier, was an association of Danish slaughterhouse companies. The claimant produced pig meat from uncastrated male pigs. When heated such meat may give off a pronounced boar taint, and there were differences over the reliability of various techniques designed to identify meat affected by that taint. In Denmark slaughterhouses identified meat affected by the taint by measuring the skatol content in their meat. **6.030**
>
> In Germany authorities favoured measuring the amount of the hormone androstenone in pig meat in order to prevent pig meat liable to be affected by the taint from reaching

55 *Brasserie* (n 16) Opinion of AG Tesauro para. 101.

56 Ibid., paras 84–85.

57 Ibid., Opinion of AG Tesauro para. 104. Oliver (n 49) 57 has similarly submitted that such rules should be permitted by the Court so as to preclude claimants from 'sitting back and waiting for the damage to occur, rather than giving the authorities the opportunity to put an end to unlawful conduct more speedily'. Piet Eeckhout, 'Liability in Damages and the Community System of Remedies' in Jack Beatson and Takis Tridimas (eds), *New Directions in European Public Law* (Hart Publishing 1998) 71, was less certain but would nevertheless concede that the reasons behind such national rules 'cannot be discarded as being clearly wrong'.

58 Case C-188/95 *Fantask A/S ea v Industriministeriet (Erhvervministeriet)* [1997] ECR I-6783 Opinion of AG Jacobs paras 82–84. The Court of Justice did not discuss this issue.

59 *Danske Slagterier* (n 53).

consumers. In 1993 Germany therefore adopted a threshold value for the amount of androstenone allowed in imported pig meat. As a result numerous consignments of pig meat exported from Denmark by members of the claimant association were rejected for exceeding the threshold for androstenone. Considering that the threshold value adopted by Germany for the amount of androstenone allowed in imported pig meat was contrary to Directive 64/433/EEC,[60] as amended, the claimant brought an action for damages against Germany.

6.031 One of the questions asked by the national court in *Danske Slagterier* was whether § 839(3) BGB was compatible with (then) Community law on actions for damages from a Member State. Under the provision at issue the obligation of the public authorities to compensate individuals for harm suffered through a breach of official duty would not arise if the injured party had wilfully or negligently failed to avert the damage sustained by using a legal remedy.[61] The Court of Justice acknowledged that the national court might inquire whether the injured person had shown reasonable diligence in order to avoid the loss or damage or limit its extent and whether, in particular, the claimant had availed her- or himself in time of all the legal remedies available. The Court however also held that it would be contrary to the principle of effectiveness to oblige injured parties to have recourse systematically to all the legal remedies available to them even if that would give rise to excessive difficulties or could not reasonably be required of them.[62] Having cited *Metallgesellschaft*[63] as an example of circumstances where it would not have been reasonable to require the injured parties to use other legal remedies available to them, the Court finally concluded that Community law did not preclude the application of a national rule such as that laid down in § 839(3) BGB provided that the use of the legal remedy in question could reasonably be required of the injured party, leaving it to the national court to make the final assessment.[64]

6.032 Circumstances were similar in the subsequent *Fuß*.[65]

60 Council Directive 64/433/EEC of 26 June 1964 on health problems affecting intra-Community trade in fresh meat [1964] OJ 121/2012. It was settled in case C-102/96 *Commission of the European Communities v Federal Republic of Germany* [1998] ECR I-6871 that the measures adopted by Germany were indeed contrary to this directive.

61 A very similar Swedish rule (3 kap 4 § skadeståndslagen) was abolished in 1990 for being unnecessary in light of a general rule on mitigation of loss, but also for being too cumbersome on claimants; prop 1989/90:42, 17–19.

62 *Danske Slagterier* (n 53) paras 60–62.

63 Joined cases C-397/98 and C-410/98 *Metallgesellschaft Ltd and Others* (C-397/98), *Hoechst AG and Hoechst (UK) Ltd* (C-410/98) *v Commissioners of Inland Revenue and HM Attorney General* [2001] ECR I-1727.

64 *Danske Slagterier* (n 53) paras 63–64.

65 *Fuß* (n 33).

Günter Fuß was a civil servant who was employed by the town of Halle. He claimed reparation for unlawful overtime work, having worked an average of 54 hours per week. However, under German case law, Mr Fuß should have submitted an application to his employer that he be employed only for the period of working time provided for by law. If such an application had been submitted reparation would have been payable in respect of working time imposed unlawfully after the making of that request.

The Court of Justice held that the obligation for the workers concerned to make a prior application to their employer in order to obtain reparation for the loss or damage suffered as a result of the infringement of EU law had the effect of enabling the German authorities concerned to shift to individuals the burden of ensuring compliance with such norms. Moreover the authorities would have a possibility of avoiding compliance with those provisions, which were EU law provisions with direct effect, where such an application had not been made. The Court would not accept such a situation as all Member State authorities were obliged to apply those provisions in their capacity as public employers. The Court of Justice therefore held that it could not be reasonable to require a worker who had suffered loss or damage as a result of the infringement by his employer of the rights conferred by EU law to make a prior application to that employer in order to be entitled to reparation for that loss or damage. The Court concluded that a requirement to make such a prior application was contrary to the principle of effectiveness.[66] **6.033**

In *Danske Slagterier* the national court also asked whether recourse to a legal remedy might be regarded as reasonable when it was likely that the national court would make a reference for a preliminary ruling under Article (now) 267 TFEU. It seemed the national court was concerned that the lapse of time during proceedings before the European Court of Justice was liable to make it unreasonable for claimants to use legal remedies that were likely to lead to a reference. In that regard the Court of Justice held that a strong likelihood that recourse to a legal remedy would give rise to a reference for a preliminary ruling was not in itself a sufficient reason for concluding that the use of that remedy was not reasonable.[67] **6.034**

Summarizing this case law on the principle of effectiveness, national rules limiting access to court in situations where the claimant should, under applicable national law, have averted harm by having recourse to another legal **6.035**

66 Ibid., paras 83–87.

67 *Danske Slagterier* (n 53) paras 58, 65–66 and Operative part para. 4. Cf. also the Opinion of AG Trstenjak paras 46–51, 128–131.

or contractual remedy are compatible with the EU law principle of effectiveness only if such recourse could reasonably be required of the claimant. The case law shows that it is not reasonable to require claimants to make use of alternative remedies where such recourse would enable the public authorities of a Member State to avoid compliance with EU law provisions with direct effect (*Fuß*), to have recourse systematically to all the legal remedies available to them even if that would give rise to excessive difficulties (*Danske Slagterier*), or to have recourse to remedies that do not effectively protect their interests (*Metallgesellschaft*). It was not unreasonable to require claimants to have recourse to remedies in circumstances where the national court or tribunal would likely refer the case to the European Court of Justice for a preliminary ruling (*Danske Slagterier*).

6.036 Continuing now to the notorious national time-limits for bringing a claim for damages against the Member State, the impact of the EU law principles of equivalence and effectiveness on such rules was discussed in *Palmisani*.[68]

6.037 The circumstances paralleled those in *Francovich* insofar as the claimant had been employed by an undertaking that was declared insolvent at the time when Italy had failed to transpose Directive 80/987 into national law.[69] Following *Francovich* the Italian Government had adopted a legislative decree providing certain detailed conditions for reparation owed by the State by reason of the belated transposition of the directive. Under the decree an action for reparation must be brought within one year from the date of entry into force of the decree. In *Palmisani* the claimant had failed, however, to submit her claim for reparation within that time-limit. The question was therefore whether Community law precluded a Member State from requiring any action for reparation of the loss or damage sustained as a result of the belated transposition of the directive to be brought within a limitation period of one year from its transposition into national law.

6.038 In the context of time-limits barring a claim it should be kept in mind that it follows from case law such as *Alassini*,[70] discussed in Section 2.D.III, that bars are one of a few typical adverse consequences of national substantive and procedural conditions which are liable to make the exercise of rights conferred by EU law virtually impossible or excessively difficult.[71] Hence the principle of effectiveness might preclude such conditions of national law. The precise

68 Case C-261/95 *Rosalba Palmisani v Istituto nazionale della previdenza sociale (INPS)* [1997] ECR I-4025.

69 Council Directive 80/987/EEC of 20 October 1980 on the approximation of the laws of the Member States relating to the protection of employees in the event of the insolvency of their employer [1980] OJ L283/23.

70 Joined cases C-317/08, C-318/08, C-319/08 and C-320/08 *Rosalba Alassini v Telecom Italia SpA* (C-317/08), *Filomena Califano v Wind SpA* (C-318/08), *Lucia Anna Giorgia Iacono v Telecom Italia SpA* (C-319/08) and *Multiservice Srl v Telecom Italia SpA* (C-320/08) [2010] ECR I-2213.

71 The other typical adverse consequences identified in *Alassini* (n 69) were impracticalities, delays, and costs. See further paras 2.072–2.073.

impact of the principle of effectiveness cannot be assessed in the abstract however, but must be decided on a case-by-case basis. In *Palmisani* for instance, the Court of Justice held that the setting of reasonable limitation periods for bringing proceedings was not as such contrary to the principle of effectiveness, inasmuch as it constituted an application of the fundamental principle of legal certainty. With reference to the existence of the decree laying down detailed conditions for the bringing of an action, the Court held that a time-limit of one year commencing from the date of the entry into force of the legislative decree could not under such circumstances be regarded as making it excessively difficult or virtually impossible to lodge a claim for reparation.[72] By comparison the Court indicated in *Danske Slagterier* that it would be incompatible with the principle of effectiveness if the limitation period at issue began to run before the injured party became aware of the loss or damage and of the identity of the person required to pay compensation.[73]

In *Palmisani* the Court of Justice continued to discuss whether the one-year time-limit was also compatible with the EU law principle of equivalence. As explained in Section 2.D.II the principle of equivalence presupposes the identification of a relevant national *comparator*, i.e., an action based on national law where the purpose, cause of action, and essential characteristics of the action are similar to those of the action based on EU law.[74] This proved to be a problem in *Palmisani*, where the national court had submitted information on time-limits in a number of potential *comparator* actions. The Court of Justice dismissed two causes of action relating to claims for social benefits because their objectives differed from the objective of an action for damages from a Member State and that those two causes of action were therefore not similar to the action for damages from a Member State within the meaning of the EU law principle of equivalence.[75] The national court had also submitted information on time-limits for bringing an action for non-contractual damages in private law. With regard to that cause of action the Court of Justice was uncertain whether it would apply to damages actions brought against the Member State at issue. The Court therefore distinguished three alternative **6.039**

72 *Palmisani* (n 68) paras 28–29; cf. *Danske Slagterier* (n 53) para. 32 and the case law there cited. In *Palmisani*, the claimant had furthermore argued that the decree left a degree of uncertainty as regards the public law body responsible for making good the loss or damage and as regards the court before which an action for reparation should be brought. However, the Court of Justice would not rule on that issue, as it had been expressly rejected by the national court; paras 30–31.

73 *Danske Slagterier* (n 53) para. 52. See also joined cases C-295/04 to 298/04 *Vincenzo Manfredi v Lloyd Adriatico Assicurazioni SpA* (C-295/04), *Antonio Cannito v Fondiaria Sai SpA* (C-296/04) and *Nicolò Tricarico* (C-297/04) and *Pasqualina Murgolo* (C-298/04) *v Assitalia SpA* [2006] ECR I-6619 paras 78–79.

74 Case C-326/96 *BS Levez v TH Jennings (Harlow Pools) Ltd* [1998] ECR I-7835 paras 41, 43. See also case C-118/08 *Transportes Urbanos y Servicios Generales SAL v Administración del Estado* [2010] ECR I-635 for an assessment where all three criteria were met. See further Section 2.D.II.

75 *Palmisani* (n 68) paras 36–37. Cf. also *Danske Slagterier* (n 53) paras 40–45.

possibilities: (a) a private law action of non-contractual liability could be brought against the public authorities for a failure to act or for having committed an unlawful act in the exercise of their powers for which they could be held liable in damages; (b) such an action could not be brought against the public authorities but there was another relevant *comparator* available to the national court; and (c) such an action could not be brought against the public authorities and there was no other relevant *comparator* available to the national court. The Court only elaborated its view with regard to the (c) alternative, holding that under such circumstances it would need to be concluded that the principle of equivalence would not preclude a Member State from laying down a time-limit for damages actions of one year from the entry into force of the legislative decree governing such actions brought against the Member State.[76] Implicitly however, it would follow from the principle of equivalence that under the (a) alternative the private law action of non-contractual liability would be a relevant *comparator* and the principle of equivalence would therefore preclude the Member State from laying down conditions governing actions brought against the Member State for a breach of EU law that were less favourable than those governing the private law action for non-contractual damages.[77] It would likewise follow from the (b) alternative that the general action for damages from the public authorities for a failure to act or for having committed an unlawful act in the exercise of their powers would be the relevant *comparator*, and hence the conditions governing actions brought against the Member State for a breach of EU law could not be less favourable than those governing such a general action for damages from the public authorities. Under both the (a) and the (b) alternatives a longer time-limit than the one-year limit laid down in the decree would therefore need to be applied also in actions for damages under the decree.

6.040 Finally some reflections on the potential impact of Article 47 of the Charter will be submitted. It was argued in Section 2.C.I that Article 47 in principle requires for national courts to grant access to claimants who wish to enforce rights guaranteed to them by EU law. This will include enforcement through an action for damages from a Member State. Nevertheless, as explained in Section 2.C.II, national limitations of the right of access to court will be compatible with the Charter insofar as they meet the conditions laid down in Article 52(1). Such national limitations must hence be provided for by law, respect the essence of the right, and meet the proportionality test prescribed by that Article. The proportionality test at issue permits only limitations which are necessary and genuinely meet objectives of a general interest recognized by

76 *Palmisani* (n 68) paras 38–39. Alternative (b) follows implicitly from the holdings of the Court.

77 See also Prechal (n 6) 300.

the EU or the need to protect the rights and freedoms of others. The details of these requirements have been discussed in Section 2.C.II and need not be repeated here. The Article 52(1) test has not been discussed yet in the context of an action for damages brought against a Member State for a breach of EU law. Nonetheless the effectiveness assessments in *Palmisani* and *Danske Slagterier* can be used to sketch an assessment under the Charter. It might in that regard not be too far-fetched to make a comparison with the criteria developed by the Strasbourg Court for the assessment of whether a limitation of a right is 'provided for by law', namely, that the limitation is identifiable, accessible, and foreseeable.[78] These criteria were not referred or even alluded to by the European Court of Justice in *Palmisani*, but it seems from the reasoning of the Court that the Italian decree would meet those criteria. In *Danske Slagterier* the principle of effectiveness triggered the same considerations as are indicated under the Strasbourg criterion of foreseeability. There the Court held that limitation periods must be fixed in advance as '[a] situation marked by significant legal uncertainty may involve a breach of the principle of effectiveness'.[79] In *Palmisani* the Court of Justice also seemed to take the view that the one-year time-limit respected the essence of the right to claim damages.[80] The Court even identified a legitimate aim for the time-limits in both cases, i.e., the fundamental principle of legal certainty.[81] The time-limit was apparently suitable for the attainment of that aim. The reasoning of the Court in *Palmisani* and *Danske Slagterier* does not however lend itself to discussions of the necessity test or proportionality assessment *sensu stricto*.[82] This lack of congruence still proves a point as it may serve to illustrate an important difference between the Article 52(1) test and the principle of effectiveness. It is hoped that future case law may further develop the Charter test and its interrelationship to the traditional effectiveness assessment.

b. Access and passing-on

In the context of passing-on it is of particular interest – irrespective of which action is applicable – whether the competent jurisdiction will allow access for Gamma claimants. This sub-section focuses on national limitations of access to court that are triggered in respect of Gamma claimants bringing an action for damages against a Member State. Case law on that issue is limited to one **6.041**

78 Bernadette Rainey, Elizabeth Wicks and Clare Ovey, *Jacobs, White and Ovey: The European Convention on Human Rights* (6th edn, Oxford University Press 2014) 312.

79 *Danske Slagterier* (n 53) para. 33.

80 Cf. *Perez de Rada Cavanilles v Spain* App No 28090/95 (ECtHR, 28 October 1998), reported in para. 2.043

81 *Palmisani* (n 68) para. 28; *Danske Slagterier* (n 53) para. 32. The mentioning of the objective in *Palmisani* was noted by Sacha Prechal, 'Community Law in National Courts: The Lessons from *van Schijndel*' (1998) 35 *Common Market Law Review* 681, 688 and 705, submitting also that a proportionality test should be included in the effectiveness assessment.

82 On the details of the assessments to be carried out in the Art. 52(1) test see Section 2.C.II.

case only: *Danfoss*. In the first part of the judgment it was settled that the right to repayment of charges levied in breach of EU law does, as such, extend to Gamma claimants.[83] The action for damages was discussed in the second part.

6.042 A summary of the facts is available in paragraph 5.030. Alongside the action for repayment of the charges paid to the Danish tax authorities the claimants also claimed compensation from the Danish state for the damage suffered as a consequence of the duty being levied. The Danish tax authorities rejected any claims for compensation, holding, inter alia, that under Danish law it was automatically ruled out that there could be a direct causal link between the levying of the excise duties and the alleged harm suffered by the claimant.

6.043 It must be noticed at the outset that the national rule at issue did not concern an assessment of the substantive issue of causation. Instead it concerned access to court. Under the national rule at issue the action was rejected (Danish: *afvist*). It was explained in Section 5.C.II that if this author correctly understands the Danish original term *afvise* the action was not admitted. In other words the national rule barred Gamma from bringing an action for damages from the Member State, as a causal link between an infringement of EU law and harm suffered by Gamma due to the passing-on of a duty was automatically ruled out.

6.044 Advocate General Kokott opined that this was not a question of fact, but one of law, as it sought to clarify 'whether the condition regarding the direct causal link is to be interpreted so narrowly that … it can be deemed to exist only in the relationship with the taxable person'. The Advocate General observed that the directness of causality should not be understood in an absolute sense but as 'sufficient directness', shielding the tortfeasor from liability to compensate every consequence of an unlawful action, 'however remote'. In that regard the Advocate General opined that the Danish notion of causality invoked was stricter than the EU law concept. The Advocate General indeed went so far as to argue that the Danish notion was tantamount to an additional condition for the action brought by Danfoss, which would be contrary to EU law as it resulted 'in the claim for compensation … being systematically withheld from those who have had to pay the charge … without each case being considered on its merits'. The Advocate General therefore concluded that the Member State might not reject a claim for damages brought by a party to whom the duty unduly paid had been passed on on the ground that a direct causal link between the levying of that duty and the damage suffered was automatically ruled out.[84]

83 *Danfoss* (n 2) paras 20–23. See para. 5.040.
84 Ibid., Opinion of AG Kokott paras 74–83.

The Court first repeated that it was not for the Court to assign a legal classification to the actions brought by the claimants and, citing *Comateb*,[85] that an action for damages might coexist with an action for the repayment of charges unduly paid. The Court then proceeded to examine the requirements to be met by individuals bringing an action for damages for a breach of EU law by a Member State. With regard to the requirement for a direct causal link, the Court found that it was for the national court to ascertain whether the loss and damage claimed flowed sufficiently directly from the breach of EU law.[86] **6.045**

Nevertheless, by way of guidance to the national court, the Court of Justice held that where a national legal system recognized a direct causal link only between the levying by the state of a duty which was not due and damage suffered by the taxable person, such a limitation might not be interpreted in such a way to make it virtually impossible or excessively difficult to obtain compensation for damage suffered. It followed, the Court further held, that such a national legal system would in principle be consistent with the principle of effectiveness only if the purchaser to whom the burden of that duty has been passed on by the taxable person was able, on the basis of national law, to bring an action for compensation for consequential damage against the taxable person. However, the Court continued, if it were to prove impossible or excessively difficult to obtain such compensation from the taxable person – in particular in the case of the insolvency of that person – the principle of effectiveness required that the purchaser was able to bring the claim for reimbursement against the state directly, without the state being legitimately able to rely on the lack of a direct causal link between the levying of the duty and the damage suffered by the purchaser.[87] **6.046**

Consequently the Court of Justice ruled that a Member State might reject a claim for damages brought by a purchaser to whom a duty unduly paid had been passed on by the taxable person, on the ground that there was no direct causal link between the levying of that duty and the damage suffered, provided that the purchaser was able on the basis of national law to bring that claim against the taxable person and provided that the compensation, by that taxable person, of the damage suffered by the purchaser was not virtually impossible or excessively difficult.[88] **6.047**

Contemplating these holdings it should be noticed first that it follows from *Danfoss* that the right to damages in compensation for harm incurred by **6.048**

85 *Comateb* (n 1).

86 *Danfoss* (n 2) paras 32–34.

87 Ibid., paras 36–38.

88 Ibid., Operative part para. 2.

reason of a breach of EU law by a Member State does extend to Gamma claimants.[89] Accordingly EU law rules and principles designed to ensure the effective judicial protection of individual rights and interests recognized by EU law will apply to restrictions facing Gamma claimants pursuant to national law. It should also be noticed that the Court of Justice was quite keen to indicate that it would not assign a legal classification to the actions brought before the national court for reimbursement of charges levied in breach of EU law or claiming compensation for damage suffered, and that an action for damages might coexist with an action for the recovery of sums unduly paid.[90] In *Danfoss* it seems from the facts that the claimants had brought an action for damages only in respect of harm incurred in the form of consequential loss, i.e., for loss in the form of decreased sales and other *lucrum cessans*.[91] Be this as it may, the holdings just cited indicate that an action for damages could also be brought as an alternative course of action with regard to the entire economic burden borne by the claimant, i.e., including loss in the form of the amounts of charges passed on to the claimants (*damnum emergens*) as well as loss suffered in the form of consequential loss.

6.049 As to the substance of the holdings in this second part of *Danfoss*, the Court of Justice followed the pattern established in the first part of the judgment. Just as in its reply to the first question asked (on access to court for a Gamma claimant bringing an action for repayment) the Court of Justice made the possibility to rule out a direct causal link between an infringement of EU law and harm caused to a Gamma claimant conditional on the possibilities for the Gamma claimant to find other redress. The legal basis for this approach was found in a pragmatic interpretation of the EU law principle of effectiveness. The essence of that interpretation was that, in the context of harm suffered due to the passing-on of a charge levied in breach of EU law, actions brought by Gamma could only be rejected if two requirements were met. First, Gamma must be able, on the basis of national law, to bring the claim for compensation against Beta. Second, it must not be virtually impossible or excessively difficult to actually obtain compensation from Beta, e.g., due to Beta being insolvent.[92] However the Court did not clarify whether the Gamma claimant had the onus of proving that it had exhausted its possibilities to obtain compensation from Beta. This was discussed in the context of the first part of the judgment, which concerned the claim for repayment of the charges levied, and has been discussed in Section 5.C.II. It was noticed in that context that such a

89 Ibid., para. 36.
90 Ibid., para. 32.
91 Ibid., para. 15. Cf. *Comateb* (n 1) para. 34.
92 *Danfoss* ibid., para. 38, and Operative part para. 2.

precondition of 'exhaustion of domestic remedies'[93] was compatible with *Unibet* and *Inuit*, where the existence of a specific remedy was not required if an alternative remedy existed in national law which made it possible to ensure the protection of the right conferred on the individual by EU law.[94] Theoretically, therefore, the contested limitation could be upheld only where an action for damages brought by Gamma against Beta has been successful. If such an action was unsuccessful, the limitation could not be upheld. It is submitted however that these theoretical alternatives are less relevant here, for reasons that deserve to be explained.

On closer scrutiny and bearing in mind the legal context, the reasoning of the Court on the issue of Gamma bringing an action for damages against Beta is intriguing. The precise wording of the Court's reasoning indicated that Gamma must be able to bring an action 'seeking compensation for the consequential damage' against Beta.[95] In Danish, the wording is '*fremsætte sit krav om erstatning af det tab, der er lidt*'; in French, it is '*son action en réparation du préjudice subi de ce fait*'; in German, it is '*seine Klage auf Ersatz des ihm hierdurch entstandenen Schadens*'. In all these language versions, some form of damages remedy seems to be indicated. The problem is the tort – what would be the tort (or fault, depending on jurisdiction) giving rise to liability in damages for Beta? The facts reported in *Danfoss* do not lend themselves to any plausible construction of tortious liability for Beta. It would follow that the possibility of upholding the bar indicated by the Court of Justice would be theoretical. In practice it would not be possible to uphold it, save perhaps for circumstances where Beta and Alpha had somehow conspired to burden Gamma with the loss at issue. For certain, passing-on as such would not suffice. Consequently the practical result of this holding would to be that the national limitation of access to bring an action for damages against the Member State could not reasonably be upheld by the national court in its final assessment. **6.050**

The logical consequence of this view can be put very simply: Gamma claimants cannot be barred from bringing an action for damages directly against the Member State for reasons related to passing-on. Further argumentative support for this conclusion can be added by noticing that the conclusion **6.051**

93 Cf. Art. 35(1) ECHR.

94 Case C-432/05 *Unibet (London) Ltd and Unibet (International) Ltd v Justitiekanslern* [2007] ECR I-2271 paras 40–41; case C-583/11 P *Inuit Tapiriit Kanatami and Others v European Parliament and Council of the European Union* EU:C:2013:625 paras 103–104.

95 *Danfoss* (n 2) para. 37.

reached is consistent with the approach chosen for the purposes of competition law damages in Directive 2014/104/EU[96] and that Member States should not in the logic of EU law be better off than private individuals in the event of a breach of EU law.

II. Substantive proximity issues for Gamma claimants

6.052 In damages the legal issue referred to here as 'substantive proximity' between the act or omission giving rise to the tort (or fault) and the alleged harm incurred is assessed as causation of the latter by the former. It will be recalled from Section 6.B that causation ('a direct causal link') is one of the three conditions laid down by the European Court of Justice for the purposes of actions for damages against a Member State for a breach of EU law by that Member State, the other two being that the rule of law infringed was intended to confer rights on individuals and that the breach of EU law was sufficiently serious. It remains somewhat controversial however whether the elements of the causation assessment are governed by EU law or by national law. This section is dedicated to case law on the condition of causation for the purposes of an action for damages from the Member State, and in particular to the balancing of EU law and national law for the purposes of the causation assessment. This general discussion is found in the general observations of sub-section 6.C.II.a. As causation tests are of particular interest in the context of Gamma claims the situation for Gamma will be discussed in detail, using the general observations as background, in sub-section 6.C.II.b.[97]

a. General observations on causation

6.053 It is well known that the Court of Justice has largely entrusted the national courts to carry out the causation assessment in actions for damages from Member States on the basis of national law.[98] The European Court of Justice had already held in *Brasserie* that it was for the national court 'to determine whether there is a direct causal link between the breach … and the damage sustained'.[99] The Court did not give any further guidance on how to carry out

96 Directive 2014/104/EU of the European Parliament and of the Council of 26 November 2014 on certain rules governing actions for damages under national law for infringements of the competition law provisions of the Member States and of the European Union [2014] OJ L349/1 Art. 14.

97 In this book, Alpha signifies a tortfeasor or enriched party, Beta a party first burdened by loss arising from Alpha's breach of EU law, and Gamma any party downstream from Beta (including all from the party dealing directly with Beta to the final consumer) to whom the burden of that loss may have been passed on; see Section 1.B.

98 A brief overview of causation tests in Germany, England and France is available in Robert Rebhahn, 'Public Liability in Comparison: England, France, Germany' in Helmut Koziol and Barbara C Steininger (eds), *Tort and Insurance Law Yearbook: European Tort Law 2005* (Springer 2006) 88–9.

99 *Brasserie* (n 16) para. 65.

the assessment in *Brasserie*. From these holdings it could seem that it was also for the national legal systems to provide the substantive causation test – and consequently it has been submitted by Aalto that this is so.[100] Tridimas on the other hand has submitted that the rules governing causation cannot depend on national law, as that would amount to a '"re-nationalization" of the conditions of liability'.[101] Biondi and Farley agree with Tridimas, arguing that 'to conclude otherwise would create great uncertainty'.[102] Notwithstanding this discussion on the division of powers with regard to the substantive legal details of the assessment, there is general consensus that it is for the national courts to make the final assessment by applying the substantive causation test to the facts.[103] As the details of causation can be crucial to Gamma claimants in a passing-on situation, it will be endeavoured here to examine the extent of EU law governance of the substantive causation test in actions for damages from a Member State.

It follows from consistent case law of the Court of Justice that the detailed conditions for reparation of loss and damage laid down by the national law of the Member States (in which the national causation test will be included) are subject to scrutiny under the EU law principles of equivalence and effectiveness.[104] Furthermore, since *Brasserie*, the Court of Justice has consistently held that the causal link must be 'direct', which is a transplant from its case law on damages actions under Article 340(2) TFEU.[105] In spite of having been asked explicitly for guidance on the condition of causation[106] the Court has otherwise consistently declined to elaborate on the causation test to be applied **6.054**

---

100 Aalto (n 13) 11.

101 Takis Tridimas, *The General Principles of EU Law* (2nd edn, Oxford EC Law Library, Oxford University Press 2006) 533. See also Takis Tridimas, 'Liability for Breach of Community Law: Growing Up and Mellowing Down?' (2001) 38 *Common Market Law Review* 301, 310.

102 Biondi and Farley (n 6) 59. To this author, the strongest argument in favour of the view that the substantive content of the condition of causation in actions for damages from a Member State is governed by EU law rather than by national law follows from a comparison of *Brasserie* case law with *Manfredi* (n 72) para. 64, where the Court of Justice held that it was for the 'domestic legal system of each Member State to prescribe the detailed rules governing … the concept of "causal relationship", provided that the principles of equivalence and effectiveness [were] observed'. Such a holding, explicitly referring to national rules governing causation, has not appeared in *Brasserie* case law. This would indicate, by its contrast to *Brasserie* case law, that the concept of causation applicable in actions for damages from a Member State is an EU law concept. However, it is submitted that the consistent unwillingness of the Court to be clear on this matter speaks against such a conclusion.

103 See, e.g., Biondi and Farley (n 6) 55, who argue that the decentralization of the causation assessment is healthy, as the Court of Justice would otherwise need to review the facts and acquire evidence, instead of focusing on the interpretation of EU law; and Tridimas (n 101 (2001)) 310.

104 E.g., *Francovich* (n 5) para. 43; *Brasserie* (n 16) paras 66–67; and more recently *Danfoss* (n 2) para. 36.

105 *Brasserie* (n 16) para. 51, and subsequent case law.

106 Case C-446/04 *Test Claimants in the FII Group Litigation v Commissioners of Inland Revenue* [2006] ECR I-11753 para. 31 (question 9); and case C-524/04 *Test Claimants in the Thin Cap Group Litigation v Commissioners of Inland Revenue* [2007] ECR I-2107 para. 21 (question 9).

for the purposes of actions for damages from a Member State. General guidance has not been offered – until *Leth*,[107] to which we will soon revert. The Court has however come close to carrying out the causation assessment itself on a few occasions, including *AGM* and *Fuß*, where it seemed on the facts presented to the Court that there was a direct causal link, but the Court stopped short of actually holding that there was.[108] The Court also came very close to holding that there was no direct causal link in the aforementioned *Leth*.[109] In *Brinkmann* the Court paid lip service to the power of national courts to determine whether the conditions for Member State liability were met, but held that, in that particular case, it had all the information necessary to determine itself whether there was a causal link between the breach by the Member State and the damage sustained by the claimant.[110]

6.055 Brinkmann Tabakfabriken GmbH (Brinkmann) had introduced a tobacco product named 'Westpoint' on the Danish market. Westpoint came in a packet resembling a normal packet of cigarettes, but contained 30 rolls of tobacco enveloped in porous cellulose that had to be wrapped in cigarette paper before they could be smoked. Brinkmann also sold cigarette-paper tubes separately into which the tobacco rolls could be inserted. The purpose of Westpoint was to offer a product that would preserve the convenience of industrially-prepared cigarettes as far as possible, but nonetheless be taxed at the lower rate applicable to smoking tobacco.

Taxes on tobacco had been harmonized through Directive 79/32/EEC.[111] Under Article 3(1) of the Directive, cigarettes were defined as '[r]olls of tobacco capable of being smoked as they are and which are not cigars or cigarillos'. Smoking tobacco was defined in Article 4(1) as 'tobacco which has been cut or otherwise split, twisted or pressed into blocks and is capable of being smoked without further industrial processing'.

In Germany Westpoint was classified as smoking tobacco. In Denmark the implementing legislation did not itself contain a transposition of these definitions, but gave power to the Danish Minister for Fiscal Affairs to lay down the provisions necessary, including definitions. At the material time no provisions had yet been laid down pursuant to that power, but the Danish authorities had given immediate effect to the relevant definitions of tobacco products in the Directive. In their application of the definitions Westpoint was classified as cigarettes however, and taxed at the higher rate, forcing the product off the market. Brinkmann brought an action before the Østre Landsret in which it claimed that the Danish fiscal authorities should be required to

107 Case C-420/11 *Jutta Leth v Republik Österreich and Land Niederösterreich* EU:C:2013:166.

108 Case C-470/03 *AGM-COS MET Srl v Suomen valtio and Tarmo Lehtinen* [2007] ECR I-2749 paras 82–83; *Fuß* (n 33) paras 59–60 (where the Court came very close to a holding).

109 *Leth* (n 107) para. 46 and Operative part.

110 Case C-319/96 *Brinkmann Tabakfabriken GmbH v Skatteministeriet* [1998] ECR I-5255 paras 26, 29.

111 Second Council Directive 79/32/EEC of 18 December 1978 on taxes other than turnover taxes which affect the consumption of manufactured tobacco [1979] OJ L10/8.

accept that Westpoint ought to be taxed as smoking tobacco, and for compensation for loss incurred by Brinkmann as a result of Westpoint being forced off the Danish market. The Østre Landsret stayed proceedings and referred questions to the European Court of Justice on the proper interpretation of Directive 79/32/EEC and on liability in damages for Denmark in the event that the interpretation made by the Danish fiscal authorities was erroneous.

The Court of Justice held that the Danish interpretation of the relevant Articles was erroneous,[112] but in light of the difficulty of fitting Westpoint into any of the categories specified in the directive, the Court held that the erroneous interpretation did not amount to a sufficiently serious breach of EU law. Consequently the Court of Justice ruled that Denmark was not bound by EU law to compensate Brinkmann for damage sustained as a result of the erroneous classification of Westpoint.[113] **6.056**

Brinkmann however also argued that the failure of Denmark to transpose the definitions in the Directive through a legislative act was *per se* a serious breach of EU law. The Court conceded that a failure to take any measure to transpose a Directive in order to achieve the result it prescribes within the period laid down for that purpose constitutes *per se* a serious breach of EU law, but would not accept that the fact that the definitions in the Directive were not implemented by ministerial decree would in itself give rise to liability on the part of the state. In that regard the Court observed that the Danish authorities had given immediate effect to the relevant definitions of tobacco products in the Directive. Therefore, the Court concluded, there was no direct causal link between the failure to transpose the definitions in the Directive and the damage allegedly suffered by Brinkmann.[114] **6.057**

This last assessment of the Court of Justice in *Brinkmann* is quite brief, and not easily interpreted, but it is submitted that it is a causation assessment. What the Court implied was that even though the definitions at issue had not been transposed into national law by any legislative act, they were nevertheless being implemented in the sense that they were in fact applied by the **6.058**

112 *Brinkmann* (n 110) paras 20–22.

113 Ibid., paras 30–31 and Operative part para. 2.

114 Ibid., paras 25–26, 28–29. As regards the erroneous interpretation given to the definitions of the Directive by the administrative authorities, the Court did not proceed to discuss causation but concluded under the circumstances that the erroneous interpretation given to the definitions of the Directive did not constitute a sufficiently serious breach to give rise to liability in damages; ibid., paras 31–32. This distinction between the failure to transpose and the erroneous interpretation was not entirely clear in the judgment, which has given rise to some confusion (see e.g. Biondi and Farley (n 6) 58). However, close reading of the judgment does disclose the sequence clarified here.

administrative authorities in the decision to classify Westpoint as cigarettes.[115] Even if the definitions had been transposed into national law through ministerial decree, the classification of Westpoint – erroneous though it was – would nonetheless have been the same. Through a comparison of the actual scenario and this hypothetical scenario the Court was thus able to conclude that there was no relevant difference to Brinkmann's position. Hence there was no direct causal link between the failure to transpose and the damage allegedly suffered.[116] In other words the Court applied the classic *conditio sine qua non* test for assessing factual causation in damages, but it must be pointed out that the test was well hidden in the Court's reasoning.

6.059 In *Rechberger* the Court of Justice was seized with arguments relating to competing causes of harm. It was argued by Austria that unlawful conduct on the part of a third party and/or exceptional and unforeseeable events, causing or at least contributing to the harm incurred, would preclude the existence of a direct causal link within the meaning of EU law.[117]

6.060 The claimants in *Rechberger* had booked trips falling within the scope of Directive 90/314/EEC[118] on package travel. The Directive had not been properly implemented in Austria. Following the bankruptcy of the travel organizer, the claimants sought reimbursement of their travel costs, but the bank guarantee issued by the travel organizer did not suffice. Therefore, the claimants brought an action against Austria before the Landesgericht Linz for compensation in damages for the harm incurred, arguing inter alia that it was caused by the failure of Austria to implement Article 7 of the Directive. The Landesgericht stayed proceedings and referred a number of questions to the European Court of Justice for a preliminary ruling.

6.061 With regard to the existence of a direct causal link, the Court of Justice noted that the national court had found that there was such a direct causal link between the conduct of the Member State (failing to transpose the Directive in full) and the harm sustained by the individuals. The question was, therefore, whether the existence of a competing cause for their harm (the negligence of the travel organizer) could preclude liability for the Member State. In that regard the Court noted that the guarantee prescribed in the Directive was specifically aimed at arming consumers against the consequences of

---

115 *Brinkmann* (n 110) para. 29. In the words of the Court the definitions of the Directive were given 'immediate effect' by the Danish authorities.

116 Brinkmann might have been more successful if it had brought an action for repayment of charges levied in breach of EU law instead, avoiding the hurdles of establishing both causation and a sufficiently serious breach.

117 Case C-140/97 *Walter Rechberger, Renate Greindl, Hermann Hofmeister and Others v Republik Österreich* [1999] ECR I-3499 paras 17, 18 (question 6).

118 Council Directive 90/314/EEC of 13 June 1990 on package travel, package holidays and package tours [1990] OJ L158/59.

bankruptcy, whatever the causes of it might be. Therefore the Court held that liability for the Member State could not be precluded by imprudent conduct on the part of the travel organizer or by the occurrence of exceptional and unforeseeable events. The Court however also indicated that such circumstances could possibly preclude the existence of a direct causal link if they presented an obstacle to the refund of money paid over or to the repatriation of consumers even if the guarantee system had been implemented by the Member State in accordance with the Directive.[119]

It seems to follow from *Rechberger* that competing events contributing to cause harm will not, for the purposes of an action for damages from the Member State, preclude liability for the Member State where a direct causal link between the breach attributable to that state and the occurrence of harm can be established. The failure of Austria to implement Article 7 of the Directive prejudiced the effects of the omission of the travel organizer to have a sufficient bank guarantee in place. Consequently Austria could be held liable irrespective of the omission of the travel organizer. To put it differently, there was no relevantly competing cause. It thus seems from *Rechberger* that competing events contributing to cause harm may preclude liability for the Member State only to the extent that those events would cause harm independently of the breach of EU law attributable to the Member State. **6.062**

It is important however to notice the final qualification added by the Court: if those competing causes of harm would still have caused the harm at issue in the event that the Directive had been properly implemented by the Member State, then they might preclude liability on the part of the Member State. As in *Brinkmann* it seems the Court was referring to the *conditio sine qua non* test: if a relevant hypothetical scenario leads to the same result as the actual scenario, the hypothetical alternative can be of no consequence to the causation assessment.[120] **6.063**

It has been mentioned above that some guidance of a substantive nature was offered in *Leth*. The holdings of the Court in that case will now be examined in some detail. **6.064**

> The claimant, Ms Leth, owned and lived on a property which was situated within the security zone of Vienna-Schwechat airport. The airport was extended and developed through a number of projects for which no environmental impact assessments were **6.065**

119 *Rechberger* (n 117) paras 73–76. Paragraph 76 is not easily interpreted, as it contains double negations.

120 Cf. *Brinkmann* (n 110) para. 29. The difference is of course that the comparison in *Brinkmann* pertained to causation between the breach of EU law by the Member State and harm incurred, while in *Rechberger* it pertained to causation between the competing cause and harm incurred.

carried out. In a decision on certain extensions of the airport the Minister-President of *Land* Niederösterreich stated that no environmental impact assessment procedure was necessary in relation to the continued development of the airport.

Ms Leth brought an action against Austria and *Land* Niederösterreich for compensation for the decrease in value of her property resulting from aircraft noise and for a declaration of liability in damages for future harm incurred. Ms Leth contended that the failure to carry out environmental impact assessments constituted a breach of Directive 85/337.[121] On appeal the Supreme Court of Austria referred the case to the European Court of Justice for a preliminary ruling on, inter alia, whether Article 3 of the Directive was to be interpreted as meaning that the environmental impact assessment serves to protect an individual against pecuniary damage as a result of a decrease in the value of property.

6.066 With regard to the objective of protection (German: *Schutzzweck*) pursued by the Directive, the Court of Justice held that the Directive conferred on the individuals concerned a right to have the effects on the environment of a project under examination assessed by the competent services, and that the prevention of pecuniary damage was covered by the objective of protection pursued by the Directive insofar as such damage was a direct economic consequence of the environmental effects of the project.[122] In respect of cases where pecuniary damage has been incurred the Court cited settled case law according to which Member States were under an obligation to nullify the unlawful consequences of a breach of EU law, e.g., through reparation in damages where the conditions for such liability were met.[123]

6.067 Further, the Court of Justice recognized that it was a matter for the national court to ascertain whether there was a direct causal link, in accordance with the guidelines laid down by the Court. To that end, the Court held, the nature of the rule breached must be taken into account. Article 3 of the Directive prescribed an assessment of the environmental impact of a public or private project, but neither laid down the substantive rules in relation to the balancing of the environmental effects with other factors nor prohibited the completion of projects which were liable to have negative effects on the environment. Those characteristics, the Court held, suggested that the failure to carry out the assessment prescribed by Article 3 of the Directive did not, in principle, by itself constitute the reason for the decrease in the value of Ms Leth's

---

121 Council Directive 85/337/EEC of 27 June 1985 on the assessment of the effects of certain public and private projects on the environment [1985] OJ L175/40, as amended by Council Directive 97/11/EC of 3 March 1997 [1997] OJ L73/5 and by Directive 2003/35/EC of the European Parliament and of the Council of 26 May 2003 [2003] OJ L156/17.

122 *Leth* (n 107) para. 36.

123 Ibid., paras 37, 40.

property.[124] The Court therefore ruled that such a breach of the Directive did not – under EU law and without prejudice to rules of national law which were less restrictive – by itself confer on individuals a right to compensation for purely pecuniary damage caused by a decrease in the value of property as a result of the environmental effects of that project. However, the Court added, it was for the national court to determine whether the requirements of EU law applicable to the right to compensation, including the existence of a direct causal link, had been satisfied.[125]

The Court evidently used a two-tier assessment in *Leth*. It was first established that pecuniary damage was covered by the objective of protection of the EU rule at issue, in accordance with the requirement laid down in national law. The Court very clearly took the view that this was a matter of interpretation of EU law. This is very interesting as it has been debated whether so-called protective scope theories included in national substantive causation assessments can be allowed to apply in actions for damages from a Member State.[126] It follows from *Leth* that they can be allowed.[127] It must accordingly be possible to conclude that where the interest harmed is not covered by the objective of protection of the EU rule breached, defendants will be able to argue that the Member State cannot be held liable in damages for harm caused to individuals by a breach.[128] For the sake of clarity however this does not mean that the Member States should all apply protective scope theories to actions for damages brought by individuals against the state for a breach of EU law. If it is not settled under national law that such a test applies to similar actions, the restriction constituted by its application to an action based on EU law – and not to similar actions based on national law – would be contrary to the EU law principle of equivalence. **6.068**

The second tier of the assessment in *Leth* was to establish whether there was a direct causal link between the breach of the rule and the harm incurred. Even though the Court indicated that the national court's assessment of whether there was a 'direct causal link' was to be carried out 'in accordance with the guidelines laid down by the Court', the guidelines offered were few. It was clear from the judgment that factual causation must be assessed: the obligation to carry out an environmental impact assessment laid down in the rule **6.069**

124 Ibid., paras 45–46.

125 Ibid., Operative part.

126 See Assimakis P Komninos, *EC Private Antitrust Enforcement* (Hart Publishing, 2008) 209.

127 However, do compare *Leth* to case C-557/12 *Kone AG and Others v ÖBB-Infrastruktur AG* EU:C:2014:1317, discussed in Section 7.D.I.

128 The precise legal meaning of this observation is not uncontroversial either. Prechal (n 6) 298 takes the view that this assessment 'is part and parcel of the first condition [for Member State liability], i.e. the (intended) grant of rights'.

breached did not in itself guarantee that the balancing of the environmental effects identified in that impact assessment against other interests would have been favourable to the claimant.[129] In other words it had to be established that the breach of the rule had in fact caused the value of the claimant's property to diminish. The Court also instructed the national court to take into account the nature of the rule breached.[130] This can be interpreted as the introduction of an element of legal causation, but the reasoning of the Court in the relevant paragraph is also open to the interpretation that the Court was simply illustrating the difficulty of establishing factual causation under the circumstances.[131] Notwithstanding which interpretation is preferred the Court did come very close to actually holding that there was no direct causal link between the breach of EU law and the harm incurred by Ms Leth, but left it to the national court to have the final say.

6.070 Finally, in *Danske Slagterier* and in *Fuß* the Court of Justice discussed German law pursuant to which damages were not payable to claimants who had failed to avert loss and harm by using other available remedies.[132] As reflected by Advocate General Tesauro such rules are not easily categorized, they can both serve as limitations of access to court or as specific causation tests.[133] Here they have been discussed in Section 6.C.I.a and reference is made to that discussion, beginning in paragraph 6.028. The rules at issue may also be categorized as pertaining to the duty to mitigate loss.[134] See paragraph 6.086 on that duty in the context of damages from a Member State.

6.071 To summarize there has been little guidance from the Court of Justice on the substantive content of the direct causal link criterion. It was held in *Leth* that the nature of the rule had to be taken into account,[135] but that holding may have been intended only to illustrate the importance of contemplating the practical consequences of the breach in order to distinguish instances of a direct causal nexus from mere sequences of events. In the cases where the Court of Justice has stepped in to make remarks on the existence of a direct causal link (i.e., *Brinkmann*, *Leth*, *AGM*, and *Fuß*) it seems to have applied a test of causal capacity, i.e., that the tortious act or omission at issue was capable of harming the claimant in the alleged way – which is arguably a *conditio sine qua non* ('but for') test although the Court has never referred to that

129 *Leth* (n 107) paras 45–46 and Operative part.
130 Ibid., para. 46.
131 On the concept of legal causation and the distinction between legal and factual causation see para. 3.056 with references.
132 See *Danske Slagterier* (n 53) paras 58–69; and *Fuß* (n 33) paras 71–90.
133 *Brasserie* (n 16) Opinion of AG Tesauro para. 100.
134 *Danske Slagterier* (n 53) Opinion of AG Trstenjak para. 123.
135 *Leth* (n 107) para. 46.

formula.[136] In that regard it further follows from *Rechberger* that competing events contributing to cause harm may preclude liability for the Member State only to the extent that those events would cause harm independently of the breach of EU law attributable to the Member State.

A certain level of correspondence between actions under Article 340(2) TFEU and actions for damages from a Member State seems to be present. Perhaps this should not be surprising, considering the alignment of the two actions in the wake of *Brasserie* and *Bergaderm*.[137] A number of cross-citations to case law on the respective actions can indeed be found in the judgments of the Court, e.g., in *FII*, where the Court held with regard to the requirement of a direct causal link that it was for the national court to assess whether the loss and damage claimed flows sufficiently directly from the breach of Community law to render the state liable to make it good, citing *Dumortier frères*.[138] However, there is an important difference between the two actions which does not only apply to the condition of causation: for the purposes of Article 340(2) TFEU only the EU – and specifically the EU Courts – have the power to put flesh on the bones of the condition of causation. It is respectfully submitted that the EU Courts should take it upon themselves to meet this challenge. For the purposes of actions for damages from a Member State it is by contrast within the power of the European Court of Justice to decide on whether to prescribe a detailed substantive content of the condition of causation, and it is for the national courts to ask the Court of Justice to do so. So far however, the Court has been content to allow the substantive causation test to be governed by national law albeit subject to the EU law principles of equivalence and effectiveness. Coming back to the issue of whether causation is governed by EU law or by national law, and the different views on that issue submitted by Aalto on the one hand and Tridimas, Biondi and Farley on the other hand, it thus seems the answer remains somewhere in the middle. **6.072**

b. *Causation and passing-on*

For Gamma claimants as well as for Beta claimants, an action for damages from the Member State may be either an alternative or a complement to an action for repayment of charges levied in breach of EU law. For the very reason of lack of a direct nexus, several EU jurisdictions will have no action for **6.073**

136 Cf. para. 3.060.

137 Case C-352/98 P *Laboratoires pharmaceutiques Bergaderm SA and Jean-Jacques Goupil v Commission of the European Communities* [2000] ECR I-5291.

138 *FII* (n 106) para. 218; joined cases 64 and 113/76, 167 and 239/78, 27, 28 and 45/79 *P Dumortier frères SA and others v Council of the European Communities* [1979] ECR 3091. It was also remarked by the Court that *Dumortier frères* concerned Art. 340(2) TFEU. Cf. also *Danfoss* (n 2) Opinion of AG Kokott paras 74–83, to be discussed in sub-section 6.C.II.b.

repayment available to Gamma.[139] Under such circumstances an action for damages from the Member State may be the only option. Therefore it may be disappointing that there is no EU case law on the condition of causation as such and the position of Gamma claimants. As in actions under Article 340(2) TFEU, in connection with which causation issues and passing-on were discussed in Section 3.D.II, it is difficult to make predictions as to the probable approach of the European Court of Justice if faced with a question on the condition of causation in the context of an action for damages from the Member State brought by a Gamma claimant. Obviously Gamma will be more vulnerable to arguments connected to the lack of proximity or the influence of competing causes for harm than Beta. In the analysis of case law on actions under Article 340(2) TFEU it was noted that the General Court emphasized the uncertainty of relevant economic parameters.[140] As the onus of proving causation rests on the claimant, Gamma will likewise need to overcome this uncertainty in order to be successful with an action for damages from a Member State. These difficulties cannot in themselves be overcome by any reference to the EU principle of effectiveness or the like.

6.074 Nevertheless it is evident from the discussion in Section 6.C.II.a that the EU law principles of equivalence and effectiveness will apply to an action for damages from the Member State brought by Gamma, and that aspects of national causation tests are subject to scrutiny under those principles. Hence national causation tests applicable in actions for damages from a Member State must not be less favourable to Gamma claimants than those applicable in similar domestic actions, and must not render the exercise of rights conferred on Gamma claimants by EU law virtually impossible or excessively difficult.[141]

6.075 In the latter regard it arguably follows from *Danfoss*,[142] discussed in some detail in Sections 5.C.II. and 6.C.I.b, that national rules that would *a priori* preclude the possibility of a direct causal link between the levy of a charge in breach of EU law by the Member State and harm incurred by Gamma, to who the burden of that charge has been passed on, would be contrary to the principle of effectiveness. *Danfoss* concerned access to court but the second question asked by the national court is relevant here too. The national court asked the Court of Justice whether a national legal rule, according to which a claim for damages brought by a Gamma claimant would be rejected (i.e., denied access to court) on the ground that the existence of a direct causal link between the levying of a charge by the Member State and the damage suffered

---

139 See para. 5.058.

140 See Section 3.D.II, e.g., the critique in para. 3.060.

141 On the EU law principles of equivalence and effectiveness see Section 2.D.

142 *Danfoss* (n 2). See paras 5.030 and 6.042 for facts and legal issues raised.

by Gamma was automatically ruled out, was compatible with EU law.[143] The Court replied that such a legal rule was compatible with EU law only if Gamma was able, on the basis of national law, to bring a corresponding claim against Beta and provided that it would not be virtually impossible or excessively difficult for Gamma to obtain compensation from Beta.[144] It would thus be contrary to the EU principle of effectiveness to reject a Gamma action under other circumstances. In that regard the Court of Justice held that if it were to prove impossible or excessively difficult for Beta to compensate Gamma – in particular in the case of the insolvency of Beta – the principle of effectiveness required that Gamma be able to bring the claim for damages against the state directly, without that state being legitimately able to rely on the lack of a direct causal link between the levying of the duty which was not due and the damage suffered by Gamma.[145]

Insofar as the substantive legal content of the national causation test applicable to an action for damages from the Member State brought by Gamma would entail an element that would *a priori* preclude causation, the practical effect of such a substantive element would be no different than a rule barring Gamma from access to court. Therefore it is submitted that it follows from *Danfoss* that such an element would likewise be contrary to the principle of effectiveness. It is interesting in this regard to notice that the Opinion of Advocate General Kokott did not as such put emphasis on the distinction between limitations of access to court and substantive causation tests, but focused on the strictness of the national rule: **6.076**

> What has to be clarified is namely whether the condition regarding the direct causal link is to be interpreted so narrowly that, as the Danish Government in particular argues, it can be deemed to exist only in the relationship with the taxable person, but not with the person to whom the excise duty levied contrary to European Union law was passed on by the taxable person. … **6.077**
>
> The criterion cited by the Danish Government is … based on a stricter concept of causality, since it results in the claim to compensation enshrined in European Union law being systematically withheld from those who have had to pay the charge levied contrary to European Union law … without each case being considered on its merits. …
>
> The fact that the number of those who can claim compensation may be indeterminate – at least initially – does not call the possibility of direct causality into question.[146]

143 Ibid., para. 18 (question 2). For a discussion of this aspect of the case see sub-section 6.C.I.b.
144 Ibid., Operative part para. 2.
145 Ibid., para. 38.
146 Ibid., Opinion of AG Kokott paras 74–81.

6.078 Consequently the Advocate General submitted that the *a priori* ruling out of a direct causal link was not compatible with EU law.[147] This view furthermore corresponds to the holding of the Court of Justice in *CMC* that it could not be ruled out that institutions of the EU, or their agents or officials, might cause damage to 'third persons' and that it should therefore be open to such persons to bring an action for damages under Article 340(2).[148] It therefore seems possible to conclude that substantive causation rules *a priori* precluding a direct causal link between the levy of a charge in breach of EU law and harm incurred by Gamma are incompatible with EU law, irrespective of whether the limitation at issue is classified as a restriction of access to court or as a substantive criterion in causation under national law. A real assessment of facts and evidence would be required.

6.079 Be this as it may, it will still be a great challenge for Gamma to produce evidence strong enough to convince the national court that there is a direct causal link between the breach of EU law by the Member State and harm incurred by Gamma. The prospects of success will depend on market conditions and other circumstances in the individual case. Ideally it can be proved that Beta has resold unaltered goods applying a simple cost-plus pricing policy.[149] In more complicated circumstances Gamma may be facing severe difficulties.

III. The defence of passing-on

6.080 The third legal issue triggered by the passing-on problem is the estimation of damages.[150] This is perhaps the area most commonly associated with passing-on, as this is the context in which the defence of passing-on can be invoked. The defence of passing-on is an argument according to which the damages payable for a breach of law should be reduced to the extent that the claimant has been able to pass on the harm incurred to the next level in the supply chain. In actions for damages from a Member State the defence of passing-on has not yet been scrutinized by the Court of Justice. Nevertheless it will be possible to make a few remarks based on findings of the Court with regard to damages actions pursuant to Article 340(2) and damages actions for a breach of competition law respectively. Before proceeding to that analysis some general observations on the estimation of damages in the context of an action

147 Ibid., Opinion of AG Kokott para. 83.

148 Case 118/83 *CMC Cooperativa muratori e cementisti and others v Commission of the European Communities* [1985] ECR 2325 para. 31.

149 Cf. Section 1.A.IV.

150 Cf. Section 1.A.III.

brought against a Member State for a breach of EU law will be submitted in order to give a fuller view.

a. General observations on the estimation of damages

EU case law on the estimation of damages in the context of actions brought against a Member State is strikingly scarce. The Court of Justice has chosen a distinct non-interventionist approach, apparent e.g. in *Fuß* where the Court was explicitly called upon to elaborate on the form of reparation due and the method of calculation of such reparation[151] but was content to observe that there was nothing in national law that seemed incompatible with the principle of effectiveness and that it was only therefore for the national court to ensure that the redress ordered was compliant with the principle of equivalence.[152] In *Combinatie Spijker Infrabouw*, the Court similarly held that 'the case-law of the Court of Justice has not yet set out, as regards review of the award of public contracts, more detailed criteria on the basis of which damage must be determined and estimated', and therefore 'it is for the legal order of each Member State to determine the criteria on the basis of which damage arising from an infringement of EU law on the award of public contracts must be determined and estimated ... provided the principles of equivalence and effectiveness are complied with'.[153] On the basis of the available case law it might therefore be concluded that the Court of Justice is content to make reference to the principle of equivalence and is reluctant to elaborate on the requirements flowing from the principle of effectiveness. It simply seems the national legal systems scrutinized have not given the Court reason to intervene. **6.081**

Brasserie stands out as the Court elaborated on 'the actual extent of reparation' payable by the Member States in that case.[154] The Court held: **6.082**

> Reparation for loss or damage caused to individuals as a result of breaches of Community law must be commensurate with the loss or damage sustained so as to ensure the effective protection for their rights.
>
> In the absence of relevant Community provisions, it is for the domestic legal system of each Member State to set the criteria for determining the extent of reparation. However, those criteria must not be less favourable than those applying to similar

151 *Fuß* (n 33) para. 91.

152 Ibid., paras 95–98.

153 Case C-568/08 *Combinatie Spijker Infrabouw-De Jonge Konstruktie and Others v Provincie Drenthe* [2010] ECR I-12655 paras 88, 90.

154 *Brasserie* (n 16) para. 81 and the preceding heading.

claims based on domestic law and must not be such as in practice to make it impossible or excessively difficult to obtain reparation.[155]

6.083 From these points of departure the Court elaborated on the implications of the principles of equivalence and effectiveness[156] and on the meaning of reparation which is 'commensurate with the loss or damage sustained'.[157] The Court's findings with the principle of effectiveness will be examined below first, and then its findings with the principle of equivalence.

6.084 With regard to the heads of damages available the Court explained that national limitations on the types of harm for which damages were payable or on the heads of damages available were subject to scrutiny under the EU law principle of effectiveness.[158] In German law reparation in damages was available only for 'certain, specifically protected individual interests, for example property' and not e.g. for loss of profit. In that regard the Court held that the '[t]otal exclusion of loss of profit as a head of damage for which reparation may be awarded in the case of a breach of Community law cannot be accepted ... in the context of economic or commercial litigation, such a total exclusion of loss of profit would be such as to make reparation of damage practically impossible'.[159] Interestingly these holdings do not prohibit the exclusion of loss of profit *per se*, in specific circumstances, only its 'total' exclusion. It is not clear from *Brasserie* under what circumstances it would be compatible with EU law to exclude loss of profit from the available heads of damages.

6.085 With regard to the estimation of damages as such the Court has held, albeit in the context of sex discrimination, that national limitations to the amount of damages payable for a breach of EU law could not be upheld 'since it limits the amount of compensation *a priori* to a level which is not necessarily consistent with the requirement of ensuring real equality of opportunity through adequate reparation'.[160] There seems to be no reason, it is submitted, to limit

155 Ibid., paras 82–83.

156 On the principles of equivalence and effectiveness see Section 2.D.

157 Cf. also case C-271/91 *M Helen Marshall v Southampton and South-West Hampshire Area Health Authority* (*Marshall II*) [1993] ECR I-4367 para. 26, where the Court held that compensation for a discriminatory dismissal contrary to Council Directive 76/207/EEC of 9 February 1976 on the implementation of the principle of equal treatment for men and women as regards access to employment, vocational training and promotion, and working conditions [1976] OJ L39/40 'must be adequate, in that it must enable the loss and damage actually sustained as a result of the discriminatory dismissal to be made good in full'.

158 Consequently it cannot be correct to submit that the heads of damages are 'all defined by national law' as in Aalto (n 13) 199.

159 *Brasserie* (n 16) paras 86–87.

160 *Marshall II* (n 157) para. 30; but cf. the Opinion of AG van Gerven paras 17–18. See also case C-180/95 *Nils Draehmpaehl v Urania Immobilienservice OHG* [1997] ECR I-2195 paras 38–43.

the scope of that holding to sex discrimination law. If this presumption is correct national limitations of the amount payable are generally incompatible with the principle of effectiveness.

It would not however be incompatible with EU law to require for injured parties to 'show reasonable diligence in limiting the extent of the loss or damage, or risk having to bear the damage himself'.[161] In principle national requirements related to the mitigation of loss, including the reduction of damages awards to the extent that a claimant has failed to show reasonable diligence, would therefore seem to be compatible with EU law.[162] By way of exception the Court of Justice held in *Metallgesellschaft* that it was incompatible with the principle of effectiveness to reject or reduce claims for reparation 'solely because the persons concerned had not applied for a tax advantage which national law denied them, with a view to challenging the refusal of the tax authorities by means of the legal remedies provided for that purpose, invoking the primacy and direct effect of Community law'.[163] Hence it was not possible for the UK to avoid liability by reference to plausible possibilities of challenging defects in its own system of taxation by reason of their incompatibility with EU law. **6.086**

The availability of interest was not covered by *Brasserie* but was brought to the attention of the Court in *Marshall II*, where it held: **6.087**

> With regard to … the award of interest, suffice it to say that full compensation for the loss and damage sustained as a result of discriminatory dismissal cannot leave out of account factors, such as the effluxion of time, which may in fact reduce its value. The award of interest, in accordance with the applicable national rules, must therefore be regarded as an essential component of compensation for the purposes of restoring real equality of treatment.[164]

The Court likewise held in *Metallgesellschaft* (citing *Marshall II*) that the circumstances were such that the award of interest was essential to reparation of the harm caused.[165] However, perhaps surprisingly, no general holding was made on the availability of interest in actions for damages from a Member State in *Metallgesellschaft* or in any other case known to this author. It has nevertheless been opined by Advocate General Cruz Villalón that effective **6.088**

161 *Brasserie* (n 16) paras 84–85.

162 This issue is closely related to issues of causation but can also in certain jurisdictions bar claimants who have failed to avert harm by using a legal remedy. For a discussion of such limitations and relevant case law see the discussion beginning at para. 6.028.

163 *Metallgesellschaft* (n 63) para. 106. See also *Danske Slagterier* (n 53) para. 63.

164 *Marshall II* (n 157) para. 31. See also the Opinion of AG van Gerven paras 22–28.

165 *Metallgesellschaft* (n 63) paras 92–95.

compensation should include an award of interest.[166] In light of recent case law on interest in actions for repayment of charges levied in breach of EU law[167] it seems reasonable to presume that the Advocate General will be proved right.

6.089 Finally we turn to the principle of equivalence. The case law shows that special heads of damages available in damages actions against the Member State based on national law must also be available in damages actions based on EU law. The Court held in *Brasserie* that 'an award of exemplary damages pursuant to a claim or an action founded on Community law cannot be ruled out if such damages could be awarded pursuant to a similar claim or action founded on domestic law'.[168]

6.090 In sum an award of damages payable by a Member State for a breach of EU law must be commensurate with the loss or damage sustained, but the Court of Justice has not been very stringent in its approach. Scrutiny of national rules against the EU law principles of equivalence and effectiveness has rarely resulted in any intervention by the Court. The main points made are that a total exclusion of loss of profit is incompatible with the principle of effectiveness and that special damages available for a breach of national law must, in accordance with the principle of equivalence, be available also for a breach of EU law. It is finally submitted, although this has not been unequivocally settled by the Court of Justice, that interest should be payable.

b. The defence of passing-on

6.091 In the context of an action for damages from a Member State the Court of Justice has not yet been seized with the issue of the defence of passing-on as such. The passing-on problem was imminent in *Danfoss*,[169] but *Danfoss* only concerned access for Gamma claimants to bring an action and consequently the defence of passing-on was not an issue. This discussion of the defence of passing-on in the context of actions for damages from a Member State must therefore be limited to making suggestions on the basis of adjacent actions. The proper point of departure to that end is, here as well as in the context of repayment of charges levied in breach of EU law,[170] that the defence of passing-on is a restriction to a right conferred on individuals by EU law. For the sake of clarity it is stressed that in the context of damages actions brought

166 *Combinatie Spijker Infrabouw* (n 153) Opinion of AG Cruz Villalón para. 111.

167 See paras 5.075–5.076.

168 *Brasserie* (n 16) para. 89.

169 *Danfoss* (n 2).

170 Case C-147/01 *Weber's Wine World Handels-GmbH and others v Abgabenberufungskommission Wien* [2003] ECR I-11365 para. 95.

against a Member State for a breach of EU law a defence of passing-on must first apply under national law. If the defence does not apply under national law, the issue of whether the defence is compatible with EU law does not, as such, arise. The legal question here is therefore if a defence of passing-on, which is available to defendants under applicable national law, would be compatible with EU law in this context.

In Sections 3.E.II and 3.E.III it was understood that for the purposes of actions under Article (now) 340(2) TFEU the European Court of Justice has accepted a defence of passing-on at law. In that context it was further settled that it was for the defendant institutions invoking the defence of passing-on to prove that the loss had or could have been passed on. It was finally noted that the Court had, in all cases brought before it, dismissed the defence of passing-on on the facts. Bearing in mind the inclination of the Court of Justice to find a consistent approach to actions for damages for a breach of EU law whether they are brought against the EU or against a Member State, it might be expected that the findings of the Court under Article 340(2) TFEU would be used as guidance if the defence of passing-on was invoked in the context of an action for damages from a Member State. The more recent Directive 2014/104/EU on competition law damages[171] likewise endorses the defence of passing-on for the purposes of competition damages actions, usually brought against private individuals (undertakings). Under Article 13 of the Directive the defence of passing-on is accepted at law but the burden of proving that an overcharge has been passed on is on the defendant.[172] Furthermore, in the context of Member State liability, the same applies (albeit with more detail) in the context of actions against Member States for the repayment of charges levied in breach of EU law.[173] **6.092**

In light of this case law and Directive 2014/104/EU it is submitted that in the interest of consistency the Court should have no choice but to accept a defence of passing-on available under national law to apply also to actions for damages from a Member State. The details of such a defence should likewise follow the patterns emerging from adjacent actions, e.g., by placing the onus of proving passing-on on the Member State. Relevant similarities and differences in the approach to the defence of passing-on chosen under EU law will be discussed further in Chapter 9. **6.093**

---

171 Directive 2014/104/EU (n 95).

172 See further sub-section 7.E.II.b.

173 See the summary of relevant case law in paras 5.164–5.168 and cf. the preceding sections for more details on the case law.

D. CONCLUSIONS AND SUGGESTIONS

6.094 An action for damages can be brought against a Member State alongside or instead of an action for repayment of charges levied in breach of EU law,[174] the latter being the more common in passing-on situations. Claimants thus have an option to bring an action for damages against the Member State as an alternative or complementary cause of action within the same proceedings as a restitutionary action. There is nevertheless very little case law which could serve to indicate how the Court would approach the passing-on problem in the context of an action for damages from the Member State. Case law is limited to the second part of *Danfoss*[175] which concerned access to court for Gamma claimants.

6.095 It has been submitted on the basis of *Danfoss* that Gamma claimants cannot be barred from bringing an action for damages directly against the Member State for reasons related to passing-on. Nonetheless it will still be a great challenge for Gamma to produce evidence strong enough to convince the national court that there is a direct causal link between the breach of EU law by the Member State and harm incurred by Gamma. The prospects of success will depend on market conditions and other circumstances in the individual case.

6.096 With regard to the defence of passing-on it has been submitted that in the interest of consistency with adjacent actions the Court should have no choice but to accept a defence of passing-on available under national law to apply also to actions for damages from a Member State. The details of such a defence should likewise follow the patterns emerging from adjacent actions, e.g., by placing the onus of proving passing-on on the Member State.

174 *Comateb* (n 1).
175 *Danfoss* (n 2).

Part IV

PASSING-ON IN HORIZONTAL ACTIONS

7

PASSING-ON IN COMPETITION DAMAGES

A. CHAPTER OUTLINE

Thus far the actions covered have concerned liability for the EU and the Member States, both being instances of liability of a public authority. Both the EU and the Member States have a direct link to the rules of the EU legal system, either as one of the Masters of the Treaties or as a creation of the Treaties. For private individuals[1] matters are more complicated and the capacity of EU law to impose legal obligations directly on private individuals has consequently been the subject of extensive scholarly debate.[2] Nevertheless **7.001**

1 The term 'private individual' will be used throughout this text (with the exception of quotes using different terminology). It is intended to serve as shorthand for any kind of natural or legal person capable of carrying rights and/or obligations pursuant to EU law, who is not an emanation of the Member State within the meaning of EU law. The criteria used for identifying legal bodies as emanations of the Member State within the meaning of EU law were laid down by the European Court of Justice in case C-188/89 *A Foster and others v British Gas plc* [1990] ECR I-3313 para. 20.

2 Contributions include Ulf Bernitz and Norbert Reich, 'Case No. A 268/04, The Labour Court, Sweden (Arbetsdomstolen) Judgment No. 89/09 of 2 December 2009, Laval un Partneri Ltd. v. Svenska Bygggnadsarbetareförbundet et al.' (2011) 48 *Common Market Law Review* 603; the critical Paul Kirchhof, 'The Legal Structure of the European Union as a Union of States' in Armin von Bogdandy and Jürgen Bast (eds), *Principles of European Constitutional Law* (Hart Publishing, 2006); Miriam Lenz, Dora Sif Tynes and Lorna Young, 'Horizontal What? Back to Basics' (2000) 25 *European Law Review* 509; Pierre Pescatore, 'The Doctrine of "Direct Effect": An Infant Disease of Community Law' (1983) 8 *European Law Review* 155;

it is well known that, on occasion, the European Court of Justice has interpreted EU law in such a way that it imposes legal obligations on individuals. For instance the Court famously held in *van Gend en Loos* that:

7.002 the Community constitutes a new legal order of international law for the benefit of which the states have limited their sovereign rights, albeit within limited fields, and the subjects of which comprise not only Member States but also their nationals. Independently of the legislation of Member States, Community law therefore not only imposes obligations on individuals but is also intended to confer upon them rights which become part of their legal heritage.[3]

7.003 One instance of such legal obligations is the liability in damages for a breach of EU competition law, which is explored in this chapter.

7.004 The rule that it must be possible to hold private individuals liable in damages for a breach of EU competition law was introduced – albeit not unequivocally – in *Courage*,[4] a judgment delivered in 2001. In 2014 Directive 2014/104/EU was adopted and now provides harmonized details of the action.[5] Directive 2014/104/EU harmonizes some aspects of the passing-on problem and further guidelines from the Commission are expected shortly.[6] In fact, the field of competition damages is where passing-on has been most intensely debated. In EU competition law it may even be said that the development of the action for damages against private individuals and the development of an approach to the passing-on problem (for the purposes of EU competition law) have been parallel and simultaneous. This is because the earliest case law and now the legislation through which the action has been developed have always included some reference or allusion to the passing-on problem. In the case law these were ambiguous hints, as we will see. In the recently adopted Directive 2014/104/EU there are provisions dealing explicitly and specifically with passing-on.

Sacha Prechal, *Directives in EC Law* (2nd edn, Oxford EC Law Library, Oxford University Press, Oxford 2006) 255–70; Takis Tridimas, 'Black, White and Shades of Grey: Horizontality of Directives Revisited' (2002) 21 *Yearbook of European Law* 327; and Bruno de Witte, 'Direct Effect, Primacy, and the Nature of the Legal Order' in Paul Craig and Gráinne de Búrca (eds), *The Evolution of EU Law* (2nd edn, Oxford University Press 2011).

3 Case 26/62 *NV Algemene Transport- en Expeditie Onderneming van Gend & Loos v Netherlands Inland Revenue Administration* [1963] ECR 1, 12.

4 Case C-453/99 *Courage Ltd v Bernard Crehan and Bernard Crehan v Courage Ltd and Others* [2001] ECR I-6297.

5 Directive 2014/104/EU of the European Parliament and of the Council of 26 November 2014 on certain rules governing actions for damages under national law for infringements of the competition law provisions of the Member States and of the European Union [2014] OJ L349/1.

6 See para. 7.182.

The three legal issues triggered by the passing-on problem (access to court, substantive proximity and the estimation of damages[7]) will be examined in turn, with a view to understand the choices made for the purposes of competition damages. Before examining these issues however, it is appropriate to trace the development of the action for damages for a breach of EU competition law in Section 7.B. The case law in which the availability of this action was established will be presented and discussed first. Thereafter there will be an overview presentation of Directive 2014/104/EU and the accompanying soft-law instruments, including a very brief legislative background. In that context a few general problems of competition damages will also be discussed, e.g., whether there is room for a national criterion of fault in damages liability for a breach of EU competition law. **7.005**

The subsequent Section 7.C will concern access to court. In that section the general impact of EU law requirements of effective judicial protection on national limitations of access to court will be addressed, in light of both Article 47 of the EU Charter of Fundamental Rights and of the dual EU law test of equivalence and effectiveness. Turning then to access for Gamma claimants[8] it will be observed that the EU approach to that issue has been developed in contrast to the approach chosen in federal US antitrust law (in which Gamma claims are barred from bringing an action for damages in respect of harm passed on to them, i.e., from invoking passing-on as a 'sword'[9]). By reason of the importance and influence of the US approach – both as an inspiration and as a deterrent – a comparative perspective will be offered in which the US approach and US debate on access for Gamma will be presented and discussed. The approach chosen for the purposes of EU law will then be juxtaposed with the US debate, introducing also the corresponding EU debate. **7.006**

In Section 7.D the element of substantive proximity (i.e., in the context of damages, causation) will be addressed. As in Chapter 6 it will be observed that this condition for liability is primarily governed not by EU law but by national law, albeit subject to the EU law principles of equivalence and effectiveness. The presentation here will therefore focus on the impact of those principles on national causation tests, and more specifically on the implications of such national causation tests on the prospects of success in actions brought by Gamma. Some attention will also be devoted to recent developments in **7.007**

---

7 See Section 1.A.III.

8 In this book, Alpha signifies a tortfeasor or enriched party, Beta a party first burdened by loss arising from Alpha's breach of EU law, and Gamma any party downstream from Beta (including all from the party dealing directly with Beta to the final consumer) to whom the burden of that loss may have been passed on; see Section 1.B.

9 On the 'sword' and 'shield' metaphors cf. para. 1.009.

respect of so-called umbrella pricing and to implications of certain provisions of the new Directive.

7.008 In Section 7.E case law on the estimation of competition damages will be presented, but emphasis will be on the provisions and guidelines included in the new harmonized regime established through Directive 2014/104/EU and the accompanying soft-law instruments. Following these general observations the EU law approach with regard to the defence of passing-on (whereby Alpha argues that the damages payable should be reduced to the extent that Beta (or Gamma) has or could have passed on the harm incurred, i.e., passing-on as a 'shield') will be discussed extensively. Beginning with a sub-section on case law, emphasis will be on the new regime in which the defence of passing-on has been explicitly endorsed. The main arguments of the passing-on debate will be presented and examined in a final sub-section.

7.009 For the convenience of the reader there will be a summary with conclusions and suggestions in Section 7.F.

B. INTRODUCTION TO COMPETITION DAMAGES

I. Case law developments

7.010 The possibilities of seeking redress for harm incurred by reason of a breach of EU competition law have long been a concern of the EU, but the Commission has traditionally been content to leave it to the national laws of the Member States to provide appropriate private enforcement remedies.[10] The case law establishing the action for damages for a breach of EU competition law still remains limited, encompassing only a few cases – although the body of case

---

10 See e.g. Commission, 'La réparation des conséquences dommageables d'une violation des articles 85 et 86 du traité instituant la CEE' (1966) 1 série concurrence, which was a comparative study of such possibilities in six Member States (Arts 85 and 86 EC are now Arts 101 and 102 TFEU); and the Commission's reply in European Parliament, 'Written Question No. 519/72 by Mr Vredeling to the Commission of the European Communities' [1973] OJ C67/54, 55. See also John Temple Lang, 'Community Antitrust Law – Compliance and Enforcement' (1981) 18 *Common Market Law Review* 335, 337–43. The conclusion of the 1966 Commission study (at p. 5) was that redress was available in national law, albeit with certain variations. Plausibly, there was little incentive to harmonize in 1966, but with subsequent enlargements of the EU, it gradually grew stronger. For a brief history of the Commission's early investigations into competition damages see Folkert Wilman, *Private Enforcement of EU Law before National Courts: The EU Legislative Framework* (Elgar European Law and Practice, Edward Elgar Publishing 2015) 202–5. For an updated overview of the national damages regimes in Europe see Marios C Iacovides, *A 'More Economic Approach' to WTO Law's Relevant Market Definition, Trade Harm, and Quantification of Trade Effects and Countermeasures: A Normative Law and Economics Comparison with EU Competition Law* (Uppsala University (diss) 2016) 368–80.

law may be expected to increase once requests for preliminary rulings on provisions of Directive 2014/104/EU begin to be submitted to the European Court of Justice.

The case in which a right to damages was acknowledged by the Court of Justice was *Courage*, delivered on 20 September 2001. However, case law developments arguably began in *BRT* where the European Court of Justice held that: **7.011**

> the prohibitions of Articles 85(1) and 86 tend by their very nature to produce direct effects in relations between individuals, these Articles create direct rights in respect of the individuals concerned which the national courts must safeguard.[11] **7.012**

How, precisely, was this safeguarding expected to be carried out? Did Community law at this point require specific remedies to be available for the private enforcement of competition law? Should, e.g., national damages remedies available between private individuals in the event of a tortious breach of national law by one of them also be made available in the event of a breach of EU competition law?[12] This was plainly arguable in light of the horizontal direct effect of the relevant Treaty Articles, settled in *BRT*, and the ruling of the Court of Justice in the *Butter Buying Cruises* case according to which Community law required that it 'must be possible for every type of action provided for by national law to be available before the national courts for the purpose of ensuring observance of Community provisions having direct effect'.[13] Nevertheless, and although it was suggested that the Commission should move to harmonize the action for damages for a breach of competition law,[14] the existence and details of the remedy remained steadfastly governed by national law albeit subject to the developing case law on equivalence and effectiveness.[15] In 1993, in his Opinion in *Banks*, Advocate General van Gerven suggested the Court introduce a Community right to compensation in damages for a breach of Articles 65 and 66(7) ECSC.[16] The Advocate **7.013**

11 Case 127/73 *Belgische Radio en Televisie and société belge des auteurs, compositeurs et éditeurs v SV SABAM and NV Fonior* [1974] ECR 51 para. 16. Arts 85 and 86 EEC are now Arts 101 and 102 TFEU.

12 Cf. Section 2.B.III.

13 Case 158/80 *Rewe-Handelsgesellschaft Nord mbH and Rewe-Markt Steffen v Hauptzollamt Kiel (Butter Buying Cruises)* [1981] ECR 1805 para. 44 and Operative part para. 7.

14 E.g., by Temple Lang (n 10) 341. Temple Lang explained that the primary concern in early discussions was whether Articles (then) 85 and 86 of the Treaty were intended to protect the interests of individuals within the meaning of German tort law (i.e., whether they were *Schutzgesetzen*, cf. paras 3.012, 3.018 and 6.019). Temple Lang reported a judgment of the German Bundesgerichtshof in 1979 settling the matter for the purposes of the Member State concerned.

15 On the EU law principles of equivalence and effectiveness see Section 2.D.

16 Case C-128/92 *H J Banks & Co Ltd v British Coal Corporation* [1994] ECR I-1209. Arts 65 and 66(7) of the Treaty establishing the European Coal and Steel Community (ECSC) correspond to Arts 101 and 102 TFEU.

General opined that the legal basis for liability of Member States found by the European Court of Justice in *Francovich*[17] would serve equally well as basis for liability in damages for private individuals, at least insofar as the EU rule breached had horizontal direct effect.[18] The Court of Justice did not grasp the issue in *Banks*. In *Guérin*, delivered on 18 March 1997, the Court still relied on damages actions being available under national law:

7.014 [a]ny undertaking which considers that it has suffered damage as a result of restrictive practices may rely before the national courts, particularly where the Commission decides not to act on a complaint, on the rights conferred on it by Article 85(1) and Article 86 of the Treaty, which produce direct effect in relations between individuals … .[19]

7.015 Nor did Advocate General Mischo argue specifically for the introduction of a Community law liability in damages for private individuals for a breach of competition law in his Opinion in *Courage*. The issue was not any lack of such an action – it was available in the applicable law, being English law – but a bar to actions brought by co-contractors. The Advocate General focused on that bar, opining that it was incompatible with the EU law principle of effectiveness,[20] however without letting go of the traditional view that the national courts were 'entrusted with ensuring the legal protection which citizens derive from the direct effect of the provisions of Community law'.[21] The Advocate General thus did not suggest that Community law actually required the availability of an action for damages for a breach of EU law, only that rights be protected by the legal means available under national law. The Court of Justice went further in its judgment, which was delivered on 20 September 2001.

7.016 In 1991 Bernard Crehan concluded a contract for the lease of two public houses (pubs) in England. The pubs were owned by Inntrepreneur Estates Ltd (IEL), a company in the business of leasing pubs to tenants like Mr Crehan. IEL was owned to 50 per cent by Courage Ltd, a brewery holding 19 per cent of the UK market in sales of beer.

IEL used a standard form agreement according to which all tenants were obliged to buy their beer from Courage Ltd exclusively. The agreement specified a minimum quantity of specified beers that had to be ordered. The agreement also provided that the prices for the beer ordered were to be set by Courage Ltd. These terms were not negotiable.

17 Joined cases C-6/90 and 9/90 *Andrea Francovich and Daniela Bonifaci and others v Italian Republic* [1991] ECR I-5357.

18 *Banks* (n 16) Opinion of AG van Gerven paras 43–45. A similar argument was submitted by Clifford A Jones, *Private Enforcement of Antitrust Law in the EU, UK and USA* (Oxford University Press 1999) 78.

19 Case C-282/95 P *Guérin Automobiles v Commission of the European Communities* [1997] ECR I-1503 para. 39. Arts 85 and 86 EC are now Arts 101 and 102 TFEU.

20 *Courage* (n 4) Opinion of AG Mischo para. 55.

21 Ibid., para. 46.

> In 1993 Courage Ltd brought an action against Mr Crehan for GBP 15 266 for unpaid deliveries of beer.
>
> Mr Crehan objected that the beer tie in his agreement with IEL was contrary to Article 85 EC (now Article 101 TFEU) and counter-claimed for damages. Mr Crehan further argued that Courage Ltd sold its beers to independent tenants of pubs at prices that were substantially lower than those in the price list applicable for IEL tenants, and that this price difference reduced the profitability of his pubs, threatening to put him out of business.
>
> The Court of Appeal (England and Wales) (Civil Division) stressed that English law would not allow a party to an illegal agreement to claim damages from the other party. The Court of Appeal had previously held that Article 85 EC was intended to protect third parties, not parties to an agreement contrary to that article. Now the Court of Appeal was concerned that this bar to Mr Crehan's claim was possibly contrary to Community law. Therefore the Court of Appeal stayed proceedings and referred the case to the European Court of Justice for a preliminary ruling.

The Court of Justice began its argumentation by explaining that the Treaty had created its own legal order, which was integrated into the legal systems of the Member States and which their courts were bound to apply. The subjects of that legal order, the Court continued, were not only the Member States but also their nationals. The Court further recalled that just as Community law imposed burdens on individuals, it also intended to give rise to rights which become part of their legal assets. Such rights, the Court held, would arise not only where they were expressly granted by the Treaty but also by virtue of obligations which the Treaty imposed in a clearly defined manner both on individuals and on the Member States and the Community institutions. The Court of Justice further held that Article 85 EC constituted a fundamental provision which was essential for the accomplishment of the tasks entrusted to the Community and, in particular, for the functioning of the internal market.[22] **7.017**

The Court of Justice stressed that any agreements contrary to Article 85 EC were automatically void. Anyone could rely on that principle of automatic nullity, the Court continued, and courts were bound by it. Moreover, the Court noted, that Article produced direct effects in relations between individuals and created rights for the individuals concerned which the national courts must safeguard. Therefore, the Court held, any individual could rely on a breach of Article 85 EC before a national court, even where that individual was a party to a contract that was liable to restrict or distort competition within the meaning of that provision.[23] **7.018**

---

22 Ibid., paras 19–20.

23 Ibid., paras 21–22, 24.

7.019 On the issue of damages, the Court of Justice observed that it was the task of national courts to apply the provisions of Community law in areas within their jurisdiction, that they must ensure that those rules take full effect, and that they must protect the rights which they confer on individuals. In this context the Court held that the full effectiveness of Article 85 EC and, in particular, the practical effect of the prohibition therein would be put at risk if it were not open to any individual to claim damages for loss caused by a contract or by conduct liable to restrict or distort competition. To the contrary, the Court held, actions for damages before the national courts could make a significant contribution to the maintenance of effective competition in the Community. Therefore, the Court ruled, there should not be any absolute bar against such actions.[24]

7.020 The Court of Justice however added that in the absence of Community rules governing the matter it was for the domestic legal system of each Member State to designate the courts and tribunals having jurisdiction and to lay down the detailed procedural rules governing actions for safeguarding rights which individuals derived directly from Community law, provided that such rules were not less favourable than those governing similar domestic actions (principle of equivalence) and that they did not render practically impossible or excessively difficult the exercise of rights conferred by Community law (principle of effectiveness). In that regard, the Court of Justice pointed out that Community law did not prevent national courts from taking steps to ensure that the protection of the rights guaranteed by Community law did not entail the unjust enrichment of those who enjoyed them.[25]

7.021 The Court of Justice moreover recognized that a litigant should not profit from his own unlawful conduct. Therefore, and provided that the principles of equivalence and effectiveness were respected, the Court held that Community law did not preclude national law from denying a party who was found to bear significant responsibility for the distortion of competition the right to obtain damages from the other contracting party. To that end the national court should take into account the economic and legal context in which the parties found themselves and the respective bargaining power and conduct of the two parties to the contract. In particular it was for the national court to ascertain whether the party who claimed to have suffered loss through concluding a contract that was liable to restrict or distort competition found himself in a

24 Ibid., paras 25–28.

25 Ibid., paras 29–30. Para. 30, in which the Court cited case law on the passing-on problem, will be discussed in paras 7.170–7.177.

markedly weaker position than the other party, such as seriously to compromise or even eliminate his freedom to negotiate the terms of the contract and his capacity to avoid the loss or reduce its extent, in particular by availing himself in good time of all the legal remedies available to him.[26]

For those reasons the Court of Justice concluded that a party to a contract liable to restrict or distort competition within the meaning of Article 85 EC could rely on the breach of that provision to obtain relief from the other contracting party; that Article 85 EC precluded a rule of national law under which such a party was barred from claiming damages for loss caused by performance of that contract on the sole ground that the claimant was a party to the contract; but that Community law did not preclude a rule of national law barring such a party from relying on his own unlawful actions to obtain damages where it was established that that party bore significant responsibility for the distortion of competition.[27] **7.022**

Courage was, in sum, a landmark case as the Court of Justice explicitly held that there was a right to obtain relief for a breach of Article 85 EC (now 101 TFEU) derived from Community law directly. The Court reached this finding through citations of case law such as *Simmenthal*[28] and *Factortame I*[29] and using private vigilance reasoning reminiscent of *van Gend en Loos*[30] and *Francovich*.[31] The right was conferred also on parties to a contract that was liable to be in breach of EU competition law, even though it would be possible to bar parties who bore significant responsibility for the distortion of competition to bring an action for relief.[32] The Court held that the full effectiveness of Article 85 EC (now 101 TFEU) and, in particular, the practical effect of the prohibition therein would be put at risk if it were not open to any individual to claim damages for loss caused by a contract or by conduct liable to restrict or distort competition. The Court indeed held that actions for damages before the national courts could make a significant contribution to the maintenance of effective competition in the Community.[33] Nonetheless the form of relief required was not specified in the Operative part of the judgment. The Court of Justice was satisfied to rule that there should not 'be any absolute bar against such an action being brought by a party to a contract **7.023**

26 Ibid., paras 31–33.
27 Ibid., Operative part.
28 Case 106/77 *Amministrazione delle Finanze dello Stato v Simmenthal SpA* [1978] ECR 629.
29 Case C-213/89 *The Queen v Secretary of State for Transport, ex parte: Factortame Ltd and others* [1990] ECR I-2433.
30 *van Gend & Loos* (n 3).
31 *Francovich* (n 17).
32 *Courage* (n 4) para. 24.
33 Ibid., paras 25–27.

which would be held to violate the competition rules'[34] – which obviously is not quite the same as saying that compensation in damages must be available as a matter of Community law. It was also apparent that the Court had refrained from developing any conditions to be applied for the purposes of such an action.

7.024 The European Commission nevertheless took the view that it was settled through *Courage* that 'effective protection of the rights granted by the Treaty requires that individuals who have suffered a loss arising from an infringement of Articles 81 or 82 have the right to claim damages',[35] and set out to harmonize the action for damages for a breach of EU competition law. This parallel process will be depicted in brief in Section 7.B.II.

7.025 The issue of whether the Court of Justice required that compensation in damages be available for a breach of Article 81 EC (now Article 101 TFEU) was unequivocally settled on 13 July 2006, by its judgment in *Manfredi*.[36]

7.026

> The defendants in the main proceedings, Lloyd Adriatico Assicurazioni SpA, Fondiaria Sai SpA and Assitalia SpA (the defendants), were Italian insurance companies who offered civil liability auto insurance, compulsory in Italy. The claimants in the main proceedings, Vincenzo Manfredi, Antonio Cannito, Nicolò Tricarico and Pasqualina Murgolo (the claimants), were private individuals who had taken out insurances for their vehicles with the defendants.
>
> On 28 July 2000 the Italian competition authority (Autorità garante per la concorrenza e del mercato, the AGCM) declared that the defendants had implemented an unlawful agreement for the purpose of exchanging information, enabling the defendants to coordinate and to fix prices for civil liability auto insurance in Italy. The AGCM held that this agreement had caused harm to final consumers through an increase in the price of insurance premiums. The AGCM estimated the average price to have been 20 per cent higher than it would have been if the defendants had not distorted competition on the relevant market.
>
> The claimants brought their respective actions before the Guidice di pace di Bitonto, claiming damages from the defendants for the increase in the cost for civil liability auto insurance by reason of the agreement declared unlawful by the AGCM. The defendants, on their part, argued that the Guidice di pace di Bitonto did not have jurisdiction under national law and that the right to restitution or compensation in damages for the alleged overcharge was out of time.

---

34 Ibid., para. 28.

35 Commission, 'Green Paper on Damages actions for breach of the EC antitrust rules' COM(2005) 672 final, 4. Arts 81 and 82 EC are now Arts 101 and 102 TFEU.

36 Joined cases C-295/04 to 298/04 *Vincenzo Manfredi v Lloyd Adriatico Assicurazioni SpA* (C-295/04), *Antonio Cannito v Fondiaria Sai SpA* (C-296/04) and *Nicolò Tricarico* (C-297/04) and *Pasqualina Murgolo* (C-298/04) *v Assitalia SpA* [2006] ECR I-6619.

The Guidice di pace di Bitonto was concerned that the relevant provisions of national law were contrary to Community law. Therefore it decided to stay proceedings and to refer the case to the European Court of Justice for a preliminary ruling.

7.027 The Court of Justice stressed that any agreements or decisions prohibited pursuant to Article 81 EC (now Article 101 TFEU) were void, that it was settled case law that this invalidity could be relied on by anyone, and that the courts were bound by it. The Court furthermore pointed out that that provision produced direct effects in relations between individuals and created rights for the individuals concerned which the national courts must safeguard. It followed, the Court held, that any individual could rely on a breach of Article 81 EC before a national court and therefore rely on the invalidity of an agreement or practice prohibited under that Article.[37]

7.028 As regards the possibility of seeking compensation for loss caused by a contract or by conduct liable to restrict or distort competition the Court of Justice emphasized that the full effectiveness of Article 81 EC and, in particular, the practical effect of the prohibition laid down in its first paragraph would be put at risk if it were not open to any individual to claim damages for loss caused to him by a contract or by conduct liable to restrict or distort competition. It followed, the Court of Justice held, that any individual could claim compensation for the harm suffered where there was a causal relationship between that harm and an agreement or practice prohibited under that provision.[38]

7.029 The Court of Justice continued to examine whether Article 81 EC must be interpreted as requiring national courts to award punitive damages greater than the advantage obtained by the offending operator, thereby deterring the adoption of agreements or concerted practices prohibited under that Article. The Court of Justice observed that the national courts, whose task it was to apply the provisions of Community law in areas within their jurisdiction, must ensure that those rules take full effect and must protect the rights which they confer on individuals. The Court repeated that the full effectiveness of Article 81 EC and, in particular, the practical effect of the prohibition laid down in its first paragraph would be put at risk if it were not open to any individual to claim damages for loss caused to him by a contract or by conduct liable to restrict or distort competition.[39]

37 Ibid., paras 56–59.
38 Ibid., paras 60–61.
39 Ibid., paras 89–90.

7.030 For those reasons the Court concluded that Article 81 EC must be interpreted as meaning that any individual could rely on the invalidity of an agreement or practice prohibited under that Article and, where there is a causal relationship between the latter and the harm suffered, claim compensation for that harm. In the absence of Community rules governing the matter it was for the domestic legal system of each Member State to prescribe the detailed rules governing the exercise of that right, including those on the application of the concept of 'causal relationship', provided that the principles of equivalence and effectiveness were observed.[40]

7.031 Furthermore the Court held that in the absence of Community rules it was for the domestic legal system of each Member State to set the criteria for determining the extent of the damages for harm caused by an agreement or practice prohibited under Article 81 EC, provided that the principles of equivalence and effectiveness were observed. In accordance with the principle of equivalence, if it was possible to award particular damages such as exemplary or punitive damages in domestic actions similar to actions founded on the Community competition rules, it must also be possible to award such damages in actions founded on Community rules. Community law did not however prevent national courts from taking steps to ensure that the protection of the rights guaranteed by Community law did not entail the unjust enrichment of those who enjoy them. The Court further ruled that it followed from the principle of effectiveness and from the right of individuals to seek compensation for loss caused by a contract or by conduct liable to restrict or distort competition that injured persons must be able to seek compensation not only for actual loss (*damnum emergens*) but also for loss of profit (*lucrum cessans*) plus interest.[41]

7.032 Proceeding to analysis it is clear, first of all, that the issue of whether compensation in damages should be available as a matter of Community law was settled through *Manfredi*. Compensation in damages should be available for a breach of Article 81 EC (now Article 101 TFEU) as a matter of (now) EU law. The Court also clarified that such an action required that there was a causal relationship between the harm and the breach. The Court thus introduced a condition of causation for such actions but left it to national law to decide how to apply the condition, albeit subject to the principles of equivalence and effectiveness.

40 Ibid., Operative part para. 2.

41 Ibid., Operative part para. 5.

The Court of Justice also laid down some details on the estimation of damages. The point of departure of the Court was that the calculation of damages would still, largely, be a matter of national law. The Court nevertheless added some substantive points on the impact of the principles of equivalence and effectiveness. It may be worth repeating that, pursuant to *Manfredi*, injured persons must be able to seek compensation not only for actual loss (*damnum emergens*) but also for loss of profit (*lucrum cessans*), plus interest.[42] It was thus established in *Manfredi* that these three heads of damages must always be taken into account by national courts. The Court moreover ruled that it must be possible to award particular damages such as exemplary or punitive damages pursuant to actions founded on EU competition rules, if such damages might be awarded pursuant to similar actions founded on domestic law.[43] This last aspect will however be legal history once the Member States have implemented Article 3(3) of Directive 2014/104/EU in which such particular damages are banned.[44] **7.033**

After *Manfredi* a few years passed before the Court of Justice was given an opportunity to develop details on competition damages in its case law. In *Otis*, delivered on 6 November 2012, it was established that the European Commission could not be precluded from bringing an action for damages on behalf of the EU against a private party in breach of EU competition law.[45] In *Kone*,[46] another case arising from the same cartel, the issue was whether damages were available by reason of harm caused by 'umbrella pricing' by competitors to the cartel. The argument was that the cartel caused prices on the relevant market to rise with the effect that prices offered by companies competing with the cartel would be higher than they would have been but for the cartel. This effect is called 'umbrella pricing'.[47] **7.034**

42 Ibid., para. 95 and Operative part para. 5.

43 Ibid., para. 93 and Operative part para. 5.

44 Directive 2014/104/EU (n 5) Art. 3(3); see further para. 7.159. Pursuant to its Art. 21 the transposition period for Directive 2014/104/EU expires 27 December 2016.

45 Case C-199/11 *Europese Gemeenschap v Otis NV and Others* EU:C:2012:684 Operative part para. 1.

46 Case C-557/12 *Kone AG and Others v ÖBB-Infrastruktur AG* EU:C:2014:1317.

47 Umbrella pricing can be intentional or unintentional, i.e., the supplier may know or may not know of the cartel. The phenomenon has received only scarce attention in EU law scholarship. Contributions include Axel Reidlinger (counsel for ThyssenKrupp Aufzüge GmbH, one of the defendants in *Kone* (n 46)), 'Cartel Damage Claims for 'umbrella pricing' – a Case for the Effectiveness Principle of EU Competition Law?' (2014) 6 *Global Competition Litigation Review* 209; Roger Gamble, 'The European Embrace of Private Enforcement: This Time With Feeling' (2014) 35 *European Competition Law Review* 469. The prospects of success with 'umbrella claims' under federal US antitrust law are uncertain; see Herbert Hovenkamp, *Federal Antitrust Policy: The Law of Competition and its Practice* (4th edn, West Publishing Co 2011) 683–4.

7.035 The defendants in the main proceedings (Kone AG, Otis GmbH, Schindler Aufzüge und Fahrtreppen GmbH, Schindler Liegenschaftsverwaltung GmbH, and ThyssenKrupp Aufzüge GmbH – the 'defendants') were parties to a network of cartels in the business of installation and maintenance of elevators and escalators in a number of Member States which had operated since at least the 1980s until 2004. The claimant in the main proceedings, ÖBB-Infrastruktur AG, was seeking compensation for damage suffered as a consequence of having been charged prices which were higher than competitive prices by suppliers who were not participating in the cartel.

The claimant brought an action for damages at an amount of EUR 1 839 239.74 against the defendants. The claimant argued that its suppliers had adapted their prices to the price level of the cartel, and that the defendants were liable to compensate the claimant for the overcharge.

The national court of first instance rejected the claim, but on appeal it was upheld by the appellate court. On appeal by the defendants the Oberster Gerichtshof observed that under Austrian case law loss due to umbrella pricing was a side effect caused by independent business considerations by third parties. It followed that it was an indirect loss and consequently there was no adequate causal link between the cartel and such loss. The Oberster Gerichtshof moreover observed that in accordance with academic writings on the protective scope (German: *Schutzzweck*) of a provision, compensation would be available only if the provision breached had as its objective the protection of the injured party's interests. As the competition law provisions breached had as their object the protection of the interests of the cartel's buyers, injured parties who were not buyers of cartel members would fall outside the protective scope of those provisions. The Oberster Gerichtshof however also observed that it was a matter of controversy whether this national law could be upheld in the context of EU competition law.

Therefore the Oberster Gerichtshof stayed proceedings and referred the case to the European Court of Justice for a preliminary ruling on whether Article 101 TFEU precluded the interpretation and application of domestic legislation enacted by a Member State which categorically excluded, for legal reasons, any civil liability of undertakings belonging to a cartel for loss resulting from the fact that an undertaking not party to the cartel, having regard to the practices of the cartel, set its prices higher than would otherwise have been expected in the absence of the cartel.

7.036 The question referred to the Court of Justice in *Kone* was essentially whether EU law required that an action for damages be available against the members of the cartel for those who have suffered loss due to umbrella pricing. In her Opinion Advocate General Kokott pointed out that the financial implications of this question were considerable.[48] The Advocate General argued that the issue of whether compensation is payable, as distinguished from the details of such claims which were (still) largely governed by national law, was a matter of EU law[49] and that liability for cartel members to compensate harm incurred

48 *Kone* (n 46) Opinion of AG Kokott para. 18.

49 Ibid., paras 21–24.

through umbrella pricing was equally a matter of EU law. The question asked should therefore, the Advocate General concluded, be given an answer creating a uniform EU law approach to the issue of damages for umbrella pricing victims.[50]

In the view of the Advocate General the problem turned on 'what specific conditions may be attached under European Union law to the establishment of a causal link between the cartel and umbrella pricing'.[51] In that regard the Advocate General submitted a few general views on causation. These will be examined in more detail in Section 7.D. For the purposes of this section suffice it to summarize that in the view of the Advocate General cartel members should be held liable in damages for loss caused by umbrella pricing where such umbrella pricing was proved.[52] **7.037**

The Court of Justice delivered its ruling in *Kone* on 5 June 2014. The judgment revolved around the issue of causation and it will therefore be analysed further in Section 7.D. In sum the Court ruled that Article 101 TFEU must be interpreted as meaning that it precluded the interpretation and application of domestic legislation enacted by a Member State which categorically excluded, for legal reasons, any civil liability of undertakings belonging to a cartel for loss resulting from the fact that an undertaking not party to the cartel, having regard to the practices of the cartel, set its prices higher than would otherwise have been expected under competitive conditions.[53] Consequently victims of umbrella pricing could not be categorically excluded from bringing an action for damages pursuant to Article 101 TFEU. **7.038**

II. The new harmonized regime

In the previous section it was noted that, in *Courage*,[54] the European Court of Justice did not go as far as to rule that compensation in damages must be available as a matter of Community law. It was also apparent that the Court had refrained from developing any conditions to be applied for the purposes of such an action. The European Commission nevertheless took the view that it was settled through *Courage* that 'effective protection of the rights granted by the Treaty requires that individuals who have suffered a loss arising from an infringement of Articles 81 or 82 have the right to claim damages'.[55] The **7.039**

---

50 Ibid., paras 28–30.
51 Ibid., para. 31.
52 Ibid., paras 83–85.
53 *Kone* (n 46) Operative part.
54 *Courage* (n 4).
55 COM(2005) 672 final (n 35) 4. Arts 81 and 82 EC are now Arts 101 and 102 TFEU.

Commission initiative importantly covered damages actions for breaches of both Article 81 and Article 82 EC (now Articles 101 and 102 TFEU) whereas *Courage* concerned Article 81 EC only. A comparative report 'on the conditions of claims for damages in case of infringement of EC competition rules' was procured, which concluded that private enforcement of competition law in Europe was in 'astonishing diversity and total underdevelopment'.[56] Considering the immensity of the harm incurred by victims of anti-competitive behaviour this was – and is – no small matter.[57] The Commission therefore considered legislating on the details of a harmonized action for damages. The Commission issued a Green Paper on 'Damages action for breach of EC antitrust rules' on 12 December 2005.[58] In this Paper the Commission requested all interested parties to consider issues such as the coordination of public and private enforcement, the choice of applicable law, consumer protection, access to evidence, the burden of proof, whether there should be a fault requirement for damages actions, definitions and methods to be used for the estimation of damages awards, and the passing-on problem.

7.040 Following *Manfredi*[59] the European Commission acted again by issuing its White Paper on damages actions for a breach of Articles 81 and 82 EC (now Articles 101 and 102 TFEU) on 2 April 2008.[60] The policy choices of the Commission in its White Paper will not be discussed at any length here.[61]

---

56 Denis Waelbroeck, Donald Slater and Gil Even-Shoshan, 'Ashurst Study on the conditions of claims for damages in case of infringement of EC competition rules: Comparative Report' (2004) <http://ec.europa.eu/competition/antitrust/actionsdamages/comparative_report_clean_en.pdf> (last accessed 31 May 2016) 1. This conclusion contrasts strongly with the conclusions of the 1966 Commission study (n 10) 5. Were conditions in the Member States in dramatic retrogression from 1966 to 2004?

57 A recent estimation by the Commission indicates that harm inflicted by hard core cartels only, operating on the internal market and/or on the domestic markets of the Member States, amounts to 'approximately €25 billion (on the most conservative assumptions) to approximately €69 billion (on the least conservative)'; Commission, 'Commission Staff Working Document: Impact Assessment Report: Damages actions for breach of the EU antitrust rules' SWD(2013) 203 final para. 65.

58 COM(2005) 672 final (n 35). The Green Paper was accompanied by the more detailed Commission, 'Staff Working Paper Annex to the Green Paper Damages action for breach of the EC antitrust rules' SEC(2005) 1732.

59 *Manfredi* (n 36).

60 Commission, 'White Paper on Damages actions for breach of the EC antitrust rules' COM(2008) 165 final. The White Paper was accompanied by Commission, 'Staff Working Paper accompanying the White Paper on Damages actions for breach of the EC antitrust rules' SEC(2008) 404; and Commission, 'Staff Working Document Accompanying document to the White Paper on Damages actions for breach of the EC antitrust rules – Impact Assessment' SEC(2008) 405.

61 For an overview of the contents of the White Paper see Veljko Milutinovic, *The 'Right to Damages' under EU Competition Law: From* Courage v. Crehan *to the White Paper and Beyond* (Wolters Kluwer 2010) 80–83. Interesting comments submitted to the Commission with regard to the White Paper include Max Planck Institute for Intellectual Property, Competition and Tax Law, 'Comments of the Max Planck Institute for Intellectual Property, Competition and Tax Law on the White Paper by the Directorate-General for Competition of April 2008 on Damages for Breach of the EC Antitrust Rules' (Munich, 15 July 2008); and American Bar Association Section of Antitrust Law, Section of International Law, and Section of Business

Suffice it to summarize that the White Paper aimed at rules that would improve the legal conditions for victims of competition law infringements to be compensated in full for all damage suffered.[62] The Commission suggested that the action be available where the claimant could show a breach by the defendant of Article 81 or 82 EC, unless the defendant was able to demonstrate that the breach was the result of a genuinely excusable error.[63] The White Paper did not include any suggestion for harmonization of the application of the requirement for a causal relationship between the breach and harm incurred. The Commission did however suggest codification of the findings of the Court in *Manfredi* with regard to the estimation of damages and the issuing of non-binding guidance for quantification of damages in antitrust cases.[64]

After the White Paper was issued time passed and little was heard. It was not until 11 June 2013 (over five years' later) that the European Commission finally submitted its 'Proposal for a Directive of the European Parliament and of the Council on Certain Rules Governing Actions for Damages under National Law for Infringements of the Competition Law Provisions of the Member States and of the European Union'.[65] Alongside the Directive proposal the Commission also issued a Communication on quantifying harm in actions for damages for a breach of EU competition law[66] accompanied by a more detailed Practical Guide on the same subject.[67] A Recommendation on **7.041**

Law, 'Joint Comments of the American Bar Association Section of Antitrust Law, Section of International Law, and Section of Business Law on the Commission of the European Communities' White Paper on Damages Actions for Breach of the EC Antitrust Rules' (30 June 2008). Both documents are available at <http://ec.europa.eu/competition/antitrust/actionsdamages/white_paper_comments.html> (last accessed 31 May 2016).

62 COM(2008) 165 final (n 60) 3.

63 Ibid., 7. If national law provided for strict liability without any requirement of fault, such liability was to be extended to damages actions for a breach of Arts 81 and 82 EC; COM(2008) 165 final (n 60) 6.

64 Ibid.

65 Commission, 'Proposal for a Directive of the European Parliament and of the Council on Certain Rules Governing Actions for Damages under National Law for Infringements of the Competition Law Provisions of the Member States and of the European Union', COM(2013) 404 final.

66 Commission, 'Communication from the Commission on quantifying harm in actions for damages based on breaches of Art 101 or 102 of the Treaty on the Functioning of the European Union' [2013] OJ C167/19.

67 Commission, 'Commission Staff Working Document – Practical Guide on quantifying harm in actions for damages based on breaches of Art 101 or 102 of the Treaty on the Functioning of the European Union', SWD(2013) 205. The Communication and Practical Guide cover breaches of Arts 101 or 102 TFEU only, unlike Directive 2014/104/EU, which covers also national competition law when applied in parallel to those Arts. As the Communication and accompanying Practical Guide are soft-law instruments, this discrepancy should not cause legal troubles – in case of a conflict, it will be for the court at issue to decide whether to what extent the guidance offered by the Commission may have an impact on its application of national law on the estimation of damages; see Communication [2013] (n 66) para. 13.

common principles for injunctive and compensatory collective redress mechanisms was also presented.[68] These instruments will all, where appropriate, be included in the discussion below.

7.042 Negotiations between the Commission, the Council and the European Parliament resulted in a political agreement on the legal contents of the Directive on 17 April 2014.[69]

7.043 The final version of Directive 2014/104/EU was published in the Official Journal on 5 December and it is to be transposed into the national laws of the Member States by 27 December 2016.[70] The Directive covers a number of issues relating to the private enforcement of competition law, some falling outside the scope of this research. The contents are the following:

Chapter I (Articles 1–4):	Subject-matter, scope and definitions
Chapter II (Articles 5–8):	Disclosure of evidence
Chapter III (Articles 9–11):	Effect of national decisions, limitation periods, joint and several liability
Chapter IV (Articles 12–16):	The passing-on of overcharges
Chapter V (Article 17):	Quantification of harm
Chapter VI (Articles 18–19):	Consensual dispute resolution
Chapter VII (Article 20–24):	Final provisions

Chapters II, VI and VII fall outside the scope of this research. Chapter III will be touched upon insofar as it is relevant. Chapters I and V will be presented in this section while the provisions of Chapter IV will mainly be discussed in sub-sections 7.E.II.b and 7.E.II.c below.

7.044 The scope of the Directive follows from its title and from its definitions. Under Article 1(1) the Directive applies to claims for compensation for 'harm caused by an infringement of competition law'. An 'infringement of competition law' is further defined for the purposes of the Directive as meaning 'an

68 Commission Recommendation 2013/396/EU of 11 June 2013 on common principles for injunctive and compensatory collective redress mechanisms in the Member States concerning violations of rights granted under Union Law [2013] OJ L201/60.

69 The agreement text version is available as European Parliament, 'Position of the European Parliament adopted at first reading on 17 April 2014 with a view to the adoption of Directive 2014/…/EU of the European Parliament and of the Council on certain rules governing actions for damages under national law for infringements of the competition law provisions of the Member States and of the European Union', T7–0451/2014 (Procedure file 2013/0185(COD)) at <http://www.europarl.europa.eu/sides/getDoc.do?type=REPORT&reference=A7–2014–0089&language=EN> (last accessed 31 May 2016).

70 Directive 2014/104/EU (n 5) Art. 21.

infringement of Article 101 or 102 TFEU, or of national competition law'.[71] The harmonization of damages law envisaged in the Directive will accordingly apply whenever Article 101 or 102 TFEU are applicable, including instances where they apply in parallel with national competition law. Consequently national damages law which may be applicable to an infringement of national competition law must not, in such instances, deviate from the rules of Directive 2014/104/EU. In other words the scope for divergent national damages law for an infringement of national competition law is limited to cases where the infringement does not have an effect on trade between Member States within the meaning of Article 101 or 102 TFEU. The Directive thus extends the primacy of EU competition law over national competition law, mainly embodied in Article 3 of Regulation (EC) No 1/2003,[72] to the field of damages for infringements. The Directive does not however address the issue of whether it is open to claimants to bring other actions for payment, instead of – or combined with, as the case may be – an action for damages. Certain claimants may for example wish to bring an alternative action for restitution where such an action is available under national law.[73]

The Articles of Directive 2014/104/EU do not cover the details of the competition law tort, i.e., how to establish that there has been an infringement of competition law which is capable of giving rise to liability in damages. It simply stipulates that 'Member States shall ensure that any natural or legal person who has suffered harm caused by an infringement of competition law is able to claim and to obtain full compensation for that harm.'[74] An 'infringement of competition law' means 'an infringement of Article 101 or 102 TFEU, or of national competition law'.[75] It follows that the details of establishing an infringement remain those developed in EU case law and secondary law. These competition law developments are much too complicated to be depicted here.[76] It is to be observed however that the Articles of the Directive do not **7.045**

71 Directive 2014/104/EU (n 5) Art. 2(1). 'National competition law' is further defined in Art. 2(3) as meaning 'provisions of national law that predominantly pursue the same objective as Articles 101 and 102 TFEU and that are applied to the same case and in parallel to Union competition law pursuant to Article 3(1) of Regulation (EC) No 1/2003' (i.e., Council Regulation (EC) No 1/2003 of 16 December 2002 on the implementation of the rules on competition laid down in Articles 81 and 82 of the Treaty [2003] OJ L1/1 (Arts 81 and 82 of the Treaty are now Arts 101 and 102 TFEU)) with the exception of some national criminal penalty provisions.

72 Regulation (EC) No 1/2003 (n 71).

73 Cf. Section 8.C.I.

74 Directive 2014/104/EU (n 5) Art. 3(1).

75 Ibid., Art. 2(1).

76 Please see any competition law textbook for details of the criteria for finding an infringement of Arts 101 or 102 TFEU, e.g., Alison Jones and Brenda Sufrin, *EU Competition Law: Text, Cases and Materials* (5th edn, Oxford University Press 2014).

mention any fault criterion or the like applying over and above the finding of an infringement of competition law. Thus, judging from the Articles, the finding of an infringement would be enough to establish that the infringing party is enough for the infringement to be capable of giving rise to liability on behalf of infringers to compensate harm caused by the infringement.[77] Under such circumstances the deliberations available pursuant to Article 101(3) TFEU (and relevant block exemptions) and their equivalents under Article 102 TFEU seem the only exonerating deliberations available to infringers of competition law for the purposes of their liability in damages. The conditions for liability in private and public enforcement of EU competition law would thus be aligned.

7.046 Matters are even more complicated however. In recital 11 it is explained that in the event applicable national law includes 'other conditions for compensation under national law, such as imputability, adequacy or culpability, they should be able to maintain such conditions in so far as they comply with the case-law of the Court of Justice, the principles of effectiveness and equivalence, and this Directive'. This sentence did not appear in the original Commission proposal for a Directive submitted on 11 June 2013[78] but was included in the 17 April 2014 compromise text negotiated with the Parliament and the Council.[79] The concept of imputability concerns the attribution of liability between parties on the defendant side and need not be addressed here. The concept of adequacy is closely related to the issue of causation and will be discussed briefly in Section 7.D. The most disturbing element is the inclusion of the concept of culpability (German: *Verschulden*, French: *culpabilité*), i.e. fault, in recital 11. This causes some uncertainty with regard to the conditions giving rise to liability for a breach of EU law. In the 2008 White Paper the Commission noted that the laws of the Member States differed with regard to fault:[80]

7.047

> Some Member States require no fault at all as a condition for an antitrust damages claim, or irrebuttably presume the existence of fault once an infringement has been proven. The Commission sees no policy grounds against such an approach.
>
> As regards the other Member States, the Court's case law on the conditions of civil liability for breaches of directly applicable Treaty rules, such as Articles 81 and 82, and the principle of effectiveness suggest that any fault requirements under national law

77 Of course, it will still be necessary to establish that the alleged harm was caused by the infringement and that the alleged harm suffered is eligible for compensation in damages.

78 See COM(2013) 404 final (n 65) rec. 10 in the proposed Directive.

79 See T7–0451/2014 (n 69) rec. 110 (misnumbered, should be 11).

80 See also Assimakis P Komninos, *EC Private Antitrust Enforcement*, (Hart Publishing 2008) 195, who argues against the acceptance of national fault criteria for the purposes of damages for a breach of competition law.

> would have to be limited. The Commission sees no reasons to relieve infringers from liability on grounds of absence of fault other than in cases where the infringer made an excusable error.
>
> The Commission therefore suggests a measure to make it clear, for Member States that require fault to be proven, that:
>
> - once the victim has shown a breach of Article 81 or 82 , the infringer should be liable for damages caused unless he demonstrates that the infringement was the result of a genuinely excusable error;
> - an error would be excusable if a reasonable person applying a high standard of care could not have been aware that the conduct restricted competition.[81]

7.048 This suggestion for a rebuttable presumption regarding fault once the infringement had been established, unless the infringer could prove that the infringement was due to an excusable error, was omitted in the 2013 proposal.[82] The reason for the omission of fault was criticism from stakeholders in the course of public consultations. The Commission reported that some business respondents argued that the fault requirement 'should not be specifically regulated in the antitrust sector, but should follow the applicable general provisions of civil law' and that 'the proposed test of "excusable error" could amount to a strict liability test, in particular in situations where self-assessment is not easy for firms'. By contrast, consumers and some Member States 'suggested that an infringer should never be allowed to escape liability on grounds of fault'.[83] Arguably the removal of the provisions on fault in the 2013 Commission proposal, compared to the proposed Directive which included no mentioning of such concepts but only of liability in damages for an infringement of competition law, suggests that liability should automatically be triggered by an infringement of Article 101 or 102 TFEU. With the introduction of the concept of culpability in recital 11 however, it seems the business respondents have won the battle. In light of the recital it seems compatible with EU law to add a national fault criterion to the assessment of whether an infringement of competition law is capable of giving rise to liability in damages. The existence of such a fault criterion will remain within the jurisdiction of the national legal systems. If this interpretation of recital 11 is correct, it threatens to undermine the harmonizing effect of Directive 2014/104/EU with regard to the conditions for liability in damages. On the other hand a Directive recital carries only so much legal significance. The wording of recital 11 moreover includes certain limits to national discretion, as national culpability conditions should be allowed to remain applicable only 'in

81 COM(2008) 165 final (n 60) 6–7. Arts 81 and 82 of the Treaty are now Arts 101 and 102 TFEU.

82 COM(2013) 404 final (n 65) 12.

83 SWD(2013) 203 final (n 57) 87.

so far as they comply with the case-law of the Court of Justice, the principles of effectiveness and equivalence, and this Directive'. In essence this must be interpreted as an example of so-called 'constructive ambiguity' whereby the EU legislature has by-passed difficult negotiations by leaving a controversial issue to be decided by the Court of Justice. It is submitted against this background that the issue of national fault criteria applicable to actions for damages for a breach of competition law should, if it arises, be referred to the Court of Justice for a preliminary ruling. To this author it seems the interest of ensuring a level playing field for competition law litigants and the interest of ensuring compliance with competition law would both be served if the Court would rule in favour of automatic liability in damages in the event of a breach of Article 101 or 102 TFEU.

7.049 In the context of criteria for liability it should be noticed also that the discussion of whether EU law, for the purposes of competition damages actions, should adopt a limiting criterion under which the alleged harm must be classified as being an 'antitrust injury' seems to have passed unheard by both the Court of Justice and the EU legislature. This concept originates from the judgment of the Supreme Court of the United States in *Brunswick* where it held, for the purposes of US federal antitrust law, that damages are payable only where the claimant has proven '*antitrust* injury, which is to say injury of the type the antitrust laws were intended to prevent'.[84] Brunswick Corp manufactured bowling equipment and had sold such equipment to bowling alleys on credit. As a large number of its customers came to be at risk of going bankrupt Brunswick Corp took over their businesses in order to avoid loss, thus becoming the largest operator of bowling alleys in the US. The claimants, who ran competing bowling alleys, complained that but for this takeover policy of Brunswick Corp competition would have been reduced and the bowling alleys run by the claimants would have been more profitable. The problem in *Brunswick* was therefore that damages were claimed for harm incurred due to an increase in competition and not, as intended, for a restriction or distortion of competition. To award damages under such circumstances would, the Supreme Court held, be 'inimical to the purposes of these laws'.[85]

7.050 It has been discussed whether such a limitation should be adopted for the purposes of EU competition damages. Jones has advised against such adoption, arguing that it follows from substantive legal differences between US antitrust law and EU competition law that the concept is superfluous for the

84 *Brunswick Corp v Pueblo Bowl-o-Mat Inc et al* 429 US 477 (1977) 489.
85 Ibid., 488.

purposes of the latter.[86] Similar arguments have been submitted by Komninos who further argues that the criterion of causation will also serve to eliminate claims without merit.[87] Milutinovic is more positive and recognizes that EU law might well have a place for such a concept in situations where claimants are 'knowingly applying [their] subjective right to compensation under Articles 101/102 of the Treaty in order to challenge an increase or improvement in competition on the relevant market'.[88] As mentioned, however, no such limitation has so far been introduced, neither by the Court nor by the EU legislature. This author agrees with Jones and Komninos that in EU competition law most situations comparable to *Brunswick* would be avoided by the differences in the standards in Article 101 TFEU as compared to the Sherman Act[89] – under Article 101 TFEU the alleged breach would not be considered a breach at all. Causation concepts might also serve to limit liability in the event of unmeritorious claims. To this author however the *Schutzzweck* notion developed in German law seems better suited for complementing Article 101(3) TFEU to this end.[90] Notwithstanding which concept is preferred in order to delimit against unmeritorious claims it must be kept in mind that such concepts remain governed by national law, albeit subject to the EU law principles of equivalence and effectiveness.[91] Their use therefore comes with a risk that the assessment may be carried out inconsistently among the Member States. This will be discussed further in Section 7.D.

C. ACCESS TO CLAIM COMPETITION DAMAGES

Article 12(1) of Directive 2014/104/EU instructs the Member States to **7.051**
'ensure that, in accordance with the rules laid down in this Chapter, compensation of harm can be claimed by anyone who suffered it, irrespective of whether they are direct or indirect purchasers from an infringer'. It follows that Gamma claimants cannot be barred from bringing an action for damages

86 Jones (n 18) 191–3.

87 Komninos (n 80) 207. Cf. *Kone* (n 46) Opinion of AG Kokott para. 40 and the discussion beginning at para. 56. Swedish readers cf. Nils Wahl, *Konkurrensskada* (Jure 2000) 187–91.

88 Milutinovic (n 61) 241.

89 Act of 2 July 1890, 15 USC §§ 1–7; amended by the Clayton Act of 15 Oct 1914, 15 USC §§ 12–27 (see n 137).

90 On the *Schutzzweck* or protective scope theory, see e.g. Cees van Dam, *European Tort Law* (2nd edn, Oxford University Press 2013) 314–16.

91 On the principles of equivalence and effectiveness in general see Section 2.D. On national causation concepts and their application in competition damages see Section 7.D.I.

against Alpha by reason of the lack of a direct nexus between the two.[92] One might therefore think that this section could be kept rather short – might it not just as well end here? It might, but if it did, the reader would remain unassisted in understanding the options and arguments brought forth in the extensive and multi-faceted debate on Gamma claims in competition damages. Moreover and importantly the reader would be deprived of a presentation of the general EU law framework surrounding the issue of access to court in competition damages actions. That framework will remain to be essential for the interpretation and application of Article 12(1) of the Directive as well as for scrutinizing other details of national law that may restrict access to the damages action, e.g., time-limits.

7.052 For these reasons the general impact of EU law on national limitations of access to bring an action for damages for a breach of EU competition law will be examined in this section. Here, as in other EU law actions to be brought before the national courts of the Member States, the balancing of powers between the EU and its Member States has an impact on the approach of the European Court of Justice. Possibly even more so here, as damages actions brought against another private individual are private law remedies for a breach of EU competition law that could previously be regarded as falling under the jurisdiction of the Member States.[93] This general discussion will follow in Section 7.C.I. The subsequent Section 7.C.II is devoted to access for Gamma claimants specifically. In EU law the problem of access for Gamma claimants has received the most attention in discussions concerning damages actions for a breach of competition law. This is arguably due to the existence of a bar against actions brought by Gamma claimants in federal US antitrust law. This bar has been vigorously discussed among both American and European legal scholars. There will therefore be a comparative perspective exploring the American case law and debate in sub-section 7.C.II.a, as a contrast to and clarification of the approach chosen for the purposes of EU law which is presented in sub-section 7.C.II.b. By reason of the mentioning of harm suffered upstream the supply chain, in Directive 2014/104/EU Article 12(4),[94] it has finally been considered appropriate to add a few comments on other remote claimants in Section 7.C.III.

92 In this book, Alpha signifies a tortfeasor or enriched party, Beta a party first burdened by loss arising from Alpha's breach of EU law, and Gamma any party downstream from Beta (including all from the party dealing directly with Beta to the final consumer) to whom the burden of that loss may have been passed on; see Section 1.B.

93 That is until the rulings of the Court of Justice in *Courage* (n 4) and *Manfredi* (n 36). Pre-*Courage*, AG van Gerven famously argued in favour of EU law damages liability for individuals in *Banks* (n 16) Opinion of AG van Gerven section V (paras 36–54). A pre-*Courage* discussion with references can also be found in Jones (n 18) 75–78 and 84–92.

94 Cf. Directive 2014/104/EU (n 5) rec. 43.

I. General observations on access

In Section 7.B.I above it was depicted how the *in pari delicto* rule of UK competition law was used by the Court of Justice to approach for the first time the possible existence of an EU law right to damages from private individuals for harm incurred due to their breach of EU competition law.[95] It followed from *Courage* that the *in pari delicto* rule, which barred damages actions for a breach of EU competition law brought by co-contractors, could not be upheld as an absolute bar, but only if qualified by further refinements.[96] The same conclusion would arguably follow from the EU fundamental right of access to court, as absolute bars are typically limitations that do not respect the essence of the right of access to court.[97] Apart from such absolute bars it is necessary also to explore the impact of EU law on less draconian limitations in national law. This section therefore endeavours to trace the details on access to court for competition damages actions. Relevant materials include Article 47 of the Charter, the EU law principles of equivalence and effectiveness, and of course Directive 2014/104/EU. **7.053**

Actions for damages for a breach of EU competition law fall under the jurisdiction of the national courts of the Member States. Not only the rules of Directive 2014/104/EU will apply, but also complementing rules of national law, albeit subject to the general requirements of EU law that follow from Article 47 of the Charter and from the principles of equivalence and effectiveness. These were presented and discussed in the abstract in Chapter 2. The relevance of the principles of equivalence and effectiveness was indicated by the Court of Justice in both *Courage* and *Manfredi* and elaborated in *Manfredi*.[98] Certain aspects of the impact of Article 47 of the Charter were discussed in *Otis*[99] but its impact in the context of damages actions for a breach of competition law is largely uncertain. **7.054**

With regard to the latter rule it was argued in Section 2.C that Article 47 of the Charter requires national courts to grant access to claimants who wish to enforce rights guaranteed to them by EU law. This will include enforcement through an action for damages for a breach of competition law. Nonetheless, as was also stressed in Section 2.C, national limitations of access to court will be **7.055**

---

95 It was noted in Section 7.B.I that the Court was not entirely clear on this matter in *Courage* (n 4) but more so in the subsequent *Manfredi* (n 36).

96 *Courage* (n 4) para. 28.

97 See Arts 47 and 52(1) of the Charter, discussed in Section 2.C.

98 *Courage* (n 4) para. 29; *Manfredi* (n 36) paras 62, 71, 77 and Operative part paras 2–5. However, that discussion did not concern access to court or any comparable rules of national law, but available heads of damages. Therefore, it will not be discussed here, but in Section 7.E.I below.

99 *Otis* (n 45), to be discussed shortly.

compatible with Article 47 if they meet the applicable criteria for such limitations. Those criteria are laid down in Article 52(1). In essence national limitations must be provided for by law, respect the essence of the right, and meet the proportionality test prescribed by that Article. The proportionality test at issue permits only limitations which are necessary and genuinely meet the objectives of a general interest recognized by the EU or the need to protect the rights and freedoms of others. The details of these requirements have been discussed in Section 2.C.II and need not be repeated here. As the Article 52(1) test has not been discussed yet in the context of an action for damages for a breach of competition law it is submitted that cases where the issue arises how to apply Article 47 of the Charter to national limitations in the context of an action for damages for a breach of EU competition law should be referred to the European Court of Justice for a preliminary ruling.

7.056 As mentioned Article 47 was discussed in *Otis* and a few comments are therefore warranted with regard to that case. The issue was not, however, whether national restrictions of access to court were compatible with that provision but whether Article 47 precluded the European Commission from bringing an action for damages, in relation to harm incurred by the EU in the form of cartel overcharges, on behalf of the EU. In brief the issue was whether Article 47 could function as a restriction of access to court. The essence of the ruling was that the Commission could not be barred from bringing an action. The relevant concerns of the national court in this context were: (1) that an action brought by the Commission might infringe the right to a fair hearing under Article 47 of the Charter as the national court was required to accept that the defendants had infringed Article (now) 101 TFEU if so decided by the claimant; (2) that the Commission would be both judge and party in its own cause, which would constitute a breach of the *nemo judex in sua causa* principle; and (3) that there would be a breach of the principle of equality of arms because the Commission itself conducted the investigation relating to the infringement in question.[100] These concerns were all acknowledged as such by the Court of Justice which stressed that 'the fundamental rights of the defendants, as safeguarded, *inter alia*, by the Charter, must be observed'.[101] Consequently the concerns were legitimate and a close reading of the holdings of the Court shows that under certain circumstances an action brought by the Commission could in fact be barred by reference to any one of them. Nevertheless, on the facts, the Court dismissed the concerns of the national court. The Commission could consequently bring an action for damages on behalf of the EU.

---

100 Ibid., paras 38–39, 68.

101 Ibid., para. 45.

Turning to the EU law principles of equivalence and effectiveness it is noted that both principles are explicitly endorsed for the purposes of Directive 2014/104/EU in its Article 4. This analysis of their potential impact on national restrictions of access to court will begin with an assessment of the principle of equivalence. Under this principle actions based on EU law must not be treated less favourably than similar actions based on national law.[102] The relevant *comparator* is a national action where the purpose, cause of action, and essential characteristics of the action based on national law are similar to those of the action based on EU law.[103] It must further be examined whether the application of a specific rule to actions based on EU law is liable to make it less favourable to pursue such an action rather than the *comparator* action, taking into account the role played by that provision in the procedure as a whole as well as the operation and any special features of that procedure before the different national courts.[104] In other words it must be shown that the practical application of different rules or conditions results in actual adverse treatment of actions based on EU law.[105] **7.057**

In the context of an action for damages for a breach of EU competition law the relevant *comparator* would typically be actions for damages for a breach of national competition law. As the intention of Directive 2014/104/EU is to harmonize damages actions for a breach of competition law whenever Article 101 or 102 TFEU are applicable (that is, whether exclusively or in parallel with national competition law) however, such a comparison will generally be irrelevant once the Directive has been transposed into national law. It will be relevant only if the Member State at issue has retained a separate damages regime for breaches of national competition law that fall under the exclusive field of application of national law. This will probably not be common.[106] If a Member State did have such a separate damages regime it follows from the principle for equivalence that damages actions falling within the field of application of Directive 2014/104/EU must be treated no less favourably than damages actions based on the special national competition damages regime. Consequently, if such a separate damages regime includes more lenient conditions for access to court than the regime designed for the implementation of Directive 2014/104/EU, those more lenient conditions must be extended to actions brought under the Directive 2014/104/EU regime. **7.058**

---

102 Elaborated in Section 2.D.II.

103 Case C-326/96 *BS Levez v TH Jennings (Harlow Pools) Ltd* [1998] ECR I-7835 paras 41, 43.

104 Ibid., para. 44.

105 See Section 2.D.II and, particularly, para. 2.066.

106 In this context cf. para. 7.159 on the prohibition against overcompensation in Directive 2014/104/EU (n 5) Art. 3(3).

7.059 The more pressing issue is whether the principle of equivalence could be pushed further by finding another relevant *comparator*, e.g., general damages law in the national legal system. If the conditions for access to court in such an action are more lenient than those applicable under the implementing regime, the principle of equivalence might require for those more lenient conditions to be extended to competition damages actions. Such a situation could plausibly occur but the necessary equivalence analysis cannot be carried out in the abstract. Instead it must be decided on a case-by-case basis whether the purpose, cause of action, and essential characteristics of a general damages action based on national law are similar to those of a competition damages action based on EU law. It should also be kept in mind that it is settled case law that the principle of equivalence does not require Member States to extend their most favourable rules to actions based on EU law.[107]

7.060 The EU law principle of effectiveness too is, as mentioned, explicitly endorsed for the purposes of Directive 2014/104/EU in its Article 4. Although there is less room for invoking the principle of effectiveness when legislative harmonization has been carried through, the principle will apply to rules and principles of national law that fill the gaps left by Directive 2014/104/EU. As Directive 2014/104/EU leaves considerable gaps with regard to access to court it is relevant to discuss the principle of effectiveness here. Under this principle the applicable substantive and procedural rules on access to court must not render it impossible or excessively difficult to exercise the right to damages for a breach of EU competition law. The details of the analysis have been described in *Peterbroeck* and *van Schijndel*.[108] It furthermore follows from *Alassini* that the question whether the principle of effectiveness will preclude the application of a national limitation of access cannot be answered in the abstract but must be decided on a case-by-case basis.[109] In that case the Court of Justice nevertheless identified a few typical adverse consequences of national substantive and procedural conditions that were liable to make the exercise of rights conferred by EU law virtually impossible or excessively difficult: bars, impracticalities, delays, and costs. Where national conditions for access to court have the effect of barring certain competition damages actions,

107 Cf. case C-231/96 *Edilizia Industriale Siderurgica Srl (Edis) v Ministero delle Finanze* [1998] ECR I-4951 para. 36.

108 Case C-312/93 *Peterbroeck, Van Campenhout & Cie SCS v Belgian State* [1995] ECR I-4599 para. 14; joined cases C-430/93 and C-431/93 *Jeroen van Schijndel* and *Johannes Nicolaas Cornelis van Veen v Stichting Pensioenfonds voor Fysiotherapeuten* [1995] ECR I-4705 para. 19. For a full quote see para. 2.070. See also para. 2.071.

109 Joined cases C-317/08, C-318/08, C-319/08 and C-320/08 *Rosalba Alassini v Telecom Italia SpA* (C-317/08), *Filomena Califano v Wind SpA* (C-318/08), *Lucia Anna Giorgia Iacono v Telecom Italia SpA* (C-319/08) and *Multiservice Srl v Telecom Italia SpA* (C-320/08) [2010] ECR I-2213 paras 54–59. See further paras 2.072–2.073.

or of making it excessively time-consuming, costly, or otherwise impractical to gain access to them, the principle of effectiveness might preclude such conditions of national law.[110]

In *Courage* the principle of effectiveness was mentioned but its impact was not elaborated upon.[111] *Manfredi* also included similar unelaborated *dicta*,[112] but the Court of Justice was also called upon to scrutinize a time-limit in national law – an issue of some relevance to access. The referring court was concerned that EU law might preclude a national rule under which the limitation period for seeking compensation for harm caused by a breach of Article (now) 101 TFEU began to run on the day when the prohibited contract or practice was adopted.[113] The Court of Justice recognized that such a rule could make it practically impossible to exercise the right to seek compensation for the harm caused by that prohibited agreement or practice, particularly if that national rule also impose a short limitation period which was not capable of being suspended. In a situation where there were continuous or repeated infringements the Court held that it was possible that the limitation period would expire even before the infringement was brought to an end, in which case it would be impossible for any individual who suffered harm after the expiry of the limitation period to bring an action. The Court of Justice left it for the national court to determine whether this was the case with regard to the national rule at issue in the main proceedings.[114] **7.061**

Circumstances were similar in the more recent *Banca Antoniana*.[115] In that case VAT had been levied in breach of EU law and the applicable time period had lapsed before the claimant had had any reason to anticipate the wrongfulness of its payment. The Court of Justice held that the principle of effectiveness precluded the application of such a national rule.[116] On the one hand this would indicate that the comparatively lax approach in *Manfredi* cannot be **7.062**

110 The question of how, exactly, the national courts are to accomplish this has not been clearly explained by the Court of Justice. It can be concluded that national courts enjoy discretion with regard to the method to be employed. However, it seems from scattered remarks in case law that the regular EU law tools are available: *invocabilité d'exclusion* (case C-147/01 *Weber's Wine World Handels-GmbH and others v Abgabenberufungskommission Wien* [2003] ECR I-11365 para. 107), and consistent interpretation (case C-432/05 *Unibet (London) Ltd and Unibet (International) Ltd v Justitiekanslern* [2007] ECR I-2271 para. 44). Obviously, in this context *invocabilité de substitution* is not possible, as the principle of effectiveness does not itself stipulate substantive or procedural conditions.

111 *Courage* (n 4) para. 29.

112 *Manfredi* (n 36) paras 62, 71.

113 Ibid., para. 73.

114 Ibid., paras 78–80.

115 Case C-427/10 *Banca Antoniana Popolare Veneta SpA v Ministero dell'Economia e delle Finanze and Agenzia delle Entrate* [2011] ECR I-13377. See paras 5.024–5.026 for a summary of facts and holdings and a discussion.

116 Ibid., para. 42 and Operative part.

guaranteed in future case law. It would also sit well with the Strasbourg jurisprudence on infringements of the 'essence of the right' of access to court, which is now embedded in the EU Charter,[117] to use Article 47 of the Charter (instead of the principle of effectiveness) in order to adopt a more stringent approach. On the other hand it might be argued that *Banca Antoniana* should be distinguished from *Manfredi*. Perhaps the Court preferred a lenient approach in cases where the legal relationship concerned was one between private individuals, as in *Manfredi*, than in cases where the legal relationship concerned was one between a private individual and a Member State, as in *Banca Antoniana*? Notwithstanding the significance of this distinction it is submitted that the better view is to see the outcome in *Manfredi* as illustrative of the discretion enjoyed by the Court of Justice with regard to how far it wishes to push the detailed requirements of EU law at the expense of rules of national law. On a close reading it is evident that the Court did not in *Manfredi* give the referring court much choice with regard to whether or not to set aside the national rule at issue. There was consequently no need to elaborate further. The Court was also able thereby to give some leeway to national law under circumstances where, in the individual case, the application of the rule would be less limiting to an action for damages for a breach of Article 101 TFEU. With this said, it admittedly remains possible to interpret the difference between *Banca Antoniana* and *Manfredi* as indicating a general development in the approach of the Court to the requirements of the principle of effectiveness.

7.063 So far the general requirements of EU law with respect to access to court have been discussed. In the context of competition damages it is of course also relevant to search for more specific directions in the text of Directive 2014/104/EU. The provisions of the Directive with regard to access for Gamma claimants will be discussed in sub-section 7.C.II.b. Here a general discussion on access drawing from the Directive focusing on other access issues than access for Gamma will be attempted.

7.064 The Directive does not, it is submitted, include any specific provisions on access to court. Article 3(1) admittedly instructs the Member States to 'ensure that any natural or legal person who has suffered harm caused by an infringement of competition law is able to claim and to obtain full compensation for that harm'. Although this Article could plausibly be interpreted as a rule on access to court, its heading ('Right to Full Compensation') indicates that the rule instead codifies the substantive right to compensation. The introduction of the words 'and to obtain' in Article 3(1) strengthens this

117 Cf. Section 2.C.II and in particular para. 2.043.

interpretation. In the view of this author Article 3(1) is a statement of policy rather than a legal rule. A provision according to which anyone who has suffered harm must 'obtain full compensation' is obviously not a black letter rule but a starting point from which it becomes necessary to continue to contemplate the limitations to, and exceptions from, that policy. Limitations on access to court are one such kind of limitation. It moreover follows from *Courage* and the findings of the Court with regard to the *in pari delicto* rule that restrictions of access to court are not *per se* contrary to EU law. The Court held that the absolute bar against claims brought by co-contractors could not be upheld but it also clarified that, provided that the principles of equivalence and effectiveness were respected, EU law did not preclude a rule of national law barring parties to contracts liable to restrict or distort competition from relying on their own unlawful actions to obtain damages where it was established that they bore significant responsibility for the distortion of competition.[118] The compatibility of such a rule with EU law was to be assessed through an examination of the details and consequences of the rule on a case-by-case basis. Consequently limitations of access to court for competition damages actions can in principle be upheld insofar as they comply with the general requirements of EU law.

7.065 For further hints on access to court in Directive 2014/104/EU we must turn to the recitals. In recital 3 it is explained that 'anyone – be they an individual, including consumers and undertakings, or a public authority – can claim compensation before national courts for the harm caused to them by an infringement' of Articles 101 and 102 TFEU. Accordingly the legal character of the claimant should be of no consequence. This reflects the findings of the Court in *Otis*.[119] Recital 13 explains that there is a right to compensation 'irrespective of the existence of a direct contractual relationship with the infringing undertaking, and regardless of whether or not there has been a prior finding of an infringement by a competition authority'. The first of these two statements both recalls the Court's refutation of the *in pari delicto* rule in *Courage*[120] and alludes to the right to damages granted to Gamma claimants in Article 12(1) of the Directive.[121] The second statement acknowledges the possibility of bringing so-called stand-alone actions, i.e., private enforcement actions that are not joined with or otherwise connected to public enforcement actions brought by the Commission or a national competition authority.[122]

118 *Courage* (n 4) paras 28, 31 and Operative part para. 3.

119 See para. 7.034.

120 See Section 7.B.I.

121 To be explained further in sub-section 7.C.II.b.

122 By contrast, private enforcement actions that are joined with or otherwise connected to public enforcement actions brought by the Commission or a national competition authority are known as 'follow-on actions'.

This last issue should not be controversial and actions brought by Gamma claimants will be discussed in sub-section 7.C.II.b.

7.066 It must consequently be concluded that, apart from the provisions on access for Gamma claimants to be presented below, Directive 2014/104/EU offers very little news on access to court. The relevant recitals are restatements of the case law and Article 3(1) is not as such a rule on access. It is thus largely left to the national laws of the Member States to decide on the details. As shown above the design of those details in national law is subject to scrutiny under Article 47 of the Charter and the EU law principles of equivalence and effectiveness. There is little guidance on the intensity of scrutiny that can be expected from the Court of Justice. Perhaps it is safe to say that the general scheme of the Directive, and in particular its rules on access to court for Gamma claimants, implies that private enforcement is to be encouraged and that the Court can therefore be expected to take a strict view. Future case law developments may tell.

II. Access and passing-on

7.067 It has already been pointed out that Article 12(1) of Directive 2014/104/EU instructs the Member States to 'ensure that, in accordance with the rules laid down in this Chapter, compensation of harm can be claimed by anyone who suffered it, irrespective of whether they are direct or indirect purchasers from an infringer' and that it follows that Gamma claimants cannot be barred from bringing an action for damages against Alpha by reason of the lack of a direct nexus between the two. This is worth repeating. With a view to explaining the options and arguments brought forth in the extensive and multi-faceted debate on Gamma claims in competition damages before the publication of the Directive we will now revisit its starting point, namely, the bar against Gamma claims in federal US antitrust law and the discussions regarding that bar. The following excursus into US antitrust discourse does not pretend to be a comprehensive presentation[123] but it is intended to highlight the most influential arguments in order to give a background picture to the subsequent European debate which will then be presented and analysed.

7.068 It should be stressed however that US and EU enforcement of competition law are not to be compared without caution. It is crucial to keep (at least) two fundamental differences in mind while reading the sub-sections below. First,

123 A full but now somewhat outdated account and comparison of the US and European approaches to Gamma claimants is available in Jones (n 18) Chs 15–16. On US federal antitrust law in general see e.g. Hovenkamp (n 47).

the traditional role of private enforcement differs. In EU competition law private enforcement is generally held to be under-developed.[124] It is beyond the scope of this inquiry to make any attempt at a complete assessment of the legal, economic, cultural and other reasons for this under-development.[125] It is simply noticed that one of the purposes of Directive 2014/104/EU is to remedy this under-development.[126] In EU competition law public enforcement by the European Commission and the national competition authorities has overshadowed private enforcement. Private enforcement of EU competition law is thus often described as a supplement or complement to the predominant public enforcement.[127] By contrast the US system is a decentralized system of parallel enforcement at federal, state, and private level.[128] US antitrust law has entailed private enforcement ever since the passage of the Sherman Act of 1890[129] and private enforcement was further encouraged by the Clayton Act of 1914.[130] Case law of the US Supreme Court on actions for damages is abundant. As a consequence EU competition law tends to trust public enforcement to satisfy the general interest of deterrence from infringements, while US discourse emphasizes the role of liability in damages in pursuing that interest.[131] This point is linked to the next. Second, namely, damages have a significant punitive function under US federal antitrust law, as successful claimants will recover 'three-fold the damages … sustained'.[132] Hence the intensity of debate in the US with regard to the passing-on problem and, in particular, access to court for Gamma claimants. In a system of treble

124 See e.g. SWD(2013) 203 final (n 57) para. 61; and Jones and Sufrin (n 76) 1187.

125 Brief pointers: the European Commission has submitted that this is due to ineffectiveness caused by 'various legal and procedural hurdles', COM(2008) 165 final (n 60) 2. On traditional aversion to private enforcement of EU competition law see Jones (n 18) 88–92. A more recent example of scepticism is found in Wouter P Wils, *Principles of European Antitrust Enforcement* (Hart Publishing 2005) Ch. 4. On the subject see also Andreas Heinemann, 'The Rise of a Private Competition Law Culture: Experience and Visions' and Robert Neruda, 'Private or Public Enforcement of Competition Law?', both in Jürgen Basedow, Jörg Philipp Terhechte and Luboš Tichý (eds), *Private Enforcement of Competition Law* (Nomos Verlagsgesellschaft 2011).

126 COM(2013) 404 final (n 65) 4; Directive 2014/104/EU (n 5) rec. 6.

127 See e.g. COM(2008) 165 final (n 60) 3; COM(2013) 404 final (n 65) 2–3; but cf. the rhetoric of interaction in Directive 2014/104/EU (n 5) rec. 6.

128 For an overview of the US system of public enforcement see Hovenkamp (n 47) Ch. 15.

129 Act of 2 July 1890, c 617, 25 Stat 209, 15 USC §§ 1–7.

130 Act of 15 Oct 1914, c 323, 38 Stat 730, 15 USC §§ 12–27.

131 Consequently, as pointed out by Ulf Bernitz, 'Introduction to the Directive on Competition Damages Actions' in Maria Bergström, Marios C Iacovides and Magnus Strand (eds), *Harmonising EU Competition Litigation: The New Directive and Beyond* (Swedish Studies in European Law vol. 8, Hart Publishing 2016) 7, 'the European system … will not function as a real counterpart to private litigation under American antitrust law'. Alison Jones, 'Private Enforcement of EU Competition Law: A Comparison with, and Lessons from, the US' in the same book includes a very useful overview of the differences between the two systems on pp. 39–41.

132 § 4 Clayton Act (n 137). The nature of this provision was discussed in an influential article by Lawrence Vold, 'Are Three-Fold Damages under the Anti-Trust Act Penal or Compensatory?' (1940) 28 *Kentucky Law Journal* 117.

damages the risk of multiple liability for infringers is more disturbing, as Alpha would risk paying treble damages to two or more claimants all claiming for the same original overcharge. This aspect is absent in the EU system. Of course there are other differences[133] but these are the most important ones for the purposes of this discussion of access to court for Gamma claimants.

7.069 One final *caveat*: much American debate over the passing-on problem has come from the law and economics perspective. The authors most cited and discussed below, Landes and Posner as well as Harris and Sullivan, are scholars of law and economics.[134] For the purposes of this inquiry there will be no analysis of their economical evidence – such analysis is left to better equipped authors. Their arguments will be presented and juxtaposed, and to the extent that they are discussed it will be with regard to consistency and normative content.[135]

a. *Comparative perspective: The Gamma bar in US antitrust law*

7.070 In its seminal ruling *Illinois Brick*,[136] delivered on 9 June 1977, the US Supreme Court held that Gamma claimants were barred from bringing an action for damages under § 4 of the Clayton Act.[137]

7.071 The State of Illinois and 700 governmental entities (Illinois) brought an action for damages against a number of concrete block manufacturers (the manufacturers) arguing that the manufacturers had engaged in an illegal price-fixing conspiracy. Illinois asserted that this conspiracy had resulted in overcharges for concrete blocks that had been passed on to Illinois when purchasing masonry structures.

---

133 For example, the US notion of 'antitrust injury'. On this notion and EU law see para. 7.050.

134 The post-*Illinois Brick* debate between these scholars is famous and influential. It started with two articles published almost simultaneously, William M Landes and Richard A Posner, 'Should Indirect Purchasers Have Standing To Sue Under the Antitrust Laws? An Economic Analysis of the Rule of *Illinois Brick*' (1979) 46 *The University of Chicago Law Review* 602; and Robert G Harris and Lawrence A Sullivan, 'Passing-on the Monopoly Overcharge: A Comprehensive Policy Analysis' (1979) 128 *University of Pennsylvania Law Review* 269. The discussion continued in 128 and 129 *University of Pennsylvania Law Review*.

135 For a European analysis of how to use economic models to determine who has borne the burden of an overcharge see Oxera, 'Quantifying Antitrust Damages. Towards Non-binding Guidance for Courts. Study Prepared for the European Commission' (Publications Office of the European Union 2010) 116–22.

136 *Illinois Brick Co et al v Illinois et al* 431 US 720 (1977). A very interesting, and entertaining, account of the discussions among the Justices of the Supreme Court before delivering its ruling in *Illinois Brick* is available in Andrew I Gavil, 'Antitrust Remedy Wars Episode I: *Illinois Brick* from Inside the Supreme Court' (2005) 79 *St John's Law Review* 553.

137 38 Stat 731, 15 USC § 15:

> Any person who shall be injured in his business or property by reason of anything forbidden in the antitrust laws may sue therefore in any district court of the United States in the district in which the defendant resides or is found or has an agent, without respect to the amount in controversy, and shall recover threefold the damages by him sustained, and the cost of suit, including a reasonable attorney's fee.

The manufacturers moved for a partial summary judgment[138] against all claimants that were indirect purchasers (i.e., Gamma claimants). The manufacturers contended that only their direct purchasers (i.e., Beta claimants) could bring an action for damages in compensation for an alleged overcharge. To this end the manufacturers relied on a previous ruling of the Supreme Court, *Hanover Shoe*,[139] where it was held that the defence of passing-on was not permitted under § 4 of the Clayton Act.

In *Hanover Shoe* the US Supreme Court had rejected the defence of passing-on as a matter of law, with an exception for situations where the parties have entered into a so-called 'cost-plus' contract.[140] But for this exception the Supreme Court held that a direct purchaser (Beta claimant) 'proved injury and the amount of its damages … when it proved that [the Alpha party] had overcharged it during the damage period and showed the amount of the overcharge; [Alpha] was not entitled to assert a passing-on defense'.[141]

In *Illinois Brick* the action was not brought by Beta, as in *Hanover Shoe*, but by Gamma. The legal question was therefore whether the bar against the defensive use of passing-on should also prompt the Supreme Court to bar the offensive use of passing-on.[142] **7.072**

The Supreme Court recognized two preliminary policy options. The first was that a consistent approach should be found where, e.g., a bar against defensive use should in consequence correspond to a bar against offensive use. Both sides in the proceedings adhered to this view, but Illinois argued that both uses should be allowed and that *Hanover Shoe* should consequently be distinguished on its facts. The second option was to interpret *Hanover Shoe* in a way that did not necessarily preclude offensive use of passing-on, i.e., so that Gamma claimants were allowed to bring evidence that the overcharge had been passed on to them.[143] **7.073**

For two reasons the Supreme Court rejected the second option and endorsed the first. First, the Supreme Court was concerned that the second option would create a risk of multiple liability for Alpha as Beta would be able to **7.074**

---

138 A summary judgment in US law is a judgment on issues of law only, designed to allow speedy disposition of a controversy without need for a full trial. A partial summary judgment is limited to certain issues in the case; see *Black's Law Dictionary* (8th edn, West Group 1990).

139 *Hanover Shoe Inc v United Shoe Machinery Corp* 392 US 481 (1968).

140 Ibid., 494. This exception implicitly recalled the so-called Oil Jobbers cases in US antitrust law, e.g., *Twin Ports Oil Co v Pure Oil Co* 119 F2d 747 (8th Cir 1941) *cert denied* 314 US 644 (1941); *NorthWestern Oil v Socony-Vacuum Oil Co* 138 F2d 967 (7th Cir 1943); and *Clark Oil Co v Phillips Petroleum Co* 148 F2d 580 (8th Cir 1945). The exception for these contracts persists, but is subject to some debate; see Hovenkamp (n 47) 677–9. See also para. 7.226.

141 *Hanover Shoe* (n 139) 494.

142 *Illinois Brick* (n 136) 726. See also 728 on differing views of Courts of Appeal on this issue.

143 Ibid., 729–30.

claim damages for the entire overcharge proven and as Gamma would likewise be able, in parallel proceedings, to claim damages for the amount of the overcharge proven to have been passed on.[144] Second, the Supreme Court observed that the principal basis for its decision in *Hanover Shoe* was that actions for damages under § 4 of the Clayton Act would be too complicated if the effects of the overcharge had to be traced. The Supreme Court held that that perception on the defensive use of passing-on applied with no less force to its offensive use. The Supreme Court also pointed out that one of the reasons for its approach in *Hanover Shoe* had been that, unless the defence of passing-on was barred, Alpha would be able to 'retain the fruits of [its] illegality' as most Gamma parties would lack the incentive to bring an action for damages. The second policy option would further the aim of disgorging Alpha, but the Supreme Court held that the underlying concern in *Hanover Shoe* was to promote the effective enforcement of antitrust law by concentrating the right to full recovery of an overcharge in Beta claimants rather than by allowing every potential claimant access to sue.[145] Therefore the Supreme Court 'decline[d] to construe § 4 [of the Clayton Act] to permit the offensive use of a pass-on theory against an alleged violator that could not use the same theory as a defense in an action by [Beta claimants]'.[146]

7.075 Following this conclusion the Supreme Court continued to identify a new set of two alternatives. It would either overrule or limit *Hanover Shoe* or, alternatively, it would preclude Illinois from seeking to recover in reliance of offensive use of passing-on. Reconsidering the *Hanover Shoe* rule the Supreme Court stressed that in the area of interpretation of statutes the principle of *stare decisis* weighed heavily, as it was open to the legislator to change the interpretations of the courts or underlying legislation at will. The Court furthermore held that even if it might seem appealing to attempt to allocate compensation for an overcharge among all potential claimants, 'it would add whole new dimensions of complexity to treble-damage suits and seriously undermine their effectiveness'. The Supreme Court continued to consider mechanisms by which to join potential claimants, but held that even if it were possible through such mechanisms to avoid the problems of multiple litigation and liability it would still transform damages actions into 'massive multiparty litigations involving many levels of distribution and including large classes of consumers remote from [Alpha]' in the effort to apportion compensation among the claimants. In the interest of effective enforcement of antitrust law the Supreme Court confirmed that it was still, as in *Hanover Shoe*, concerned

144 Ibid., 730–31. The Supreme Court cited a *dictum* rejecting 'duplicative recoveries' in *Hawaii v Standard Oil Co of California et al* 405 US 251 (1972) 263–4.

145 Cf. *Hanover Shoe* (n 139) 493–4.

146 *Illinois Brick* (n 136) 731–5.

to avoid weighing down antitrust damages actions with 'massive evidence and complicated theories'.[147] The Supreme Court further dismissed in principle the possibility of calculating the distribution of an overcharge among the potential claimants, and the option of creating special rules for different markets, depending on the price elasticity or other particularities of markets. The Supreme Court instead held that the *Hanover Shoe* rule served to encourage vigorous private enforcement of antitrust law, as Beta was spared the intricacies of the passing-on problem and allowed to recover the full amount of the overcharge.[148]

The Supreme Court nevertheless recognized that some Beta parties might refrain from bringing an action against Alpha under circumstances where Beta was more concerned to maintain business relations with Alpha. The Supreme Court moreover recognized that the *Hanover Shoe* rule denied recovery to Gamma parties who might have been injured by the antitrust violation, and that it made no difference to the general interest of deterrence to whom damages were paid – as long as someone brought an action.[149] The Supreme Court nonetheless held that, on balance and until directed otherwise by the legislator, the aim of effective private enforcement was better served by holding Beta to be injured to the full extent of the overcharge. The Supreme Court observed that the *Hanover Shoe* rule did serve the principle of compensation inasmuch as Beta had absorbed the overcharge. Moreover the Supreme Court was 'unwilling to carry the principle of compensation to its logical extreme' as many Gamma claimants would not have an incentive even to come forward to collect damages awarded to them as part of a class. Therefore, the Supreme Court concluded, there was little basis for believing that the amount of recovery would reflect the actual injury suffered at the Gamma level.[150] For these reasons the Supreme Court did not overrule or limit *Hanover Shoe* but chose instead to preclude Illinois from seeking to recover in reliance on offensive use of passing-on.[151] **7.076**

Controversy over *Hanover Shoe* and *Illinois Brick* has continued in US antitrust discourse and has influenced European competition law debate on private enforcement issues in general and the issue of access to court for Gamma claimants in particular. For the purposes of this presentation five typical arguments have been extracted from the American debate over access to court for Gamma claimants. Most of these were identified by the Supreme Court **7.077**

147 Cf. *Hanover Shoe* (n 139) 493.
148 *Illinois Brick* (n 136) 736–46.
149 On the last point, cf. also the dissent of J Brennan, 760.
150 *Illinois Brick* (n 136) 746–7.
151 Ibid., 736.

itself (majority opinion delivered by J White) in *Illinois Brick*. The fifth was voiced by J Brennan, dissenting, in the same judgment. It is interesting to notice that these arguments have ever since remained at the fore of the continuing discussions. By and large they are also mirrored in the EU debate, as will be seen below.

Argument 1

7.078 As mentioned the Supreme Court was careful to avoid multiple liability for Alpha.[152] Therefore, it argued, it was necessary either to deny access for Gamma or to reverse *Hanover Shoe*.

7.079 J Brennan, dissenting, was less concerned with multiple liability. Although J Brennan recognized 'some abstract merit in the argument' he perceived the risk of multiple liability as too limited in practice to have any substantial impact on a passing-on policy. J Brennan argued that the problem would only arise in two situations. The first was when Beta and Gamma both brought actions at the same time but in different courts. Under such circumstances J Brennan pointed out that there were mechanisms that could and should be used to join the actions and apportion an award of damages between the respective claimants. The second situation was when Beta and Gamma both brought actions but did so consecutively, making it impossible to join them. These were the difficult cases, but in the view of J Brennan they were quite unlikely to occur because of the time-consuming nature of antitrust litigation and the applicable time bars.[153]

7.080 Commentators seem to have agreed with the Supreme Court majority that multiple liability is undesirable.[154] Harris and Sullivan have distinguished 'excessive' liability from 'duplicative' liability. Excessive liability, in their terminology, indicates cases where Alpha would be held liable in treble damages for the entire amount of the aggregate overcharges (i.e., all overcharges along every chain of distribution originating from Alpha) by all prospective Beta claimants plus a number of Gamma claimants. Harris and Sullivan found this situation to be unrealistic. Duplicative liability, on the other hand, would occur where courts deliver inconsistent judgments in response to actions brought by Beta and Gamma respectively. Under such circumstances none of the actions would normally pertain to the entire aggregate of overcharges, but only to those overcharges that were absorbed by the particular chain of distribution along which the Beta and Gamma claimants at issue were found. Harris and Sullivan recognized the possibility of

152 Ibid., 730.
153 Ibid., dissent of J Brennan, 761–3.
154 E.g., Landes and Posner (n 134) 603; Harris and Sullivan (n 134) 345.

allowing such duplicative liability in the interest of disgorging Alpha, but argued that such an approach was undesirable as it would lead to windfall awards (i.e., arbitrary awards in excess of harm actually sustained).[155] They consequently endorsed the view of the majority in this regard. Jones has observed that in the period between *Hanover Shoe* and *Illinois Brick* several US circuits took the view that Beta did have a right to claim damages corresponding to the entire amount of the overcharge paid by them and that Gamma did all the same have access to bring an action for damages for harm caused by the passing-on of the overcharge to them. Notwithstanding this exposure to multiple liability for Alpha, Jones reported that duplicative liability had not occurred in any single case.[156] Jones seemed to imply, citing Sarris to that end, that the rare occasion of such duplicative liability might be preferable over the potential under-deterrence resulting from *Illinois Brick*.[157]

In April 2007 the US Antitrust Modernization Commission (the AMC) presented its Report and Recommendations on a reform of the US antitrust system.[158] The AMC recommended Congress overrule the decisions in both *Hanover Shoe* and *Illinois Brick*. So far it seems this recommendation has fallen into the now rather long list of US legislative initiatives that have made that specific recommendation to no avail. The reasoning of the AMC is nevertheless worth considering. Albeit implicitly, the AMC seemed to share the view that Alpha should not be liable to pay multiple damages.[159] The EU legislature has endorsed the same view for the purposes of Directive 2014/104/EU and has explicitly provided that multiple liability is to be avoided in its Article 15(1).[160] **7.081**

Argument 2

The Supreme Court cited *Hanover Shoe* in which it had held that 'in the real economic world rather than in an economist's hypothetical model' it was uncertain and difficult to determine whether Beta had passed on an overcharge. It had therefore rejected the defence of passing-on. The Supreme Court now held that this applied *a fortiori* to **7.082**

155 Harris and Sullivan (n 134) 343–5. Curiously, Harris and Sullivan later contradict themselves by arguing (on the issue of allocating the burden of proving to whom the overcharge has been passed on) that it is preferable that Beta claimants receive windfall benefits in situations where the only alternative is to allow Alpha to retain the same windfall; see 347–8.

156 Jones (n 18) 198, citing *Effective Enforcement of the Antitrust Laws, 1977: Hearings on HR 8359 Before the Subcomm on Monopolies and Commercial Law of the House Committee on the Judiciary*, 95th Cong 1st Sess 41 (1977) (testimony of Kenneth Reed, Assistant Attorney General for Antitrust, State of Arizona).

157 Jones (n 18) 198, citing Valerie Sarris, *The Efficiency of Private Antitrust Enforcement: The 'Illinois Brick' Decision* (Harland Publishing 1984) 161.

158 Antitrust Modernization Commission, 'Report and Recommendations' (2007) <http://govinfo.library.unt.edu/amc/report_recommendation/toc.htm> (last accessed 31 May 2016).

159 AMC Report and Recommendations (n 158) 271 and 274.

160 In *travaux préparatoires*, see COM(2008) 165 final (n 60) 8.

actions where Gamma claimants wished to prove that an overcharge had been passed on to them through a number of links in the chain of distribution.[161]

7.083 Harris and Sullivan disagreed on this point, arguing that it was inappropriate to rule out the possibility of tracing an overcharge. Instead, Harris and Sullivan suggested, an assessment of the possibility of tracing an overcharge should be made in each individual case. They asserted that it would not be difficult as such to determine how far down the chain such an inquiry could be pursued, arguing that 'the instances in which difficulties are present are readily distinguishable from those in which they are not'. Harris and Sullivan thus seemed to identify three distinct questions to be asked: first, whether the chain of distribution was discernible as such; second, how far down that chain an overcharge could be traced before it became 'an indirect cost of a multiproduct firm' (which would be the point at which it became untraceable); and third, whether and how far the overcharge had in fact been passed on.[162] Landes and Posner opposed Harris and Sullivan on this point and supported the view of the Supreme Court, arguing that the economic analyses necessary were indeed quite difficult. Landes and Posner argued in particular that it was difficult to determine the harm incurred by an enterprise as its absorption of an overcharge was dependent on complicated interplay between short- and long-term elasticity on the market.[163]

7.084 To the non-economist the very existence of disagreement between economists seems to illustrate the point made by J White in *Illinois Brick*, that it is difficult to determine whether (and, it should be added, to what extent) an overcharge has been passed on. The Supreme Court in fact anticipated some of this debate. In *Illinois Brick* it recognized that the difficulties and uncertainties with which it was concerned would be more or less pronounced depending on the structure of the market at issue. The Supreme Court was nonetheless clear that it wanted to create one simple rule to encompass all markets, in order to avoid 'massive evidence and complicated theories' in antitrust litigation.[164]

7.085 More recently the AMC concluded that even though experts had submitted before it that 'recent advances in econometrics and other methodologies have made such assessments somewhat more manageable', with the result of making 'at least some' Gamma claims determinable, it remained problematic to manage the complexity of damage calculation for both Beta and Gamma

161 *Illinois Brick* (n 136) 731–2, citing *Hanover Shoe* (n 139) 493.

162 Harris and Sullivan (n 134) 338–9. For details on how to make this assessment see 315–21.

163 William M Landes and Richard A Posner, 'The Economics of Passing-On: A Reply to Harris and Sullivan' (1980) 128 *University of Pennsylvania Law Review* 1274, 1276–7. Cf. the comment of the Supreme Court on the value of elasticity studies in *Illinois Brick* (n 136) 742.

164 *Illinois Brick* (n 136) 743–5, quoting *Hanover Shoe* (n 139) 493.

claimants.[165] The European Oxera report of 2010 seemed more optimistic, but pointed at difficulties at collecting the data necessary for making the calculation.[166] By and large, therefore, it seems the view of the Supreme Court still holds water. Directive 2014/104/EU nevertheless allows Gamma claims and the European Commission seems in its Practical Guide on quantifying harm to endorse the Harris and Sullivan position that the existence and extent of passing-on is indeed to be assessed in the individual case.[167]

Argument 3

> The Supreme Court held that antitrust law would be more effectively enforced if the right to recover the overcharge was concentrated at the Beta level rather than distributed among all potential claimants.[168] **7.086**

The issue of effective enforcement constitutes a centre of gravity for the American debate. For clarity however, three different conceptions of effective enforcement should be distinguished. The first is effective deterrence from anti-competitive behaviour. The second is effective reparation of harm incurred as a result of anti-competitive behaviour. The third is effective management of antitrust litigation. What is at issue here is the first of these conceptions, i.e., the effective deterrence from anti-competitive behaviour. To understand the discussion between Landes and Posner, on the one side, and Harris and Sullivan, on the other, it is furthermore crucial to keep in mind the options envisaged by the participants: either to endorse both *Hanover Shoe* and *Illinois Brick* or to overrule both cases. The latter alternative is to allow the defence of passing-on and to grant Gamma claimants access to bring an action for damages (i.e., the EU law approach). **7.087**

Landes and Posner argued that the Supreme Court was correct and that the *Illinois Brick* rule contributes to effective deterrence. They argued that the proximity of Beta to Alpha puts Beta in a better position to detect an antitrust violation.[169] Landes and Posner recognized the common counterargument that Beta will lack incentive to bring an action against Alpha under circumstances where it is more beneficial to maintain good business relations with Alpha,[170] but dismissed it as unrealistic. In their view Beta would always seek to maximize profit. Therefore Beta would bring an action unless it was economically preferable not to. In support of this view Landes and Posner also **7.088**

165 AMC Report and Recommendations (n 158) 274.

166 Oxera (n 135) 122. See also Simon Bishop and Mike Walker, *The Economics of EC Competition Law: Concepts, Application and Measurement* (Sweet & Maxwell 2010) 719–20.

167 Directive 2014/104/EU (n 5) Art. 14; SWD(2013) 205 (n 67) para. 168.

168 *Illinois Brick* (n 136) 733–5.

169 Landes and Posner (n 134) 609.

170 Cf. *Illinois Brick* (n 136) 746.

submitted statistical evidence suggesting that Beta claimants were not hesitant to bring actions against Alpha. Landes and Posner further asserted that Gamma claimants, by contrast, had less incentive than Beta to bring an action. Gamma claimants would need to use a class action, and Landes and Posner argued that these were not effectively deterrent. The administration of a class action tended to 'eat up' any award of damages and attorneys were paid higher fees if the claim was settled than if it was brought to court, giving them an incentive to reach settlement rather than pushing for maximum damages.[171] Finally Landes and Posner argued that the more claimants had a right to bring an action the fewer probably would, because the potential claim of each claimant would be too small to outweigh the cost of bringing an action and deciding how to allocate damages awarded among the claimants.[172]

7.089 Harris and Sullivan took the opposite view, arguing that Beta would have little incentive to bring an action inasmuch as Beta had been able to pass on the overcharge, thereby avoiding the suffering of any loss.[173] Harris and Sullivan recognized that *Illinois Brick* (and, one might add, *Hanover Shoe*) encouraged Beta to bring an action, and that it would be equally discouraging if the case law was overruled. They were nonetheless convinced that it did not follow from the fact that Beta claimants did bring actions that Beta claimants were effective 'private attorneys general', as there was no data that could tell the percentage of instances in which an overcharge known to Beta would prompt Beta to bring an action. Instead, they argued, deterrence would be served if *Illinois Brick* was repealed by legislation, as this (relatively small, in their view) discouragement to Beta would by far be outweighed by the encouragement to Gamma to bring actions. Harris and Sullivan also presented statistics showing that a substantial portion of antitrust actions since 1960 had been brought by Gamma claimants. This suggested that Gamma claimants could be effective private enforcers of antitrust law if *Illinois Brick* – which constituted an absolute discouragement to all Gamma claimants – was repealed.[174]

7.090 Harris and Sullivan also recognized that the incentive of Beta to bring an action would be small if its business relationship to Alpha was important. Although Harris and Sullivan recognized that the proximity of Beta to Alpha might put Beta in a better position to become aware of the antitrust violation, they therefore remained unconvinced that this would outweigh Beta's dependence on Alpha. They particularly opposed the view of Landes and Posner that

---

171 Landes and Posner (n 134) 612–14. Cf. *Illinois Brick*, 746–7.

172 Landes and Posner (n 134) 607, 609. Landes and Posner also submitted a related argument based on economic theory; see 621–5.

173 Harris and Sullivan (n 134) 277.

174 Ibid., 349–54. Cf. *Illinois Brick* (n 136) dissent of J Brennan, 749.

Beta would always bring an action if that was the economically preferable option. According to Harris and Sullivan such a view disregarded the mentality of American managers, who would rather earn their profits by selling products than by pushing for windfall gains.[175] They took the view that Beta parties were more likely to instigate a Gamma action against Alpha by disclosing the overcharge to Gamma – provided that *Illinois Brick* was repealed. Without such repeal Harris and Sullivan concluded that in many instances no action at all would be brought against Alpha.[176]

In a reply Landes and Posner maintained that Beta's possible dependence on Alpha did not support the conclusion that Beta would have less incentive to bring an action. To avoid an action Alpha would need to pay Beta a functional equivalent of a treble damages award. Under such circumstances, Landes and Posner seemingly implied, justice would have been served. Landes and Posner also maintained that the omission to bring an action for damages would economically be equivalent to a business cost, irrespective of whether an award could be characterized as a windfall.[177] In response Harris and Sullivan counterargued that it followed from the facts of *Illinois Brick* itself, where Gamma (the state of Illinois) was in an excellent position to detect the antitrust violation and bring an action for damages while it was uncertain whether Beta had detected the violation at all, that the interest of deterrence would be best served if *Illinois Brick* was repealed. Harris and Sullivan further argued that the 'automatic' compensation envisaged by Landes and Posner did not amount to justice, but injustice, and ruled out any possibility of deterrence by private enforcement. Harris and Sullivan also maintained that although managers were economically rational, that rationality would not extend to the extreme of becoming 'bounty hunter[s]'.[178] **7.091**

It is respectfully submitted that this debate entails a number of good arguments, and a number of not so good ones – not all of which have been included in this survey. The argument that Beta is in a better position than Gamma to detect the overcharge[179] is effectively falsified by Harris and Sullivan by pointing out a 'black swan': *Illinois Brick*.[180] If it cannot be generally assumed that Beta is in such a better position, the proximity argument must be abandoned. **7.092**

175 Harris and Sullivan (n 134) 352 n 158a.

176 Ibid., 352.

177 Landes and Posner (n 163) 1278–9.

178 Robert G Harris and Lawrence A Sullivan, 'Passing-on the Monopoly Overcharge: A Response to Landes and Posner' (1980) 128 *University of Pennsylvania Law Review* 1280, 1287–9.

179 Landes and Posner (n 134) 609.

180 Harris and Sullivan (n 178) 1287.

7.093 The argument on rational choice brought by Landes and Posner, according to which Beta will always bring an action if this is economically preferable,[181] also seems over-simplified. It considers neither the bigger context of business relations and goodwill to complete the picture of how to determine what is economically preferable, nor the social, cultural and other human considerations that will influence the decision of whether or not to bring an action. Admittedly however, the rational choice argument illustrates the considerations that would be relevant if all these human factors were cut away with Occam's razor. For the sake of argument let us accept this model and proceed to review the analysis. Landes and Posner argue that Beta will choose not to bring an action only if Alpha has already paid Beta the functional equivalent of antitrust damages. Otherwise Landes and Posner maintain that Beta will unavoidably bring an action. Assuming that Alpha is also acting economically rationally this means that Alpha will violate antitrust law and pay Beta the functional equivalent of antitrust damages if this is economically preferable over the alternative, i.e., the option to comply with antitrust law. In the interest of deterrence from violations of law it is plainly unacceptable to allow the parties such corruption. Perhaps Landes and Posner implicitly wished to show that it would probably never be economically preferable for Alpha to pay the functional equivalent of treble damages to its customers, and consequently Beta would always bring an action against Alpha when Beta detected an antitrust violation. If so, this argument is relevant to the distribution of legal powers between Beta and Gamma but would need clarification and supporting empirical evidence. Otherwise this argument may illustrate that economic incentives to bring an action may contribute to the deterrent effect of antitrust actions but does not bring the conclusion that actions should be brought by Beta rather than Gamma.

7.094 The next argument of Landes and Posner was that Gamma claimants have less incentive to bring an action, as the benefits obtainable will not suffice to outweigh their costs and efforts for bringing an action (typically a class action).[182] Harris and Sullivan argued against this, showing with statistics that Gamma can contribute to private antitrust enforcement.[183] It is submitted that the evidence produced by Harris and Sullivan is more convincing in this context, while the evidence produced by Landes and Posner seems weak and speculative. Even the statistics that Landes and Posner themselves submitted

181 Landes and Posner (n 134) 613–14.

182 Ibid., 607, 609.

183 Harris and Sullivan (n 134) 349–51, 353–4.

suggest that Gamma claimants had contributed substantially to private antitrust enforcement.[184] Admittedly it cannot be ruled out that there will be situations where the class of potential Gamma claimants, as a whole, will have little incentive to bring an action, in particular where the Gamma class is scattered and each potential claimant has very little to gain from an award of damages.[185] Nevertheless, if deterrence from anticompetitive behaviour is the aim pursued, it still seems reasonable against this background to agree with Harris and Sullivan that Gamma claimants should be allowed to bring actions for antitrust damages when they themselves find it worthwhile to do so – it must be better to give the opportunity than to withdraw it.[186] It must however be remembered that in the common US perspective this would consequently mean that *Hanover Shoe* must also be overruled, as Alpha should not be held liable in multiple damages.[187] As Alpha would consequently be able to raise the defence of passing-on this might substantially lessen the incentive of Beta to bring actions against Alpha. The crucial question from the point of view of the US context is, therefore, one of fact. Under what circumstances is deterrence best served? Is more private antitrust enforcement to be expected if *Hanover Shoe* and *Illinois Brick* remain intact, or if they are repealed? For lack of evidence that question of fact cannot be answered here.

Hovenkamp has not entered into the details of this debate as such but has simply noticed that views for and against the *Illinois Brick* ruling generally coincide with views on the priority between the antitrust goals of deterrence and reparation. Hovenkamp thus reports that commentators who are exclusively concerned with effective deterrence will support *Illinois Brick*, while those who favour full compensation of victims argue for its repeal.[188] Landes and Posner recognize both interests, but give explicit priority to deterrence.[189] Harris and Sullivan view deterrence as the 'second salient feature' of private antitrust enforcement, the first being compensatory justice.[190] This may **7.095**

184 See Landes and Posner (n 134) 614 n 30.

185 Daniel Beard and Alison Jones, 'Co-Contractors, Damages and Article 81: The ECJ Finally Speaks' (2002) 23 *European Competition Law Review* 246, 255, memorably captured this when arguing that, in the *Courage* litigation, it was unlikely that 'even the most hardened drinkers would contemplate their losses being sufficient to make proceedings against the brewers worthwhile'.

186 The views of Landes and Posner in this regard should be read in light of their view that Gamma parties actually benefit from the *Illinois Brick* bar, see para. 7.100 below.

187 J Brennan (*Illinois Brick* (n 136) dissent of J Brennan, 751–4) did not however share this view of the link between *Hanover Shoe* and *Illinois Brick*. Questioning the 'consistency' approach of the majority, he argued that it did not follow from *Hanover Shoe* that Gamma claimants should be barred. In other words J Brennan took the view that it might be possible both to allow Gamma claims and to deny the defence of passing-on in actions brought by Beta. Jones (n 18) 197–8, citing Sarris (n 157) 133–4, 138, supported this view but recognized that this solution increases the risk liability to pay multiple damages.

188 Hovenkamp (n 47) 681.

189 Landes and Posner (n 134) 605.

190 Harris and Sullivan (n 178) 1286. Cf. Harris and Sullivan (n 134) 276–7.

account for some of their differences. The Supreme Court itself explicitly favoured deterrence over reparation in *Illinois Brick*.[191] By contrast Directive 2014/104/EU is committed to the interest of reparation.[192] It is therefore no surprise that it will allow Gamma claims.[193]

Argument 4

7.096 The Supreme Court was concerned that if Gamma was not barred from bringing an action against Alpha it would be consumed with 'massive efforts to apportion the recovery among all potential plaintiffs' that would undermine the effectiveness of private antitrust enforcement.[194]

7.097 This is an issue of effective management of antitrust litigation. The worry of the Supreme Court pertains not to the award of damages to Gamma as such, but to the apportionment of the award among the heterogeneous classes of Beta and Gamma claimants. The implications of this fourth argument are almost identical to the second above and the considerations at issue are alike. Reference is therefore made to that discussion, but it may be recalled that it was concluded that the advances of economic theory and analysis since *Illinois Brick* do not seem able to overcome all the difficulties envisaged by the Supreme Court.[195]

Argument 5

7.098 J Brennan, dissenting, was concerned that the majority did not pay sufficient attention to the interest of reparation underlying § 4 of the Clayton Act. In many instances, he argued, 'the brunt of antitrust injuries' was borne by Gamma.[196]

7.099 The majority recognized that Gamma would be denied recovery but held that its approach would still serve the interest of reparation 'to the extent that [Beta] absorbs at least some and often most of the overcharge'. The majority was furthermore 'unwilling to carry the compensation principle to its logical extreme' as it held that Gamma actions were liable to 'deplet[e] the overall recovery in litigation over pass-on issues' rather than repair actual harm suffered.[197] In this context, however, the issue is not whether Beta or Gamma is the more effective private antitrust enforcer but whether it is equitable to deny Gamma the opportunity to seek reparation. The holdings of the Supreme Court majority hence miss the mark if intended as a reply to this

191 *Illinois Brick* (n 136) 746–7.
192 Directive 2014/104/EU (n 5) Arts 3, 12, 15.
193 Ibid., Art. 14.
194 *Illinois Brick* (n 136) 737.
195 See para. 7.085.
196 *Illinois Brick* (n 136) dissent of J Brennan, 749.
197 Ibid., 746–7.

argument by J Brennan. It may well be that *Illinois Brick* promotes effective enforcement in the sense of effective deterrence[198] but the issue here is whether it promotes effective reparation.[199]

With regard to the third argument listed above, the reasoning of Landes and Posner was similar to that of the Supreme Court majority. Landes and Posner however also submitted that the *Illinois Brick* solution would promote effective reparation for all. Landes and Posner came to this conclusion by arguing that whenever Beta knew about or suspected an overcharge, the contingent treble damages claim would be 'equivalent to a valuable, though risky, asset' held by Beta. Beta would therefore, according to Landes and Posner, lower the expected marginal costs for its own production, which would generate a spill-over effect of lower prices to be paid by Gamma – hence compensating Gamma. If *Illinois Brick* were repealed, Landes and Posner argued that the expected marginal costs for Beta's production would rise, increasing prices to be paid by Gamma. Landes and Posner recognized that this model would work only if Beta anticipated and took account of the overcharge. Nevertheless they maintained that the instances of this model would work better than a repeal, e.g., because the benefits spreading from their model might also benefit those more remote parties – even upstream – who would not benefit from a repeal.[200] **7.100**

Harris and Sullivan unsurprisingly took the opposite view, arguing that the passing-on of overcharges '*is not the exception: it is the rule*'.[201] Therefore, they asserted, to deny Gamma the opportunity of compensation while granting it to Beta was inequitable.[202] Harris and Sullivan also disagreed with the economic model of automatic compensation submitted by Landes and Posner. According to Harris and Sullivan it was unlikely that any real or contingent award of damages would be 'passed back' as argued by Landes and Posner. Instead it would remain with Beta as a windfall award.[203] Harris and Sullivan further added in a later comment that if it was so difficult for courts to relate damages awards to price effects in the form of overcharges, Beta could not reasonably have the precision expected by Landes and Posner in anticipating **7.101**

198 It has been submitted in the context of the third argument here listed that, in the US context and accepting that *Hanover Shoe* and *Illinois Brick* are inseparably intertwined, this is a question of fact that the available evidence does not answer.

199 Cf. para. 7.087 on the different notions of effectiveness at issue here.

200 Landes and Posner (n 134) 605–7.

201 Harris and Sullivan (n 134) 276 (italics in original). Similarly in Directive 2014/104/EU (n 5) Art. 14(1), but cf. SWD(2013) 205 (n 67) para. 168.

202 Harris and Sullivan (n 134) 277, 346–7 where this is called 'blatantly unfair'. See also *Illinois Brick* (n 136) dissent of J Brennan, 761.

203 Harris and Sullivan (n 134) 298–9 n 67.

contingent damages awards in its pricing policy.[204] It is submitted that the arguments submitted by Harris and Sullivan are convincing. It also speaks to common sense that Beta will not lower its prices in light of the remote possibility of an award of damages. The only imaginable instance in which the benefit of an award would be 'passed back' from Beta to Gamma seems to be where Beta uses the award to create an opportunity to temporarily drop prices in order to gain new market shares. That scenario does not, however, support any policy with regard to *Illinois Brick*. This author therefore remains unconvinced that a bar against Gamma claims could in any way benefit Gamma or other remote claimants.

7.102 The AMC later argued that '[t]he most fundamental criticism of the *Illinois Brick* rule' was that Gamma claimants were not permitted by federal law to recover compensation for harm suffered because of antitrust violations.[205] Hovenkamp too has observed that the most serious problem with *Illinois Brick* is that it does not appear to be consistent with the compensatory objective of § 4 of the Clayton Act.[206] It indeed seems that J Brennan was correct in finding that *Illinois Brick* does not serve the interest of reparation. Many US state legislators have accordingly taken the view that *Illinois Brick* unfairly bars Gamma from recovering. In the years following *Illinois Brick* several states therefore adopted '*Illinois Brick* repealers' for the purposes of state antitrust law.[207] In *ARC America* the Supreme Court held that federal antitrust law did not pre-empt such legislation.[208] This discord between federal and state law created new problems, however. The AMC report described a situation where the judicial system was unnecessarily burdened by multiple and wasteful parallel proceedings, where defendants suffered costs for uncoordinated discovery in several courts and where claimants lacked access to the findings of other claimants. This also made it difficult to negotiate global settlements. It furthermore caused inequality among Gamma claimants depending on the policy chosen by the state in which they wished to bring their action. The AMC also expressed fear that under the present circumstances defendants would be inequitably liable to pay multiple damages. Against this background the AMC recommended Congress follow the displayed preference of the majority of states and consequently to overrule *Illinois Brick*.[209] Congress has not yet followed this recommendation.

---

204 Harris and Sullivan (n 178) 1283.

205 AMC Report and Recommendations (n 158) 273.

206 Hovenkamp (n 47) 681.

207 AMC Report and Recommendations (n 158) 269 counted more than 35 states with such diverging antitrust legislation in 2009.

208 *California et al v ARC America Corp et al* 490 US 93 (1989).

209 AMC Report and Recommendations (n 158) 271–5.

7.103 It has already been mentioned that the EU legislature has favoured the interest of reparation over the interest of deterrence in the drafting of Directive 2014/104/EU. Moreover, as the Directive covers all situations where Article 101 or 102 TFEU are applicable (including those situations where they apply in parallel with national competition law), there is little room for divergent national law. Hence the problem outlined by the AMC seems not to be relevant in the EU context. A similar situation could theoretically arise if the national competition law of a Member State would bar Gamma from bringing an action for damages in cases where Article 101 or 102 TFEU did not apply. This would not be a policy problem for EU law however, but only for the Member State concerned.

7.104 To summarize this comparative perspective, and its discussion of the reasons for and against access to court for Gamma, it can be submitted that the *Illinois Brick* wall against Gamma claims is designed to serve deterrence but not to serve reparation. It has not been proved that it would be manageable for courts to assess whether and to what extent Beta has passed on the burden of the overcharge to Gamma, although it seems this will largely depend on circumstances on the individual markets – which might of course be taken as support for the approach chosen by the Supreme Court in *Illinois Brick*. Some Americans also worry that if Gamma were granted access to court, Alpha might be liable to pay multiple treble damages. Empirical evidence however seems to suggest that this risk is exaggerated.[210]

b. Access for Gamma claimants in EU law

7.105 It is now time to examine the approach chosen for the purposes of EU competition law. Before the adoption of Directive 2014/104/EU it was sometimes argued that *Courage* and *Manfredi* had implications for the issue of access for Gamma claimants.[211] Such interpretations took their point of departure in the holding of the Court in *Courage* that the full effectiveness of Article 85 EC (now 101 TFEU) and in particular the practical effect of the prohibition therein would be put at risk if it were not open to 'any individual' to claim damages for loss caused by a contract or by conduct liable to restrict or distort competition, and that therefore there should not be any absolute bar against such actions.[212] The Court furthermore held in *Manfredi* that 'any individual' could claim compensation for the harm suffered where there was a causal relationship between that harm and an agreement or practice prohibited

210 Jones (n 18) 198, see para. 7.080.

211 E.g., COM(2008) 165 final (n 60) 4.

212 *Courage* (n 4) paras 26, 28.

under that provision,[213] adding details on such actions in the following paragraphs. The interpretation that the 'any individual' concept had cleared the path for Gamma claimants was reinforced by the inclusive policy chosen by the Court of Justice in subsequent case law. For example the Commission was allowed to bring an action for damages on behalf of the EU in *Otis*,[214] and victims of umbrella pricing were allowed to bring an action against members of a cartel in *Kone*.[215] Nevertheless these were *ad hoc* rulings, and it was not possible to draw certain conclusions with regard to Gamma claimants neither from them nor from the ambiguous 'any individual' phrase.

7.106 Now clarity has been achieved through Directive 2014/104/EU which grants access to court for Gamma claimants in order for them to be able to bring an action for damages seeking compensation for harm incurred due to a breach of competition law. The relevant rule is laid down in Article 12(1):

7.107

> Article 12: Passing-on of overcharges and the right to full compensation
>
> 1. To ensure the full effectiveness of the right to full compensation as laid down in Article 3, Member States shall ensure that, in accordance with the rules laid down in this Chapter, compensation of harm can be claimed by anyone who suffered it, irrespective of whether they are direct or indirect purchasers from an infringer … .

7.108 'Indirect purchaser' is defined in Article 2(24):

> 'indirect purchaser' means a natural or legal person who acquired, not directly from an infringer, but from a direct purchaser or a subsequent purchaser, products or services that were the object of an infringement of competition law, or products or services containing them or derived therefrom.

7.109 It thus follows explicitly from Directive 2014/104/EU that Gamma claimants (here 'indirect purchasers', the common term in competition law discourse) must be granted access to bring an action before the competent national court. It is of no consequence to this rule how many levels of the supply chain separate the Gamma claimant from Alpha, or whether the products or services bought by Gamma have been altered along the way.

7.110 Of course it does not follow that any Gamma action must be successful. Success still requires for the Gamma claimant to prove several other points, e.g., that harm was indeed passed on to the Gamma claimant. These points are addressed in subsequent Articles, to be discussed in Section 7.D.II and

213 *Manfredi* (n 36) para. 61.
214 *Otis* (n 45).
215 *Kone* (n 46).

sub-section 7.E.II.b. Suffice it here to indicate that the rules of the Directive are designed to promote the interest of reparation and that they may serve the interest of deterrence from anticompetitive behaviour to a lesser extent.[216] In this section the European debate over the policy options with regard to Gamma claimants will be discussed. In the interest of assisting the reader the discussion has been structured so as to mirror the major points of controversy in the US debate listed above. A specifically European concern will however be added.

The first concern listed above was multiple liability for Alpha.[217] This concern is shared in Directive 2014/104/EU, as Article 15(1) instructs the Member States to take steps to 'avoid that actions for damages by claimants from different levels in the supply chain lead to a multiple liability ... of the infringer'.[218] As seen above, some American critics of *Illinois Brick* did not rule out the option of upholding *Hanover Shoe* while overruling *Illinois Brick*,[219] i.e., to preclude the defence of passing-on (passing-on as 'shield') while nonetheless allowing Gamma claims with regard to harm passed on to them (passing-on as 'sword').[220] Such a solution would contribute to deterrence but might lead to over-deterrence and multiple liability for Alpha.[221] **7.111**

The evidence presented by Jones, and the arguments of J Brennan as well as those of Harris and Sullivan, put the reasonability of this fear into question however, most importantly as it would not be common for all potential claimants to bring an action.[222] In this regard Jones has recognized, on the one hand, that a 'theoretical possibility of double recovery is inherent' if Gamma claimants are granted access to court, but only if the defence of passing-on is simultaneously banned. Jones also noticed, on the other hand, that if the defence of passing-on is allowed and not all Gamma claimants bring an action, Alpha will retain at least some of the fruits of its breach of competition **7.112**

216 The role of deterrence in EU competition damages will be discussed further in Section 9.E.II. Cf. also para. 7.227.

217 *Illinois Brick* (n 136) 730.

218 See also COM(2008) 165 final (n 60) 7–8; and SEC(2008) 404 (n 60) para. 210.

219 *Illinois Brick* (n 136) dissent of J Brennan, 751–4; Jones (n 18) 197–8, citing Sarris (n 157) 133–4, 138.

220 The 'sword' and 'shield' metaphors were introduced in para. 1.009. A nice overview of the options with regard to the defence of passing-on and access for Gamma is available in Süleyman Parlak, 'Passing-on Defence and Indirect Purchaser Standing: Should the Passing-on Defence Be Rejected Now the Indirect Purchaser Has Standing after *Manfredi* and the White Paper of the European Commission?' (2010) 33 *World Competition* 31, 41–3.

221 This was feared in AMC Report and Recommendations (n 158) 271.

222 See para. 7.079. Cf. also case C-94/10 *Danfoss A/S and Sauer-Danfoss ApS v Skatteministeriet* [2011] ECR I-9963, where Beta did not bring an action for repayment of charges levied in breach of EU law, as those charges had been passed on.

law. Therefore both options 'have aspects which are unsatisfactory'.[223] It would seem necessary to make a choice between the two. To that end van Gerven has argued that 'over-recovery at the charge of the wrongdoer' should be avoided.[224] By contrast, Bulst has submitted that 'one must not take the avoidance of multiple liability as a starting point, but rather focus on achieving compensation of the victims'.[225] Seeking what might be a middle way, Bulst would thus allow claimants to benefit from the complexity of the situation rather than allow the infringer to do so, as long as no excessive liability was inflicted on the infringer.[226] Technically the solution implied by Bulst would probably be workable only if realized through some form of class action.[227] Another option, very similar to class actions, would be to subrogate the mass of claims pertaining to a certain supply chain to a joint claimant body.[228]

7.113 It should also be recalled that in the US context Alpha would fear multiple treble damages. In EU competition law only single damages are awarded, and the risk of over-deterrence is therefore much less in the EU than in the US.[229] From the European perspective treble damages in itself constitutes multiple liability. If it is accepted that not all potential claimants will bring an action,[230] the risk of multiple liability for Alpha should perhaps not be a significant policy consideration in a system of single damages awards. On balance it is accordingly submitted that the fear of multiple liability should not dictate the EU law approach to access to court for Gamma claimants. Beard and Jones have similarly submitted that 'the risk of double recovery is outweighed by the public interest in ensuring that anti-competitive behaviour is deterred'.[231] To promote that interest in private enforcement of competition law in the EU it

223 Jones (n 18) 198.

224 Walter van Gerven, 'Private Enforcement of EC Competition Rules in the ECJ – Courage v. Crehan and the Way Ahead' in Jürgen Basedow (ed.), *Private Enforcement of EC Competition Law*, (Kluwer Law International 2007) 35.

225 Friedrich Wenzel Bulst, 'Passing-on' in Jürgen Basedow, Jörg Philipp Terhechte and Luboš Tichý (eds), *Private Enforcement of Competition Law* (Nomos Verlagsgesellschaft 2011) 78.

226 Ibid. It is not clear whether Bulst uses the term 'excessive liability' with the same meaning as Harris and Sullivan (n 134) 343–4. However, since Bulst cites Harris and Sullivan in an earlier footnote (54), this may be so.

227 It may be doubted in that regard whether the model recommended in Recommendation 2013/396/EU (n 68) is strong enough to do the trick; see European Law Institute, 'Statement of the European Law Institute on Collective Redress and Competition Damages Claims' (2014) <http://www.europeanlawinstitute.eu/fileadmin/user_upload/p_eli/Projects/S-5-2014_Statement_on_Collective_Redress_and_Competition_Damages_Claims.pdf> (last accessed 31 May 2016) 42–4.

228 This is a growing business idea in the EU. A well-known example is CDC Consulting SCRL, aka Cartel Damages Claims.

229 See Jones (n 18) 198.

230 Cf. Harris and Sullivan (n 134) 343–4.

231 Beard and Jones (n 185) 255.

might even have been reasonable to contemplate a *Hanover Shoe* rule for Beta actions while nevertheless allowing access for Gamma.[232]

The second concern of the US Supreme Court was that it was too difficult to ascertain whether and to what extent harm was passed on down the supply chain. For the Supreme Court it seems this was the paramount reason for its approach in *Illinois Brick*.[233] The Supreme Court did recognize that the complexity would differ between markets but insisted on finding a universal rule.[234] It has been pointed out by Ashton and Henry that European courts would likewise suffer from the difficulties of tracing the exact extent of harm suffered at various points in the supply chain.[235] Parlak has similarly submitted that although it may to some extent be possible to estimate passing-on, that task seems to be 'an insurmountable task for judges'.[236] The Commission has by contrast been more optimistic with regard to the possibility of overcoming complexities than the US Supreme Court,[237] and is presently drafting guidelines to assist the national courts in the estimation of passing-on.[238] Accordingly the EU legislature has opted for an almost converse rule to solve the same problem: that Gamma claimants be able to rely on a rebuttable presumption that the entire overcharge has been passed on to them.[239] The reasons for this choice were, first, a recognition of the complexity that may be involved, second, a reluctance to allow Alpha to 'retain an unjust enrichment', and third, a pursuit of the interest of reparation of Gamma parties 'at, or near the end of the distribution chain [who] are often those most harmed by antitrust infringements'.[240] Kloub has submitted that this approach will produce new problems, especially regarding the standard of proof for rebuttal.[241] This presumption and its rebuttal will be discussed further in paragraphs 7.196–7.197. 7.114

232 As indicated by Jones (n 18) 197. The plausible possibility for Beta to circumvent the passing-on rules in Directive 2014/104/EU in certain situations is contemplated by this author in Magnus Strand, 'Beyond the Competition Damages Directive: What Room for Competition Law Restitution?' in Maria Bergström, Marios C Iacovides and Magnus Strand (eds), *Harmonising EU Competition Litigation: The New Directive and Beyond* (Swedish Studies in European Law vol. 8, Hart Publishing 2016).

233 *Illinois Brick* (n 136) 731–2.

234 Ibid., 743–4.

235 David Ashton and David Henry, *Competition Damages Actions in the EU: Law and Practice* (Edward Elgar Publishing 2013) 45.

236 Parlak (n 220) 53.

237 See SWD(2013) 205 (n 67) para. 168.

238 COMP/2015/011 – 'Study on the passing-on of overcharges', see <http://ec.europa.eu/competition/antitrust/actionsdamages/index.html>.

239 Directive 2014/104/EU (n 5) Art. 14(2).

240 COM(2008) 165 final (n 60) 8.

241 See Jindřich Kloub, 'Standing and Pass-on Defense in Antitrust Damage Suits: Guided by Corrective Justice or Efficiency?' in Jürgen Basedow, Jörg Philipp Terhechte and Luboš Tichý (eds), *Private Enforcement of Competition Law* (Nomos Verlagsgesellschaft 2011) 96.

7.115 The third argument of the US Supreme Court was that an exclusive right to damages for Beta claimants would serve the interest of effective enforcement of federal antitrust law, as the risk of facing treble damages claims from Beta would deter Alpha from infringements.[242] As seen in paragraph 7.114 it was admitted by the Supreme Court majority that the *Illinois Brick* wall against Gamma claimants would deny compensation for harm incurred by Gamma claimants and that this was an unfortunate side effect. However, as they would give priority to deterrence over reparation, this side effect had to be tolerated.[243] This insistence on deterrence must be seen in light of the importance of private enforcement in the overall enforcement system of US antitrust law. In EU competition law the interest of deterrence is served first and foremost by public enforcement, although it is generally agreed that private enforcement can contribute to deterrence, especially when private individuals bring standalone actions.[244] It follows that the interest of designing the rules of private enforcement in a manner that will achieve optimal deterrence is not as strong in the EU as it is in the US. It has indeed been submitted by Nebbia that 'the primary aim of private enforcement [in the EU] should be compensation'.[245] This bias is quite evident in Directive 2014/104/EU.[246] As observed by Hovenkamp a policy designed primarily to serve the interest of reparation will generally coincide with a rejection of the *Illinois Brick* rule.[247] Hovenkamp's observation holds true with regard to Directive 2014/104/EU.

7.116 Continuing with the fourth issue listed in the previous section, the US Supreme Court was concerned that if Gamma was not barred from bringing an action against Alpha, it would be consumed with 'massive efforts to apportion the recovery among all potential plaintiffs' that would undermine the effectiveness of private antitrust enforcement.[248] In the European context it has similarly been argued by Wahl that the *Illinois Brick* rule (or similar)

242 *Illinois Brick* (n 136) 733–5.

243 Ibid., 746–7; Landes and Posner (n 134) 605–6 even argued that the *Illinois Brick* wall would result in indirect compensation for Gamma.

244 See Directive 2014/104/EU (n 5) rec. 6; SWD(2013) 203 final (n 57) paras 29, 68, and pp. 26–7; SEC(2008) 404 (n 60) paras 15, 17–21; and most especially Communication [2013] (n 66) paras 1–2. See also Komninos (n 80) 6–7 and 'The Relationship between Public and Private Enforcement: *quod Dei Deo, quod Caesaris Caesari*' in Philip Lowe and Mel Marquis (eds), *European Competition Law Annual 2011: Integrating Public and Private Enforcement of Competition Law – Implications for Courts and Agencies* (Hart Publishing 2014) 142–5; and Renato Nazzini, 'The Objective of Private Remedies in EU Competition Law' (2011) 4 *Global Competition Litigation Review* 131, 140. For a critical discussion see Wils (n 125) 116–27. Of course, as already mentioned, it is nevertheless open for the EU to boost the deterrent effect of its private enforcement system by taking specific measures to that effect. Compensation and deterrence are not in binary opposition.

245 Paolisa Nebbia, 'Damages Actions for the Infringement of EC Competition Law: Compensation or Deterrence' (2008) 33 *European Law Review* 23, 36.

246 See Directive 2014/104/EU (n 5) Arts 3, 12–15.

247 Hovenkamp (n 47) 681.

248 *Illinois Brick* (n 136) 737.

should be adopted in the interest of effective litigation.[249] In other words the argument was that access for Gamma claimants would come at the expense of litigation management, increasing the risk for flaws and mistakes in the service of justice. It was seen in paragraph 7.085 that, according to experts, this seems to remain true.[250] Directive 2014/104/EU does include a number of measures designed to address the problem of complexity, including presumptions, approximations and rules on the disclosure of evidence. These will be discussed further in sub-section 7.E.II.c.

The fifth issue discussed in the previous section was the one most often returned to by those who oppose the *Illinois Brick* rule, namely that Gamma claimants are not compensated for harm actually incurred by them. In European discourse this argument is the principal argument used to distance our approach from the US approach. For instance Beard and Jones have submitted that the *Illinois Brick* rule undermines 'the operation of the principle that an individual who has suffered loss in consequence of a breach of the competition rules is entitled to compensation'.[251] As pointed out by Wahl, market conditions may be such that all harm has been passed on from Beta to the Gamma class.[252] Under such circumstances, Bulst has observed, 'private enforcement would be paralyzed whenever [Beta is] unwilling or unable to actually bring a claim'.[253] Nevertheless it has also been recognized by European commentators that Gamma claimants who have suffered insignificant losses will have little incentive to bring an action,[254] or may be too remote even to detect the infringement and the implications of it for themselves.[255] The pulverization of harm may thus ultimately lead to an absence of private enforcement, under which circumstances Alpha will retain benefits earned through a breach of competition law. Even though the interest of reparation for Gamma has been safeguarded by Directive 2014/104/EU, this remains a real problem in the EU law context and will be discussed further in sub-section 7.E.II.c. **7.117**

Finally, a concern particular in the EU context has been voiced by e.g. Beard and Jones, arguing that a bar against Gamma claimants 'would be inconsistent with direct effect of Articles 81 and 82'.[256] Komninos has similarly stressed the constitutionality of Articles 101 and 102 TFEU and the protection of rights **7.118**

249 Wahl (n 87) 253–6.
250 Cf. Directive 2014/104/EU (n 5) rec. 45.
251 Beard and Jones (n 185) 255.
252 Wahl (n 87) 252.
253 Bulst (n 225) 78.
254 Ashton and Henry (n 235) 42.
255 Wahl (n 87) 252.
256 Beard and Jones (n 185) 255. Arts 81 and 82 are now Arts 101 and 102 TFEU.

conferred on individuals by the EU Treaties.[257] Jones has likewise argued that a right to damages 'would be without meaning if an additional corollary to direct effect is not the existence of *locus standi*'.[258] To this author these arguments seem to jump to conclusions. It may be true that *ubi ius, ibi remedium*, but that maxim can also be read *e contrario*: where there is no right, there will be no remedy.[259] Direct effect as such does not indicate an all-encompassing *ratione personae* of the rule at issue. Naturally it is important that Articles 101 and 102 TFEU have direct effect and that the rights conferred on individuals by them are to be protected, but it is then crucial to remember the next step, i.e., to determine who are in fact protected.[260]

7.119 The European Court of Justice has not ruled that the right to damages for a breach of Article 101 and/or 102 TFEU extends to Gamma claimants. This was not settled until the adoption of Directive 2014/104/EU, from which it follows that Gamma will have a right to damages for harm incurred due to a breach of competition law and that no Gamma claimant can be denied access to court by reason of remoteness from Alpha.[261] It further follows from the existence of such a right that Gamma actions will fall under the scope of application of Article 47 of the Charter and the EU law principles of equivalence and effectiveness. It is well known however that a right to damages laid down in a Directive cannot as such be exercised in horizontal legal relationships.[262] Unless it is settled by the Court of Justice that the right to damages for a breach of Article 101 and/or 102 TFEU established in *Courage* and *Manfredi* extends to Gamma, the right enjoyed by Gamma under Directive 2014/104/EU may become fraught with substantial limitations in the event of incomplete national implementation of the Directive. More precisely it will be possible for Gamma to exercise its right to compensation against Alpha only if the applicable national jurisdiction has properly implemented those aspects of Directive 2014/104/EU. When the transposition period for the Directive has expired[263] Gamma will also be able to exercise its right to compensation against Alpha if Alpha is an emanation of a Member

---

257 Komninos (n 80) 203.

258 Jones (n 18) 186.

259 See Section 2.A on the right-remedy-procedure sequence.

260 See also Jones (n 18) 191, submitting that 'in the Community *locus standi* rules at least will be coextensive with the substantive reach of the competition rules'.

261 Directive 2014/104/EU (n 5) Arts 12(1), 2(24), quoted above.

262 On the necessity of horizontal direct effect for horizontal damages claims based exclusively on EU law to be successful see Section 8.B.I.

263 Under Directive 2014/104/EU (n 5) Art. 21(1) the transposition period expires 27 December 2016.

State within the meaning of EU law.[264] If Alpha is not an emanation of the Member State in this sense, incomplete implementation of Directive 2014/104/EU risks leaving Gamma with no legal basis for its claim as a Directive is not capable of itself of producing legal obligations for private individuals – unless the Court of Justice is given the opportunity to deliver a preliminary ruling providing that Gamma claimants fall within the *ratione personae* of Article 101 and/or 102 TFEU and that their rights are horizontally enforceable through an action for damages. It is indeed very likely that the Court would rule to that effect,[265] but the comments here submitted nevertheless serve to illustrate that the direct effect of Article 101 and/or 102 does not short-circuit the intricacies of EU law.

In sum none of the policy arguments submitted in US and EU discourse have managed to give rise to consensus on the better view with regard to access to court for Gamma in the context of competition damages. Views differ and, as observed by Hovenkamp, those who would give priority to the interest of universal compensation will support access for Gamma.[266] Although those who favour a bar against Gamma claims seem invariably to suggest that this would serve the interest of deterrence, it has been demonstrated above that preference for the interest of deterrence from infringements of competition law is still perfectly compatible with access for Gamma. Deterrence can be served by prohibiting the defence of passing-on while granting access for Gamma if one is prepared to accept rare instances of duplicate recoveries. Alternatively deterrence can be served by introducing other deterring elements in the damages regime such as presumptions or the publication of judgments. The legal issue of whether Gamma should have access to court has been settled for the purposes of EU law through Articles 12(1) and 2(24) of Directive 2014/104/EU, but it has been pointed out that the enforceability of that right may remain limited unless it is settled by the Court of Justice that this right for Gamma also follows from Article 101 and/or 102 TFEU. **7.120**

264 On such 'vertical' direct effect of Directives see e.g. case 41/74 *Yvonne van Duyn v Home Office* [1974] ECR 1337 paras 12–13; and case 152/84 *M H Marshall v Southampton and South-West Hampshire Area Health Authority (Teaching)* [1986] ECR 723 paras 46–47. On the concept of the 'State' in EU law see e.g. *Foster* (n 1) para. 20.

265 Cf. the 'any individual' rhetoric in *Courage* (n 4) para. 26, and *Manfredi* (n 36) para. 90, but also the implicit extension of the right to damages to victims of umbrella pricing in *Kone* (n 46). In this context, notice also the vexed interaction of primary EU law rights and secondary EU law instruments in case C-144/04 *Werner Mangold v Rüdiger Helm* [2005] ECR I-9981 and case C-555/07 *Seda Kücükdeveci v Swedex GmbH & Co KG* [2010] ECR I-365.

266 Hovenkamp (n 47) 681.

III. Access for other remote claimants

7.121 It does not follow from a policy of granting access to all Gamma claimants that anyone and everyone should be granted access to bring an action for competition damages. There are still potentially individuals who do not come within the scope of the definition in Article 2(24) of Directive 2014/104/EU but who may have suffered loss. Bishop and Walker have identified three more classes of potentially harmed persons.[267] The first class identified is non-purchasers, i.e., consumers who, because of increased prices, have chosen not to buy a product they would otherwise have bought. Bishop and Walker submitted that non-purchasers may suffer harm in the form of lost consumer surplus but admitted that it is generally very difficult to prove and to estimate such harm incurred by non-purchasers. The second class is purchasers in parallel distribution networks, typically purchasers in supply chains downstream from Alpha's competitors. Prices in such parallel networks may have risen in response to the relaxation in competition that has followed in the wake of increased prices. This phenomenon is known as 'umbrella pricing'.[268] Alpha's violation might indirectly harm such parallel purchasers even though the sellers, who are in competition with Alpha, have not themselves infringed competition law. Bishop and Walker argue that the harm incurred by these purchasers is 'conceptually clear and should in principle be quantifiable'. The third class identified is suppliers to those whose spending power is lessened by increased prices. Such suppliers may suffer a decline in sales. Bishop and Walker argue that it should be possible to estimate this reduction for the purposes of damages calculation.

7.122 Bishop and Walker however seem to overlook what is probably the most relevant class of suppliers in this context: suppliers to Alpha where the infringement of competition law committed by Alpha is aimed at those suppliers specifically. Alpha may for instance be part of a buying cartel or may abuse a dominant position on the buying market by forcing prices excessively low. Directive 2014/104/EU explicitly recognizes a right for such upstream claimants to bring an action by providing, in Article 12(4), that its rules on the passing-on of overcharges 'apply accordingly where the infringement of competition law relates to a supply to the infringer'. In other words not only direct suppliers may bring an action, but also indirect suppliers – a mirror image of the passing-on problem. It is not intended here to conduct a full assessment of the particularities of such 'passing-up' of harm. Suffice it to notice that the Directive recognizes a right to compensation for such claimants

267 Bishop and Walker (n 166) 720–21.

268 Cf. *Kone* (n 46). On umbrella pricing see also Hovenkamp (n 47) 683–4.

and that the rules on passing-on apply. It is added that the *caveat* in paragraph 7.119 will likewise apply.

What of the classes of potential claimants identified by Bishop and Walker? These are not mentioned in Directive 2014/104/EU and consequently it is more difficult to decide whether they should fall within the *ratione personae* of the right to compensation. Indeed the *ratione personae* is not easily defined in the abstract – it is even doubted whether this is at all possible. It will be for the Court of Justice to decide, and most likely the properties of the relevant markets and the particularities of the individual cases will be significant. 7.123

There has been one such assessment by the Court of Justice. It concerned victims of umbrella pricing, i.e., the second class of claimants identified by Walker and Bishop. In *Kone* the Court thus ruled that civil liability for cartel members (i.e., for Alpha and its cartel partners, not for the parallel sellers who had raised their prices without infringing competition law) for harm suffered by such purchasers in parallel distribution networks could not be categorically excluded.[269] It follows that the Court has included such claimants in the *ratione personae* of Article 101 TFEU. The Court also implicitly required that national courts grant access to court for such claimants, although the limiting rule at issue in *Kone* was a rule concerning legal causation.[270] 7.124

With regard to the first and third classes identified it remains to be seen whether the Court will include them in the *ratione personae* of Article 101 and/or 102 TFEU. If the 'any individual' *dictum* in *Courage* and *Manfredi* is to be interpreted to its extreme, no *a priori* limit to the circle of potential claimants should apply under Articles 101 and 102 TFEU.[271] The merits of such an extreme interpretation are dubious however. In the interest of finding a way forward a test of general application has been suggested by Jones: 7.125

> (1) The defendant or defendants have infringed Article [101 or 102 TFEU]; and 7.126
>
> (2) The infringement is likely adversely to affect the legitimate interests of the plaintiff or adversely has affected the legitimate interests of the plaintiff.[272]

---

269 *Kone* (n 46) Operative part. A summary of facts and holdings is available in paras 7.035–7.038.

270 The significance of *Kone* with regard to national causation tests is discussed in Section 7.D.I.

271 A similarly extensive interpretation is possible under Art. 340(2) TFEU as the Court held in case 118/83 *CMC Cooperativa muratori e cementisti and others v Commission of the European Communities* [1985] ECR 2325 para. 31 that '[a]ny person must ... have the possibility of bringing an action, if he is able to establish ... the existence of damage caused by an illegal act or by illegal conduct on the part of the [Union]'. See further paras 3.033–3.036. No similar *dicta* apply to actions for repayment of charges levied in breach of EU law.

272 Jones (n 18) 186.

7.127 This test was inspired by the legitimate interest test now laid down in Article 7(2) of Regulation (EC) No 1/2003[273] which has been explained by the Commission as meaning that 'undertakings … can claim a legitimate interest where they are operating in the relevant market or where the conduct complained of is liable to directly and adversely affect their interests'.[274] It has been added by Milutinovic that such a legitimate interest must be economic or market-based rather than, e.g., emotional or political. In other words claimants must be 'users or buyers of goods or services, or representative associations thereof'.[275]

7.128 The test suggested by Jones and Milutinovic does seem capable of encompassing the first and third class of remote claimants identified by Walker and Bishop. If the right to damages for a breach of competition law would be extended to these remote claimants, Article 47 of the Charter and the EU law principles of equivalence and effectiveness will also apply to actions brought by them. In principle therefore, the point of departure should be that they should have access to court, although specific limitations may be compatible with EU law. For many remote claimants it will certainly be quite difficult to prove causation, although the level of difficulty depends on the conditions of the relevant market. That issue will be discussed next.

D. SUBSTANTIVE PROXIMITY IN EU COMPETITION DAMAGES

7.129 In the context of damages substantive proximity is addressed in the context of factual and legal causation.[276] To Komninos 'causation is by far the most serious problem' in private enforcement of EU competition law.[277] In this section the condition of causation in actions for damages for a breach of EU competition law will be examined in general as well as with regard to the

273 Regulation (EC) No 1/2003 (n 71).

274 Commission Notice on the handling of complaints by the Commission under Articles 81 and 82 of the EC Treaty [2004] OJ C101/65 para. 36.

275 Milutinovic (n 61) 224.

276 For clarity causation between an infringement of competition law and harm incurred must not be confused with EU case law on the causal connection between a concerted practice and market conduct of the participating undertakings (see e.g., case C-8/08 *T-Mobile Netherlands BV, KPN Mobile NV, Orange Nederland NV and Vodafone Libertel NV v Raad van bestuur van de Nederlandse Mededingingsautoriteit* [2009] ECR I-4529).

277 Komninos (n 80) 208. See also Milutinovic (n 61) 137. Swedish readers may enjoy the deconstruction of the 'causation language-game' in Håkan Andersson, *Gränsproblem i skadeståndsrätten: Skadeståndsrättsliga utvecklingslinjer bok II* (Iustus förlag 2013) 23–56 (and thereafter with further specification). The main thrust of this critique is that 'causation' is shorthand for a variety of legal problems pertaining to the delimitation of compensatory liability, and that these legal problems are not as closely related to factual causation as they are to legal/normative evaluation of the situation at hand.

position of Gamma.[278] Here, as in actions for damages from a Member State, the balancing of EU law and national law will be relevant. The condition of causation applicable to actions for damages for a breach of EU competition law has not been harmonized through Directive 2014/104/EU and case law is scarce. In principle, therefore, national law governs the causation assessment.[279] As in Section 6.C.II on causation in damages actions brought against Member States for a breach of EU law it will be discussed here to what extent EU law nevertheless governs the application of national causation tests in the context of competition damages.

I. General observations on causation

The right for any individual to claim compensation for damage caused by a breach of EU competition law was established in *Courage*.[280] The word 'caused' did indicate that causation in some form should be established in order for a damages action to be successful, but causation was not explicitly identified as a condition. This however occurred in the subsequent *Manfredi*.[281] Thus, to bring a successful action for damages, it will be necessary to establish that the alleged injury sustained was caused, in one sense or other, by the wrongful conduct. The Court did not however provide any guidance with regard to the substantive content of the causation test to be applied. Instead the Court was satisfied to leave the substantive content of the causation test to the national legal systems, albeit subject to the EU law principles of equivalence and effectiveness:[282] **7.130**

> In the absence of Community rules governing the matter, it is for the domestic legal system of each Member State to prescribe the detailed rules governing the exercise of that right, including those on the application of the concept of 'causal relationship', provided that the principles of equivalence and effectiveness are observed.[283] **7.131**

This holding, which spoke of national 'rules' governing the exercise of the right to compensation for a breach of EU competition law such as 'the notion of **7.132**

278 In this book, Alpha signifies a tortfeasor or enriched party, Beta a party first burdened by loss arising from Alpha's breach of EU law, and Gamma any party downstream from Beta (including all from the party dealing directly with Beta to the final consumer) to whom the burden of that loss may have been passed on; see Section 1.B.

279 For an overview of certain national jurisdictions and their approach to causation see Ioannis Lianos, Peter Davis and Paolisa Nebbia, *Damages Claims for the Infringement of EU Competition Law* (Oxford University Press 2015) 91–116.

280 *Courage* (n 4) para. 26. For a summary of facts and holdings see paras 7.016–7.022.

281 *Manfredi* (n 36) paras 60–61, and Operative part para. 2. For a summary of facts and holdings see paras 7.026–7.031.

282 On the EU law principles of equivalence and effectiveness see Section 2.D.

283 *Manfredi* (n 36) para. 64, and Operative part para. 2.

causal relationship between the infringement and the harm', indicated that it would be for national law to provide the substantive content of the condition of causation. However, following *Kone*,[284] it has become evident that the Court's initial deference to national concepts of causation in the context of competition damages has its limits.

7.133 The question is therefore just how tight those limits are. The EU legislature had the opportunity to harmonize the notion of causation in Directive 2014/104/EU, but opted not to include any provisions on either factual or legal causation. In recital 11 it instead explicitly stated that 'the notion of causal relationship' is 'not dealt with in this Directive' but remains governed by national law, subject to the principles of equivalence and effectiveness. This part of the recital seems to be modelled on the *Manfredi* holding on causation quoted above.[285] It is furthermore stated in recital 11 that Member States should be able to maintain national concepts such as 'adequacy', albeit insofar as such conditions 'comply with the case-law of the Court of Justice, the principles of effectiveness and equivalence, and this Directive'.[286] The concept of adequacy pertains to legal causation, i.e., the legal evaluation of the factual chain of events in order to determine whether certain alleged harm was 'adequately' caused by the conduct or omission. This concept thus signifies the delineation of a class of adequate harmful consequences that fall within the scope of liability in damages. Inadequate harmful consequences will not be compensated.[287] With regard to such a concept it is submitted that the tolerance indicated in recital 11 is likely to prevail as long as the national interpretation of adequacy does not include the automatic exclusion of certain classes of claims.[288]

---

284 *Kone* (n 46).

285 *Manfredi* (n 36) para. 64, and Operative part para. 2.

286 It was noted in para. 7.048 that this passage seems to be an example of so-called 'constructive ambiguity' whereby the EU legislature has by-passed difficult negotiations by leaving a controversial issue to be decided by the Court of Justice, and that difficult issues related to the national legal concepts there mentioned should be referred to the Court of Justice for a preliminary ruling when an opportunity thereto arises.

287 See e.g. Konrad Zweigert and Hein Kötz, *An Introduction to Comparative Law* (3rd edn, Oxford University Press 1998) 601–2; and Walter van Gerven, Jeremy Lever and Pierre Larouche (eds), *The Common Law of Europe Casebooks: Tort Law* (Hart Publishing 2000) 399–403. Adequacy is often connected to foreseeability. On that concept see European Group on Tort Law, *Principles of European Tort Law: Text and Commentary* (Springer 2005) 61–2. Swedish readers see also Andersson (n 277) 48–50, who stresses that the concept of adequacy is neither more nor less than a symbol for a multi-faceted field of inquiries that share the purpose of delineating compensatory liability.

288 Cf. paras 7.145–7.146 below. It might be discussed whether Art. 17(2) is intended to include a presumption of causation with regard to harm caused by cartels; see e.g. Lianos, Davis and Nebbia (n 279) para. 4.140. Such an interpretation is possible if the rule is taken out of context, but rec. 11 as well as the heading of Art. 17 speak against it. Moreover the scope of the presumption would be very vague. E.g., does it apply to Gamma claimants or only Beta claimants? If intended to be a presumption for causation Art. 17(2) should have been clearer. On balance it should therefore be presumed that Art. 17(2) was not intended as a rule on causation.

In the absence of provisions on causation in the Directive we must return to case law for hints on how to balance national law against the standards of EU law. As suggested above this discussion of the interface of EU law and national law with regard to causation in competition damages actions parallels the same discussion in damages from a Member State. There is however a difference in wording that emerges in a comparison of the relevant holdings in competition law cases to those in cases concerning damages from Member States (and in cases concerning damages from the EU). In case law on the action for damages from a Member State the national court's assessment of whether there is a 'direct causal link' is to be carried out 'in accordance with the guidelines laid down by the Court'.[289] Similarly, in case law on actions for damages under Article 340(2) TFEU, the EU Courts have consistently held that the causal link must be 'direct'.[290] In *Manfredi* there was by contrast no mention of the 'direct' element of the requirement, seemingly implying that a comparatively lax requirement for a 'causal relationship' would apply in competition damages.[291] In the subsequent *Otis*, which also concerned competition damages, the 'direct' element was however reintroduced by the Court.[292] Should *Otis* therefore be interpreted as indicating that the Court of Justice was seeking to align the conditions for liability in damages for a breach of EU competition law to those used for the purposes of Article 340(2) TFEU and actions for damages from a Member State? 7.134

On the one hand such an interpretation is supported by two circumstances. First, the Court of Justice has been known before to introduce adjustments to its case law somewhat covertly. Gradual changes to its approach can be traced in many instances, such as in its interpretation(s) of the principle of effectiveness[293] and, as seen, with regard to the passing-on defence in actions for the 7.135

---

289 Case C-420/11 *Jutta Leth v Republik Österreich and Land Niederösterreich* EU:C:2013:166 para. 45. See further paras 6.064–6.069.

290 See e.g. case C-352/98 P *Laboratoires pharmaceutiques Bergaderm SA and Jean-Jacques Goupil v Commission of the European Communities* [2000] ECR I-5291 para. 42. See further Section 3.D.I.

291 *Manfredi* (n 36) para. 61, and Operative part para. 2. The same wording was used in the subsequent case C-421/05 *City Motors Groep NV v Citroën Belux NV* [2007] ECR I-653 para. 33. Cf. Komninos (n 80) 209 with references, who identifies a specific direct causal link theory which would be designated by the Court of Justice in its case law on Art. 340(2) TFEU and actions for damages from a Member State, but not in the context of competition law damages.

292 *Otis* (n 45) para. 65. The element of 'direct' is included in all language versions comprehensible to this author. On the ambiguity caused by the inclusion of the word 'direct' in *Otis* see also Katri Havu, 'Issues Emanating from the Interface of EU and National Law – the Finnish Experience and Beyond' in Maria Bergström, Marios Iacovides and Magnus Strand (eds), *Harmonising EU Competition Litigation: The New Directive and Beyond* (Swedish Studies in European Law vol. 8, Hart Publishing 2016).

293 On three phases in the case law on the principle of effectiveness see Anthony Arnull, *The European Union and its Court of Justice* (2nd edn, Oxford EC Law Library, Oxford University Press 2006) Ch. 9; and Takis Tridimas, *The General Principles of EU Law* (2nd edn, Oxford University Press 2006) 420–22. A fourth

repayment of charges levied in breach of EU law.[294] Second, Judge Rosas and Judge Ó Caoimh have been included in the composition of the Court of Justice in all three cases where the Court of Justice has referred to the condition of causation for the right to damages for a breach of EU competition law.[295] It is not likely that they would accidently overlook this new addition. On the other hand the holding at issue was undeniably an *obiter dictum* within a line of reasoning that concerned the division of powers between the EU and the Member States and, in particular, between the Commission and the national courts pursuant to Article 16 of Regulation (EC) No 1/2003.[296] Moreover the Court of Justice referred to the existence of a 'causal relationship', without the 'direct' element, in an earlier paragraph in *Otis*.[297] It is therefore submitted that the inclusion of the 'direct' element in *Otis* may at most be interpreted as signalling a wish on behalf of the Court to seize some control over the condition of causation for the purposes of competition damages.

7.136 Notwithstanding whether causation in competition damages must be 'direct' or not, the Court of Justice did seize some control over the assessment in *Kone*. In that case the national court had explained that under national law compensation would be available only if the provision breached had as its objective the protection of the injured party's interests. As the competition law provisions breached had as their object the protection of the interests of the cartel's buyers, injured parties who were not buyers of cartel members would fall outside the protective scope of those provisions.[298] The question referred to the Court of Justice in *Kone* was, essentially, whether EU law required that an action for damages be available against the members of the cartel for those who have suffered loss due to umbrella pricing.

7.137 Advocate General Kokott submitted a detailed Opinion in *Kone* which deserves to be presented extensively.[299] She opined that the problem turned on

---

neo-interventionist phase would be added by Katri Havu, 'Horizontal Liability for Damages in EU Law – the Changing Relationship of EU and National Law' (2012) 18 *European Law Journal* 407, 410.

294 Evident in the overview of the case law in Section 5.E.II.

295 I.e., *Manfredi* (n 36); *City Motors* (n 291); and *Otis* (n 45).

296 Regulation (EC) No 1/2003 (n 71).

297 *Otis* (n 45) para. 43.

298 For a summary of the facts in *Kone* (n 46) see para. 7.035. It seems Austria had omitted to avoid this problem by introducing special legislation for the purposes of competition law damages while Germany has; cf. Christian Andrelang, 'Damages for the Infringement of Art. 81 EC by Cartel Agreements according to sec. 33(3) GWB: The Changes of Law concerning the 'Protective Law' Requirement and the 'Passing On' Defence' (2007) 30 *World Competition: Law and Economics Review* 573 on relevant German law.

299 The Opinion of AG Kokott has attracted a fair amount of scholarly attention, cf. e.g. Niamh Dunne, 'It Never Rains but it Pours? Liability for 'Umbrella effects' under EU Competition Law in *Kone*' (2014) 51 *Common Market Law Review* 1813, 1820–27; and Lianos, Davis and Nebbia (n 279) 121–8.

'what specific conditions may be attached under European Union law to the establishment of a causal link between the cartel and umbrella pricing'. The Advocate General submitted five points on those conditions. First, in view of the 'any individual' phrase used by the Court, the obligation to pay compensation should not be interpreted narrowly but it was nevertheless perfectly legitimate to ensure that cartel members were not 'subject to unlimited liability to provide compensation for any losses, however remote, for which their anti-competitive behaviour may have been the cause in the sense of a '*conditio sine qua non*'. Second, EU case law under Article 340(2) TFEU requiring a sufficiently direct causal nexus between the alleged breach of EU law and the harm incurred should, for the sake of consistency, be applied 'to all other cases involving claims to compensation for infringement of European Union law'. Third, the Advocate General opined that a sufficiently direct causal nexus could finally be established only through 'normative examination' – i.e., an assessment of legal causation. Fourth, the Advocate General submitted that a sufficiently direct causal nexus was not excluded under EU law where there were other contributory causes, but that it was enough that the causal chain was traceable back to the cartel.[300] Fifth and finally, she opined that the criterion of a sufficiently direct causal nexus was designed to (a) limit liability to losses that the infringers could reasonably have foreseen and (b) limit liability to losses 'the compensation of which is consistent with the objectives of the provision of law [infringed]'.[301]

These points then guided the Advocate General's assessment of the facts of the case. Beginning with foreseeability the Advocate General further specified that '[a]ny loss the incurrence of which the cartel members ought reasonably to take into consideration on the basis of practical experience is foreseeable (or ensues via an adequate causal link)'.[302] The Advocate General then opined that undertakings in a market economy will typically keep an eye on the market behaviour of their competitors, that there was nothing to indicate the contrary for the relevant market in the main proceedings, and that successful anti-competitive agreements in a cartel must presuppose umbrella pricing. For those reasons the Advocate General submitted that umbrella pricing was not unforeseeable, and therefore that compensation for loss due to umbrella **7.138**

300 *Kone* (n 46) Opinion of AG Kokott paras 31–37. The Advocate General recognized that in case C-440/07 P *Commission of the European Communities v Schneider Electric SA* [2009] ECR I-6413 Opinion of AG Ruiz-Jarabo Colomer para. 140, a different view had been submitted.

301 Ibid., para. 40. In this context, this last remark is related to the discussion on a criterion for the harm incurred to be an 'antitrust injury' within the meaning of US federal antitrust law; see Hovenkamp (n 47) 654–61, in particular 659–60. On the adoption of such a criterion for the purposes of EU competition law see para. 7.050.

302 *Kone* (n 46) Opinion of AG Kokott para. 42.

pricing could not be precluded under Article (now) 101 TFEU by reference to the criterion of an adequate causal link.[303]

7.139 Continuing with the issue of whether compensation was consistent with the objectives pursued by Article (now) 101 TFEU the Advocate General clarified that this issue concerned the protective scope (German: *Schutzzweck*) of that provision. In that regard the defendants had argued that there was no 'context of unlawfulness' (German: *Rechtswidrigkeitszusammenhang*) in the situation at hand. The Advocate General took the opposite view, arguing that the aim of creating and maintaining a system of undistorted competition on the internal market was not incompatible with the recognition of liability to compensate harm incurred due to umbrella pricing. In support of her view the Advocate General dismissed a number of arguments that such liability would risk to reduce competition on the internal market or would not be cost-efficient, stressing instead that injured parties 'should not be denied the possibility of instituting such judicial proceedings on the ground that the costs are alleged to be too high' and that 'the second subparagraph of Article 19(1) of the EU Treaty and Article 47(1) of the Charter of Fundamental Rights require the Member States to provide, within the field of application of EU competition law, remedies sufficient to ensure adequate legal protection.'[304]

7.140 The Advocate General further argued that it was of no consequence that harm caused by umbrella pricing was unintended by the members of the cartel, or that compensation in damages did not necessarily lead to total disgorgement of profits earned through the infringement of competition law. Finally the Advocate General did not accept that liability to pay compensation for harm incurred due to umbrella pricing would constitute punitive damages. For those reasons Advocate General Kokott concluded that liability in damages for cartel members for loss caused by umbrella pricing was consistent with the objectives of EU competition law and that such claims could not therefore be precluded from the outset. She nonetheless stressed that it would 'always be necessary to carry out a comprehensive assessment of all the relevant circumstances in order to determine whether the cartel in the case in question has given rise to umbrella pricing'.[305]

7.141 The Court of Justice pointed out that Articles 101(1) and 102 TFEU produced direct effects in relations between individuals and created rights for

303 Ibid., paras 46–52.
304 Ibid., paras 54–70.
305 Ibid., paras 72–85.

the individuals concerned which the national courts must safeguard,[306] but also recognized that in the absence of EU rules governing the matter it was for the domestic legal system of each Member State to lay down the detailed rules – e.g., rules on the application of the concept of 'causal relationship' – governing the exercise of the right to claim compensation for the harm resulting from an agreement or practice prohibited under Article 101 TFEU. The Court however stressed that the national rules at issue were subject to scrutiny under the principles of equivalence and effectiveness, and must not jeopardize the effective application of Articles 101 and 102 TFEU.[307]

The defendants had argued that it would be inappropriate to interpret EU law **7.142**
as meaning that it would permit claims for damages based on the existence of umbrella pricing. In that regard the Court of Justice held that it could not be ruled out that a competing undertaking, outside the cartel in question, might choose to set the price of its offer at an amount higher than it would have chosen under normal conditions of competition (i.e., in the absence of that cartel). Even if the determination of an offer price was regarded as a purely autonomous decision taken by the undertaking not party to a cartel such a decision had nonetheless been taken by reference to a market price distorted by that cartel and, as a result, contrary to the competition rules. It followed, the Court held, that loss suffered due to umbrella pricing was one of the possible effects of the cartel that the members thereof could not disregard.[308]

The Court of Justice explained that national legislation must ensure that EU **7.143**
competition law was fully effective, must specifically take into account the objective pursued by Article 101 TFEU which aims to guarantee effective and undistorted competition in the internal market, and must recognize the right of any individual to claim compensation for loss sustained. In *Kone* the individual concerned had no contractual links with any member of the cartel but with an undertaking, not party thereto, whose pricing policy however was a result of the cartel that contributed to the distortion of price formation mechanisms governing competitive markets. In such a situation the Court held that the full effectiveness of Article 101 TFEU would be put at risk if the right of such an individual to claim compensation was subject in national law, categorically and regardless of the particular circumstances of the case, to a rule that would exclude that right by reference to a national understanding of what constitutes a necessary direct causal link. The Court of Justice therefore ruled that the victim of umbrella pricing might obtain compensation for the

306 *Kone* (n 46) paras 20–22.
307 Ibid., paras 24–26.
308 Ibid., paras 28–30.

loss caused by the members of a cartel even if it did not have contractual links with them, where it was established: (1) that the cartel at issue was, in the circumstances of the case and in particular the specific aspects of the relevant market, liable to have the effect of umbrella pricing being applied by third parties acting independently; and (2) that those circumstances and specific aspects could not be ignored by the members of that cartel. The Court left it to the national court to determine whether those conditions were satisfied.[309]

7.144 On those grounds the Court of Justice ruled that Article 101 TFEU must be interpreted as meaning that it precluded the interpretation and application of domestic legislation enacted by a Member State which categorically excluded, for legal reasons, any civil liability of undertakings belonging to a cartel for loss resulting from the fact that an undertaking not party to the cartel set its prices higher than would otherwise have been expected under competitive conditions.[310] *Kone* thus effectively settled that victims of umbrella pricing could not be categorically excluded from bringing an action for damages pursuant to Article 101 TFEU.

7.145 However, although the Court of Justice was not as clear on this point as Advocate General Kokott was, it will still be 'necessary to carry out a comprehensive assessment of all the relevant circumstances in order to determine whether the cartel in the case in question has given rise to umbrella pricing'.[311] In other words the ruling of the Court in *Kone* does not mean that the criterion of causation was eliminated from the assessment but by contrast that the assessment of causation could not be reduced to categorical rules. The Court of Justice did not pick up on the details on causation submitted in the Opinion of Advocate General Kokott. It is likely that this was so because the issue in *Kone* was not so much the details of the criterion of causation in damages for a breach of EU competition law, but the existence of an automatic exclusion of claims for reasons related to proximity and causation that in practice had the effect of denying certain claimants access to court. In this way *Kone* is reminiscent of the holdings of the Court on automatic exclusion for reasons relating to causation in *Danfoss*.[312] It is nevertheless apparent that *Kone* signals a step away from the non-interventionist approach of the Court in *Manfredi*. It has now been clarified that the principles of equivalence and effectiveness and the particular character and function of Articles 101 and 102

---

309 Ibid., paras 32–34. The Court also dismissed two alternative arguments submitted by the defendants in the main proceedings, see paras 35 and 36.

310 Ibid., Operative part.

311 Ibid., Opinion of AG Kokott para. 84.

312 Cf. sub-section 6.C.II.b.

TFEU will set certain standards for causation assessments in competition damages actions.

The findings of the Court in *Kone* may be indicative with regard to the general approach of the Court of Justice to national concepts and traditions in causation. It was for instance noted in paragraph 7.133 that, pursuant to recital 11 of Directive 2014/104/EU, the review of such national concepts against the standards of EU law should be rather lenient. Nonetheless it is evident from *Kone* that they are indeed subject to such review. A reading of recital 11 in light of *Kone* thus suggests, it is submitted, that national concepts and traditions in causation will be tolerated for the purposes of competition damages actions as long as they do not include the automatic exclusion of certain classes of claims. If such exclusionary practices are maintained in national law, odds are that they will be held to be incompatible with EU law. As mentioned above the message is that the assessment of causation cannot be reduced to categorical rules but must be carried out in the individual case. **7.146**

II. Causation and passing-on

It has been noticed in Sections 3.D.II and 6.C.II.b that it is generally difficult for Gamma claimants bringing an action for damages to prove causation. In the context of competition damages this difficulty for Gamma was noticed by the Commission in its 2005 Green Paper.[313] It may first and foremost be difficult to trace harm down the supply chain. It was pointed out by Toth, quoted in the context of damages under Article 340(2) TFEU, that 'the cause of an event can usually be traced back to a number of factors ... operating simultaneously or successively and producing direct as well as indirect effects'.[314] The farther from the infringement of competition law a claimant is positioned, the more difficult it will typically be for the claimant to prove causation. This is however also dependent on the particularities of the market at issue. On some markets causation is easier to establish, on other markets it will be more difficult. **7.147**

There is as yet no case law on competition damages that touches on how to approach the causation assessment in the context of passing-on. Hence it is difficult to make predictions, especially with regard to actions brought by a Gamma claimant. It is obvious that Gamma will typically be more vulnerable **7.148**

313 COM(2005) 672 final (n 35) 8.

314 Akos George Toth, 'The Concepts of Damage and Causality as Elements of Non-Contractual Liability' in Ton Heukels and Alison McDonnell (eds), *The Action for Damages in Community Law* (Kluwer Law 1997) 192, quoted in para. 3.054.

to arguments connected to the lack of proximity or the influence of competing causes for harm than Beta. If the 'direct' element would find its way into the condition of causation for the right to damages for a breach of EU competition law, the position of Gamma on such actions for damages should be no different from the position of Gamma when bringing an action for damages from a Member State. Under such circumstances the discussion in sub-section 6.C.II.b on the requirement of causation and Gamma claimants bringing an action for damages from a Member State should *mutatis mutandis* serve to point out the general directions with regard to Gamma claimants bringing an action for damages for a breach of competition law. If by contrast the 'direct' element is not adopted in future case law on competition damages, the substantive content of the causation test arguably remains more exclusively governed by national law albeit subject to scrutiny as in *Kone*.

7.149 An inevitable effect of leaving the concept of causation to be governed by national law is that the possibilities for Gamma to bring a successful action will vary between Member States.[315] Although this variance may be seen as a disadvantage, any negative effects may arguably be outweighed by the advantage of allowing the national courts to use the causation tests that have been carefully developed in their own legal cultures over long periods of time. In other words the service of justice may gain from national autonomy with regard to causation even though formal justice across the EU – i.e., the equal treatment of equal cases – may suffer. It is also plausible for the Court of Justice to intervene on a case-by-case basis, as it did in *Kone*, in order to preclude elements of national causation tests that are liable to impede the effective private enforcement of competition law. Such intervention could e.g. be for the benefit of Gamma claimants. It remains to be seen which of these alternatives – if any – will be pursued in future case law.

7.150 Although it has been stressed that Directive 2014/104/EU leaves causation to be governed by national law, it should finally be noticed that Article 14(2) of the Directive will arguably have an indirect impact on the allocation of the burden of proof in the causation assessment insofar as it covers the existence of a causal relationship between the breach of EU competition law and harm passed on to Gamma. In Article 14(2) the Commission wishes to introduce a rebuttable presumption that the burden of an overcharge has been passed on. The provision reads:

315 Komninos (n 80) 208–9 offers a brief overview of causation tests applied in England and Germany.

In the situation referred to in paragraph 1, the indirect purchaser shall be deemed to have proven that a passing-on to that indirect purchaser occurred where that indirect purchaser has shown that: 7.151

(a) the defendant has committed an infringement of competition law;
(b) the infringement of competition law has resulted in an overcharge for the direct purchaser of the defendant; and
(c) the indirect purchaser has purchased the goods or services that were the object of the infringement of competition law, or has purchased goods or services derived from or containing them.

This paragraph shall not apply where the defendant can demonstrate credibly to the satisfaction of the court that the overcharge was not, or was not entirely, passed on to the indirect purchaser.

Such a presumption must include a presumption for causation with regard to the passing-on of the overcharge. This presumption does not however offer guidance with regard to the rate of passing-on, i.e., the extent at which the overcharge was passed on. In this and all other aspects (e.g., the existence and estimation of harm incurred due to decreased sales) save for the existence of passing-on as such, the Directive is satisfied to leave the element of causation to be governed by national law. If a specific rebuttable presumption on the requirement of causation had been included it could have been given a wider scope than Article 14(2) in order to facilitate actions by Gamma claimants.[316] 7.152

In sum the guidance available in respect of the condition of causation in actions for damages for a breach of EU competition law is scarce indeed. Therefore national courts adjudicating such actions should arguably make a reference to the European Court of Justice, giving the Court the opportunity to decide on whether and to what extent to engage in the substantive content of the applicable causation test. Demonstrating causation will also trigger the need to obtain evidence. It follows that future litigation will put the disclosure mechanisms in Directive 2014/104/EU to the test. 7.153

---

316 Some suggestions on how to facilitate for claimants to overcome the condition of causation, through new case law and by harmonization, are submitted by Milutinovic (n 61) 139–40. Art. 14(2) should moreover be read in conjunction with Ch. II on disclosure of evidence, and in particular Art. 5, which serves to ease the burden of proof for litigants by introducing opportunities for national courts to order the disclosure of specified pieces of evidence which are under the control of their adversaries or third parties. Art. 5 further includes a number of specific qualifications to this possibility which will not be analysed in detail here. On Art. 14(2) see also paras 7.195–7.197.

E. ESTIMATING COMPETITION DAMAGES

7.154 The third legal issue triggered by the passing-on problem is the estimation of damages. This is perhaps the area most commonly associated with passing-on, simply because this is the context in which Alpha's defence of passing-on belongs.[317] As has been explained the defence of passing-on is an argument according to which the damages payable for a breach of law should be reduced to the extent that the claimant has been able to pass on the harm incurred to the next level in the supply chain. This section will begin with some general observations on the estimation of damages in the context of EU competition damages actions. Thereafter focus will be on the defence of passing-on specifically. Relevant case law of the European Court of Justice will be discussed and it will be submitted that, contrary to the interpretations made by the European Commission, the Court of Justice has not yet ruled on the defence of passing-on in the context of competition damages. Thereafter there will be an examination of provisions on passing-on in Directive 2014/104/EU, highlighting also relevant paragraphs in the accompanying soft-law instruments in the competition damages package. In the final discussion the approach chosen by the EU legislature will be discussed in light of US federal antitrust law and the EU debate. The discussion has been sub-divided thematically, each theme focusing on a particular policy problem.

I. General observations on the estimation of damages

7.155 The estimation of damages entails the issues of: (1) what heads of damages should be recognized; and (2) the quantification of harm. The latter question also entails the issue of whether or not to take passing-on into consideration for the purposes of the quantification of harm. The detailed rules and guidance on passing-on laid down in Directive 2014/1204/EU and the accompanying soft-law instruments is presented in sub-section 7.E.II.b below. This first section focuses instead on more general issues with regard to available heads of damages and the quantification of harm.[318]

---

317 In this book, Alpha signifies a tortfeasor or enriched party, Beta a party first burdened by loss arising from Alpha's breach of EU law, and Gamma any party downstream from Beta (including all from the party dealing directly with Beta to the final consumer) to whom the burden of that loss may have been passed on; see Section 1.B.

318 This presentation will focus on case law and the instruments of the new regime. Readers searching for further reading on the estimation of competition damages are recommended to see Lianos, Davis and Nebbia (n 279) Ch. 6. A detailed discussion on the quantification of harm caused by an infringement of Art. 102 TFEU, with an account of differences between infringements of Arts 101 and 102 TFEU respectively, is available in Robert O'Donoghue and Jorge Padilla, *The Law and Economics of Article 102 TFEU* (2nd edn, Hart Publishing 2013) 963–75.

In the scarce case law on competition damages the issue of how to estimate such a damages award has been addressed only in *Manfredi*.[319] To be precise the Court discussed the heads of damages that should be available in the context of an EU competition damages action but did not in any detail engage in how to quantify the harm suffered. The referring court was uncertain whether EU law required for an award of damages for an infringement of EU competition law to be higher than the advantage gained by the infringing party in order to deter from infringements.[320] The European Court of Justice replied that, in the absence of EU rules governing the estimation of damages (an absence which has since been addressed through Directive 2014/104/EU), it was for the domestic legal system of the Member State to set relevant criteria which were nonetheless subject to scrutiny under the EU principles of equivalence and effectiveness. With regard to the principle of equivalence the Court of Justice established that if exemplary or punitive damages were available to actions under national law, which were similar to actions for damages for an infringement of EU competition law, an award of such damages had to be available also in the latter actions.[321] With regard to the principle of effectiveness the Court of Justice ruled that injured persons must be able to seek compensation for actual loss (*damnum emergens*) and also for loss of profit (*lucrum cessans*) plus interest.[322] The Court thus required for two heads of compensatory damages, and for interest on the amounts payable, to be available as a matter of EU law. The Court did not however elaborate on the criteria for calculating harm or interest under these heads of damages. **7.156**

As mentioned the 'absence of EU rules governing the estimation of damages' referred to by the Court in *Manfredi* is no more, as Directive 2014/104/EU sets out to harmonize at least the general points of departure for the estimation of damages. The main thrust of the Directive is explained in Article 3: **7.157**

> Right to full compensation **7.158**
>
> 1. Member States shall ensure that any natural or legal person who has suffered harm caused by an infringement of competition law is able to claim and to obtain full compensation for that harm.
>
> 2. Full compensation shall place a person who has suffered harm in the position in which that person would have been had the infringement of competition law not been

319 *Manfredi* (n 36). A summary of facts and holdings is available in paras 7.026–7.031.

320 Ibid., para. 20 (question 4).

321 Ibid., Operative part para. 5. On the principle of equivalence see Section 2.D.II. See the discussion in para. 7.058 on the appropriate *comparator* in the context of competition law damages. It is discussed in para. 7.159 whether this element of *Manfredi* is now overruled by Directive 2014/104/EU (n 5) Art. 3(3).

322 *Manfredi* (n 36) Operative part para. 5. On the principle of effectiveness see Section 2.D.III.

committed. It shall therefore cover the right to compensation for actual loss and for loss of profit, plus the payment of interest.

3. Full compensation under this Directive shall not lead to overcompensation, whether by means of punitive, multiple or other types of damages.

7.159 Article 3(1) captures the essence of the approach adopted through the Directive, namely to provide full compensation to anyone harmed. Article 3(2) is a codification of certain findings of the Court of Justice in *Manfredi*[323] but Article 3(3) partly overrules that same judgment. In *Manfredi* the Court of Justice ruled, as reported in paragraph 7.031, that it followed from the EU law principle of equivalence that it must be possible to award particular damages, such as exemplary or punitive damages, pursuant to actions founded on EU competition rules if such damages might be awarded pursuant to similar actions founded on domestic law.[324] These are heads of damages designed to serve the interest of deterrence rather than the interest of reparation, which is served by compensatory damages. Article 3(3) introduces a ban on punitive, exemplary and multiple damages within the scope of Directive 2014/104/EU.[325] Although the reasons for this ban are not clearly explained in the *travaux préparatoires* it seems the EU legislature has been persuaded by stakeholders in business that single and strictly compensatory damages are preferable to deterrent heads of damages.[326] As punitive, exemplary and multiple damages serve the interest of deterrence, they will be unwanted in a damages regime designed primarily to serve the interest of reparation. It is indeed explicitly stated in the accompanying Communication on quantifying harm in actions for damages for a breach of EU competition law that the objective of private enforcement of EU competition law is reparation, and that deterrence will continue to be served through the EU system of public enforcement.[327] In the background of this discussion one glimpses apprehension of the US federal antitrust damages system in which treble (threefold)

323 See ibid., para. 95 and Operative part para. 5.

324 Ibid., para. 93 and Operative part para. 5.

325 See also Recommendation 2013/396/EU (n 68) para. 31. The ban on punitive damages has been lamented in Erdem Büyüksagis, Ina Erbert, Duncan Fairgrieve, Renée Charlotte Meurkens and Fransesco Quarta, 'Punitive Damages in Europe and Plea for the Recognition of Legal Pluralism' (2016) 27 *European Business Law Review* 137. This author has raised the issue whether there might still be room for the *Manfredi* rule if an application of the principle of equivalence should not properly be understood as 'compensation under this Directive' within the meaning of Directive 2014/104/EU (n 5) Art. 3(3); see Magnus Strand, 'Indirect Purchasers, Passing-On and the New Directive on Competition Law Damages' (2014) 10 *European Competition Journal* 361, 378–9. However, such an interpretation does seem to run contrary to the harmonization intended through the Directive.

326 See SWD(2013) 203 final (n 57) 26; and cf. Table 1 (p. 31): no alternative to single damages was included in the impact assessment.

327 Communication [2013] (n 66) paras 1–2.

damages are paid for the harm sustained by claimants.[328] It may be that over-deterrence was feared if the EU was to maintain a stringent system of public enforcement and add to it a severe private enforcement regime. Irrespective of the reasons it seems punitive, exemplary and multiple damages were already quite rare among the Member States,[329] which may in itself partly explain why they have been excluded in an effort to harmonize. The role of deterrence in damages will be explored further in sub-section 7.E.II.c and in Section 9.E.II.

National jurisdictions may moreover offer restitutionary damages.[330] Articles 12 and 13 of Directive 2014/104/EU (which concern passing-on) however preclude any possibility to award restitutionary damages for a breach of competition law.[331] This leaves compensatory heads of damages as the only heads of damages available. The Communication and Practical Guide on quantifying harm in actions for damages for a breach of EU competition law also stay within the compensatory heads of damage identified in the Directive.[332] **7.160**

The restrictions on multiple, exemplary, punitive or restitutionary damages in Directive 2014/104/EU may give rise to certain unexpected problems. Where national law traditionally offers such heads of damages, some claimants will have an incentive to argue that an infringement of competition law which has caused them harm did not have an effect on trade between Member States within the meaning of Article 101 or 102 TFEU. Such claimants might wish to argue that the infringement was isolated to a geographic market confined to the Member State in which such heads of damages are available, thereby escaping the restrictions. Although the significance of the problem should not be exaggerated, incentives for fragmentation are bad news for the endeavour to create a level playing field in competition damages. Political pressure for the **7.161**

---

328 § 4 Clayton Act (n 137). In AMC Report and Recommendations (n 158) 243–4, the American Antitrust Modernization Commission reviewed this rule but did not recommend for it to be changed. The difference between the US and the EU systems is mainly due to the fact that while the EU system is primarily enforced by public authorities (the Commission and the national competition authorities), the US federal system is mainly enforced through private litigation. On the litigation orientation of US antitrust law see Jones (n 18) 14–20.

329 The Ashurst Study (n 56) 84 reported exemplary damages to be available in Cyprus, the UK, and in Ireland, but also that they were rarely awarded. Punitive damages were available only in Cyprus but seemed to be awarded more commonly there than exemplary damages.

330 Some thoughts on restitutionary damages in the context of competition law damages have been submitted by Walter van Gerven, 'Substantive Remedies for the Private Enforcement of EC Antitrust Rules before National Courts' in Jules Stuyck and Hans Gilliams (eds), *Modernisation of European Competition Law* (Leuven Centre for a Common Law of Europe, Intersentia 2002) 105–6.

331 Notwithstanding Directive 2014/104/EU (n 5) Arts 12–13 restitution, as an alternative course of action, may be an option in certain circumstances; see Section 8.C.I and Strand (n 232).

332 Communication [2013] (n 66); SWD(2013) 205 (n 67).

abolition of these deterrent heads of damages by the Member States at issue might therefore ensue.

7.162 Turning to the rules on quantification of harm, Directive 2014/104/EU includes very little hard law. The relevant provision is Article 17:

7.163 Quantification of harm

> 1. Member States shall ensure that neither the burden nor the standard of proof required for the quantification of harm renders the exercise of the right to damages practically impossible or excessively difficult. Member States shall ensure that the national courts are empowered, in accordance with national procedures, to estimate the amount of harm if it is established that a claimant suffered harm but it is practically impossible or excessively difficult precisely to quantify the harm suffered on the basis of the evidence available.
>
> 2. It shall be presumed that cartel infringements cause harm. The infringer shall have the right to rebut that presumption.
>
> 3. Member States shall ensure that, in proceedings relating to an action for damages, a national competition authority may, upon request of a national court, assist that national court with respect to the determination of the quantum of damages where that national competition authority considers such assistance to be appropriate.

7.164 All three paragraphs of Article 17 are intended to facilitate the task of quantifying harm suffered. It should be noticed that these are not legal rules governing the assessment as such. As indicated in recital 46 of the Directive it will still be for the Member States to determine their own rules on quantifying harm and to determine the applicable requirements to be met by claimants in order to prove the amount of harm suffered, subject to the principles of equivalence and effectiveness.[333] The provisions of Article 17 are not intended to intensify the level of EU law scrutiny but rather to offer some assistance to the national assessment. First, by virtue of Article 17(3), national competition authorities are empowered to assist national courts 'with respect to the determination of the quantum of damages' upon request of the national court and subject to the consent of the national competition authority. The expertise of national competition authorities can thus be put to use in the quantification of harm. Second, where it is nevertheless established that it is 'practically impossible or excessively difficult precisely to quantify the harm suffered on the basis of the evidence available', the Member States are instructed in Article 17(1) to empower their courts to approximate the amount of harm incurred by claimants. Article 17(2), finally, introduces a rebuttable presumption that a

333 See also Communication [2013] (n 66) paras 8–9.

cartel infringement causes harm.[334] None of these provisions provide guidelines for the quantification of the harm as such. The procedural details surrounding these provisions are equally left for the Member States to flesh out, although it must – as always – be kept in mind that national law applies subject to the EU law principles of equivalence and effectiveness.

National courts looking at EU level for more detailed guidance for the estimation of damages will instead have to find it in the non-binding soft-law instruments issued in 2013 alongside the original Commission proposal for a Directive, e.g., the Communication and Practical Guide on quantifying harm in actions for damages for a breach of EU competition law.[335] The Communication as such does not contain much specific guidance. The holdings of the Court of Justice in *Manfredi* are recalled, and the Practical Guide is introduced. It is thus explained that substantive guidance will be offered in the Practical Guide.[336] The Communication nevertheless provides important starting points for the understanding of the Practical Guide. It is thus stated in the Communication that the principles established in *Manfredi* serve the purpose of placing the injured parties in the position they would have been in had there been no infringement of EU competition law, and that parties harmed 'should therefore have the full real value of their losses restored'.[337] It is also stressed in the Communication that this is an ideal that cannot be accomplished in reality, but that quantification of harm seeks to find an estimate of a hypothetical scenario. It is finally underlined that the guidance offered in the Practical Guide is not binding on national courts: 'The practical guide is intended to provide information that can be used within the framework of national legal rules and practices, not instead of them.'[338] It can thus be concluded from the Communication that the objective of the guidance offered in the Practical Guide is to assist in the endeavour for compensatory justice in the traditional sense of damages, expressed in Article 3(2) in Directive 2014/104/EU.[339] **7.165**

A detailed survey of the methods for quantifying harm included in the Practical Guide is not intended here. Suffice it to notice that comparator-based methods and other methods are distinguished in the Practical Guide, **7.166**

334 Cf. n 288. On this presumption and its role in the estimation of harm see Marios C Iacovides, 'The Presumption and Quantification of Harm in the Directive and the Practical Guide' in Maria Bergström, Marios Iacovides and Magnus Strand (eds), *Harmonising EU Competition Litigation: The New Directive and Beyond* (Swedish Studies in European Law, vol. 8, Hart Publishing 2016).

335 Communication [2013] (n 66); SWD(2013) 205 (n 67).

336 Communication [2013] (n 66) para. 10.

337 Ibid., para. 6.

338 Ibid., para. 13.

339 See para. 7.158 for a full quote of Art. 3(2).

that more attention is devoted to comparator-based methods, and that its recommendations serve the interest of reparation.[340] Comparator-based methods include the establishment of a hypothetical scenario in which the infringement of competition law had not occurred. This can be done by studying data from the relevant market over time (in particular, studying pre-infringement and post-infringement prices),[341] by comparing data from the relevant geographic market with data from other geographical markets,[342] by comparing data from the relevant product market with data from similar product markets,[343] and combinations of these methods.[344] Methods other than comparator-based methods include simulations using economic models of market behaviour,[345] cost-based methods using an estimated production cost and reasonable profit margin per unit produced,[346] and finance-based methods studying the financial performance of the allegedly injured party.[347] Pragmatic techniques used to approximate harm are also mentioned but are not discussed in detail.[348] In paragraphs 7.209–7.211 sections in the Practical Guide which specifically address passing-on will be discussed.

7.167 Over and above the issues of what heads of damages are available and how to quantify harm, it is warranted also to submit some brief comments on Chapter III of Directive 2014/104/EU and in particular the issues of limitation periods and of joint and several liability. As regards limitation periods for bringing actions for damages Member States are instructed in Article 10(3) to ensure that such limitation periods are at least five years. Under Article 10(4) the limitation period shall be suspended or interrupted (the choice of which is left to be decided on the basis of national law) if the Commission or a national competition authority takes action for the purpose of investigation or proceedings in respect of the infringement to which the action for damages at issue relates. Under Article 10(2), which is important, the limitation period shall not begin to run until the infringement has ceased and the claimant 'knows, or can reasonably be expected to know' of the infringing behaviour, that it constitutes an infringement of competition law, that it has caused the claimant harm, and the identity of the infringer. Other issues are left to be decided on the basis of national law by virtue of Article 10(1).

340 Accordingly, the Practical Guide does not make any suggestions along the lines of the US 'Optimal Deterrence Model' for damages. On that model see Hovenkamp (n 47) 711–20.

341 SWD(2013) 205 (n 67) paras 38–48.

342 Ibid., paras 49–53.

343 Ibid., paras 54–55.

344 Ibid., paras 56–58.

345 Ibid., paras 97–105.

346 Ibid., paras 107–113.

347 Ibid., paras 114–118.

348 Ibid., para. 120.

As regards joint and several liability the main rule in Article 11(1) of the Directive is that where undertakings have infringed competition law through joint behaviour, they are jointly and severally liable for the harm caused. Hence each undertaking is liable to pay damages for the full amount of harm caused. There are two exceptions to the main rule: one for small- or medium-sized enterprises (SMEs);[349] and one for whistleblowers. It follows from Article 11(2) and (3) that an SME which holds a market share smaller than 5 per cent, which would be economically jeopardized by the main rule, which has not led the infringement or coerced other undertakings to participate in it, and which has not previously infringed competition law, is liable to pay damages only to its own direct and indirect purchasers (Beta and Gamma parties down the supply chain from that particular SME). This exception however applies 'without prejudice to the right of full compensation as laid down in Article 3' of the Directive. It therefore seems that in case it becomes difficult for claimants to secure compensation from other infringers the exception for SMEs will yield to the claimant's interest in compensation. Whistleblowers, who have been granted immunity (immunity recipients) from fines under a leniency programme of the Commission or a national competition authority, are under Article 11(4) jointly and severally liable only to their direct and indirect purchasers or providers. The inclusion of providers here, by contrast to the liability of SMEs, concerns liability for harm caused to direct and indirect providers (i.e., upstream) for the participants in a buying cartel. Similarly with SMEs immunity recipients are liable to other injured parties only where full compensation cannot be obtained from the other infringing undertakings. Article 11(5) and (6), finally, concern the recovery of contributions among infringing undertakings in light of their respective responsibility for the harm caused. **7.168**

II. The defence of passing-on

It has been reported by the European Commission that, prior to the transposition of Directive 2014/104/EU, the laws of the Member States with regard to the defence of passing-on differed substantially. Some had no legislation or case law on the defence, some had rejected it, and some had endorsed it.[350] Directive 2014/104/EU includes a number of provisions addressing passing-on specifically and sets out to harmonize the laws of the Member States on the defence. The accompanying soft-law instruments also **7.169**

---

349 Pursuant to Directive 2014/104/EU (n 5) Art. 11(2) the definition of small- or medium-sized enterprises in Commission Recommendation of 6 May 2003 concerning the definition of micro-, small- and medium-sized enterprises C(2003) 1422 shall apply.

350 See SWD(2013) 203 final (n 57) 16–17.

offer some guidance relevant to the defence of passing-on.[351] This section presents and discusses this harmonization and the alternatives to the approach chosen that were available. First, there will be a presentation and analysis of relevant remarks made by the Court of Justice in its case law in sub-section 7.E.II.a. Thereafter the rules in Directive 2014/104/EU and relevant soft-law provisions will be examined in sub-section 7.E.II.b. Finally, in sub-section 7.E.II.c, the policy choices made will be discussed in light of US federal antitrust law and the EU debate.

a. Case law relevant to the defence of passing-on

7.170 *Courage* included a somewhat laconic paragraph in which the Court of Justice reminded us that Community law did not prevent national courts from taking steps to ensure that the protection of the rights guaranteed by Community law did not entail the unjust enrichment of those who enjoyed them.[352] The point intended in this *dictum* was not entirely clear. It is worth noticing, perhaps, that the national court had asked no question on the issue of passing-on. Indeed it should be questioned whether the Court had the passing-on problem in mind at all. To attempt an answer it is appropriate to turn first to the Opinion submitted by Advocate General Mischo. The Advocate General mentioned there that a party to an unlawful agreement should not obtain more than they have lost by reason of the unlawful agreement, so as to avoid unjust enrichment. The connection from this statement to the defence of passing-on is however quite weak, as becomes apparent on contemplation of the full quote:

7.171

> I therefore agree with the United Kingdom Government when it states that it does not advocate that the party to the unlawful agreement should obtain more than it has lost by reason of the unlawful agreement. In certain cases the claimant, even if in a weaker bargaining position, may have obtained benefits from the unlawful provisions of the agreement, and, to avoid unjust enrichment and the imposition of penal damages on the defendant, such benefits should in principle be taken into account in the assessment of damages. The precise quantification of the damages is, of course, a matter for national courts.[353]

7.172 The Advocate General did not seem concerned with the passing-on of an overcharge, but rather with benefits obtained by reason of the distortion or restriction of competition caused by the agreement at issue. In other words the Advocate General was illustrating that in order to avoid unjust enrichment of

---

351 Specific guidelines on how to estimate the share of an overcharge passed on is presently being drafted by the Commission; see para. 7.182.

352 *Courage* (n 4) para. 30. A summary of the facts in *Courage* is available in para. 7.016.

353 Ibid., Opinion of AG Mischo para. 59.

claimants, damages should not be awarded in excess of an amount corresponding to harm inflicted by the contract minus any benefits earned from the contract.[354] If the holding of the Court of Justice is interpreted in the light of the Opinion it is consequently arguable that the unjust enrichment *dictum* was not intended as an acknowledgement of a defence of passing-on for the purposes of EU competition law. It would instead seem intended as an indication that the national court is free, in its assessment of whether to allow recovery, to take into consideration such circumstances that may have enriched the claimant.

Alternatively however, the *dictum* of the Court of Justice could be read in the light of the case law cited by the Court of Justice in the relevant paragraph, namely *Ireks-Arkady*,[355] *Just*[356] and *Michaïlidis*.[357] The cited paragraph in the quellmehl case *Ireks-Arkady* explicitly concerned the passing-on problem, stating that when the loss caused by an abolition of refunds had been or could have been passed on such a price increase would take the place of refunds, compensating the producer of quellmehl.[358] The cited paragraph in *Just* contained the crucial point that Community law did not require an order for the recovery of charges improperly made to be granted in conditions which would involve the unjust enrichment of those entitlement and that, therefore, there was nothing in Community law to prevent national courts from taking into account the fact that it was possible for charges unduly levied to be incorporated into prices and passed on.[359] The cited paragraph in *Michaïlidis* reiterated and cited the same paragraph in *Just*. It would follow from such a reading that the Court of Justice in *Courage* was indeed aiming to make a statement on the applicability *mutatis mutandis* of previous case law concerning the passing-on problem in the context of competition damages actions. **7.173**

A third reading is also possible in which the relevant paragraph is placed in the bigger argumentative pattern emanating from a close reading of *Courage*. At this point in its line of argument the Court had established that there should be no absolute bar against an action being brought by a party to a contract liable to violate competition law.[360] The Court then continued to hold that the **7.174**

354 Ibid.

355 Case 238/78 *Ireks-Arkady GmbH v Council and Commission of the European Communities* [1979] ECR 2955. In *Courage*, the Court cited *Ireks-Arkady* para. 14.

356 Case 68/79 *Hans Just I/S v Danish Ministry for Fiscal Affairs* [1980] ECR 501. In *Courage*, the Court cited *Just* para. 26.

357 Joined cases C-441/98 and C-442/98 *Kapniki Michaïlidis AE v Idryma Koinonikon Asfaliseon (IKA)* [2000] ECR I-7145. In *Courage*, the Court cited *Michaïlidis* para. 31.

358 Cf. para. 3.090.

359 Cf. para. 5.136.

360 *Courage* (n 4) para. 28.

details of the action were governed by national law, subject to the EU law principles of equivalence and effectiveness.[361] After this general holding the unjust enrichment paragraph appeared. The Court thereafter continued:

7.175 Similarly, ... Community law does not preclude national law from denying a party who is found to bear significant responsibility for the distortion of competition the right to obtain damages from the other contracting party. Under a principle which is recognised in most of the legal systems of the Member States and which the Court has applied in the past ... , a litigant should not profit from his own unlawful conduct, where this is proven.

In that regard, the matters to be taken into account by the competent national court include the economic and legal context in which the parties find themselves and, as the United Kingdom Government rightly points out, the respective bargaining power and conduct of the two parties to the contract.[362]

7.176 The Court then concluded that 'Community law does not preclude a rule of national law barring a party to a contract liable to restrict or distort competition from relying on his own unlawful actions to obtain damages where it is established that that party bears significant responsibility for the distortion of competition.'[363] Read in this bigger context the unjust enrichment remark in *Courage* illustrated that since a possible award of damages to claimants who bore significant responsibility for the distortion of competition could reasonably be perceived as an unjust enrichment of them, EU law would permit a bar against actions brought by such claimants. It was not, under this interpretation, an indication on the status of the defence of passing-on within the context of damages actions for a breach of EU competition law. Such a reading is also easily compatible with the first reading here suggested.

7.177 Plausibly the Court framed its unjust enrichment remark in *Courage* so as to keep its future options open to all these possible interpretations. The Court cannot reasonably have been blind to the likelihood of readers interpreting the unjust enrichment holding as a hint on the defence of passing-on.[364]

---

361 Ibid., para. 29.

362 Ibid., paras 31–32.

363 Ibid., Operative part para. 3.

364 The insightful Komninos would not take the view that this *dictum* was a hint on passing-on; see Assimakis P Komninos, 'New Prospects for Private Enforcement of EC Competition Law: Courage v. Crehan and the Community Right to Damages' (2002) 39 *Common Market Law Review* 447, 478, where he submitted that it would have been 'inappropriate' for the Court to engage in premature discussion of passing-on in *Courage*.

Manfredi included a *dictum* on unjust enrichment which was essentially identical to the one in *Courage*,[365] but passing-on was neither discussed any more explicitly by the Court in *Manfredi* than in *Courage* nor mentioned in the Opinion submitted by Advocate General Geelhoed.[366] Again the national court had asked no question on the issue of passing-on – and indeed it could not reasonably have asked any such question for there were no Gamma parties in *Manfredi*: the Beta claimants at issue were final consumers. In *Manfredi* it consequently becomes apparent that the unjust enrichment *dictum* could not logically have been included in the judgment in order to instruct the national court to take into consideration any passing-on of the overcharge. Reading the relevant paragraph in the light of the case law cited (the second alternative above) does not, therefore, yield a strong interpretation of its legal meaning. Another interpretation must accordingly be chosen. Since Advocate General Geelhoed did not mention the issue the option of close reading of the relevant paragraph in its context in the judgment is the most rewarding approach. The unjust enrichment *dictum* in *Manfredi* appeared in the context of the fourth and fifth questions asked by the national court, which concerned the estimation of damages and more specifically whether Article 81 EC (now Article 101 TFEU) required that punitive damages be available for a breach of that provision. Having pointed out that the availability of compensation in damages as such followed from the need to ensure the full effectiveness of Article 81 EC, the Court held that it was for the national legal systems of the Member States to set the applicable criteria for the estimation of damages, subject to the EU law principles of equivalence and effectiveness.[367] The Court then held: **7.178**

> In that respect, first, in accordance with the principle of equivalence, it must be possible to award particular damages, such as exemplary or punitive damages, pursuant to actions founded on the Community competition rules, if such damages may be awarded pursuant to similar actions founded on domestic law … . **7.179**
>
> However, it is settled case-law that Community law does not prevent national courts from taking steps to ensure that the protection of the rights guaranteed by Community law does not entail the unjust enrichment of those who enjoy them … .
>
> Secondly, it follows from the principle of effectiveness and the right of any individual to seek compensation for loss caused by a contract or by conduct liable to restrict or

365 *Manfredi* (n 36) para. 94, citing *Ireks-Arkady* (n 355) para. 14, *Michaïlidis* (n 357) para. 31, and *Courage* (n 4) para. 30. A summary of the facts in *Manfredi* is available in para. 7.026.

366 But cf. ibid., Opinion of AG Geelhoed paras 69–70, which could be construed as significant to the passing-on problem.

367 Ibid., paras 89–92.

distort competition that injured persons must be able to seek compensation not only for actual loss (*damnum emergens*) but also for loss of profit (*lucrum cessans*) plus interest.[368]

7.180 The sequence of these holdings reveals that the unjust enrichment *dictum* forms an integral part of the Court's reasoning on the impact of the principle of equivalence. The meaning of that reasoning is to instruct the national court to extend any availability of punitive damages in similar actions in national law to the action for damages for a breach of EU competition law.[369] The unjust enrichment *dictum* seems, read this way, to underline the autonomy of the Member States in the estimation of damages. Punitive damages in similar actions should be extended to EU law actions pursuant to *Manfredi*, but where punitive damages were not available they needed not be introduced. In jurisdictions where punitive damages were not available it was likely that the reparative function of compensation in damages was traditionally underlined. In such jurisdictions overcompensation, e.g. through punitive damages, could be perceived as causing the claimant to be unjustly enriched (to the amount of the excess). Read this way the unjust enrichment *dictum* clarified that even if punitive damages should be extended to EU law actions whenever available, punitive damages were by no means required by EU law – which was indeed what the national court had asked.

7.181 It must therefore be concluded that the unjust enrichment *dictum* in *Manfredi* did not as such concern the passing-on problem even though (as mentioned in connection to *Courage*) the Court cannot reasonably have been blind to the likelihood that readers might see the unjust enrichment *dictum* as a hint on the defence of passing-on.

b. The new regime and the defence of passing-on

7.182 Chapter IV (Articles 12–16) of Directive 2014/104/EU specifically concerns the passing-on problem. Article 12 sets out the overall principles chosen with regard to passing-on. Article 13 explicitly endorses a right for Alpha (defendants) to invoke the passing-on defence, but also gives them the onus of proving that harm has in fact been passed on. Article 14 addresses the position of Gamma claimants when invoking passing-on as a 'sword', i.e., to demonstrate that harm has been passed on to them.[370] Article 15 concerns the interrelationship of claims from different levels of the supply chain, i.e., between

368 Ibid., paras 93–95. Citations omitted.

369 The similar action would typically be an action for damages for a breach of national competition law. On the principle of equivalence in general see Section 2.D.II. On punitive damages, cf. para. 7.159.

370 Causation aspects of Art. 14(2) were discussed briefly in paras 7.150–7.152. The 'shield' and 'sword' metaphors were introduced in para. 1.009.

Beta claims and Gamma claims at different levels. Finally Article 16 orders the Commission to issue guidelines on how to estimate the extent of passing-on. Work on these guidelines has begun by commissioning an expert study on the passing-on of overcharges, the results of which became public in the autumn of 2016.[371] This section seeks to present the provisions of the Directive and, where relevant, those of the accompanying soft-law instruments. An extensive critical analysis in light of the relevant policy considerations discussed by the Commission in the *travaux préparatoires* and by legal writers is offered in sub-section 7.E.II.c.

It was noted in sub-section 7.C.II.b that the issue of access to court for Gamma claimants is settled through Articles 12(1) and 2(24) of Directive 2014/104/EU. Here other aspects of Article 12 will be discussed. In its entirety Article 12 of the Directive reads as follows: **7.183**

> Passing-on of overcharges and the right to full compensation **7.184**
>
> 1. To ensure the full effectiveness of the right to full compensation as laid down in Article 3, Member States shall ensure that, in accordance with the rules laid down in this Chapter, compensation of harm can be claimed by anyone who suffered it, irrespective of whether they are direct or indirect purchasers from an infringer, and that compensation of harm exceeding that caused by the infringement of competition law to the claimant, as well as the absence of liability of the infringer, are avoided.
>
> 2. In order to avoid overcompensation, Member States shall lay down procedural rules appropriate to ensure that compensation for actual loss at any level of the supply chain does not exceed the overcharge harm suffered at that level.
>
> 3. This Chapter shall be without prejudice to the right of an injured party to claim and obtain compensation for loss of profits due to a full or partial passing-on of the overcharge.
>
> 4. Member States shall ensure that the rules laid down in this Chapter apply accordingly where the infringement of competition law relates to a supply to the infringer.
>
> 5. Member States shall ensure that the national courts have the power to estimate, in accordance with national procedures, the share of any overcharge that was passed on.

A preference for reparation has evidently guided the approach to the passing-on problem that emerges from Articles 3 and 12 of the Directive.[372] The Member States are thus instructed in Article 12(1) both to avoid overcompensation and to ensure that the absence of liability of the infringer is **7.185**

---

371 COMP/2015/011 (n 238). The study became available on <http://ec.europa.eu/competition/antitrust/actionsdamages/index.html> as this book was being finalized for print.

372 For a full quote of Art. 3 see para. 7.158.

avoided. The Directive is silent however with regard to situations where the choice is to either overcompensate or allow the infringer to escape liability. Such situations are arguably at the heart of the passing-on problem. It seems to follow that it will be for the national courts to make the choice – or perhaps to refer the issue to the Court of Justice for a preliminary ruling.

7.186 The Member States are instructed in Article 12(2) to enact the 'procedural rules appropriate' to procure compensation and to avoid overcompensation. It is not clear what the procedural rules at issue would be like. If rules on the estimation of damages are intended, such rules are not necessarily to be viewed as procedural in character. Perhaps Article 12(5) can be read as providing an example: court power to make estimations of which share of the overcharge was passed on at the different levels of the supply chain. More details on the coordination of claims follow from Article 15, which will be discussed below. Suffice it here to conclude that the instruction in Article 12(2) must be read in conjunction with Article 15 and that it will be for the Member States to ensure in accordance with both Articles that not only substantive rules but also procedural mechanisms for the coordination of claims must be put into place for the implementation of Directive 2014/104/EU.

7.187 It is acknowledged in Article 12(3) that the rules of Chapter IV do not as such apply to other harm than harm incurred through an overcharge and the passing-on of an overcharge. In other words an overcharge will spread down the supply chain and may cause harm at any level, but other harm, e.g., loss of profits, does not spread in this way – at least the common view is that it does not.[373] The Directive codifies this common view.

7.188 It is clarified in Article 12(4) that the Directive provisions on passing-on apply also to the upstream mirror image of passing-on, where suppliers incur harm due to, e.g., a buying cartel. Although it is less common to think of such harm passing back up the supply chain, and if so how this happens in practice, such a possibility is still accounted for in Article 12(4).[374]

7.189 In sum it is endeavoured through the provisions in Article 12 of Directive 2014/104/EU to ensure that full reparative compensation for harm is available to claimants for overcharge harm incurred at their level of the supply chain, but not for overcharge harm absorbed above their level or for overcharge harm passed further on. The problem is how to prove to what extent harm was

373 See e.g. SEC(2008) 404 (n 60) para. 202. This view is of course open to discussion; see Strand (n 325) 385 and Section 1.A.IV.

374 See also para. 7.122 on access for such claimants.

absorbed at the different levels. This is addressed by Articles 13 and 14 which read as follows:

Article 13: Passing-on defence 7.190

Member States shall ensure that the defendant in an action for damages can invoke as a defence against a claim for damages the fact that the claimant passed on the whole or part of the overcharge resulting from the infringement of competition law. The burden of proving that the overcharge was passed on shall be on the defendant, who may reasonably require disclosure from the claimant or from third parties.

Article 14: Indirect purchasers 7.191

1. Member States shall ensure that, where in an action for damages the existence of a claim for damages or the amount of compensation to be awarded depends on whether, or to what degree, an overcharge was passed on to the claimant, taking into account the commercial practice that price increases are passed on down the supply chain, the burden of proving the existence and scope of such a passing-on shall rest with the claimant, who may reasonably require disclosure from the defendant or from third parties.

2. In the situation referred to in paragraph 1, the indirect purchaser shall be deemed to have proven that a passing-on to that indirect purchaser occurred where that indirect purchaser has shown that:
(a) the defendant has committed an infringement of competition law;
(b) the infringement of competition law has resulted in an overcharge for the direct purchaser of the defendant; and
(c) the indirect purchaser has purchased the goods or services that were the object of the infringement of competition law, or has purchased goods or services derived from or containing them.

This paragraph shall not apply where the defendant can demonstrate credibly to the satisfaction of the court that the overcharge was not, or was not entirely, passed on to the indirect purchaser.

Under Article 13 Alpha defendants who invoke the defence of passing-on – 7.192 i.e., passing-on as a shield – have the onus of proving the extent to which the overcharge was in fact passed on down the supply chain. The defence of passing-on is thus endorsed as such for the purposes of EU competition damages actions. The merits of this choice will be discussed in sub-section 7.E.II.c.

Under Article 14(1) Gamma claimants arguing that overcharge harm has been 7.193 passed on to them – i.e., passing-on as a sword – will have the onus of proving 'the existence and scope of such a passing-on'. In both instances the litigant bearing the onus of proving passing on may 'reasonably require disclosure' from its adversary or from third parties (more often than not, this will be

Beta). Therefore Articles 13 and 14 should be read in conjunction with Chapter II on disclosure of evidence and in particular Article 5, which serves to ease the burden of proof for litigants by introducing opportunities for national courts to order the disclosure of specified pieces of evidence which are under the control of defendants or third parties.[375] Further opportunities to obtain evidence held by the Commission or national competition authorities are offered in Article 6.

7.194 National courts are further instructed in Article 14(1) to take into account 'the commercial practice that price increases are passed down the supply chain'. This phrase, which was not in the original Commission proposal for a Directive[376] but was included after negotiations with the Parliament and the Council, is arguably obscure. Its legal content is vague and its empirical truth can be questioned. The Commission has indeed argued the contrary.[377] The same issue is presented in a more balanced way in recital 41 where it is explained that it 'may' be commercial practice to pass on price increases down the supply chain, depending on the conditions of the relevant market. Read in context it seems the phrase at issue in Article 14(1) may have been intended to relax the burden of proof on Gamma with regard to passing-on (to the Gamma claimant), but it is doubtful whether it will be able to have any influence on the assessment under Article 14. It can be speculated that this phrase was inserted as part of a political compromise, and it can be feared that it will influence the interpretation of Article 13 more than the interpretation of Article 14.

7.195 In respect of evidence demonstrating the existence and extent of passing-on, Gamma claimants have the advantage of some assistance made available through Article 14(2). For Gamma in particular the burden of proving the existence and scope of passing-on might otherwise be difficult to meet. On the other hand, as expressed in Article 15(1),[378] if the burden of proof for Gamma claimants is eased too much the risk for multiple liability increases.[379] Directive 2014/104/EU therefore strikes a balance by introducing in Article 14(2) a rebuttable presumption in favour of passing-on of overcharge harm to the Gamma claimant where the Gamma claimant has successfully proved three points: first, it must prove that 'the defendant has committed an infringement of competition law'; second, Gamma must prove that 'the

375 Directive 2014/104/EU (n 5) Art. 5 further includes a number of specific qualifications to this possibility, which will not be analysed in detail here.

376 Cf COM(2013) 404 (n 65) Art. 13(1).

377 SWD(2013) 205 (n 67) para. 168. See further paras 7.214–7.217.

378 Directive 2014/104/EU (n 5) Art. 15 follows below.

379 For policy considerations of the Commission in this regard see SWD(2013) 203 final (n 57) paras 157–171.

infringement of competition law has resulted in an overcharge for the direct purchaser'; and third, it must prove that Gamma 'purchased the goods or services that were subject to the infringement of competition law' or 'goods or services derived from or containing them'. In the event that the overcharge resulted from a cartel infringement, it seems to follow from Article 17(2) of the new Directive that Gamma claimants will not need to prove the second element of Article 14(2), but would be able to rely on the presumption for harm laid down in Article 17(2) for the purposes of harm caused by cartel infringements.[380]

It was noted in sub-section 7.C.II.b that Kloub has identified new problems potentially arising from the presumption in Article 14(2), especially regarding the standard of proof for rebuttal.[381] A literal interpretation of Article 14(2)(2) suggests that a presumption would be rebutted in its entirety if Alpha is able to demonstrate to the satisfaction of the court that some portion of the overcharge was not passed on. However, it is submitted, the better view is to interpret Article 14(2)(2) as setting the standard of proof pertaining to the extent at which an overcharge has been passed on rather than pertaining to the existence of passing-on or to the amount claimed to have been passed on. If this view is accepted the presumption established by the Gamma claimant will be rebutted only to the extent that Alpha can demonstrate to the satisfaction of the court that a certain portion of the overcharge was not passed on. The presumption would remain unaffected with regard to other portions of the overcharge. **7.196**

Notwithstanding this preliminary interpretative problem, the standard of 'demonstrating credibly to the satisfaction of the court' is liable to be understood in differing ways among the Member States. For instance the Swedish language version uses a terminology (*'på ett trovärdigt sätt enligt domstolen kan visa'*) which does not connect to any of the traditional Swedish standards of proof.[382] Under such circumstances it becomes difficult to foresee how the standard envisaged by the Directive will be applied by the national courts. Kloub has submitted in that regard that if the standard of proof is of the same degree as required of Alpha to prove passing-on when using it as a defence, the presumption will be virtually irrebuttable unless Alpha is able to obtain evidence held by Beta. This problem has however been addressed in Article 5 of the Directive under which Alpha should be able to request the national court to order Beta to disclose relevant evidence. Kloub was further **7.197**

380 On Directive 2014/104/EU (n 5) Art. 17(2) cf. n 288.

381 See Kloub (n 241) 96.

382 The German language version reads 'gegenüber dem Gericht glaubhaft machen kann'. The French language version reads 'peut démontrer de façon crédible, à la satisfaction de la juridiction'.

rightly concerned that a low standard of proof would render the presumption useless.[383] It thus seems it will be for the national courts to strike the proper balance between the presumption and the standard of proof for rebuttal in cooperation with the Court of Justice. As pointed out by Kloub this balancing exercise is furthermore dependent on the effectiveness of the disclosure mechanisms prescribed by Directive 2014/104/EU.[384]

7.198 It should finally be noted that the estimation of *damnum emergens* at various levels of the supply chain is without prejudice to the issue of *lucrum cessans* at that level, which must be proved as such. Reduced sales constitute harm for which damages are payable under Directive 2014/104/EU at an amount which cannot be decreased with reference to passing-on of such harm.[385] The issues are nevertheless connected as the estimation of reduced sales at any level of the supply chain requires evidence of the extent of passing-on to and/or from that level. It therefore seems impossible to determine the total amount of damages payable to a claimant without first determining the extent of passing-on to each Gamma level of the supply chain.

7.199 Article 15 of the Directive, next, primarily concerns the legal effect of parallel proceedings relating to the same competition law infringement. It should be read in conjunction with Article 9 on the effect of decisions by national competition authorities and review courts (and Regulation (EC) No 1/2003[386]). Article 15 reads as follows:

7.200 Actions for damages by claimants from different levels in the supply chain

1. To avoid that actions for damages by claimants from different levels in the supply chain lead to a multiple liability or to an absence of liability of the infringer, Member States shall ensure that in assessing whether the burden of proof resulting from the application of Articles 13 and 14 is satisfied, national courts seized of an action for damages are able, by means available under Union or national law, to take due account of any of the following:
(a) actions for damages that are related to the same infringement of competition law, but that are brought by claimants from other levels in the supply chain;
(b) judgments resulting from actions for damages as referred to in point (a);
(c) relevant information in the public domain resulting from the public enforcement of competition law.

383 Kloub (n 241) 96.
384 Ibid.
385 See Directive 2014/104/EU (n 5) rec. 40 and Section 1.A.IV.
386 Regulation (EC) No 1/2003 (n 71).

2. This Article shall be without prejudice to the rights and obligations of national courts under Article 30 of Regulation (EU) No 1215/2012.[387]

It is not explained in Article 15 how to make priorities among the aims pursued. More often than not a national court seized with competition damages will need to resort to approximations, as instructed by Article 12(5). Should the approximation give priority to the avoidance of liability for the infringer to pay multiple damages or to the avoidance of absence of liability? Moreover, let us assume that a Beta claimant has successfully claimed damages to an amount equivalent to the full overcharge. Then a class of Gamma claimants bring an action, demonstrating to the full satisfaction of the court that at least half the overcharge was passed on to them. Should the national court take refuge in Article 15(1)(b) and dismiss the action in the interest of avoiding liability for the infringer to pay multiple damages? Would that not frustrate the rights of the Gamma claimants under Article 2 of the Directive? These questions need to be resolved and it remains to be seen in the case law on Directive 2014/104/EU how to fill the gaps. **7.201**

Article 15 also has the more specific function of ensuring that national courts seized with competition damages litigation take into account the conclusions drawn in parallel proceedings with regard to the points to be proved under Articles 13 and 14. It is clear in Article 15(1)(a) and (b) that national courts are instructed to 'take due account of' parallel proceedings and judgments relating to the same infringement but originating from different levels in the supply chain. It is by contrast less clear in what legal and/or procedural manner such parallel proceedings and judgments should be taken into due account. It is suggested in recital 44 that on-going parallel proceedings could be joined, even in cross-border cases. One might also imagine a partial joinder of claims for the purposes of determining some of the issues that will be under dispute in all of them, e.g., whether there was an infringement of competition law and whether that infringement was capable of causing harm. Article 15(1)(c) further provides that national courts should 'take due account of' information from public enforcement cases, typically regarding the same infringement. Although this is not specified it thus seems Article 15(1) is designed for stand-alone actions. **7.202**

Irrespective of whether the action is a stand-alone or follow-on action it should be noticed that 'taking due account of' information from public **7.203**

387 Regulation (EU) No 1215/2012 of the European Parliament and of the Council of 12 December 2012 on jurisdiction and the recognition and enforcement of judgments in civil and commercial matters (recast) [2102] OJ L351/1.

enforcement cases will include the effects of decisions in public enforcement cases prescribed in Article 9(1) of the Directive, i.e., that the establishment of an infringement of competition law in public enforcement cases arising from the same infringement is accepted for the purposes of private enforcement proceedings in the same jurisdiction. Also, in accordance with Article 9(2), the establishment of an infringement of competition law in public enforcement cases in one Member State will serve at least as *prima facie* evidence of an infringement for the purposes of private enforcement proceedings, arising from the same infringement, in other Member States. In situations not covered by Article 9 however, Article 15 is not clear on how national courts are expected to use the information gathered. It is submitted that the gathering of information should be used in accordance with the explicit aims of Article 15. First, the information should be used to avoid multiple liability and absence of liability for the infringer.[388] Accordingly the information gathered should be used to avoid situations where the infringer is held liable to pay multiple damages and situations where the infringer is not held to pay any damages (in essence, situations where the total amount of damages payments ordered do not correspond to the harm caused). Second, the information gathered should be used to assess 'whether the burden of proof resulting from the application of Articles 13 and 14 is satisfied'. This second point is essentially a practical method for the purposes of the first point. It follows that Article 15 is intended to be read in conjunction with Articles 13 and 14. As a package these Articles (indeed, Chapter IV of the Directive in its entirety) apparently endeavour to put in place rules that will facilitate the achievement of full reparative justice through compensation for all harm at all levels of the supply chain that has been caused by an infringement of competition law – or at least as close as possible an approximation.

7.204 It is also interesting to read Article 15 in light of its legislative history. In its 2013 proposal for a Directive the Commission included a provision intended to prohibit the defence of passing-on in situations where national law would preclude Gamma claimants of the next level of the supply chain (i.e., the next level downstream from the claimant bringing proceedings) to bring an action, e.g., for reasons of remoteness.[389] This limited prohibition of the defence of passing-on was included in order to avoid situations where Alpha would not be held liable to compensate any claimant. The proposed provision did not make the final Directive, but it is worth noticing that the inclusion of the aim of 'avoiding absence of liability of the infringer' in Article 15 was not included in the 2013 proposal either. It seems therefore that the elimination of the

388 Directive 2014/104/EU (n 5) Art. 15(1).

389 See COM(2013) 404 final (n 65) 17–18 and Art. 12(2).

limited prohibition of the defence of passing-on here described and the inclusion of this aim in Article 15 are connected, and that this aim was included in Article 15 in the hope of achieving the purpose intended through the proposed provision. It remains to be seen if Article 15 will be interpreted as having the effect of prohibiting the defence of passing-on in circumstances where Gamma claimants belonging to the next level of the supply chain are precluded from bringing an action under applicable national law, as the Commission originally intended.

In the context of mechanisms for the coordination of claims, it is appropriate also to highlight the relevance of Recommendation 2013/396/EU on collective redress.[390] This recommendation applies to actions for compensation in mass harm situations caused by violations of rights granted under Union law generally, i.e., its scope of application is not limited to competition law. Pursuant to the recommendation a claimant party formed for the purposes of collective redress 'should be formed on the basis of express consent of the natural or legal persons claiming to have been harmed ("opt-in" principle)'. It is accepted under the recommendation for national rules to use other ways to form a claimant party, e.g., by using the opt-out principle whereby natural or legal persons that have been harmed are automatically represented by the claimant party unless they have actively opted not to be represented by it. Such alternatives to the opt-in principle are however accepted only if 'duly justified by reasons of sound administration of justice'.[391] Even though the recommendation is a soft-law instrument, it is comparatively stringently written and explains that its provisions 'should' be implemented by the Member States by 26 July 2015.[392] Consequently its emphasis on the opt-in principle cannot be disregarded by Member States. The Commission seems rather to have envisaged a 'comply or explain' approach to its recommendation. **7.205**

The choice of the opt-in alternative has been criticized for not taking into sufficient consideration the interest of deterrence. In that regard, according to the European Law Institute, behavioural science has proved that potential claimants are largely guided by so-called 'inertia bias', i.e., an inclination not to choose actively but to follow the default option. It would follow that collective redress mechanisms based on the opt-in principle risk being less effective than **7.206**

390 Commission Recommendation 2013/396/EU (n 68). For further reading on the recommendation see European Law Institute (n 227). A critical assessment of the recommended rules, with a comparative look at some European collective redress mechanisms, is available in Arianna Andreangeli, *Private Enforcement of Antitrust: Regulating Corporate Behaviour through Collective Claims in the EU and US* (Edward Elgar Publishing 2014); unfortunately brought to this author's attention too recently to receive proper attention in this brief analysis.

391 Commission Recommendation 2013/396/EU (n 68) 21.

392 Ibid., 38.

those based on the opt-out principle. The European Law Institute nonetheless acknowledged that views on the two principles differed and that empirical research on the pros and cons of the two principles was needed.[393]

7.207 Article 16 of the Directive, finally, reads as follows:

> The Commission shall issue guidelines for national courts on how to estimate the share of the overcharge which was passed on to the indirect purchaser.

7.208 As mentioned in paragraph 7.182 work on these guidelines has begun by commissioning an expert study on the passing-on of overcharges, the results of which have recently been published. Unfortunately, however, the study was not available in time for presentation and analysis in this book. The Practical Guide on quantifying harm nevertheless includes a detailed explanation of the passing-on problem, the factors to be taken into account in an assessment of to what extent an overcharge has been passed on and the extent of profit lost by reason of decreased sales, and suggestions on the methods to use for an economic analysis of passing-on for the purposes of quantifying harm for which damages may be payable.[394] A few comments will therefore be submitted on the statements in the Practical Guide.

7.209 Two main ways of quantifying the extent of harm passed on are identified in the Practical Guide. In the first method the initial overcharge is quantified and the extent of passing-on to relevant levels of the supply chain is determined by use of econometrics. In the second method a comparative model is used in order to determine whether Gamma has paid an overcharge. There may for example be a difference between prices paid before and during the infringement. Such a price increase can be held to be equivalent to the overcharge passed on, making it unnecessary to investigate the extent to which the initial overcharge was passed on.[395] Comparing these methods with Article 14(2) in Directive 2014/104/EU, and Article 14(2)(b) in particular, it seems that Gamma claimants might in future litigation focus on bringing evidence on the initial overcharge (paid by Beta) in order to establish a presumption. It will then be for Alpha to rebut the presumption, by using the methods suggested in the Practical Guide (or other methods – the Practical Guide is not binding). Gamma will likely attack the evidence presented by Alpha, perhaps by presenting alternative studies using other methods.

393 European Law Institute (n 227) 43–44. The European Law Institute also interestingly noted that the opt-out principle in collective redress for the purposes of private enforcement of competition law is not appreciated by the business sector: 12–14.

394 SWD(2013) 205 (n 67) paras 161–179.

395 Ibid., paras 166–167.

It is submitted that the comparative method suffers from two significant disadvantages. First, it is vulnerable to the counterargument that the price rise was due to other factors on the market. Second, where the indirect purchaser is not the final consumer, it does not provide guidance on the extent to which the indirect purchaser in turn passed on the overcharge to the next link in the supply chain. To that end it would be necessary to carry out another comparison with regard to the next link. For these reasons it may be that the econometric method in the Practical Guide will come to be preferred over comparative methods. **7.210**

It should furthermore be kept in mind that assessments of the amount of overcharge passed on are not the end of the story. All operators down the supply chain from Alpha are also liable to suffer harm caused by the 'volume effect', i.e., loss of profit through decreased sales.[396] With regard to this category of harm the Practical Guide recommends a comparative method.[397] This method will still be vulnerable to counterarguments that the volume effect was due to other factors on the market. In this context, however, it is not likely to be vulnerable to arguments that the harm at issue was passed on to the next link in the supply chain, as we do not commonly imagine undertakings to respond to a decrease in sales by increasing prices.[398] Therefore a comparative model may be more successful for the estimation of harm caused by the volume effect than for the estimation of to what extent an overcharge has been passed on. **7.211**

c. *Analysis*

For the purposes of competition damages the EU legislature has chosen a policy on the defence of passing-on which, it is submitted, harmonizes quite well with its choices for the purposes of damages actions pursuant to Article 340(2) TFEU and for repayment actions against a Member State.[399] Nevertheless the EU policy is the extreme opposite of the policy chosen by the US Supreme Court for the purposes of federal antitrust law. This section will explore the reasons presented for the policy chosen by the EU legislature, and compare those reasons with arguments presented in both EU and US discourse on passing-on in competition damages. **7.212**

---

396 Also known as 'deadweight loss'. See e.g. Ingeborg Simonsson, 'Challenges for Swedish Courts: Will the New Directive on Antitrust Damages Actions Help?' in Maria Bergström, Marios Iacovides and Magnus Strand (eds), *Harmonising EU Competition Litigation: The New Directive and Beyond* (Swedish Studies in European Law, vol. 8, Hart Publishing 2016), citing Christopher R Leslie, 'Antitrust Damages and Deadweight Loss' (2006) 51 *The Antitrust Bulletin* 521.

397 SWD(2013) 205 (n 67) para. 166.

398 See Section 1.A.IV.

399 Cf. Section 3.E.III and sub-section 5.E.II.d respectively.

7.213 Discourse on the defence of passing-on has included a range of arguments. These cannot be presented and discussed in their entirety. It will instead be endeavoured below to cover the most important arguments and to discuss these in depth. By and large the arguments chosen are those that have been discussed by the Commission in its Green and White Papers,[400] the holdings of the US Supreme Court, and some submissions by legal commentators. Rather than listing every argument individually it has been endeavoured to juxtapose arguments *pro et contra* where they relate to the same policy problem. Therefore the discussion below will depart from policy problems rather than arguments as such. Arguments will nevertheless overlap, as the various policy problems are interrelated. The arguments discussed will also partially overlap arguments discussed in Section 7.C.II. This will be indicated in footnotes in order to highlight the close interrelationship between the defence of passing-on and the issue of access for Gamma claimants. The sequence of the issues discussed has also – to some extent – been aligned so as to be compatible with the sequence in sub-section 7.C.II.b. Due to inherent differences it has not been appropriate to do so strictly, however. For instance problems numbers 1 and 2 below do not exactly correspond to any specific argument in the sequence used in sub-section 7.C.II.b. Problem number 3 nonetheless roughly corresponds to argument number 1 in sub-section 7.C.II.b, problem number 4 below roughly to argument number 2, and problem number 5 below connects to argument number 3 in that section.[401]

1. Is passing-on common enough to be a concern in law?

7.214 Let us begin the analysis with a question of fact and legal policy. The US Supreme Court held in *Hanover Shoe* that the supposition underlying the defence of passing-on (i.e., that costs were passed on in prices) was flawed. The Commission has been inclined to agree.[402] Nevertheless, as mentioned in paragraph 7.194, it is now stated in Article 14(1) of Directive 2014/104/EU that the passing-on of price increases is 'commercial practice'.[403] Harris and Sullivan have submitted in that vein that the passing-on of overcharges '*is not the exception: it is the rule*'.[404] It must consequently be acknowledged that views

---

400 The legal certainty argument stressed in SWD(2013) 203 final (n 57) para. 158 will not be included, as it is not an argument on which policy to choose, but only on the need to harmonize.

401 Readers may recall a similar list of arguments in para. 5.144. Although some arguments overlap, the arguments in legal debate over the defence of passing-on in repayment of charges levied by Member States in breach of EU law are mostly of a public law character. Therefore it has not been attempted to compare those arguments systematically with the arguments in this chapter. See however the summaries and comparative analysis in Ch. 9.

402 SWD(2013) 205 (n 67) para. 168, noted in para. 7.194.

403 The statement in Art. 14(1) is somewhat softened by rec. 41 where it is acknowledged that the existence of such a practice depends on conditions on the relevant market.

404 Harris and Sullivan (n 134) 276 (italics in original).

differ. The US Supreme Court explained in *Hanover Shoe* why it was 'not impressed' with this presumption regarding commercial practice:

> A wide range of factors influence a company's pricing policies. Normally the impact of a single change in the relevant conditions cannot be measured after the fact ... there would remain the nearly insuperable difficulty of demonstrating that the particular plaintiff could not or would not have raised his prices absent the overcharge or maintained the higher price had the overcharge been discontinued.[405] **7.215**

In other words the pricing policy of an undertaking should not be supposed to operate on a simple cost-plus basis without regard to market conditions.[406] In *San Giorgio* Advocate General Mancini similarly reported that the Commission's representative had submitted at the hearing that '[i]n order to be certain that charges were passed on, supply would have to be elastic and demand would have to be ... rigid, but I believe the only product for which both those conditions are fulfilled is salt'.[407] The US Supreme Court moreover pointed out in *Hanover Shoe* that in order for product demand to be sufficiently inelastic the overcharge must be 'imposed equally on all ... competitors'.[408] The sum of these observations, if accepted, is that the defence of passing-on should be allowed only on salt markets controlled by a monopolist. A more pragmatic (and, it is submitted, better) view is to acknowledge that the accuracy of the presupposition that costs can be passed on in prices is an empirical issue which must be assessed on the evidence in the individual case. Such a pragmatic approach is represented by Bishop and Walker, submitting that 'it is almost never correct to assume that none of the input cost increase was passed on' but adding that 'the degree of pass-through is an empirical question that requires an empirical answer'.[409] **7.216**

In sum views differ on this point. It is beyond this author to evaluate the economic evidence presented in support of each view. Nevertheless it is appropriate for the purposes of this inquiry to make two observations on the basis of these discussions. First, notwithstanding whether one takes the view that passing-on is an exception or the rule, there seems to be consensus that the conditions of the relevant market are crucial to the existence and extent of **7.217**

405 *Hanover Shoe* (n 139) 492–3.

406 Cf. the discussion on submissions by Toth (n 314) 189 in paras 3.101–3.105; and *Ireks-Arkady* (n 355) Opinion of AG Capotorti para. 11.

407 Case 199/82 *Amministrazione delle Finanze dello Stato v SpA San Giorgio* [1983] ECR 3595 Opinion of AG Mancini para. 6.

408 *Hanover Shoe* (n 139) 492.

409 Bishop and Walker (n 166) 709–10, offering also some economic models for the quantification of passing-on on 711–12.

passing-on.[410] Second, even where market conditions would be such that passing-on is possible, the actual existence and extent of passing-on by the individual claimant must be proved by the defendant pursuant to Article 13 of Directive 2014/104/EU. Therefore, notwithstanding the assertion in Article 14(1), the pragmatism of Bishop and Walker seems at the end of the day to be closest to the approach chosen by the EU legislature and to the guidance offered by the Commission.[411] To analyse the existence and extent of passing-on in every individual case inevitably complicates litigation, however. This will be discussed below.

2. *Windfalls*

7.218 In its 2008 White Paper the Commission was careful to stress reparation as the primary aim pursued in EU competition damages actions. The Commission thus argued:

7.219 Against this background, infringers should be allowed to invoke the possibility that the overcharge might have been passed on. Indeed, to deny this defence could result in unjust enrichment of purchasers who passed on the overcharge and in undue multiple compensation for the illegal overcharge by the defendant.[412]

7.220 The Commission similarly indicated in its 2005 Green Paper that the defence of passing-on was a variation of the duty to mitigate loss.[413] This is a plausible view, as damages awards will commonly be lessened to the extent that claimants have successfully taken steps to mitigate their loss.[414] The passing-on of an overcharge – when possible under present market conditions – can indeed be seen as a way of mitigating loss. By contrast the argument in the White Paper, that overcompensation would constitute an unjust enrichment of the recipient, is flawed. It is evident that the legal concept of unjust

410 Milutinovic (n 61) 183–6 lists 'likely pass-on scenarios'. Relevant factors are also discussed (in Swedish) by Wahl (n 87) 310–11. An overview of economic literature on the passing-on of overcharges is available in Emily Clark, Mat Hughes and David Wirth, 'Ashurst Study on the Conditions of Claims for Damages in Case of Infringement of EC Competition Rules: Analysis of Economic Models for the Calculation of Damages' (2004) <http://ec.europa.eu/competition/antitrust/actionsdamages/economic_clean_en.pdf> (last accessed 31 May 2016) 31–34.

411 Cf. Komninos (n 80) 201, submitting that the European Court of Justice has preferred to 'deal with the issue on an ad hoc basis', citing joined cases 331/85, 376/85 and 378/85 *SA Les Fils de Jules Bianco and J Girard Fils SA v Directeur Général des Douanes et Droits Indirects* [1988] ECR 1099 para. 17, where it was stressed by the Court (in the context of repayment of charges levied in breach of EU law) that 'actual passing on … in whole or in part, depends on various factors in each commercial transaction'. On *Bianco* see paras 5.101–5.105.

412 COM(2008) 165 final (n 60) 7–8; see also SEC(2008) 404 (n 60) paras 209–210.

413 COM(2005) 672 final (n 35) 7.

414 See e.g. Harvey McGregor, *McGregor on Damages* (18th edn, The Common Law Library, Sweet & Maxwell 2009) 236. Cf. para. 6.086 on national rules on mitigation of loss in the context of damages from a Member State.

enrichment would not commonly apply to an order for compensation in excess of harm suffered. An action for restitution by reason of unjust enrichment applies where there is no legal basis for a transaction, but the payment of an amount of damages will by contrast have a legal basis in the court order.[415] Therefore this argument submitted by the Commission should be read as a policy argument connecting to the case law of the Court of Justice with regard to the defence of passing-on in actions for repayment of charges levied in breach of EU law. The argument is that the amount of compensation in damages should be equal to the harm sustained and absorbed by the claimant, and accordingly that damages should not be payable in excess of such absorbed harm. When referring to such overcompensation the less value-laden 'windfall' is preferable to 'unjust enrichment'.

The view that damages should not be payable in excess of absorbed harm was submitted before the US Supreme Court by the defendant in *Hanover Shoe*. The Supreme Court discussed this in some detail: **7.221**

> If in the face of the overcharge the buyer does nothing and absorbs the loss, he is entitled to ... damages. This much seems conceded. ... It is also clear that if the buyer, responding to the illegal price, maintains his own price but takes steps to increase his volume or to decrease other costs, his right to damages is not destroyed. ... We hold that the buyer is equally entitled to damages if he raises the price for his own product. As long as the seller continues to charge the illegal price, he takes from the buyer more than the law allows. At whatever price the buyer sells, the price he pays the seller remains illegally high, and his profits would be greater were his costs lower.[416] **7.222**

The Supreme Court accordingly rejected the defence of passing-on and granted Beta damages to the full amount of the overcharge, trebled. The Supreme Court found support for its view in previous case law, e.g., *Chattanooga Foundry & Pipe Works* where it had held that a claimant 'whose property is diminished by a payment of money wrongfully induced is injured in his property [within the meaning of § 7 of the Sherman Act[417]]'.[418] The Supreme Court also referred to *Southern Pac Co*, a case on damages for excessive interstate railway charges, where it had held that harm in the form of **7.223**

415 See e.g. Draft Common Frame of Reference (Christian von Bar and Eric Clive (eds), *Principles, Definitions and Model Rules of European Private Law: Draft Common Frame of Reference (DCFR) Full Edition* (6 vols, Sellier European Law Publishers 2009)) Art.VII. – 2:101(1)(a). Jones (n 18) 196 similarly questions the aptitude of the 'unjust enrichment' notion in this context, albeit emphasizing policy deliberations.

416 *Hanover Shoe* (n 139) 489.

417 Sherman Act (n 89).

418 *Chattanooga Foundry & Pipe Works v. City of Atlanta* 203 US 390 (1906) 396.

an overcharge was suffered when it was paid, irrespective of later events.[419] This point comes across even more clearly in *Adams v Mills*, another interstate railway case:

7.224 If the defendants exacted from them an unlawful charge, then the exaction was a tort, for which the plaintiffs are entitled, as for other torts, to compensation from the wrongdoer.[420]

7.225 Under this US approach the harm incurred consequently equals the overcharge illegally exacted. It seems this approach is the extreme opposite of the one chosen for the purposes of EU competition damages, and it is noticed that they coincide with the respective systematic emphasis on reparation in private enforcement of EU competition law and on deterrence in private enforcement of federal US antitrust law. It should however also be noticed that the US approach is more reminiscent of traditional concepts of restitution or restitutionary damages, while the EU approach sticks more closely to traditional reparatory damages. In the US approach the concept of compensation in damages has covered repayments of interstate railway charges levied in breach of law. This case law has in turn influenced the Supreme Court with regard to overcharges exacted in breach of antitrust law, as shown by the citations made by the Supreme Court in *Hanover Shoe*. In EU law actions of a restitutionary character have been distinguished from damages actions in the context of passing-on,[421] but just as the US Supreme Court the European Court of Justice has cross-cited across contexts[422] and the approaches chosen have thus far been equivalent in both contexts.

7.226 It should be added that the Supreme Court has recognized an exception to its approach in 'cost-plus arrangements'. This exception is related to the so-called Oil Jobbers cases in the antitrust case law of lower federal US courts, none of which made it to the Supreme Court but one of which was nevertheless cited in *Hanover Shoe*.[423] It has been explained by Hovenkamp that this exception (within which the defence of passing-on is allowed and Gamma claimants may have access to bring an action for damages before federal courts)

419 *Southern Pac Co v Darnell-Taenzer Lumber Co* 245 US 531 (1918) 533–4. Interestingly, in *Southern Pac Co* 534, one of the reasons presented was that '[Alpha] ought not to be allowed to retain his illegal profit, and the only one who can take it from him is [Beta]'.

420 *Adams v Mills* 286 US 397 (1932) 407.

421 See joined cases C-192/95 to 218/95 *Société Comateb and others v Directeur Général des Douanes et Droits Indirects* [1997] ECR I-165 para. 34 and subsequent case law.

422 See *Courage* (n 4) para. 30 and *Manfredi* (n 36) para. 94. Jones (n 18) 196 questions the pertinence of such cross-referencing across contexts.

423 Namely *Twin Ports Oil Co* (n 140); see *Hanover Shoe* (n 139) 492. For other cases belonging to this group see n 140.

encompasses only '*fixed quantity, fixed mark-up* contracts that existed *before* the cartel price took effect'.[424]

Article 12(2) of Directive 2014/104/EU very clearly makes it an EU law policy to avoid windfalls in competition damages. Jones has submitted that EU competition lawyers should be less concerned with possible windfall awards (i.e., damages awards in excess of harm absorbed by the claimant) than US antitrust lawyers. As the EU system does not award treble damages, Jones argued that European windfalls should be less troublesome than US windfalls.[425] There seem to be two reasons for the disinclination of the EU legislature to allow windfall awards. First, the view of the Commission that Gamma actions cannot be encouraged unless the defence of passing-on is simultaneously allowed.[426] This connection between the defence and access for Gamma echoes the US view that *Illinois Brick* and *Hanover Shoe* must both be maintained or both overruled. That view has been debated in US antitrust law and is even more debatable in EU law, as discussed in paragraphs 7.111–7.113. Reference is made to that discussion. Second the EU legislature has opted to leave the interest of deterrence to public enforcement of EU law, settling for reparation in private enforcement. To allow windfalls while nevertheless allowing claimants downstream to claim the full amount passed on to them could boost deterrence, but the EU simply has not been interested. The issue of deterrence and its role in the bigger picture will be elaborated in Section 9.E.II. **7.227**

3. *Multiple liability for Alpha*

In its 2008 White Paper the Commission was concerned that Alpha could be held liable to pay multiple damages awards unless the defence of passing-on was allowed in EU competition damages.[427] In the accompanying Staff Working Paper the Commission clarified that it wished to promote Gamma actions. There was therefore, in the view of the Commission, an inherent risk that claimants from different levels of the supply chain were 'to claim antitrust damages for the same illegal price increase' unless, for balance, the defence of passing-on was allowed.[428] The Commission did not however see the risk of multiple liability as particularly alarming in practice: **7.228**

424 Hovenkamp (n 47) 677. Italics in original. See also *Kansas & Missouri v UtiliCorp United* 497 US 199 (1990) 218.

425 Jones (n 18) 196.

426 SEC(2008) 404 (n 60) para. 212.

427 COM(2008) 165 final (n 60) 7–8.

428 SEC(2008) 404 (n 60) paras 210–212.

7.229 Indeed, for the defendant to face multiple liability, three conditions are to be fulfilled. First, he is sued for compensation of the same (part of the) overcharge by both direct and other purchasers, while only one has suffered the harm due to that given overcharge; second, the defendant cannot successfully invoke the passing-on defence; and third, the court acting in a joint, parallel or subsequent action does not offset the damages already awarded/paid to another claimant.[429]

7.230 According to the Commission it was relatively unlikely that all three conditions would be fulfilled. The Commission was therefore, at this point, more concerned with the risk of absence of liability for Alpha.[430] Nevertheless the interest of avoiding multiple liability for Alpha found its way into Directive 2014/104/EU.[431]

7.231 Multiple liability was discussed further in sub-sections 7.C.II.a and 7.C.II.b. It may be recalled that it was questioned in US antitrust discourse whether the fear of multiple liability was at all warranted, and that reasons to avoid multiple liability are less strong in the EU than in the US. Jones has thus suggested that it would be open for the EU system of single damages to prohibit Alpha from using the defence of passing-on as a shield but to allow Gamma claimants to prove passing-on as a sword nevertheless. This would increase the risk of multiple liability for Alpha, but Jones submitted that multiple liability should be of less concern in a single damages system and that 'the rare or occasional occurrence of multiple liability is preferable to ... consistent under-deterrence'.[432] It has very similarly been suggested by Bulst that Alpha should be prohibited from using the defence of passing-on in actions brought by Beta but that Alpha should be allowed to use it in actions brought by Gamma.[433] Such rules would admittedly boost the deterrent effect of private enforcement of EU competition law. The EU legislature has nevertheless chosen to remain faithful to the paradigm of reparation in private enforcement of competition law, saving deterrence to be served by public enforcement actions mainly.

4. *The complexity of proceedings*

7.232 The complexity of proceedings caused by the need to trace harm down the supply chain is one of the main arguments against allowing the defence of passing-on in US federal antitrust law. The US Supreme Court feared in *Hanover Shoe* that:

---

429 Ibid., para. 218.

430 Ibid., para. 218.

431 Directive 2014/104/EU (n 5) Arts 3(3), 12(1)–(2), 15(1).

432 Jones (n 18) 196–8, quote from 198. On deterrence see further Section 9.E.II.

433 Bulst (n 225) 81.

> The applicability of the passing-on defense would require a convincing showing of … virtually unascertainable figures, [which] would normally prove insurmountable. … [This] would often require additional long and complicated proceedings involving massive evidence and complicated theories.[434] 7.233

In *Illinois Brick* the US Supreme Court confirmed that it would not tolerate for proceedings to turn: 7.234

> into massive efforts to apportion the recovery among all potential plaintiffs … from direct purchasers to middlemen to ultimate consumers. However appealing this attempt … might seem in theory, it would add whole new dimensions of complexity to [damages actions] and seriously undermine their effectiveness.[435]

For this reason and others, the Supreme Court was 'unwilling to carry the principle of compensation to its logical extreme'.[436] 7.235

It interestingly seems from the *travaux préparatoires* leading up to Directive 2014/104/EU that the Commission was inclined to agree with the US Supreme Court in 2005, but had a change of heart somewhere between there and the 2008 White Paper. The Commission noticed in the 2005 Green Paper that allowing the defence of passing-on 'substantially increases the complexity of damages claims as the exact distribution of damages along the supply chain could be exceedingly difficult to prove'.[437] In the accompanying Staff Working Paper it was elaborated that the existence and extent of passing-on would need to be assessed at every level of the supply chain and would risk causing conflicts among the various claimants and/or potential claimants.[438] The Commission argued that it 'does not appear possible to construct a model which accurately identifies, at reasonable cost, the harm suffered by players at different levels of the supply chain'. Although the Commission recognized that the European Court of Justice had allowed the defence of passing-on for 7.236

434 *Hanover Shoe* (n 139) 493. It has been submitted by Milutinovic (n 61) 180–81, citing Earl E Pollock, 'Automatic Treble Damages and the Passing-on Defense: The *Hanover Shoe* Decision' (1968) 13 *Antitrust Bulletin* 1183, 1208–9, that the US Supreme Court contradicts itself in this context, as it asserts both that it will be insurmountable to prove passing-on and that defendants will be inclined to do so. To this author, these do not seem to be logically incompatible statements, as the concern of the US Supreme Court may have been ineffective litigation management rather than cumbersome burdens of proof for litigants.

435 *Illinois Brick* (n 136) 737.

436 Ibid., 746.

437 COM(2005) 672 final (n 35) 8. Cf. Bernard Rudden and William Bishop, 'Gritz and Quellmehl: Pass It On' (1981) 6 *European Law Review* 243, 253–6, discussed from para. 3.106. Cf. also Peter Oliver, 'Enforcing Community Rights in the English Courts' (1987) 50 *Modern Law Review* 881, 889–90; *Comateb* (n 421) Opinion of AG Tesauro para. 20; and Andrea Biondi and Lindsay Johnson, 'The Right to Recovery of Charges levied in Breach of Community Law: No Small Matter' (1998) 4 *European Public Law* 313, 317, discussed from para. 5.155.

438 SEC(2005) 1732 (n 58) para. 159, citing Clark, Hughes and Wirth (n 410) 30.

the purposes of actions for damages under Article 340(2) and actions for the repayment of charges levied in breach of EU law, it submitted that wider effects of anticompetitive behaviour could make the apportionment of awards in competition law cases more complex than it was in those other contexts.[439]

7.237 By contrast complexity concerns were almost completely absent in the 2008 White Paper and accompanying Staff Working Paper.[440] Instead the 'compensatory principle' in the case law of the Court of Justice was stressed in the White Paper, suggesting against that background that the defence of passing-on should be allowed against a claim for competition damages[441] even though it therefore became necessary to coordinate actions from different levels of the supply chain.[442]

7.238 In order to overcome the complexities of multiple and parallel proceedings Directive 2014/104/EU includes a number of legal mechanisms such as presumptions, approximations and rules on the disclosure of evidence. Article 15 in particular is devoted to the endeavour to join or otherwise coordinate actions relating to the same infringement. It was argued in sub-section 7.E.II.b that Chapter IV of the Directive, including Articles 12–16, form a package intended to facilitate the reparation of harm at all levels of the supply chain. Ideally this could be accomplished without causing multiple liability or absence of liability for Alpha. It was also briefly described how the rules of Chapter IV interrelate to, e.g., Chapter II on the disclosure of evidence and Article 9 on the effect of decisions of national competition authorities and review courts. These rules mainly aim at satisfying the interest of reparation but it has been maintained by the Commission that effective compensation will contribute also to deterrence by providing 'an incentive for better compliance with the EU competition rules'.[443] It has already been noted that this endeavour at contributing to deterrence comes across in Articles 12(1) and 15(1) where it is provided that absence of liability for infringers must be avoided. All in all, Directive 2014/104/EU sets out to attain the ideal or at least to ensure that the national courts endeavour to come as close as possible to the ideal. At the end of the day it may well be that the powers of national courts to approximate harm and passing-on, under Articles 17(1) and 12(5) of the Directive, will more often than not be put to use.

---

439 SEC(2005) 1732 (n 58) paras 161, 165–167, 174.

440 To the best of this author's efforts, the only references to complexity and difficulty in the White Paper and accompanying documents are found in SEC(2008) 404 (n 60) paras 27 and 217, both concerning Gamma claimants. There are also a number of references to the general complexity of competition law litigation.

441 COM(2008) 165 final (n 60) 7–8.

442 A discussion on such coordination are found in SEC(2008) 404 (n 60) paras 221–225.

443 COM(2013) 404 final (n 65) 4.

Some commentators had wished for stronger emphasis on the interest of deterrence in the detailed rules. Kloub, for instance, has argued that efficiency should be 'of serious concern' in designing private enforcement of competition law, and that it should be endeavoured to 'satisfy the requirements of both corrective justice and efficiency'.[444] To that end Kloub suggested for the Commission or national competition authorities to intervene with regard to the amount of damages payable.[445] A possibility for national competition authorities to contribute, which is reminiscent of (but weaker than) the second suggestion submitted by Kloub, is indeed included in Directive 2014/104/EU.[446] Kloub further suggested a two-step class-action solution whereby a total amount of damages is first awarded to all claimants, and then distributed among the claimants in a second proceeding.[447] Such a model has been suggested by others too, e.g., by the US Antitrust Modernization Commission which made a very similar recommendation to the US Congress in 2007.[448] In Germany Beta has similarly been able to bring an action against Alpha for the total amount of the overcharge paid but is thereafter liable to distribute the award to Gamma claimants to the extent that the overcharge was passed on to them.[449] One of the merits of such a solution would be to postpone conflicts of interests within the class of claimants until the second stage of proceedings. Nonetheless the two-step class action solution has been endorsed by neither the US Congress nor the EU legislature. **7.239**

The optimal solution would plausibly be a three-stage model under which the total overcharge was estimated first. Thereafter the overcharge would be traced among the claimants in a second stage. Finally harm in the form of reduced sales at each level could be estimated. Alpha would consequently be held liable to pay damages to the amount of the total overcharge plus total harm in the form of reduced sales, and interest. Such an ideal solution would require a massive effort of coordination however, and most probably would also require opt-out collective redress mechanisms that are not envisaged at present.[450] **7.240**

---

444 Kloub (n 241) 98. It seems from COM(2013) 404 final (n 65) 2–5 that the Commission would agree in principle.

445 Kloub (n 241) 97. This suggestion has been criticized by Komninos (n 244) 154–7, albeit not mentioning Kloub.

446 Directive 2014/104/EU (n 5) Art. 17(3).

447 Kloub (n 241) 97.

448 AMC Report and Recommendations (n 158) 277. Another similar suggestion was made by van Gerven (n 224) 34–5.

449 Anne Howard and Anneliese Blackwood, 'Litigating Infringements in the National Courts' in Vivien Rose and David Bailey (eds) *Bellamy & Child: European Union Law of Competition* (7th edn, Oxford University Press 2013) 1257.

450 Cf. Commission Recommendation 2013/396/EU (n 68) 21 and the discussion in paras 7.205–7.206.

5. *The risk of absence of liability*

7.241 It has been pointed out by Wahl that one of the significant traits of infringements of competition law is that they do not only cause harm for Beta and Gamma (and/or Alpha's competitors), but also give rise to a gain for Alpha. Therefore Wahl argued that one of the aims of competition damages should be the disgorgement of Alpha.[451] Directive 2014/104/EU does not explicitly aim at disgorgement but does provide in Articles 12(1) and 15(1) that its rules should be implemented and applied in a manner that seeks to avoid absence of liability for Alpha. The Commission further intended, as discussed in sub-section 7.E.II.b, to include a provision prohibiting the defence of passing-on in situations where national law made it impossible for Gamma claimants of the next level of the supply chain to bring a successful action.[452] The underlying reason was the avoidance of absence of liability for Alpha. The provision was not included, but it seems intended that the same interest should now be pursued by Article 15(1).

7.242 Where the defence of passing-on is allowed the harm caused may furthermore be pulverized to the extent that not all potential claimants will have an incentive to bring an action for damages. In the extreme there may be little incentive for any one potential claimant to bring an action. The problem was memorably captured by Beard and Jones:

7.243

> In a case like [Courage], for example, the public-tenants may have passed on some of their loss down the chain to their customers. It seems unlikely, however, that even the most hardened drinkers would contemplate their losses being sufficient to make proceedings against the brewers worthwhile.[453]

7.244 In *Hanover Shoe* one of the reasons why the US Supreme Court rejected the defence of passing-on was that harm was pulverized as it was passed on down the supply chain. Consequently the harm absorbed at each level, from Beta to the final consumers, might be too small for each to have an incentive to bring an action for damages. If too few brought an action 'those who violate the antitrust laws by price fixing or monopolizing would retain the fruits of their illegality because no one was available who would bring suit against them'. It would follow also that the deterrent effect of private enforcement of US antitrust law would suffer.[454]

---

451 Wahl (n 87) 308–9.

452 See COM(2013) 404 final (n 65) 17–18 and Art. 12(2).

453 Beard and Jones (n 185) 255. A summary of the facts in *Courage* (n 4) is available in para. 7.016.

454 *Hanover Shoe* (n 139) 494.

This point has been heard by the European Commission. In the Staff Working Paper accompanying its 2005 Green Paper, the Commission discussed this in the context of the proper balancing of the interests of reparation and deterrence. At that time the Commission was inclined to argue that 'the main objective must be the efficient and effective enforcement of the antitrust rules', and that in the 'trade-off between justice (in the sense of full recovery for all those who have suffered a loss from an illegal practice) and efficiency ... it might be necessary to determine what rights must be facilitated to ensure an effective enforcement system rather than insisting on the absolute protection of all private rights'.[455] **7.245**

In the subsequent Staff Working Paper accompanying the 2008 White Paper the Commission similarly argued that the absence of liability 'would not only be contrary to the objective of effective and full compensation of the harm caused by a competition law infringement, but it can also be qualified as an unjust enrichment of the defendant'.[456] Nevertheless, as seen above, the Commission would not at this point give priority to deterrence over reparation. The reluctance to boost deterrence at the risk of incidental windfalls prevailed and guided the drafting of Directive 2014/104/EU thereafter. **7.246**

6. *The volume effects problem*

A specific aspect of the passing-on problem is the decrease in sales that may follow from an increase in prices where an overcharge is passed on. In *Hanover Shoe* the US Supreme Court stressed that such sales volume effects of passing-on were just as difficult to determine as the extent of passing-on itself.[457] In Directive 2014/104/EU harm in the form of volume effects (*lucrum cessans*) is distinguished from harm in the form of an overcharge (*damnum emergens*).[458] It is further stated in recital 40 that the right to compensation for harm in the form of loss of profits (e.g., volume effects) should remain unaffected by any passing-on of other harm. However, no further details on how to compensate harm suffered through decreased sales are offered, save for the general provision in Article 3(2) that such harm is to **7.247**

455 SEC(2005) 1732 (n 58) paras 179–180.

456 SEC(2008) 404 (n 60) para. 217. In this context, the notion of unjust enrichment is more easily acceptable in the legal sense than in the discussion of windfall gains by claimants, as there is no valid legal basis for the enrichment of Alpha through an infringement while there is a valid legal basis of the enrichment of a claimant who has been awarded damages. From the policy perspective, Wahl (n 87) 309 has stressed that 'unjust enrichment' of claimants should be preferred over unjust enrichment of Alpha.

457 *Hanover Shoe* (n 139) 493.

458 Directive 2014/104/EU (n 5) Arts 3(2) and 12(3) read with recs 12 and 39–40. See also COM(2013) 404 final (n 65) 17; and SWD(2013) 205 (n 67) para. 128.

be compensated (with interest) and the provision in Article 12(3) that the rules on passing-on are 'without prejudice' to the right to such compensation.[459]

7.248 For further guidance, it is necessary to consult the soft-law Practical Guide offered by the Commission. As explained in the Practical Guide:

7.249 A rise in prices for a particular product leads to less demand. The degrees to which both prices rise and quantities decrease following an infringement depend on the same cost and demand parameters, and are determined jointly. Hence, the overcharge and volume effects are intrinsically linked.[460]

7.250 It is consequently recommended, in principle, that the same methods are used for the quantification of harm in the form of reduced sales as for the quantification of an overcharge, i.e., econometric methods or comparator-based methods. With regard to harm in the form of reduced sales it particularly recommends comparator-based methods.[461] It can be added that claimants will be able to use the opportunities to obtain evidence for these purposes that are provided for in Chapter II of Directive 2014/104/EU.

7. *Conclusions from the analysis*

7.251 The aim of Directive 2014/104/EU is that 'any natural or legal person who has suffered harm caused by an infringement of competition law is able to claim and to obtain full compensation for that harm',[462] placing them 'in the position in which that person would have been had the infringement of competition law not been committed'[463] while nevertheless ensuring 'that compensation of harm exceeding that caused by the infringement of competition law to the claimant, as well as the absence of liability of the infringer, are avoided'.[464] The Directive has thus focused on the reparation of harm. The disgorgement of Alpha is a lesser priority – but it is still a priority that Alpha be held liable in damages for harm caused by its infringement of competition law.[465]

7.252 As the pulverization of harm makes it less likely that all potential claimants will bring an action, it is submitted that this choice of approach is a missed

459 Of course, there other forms of loss of profit than harm in the form of reduced sales. For a framework on the quantification of lost profits where an undertaking is harmed through anti-competitive behaviour by a competing undertaking see Clark, Hughes and Wirth (n 410) 35–41.

460 SWD(2013) 205 (n 67) para. 175.

461 Ibid., paras 177–178.

462 Directive 2014/104/EU (n 5) Art. 2(1).

463 Ibid., Art. 2(2).

464 Ibid., Art. 12(1).

465 See e.g., Directive 2014/104/EU (n 5) Art. 15(1).

opportunity to enhance the deterrent effect of private enforcement of EU competition law. The opt-in model chosen for collective redress in Recommendation 2013/396/EU does not help to raise the incentive to litigate.[466] It must moreover be kept in mind that Gamma claimants may face difficulties with regard to proving a causal link between the infringement and the harm incurred by them.[467] The result of this is a strong likelihood that less than all claimants will bring a successful action. As a result Alpha will retain some of the fruits of its infringement, unless successfully disgorged through public enforcement proceedings.

It has been argued, in favour of the approach chosen by the EU legislature, that to prohibit the defence of passing-on would create windfall awards for claimants and that such windfalls might be described as an unjust enrichment. If the defence of passing-on were to be prohibited without denying access to court for Gamma claimants, Alpha would also risk paying multiple damages awards. It has been counterargued above that overcompensation to claimants is preferable to unjust enrichment of Alpha and that the risk of multiple liability is exaggerated. **7.253**

The pursuit of compliance with EU competition law and the pursuit of justice do both require that Alpha be disgorged of any gains arising from its infringement of competition law and that Beta as well as Gamma are compensated for harm incurred. It is not yet clear whether the approach chosen with regard to the defence of passing-on is suitable for the attainment of those aims. On the one hand it may be possible for public enforcement to achieve disgorgement of Alpha to the extent that this is not attained through private enforcement. On the other hand it may be that even the combined force of both is unable sufficiently to deter from infringements of EU competition law.[468] It would be desirable for the Commission to include an assessment of this in its review report due on 27 December 2020.[469] If the deterrent effect of the combined public and private enforcement systems should prove insufficient, it is submitted that the risk of multiple liability for Alpha and the risk of damages awards in excess of harm absorbed should not discourage the EU legislature from discarding the defence of passing-on for the purposes of EU competition damages while nevertheless retaining the opportunity for Gamma to bring an independent action for compensation for harm passed on. **7.254**

466 Commission Recommendation 2013/396/EU (n 68) 21.
467 See further Section 7.D.II.
468 Jones (n 131) 37–8 is concerned that the new harmonized regime may not be enough to achieve this aim.
469 Directive 2014/104/EU (n 5) Art. 20.

F. CONCLUSIONS AND SUGGESTIONS

7.255 The European Commission's endeavours to bring about a new harmonized regime for the private enforcement of EU competition law has resulted in Directive 2014/104/EU, which is to be transposed into the national laws of the Member States by 27 December 2016,[470] and which is also accompanied by a number of soft law instruments.[471] For the purposes of this inquiry the crucial property of the new regime is its emphasis on compensatory justice for anyone harmed by an infringement of competition law.

7.256 Article 12(1) of Directive 2014/104/EU instructs the Member States to 'ensure that, in accordance with the rules laid down in this Chapter, compensation of harm can be claimed by anyone who suffered it, irrespective of whether they are direct or indirect purchasers from an infringer'. It follows that Gamma claimants cannot be barred from bringing an action for damages against Alpha by reason of the lack of a direct nexus between the two. It has nevertheless been pointed out that a Directive cannot under EU law by itself give rise to legal obligations for private individuals. In the event of insufficient transposition of Directive 2014/104/EU by a Member State the enforceability of Gamma's right to reparation under the Directive may consequently remain limited, unless it is settled by the Court of Justice that this right for Gamma also follows from Articles 101 and/or 102 TFEU.

7.257 Concepts of causation are not harmonized through Directive 2014/104/EU. Nor is there as yet any case law on competition damages that touches on how to approach causation in the context of passing-on. It is clear that the dual test of the EU law principles of equivalence and effectiveness will apply to national causation standards but the details of such scrutiny are difficult to predict, especially with regard to actions brought by a Gamma claimant. National courts adjudicating such actions should arguably make a reference to the European Court of Justice, giving the Court the opportunity to decide on whether and to what extent to engage in the substantive content of the applicable causation test.

7.258 The rules on passing-on in Directive 2014/104/EU are designed to offer reparation for harm rather than to contribute to deterrence from infringements. It has been submitted that this is a missed opportunity and that the

470 Ibid., Art. 21.

471 See para. 7.041 for an overview of these instruments.

Commission should review the approach chosen in its report due on 27 December 2020.[472] If the deterrent effect of the combined public and private enforcement systems should prove insufficient, it is submitted that the risk of multiple liability for Alpha and the risk of damages awards in excess of harm absorbed should not discourage the EU legislature from discarding the defence of passing-on for the purposes of EU competition damages while nevertheless retaining the opportunity for Gamma to bring an independent action for compensation for harm passed on.

Irrespective of the pros and cons of the approach chosen with regard to the defence of passing-on it is finally to be noticed that the entire problem can be circumvented if all claimants in a certain supply chain subrogate their claims to a joint claimant body. The deterrent effect of private enforcement is consequently not necessarily in the hands of the EU legislature only, but may be boosted by independent choices to be made by potential litigants. **7.259**

472 Directive 2014/104/EU (n 5) Art. 20.

8

PASSING-ON IN OTHER HORIZONTAL ACTIONS?

A. CHAPTER OUTLINE

8.001 In the previous chapter liability in damages for private individuals for a breach of EU competition law was examined.[1] It has been debated whether there is any possibility that a breach of other EU law provisions could lead to liability in damages or restitution for private individuals, i.e., liability outside the confines of competition damages.[2] The views of scholars differ.[3]

1 The term 'private individual' will be used throughout this text (with the exception of quotes using different terminology). It is intended to serve as shorthand for any kind of natural or legal person capable of carrying rights and/or obligations pursuant to EU law, who is not an emanation of the Member State within the meaning of EU law. The criteria used for identifying legal bodies as emanations of the Member State within the meaning of EU law were laid down by the European Court of Justice in case C-188/89 *A Foster and others v British Gas plc* [1990] ECR I-3313 para. 20.

2 There are of course instances where liability in damages for private individuals is prescribed in an EU Directive, e.g., Directive 2004/48/EC of the European Parliament and of the Council of 29 April 2004 on the enforcement of intellectual property rights [2004] OJ L157/45 Art. 13. Such provisions in Directives cannot however as such give rise to liability in damages for private individuals but must first be transposed into national law; cf. para. 7.119.

3 The discussion has generally focused on liability in damages. Proponents include Andrea Biondi and Martin Farley, *The Right to Damages in European Law* (Kluwer European Law Collection, Kluwer Law International 2009) 75–6; Michael Dougan, *National Remedies before the Court of Justice: Issues of Harmonisation and Differentiation* (Modern Studies in European Law, Hart Publishing 2004) 385–6; Sara Drake, 'Scope of Courage and the Principle of 'Individual Liability' for Damages: Further Development of the Principle of Effective Judicial Protection by the Court of Justice' (2006) 31 *European Law Review* 841, 858–61; Norbert Reich, *General Principles of EU Civil Law* (Intersentia 2014) 117–20; and Takis Tridimas, *The General*

To illustrate circumstances where such damages or restitution might be claimed, consider *Laval*.[4] Collective action was instigated against a Latvian company which had been contracted for construction work in Sweden. Under the circumstances, which will not be explained in detail here, the European Court of Justice held that the collective action taken was contrary to Article (now) 56 TFEU. In the thereafter re-opened national proceedings the Latvian company claimed damages for harm incurred by reason of the collective action. The Swedish Labour Court, adjudicating at last instance, refrained from making a second reference on the specific issue of horizontal liability in damages for a breach of EU law and held instead – as the first court in Europe to do so – that the Latvian company had a right to damages from the trade unions at issue for the harm incurred by reason of the latter's breach of other EU law than competition law.[5] Similar damages claims can be envisaged for a breach of, e.g., Articles 45 and 49 TFEU by private individuals. In restitution one can imagine the payment of fees contrary to the same Articles that are charged by a private entity. Is the repayment of such charges a consequence of, and an adjunct to, the rights conferred on individuals by the EU law provisions prohibiting such charges if the claim must be brought against another private individual rather than against a Member State?[6] **8.002**

For the purposes of this discussion damages and restitution must be distinguished, for several reasons. The legal bases for the two courses of action are different: in damages liability will arise from a tort, but in restitution the absence of a legal basis for a transaction may be sufficient to give rise to liability. Moreover the particular conditions for the exercise of the two actions are different. The systematic differences between damages and restitution also have a decisive impact on the approach to be chosen for the purposes of the passing-on problem. The discussion in this chapter of the three legal issues triggered by the passing-on problem (access to court, substantive proximity and the estimation of damages[7]) must therefore be carried out separately for damages and restitution. Consequently EU law damages actions against private individuals (outside competition damages) are discussed in Section **8.003**

Principles of EU Law (2nd edn, Oxford EC Law Library, Oxford University Press 2006) 544. Sceptics include Angela Ward, *Judicial Review and the Rights of Private Parties in EU Law* (2nd edn, Oxford University Press 2007) 249–52.

4 Case C-341/05 *Laval un Partneri Ltd v Svenska Byggnadsarbetareförbundet, Svenska Byggnadsarbetareförbundets avdelning 1, Byggettan and Svenska Elektrikerförbundet* [2007] ECR I-11767.

5 AD 2009 nr 89 (Swedish Labour Court). For a positive comment to the judgment of the Labour Court see Ulf Bernitz and Norbert Reich, 'Case No. A 268/04, The Labour Court, Sweden (Arbetsdomstolen) Judgment No. 89/09 of 2 December 2009, Laval un Partneri Ltd. v. Svenska Bygggnadsarbetareförbundet et al.' (2011) 48 *Common Market Law Review* 603. For a critical comment see Jonas Malmberg, 'Trade Union Liability for 'EU-Unlawful' Collective Action' (2012) 3 *European Labour Law Journal* 5.

6 Cf. Section 5.B on the repayment of charges levied by Member States.

7 See Section 1.A.III.

8.B, and EU law restitutionary actions against private individuals are discussed in Section 8.C. Both sections will begin with an analysis of whether and when the action might be available and thereafter continue to contemplate the three legal issues triggered by the passing-on problem in turn. Conclusions and suggestions for both courses of action are submitted together in the final Section 8.D.

B. PASSING-ON IN OTHER DAMAGES FROM A PRIVATE INDIVIDUAL?

I. Is other horizontal damages liability possible?

8.004 In this section it will be attempted to answer whether and under what conditions it could and, perhaps, should be possible to hold private individuals liable in damages for a breach of EU law (other than a breach of competition law). It is beyond the scope of this book to carry out a detailed discussion of that issue,[8] but a brief discussion is warranted.

8.005 In Chapter 2 the many guises of effective judicial protection were discussed, drawing on the classic model of van Gerven according to which one must first identify the existence of a right or interest protected by EU law in order to trigger the effective judicial protection 'package' of EU law.[9] For an analysis of liability for private individuals it becomes crucial to determine who holds the legal obligation corresponding to the right or interest conferred on an individual by EU law. The detailed remedies, rules and conditions applicable, and with them the detailed contents of the follow-on EU law requirements, vary quite considerably depending on whether an action is enforceable against the EU, a Member State, or other private individuals. As has been pointed out in Chapters 3 and 4 the EU has full jurisdiction over what remedies and what rules apply to actions brought against the EU. By contrast actions against Member States and against private individuals fall under the jurisdiction of the competent national courts of the Member States. Therefore the remedies and rules applicable to actions brought against Member States and against private individuals will (in the absence of EU law harmonization) be those of national law, albeit subject to the EU law requirements that have been assessed in Chapter 2. Passing-on issues appear in the context of the overall conditions for

8 Central contributions were cited in fn 3. An extended discussion by this author is available in Magnus Strand, *The Passing-On Problem in EU Law Damages and Restitution* (Uppsala University (diss) 2015) Ch. 10.

9 See Walter van Gerven, 'Of Rights, Remedies and Procedures' (2000) 37 *Common Market Law Review* 501, 502–4 (and see further Section 2.A with more references).

the exercise of the damages remedy and will consequently be addressed below. This section is concerned with the possibility of horizontal damages liability as such.

It was seen in paragraph 3.020 that the EU itself has been held liable for civil **8.006** wrongs. The main rule is however that the EU can be liable in damages pursuant to Article 340(2) TFEU only for an infringement of a rule of law intended to confer rights on individuals.[10] The same is true for liability in damages for Member States.[11] As it does not make constitutional sense for horizontal liability to be broader than that of the EU and of the Member States, it is concluded that horizontal liability can only arise in the event of an infringement, by a private individual, of a rule of EU law intended to confer rights on individuals.

The existence of a right of course also corresponds to the first in the three-tier **8.007** model of EU law enforcement examined in Chapter 2. If the EU law rule at issue does not confer any right on any particular identifiable person, the requirements embodied in the principle of effective judicial protection will not be triggered by an infringement of that rule. It was noticed in paragraphs 3.021 and 6.019 that the 'right' criterion also implies that the EU law rule at issue must have a protective purpose (i.e., be a *Schutzgesetz*)[12] in order for an infringement to give rise to liability in damages. This should apply to horizontal damages too.

Before proceeding to discuss the next tier of the van Gerven model, i.e., the **8.008** existence of remedies, we should return to the allocation of legal obligations by EU law. The mirror image of the conferred right is a conferred obligation. It was hinted above that horizontal liability in damages for a breach of EU law cannot be possible unless the EU law rule infringed confers an obligation on private individuals: there can be no legal consequences for a person acting contrary to a norm unless the norm is binding on that person. It is consequently crucial to this section to examine under what circumstances EU law may, of itself, confer legal obligations on private individuals.

10 See paras 3.015–3.018.

11 See paras 6.018–6.019.

12 This concept is used here without prejudice to the precise meaning given to that concept in German law. See further Sacha Prechal, *Directives in EC Law* (2nd edn, Oxford EC Law Library, Oxford University Press 2005) 284–5 and cf. paras 3.012 and 3.018. For a detailed analysis of the types of rules capable of being identified as a 'right' in the Member State liability context see Pekka Aalto, *Public Liability in EU Law:* Brasserie, Bergaderm *and Beyond* (Hart Publishing 2011) 162–75.

8.009 It has been settled since *BRT* that Articles (now) 101 and 102 TFEU 'produce direct effects in relations between individuals',[13] i.e., have horizontal direct effect. For EU law to confer legal obligations on private individuals, the legal rule at issue must be capable, of itself, to have horizontal direct effect.[14] The search for EU law provisions that meet the established criteria for having direct effect and that are capable of producing such effects in horizontal legal relationships can, pursuant to settled case law,[15] be limited to primary law,[16] Regulations,[17] and Decisions addressed to the private individual at issue.[18]

8.010 It has been debated, at least with regard to primary law provisions, whether horizontal direct effect is enough or whether the EU law provisions at issue must satisfy further criteria in order to be binding for private individuals. In this regard commentators have discussed the significance of the Court's insistence in *Courage* that Article (now) 101 TFEU constituted 'a fundamental provision which is essential for the accomplishment of the tasks entrusted to the Community and, in particular, for the functioning of the internal market'.[19] The *dictum* is inconclusive, however. It is moreover submitted that such a criterion would be difficult to manage, since it is rather unclear against what standard the 'fundamentality' of EU law provisions should be measured. There are no other hints in *Courage* or subsequent case law that point out other additional criteria that could plausibly apply.

---

13 Case 127/73 *Belgische Radio en Televisie and société belge des auteurs, compositeurs et éditeurs v SV SABAM and NV Fonior* [1974] ECR 51 para. 16.

14 See e.g. Drake (n 3) 858; and Katri Havu, 'Horizontal Liability for Damages in EU Law – the Changing Relationship of EU and National Law' (2012) 18 *European Law Journal* 407, 412.

15 With regard to the lack of horizontal direct effect but prevalence of other effects of Directives suffice it here to cite the recent case C-441/14 *Dansk Industri (DI), acting on behalf of Ajos A/S v Estate of Karsten Eigil Rasmussen* EU:C:2016:278 which explains the various effects and the lack of horizontal direct effect of Directives, citing a multitude of relevant case law.

16 Horizontal direct effect of primary law rules (other than Arts 101 and 102 TFEU) has been acknowledged with regard to the principle of non-discrimination on grounds of sex in Art. 157 TFEU (case 43/75 *Gabrielle Defrenne v Société anonyme belge de navigation aérienne Sabena (Defrenne II)* [1976] ECR 455 paras 39–40). Horizontal direct effect has also been acknowledged in semi-vertical legal relationships where the obligated party has enjoyed some normative autonomy under national law. See further para. 8.011.

17 Case C-253/00 *Antonio Muñoz y Cia SA and Superior Fruiticola SA v Frumar Ltd and Redbridge Produce Marketing Ltd* [2002] ECR I-7289 paras 27–30. The capacity of Regulations to include provisions with horizontal direct effect should be constitutionally unsurprising, as Regulations are designed specifically to be binding and directly applicable in all Member States (as if they were national legislative instruments); see Art. 288(2) TFEU.

18 There is no case law on the horizontal direct effect of provisions in a Decision conferring legal obligations on private individuals, but it is commonly accepted that a Decision addressed to one or more private parties will be binding on them and that it should be possible to invoke a breach of such a Decision against them within the meaning of horizontal direct effect. See e.g. Paul Craig and Gráinne de Búrca, *EU Law: Text, Cases, and Materials* (6th edn, Oxford University Press 2015) 200.

19 Case C-453/99 *Courage Ltd v Bernard Crehan and Bernard Crehan v Courage Ltd and Others* [2001] ECR I-6297 para. 20. Drake (n 3) 858–9 and Dougan (n 3) 385–6 do seem to include the fundamental character of the provision as a criterion for liability in damages for private individuals. It is also mentioned by Havu (n 14) 413–14.

Certain other factors might also have an impact on the capacity of primary law **8.011** to be binding on private individuals. Such factors could be the legal certainty of private individuals and the regulatory power of the private individual on the market.[20] The case law remains inconclusive, but the allocation of regulatory and/or economic power on the relevant market between the litigating parties does seem relevant. In 'purely' horizontal situations, i.e., where there is no significant difference in the allocation of power between the parties, it seems to have been established that Articles 101 and 102 TFEU are binding on private individuals (undertakings) notwithstanding their respective power on the relevant market.[21] It is also established through *Muñoz* that provisions in EU Regulations that are capable of having horizontal direct effect are binding on private individuals addressed by the Regulation at issue.[22] In case law on the horizontal direct effect of TFEU Articles other than 101 and 102 however, the tendency is that one of the parties has enjoyed a significant normative autonomy. In *Walrave*, *Donà* and *Bosman* the private individuals who were legally bound by Articles (now) 18, 45 and 56 TFEU were sports federations who enjoyed normative autonomy to regulate sports activities and affiliations for all athletes and organizations connected to the federation.[23] In *Defrenne II*, *Angonese* and *Viking Line* the Court of Justice reviewed the compatibility of collective agreements with Articles (now) 18, 45 and 157 TFEU.[24] In *Wouters*, the Court reviewed the internal rules of the Bar of the Netherlands.[25] The Court of Justice has nonetheless explicitly rejected the notion that the horizontal direct effect of Article (now) 49 TFEU would apply 'only to quasi-public organisations or to associations exercising a regulatory task and

20 On the latter issue see n 16 on the semi-vertical character of the legal relationship in much of the case law on horizontal direct effect of TFEU Articles. Pursuant to case C-199/11 *Europese Gemeenschap v Otis NV and Others* EU:C:2012:684 the relative market strength of the infringer does not seem relevant under Art. 101 TFEU.

21 See e.g., *BRT* (n 13) and *Otis* (n 20). On the definition of the concept of an 'undertaking' in competition law see any textbook; e.g., Alison Jones and Brenda Sufrin, *EU Competition Law: Text, Cases and Materials* (5th edn, Oxford University Press 2014) 127–47.

22 *Muñoz* (n 17) paras 27–30.

23 Case 36/74 *BNO Walrave and LJN Koch v Association Union cycliste internationale, Koninklijke Nederlandsche Wielren Unie and Federación Española Ciclismo* [1974] ECR 1405; case 13/76 *Gaetano Donà v Mario Mantero* [1976] ECR 1333; and case C-415/93 *Union royale belge des sociétés de football association ASBL v Jean-Marc Bosman, Royal club liégeois SA v Jean-Marc Bosman and others and Union des associations européennes de football (UEFA) v Jean-Marc Bosman* [1995] ECR I-4921.

24 *Defrenne II* (n 16); case C-281/98 *Roman Angonese v Cassa di Risparmio di Bolzano SpA* [2000] ECR I-4139; and case C-438/05 *International Transport Workers' Federation and Finnish Seamen's Union v Viking Line ABP and OÜ Viking Line Eesti* [2007] ECR I-10779. With regard to *Viking Line*, it is noticeable that although no collective agreement was in force at the relevant time, the Court held that collective action was inextricably linked to the collective agreement the conclusion of which the action seeks to accomplish; *Viking Line* para. 36.

25 Case C-309/99 *J C J Wouters, J W Savelbergh and Price Waterhouse Belastingadviseurs BV v Algemene Raad van de Nederlandse Orde van Advocaten, intervener: Raad van de Balies van de Europese Gemeenschap* [2002] ECR I-1577.

having quasi-legislative powers'.[26] The case law does not therefore lend itself to any certain conclusion that the TFEU Articles at issue cannot be binding on private individuals in 'purely' horizontal legal relationships. The tendency as such must however serve as a *caveat*: the capacity of TFEU Articles of having horizontal direct effect may not automatically lead to those Articles having legally binding force for every private individual. Such legally binding force must be assessed in the individual case, where necessary with the assistance of the European Court of Justice. Consequently, for an infringement of an EU law rule by a private individual to be able to give rise to liability in damages for the infringer as a matter of EU law, the EU law rule must not only have horizontal direct effect but also be legally binding on the specific infringer at issue.

8.012 In order for an infringement of an EU law rule to be eligible as basis for a horizontal claim for damages it is concluded from the above that the rule at issue must confer a right on the claimant and have a protective purpose with regard to that right. It is further concluded that the EU law rule must have horizontal direct effect and be legally binding on the defendant specifically. It is also to be noted that horizontal damages claims fall under the jurisdiction of the competent national courts of the Member States. From these points of departure it is time to continue to discuss the effective judicial protection of the right at issue.

8.013 The first issue in that regard is whether the claimant can avail her- or himself of any remedy in order to protect the right conferred.[27] EU law largely relies on national remedies for the enforcement of EU law rights. It is accordingly presupposed that in most cases a breach of EU law for which a private individual can be held responsible will be taken care of by use of such national remedies, and the rules and conditions applicable thereto. The Court of Justice has accordingly required, in *Butter-Buying Cruises*, that remedies available to claimants whose claims were based on national law were equally available to claimants whose claims were based on an EU law provision with direct effect.[28] It seems safe to presume that a damages action against private individuals should be available in all Member States.[29] Consequently this national 'horizontal' damages remedy is to be made available to claimants who

26 *Viking Line* (n 24) para. 64.

27 The details of EU law in this regard have been explained in Section 2.B.

28 Case 158/80 *Rewe-Handelsgesellschaft Nord mbH and Rewe-Markt Steffen v Hauptzollamt Kiel (Butter Buying Cruises)* [1981] ECR 1805 para. 44 and Operative part para. 7. See further Section 2.B.III.

29 If, for the sake of argument, a damages remedy was not available under national law, EU law might still require it to be made available if the claimant was unable to protect her or his rights by using any other effective remedy; see case C-583/11 P *Inuit Tapiriit Kanatami and Others v European Parliament and Council of the European Union* EU:C:2013:625 para. 104 and Section 2.B.I.

bring an action for damages for an infringement of an EU law provision that meets the criteria identified above.

Assuming that this tier of effective judicial protection has been satisfied the next issue, in the absence of EU law harmonization, is to assess the precise national rules and conditions that govern the damages action. Suffice it here to repeat that national rules and conditions are subject to scrutiny under the EU law requirements following from Article 47 of the EU Charter and the principles of equivalence and effectiveness.[30] This scrutiny will encompass rules and conditions that are of the essence to the passing-on problem, namely access to court, substantive proximity (in damages i.e. causation), and the estimation of damages. The potential impact of EU law on those issues will be discussed in Section 8.B.II. **8.014**

Before continuing to the passing-on issues however, this discussion of the possibility of horizontal EU law damages (other than competition damages) should be complemented by a few remarks on plausible further EU law conditions that might apply. The debate on horizontal liability has focused on two plausible additional conditions: fault, or in the alternative, that the infringement of the EU law constituted a 'sufficiently serious breach' of EU law. By contrast the existence of a causal link between the infringement of EU law and the alleged harm suffered has attracted little attention, but that is probably because the addition of that criterion to horizontal liability has been considered too plain to be discussed. **8.015**

Beginning with fault, it was observed – not without criticism – in paragraph 7.048 that it seemingly remains within the jurisdiction of the national legal systems to decide whether a fault criterion should apply in competition damages. It has been submitted by Reich that a fault criterion would not be suitable to more general horizontal liability for private individuals in EU law.[31] This author agrees, for the sake of consistency but also because the concept of fault is laden with national preconceptions that will probably result in inconsistent application of such a criterion (or to an overload of references to the Court of Justice). In light of recital 11 of Directive 204/104/EU[32] it will **8.016**

30 These tests were described in detail in Sections 2.C and 2.D.

31 Norbert Reich, 'Horizontal Liability in EC Law: Hybridization of Remedies for Compensation in Case of Breaches of EC Rights' (2007) 44 *Common Market Law Review* 705, 714, implying that it follows from joined cases C-46/93 and C-48/93 *Brasserie du Pêcheur SA v Bundesrepublik Deutschland* and *The Queen v Secretary of State for Transport, ex parte: Factortame Ltd and others* [1996] ECR I-1029 para. 79, that 'reparation cannot depend upon a condition based on any concept of fault'.

32 Directive 2014/104/EU of the European Parliament and of the Council of 26 November 2014 on certain rules governing actions for damages under national law for infringements of the competition law provisions of the Member States and of the European Union [2014] OJ L349/1.

however be difficult to argue that national fault criteria should not apply to horizontal damages based on an infringement of EU law other than competition law. It would be counterargued that a discretionary power of the Member States under Directive 2014/104/EU should be equally motivated in other horizontal damages liability. In other words recital 11 may have a spill-over effect on other horizontal damages claims.

8.017 The 'sufficiently serious breach' condition (as in EU liability under Article 340(2) TFEU and as in Member State liability for a breach of EU law[33]) contrasts against fault insofar as it is – in those public law contexts – an EU law criterion, whereas fault would be a national criterion added to the applicable EU law criteria. The 'sufficiently serious breach' criterion has not, however, been discussed by the Court of Justice in competition damages case law. It has neither been recommended by Advocate Generals[34] nor was it seriously considered for the purposes of Directive 2014/104/EU.[35] Irrespective of its dismissal for the purposes of competition damages it been submitted by Reich that a criterion of 'sufficiently serious breach' should be adopted for the purposes of EU law liability in damages for private individuals. Reich observes in this context that the condition of sufficiently serious breach is not based on fault or negligence but constitutes a certain threshold with regard to the violation of an obligation under EU law.[36] Reich further points out the risk for legal uncertainty in delicate situations. If liability for private individuals to pay damages for a breach of EU law is extended from its present confines, it is not self-evident that such liability should follow automatically from a breach of a provision of EU law with horizontal direct effect – other interests will need to be taken into account. For example, Reich mentions situations where a private individual has relied on applicable national law which is incompatible with a provision of EU law with horizontal direct effect.[37] This occurred in *Laval*, where trade unions relied on Swedish law permitting industrial action in the circumstances of the case, but where the Court of Justice ruled that the

33 See paras 3.015–3.019 and 6.018–6.022, respectively.

34 The only mention is in case C-128/92 *H J Banks & Co Ltd v British Coal Corporation* [1994] ECR I-1209 Opinion of AG van Gerven para. 53, where the Advocate General explicitly argued that there would be no need for the establishment of a 'sufficiently serious breach' since 'the relevant rules of competition impose on undertakings precise, directly effective obligations which are reflected in rights conferred on individuals'.

35 The inclusion of such a criterion (as well as fault) was dismissed in Commission, 'Staff Working Paper accompanying the White Paper on Damages actions for breach of the EC antitrust rules' SEC(2008) 404 paras 172–188 but otherwise rarely touched upon in the *travaux préparatoires*.

36 Reich (n 31) 713–14. Reich finds support for his view in Cees van Dam, *European Tort Law* (2nd edn, Oxford University Press 2013) 559 (1805–1). However, in the cited paragraph, van Dam seems to have included a mention of private individuals by mistake. In the paragraph concerned with liability for private individuals specifically, 47–49 (205–4), van Dam observes that the 'sufficiently serious breach' criterion does not seem to apply to horizontal liability in EU law. See also Bernitz and Reich (n 5).

37 Reich (n 31) 716.

national legislation relied on was contrary to Articles 49 and 50 EC (now Articles 56 and 57 TFEU).[38] The trade union was subsequently held liable to pay damages to the claimant for its breach of Article 49 EC (and Article 3 of Directive 96/71/EC[39]).[40] As suggested by Reich it might be preferable under such circumstances to exempt a private individual from liability to pay damages, and to instruct the claimant to bring the action against the Member State instead.[41] Reich further argues that private individuals should not be liable in damages where EU law 'presents uncertainties which can only be settled by case law' of the Court of Justice.[42] In other words the breach of EU law may in some circumstances be excusable for reasons of legal certainty.

By contrast it has been submitted by Tridimas and van Gerven that the 'sufficiently serious breach' criterion is designed to take into account the margin of discretion enjoyed by EU and Member State institutions, respectively, and should be reserved for that purpose. It would follow that it should not apply to liability for private individuals.[43] It is submitted however that this remark does not as such exclude the possibility of some mechanism to make sure that private individuals are not held liable in damages for excusable infringements of EU law provisions, notwithstanding the direct effect of that provision in the legal relationship at issue. The 'sufficiently serious breach' criterion might furthermore be more easily transferrable to liability in damages for private individuals with some normative power in the legal relationship at issue. **8.018**

It remains to be seen whether the Court of Justice will be called upon to develop specific conditions for horizontal damages liability outside competition damages. If so, it has been submitted that the Court can be expected to reserve horizontal damages to situations where the EU law rule infringed confers a right on the claimant and has a protective purpose with regard to that right. It has further been submitted that the EU law rule must have horizontal direct effect and be legally binding on the defendant specifically. Whether a 'sufficiently serious breach' condition will be added, and whether **8.019**

---

38 *Laval* (n 4) Operative part para. 2.

39 Directive 96/71/EC of the European Parliament and of the Council of 16 December 1996 concerning the posting of workers in the framework of the provision of services [1997] OJ L18/1.

40 AD 2009 nr 89 (n 5).

41 Reich (n 31) 716. Another option, not discussed by Reich, could be to grant private individuals, who have been held liable to pay damages for a breach of EU law even though they have acted in accordance with national law, an action of recourse against the Member State.

42 Reich (n 31) 714. See also Bernitz and Reich (n 5) 618.

43 Tridimas (n 3) 544–5; Walter van Gerven, 'Private Enforcement of EC Competition Rules in the ECJ – Courage v. Crehan and the Way Ahead' in Jürgen Basedow (ed.), *Private Enforcement of EC Competition Law* (Kluwer Law International 2007) 28.

national fault notions will be allowed, is more difficult to foresee. It should also be stressed that the Court might prefer an *ad hoc* approach, establishing specific horizontal liability criteria for the breach of specific rules (as it has in competition law), to the setting of uniform standards of horizontal liability. As submitted by Havu this would open up for variation between sectors, but cross-analogies could nonetheless align such sector-specific liability over time.[44]

II. Passing-on issues in other horizontal damages actions

8.020 If horizontal liability in damages for a breach of EU law other than competition law is possible it may, irrespective of the problems concerning the legal basis of the action discussed in the previous section, also become necessary to approach passing-on issues. It is time to consider those.

8.021 In the event of liability for private individuals for a breach of EU law, other than competition law, the EU law 'effective judicial protection package' would be triggered.[45] Issues pertaining to the right to an effective remedy have been covered in the previous section.[46] With regard to passing-on issues the discussion concerns EU law scrutiny of national conditions – the third level of the 'effective judicial protection' model used.

8.022 In the absence of EU law harmonization of the remedies and conditions to apply, national rules and conditions would govern the action. Such national rules and conditions would nevertheless be subject to the EU law requirements following from Article 47 of the EU Charter and from the principles of equivalence and effectiveness. This would encompass rules and conditions that are of essence to the specific legal issues triggered by the passing-on problem, namely access to court, substantive proximity (in damages i.e. causation), and the estimation of damages. This section very briefly examines the potential contours of these legal issues in horizontal damages for a breach of EU law other than competition law, beginning with access issues for Gamma claimants.[47]

---

44 Havu (n 14) 411, 425–6. For a discussion of the pros and cons of sector-specific and uniformity-seeking approaches respectively, see Dougan (n 3) 212–26.

45 The EU law principle of effective judicial protection was the topic of Chapter 2. On the model referred to in this paragraph see in particular Section 2.A.

46 See para. 8.013.

47 In this book Alpha signifies a tortfeasor or enriched party, Beta a party first burdened by loss arising from Alpha's breach of EU law, and Gamma any party downstream from Beta (including all from the party dealing directly with Beta to the final consumer) to whom the burden of that loss may have been passed on; see Section 1.B.

a. *Access issues for Gamma claimants*

If a horizontal action for damages were brought before a national court or tribunal, the conditions on access to court would be governed by national law subject to the general EU law requirements just mentioned. The potential impact of those requirements will now be commented on in turn. **8.023**

Article 47 of the EU Charter requires national courts to grant access to claimants who wish to enforce rights guaranteed for them by EU law.[48] This would include actions for damages for a breach of EU law other than competition law. Nonetheless national limitations of access to court would be compatible with Article 47 if they met the applicable conditions for such a limitation in Article 52(1). Under the latter Article the limitation must be provided for by law, respect the essence of the right, and meet the proportionality test prescribed by that Article. The proportionality test at issue permits only limitations which are necessary and genuinely meet objectives of a general interest recognized by the EU or the need to protect the rights and freedoms of others.[49] In the absence of relevant case law of the European Court of Justice it is submitted that cases where the issue arises how to apply Article 47 of the Charter in the context of an action for damages from a private individual for a breach of EU law should be referred to the Court of Justice for a preliminary ruling. **8.024**

As regards the EU law principle of equivalence it has been noticed above that claims based on a breach of EU law must be treated no less favourably than 'similar domestic actions'. The relevant *comparator* is an action where the purpose, cause of action, and essential characteristics of the action based on national law are similar to those of the action based on EU law.[50] Further, it must be examined whether the application of a specific rule to actions based on EU law is liable to make it less favourable to pursue such an action rather than the *comparator* action, taking into account the role played by that provision in the procedure as a whole, as well as the operation and any special features of that procedure before the different national courts.[51] It must consequently be shown that the practical application of different rules or conditions results in actual adverse treatment of actions for the exercise of rights conferred by EU law. In the context of an action for damages against private individuals for a breach of EU law the relevant *comparator* would typically be actions for damages for a breach of national statutory law, e.g., the **8.025**

---

48 See further Section 2.C.

49 See further Section 2.D.II.

50 Case C-326/96 *BS Levez v TH Jennings (Harlow Pools) Ltd* [1998] ECR I-7835 paras 41, 43.

51 *Levez* (n 50) para. 44.

English tort of breach of statutory duty. In the absence of such a specific *comparator* action the relevant *comparator* would be the general private law damages action.

8.026 Under the EU law principle of effectiveness the applicable substantive and procedural rules on access to court must not render it impossible or excessively difficult to exercise the right to damages for a breach of EU competition law.[52] The details of the analysis have been described in *Peterbroeck* and *van Schijndel*.[53] It furthermore follows from *Alassini* that the question whether the principle of effectiveness will preclude the application of a national limitation of access cannot be answered in the abstract but must be decided on a case-by-case basis.[54] In *Alassini* the Court of Justice still identified a few typical adverse consequences of national substantive and procedural conditions, liable to make the exercise of rights conferred by EU law virtually impossible or excessively difficult: bars, impracticalities, delays, and costs.

8.027 With regard to the passing-on problem and the situation for Gamma claimants the common problem is the existence of bars, or rules equivalent in practice to bars, in national law. Suffice it to notice that the requirements of EU law described above would apply to any national limitations of the right of access to court that could have the effect of barring actions for damages brought by Gamma by virtue of the lack of a nexus between Gamma and Alpha. Argumentative support for the setting aside of such bars in national law could be drawn from the fact that similar bars are prohibited under Directive 2014/104/EU.[55] It could also be argued that such bars should at least be subject to the same level of scrutiny as in the context of damages liability for Member States. In that regard it was submitted in paragraph 6.051, following analysis of *Danfoss*,[56] that Gamma claimants cannot be barred from bringing an action for damages directly against a Member State for reasons related to passing-on. If that analysis is correct, the combined effect of that view and the explicit rule to the same effect in Directive 2014/104/EU should, it is submitted, lead to the conclusion that Gamma claimants cannot be barred from bringing a direct action for damages against Alpha in the context of other horizontal damages either.

---

52 See further Section 2.D.III.

53 Case C-312/93 *Peterbroeck, Van Campenhout & Cie SCS v Belgian State* [1995] ECR I-4599 para. 14; joined cases C-430/93 and C-431/93 *Jeroen van Schijndel* and *Johannes Nicolaas Cornelis van Veen v Stichting Pensioenfonds voor Fysiotherapeuten* [1995] ECR I-4705 para. 19.

54 Joined cases C-317/08, C-318/08, C-319/08 and C-320/08 *Rosalba Alassini v Telecom Italia SpA* (C-317/08), *Filomena Califano v Wind SpA* (C-318/08), *Lucia Anna Giorgia Iacono v Telecom Italia SpA* (C-319/08) and *Multiservice Srl v Telecom Italia SpA* (C-320/08) [2010] ECR I-2213 paras 54–59.

55 Directive 2014/104/EU (n 32) Art. 12(1).

56 Case C-94/10 *Danfoss A/S and Sauer-Danfoss ApS v Skatteministeriet* [2011] ECR I-9963.

b. *Causation issues for Gamma claimants*

It was noted in paragraph 8.015 that horizontal damages liability outside competition law would obviously include a criterion of causation. With regard to the details of the causation assessment it is expected that the Court of Justice would be satisfied to leave the substantive content of the causation test to the national legal systems, albeit subject to the EU law principles of equivalence and effectiveness, as it did for the purposes of competition damages in *Manfredi*.[57] However, in light of *Kone*,[58] it is equally expected that the Court would take seriously the potential impact of the EU law principles of equivalence and effectiveness. **8.028**

Notwithstanding the findings of the Court of Justice in *Kone* it was concluded in Section 7.D that, in the context of damages for a breach of EU competition law, the guidance available in respect of the condition of causation was scarce and did not lend itself to conclusions relevant to the passing-on problem. The same of course applies *a fortiori* to any possible horizontal liability in damages for a breach of EU law other than competition law. It might nevertheless be commented on in parallel with paragraph 7.146, that if an applicable national causation test practically constituted a bar against Gamma claims there would be a strong argument for the setting aside of such a bar. **8.029**

c. *The defence of passing-on*

In the absence of EU rules governing the estimation of damages the details of estimating the award of damages payable for a breach of EU law by a private individual would also be determined by national law subject to the EU law principles of equivalence and effectiveness. Therefore the standards outlined by the Court of Justice in *Manfredi* are a more plausible option than, by any analogy, the standards laid down in Directive 2014/104/EU on competition law damages and the soft-law instruments accompanying the directive.[59] Although spill-over effects from the latter cannot be *a priori* excluded, the Directive cannot as such harmonize the estimation of damages awards outside its scope of application. The *Manfredi* findings, by contrast, were derived from an interpretation of primary EU law with horizontal direct effect and the general EU law principles of equivalence and effectiveness, for the purposes of liability in damages for private individuals in a situation where (at the time) **8.030**

57 Joined cases C-295/04 to 298/04 *Vincenzo Manfredi v Lloyd Adriatico Assicurazioni SpA* (C-295/04), *Antonio Cannito v Fondiaria Sai SpA* (C-296/04) and *Nicolò Tricarico* (C-297/04) and *Pasqualina Murgolo* (C-298/04) *v Assitalia SpA* [2006] ECR I-6619 para. 64 and Operative part para. 2. The EU legislature has continued that approach to causation under Directive 2014/104/EU (n 32), see rec. 11. See however the discussion of certain details in Section 7.D.

58 Case C-557/12 *Kone AG and Others v ÖBB-Infrastruktur AG* EU:C:2014:1317.

59 See para. 7.041.

there were no EU rules governing the estimation of damages. It follows that those findings have a closer connection to the potential situations discussed here.

8.031 It would consequently be for the domestic legal system of each Member State to set the criteria for determining the extent of the damages for harm caused by a breach of EU law, provided that the principles of equivalence and effectiveness were observed. Pursuant to the principle of effectiveness injured persons should be able to seek compensation not only for actual loss (*damnum emergens*) but also for loss of profit (*lucrum cessans*) plus interest. If it were possible to award particular damages such as exemplary or punitive damages in domestic actions similar to the EU law action brought, the availability of such damages for the purposes of the EU law action should furthermore be required pursuant to the principle of equivalence.[60]

8.032 As to the defence of passing-on it was submitted in Section 7.E.II.a that the relevant holdings in *Courage* and *Manfredi* indicated Member State autonomy on the issue.[61] In this regard a spill-over effect from Directive 2014/104/EU would arguably be more plausible, potentially causing the Court to require national courts to allow the defence of passing-on in actions for damages against private individuals for other breaches of EU law. This author can find no convincing reason for such an intervention in national autonomy, however. It is therefore submitted that it would be better for the Court to maintain a non-interventionist approach outside the scope of application of the Directive, leaving the issue to be decided on the basis of national law on damages.

C. PASSING-ON IN RESTITUTION FROM A PRIVATE INDIVIDUAL?

I. Is horizontal restitutionary liability possible?

8.033 The concern in this section is the legal basis and possible conditions to apply to a general restitutionary liability for private individuals by reason of a breach of EU law. As with the previous section on damages it is beyond the scope of this book to present a complete discussion, but a few pointers are necessary to explain the context.

8.034 It was explained in paragraph 8.002 that the payment of fees charged by a private entity may be contrary to, e.g., Articles 45, 49 or 56 TFEU. If the

60 *Manfredi* (n 57) paras 92–100, and Operative part para. 5.
61 Cf. *Courage* (n 19) para. 30; and *Manfredi* (n 57) para. 94.

charge had been levied by a Member State the repayment of such charges would be a consequence of, and an adjunct to, the rights conferred on individuals by the EU law provisions prohibiting such charges.[62] But what if the charge was levied by a private individual, e.g., an undertaking or a trade union? Similarly, what if the charge constituted abuse by a private undertaking of its dominant position contrary to Article 102 TFEU? Under such circumstances the crucial issue, from the perspective of EU law, is whether the breach of EU law can be directly relied on against a private individual, who has exacted such a charge, in order to claim restitution of the charge.

In the abstract, horizontal restitution would come into play where a transaction had taken place in accordance with national law acknowledging a right for the beneficiary of that transaction and a corresponding obligation for the individual paying. If it was then established that the national legal basis for the transaction was contrary to some provision of EU law, the crucial issue is whether the payer should be able to rely on the right conferred by that provision of EU law in order to have the transaction reversed. An argument for such restitution can easily be construed: the transaction would be *sine causa* and reversible under the *condictio indebiti* which, or at least an equivalent of which, is presumably available in every Member State.[63] Under EU law the remedies available in the Member States for the enforcement of national rights must be available also to claimants seeking to enforce the rights conferred on them by EU law.[64] Other aspects of the EU law effective judicial protection package, including Article 47 of the Charter and the principles of equivalence and effectiveness, would moreover become applicable in respect of the national conditions that would apply to the use of the restitutionary remedy.[65] It would consequently also become possible to examine the impact of the various aspects of the EU law effective judicial protection package on the legal issues triggered by the passing-on problem (access to court, substantive proximity **8.035**

62 Cf. Section 5.B.

63 For a very brief history and overview see Sonja Meier, 'Unjust Factors and Legal Grounds' in David Johnston and Reinhard Zimmermann (eds), *Unjustified Enrichment: Key Issues in Comparative Perspective* (Cambridge University Press 2002) 38–9. For clarity repayment in the form of *condictio indebiti* and the like is only one form of restitution. One might also consider restitution in kind (the unwinding of performances) when a contract is null and void by reason of a breach of EU law. An *actio de in rem verso* scenario is more difficult to design. Possibly there could be circumstances where, say, a company (A) has been enriched through another company's (B) breach of competition law without the two companies being part of the same undertaking within the meaning of competition law. Subsequently company B is declared bankrupt. Company C, which by reason of the infringement of competition law has suffered loss corresponding to the enrichment of A but being unable under the circumstances to find redress from B, brings an *actio de in rem verso* against A for its enrichment. Notwithstanding these possibilities the more common repayment action will be focused upon in this chapter.

64 See Section 2.B.III.

65 See Sections 2.C and 2.D.

and the estimation of damages).[66] Passing-on issues of this kind will be discussed in Section 8.C.II. Before going that far, however, there should be a few more comments of how horizontal restitution might come into play – beginning with a look at the support for horizontal restitution in EU case law.

8.036 Restitution by reason of a breach of competition law was touched upon by the Court of Justice in *GT-Link*.[67] The defendant was not a private individual however, but a Member State (Denmark). Consequently the Court approached the circumstances in accordance with its case law on the repayment of charges levied in breach of EU law. Otherwise hints in case law indicate that the issue will be left to be decided on the basis of national law.[68] Notwithstanding its limits *GT-Link* does prove that restitution is, as such, a plausible remedy in the event of a breach of competition law.[69] Furthermore Directive 2014/104/EU does not explicitly exclude the possibility of bringing other actions for payment instead of, or combined with, an action for damages. The circumstances in which restitution would be a practically viable option to damages are rather few, however. The nullity of horizontal agreements contrary to Article 101 TFEU pertains to the cartel agreement and not, in principle, to any contracts linked to that cartel agreement. Therefore an overcharge caused by the cartel may be part of sales contracts entered into by a cartel company and its customers, but the overcharge can only very rarely be remedied by reference to the nullity of the cartel agreement.[70] By contrast the nullity of a vertical agreement that includes, e.g., a tying clause might provide claimants with an opportunity to use a restitutionary remedy – unless the illegality of the contract renders restitution unavailable under national law. Under such circumstances the findings of the Court of Justice in *Courage* might however offer a strong argument for the setting aside of such a national rule unless the claimant bears significant responsibility for the illegality of the contract.[71] Under Article 102 TFEU the situation would be similar to vertical agreements contrary to Article 101 TFEU – provided of course that the vexed

---

66 See Section 1.A.III.

67 Case C-242/95 *GT-Link A/S v De Danske Statsbaner (DSB)* [1997] ECR I-4449.

68 Case 10/86 *VAG France SA v Établissements Magne SA* [1986] ECR 4071 paras 14–15; cf. Operative part. Cf. also the Opinion of AG Mischo para. 4.

69 This discussion of restitution for a breach of competition law is based upon this author's article 'Beyond the Competition Damages Directive: What Room for Competition Law Restitution?' in Maria Bergström, Marios C Iacovides and Magnus Strand (eds), *Harmonising EU Competition Litigation: The New Directive and Beyond* (Swedish Studies in European Law vol. 8, Hart Publishing 2016).

70 On instances where this might be possible under the national laws of some Member States see Caroline Cauffman, 'The impact of voidness for infringement of Article 101 TFEU on linked contracts' (2013) Maastricht European Private Law Institute Working Paper No 2013/3 <http://ssrn.com/abstract=2204954>, last accessed 31 May 2016.

71 See *Courage* (n 19) para. 31 and Strand (n 69) 287–8.

issue of nullity pursuant to a breach of Article 102 TFEU is resolved.[72] Notwithstanding its relatively small importance in practice – that is, seen in relation to competition damages – restitution has been acknowledged as a possible alternative remedy in those situations where it might apply and be a preferable option for the purposes of the claimant.[73]

As regards restitution from private individuals based on a breach of other provisions of EU law, Jones has submitted that restitutionary actions should be available also for a breach of other EU law provisions with horizontal direct effect, citing *Walrave* and *Barra*.[74] It should be recognized that there is no case law explicitly supporting such a conclusion. Nevertheless, with regard to EU law provisions with horizontal direct effect, this author can see no reason why the arguments submitted in Section 8.B.I for the availability of damages for breaches of such EU law provisions, even when committed by private individuals, should not be equally sound for the availability of restitutionary awards. For instance, trade unions may have a right to order payments under a collective bargaining agreement and that right may be protected by national law. If, however, an employer has been coerced into signing the agreement by collective action which is contrary to Article 56 TFEU, as in *Laval*,[75] the legal basis for payments ordered and paid might be called into question. A situation of this kind (albeit without the element of payments here suggested) has occurred in Sweden where the Labour Court recently ruled that the clauses on pay in a collective bargaining agreement, into which employers had been coerced through collective action contrary to Article 56 TFEU, were unreasonable by reason of those circumstances. Due to the pivotal role of those clauses in the agreement the Labour Court further ruled that the collective bargaining agreement was avoidable in its entirety under Swedish law.[76] In other situations voidness may pertain only to a specific contractual clause. **8.037**

It is a more complex issue to decide whether the mere exclusionary effect (*invocabilité d'exclusion*) of an EU law provision could make way for restitution **8.038**

---

72 See e.g. Ulf Bernitz, 'The Sanction of Voidness under Article 102 TFEU and its Relation to Damages' in Ulf Bernitz, *Europarättens genomslag* (Norstedts Juridik 2012) 276–7 (this article is available also in Ariel Ezrachi (ed.), *Article 82 EC: Reflections on its Recent Evolution* (Studies of the Oxford Institute of European and Comparative Law, Hart Publishing 2009)); Jones and Sufrin (n 21) 1100; and Anne Howard and Anneliese Blackwood, 'Litigating Infringements in the National Courts' in Vivien Rose and David Bailey (eds) *Bellamy & Child: European Union Law of Competition* (7th edn, Oxford University Press 2013) 1232 n 187.

73 E.g., by Howard and Blackwood (n 72) 1254; and by Assimakis P Komninos, *EC Private Antitrust Enforcement* (Hart Publishing 2008) 219.

74 Alison Jones, *Restitution and European Community Law* (Mansfield Press 2000) 61–2; *Walrave* (n 23); case 309/85 *Bruno Barra v Belgian State* and *City of Liège* [1988] ECR 355.

75 *Laval* (n 4).

76 Swedish Labour Court judgment 25 November 2015, AD 2015 nr 70.

in the manner described in paragraph 8.035.[77] The capacity of certain EU law provisions to cause a conflicting rule of national law to be set aside has been increasingly recognized by the Court of Justice in recent case law,[78] but it remains somewhat unclear what the criteria for such exclusionary effect are.[79] If such an exclusionary effect would suffice then the logic of horizontal restitution would nonetheless be plain: the setting aside of a national law provision, by reason of its incompatibility with EU law, might lead to the lack of a legal basis for a transaction, and if so that transaction should be reversed. It remains to be seen whether the Court of Justice will be willing to go quite as far as that. The Court might, if pressed on the issue, leave the consequences of the inapplicability of a national rule to be decided on the basis of national law.[80]

8.039 An even more vexing issue is whether an EU law provision capable of having exclusionary effect can be relied on in order to avoid a clause in a contract entered into by private individuals. It could be argued that the same logic as in the previous paragraph should apply in respect of clauses in such a contract, if the clause is contrary to EU law. However, in the view of this author, this is

---

77 The concept *invocabilité d'exclusion* has been coined in French EU law debate and picked up through AG Léger; see case C-287/98 *Grand Duchy of Luxemburg v Berthe Linster, Aloyse Linster and Yvonne Linster* [2000] ECR I-6917 Opinion of AG Léger paras 57 (and following). It is often used to pinpoint the capacity of an EU law norm to 'knock out' a national law norm, without the former taking the place of the latter (which is the essence of direct effect or *invocabilité de substitution*). I will however use the English term exclusionary effect.

78 E.g., case C-176/12 *Association de médiation sociale v Union locale des syndicats CGT and Others* EU:C:2014:2; and *Dansk Industri* (n 15).

79 The point of departure, here as otherwise, must be that it should first be established whether the claimant holds a right or interest protected by EU law; see *Dansk Industri* (n 15) para. 36 (and cf. Section 2.A). If so, the case law suggests that exclusionary effect is subsidiary to direct effect and to consistent interpretation, which should consequently be tried first; see case C-555/07 *Seda Kücükdeveci v Swedex GmbH & Co KG* [2010] ECR I-365 paras 46–53; *Association de médiation sociale* (n 78) paras 36–41; and *Dansk Industri* paras 30–35. When those methods are not available, and the effective judicial protection of the individual is consequently at risk by reason of a provision of national law which is incompatible with a rule or principle of EU law, the national provision must be set aside; *Kücükdeveci* para. 51; and more clearly in *Dansk Industri* paras 35–37. It remains unclear what categories of EU law norms are capable of exclusionary effect. Jones (n 74) 149 n 2 has suggested, for instance, that restitution should be available also for a breach of EU law provisions in a Directive. Such exclusionary effect of provisions in a Directive has some support in case law (e.g., case C-201/02 *The Queen, on the application of Delena Wells v Secretary of State for Transport, Local Government and the Regions* [2004] ECR I-723 para. 57) but is debated; see e.g., Takis Tridimas, 'Black, White and Shades of Grey: Horizontality of Directives Revisited' (2002) 21 *Yearbook of European Law* 327; Prechal (n 12) 261–70; Koen Lenaerts and Tim Corthaut, 'Of Birds and Hedges: The Role of Primacy in Invoking Norms of EU Law' (2006) 31 *European Law Review* 287; Michael Dougan, 'When Worlds Collide! Competing Visions of the Relationship between Direct Effect and Supremacy' (2007) 44 *Common Market Law Review* 931; and Florian Becker and Angus Campbell, 'The Direct Effect of European Directives: Towards the Final Act?' (2007) 13 *Columbia Journal of European Law* 401. In the cited case law the Court has however clearly refrained from holding that provisions of a Directive can have an exclusionary effect against provisions of national law, relying instead on the exclusionary effect of the general principle of non-discrimination on grounds of age (which is a primary law norm).

80 Cf. *VAG France* (n 68) paras 14–15.

only possible if the EU law norm at issue has horizontal direct effect. The exclusionary effect of an EU law norm (on which it is *per se* possible to rely against a private individual) should rightly be understood as a collision of norms rule.[81] Consequently it applies in the event of a conflict between legal provisions of EU law and national law respectively. Under the doctrine of EU law precedence the national law provision must yield. Accordingly the case law on exclusionary effect so far suggests no more than that EU law may be relied on, in civil litigation between individuals, to preclude provisions of national law.[82] For the next step to be possible, i.e., for the EU law norm to enter into and to modify a contract entered into by private individuals, the norm must be able to create legal obligations for individuals. That capacity is, it was submitted in paragraph 8.009, what we know as horizontal direct effect. The issue of exclusionary effect vis-à-vis clauses in a contract is nonetheless intriguing and should therefore, in the event of an opportunity, be referred to the European Court of Justice for a preliminary ruling.

In sum the incompatibility of a rule of national law with a rule of EU law may render the former inapplicable. A performance in accordance with the national rule would consequently be *sine causa* and reversible, even where the party liable to make restitution is a private individual. It has been submitted that such a restitutionary liability for private individuals should at least apply where the EU law rule at issue has the properties defined for the purposes of horizontal liability in damages in Section 8.B.I, but also that it may apply by reason of the exclusionary effect of the EU law rule at issue. Clarifications by the Court of Justice would be most welcome. **8.040**

II. Passing-on issues in horizontal EU law restitution

a. Access issues for Gamma claimants

In restitution passing-on will occur if the disadvantage or 'impoverishment' of Beta – which should correspond to an enrichment of Alpha – is somehow passed on to Gamma, leaving Beta 'disimpoverished'.[83] As is apparent from the above there is no EU case law on the passing-on problem in the context of horizontal restitution. In respect of access to court, the main concern is whether Gamma claimants could have such access. The problem for Gamma is, essentially, that it is not the general view of the Member States that Gamma **8.041**

81 On this much there seems to be consensus even between antagonists; compare Lenaerts and Corthaut (n 79) 289 with Dougan (n 79) 934–5.

82 See e.g. *Dansk Industri* (n 15).

83 See Peter Birks, *Unjust Enrichment* (2nd edn, Clarendon Law Series, Oxford University Press 2005) 219 and Michael Rush, *The Defence of Passing On* (Hart Publishing 2006) 10–11.

should be able to bring an action for restitution against Alpha, leapfrogging Beta. On the contrary the concept of restitution will commonly presuppose a direct transaction from the claimant to the defendant.[84] As Gamma has no direct nexus to Alpha, Gamma will be vulnerable to national rules the effect of which is to dismiss the action as being manifestly unfounded. It does seem very difficult to overcome such national rules by use of EU law argumentation. To this author it therefore seems that the best possibility for Gamma is to try to win damages instead of restitution. If Gamma insists on attempting a restitutionary action against a private Alpha, searching for support in EU law, it could be contemplated whether there are any possibilities of using Article 47 of the Charter and/or the EU law principle of effectiveness to that end. EU law does not usually embrace absolute bars, as is evident from case law on Article 47 and on the principle of effectiveness that was analysed in Chapter 2.[85] That is not to say, however, that an action could never be dismissed.[86]

8.042 An argument drawing from Article 47 of the Charter would need to focus on the compatibility of the national law bar with the requirements in Article 52(1) that set the standard for permissible limitations to Charter rights.[87] It is expected that an argumentation on the criteria in Article 52(1) would focus on the circumstances of the individual case and, at the end of the day, turn on the possibilities for Gamma to use a damages remedy.

8.043 As regards the EU law principle of effectiveness, a comparison with restitution from a Member State of charges levied in breach of EU law would offer what might be Gamma's best opportunity for success in respect of access to court. In *Danfoss* the Court of Justice allowed Gamma to leapfrog Beta if it were virtually impossible or excessively difficult to obtain redress from Beta.[88] Should the Court of Justice therefore order national courts to allow Gamma actions to be brought against Alpha in the context of horizontal restitutionary actions, where it is virtually impossible or excessively difficult to obtain redress from Beta? That conclusion is tempting, but public law restitution from a

84 See Christian von Bar and Eric Clive (eds), *Principles, Definitions and Model Rules of European Private Law: Draft Common Frame of Reference (DCFR) Full Edition* (6 vols, Sellier European Law Publishers 2009) 4036, 4039–42. Cf. also Section 4.D.II.

85 On Art. 47 of the Charter in general see Section 2.C. On the principle of effectiveness see Section 2.D.III. The principle of equivalence (see Section 2.D.II) does not seem relevant in this context.

86 Cf. case 33/76 *Rewe-Zentralfinanz eG and Rewe-Zentral AG v Landwirtschaftskammer für das Saarland* [1976] ECR 1989 Opinion of AG Warner, 2004; cited by Daniel Beard and Alison Jones, 'Co-Contractors, Damages and Article 81: The ECJ Finally Speaks' (2002) 23 *European Competition Law Review* 246 n 38.

87 For details see Section 2.C.II.

88 *Danfoss* (n 56) para. 28 and Operative part para. 1. Notice that the requirement to allow the direct Gamma action applied only if Gamma were not able, on the basis of national law, to bring a civil action against Beta for recovery of the sum unduly paid, or if it were virtually impossible or excessively difficult for Gamma to obtain reimbursement from Beta, e.g., due to Beta being insolvent.

Member State by reason of charges levied in breach of EU law must be carefully distinguished from private law restitutionary actions brought against another private individual. Even if the latter action might be available as a matter of EU law it does not follow that the conditions applicable to both should be alike. In the field of private law *sensu stricto* the Court of Justice has traditionally proceeded with caution, allowing the Member States to retain a wide margin of discretion.[89] The Court is usually satisfied to preclude national law which is discriminatory on one of the grounds prohibited by EU law.[90] The counterargument to a *Danfoss* comparison is therefore that the findings of the Court in *Danfoss* should not be regarded as indications that could apply *mutatis mutandis* in private law restitution.

In conclusion national rules barring a Gamma action will not be easily overcome by use of EU law arguments, but the particular circumstances of the individual case will be significant. If a national bar is set aside (and, of course, if there is no such bar in national law) the problem will be to establish sufficient substantive proximity between the loss of Gamma and the enrichment of Alpha. **8.044**

b. Substantive proximity issues for Gamma claimants

Substantive proximity can be expected to be a high hurdle to jump for Gamma claimants seeking horizontal restitution. The issue has not been discussed by the European Court of Justice, but there are hints to be found in the context of repayment of charges levied in breach of EU law that are of interest. These will be compared with relevant European private law materials. **8.045**

The Court of Justice held in *FII* that an action against a Member State would qualify as an action for repayment only if the loss, on behalf of the claimant, was the 'inevitable consequence' of the breach of EU law on behalf of the Member State.[91] In *Danfoss* Advocate General Kokott opined that if the 'real meaning' of the criterion of inevitable consequence was applied, it would not be fulfilled with respect to claimants downstream from Beta, because the charge was not passed on automatically but through an entrepreneurial decision taken by Beta. In *San Giorgio* Advocate General Mancini similarly opined that there was no basis for an action of unjust enrichment (other than a **8.046**

89 *Manfredi* (n 57), where the Court interpreted the impact of the EU law principles of equivalence and effectiveness in respect of the estimation of competition law damages, is perhaps the most far-reaching EU judgment in private law.

90 For an overview see Arthur Hartkamp, *European Law and National Private Law: Effect of EU Law and European Human Rights Law on Legal Relationships between Individuals* (Kluwer 2012) 28–37.

91 Case C-446/04 *Test Claimants in the FII Group Litigation v Commissioners of Inland Revenue* [2006] ECR I-11753 para. 207.

repayment action) in passing-on situations.[92] A strict 'inevitable consequence' test along these lines would consequently prevent Gamma claimants from being able to establish sufficient substantive proximity to Alpha for the action to be successful. Advocate General Kokott however also stressed in *Danfoss* that the case law was not clear on this point.[93]

8.047 This 'inevitable consequence test' used by the Court in *FII* could plausibly be applied as an EU law standard of substantive proximity in restitutionary actions brought against private individuals just as well as against Member States. The test seems to give very little room for Gamma claims.

8.048 The 'inevitable consequence test' furthermore seems to match the approach to substantive proximity in European private law materials on private law restitution. Under Article VII. – 4:101 of the Draft Common Frame of Reference (DCFR) enrichment is attributable to another's disadvantage in circumstances where an asset of the disadvantaged person is transferred to the enriched person and in a number of other circumstances. The situations covered all share the common trait that the nexus between the two parties is direct.[94] With regard to the transfer of assets (which encompasses the payment of a price which includes an overcharge) it is explained that an enrichment is sufficiently connected to the disadvantage of another only if 'the asset which has become vested in the enriched person was the asset of the disadvantaged person'. By contrast it 'does not apply where the enriched person's gain is the effect of a transfer by a third party of an asset of the third party unless … the third party is acting only as a cipher who in material terms is merely forwarding on an asset of the disadvantaged person'.[95]

8.049 German law similarly requires that the claimant has performed towards the defendant, thus causing the latter to be enriched.[96] In common law, a nexus is also required.[97] In French law the action of *enrichissement sans cause* is distinguished from *répétition de l'indu* which covers repayment of money paid but not due. In *répétition de l'indu* it follows from the wording of Article 1376 of the Code civil that a Gamma action is not possible.[98] In *enrichissement sans*

92 Case 199/82 *Amministrazione delle Finanze dello Stato v SpA San Giorgio* [1983] ECR 3595 Opinion of AG Mancini para. 7.

93 *Danfoss* (n 56) Opinion of AG Kokott paras 53–55.

94 DCFR (n 84) Art. VII. – 4:101.

95 DCFR (n 84) 4036. See also 4037 and the accompanying Notes.

96 Gerhard Dannemann, *The German Law of Unjustified Enrichment and Restitution* (Oxford University Press 2009) 34.

97 Rush (n 83) 210–11.

98 Article 1376 reads: 'Celui qui reçoit par erreur ou sciemment ce qui ne lui est pas dû s'oblige à le restituer *à celui de qui l'a indûment reçu*' (emphasis added).

cause, which is the subsidiary action, evidence of a causal nexus between the enrichment of the defendant and the impoverishment of the claimant is required. It is stated in the DCFR that this requirement of a causal nexus in French restitution law will be met in circumstances where 'one and the same intervening event caused the enrichment as well as the impoverishment'.[99] This is sometimes called the doctrine of 'indivisibility of origin', under which an action for restitution is available only if both the enrichment and the corresponding impoverishment have flown from the same event and the one would not exist without the other.[100] It has been reported that French, Belgian, Spanish and Italian law will at times interpret this requirement leniently, and accept claims for the restitution of enrichments that have passed through patrimonies to the enriched defendant.[101] However, it is not reported that the reverse situation, i.e., for the disadvantage (or impoverishment) to pass through patrimonies to the claimant, would satisfy the doctrine of indivisibility of origin even in these jurisdictions.

In sum both EU law and European private law materials seem to require the existence of a direct nexus between the impoverished claimant and the enriched defendant. Under such circumstances it seems Gamma claimants will be unable to use EU law argumentation to overcome national concepts of substantive proximity that require a direct nexus to the enrichment of Alpha. Gamma actions will consequently be unsuccessful unless particular circumstances or particular national law disperses the proximity problem. **8.050**

Notwithstanding the difficulties for Gamma to find redress against Alpha directly, the option of restitutionary redress from Beta deserves to be briefly reconsidered. In paragraph 4.030 it was noted that Rush has suggested a solution under which Beta is allowed to claim the entire enrichment from Alpha, rejecting any defence of passing-on tried by Alpha, and under which Gamma will thereafter be allowed to bring a subsequent action against Beta with regard to the amount passed on.[102] A similar possibility was indicated by the European Court of Justice in *Comateb*,[103] albeit for the purposes of actions against a Member State for repayment of charges levied in breach of EU law. **8.051**

99 DCFR (n 84) 3850–3851.

100 See Jack Beatson and Eltjo Schrage (eds), *Cases, Materials and Texts on Unjustified Enrichment* (Hart Publishing, 2003) 207.

101 Rebecca Williams, *Unjust Enrichment and Public Law: A Comparative Study of England, France and the EU* (Hart Publishing, 2011) 173; DCFR (n 84) 3851–3852.

102 Rush (n 83) 218, with an extensive discussion of different constructions to this end at 211–17. See also Andrew Burrows, *The Law of Restitution* (3rd edn, Oxford University Press 2011) 617–18.

103 Joined cases C-192/95 to 218/95 *Société Comateb and others v Directeur Général des Douanes et Droits Indirects* [1997] ECR I-165 para. 24.

It is open for the Court of Justice to adopt a similar approach for the purposes of horizontal restitutionary claims based on EU law.

c. *The defence of passing-on*

8.052 The third legal issue triggered by the passing-on problem is the estimation of the award, and more specifically whether passing-on can be relevant in the estimation of the award. In the absence of EU law materials the issue will be discussed in light of European private law materials.

8.053 The defence of passing-on is not mentioned explicitly in the DCFR.[104] Nevertheless, interestingly, the DCFR seems to dismiss the defence of passing-on in Article VII. – 3:102(2), in which 'disadvantage' is defined. The Article reads:

8.054

> In determining whether and to what extent a person sustains a disadvantage, no regard is to be had to any enrichment which that person obtains in exchange for or after the disadvantage.

8.055 It is further explained that disadvantage, within the meaning of Book VII, is the individual negative item on a balance sheet rather than 'the "bottom line" figure representing the balance itself (i.e. the aggregate of all positive and negative entries)'.[105] Dannemann has reported that the defence of passing-on is alien to German restitution law, as financial loss on behalf of the claimant is irrelevant.[106] In English law there has been some hesitation, but authorities now seem to agree that the defence of passing-on has been rejected at common law although it remains available under statutory law on the recovery of undue tax payments.[107]

8.056 It thus seems that most Member State jurisdictions reject the defence of passing-on in private law restitution. EU law will take no issue with this. The situation in horizontal restitution is parallel to the situation in actions brought against a Member State, where the defence of passing-on is neither prohibited nor imposed by EU law. Rather it is tolerated, if available in national law.

---

104 Notice in DCFR (n 84) 4017 the discussion on disenrichment in Art. VII. – 3:101(2) which is not mirrored by any discussion on 'disimpoverishment'. The latter term has been suggested to replace 'passing-on' for the purposes of restitution law by Birks (n 83) 219–21; and Rush (n 83) 11–17.

105 DCFR (n 84) 4004, 4016–4017.

106 Dannemann (n 96) 103.

107 For an in-depth study of the case law and statutory law see Rush (n 83) Chs 3–4. See also e.g. Birks (n 83) 219–21, 230–32; and Burrows (n 102) 614–18 with references, reporting for instance that the Supreme Court of Canada first allowed the defence of passing-on in *Air Canada v British Columbia* (1989) 59 DLR (4th) 161 before rejecting it in *Kingstreet Investments Ltd v New Brunswick (Department of Finance)* [2007] SCC 1.

Consequently the relevant question to be asked is likewise whether, and if so under what conditions, EU law should tolerate a defence of passing-on in the context of horizontal restitution.

To this author the proper point of departure is to allow the Member States a margin of discretion in private law restitution. That margin of discretion should not be narrower in private law restitution than it is in public law restitution (i.e., repayment of charges levied by Member States in breach of EU law). It could reasonably be wider, however. This author would therefore prefer for the Court of Justice to adopt a non-interventionist approach, leaving the issue of the defence of passing-on to be decided by the Member States. Any differences that might result should be acceptable, bearing in mind that there has been no harmonization in respect of restitution from Member States, which should be a greater concern.[108] Admittedly this author would also prefer for the Member States to reject the defence of passing-on and adopt the Rush solution, making Beta subsequently liable to distribute portions of the award to Gamma claimants at the next level of the supply chain to the extent that the original unlawful charge or overcharge has been passed on to them. Successful Gamma claimants should then in turn be liable to distribute to the next level of Gamma claimants, and so on. The door to acknowledging a defence of passing-on could be left ajar in the event of cases where the sum charged in breach of EU law could be shown to be directly attributable to that breach and identifiable as a specific item on invoices along the supply chain, or with equivalent precision – in other words, in circumstances where a direct Gamma action leapfrogging Beta might deserve consideration. However, with this said, it would be for the Member States to find a proper approach in accordance with national law, albeit subject to the EU law principles of equivalence and effectiveness in the individual case. **8.057**

In restitution by reason of a breach of competition law it might however be argued that it does not serve to have Beta claimants circumventing the rules on passing-on in Directive 2014/104/EU by bringing an action for restitution instead of an action for damages. According to this argument the Court of Justice should safeguard the harmonizing effect on private enforcement in the EU, making certain that the playing field is not unlevelled by reason of national differences in restitution law and the legal ingenuity of claimants. Proponents of this view might wish for this to be done by interpreting Article 12 of the Directive as a preclusion of restitutionary actions, or by ensuring that the substantive content of the Directive is applied *mutatis mutandis* in **8.058**

108 Such harmonization has been suggested in Andrea Biondi and Lindsay Johnson, 'The Right to Recovery of Charges levied in Breach of Community Law: No Small Matter' (1998) 4 *European Public Law* 313.

restitution. It could however be counterargued that although it is true in theory that Beta claimants who wish to avoid facing a defence of passing-on might prefer to claim restitution of an overcharge rather than damages, in practice the circumstances in which restitution is a viable option to damages are scarce.[109] Moreover a claim for restitution would not include compensation for losses due to a decrease in sales. Therefore, as Beta will commonly have suffered such loss in a passing-on context, an action for damages under the rules of the Directive has substantive benefits.[110] Any detriment to the harmonizing effect of Directive 2014/104/EU that could supposedly be caused by allowing alternative restitutionary actions will therefore be quite small. In the few situations where restitution may be a viable option circumstances are moreover likely to be rather particular, and it will likely be fair under such circumstances to entrust the national courts with the finding of a proper solution subject to the EU law principles of equivalence and effectiveness. To this author these counter arguments seem more convincing than the ones suggesting EU law intervention.

D. CONCLUSIONS AND SUGGESTIONS

8.059 With regard to liability in damages for a private individual by reason of a breach of EU law by that individual, it has been submitted that the Court can be expected to reserve horizontal damages to situations where the EU law rule infringed confers a right on the claimant and has a protective purpose with regard to that right. It has further been submitted that the EU law rule must have horizontal direct effect and be legally binding on the defendant specifically. Whether a 'sufficiently serious breach' condition will be added, and whether national fault notions will be allowed, is more difficult to foresee.

8.060 Under such a horizontal damages action it was submitted that Gamma claimants could not be barred from bringing a direct action for damages against Alpha. This should apply irrespective of whether such a bar was construed under national law as a rule on access to court or as a very stringent requirement of causation. Otherwise it was submitted, with regard to causation specifically, that the available materials did not lend themselves to conclusions relevant to the passing-on problem. In respect of the defence of passing-on it was submitted that a spill-over effect from Directive 2014/

---

109 See para. 8.037.

110 Contemplating these matters, Beta claimants in the rare circumstances where restitution is a good option might consider cumulating an action for restitution of the overcharge with an action for damages for loss caused by decreased sales.

104/EU was plausible, potentially causing the Court to require national courts to allow the defence of passing-on in actions for damages against private individuals for other breaches of EU law. Nonetheless it was recommended that the Court maintain a non-interventionist approach outside the scope of application of the Directive, leaving the issue to be decided on the basis of national law on damages.

With regard to liability in restitution for a private individual it was concluded that the incompatibility of a rule of national law with a rule of EU law will, under the doctrine of EU law precedence, render the former inapplicable. A performance in accordance with the national rule may consequently be *sine causa* and therefore reversible, even where the party liable to make restitution is a private individual. It was submitted that such a restitutionary liability for private individuals should at least apply where the EU law rule at issue has the properties defined for the purposes of horizontal liability in damages, but also that it may apply by reason of the exclusionary effect of the EU law rule at issue. **8.061**

In contrast with the conclusions on damages it was concluded in restitution that national rules barring a Gamma action would not be easily overcome by use of EU law arguments, notwithstanding if those national rules were construed under national law as rules on access to court or as a requirement of a direct nexus between the loss of the claimant and the enrichment of the defendant. It was therefore submitted that Gamma actions would probably be unsuccessful unless particular circumstances or particular national law dispersed the proximity problem. It was further submitted that it should be for the Member States to find a proper approach to the defence of passing-on in accordance with national law, albeit subject to the EU law principles of equivalence and effectiveness. **8.062**

Part V

PERSPECTIVES AND CONCLUSIONS

9

COMPARISON AND ANALYSIS

A. CHAPTER OUTLINE

It was demonstrated in Section 1.A.III that the legal issues triggered by the passing-on problem subdivide into three main legal issues. The first issue was access to court, under which it is asked whether access to claim damages or restitution, as the case may be, should be limited to certain classes of claimants based on the fact that the burden of a charge may have been passed on. The second issue concerned substantive proximity (causation or attribution) in respect of the lack of a direct nexus between the defendant and such claimants that have not dealt with the defendant directly, but are found down the supply chain. The third issue identified was estimating the amount of damages or restitution payable to the respective claimants along the supply chain, and whether courts should take account of the fact that a financial burden – or any portion of it – has or could have been passed on. **9.001**

In the previous Chapters 3–8 these three identified aspects of the passing-on problem have been presented and analysed in the context of the relevant actions in which the passing-on problem has, or may, occur. This chapter proceeds to summarize the analyses submitted in the previous chapters and to compare them. Summaries are available in Sections 9.B, 9.C, and 9.D. Thereafter, in section 9.E, it will also be discussed how actions from various **9.002** levels of a supply chain might be coordinated in order to find a comprehensive approach to the passing-on problem. In Section 9.E.I it will be discussed how the interests of the parties can be reconciled in a comprehensive solution that seeks to satisfy the interest(s) of reparation. In Section 9.E.II the general interest of deterrence will be added to the assessment, and it will be highlighted that the existence and effectiveness of parallel public enforcement may be of essence to the need for deterrence in private enforcement. In the final Section 9.F it is endeavoured to find a way to reconcile the interests discussed into a comprehensive blueprint that is capable of being compatible with settled EU law throughout the contexts discussed in this book. Some suggestions for how to find such a comprehensive approach are respectfully submitted.

B. ACCESS TO COURT FOR GAMMA CLAIMANTS: SUMMARY

9.003 When prompted to address the issue of access to court for Gamma claimants the European Court of Justice and the EU legislature have required for Gamma claimants to be granted access to bring an action against Alpha before the competent court.[1] The opportunity thus granted is not without its limits, however.

9.004 In *Danfoss*, for instance, the Court ruled that a Member State may oppose a claim for reimbursement of a duty unduly paid, brought by the party to whom that duty has been passed on (i.e., Gamma), on the ground that it was not that party who had paid the duty to the tax authorities, provided that Gamma was able on the basis of national law to bring a civil action against the taxable person (i.e., Beta) for recovery of the sum unduly paid and provided that the reimbursement, by Beta, of the duty unduly paid was not virtually impossible or excessively difficult.[2] It follows that the EU law requirement of access for Gamma was conditional in the sense that it was subject to the occurrence of a number of specific circumstances.

9.005 In *Danfoss* the Court of Justice also addressed the same issue for the purposes of an action for damages brought against the Member State. The wording chosen in this part of the ruling was quite similar to the one cited above. The Court settled that a Member State might reject a claim for damages brought

1 In this book, Alpha signifies a tortfeasor or enriched party, Beta a party first burdened by loss arising from Alpha's breach of EU law, and Gamma any party downstream from Beta (including all from the party dealing directly with Beta to the final consumer) to whom the burden of that loss may have been passed on; see Section 1.B.

2 Case C-94/10 *Danfoss A/S and Sauer-Danfoss ApS v Skatteministeriet* [2011] ECR I-9963 Operative part para. 1. See further Section 5.C.II.

by Gamma on the ground that there was no direct causal link between the levying of that duty and the damage suffered provided that Gamma was able, on the basis of national law, to bring that claim against Beta and provided that the compensation, by Beta, of the damage suffered by Gamma was not virtually impossible or excessively difficult.[3] Accordingly the EU law requirement of access for Gamma is contingent on the occurrence of specific circumstances in this context too.

In the context of competition law damages the requirement is not contingent on circumstances in the same way. Directive 2014/104/EU straightforwardly requires for compensation to be available for 'anyone who suffered it',[4] including any 'natural or legal person who acquired, not directly from an infringer, but from a direct purchaser or a subsequent purchaser, products or services that were the object of an infringement of competition law, or products or services containing them or derived therefrom'.[5] It was noted in sub-section 7.C.II.b that this policy was chosen notwithstanding the many counterarguments to access for Gamma claimants that have been submitted in both US and EU competition law discourse. The problem for Gamma in this context will most likely be to convince the court that Gamma is not too remote from the infringement to be able to satisfy the applicable causation test. That, however, is (here labelled) a substantive proximity problem and has been discussed in that context. **9.006**

In the other contexts discussed in this book there is no legislation or case law on access to court for Gamma claimants. It has nevertheless been submitted that the policy choices in *Danfoss* should apply with no less stringency to actions for damages brought against the EU under Article 340(2) TFEU for a breach of EU law by its institutions or agents, and that this suggestion finds support in the case law on such liability as well as in Article 47 of the EU Charter.[6] By contrast it has been observed that Gamma claimants bringing a restitutionary action against the EU, or against a private individual,[7] might find themselves struggling for access. It is not the general view of the Member **9.007**

---

3 Ibid., Operative part para. 2.

4 Directive 2014/104/EU of the European Parliament and of the Council of 26 November 2014 on certain rules governing actions for damages under national law for infringements of the competition law provisions of the Member States and of the European Union [2014] OJ L349/1, Art. 12(1).

5 Ibid., Art. 2(24).

6 See further Section 3.C.II.

7 The term 'private individual' will be used throughout this text (with the exception of quotes using different terminology). It is intended to serve as shorthand for any kind of natural or legal person capable of carrying rights and/or obligations pursuant to EU law, who is not an emanation of the Member State within the meaning of EU law. The criteria used for identifying legal bodies as emanations of the Member State within the meaning of EU law were laid down by the European Court of Justice in case C-188/89 *A Foster and others v British Gas plc* [1990] ECR I-3313 para. 20.

States that Gamma should be able to bring an action for restitution against Alpha, leapfrogging Beta. On the contrary the concept of restitution will commonly presuppose a direct transaction from the claimant to the defendant.[8]

9.008 To conclude, therefore, Gamma's prospects of gaining access to court are dependent on the legal context, ranging from great difficulty to an EU law requirement of access. It will be discussed in sections 9.E and 9.F how to reconcile such divergences between contexts.

C. SUBSTANTIVE PROXIMITY PROBLEMS FOR GAMMA CLAIMANTS: SUMMARY

9.009 The lack of a direct nexus between Alpha and Gamma may be the biggest problem facing Gamma claimants attempting to pursue their claims against Alpha, regardless of whether the action is for restitution or for damages. Besides giving rise to procedural bars denying Gamma access to court, the lack of a direct nexus may also be a problem in the substantive assessment of whether there is sufficient proximity between the original unlawful transaction (or unlawfully omitted transaction) and the loss sustained by the Gamma claimant at issue for Gamma to be able to bring a successful claim against Alpha. In damages the common term for this complex of issues is causation. In restitution different terms are used, e.g., attribution.[9] In this book the concept 'substantive proximity' has been used as shorthand for these problems.

9.010 Substantive proximity in the context of passing-on has not been addressed as such by the Court of Justice. The discussions of substantive proximity in the previous chapters nevertheless reveal that EU law does not suffer automatic exclusion gladly. Therefore substantive proximity rules that are designed to or have the effect of excluding certain classes of claimants automatically, i.e., without assessing the circumstances of the individual case, have on several occasions and in various contexts been found to be incompatible with EU law.[10] It will nonetheless remain for Gamma to establish substantive proximity, in the assessment of the facts thus required, in order to bring a successful action.

---

8 See further Section 4.D.I and sub-section 8.C.II.a.

9 The term 'attribution' is used in Christian von Bar and Eric Clive (eds), *Principles, Definitions and Model Rules of European Private Law: Draft Common Frame of Reference (DCFR) Full Edition* (6 vols, Sellier European Law Publishers 2009) Book VII Ch. 4.

10 E.g., in case 118/83 *CMC Cooperativa muratori e cementisti and others v Commission of the European Communities* [1985] ECR 2325 (see Section 3.C.II and para. 3.062) and case C-557/12 *Kone AG and Others v*

9.011 In damages the prospects of such success seem largely to depend on the conditions of the relevant market. In the context of damages claims against the EU it follows from the case law of the General Court that the economic complexity of a situation may be detrimental to the prospects of bringing a successful action. Gamma claimants operating on a very complex buying market will therefore have little chance of success.[11] In the context of damages claims against a Member State it is for the national courts to assess causation in accordance with national law, albeit subject to the EU law principles of equivalence and effectiveness.[12] Advocate General Kokott has argued in *Danfoss* that it should not be compatible with the effective protection of rights recognized by EU law to exclude the existence of a direct causal link between an infringement of Alpha and harm incurred by Gamma claimants,[13] but guidance from the Court itself has been scarce. Directive 2014/104/EU similarly leaves the element of causation in competition law damages to be decided on the basis of national law.[14] Nevertheless, as in damages actions against a Member State, the assessment will be subject to the principles of equivalence and effectiveness – the potential impact of which was illustrated in *Kone*.[15] It was furthermore submitted in section 7.D.II that Article 14(2) of Directive 2014/104/EU will have an impact on the allocation of the burden of proof in the causation assessment.

9.012 In restitution substantive proximity seems an almost insurmountable problem for Gamma claimants, save possibly for rather particular markets and circumstances. This has not been addressed by the Court of Justice but it has been submitted that it follows from the EU principle of effectiveness as interpreted by the Court in *Danfoss* that national courts should not be able to reject *a priori* a restitutionary action brought by Gamma with reference to the lack of a nexus between Alpha and Gamma, even where such an *a priori* conclusion formally follows from substantive proximity concepts rather than from a procedural law bar. Nevertheless an examination of European private law materials demonstrates that it is commonly required that the claimant bringing a restitutionary action has transferred the enrichment to the defendant her- or himself.[16] This

---

ÖBB-Infrastruktur AG EU:C:2014:1317 (see Section 7.D.I). See also *Danfoss* (n 2) Opinion of AG Kokott para. 83, cited in sub-section 6.C.II.b.

11 Cf. case T-351/03 *Schneider Electric SA v Commission of the European Communities* [2007] ECR II-2237 paras 283, 285–286.

12 It is a matter of some controversy whether this element is governed primarily by EU law or primarily by national law; see para. 6.053.

13 *Danfoss* (n 2) Opinion of AG Kokott paras 79–83.

14 Directive 2014/104/EU (n 4) rec. 11. See further Section 7.D.I.

15 *Kone* (n 10).

16 DCFR (n 9) Art. VII. – 4:101(a), 4036–4037 and 4039–4042; Gerhard Dannemann, *The German Law of Unjustified Enrichment and Restitution* (Oxford University Press 2009) 34; and Michael Rush, *The Defence of Passing On* (Hart Publishing 2006) 209–10.

seems to apply notwithstanding whether the action is brought against the EU, against a Member State, or against a private individual pursuant to a breach of EU competition law.[17] Therefore prospects of success for Gamma seem small in restitution, unless the action can be brought against Beta instead of against Alpha.[18]

D. THE DEFENCE OF PASSING-ON: SUMMARY

9.013 The defence of passing-on is perhaps the passing-on problem *par excellence*. The defence of passing-on is an argument on the amount of the award of damages or restitution payable to Beta claimants. The defence can also be raised against Gamma claimants – it potentially applies as long as the claimant is not a final consumer.

9.014 The first EU case law on the defence of passing-on was developed in the context of damages actions brought against the EU under Article (now) 340(2) TFEU by reason of refunds due but not paid. In the gritz and quellmehl cases the Court of Justice thus held that where the absence of refunds was compensated by way of increased prices, such price increases would take the place of the refunds and the interest of compensation would accordingly be extinguished.[19] There is no case law on the defence in damages against a Member State and it was argued in sub-section 7.E.II.a that comparisons with other actions yield little.[20] Directive 2014/104/EU has however settled this issue for the purposes of competition law damages by requiring for the defence of passing-on to be available to defendants in the context of such actions.[21] In the case law under Article 340(2) TFEU and in

---

17 See Sections 4.D.II, 5.D.II and sub-section 8.C.II.b respectively.

18 Along those lines, Rush (n 16) 217–18 has suggested to allow Beta to claim the entire enrichment from Alpha, rejecting any defence of passing-on tried by Alpha, and to allow Gamma to bring a subsequent action against Beta.

19 Case 238/78 *Ireks-Arkady GmbH v Council and Commission of the European Communities* [1979] ECR 2955 para. 14; joined cases 261 and 262/78 *Interquell Stärke-Chemie GmbH and Diamalt AG v Council and Commission of the European Communities* [1979] ECR 3045 para. 17: joined cases 64 and 113/76, 167 and 239/78, 27, 28 and 45/79 *P Dumortier frères SA and others v Council of the European Communities* [1979] ECR 3091 para. 15; and joined cases 241, 242, 245 to 250/78 *DGV, Deutsche Getreideverwertung und Rheinische Kraftfutterwerke GmbH and others v Council and Commission of the European Communities* [1979] ECR 3017 para. 15.

20 The parallel discussed was with the holdings of the Court of Justice in competition law cases, namely case C-453/99 *Courage Ltd v Bernard Crehan and Bernard Crehan v Courage Ltd and Others* [2001] ECR I-6297 para. 30; and joined cases C-295/04 to 298/04 *Vincenzo Manfredi v Lloyd Adriatico Assicurazioni SpA* (C-295/04), *Antonio Cannito v Fondiaria Sai SpA* (C-296/04) and *Nicolò Tricarico* (C-297/04) and *Pasqualina Murgolo* (C-298/04) *v Assitalia SpA* [2006] ECR I-6619 para. 94 and Operative part para. 5.

21 Directive 2014/104/EU (n 4) Art. 13. See further sub-section 7.E.II.b.

Directive 2014/104/EU alike the burden of proving that harm has been passed on is on the defendant.[22]

In the scarce – almost non-existent – case law on restitution from the EU and horizontal restitution the defence of passing-on has not been touched upon. The most developed EU case law on this defence is nonetheless found in the context of restitution, namely actions for the repayment of charges levied by a Member State in breach of EU law. In that context the Court of Justice has consistently held that EU law neither prevents nor requires national courts to take into account, in accordance with their national law, the fact that the burden of charges unlawfully levied may have been passed on. The case law however allows Member States to resist repayment only where the charge has been borne, in whole or in part, by someone other than the claimant, and reimbursement must constitute unjust enrichment of the claimant notwithstanding any reduction of sales suffered by the claimant. To avail itself successfully of the defence of passing-on the Member State at issue must furthermore prove the existence and extent of passing-on. The Court has been less clear on the burden of proving that unjust enrichment is excluded by reason of reduced sales.[23] **9.015**

All this EU case law and Directive 2014/104/EU arguably follow – or are at least compatible with – a two-tier assessment of whether a defence of passing-on can be upheld. In sum the point of departure is that the defence of passing-on can be upheld only to the extent that an award of damages or restitution would constitute a windfall award for the claimant. To determine whether it would, it is first examined whether the economic burden of the EU law infringement committed by Alpha has been passed on. To the extent that it has not been passed on the award is no windfall. It is then examined whether the amount which could potentially constitute a windfall (as determined in the first tier of the test) is nevertheless not to be regarded as a windfall due to factors such as consequential loss, e.g., reduced sales. **9.016**

Simplifying this approach even further it could be restated in a formula. The award (A) equals the amount of the unlawful charge (C) paid by the claimant, minus the amount passed on (P) plus other loss (L) incurred: or A=C−P+L. In restitution one might prefer A=E, the latter (E) meaning the enrichment of Alpha at the expense of the claimant. Although this may seem very appealing in its simplicity, it begs the question, namely: to what extent has Alpha been **9.017**

22 See joined cases 256, 257, 265, 267/80, 5 and 51/81 and 282/82 *Birra Wührer SpA and others v Council and Commission of the European Communities* [1984] ECR 3693 para. 28, and Directive 2014/104/EU (n 4) Art. 13, respectively.

23 For a summary of all these findings with references see sub-section 5.E.II.d.

enriched at the expense of the particular claimant who is bringing an action? Contemplating that question in light of the EU law approach to the defence of passing-on in restitution (from a Member State), it soon becomes apparent that if it is accepted that an enrichment of Alpha is at the expense of Beta only to the extent that the corresponding impoverishment has not been passed on, then E=C−P but the +L element has been lost.[24] The A=E solution therefore seems unhelpful as long as the defence of passing-on is not rejected. Of course one might wish to consider A=E+L, but that would not solve the problem of tracing at whose expense Alpha has been enriched. Furthermore it might be more relevant to address the L element through an action for damages instead of restitution.

9.018 Nevertheless, as long as the defence of passing-on is not rejected, it follows that A=C−P+L will apply in restitution as well as in damages. By contrast, if the defence of passing-on is rejected,[25] then it becomes possible in restitution to adopt A=E, or, if restitution and damages are combined, even A=E+L.

E. COORDINATION, DETERRENCE, AND THE PASSING-ON PROBLEM

9.019 In this section focus will be on the pivotal issue of how to coordinate litigation where the passing-on problem arises.[26] The EU law approach summarized above seems to have been designed to satisfy an ideal conception of reparation. As highlighted in Directive 2014/104/EU 'any natural or legal person who has suffered harm ... [should] obtain full compensation',[27] but 'compensation of harm exceeding that caused ... to the claimant' should be avoided[28] as well as both 'multiple liability [and] absence of liability of the infringer'.[29] The Directive seeks to accomplish this ideal by allowing the defence of passing-on and requiring Gamma claimants to have access to claiming damages.[30] It

24 Sometimes, it may occur that E>C if Alpha has enjoyed any fruits, use, or savings from having possession of the enrichment; cf. DCFR (n 9) Art. VII. – 5:104.

25 It has been submitted that the Court of Justice is at liberty to do so in the contexts of restitutionary actions against the EU (see Section 4.D.III) and that the Member States should be given discretion to do so for the purposes of horizontal restitutionary actions (see sub-section 8.C.II.c).

26 On a more general level of coordination in litigation it should be mentioned again that Directive 2014/104/EU (n 4) Arts 9 and 15 include provisions on the legal effect of decisions and judgments concerning an infringement of competition law for national courts seized with litigation related to the same infringement of competition law. These provisions were discussed in paras 7.199–7.204.

27 Directive 2014/104/EU (n 4) Art. 3(1).

28 Ibid., Art. 12(1).

29 Ibid., Art. 15(1).

30 Ibid., Arts 13 and 12(1).

moreover seeks to avoid multiple and possibly contradictory parallel proceedings where harm has been suffered at various levels of the supply chain.[31] A comprehensive analysis of the case law on repayment actions against a Member State, notably *Comateb* and *Danfoss*, reveals a very similar pattern.[32] Case law on the passing-on problem under Article 340(2) TFEU is less detailed but arguably quite similar. The question is, however, to what extent can this approach be reconciled with the interest of coordinating litigation arising from the same infringement of EU law, and to what extent does it satisfy the general interests at stake?

In Section 9.E.I the implications of the findings in previous chapters will be discussed with a view to find a manageable 'optimal reparation' model for the coordination of actions brought by claimants at different levels of the supply chain. In Section 9.E.II the interest of deterrence from breaches of EU law will be added to the discussion. **9.020**

I. Coordinating in the interest of reparation

a. Liability for Alpha

The EU law approach to the passing-on problem seems to have arisen from a concern to avoid overcompensation or overrestitution, i.e., to avoid windfall awards to claimants.[33] It is submitted however that the main conflict in the passing-on problem is between the pursuit of restitution or compensation by claimants from multiple levels of the supply chain, on the one hand, and the avoidance of multiple liability for defendants, on the other hand. Defendants will fear multiple claims for the same overcharge while claimants fear that awards will not sufficiently cover their losses. The possibility of windfall awards is a side-effect in the event of bias – intentional or unintentional – to the protection of the interests of claimants. Similarly the possibility of lingering unlawful gains in the hands of defendants is a side effect in the event of intentional or unintentional bias to the protection of the interests of defendants. These side effects however are arguably risked in any restitution or damages litigation, often by reason of lacking or insufficient evidence. By contrast the multi-level character of the passing-on situation is a specific trait **9.021**

31 Ibid., Art. 15.

32 Cf. joined cases C-192/95 to 218/95 *Société Comateb and others v Directeur Général des Douanes et Droits Indirects* [1997] ECR I-165; *Danfoss* (n 2); and the discussion in sub-section 5.E.II.d.

33 While the reasoning of the Court of Justice in the gritz and quellmehl cases seems to have been based on the concept of mitigation of loss (see *Ireks-Arkady* (n 19) para. 14; *Interquell Stärke-Chemie* (n 19) para. 17; *Dumortier frères* (n 19) para. 15; *DGV* (n 19) para. 15; and the joined Opinion of AG Capotorti para. 11), in the repayment of charges cases it is based on indulgence towards national concepts of unjust enrichment (see e.g. case 68/79 *Hans Just I/S v Danish Ministry for Fiscal Affairs* [1980] ECR 501 para. 26).

of that complex legal problem and the legal analysis of liability for Alpha should therefore focus on this trait.

9.022 The European Court of Justice has not concerned itself with the multi-level character of the passing-on situation as such. Instead it has been content to approach the specific situations brought before it. As a consequence of this casuistry it is difficult to assess whether the rulings of the Court have been designed to fit into any overall view on how to coordinate multiple and parallel claims in the passing-on situation. The general impression of this author is that the case law has developed on an *ad hoc* basis, and that the need to consider the bigger passing-on picture has arisen only recently in repayment cases such as *Reemtsma* and *Danfoss*.[34] Nevertheless it is possible to extract an abstract approach to the coordination of multiple claims, which is furthermore reflected also in Directive 2014/104/EU and compatible with the case law under Article 340(2) TFEU. The structure of the approach in the latter two EU law regimes will be addressed shortly.

9.023 Focusing for now on restitution from Member States, the structure of the approach is as follows:

1. If the defence of passing-on is available under applicable national law, Alpha is allowed to use that defence against all claimants.[35]
2. If Alpha is able to use the defence of passing-on, Alpha must however prove the existence and extent of passing-on.[36]
3. Notwithstanding any passing-on of an economic burden, consequential loss of profit must be compensated by Alpha.[37]
4. Gamma cannot be automatically barred from bringing an action against Alpha, but it is permitted for the national jurisdiction to take measures to prevent multiple proceedings arising from the same infringement of EU law from leading to awards in excess of the disadvantage sustained by claimants.[38]

34 Case C-35/05 *Reemtsma Cigarettenfabriken GmbH v Ministero delle Finanze* [2007] ECR I-2425; and *Danfoss* (n 2).

35 *Just* (n 33) para. 26, and case 61/79 *Amministrazione delle Finanze dello Stato v Denkavit Italiana Srl* [1980] ECR 1205 para. 31.

36 *Comateb* (n 32) paras 26–28.

37 *Comateb* (n 32) para. 32; and case C-147/01 *Weber's Wine World Handels-GmbH and others v Abgabenberufungs-kommission Wien* [2003] ECR I-11365 para. 100.

38 *Danfoss* (n 2) paras 20–28, and Operative part para. 1.

In the context of repayment actions against a Member State the Court of Justice has thus left it to the national jurisdictions to coordinate multiple and parallel litigation arising from a passing-on situation in accordance with applicable national law and procedure, albeit subject to a few EU law requirements. In the case law it seems the Court has envisaged a level-by-level model of coordination as the most expected choice of national jurisdictions. Accordingly, in *Comateb*, the Court held that if Gamma was able to obtain reimbursement from Beta for the portion of an unlawful charge passed on to Gamma by Beta,[39] then Beta must in turn be able to obtain reimbursement (with regard to its repayment to Gamma) from Alpha.[40] Similarly, in *Danfoss*, the Court held that a national legal system which allowed Beta to seek reimbursement from Alpha, and which allowed Gamma to bring a civil law action against Beta for recovery of the sums paid but not due, was compatible with EU law.[41] **9.024**

The Court has also recognized the possibility of direct actions brought by Gamma against Alpha. The Court held in *Comateb* that if Gamma could obtain reimbursement directly from Alpha for the portion of an unlawful charge passed on to Gamma by Beta, then the issue of reimbursing Beta (for that same portion of the unlawful charge) should not arise.[42] Conversely, in *Danfoss*, the Court held that in situations where it was virtually impossible or excessively difficult for Gamma to obtain reimbursement from Beta, Alpha could not oppose claims brought by Gamma directly against Alpha.[43] For the purposes of actions for repayment of charges levied by a Member State in breach of EU law, emphasis in EU case law is thus on providing rules and procedures empowering all to claim reimbursement from Alpha, who may in turn use the defence of passing-on if available under national law. If national courts follow those guidelines it seems the Court of Justice has expected that the interest of reparation will be served. It is nonetheless quite clear that this case law also requires national courts to engage in complex tracing of unlawful charges passed on down the supply chain. **9.025**

In the context of a damages action against the EU under Article 340(2) TFEU the defence of passing-on has been recognized at law, and Alpha must prove the existence and extent of passing-on. It remains to be seen whether consequential losses of profit must be compensated by Alpha in that context[44] **9.026**

---

39 This type of claim will be discussed in sub-section 9.E.I.b.

40 *Comateb* (n 32) para. 24.

41 *Danfoss* (n 2) para. 26.

42 *Comateb* (n 32) para. 24.

43 *Danfoss* (n 2) paras 27–28 and Operative part para. 1.

44 But see *Ireks-Arkady* (n 19) 2166–7.

and whether the Court will be called upon to take a stance with regard to access to court for Gamma claimants.[45] At present, therefore, any predictions on the coordination of multiple and parallel litigation arising from a passing-on situation under Article 340(2) TFEU are speculative. It might be predicted that the third point above would be accepted under Article 340(2) TFEU, as it was argued in paragraphs 3.080–3.082 that damages were available for loss of profit under Article 340(2) TFEU. The case law however suggests that the onus of proving such harm is on the claimant. It was further argued in Section 3.C.II that Gamma claimants should not be automatically barred from bringing proceedings under Article 340(2) TFEU. The EU will of course have an interest in preventing multiple proceedings arising from the same infringement of EU law from leading to awards in excess of the disadvantage sustained by claimants at the various levels of a supply chain, but the Court has not yet been called upon to design more precisely any measures to that end.

9.027 By contrast, in Directive 2014/104/EU on competition law damages, the EU legislature has made an effort in that direction. Although the Directive does not give precise details on the coordination of multiple claims,[46] it does pinpoint the interests to be safeguarded by the national legislators and courts. These are to ensure full compensation to any natural or legal person who has suffered harm caused by an infringement of competition law,[47] irrespective of whether the claimant is a Beta or Gamma claimant.[48] They are further instructed to avoid compensation in excess of harm caused to the individual claimant[49] and to avoid that actions for damages by claimants from different levels in the supply chain lead to multiple liability or to absence of liability of the infringer.[50] Consequently full reparation but nothing in excess of reparation is what is requested. In essence Directive 2014/104/EU is thus telling us that there will be no short cuts: it will be necessary to trace the passing-on of illegal charges down the supply chain.

9.028 The tracing of a charge down the supply chain is a matter of evidence. To that end Directive 2014/104/EU offers a number of rules on the allocation of the burden of proof and on the disclosure of evidence. Litigants have the opportunity (within certain limits) to request the disclosure of evidence held

45 For a discussion of that issue see Section 3.C.II.

46 More detailed albeit non-binding guidance is expected in the forthcoming guidance on passing-on which is presently being drafted by the Commission.

47 Directive 2014/104/EU (n 4) Art. 3(1).

48 Ibid., Art. 12(1).

49 Ibid.

50 Ibid., Art. 15(1).

by their adversaries or by third parties,[51] and evidence held by the Commission or national competition authorities.[52] With regard to evidence held by adversaries or by third parties the most important provision is Article 5(3), which sets certain limits to the disclosure of evidence. It reads:

> Member States shall ensure that national courts limit the disclosure of evidence to that which is proportionate. In determining whether any disclosure requested by a party is proportionate, national courts shall consider the legitimate interests of all parties and third parties concerned. They shall, in particular, consider: **9.029**
>
> (a) the extent to which the claim or defence is supported by available facts and evidence justifying the request to disclose evidence;
> (b) the scope and cost of disclosure, especially for any third parties concerned, including preventing non-specific searches for information which is unlikely to be of relevance for the parties in the procedure;
> (c) whether the evidence the disclosure of which is sought contains confidential information, especially concerning any third parties, and what arrangements are in place for protecting such confidential information.

Litigants trying to produce evidence on the existence and extent of passing-on **9.030** will wish to trace the effect of certain cost increases on selling prices and sold quantities. Relevant documentary evidence to that end would be sheets showing the fluctuation of specific costs, selling prices and sold quantities over time.[53] Such sheets and figures do not tell the whole story, however. Although the fluctuation of specific costs should reliably reflect the increases or decreases of the charges or prices paid, the fluctuation of selling prices may well be due to other factors. As pointed out by Advocate General Capotorti in 1979 (albeit in the context of damages actions under Article 340(2) TFEU), prices cannot generally be set through the passing-on of costs plus a profit margin. Rather, he argued, 'undertakings act according to the logic inspired by the profit motive and on the basis of the market conditions'. Therefore 'where the market does not permit of price increases, they must refrain from making such increases ... when a public financial aid ceases to be paid' as to do otherwise 'might constitute a grave commercial error'. Fluctuations in sold quantities can, moreover, just as well be due to achievements of the management of the undertaking at issue.[54] Also, finally, sheets and figures do not help establish how the claimants would have acted if the unlawful charge or overcharge had

51 Ibid., Art. 5.

52 Ibid., Arts 6–7.

53 Detailed methods on how to use such data are described in Commission, 'Staff Working Document – Practical Guide on quantifying harm in actions for damages based on breaches of Art 101 or 102 of the Treaty on the Functioning of the European Union' SWD(2013) 205.

54 *Ireks-Arkady* (n 19) Opinion of AG Capotorti para. 11.

not been paid; 'perhaps they would have used [the sums retained] to renew their plant ... or to fix their selling prices at more competitive levels'.[55]

9.031 Consequently sheets and figures must be complemented. Unless documentary evidence addressing the problems identified above can be obtained (e.g., in the form of marketing analyses or written pricing policies) it will be necessary to hear financial and/or marketing officers of the adversary or third-party company on their business strategies and in particular on their pricing policies.

9.032 It is on the basis of such evidence that the court must decide to what extent the parties have proven or rebutted the existence and extent of passing-on, at each relevant level of the supply chain. The further away from the original infringement, the more complicated this will generally become. At some point courts will need to draw the line to say that passing-on can no longer be proved. This will inevitably be to the disadvantage of any potential claimants further down the supply chain. The precise point at which this will occur cannot – and should not – be discussed in the abstract but must be assessed in the individual case. Still, as long as the passing-on of a specific charge or cost can be traced as a specific cost item in invoices, as is the case with VAT, or somehow with equivalent certainty, Directive 2014/104/EU seems to require courts to refrain from drawing the line in this way.[56] The possibility in Article 12(5) to 'estimate, in accordance with national procedures, the share of any overcharge that was passed on' is, it is submitted, a last resort.

b. *Liability for Beta*

9.033 It was noted above that, in the context of repayment of charges levied by a Member State in breach of EU law, the Court of Justice seems to have expected for a level-by-level model of coordination to be the first choice of national jurisdictions. In *Comateb* the Court thus held that if Gamma was able to obtain reimbursement from Beta for the portion of an unlawful charge passed on to Gamma by Beta, then Beta must in turn be able to obtain reimbursement (covering its expenses for the repayment to Gamma) from Alpha.[57] Similarly, in *Danfoss*, the Court held that a national legal system which allowed Beta to seek reimbursement from Alpha, and which allowed Gamma to bring a civil law action against Beta for recovery of the sums paid

---

55 Ibid., para. 9.

56 Cf. Directive 2014/104/EU (n 4) Art. 12(1); and *Danfoss* (n 2).

57 *Comateb* (n 32) para. 24.

but not due, was compatible with EU law.[58] Problems of the kind addressed in *Danfoss* will arise where there is no action available to Gamma against Beta.[59]

Directive 2014/104/EU does not account for the possibility of an action brought by Gamma against Beta. Such an action would seem incommensurable with the prerequisite of fault or tort in damages liability, but could function if some form of strict liability was introduced for Beta in this context. This author however fails to imagine any convincing reasons for such strict liability in damages for Beta in the competition law context or any other context.[60] By contrast one might consider restitutionary liability for Beta against Gamma, which could be triggered if it was proven by Gamma that Beta had obtained a windfall award through litigation against Alpha. **9.034**

In sum, the focus on EU law has been on liability for Alpha. Liability for Beta has been discussed as a possibility in national law, but seems to have been discussed only in order to outline possible consequences of different approaches in respect of Alpha's overarching liability towards claimants of all levels of the supply chain. It is submitted that this possibility deserves more attention. **9.035**

c. *Coordination by sequences or collective redress*

A number of mechanisms have been suggested to aid the pursuit of reparation for all in the passing-on context. Rush has suggested for the defence of passing-on to be abandoned in actions for restitution, thus allowing Beta to reclaim the full amount paid but not due to Alpha. It would then be for Gamma to consider whether it had incentive enough to bring an action against Beta for restitution of amounts passed on down the supply chain. A successful Gamma claimant would then in turn be vulnerable to actions brought by Gamma claimants belonging to the next level of the supply chain, and so on.[61] This solution thus coordinates multiple claims by ordering them in sequences. Such a solution could plausibly solve the problem of delimiting restitutionary liability, simply by leaving it to potential claimants at the respective levels of the supply chain to contemplate their prospects of success. Rush has further submitted that his solution would make it unnecessary for Gamma to attempt leapfrogging Beta. The mechanism envisaged by Rush does not however seem able to solve situations where Beta omits to bring the initial action against **9.036**

58 *Danfoss* (n 2) para. 26.

59 Cf. para. 5.180.

60 But cf. – with regard to the position of the Court of Justice – the discussion on this aspect of *Danfoss* (n 2) in para. 6.075.

61 Rush (n 16) 217–18.

Alpha – for instance because Beta has no incentive to do so or because Beta is careful not to disturb business relations with Alpha.[62] Under such circumstances the anticipated chain of actions would never kick off. Therefore leapfrogging would still be necessary whenever any level of potential claimants would omit to bring an action. Unless leapfrogging is allowed under such circumstances the model suggested by Rush would in fact be incompatible with the approach so far chosen for the purposes of EU law.[63]

9.037 A quite similar sequence solution has been adopted by the Berlin Kammergericht for the purposes of competition damages actions. Under the Berlin model Beta and Gamma claimants alike can bring actions for damages in respect of harm incurred by each. Beta is furthermore able to bring an action for competition damages against Alpha for the total amount of the overcharge paid. If such an award is obtained, Beta is subsequently liable to distribute portions of the award to Gamma claimants to the extent that the overcharge was passed on to them.[64] It seems the Berlin solution avoids barring Gamma claimants, making it more easily compatible with EU law than the model suggested by Rush. It must nonetheless be stressed that this model does not in itself account for losses suffered in the form of reduced sales. Actions for the recovery of such losses of profit would accordingly have to be brought against Alpha in parallel to the sequence of actions pertaining to recovery and redistribution of the overcharge as such. Moreover, in light of the rules of Directive 2014/104/EU, this model can no longer be upheld in the context of competition damages. If transplanted into a model for horizontal restitution however (merging this model with the Rush model, if you will), the Berlin model is still compatible with EU law.

9.038 Alternatively one might consider various collective redress solutions.[65] Kloub has suggested a two-step class-action solution for the purposes of competition law damages that was discussed in paragraph 7.239. Under this solution a total amount of damages would first be awarded to the claimants collectively, and in

62 For instance, Beta seems to have had no such incentive in *Danfoss* (n 2).

63 It might however still be adopted for the purposes of restitution from the EU or from an individual, by reason of the lack of case law in those contexts. See further paras 4.030–4.031 and para. 8.051, respectively.

64 Anne Howard and Anneliese Blackwood, 'Litigating Infringements in the National Courts' in Vivien Rose and David Bailey (eds) *Bellamy and Child: European Union Law of Competition* (7th edn, Oxford University Press 2013) 1257. See also Assimakis P Komninos, 'Private Enforcement in the EU with Emphasis on Damages Actions' in Ioannis Lianos and Damien Geradin (eds), *Handbook on European Competition Law: Enforcement and Procedure* (Edward Elgar Publishing 2013) 249.

65 Commission Recommendation 2013/396/EU of 11 June 2013 on common principles for injunctive and compensatory collective redress mechanisms in the Member States concerning violations of rights granted under Union Law [2013] OJ L201/60, discussed briefly in paras 7.205–7.206, is less relevant here as it does not discuss the allocation of awards among those who have joined the collective claimant party.

the next step that sum would be distributed among the claimants.[66] The solution is thus similar to the Berlin model discussed above, with the difference that the Kloub suggestion would integrate the redistribution of overcharges into the collective redress mechanism as a second step within it. This solution has the merit of postponing conflicts of interests within the class of claimants until the second stage of proceedings. It does not, however, take into account the issue of reduced sales at various levels of the supply chain.

It was noted in paragraph 7.198 that reduced sales at any specific level of the supply chain cannot be compensated without it first being established to what extent the original overcharge has been passed on to and/or from that level. It was therefore suggested that the optimal solution for reparation would be a three-stage model under which the total overcharge was quantified first. Thereafter the overcharge would be traced among the claimants in a second stage. Finally harm in the form of reduced sales was quantified at each level. Alpha would consequently be held liable to pay damages to the amount of the total overcharge plus total harm in the form of reduced sales, and interest. If EU law should pursue reparation to its extreme such a solution might be the best option. However, as noticed by the US Supreme Court, this solution comes at a cost: it may transform passing-on litigation into 'massive multiparty litigations involving many levels of distribution and including large classes of consumers remote from [Alpha]' in the effort to recover and redistribute overcharges among the various claimants.[67] **9.039**

It was finally highlighted in paragraph 7.112 that there is also the option, very similar to class actions, to subrogate the mass of claims pertaining to a certain supply chain to a joint claimant body.[68] Such a joint litigant could gather all claims, pertaining to both *damnum emergens* (e.g., an overcharge) and *lucrum cessans* (e.g., reduced sales), and pursue them in one single action against Alpha. The amount of damages that may be obtained from Alpha will then be redistributed among the claimants in accordance with the subrogation contract. Like the Kloub solution this solution too neutralizes conflicts of interests within the class of claimants in respect of their parallel claims against Alpha, **9.040**

---

66 Jindřich Kloub, 'Standing and Pass-on Defense in Antitrust Damage Suits: Guided by Corrective Justice or Efficiency?' in Jürgen Basedow, Jörg Philipp Terhechte and Luboš Tichý (eds), *Private Enforcement of Competition Law* (Nomos Verlagsgesellschaft 2011) 97; cf. Antitrust Modernization Commission, 'Report and Recommendations' (2007) <http://govinfo.library.unt.edu/amc/report_recommendation/toc.htm 277> (last accessed 31 May 2016); and Walter van Gerven, 'Private Enforcement of EC Competition Rules in the ECJ – Courage v. Crehan and the Way Ahead' in Jürgen Basedow (ed.), *Private Enforcement of EC Competition Law*, (Kluwer Law International 2007) 34–5.

67 *Illinois Brick Co et al v Illinois et al* 431 US 720 (1977) 740.

68 This is a growing business idea in the EU. A well-known example is CDC Consulting SCRL, aka Cartel Damages Claims.

but unlike the Kloub model this solution will necessitate an agreement on redistribution between the various claimants in the subrogation contract. The success of this model will therefore be contingent on the willingness of claimants to agree on the principles of redistribution in order to gain the benefits of this model.

9.041 From a legislative perspective the incentive-driven Rush/Berlin model therefore seems the more manageable option in the pursuit of an 'optimal reparation model'. The subrogation of claims to a joint claimant body should nevertheless be encouraged.

II. Safeguarding the interest of deterrence

9.042 From time to time it has been suggested that the EU law focus on reparation should be complemented by mechanisms emphasizing deterrence. Commentators have pointed out that the more an initial unlawful charge is pulverized by being passed on down the supply chain, the less incentive will each potential claimant have to bring an action against Alpha.[69] As recognized by Directive 2014/104/EU this creates a risk for absence of liability for the infringer (Alpha) which is shared in the contexts of actions against the EU and against a Member State.[70] Therefore it is discussed in this section whether EU law should introduce measures safeguarding the interest of deterrence in passing-on situations.

a. Introducing deterrence

9.043 If a counterfactual situation is contemplated in which litigation costs are none, where there can be no recovery for loss in the form of reduced sales, and where there is no public enforcement, it could be beneficial for Alpha to exact money from Beta in breach of EU law as soon as less than 100 per cent of the sum exacted would be claimed back by Beta or Gamma claimants. This counterfactual scenario may seem to illustrate only that concerns for deterrence are exaggerated (as such a situation will never occur). It is submitted however that this counterfactual scenario rather serves to highlight the factors to be accounted for in a comprehensive assessment of how to safeguard deterrence from breaches of EU law. The approach chosen with regard to the passing-on

69 See e.g. *Hanover Shoe Inc v United Shoe Machinery Corp* 392 US 481 (1968) 494; Commission, 'Staff Working Paper Annex to the Green Paper Damages action for breach of the EC antitrust rules' SEC(2005) 1732 paras 179–180; and Commission, 'Staff Working Paper accompanying the White Paper on Damages actions for breach of the EC antitrust rules' SEC(2008) 404 para. 217.

70 Directive 2014/104/EU (n 4) Arts 12(1) and 15(1); cf. Bernard Rudden and William Bishop, 'Gritz and Quellmehl: Pass It On' (1981) 6 *European Law Review* 243, 254–5; and *Comateb* (n 32) Opinion of AG Tesauro para. 21.

problem in private enforcement cannot be seen in isolation. Instead it is necessary to take into account the effectiveness of alternative enforcement (e.g., public enforcement of competition law) and the possibility of recovering loss suffered in the form of reduced sales.[71] The counterfactual scenario above further illustrates that if a system of enforcement aims at the disgorgement of unlawful profits it must take into account the possibility that not all potential claimants will bring a private enforcement action. Indeed it must take into account the possible situation that none of the potential claimants will bring a private enforcement action. In any event, to deter from breaches of EU law, the combined effect of applicable sanctions should at the very least disgorge from infringers all profits earned by virtue of the breach.

Against this background the role of deterrence in the enforcement of EU law is discussed in this section. It will be shown that actions for damages and restitution could be designed to serve the interest of deterrence, but that the need for such added deterrence must be assessed in context. It has indeed been submitted by Wilman that 'private enforcement of EU law cannot be properly understood without having regard to the public law context'.[72] In other words, where alternative mechanisms serve to deter sufficiently from infringements it will not be necessary also to design damages and restitution for that purpose. **9.044**

b. *Deterrence and infringements of EU law by public bodies*

Although deterrence is regarded as one of the basic functions of private law liability in damages,[73] it is not commonly regarded as one of the basic functions of public damages liability.[74] While the institutions and agents of the EU and the Member States certainly do concern themselves with the preservation of public fiscal integrity in the context of actions for damages or restitution brought against them,[75] public liability in damages has been legitimized by the European Court of Justice by reference to the effective judicial protection of rights and interests conferred on individuals by EU law **9.045**

---

71 One might wish to add that the threat of litigation as such can be a deterrent factor. Litigation consumes time and energy, may give rise to bad publicity and loss of goodwill, is costly in itself and the loser may also have to pay the winner's costs. However, it swings both ways: it deters claimants from bringing an action as well as it deters from infringements. Arguably, it dissuades financially weaker parties more than it dissuades financially stronger parties. The deterrent effect of litigation as such will consequently be overlooked here.

72 Folkert Wilman, *Private Enforcement of EU Law before National Courts: The EU Legislative Framework* (Elgar European Law and Practice, Edward Elgar Publishing 2015) 44.

73 Walter van Gerven, Jeremy Lever and Pierre Larouche (eds), *The Common Law of Europe Casebooks: Tort Law* (Hart Publishing 2000) 18.

74 Pekka Aalto, *Public Liability in EU Law:* Brasserie, Bergaderm *and Beyond* (Hart Publishing 2011) 61–2.

75 See e.g. joined cases C-46/93 and C-48/93 *Brasserie du Pêcheur SA v Bundesrepublik Deutschland* and *The Queen v Secretary of State for Transport, ex parte: Factortame Ltd and others* [1996] ECR I-1029 para. 97.

rather than by reference to deterrence from unlawful behaviour.[76] As pointed out by van Dam, public bodies 'work (or are supposed to work) for the benefit of everyone'.[77] Nevertheless the interest of deterring Member States from a breach of EU law has remained a concern in legal debate. Advocates General Mancini and Tesauro have both expressed fear that the acceptance of a defence of passing-on in actions for repayment of charges levied by Member States in breach of EU law would lead to non-compliance with EU law among the Member States.[78] Indeed, as shown by the notorious French and Italian rules on passing-on of charges levied by national authorities introduced after *Just*,[79] Member States will sometimes give priority to the interests of their own public finances over the effective reparation of a breach of EU law by their institutions and agents. It follows that the interest of deterrence from a breach of EU law is not irrelevant in the context of public liability in EU law – at least not in the context of Member State liability in damages and/or restitution.

9.046 It was submitted in paragraph 5.149 that the interest of deterrence was served also by infringement actions against Member States pursuant to Articles 258 and 259 TFEU.[80] The existence and effectiveness of those infringement actions should therefore be taken into account. It is particularly significant that, since the Treaty of Maastricht, there has been a possibility for the Court of Justice, upon an initiative by the Commission, to penalize Member States in accordance with Article 260(2) TFEU. Penalty payments ordered can be quite severe.[81] By contrast no similar sanctions are available against the institutions

---

76 Cf. e.g. joined cases C-6/90 and 9/90 *Andrea Francovich and Daniela Bonifaci and others v Italian Republic* [1991] ECR I-5357 para. 33; and case C-47/07 P *Masdar (UK) Ltd v Commission of the European Communities* [2008] ECR I-9761 para. 50.

77 Cees van Dam, *European Tort Law* (2nd edn, Oxford University Press 2013) 530. By contrast, private undertakings are expected to work for their own profit. In this respect, Håkan Andersson, *Ansvarsproblem i skadeståndsrätten: Skadeståndsrättsliga utvecklingslinjer bok I* (Iustus 2013) 345–6 has observed that the prospect of profit is capable of legitimizing liability to compensate harm caused by commercial risk-taking.

78 *San Giorgio* (n 79) Opinion of AG Mancini para. 10; *Comateb* (n 32) Opinion of AG Tesauro para. 21. See also Gerhard Bebr, 'Joined Cases C-6/90 and 9/90, Francovich v. Italy, Bonifaci v. Italy Judgment of the Court of Justice of 19 November 1991, not yet reported' (1992) 29 *Common Market Law Review* 557, 558–9, and 582–4 on *Francovich* (n 76) as a means 'for enforcing the respect and execution of Community obligations' (582) of Member States.

79 See case 199/82 *Amministrazione delle Finanze dello Stato v SpA San Giorgio* [1983] ECR 3595 Opinion of AG Mancini para. 3; and joined cases 331/85, 376/85 and 378/85 *SA Les Fils de Jules Bianco and J Girard Fils SA v Directeur Général des Douanes et Droits Indirects* [1988] ECR 1099 Opinion of AG Sir Gordon Slynn 1108.

80 Due to the special task of the Commission to be the 'guardian of the Treaties', Art. 258 TFEU is usually in focus in discussions on infringement actions. However, other Member States may equally have an interest in bringing an action under Art. 259 TFEU, e.g., by reason of the levying of charges in breach of EU law where such charges have significant adverse effects on their exports.

81 The details of calculation can be found in Commission, 'Communication from the Commission – Application of Article 228 of the EC Treaty' SEC(2005) 1658. See Alan Dashwood et al, *Wyatt and Dashwood's European Union Law* (6th edn, Hart Publishing 2011) 149–52 for a more accessible overview of Commission practices and EU case law.

and agents of the EU for a breach of EU law. Public enforcement against the institutions and agents of the EU is thus limited to political review and the watching eye of the European Ombudsman.

Infringement actions against Member States pursuant to Articles 258 and 259 TFEU, as well as the more particular public enforcement actions against the institutions and agents of the EU in Articles 263 and 265 TFEU, naturally differ from private enforcement actions for damages and restitution in many ways. For example, the Article 260(2) TFEU sanction is intended to compel Member States to comply with their duties under EU law, while liability to pay damages or restitution is intended to repair an injustice caused to the individual because of the non-compliance of the Member State. It is nevertheless submitted that insofar as effective infringement actions will serve to deter from a breach of EU law it will be less important to pursue the interest of deterrence in the context of EU law requirements on national rules and conditions governing the repayment of charges levied in breach of EU law, e.g., national rules that limit awards to the extent that such charges have been passed on. The concerns of Advocates General Mancini and Tesauro will, under such circumstances, be attended to by the Commission (and on occasion by other Member States). Needless to say, perhaps, this is without prejudice to the reparatory functions of damages and restitution. **9.047**

For these reasons the existence of a public enforcement mechanism deterring Member States from infringements of EU law makes it less important in that context to use actions for damages or restitution against Member States in the interest of deterrence. The case law of the European Court of Justice on passing-on in the context of repayment of charges levied in breach of EU law is therefore not particularly vulnerable to the argument that the defence of passing-on should be rejected in the interest of deterrence. To repeat, this is without prejudice to other arguments, e.g., arguments related to the reparatory functions of damages and restitution. **9.048**

By contrast it has been noticed that there is no effective public enforcement mechanism deterring the institutions and agents of the EU from infringements of EU law. As long as it holds water to presume that these institutions and agents work for the common good and do their best to comply with EU law and avoid harming individual rights and interests, all will be well. But should the circumstances of an individual case reveal that deterrence is of the essence it could be relevant to adjust the case law of the Court of Justice under Article 340(2) TFEU in order to safeguard the interest of deterrence. For example, deterrence could be served by rejecting the defence of passing-on in actions for damages brought against the EU pursuant to Article 340(2) TFEU. **9.049**

If Gamma claimants would simultaneously be granted access to court to bring an action in respect of harm passed on to them and for harm in the form of reduced sales, plus interest, the deterring capacity of private enforcement actions brought against the EU could be increased. This would of course require the reversal of previous case law on the defence of passing-on in damages actions under Article 340(2) TFEU. This might be possible if the facts in the new case were indeed such as to require its distinguishing against previous case law.

c. *Deterrence in competition law and other horizontal actions*

9.050 In EU competition law deterrence is traditionally entrusted to public enforcement by the Commission and the national competition authorities. Much has been said on the interrelationship between public and private enforcement of EU competition law and it is not intended here to give any comprehensive overview of this debate.[82] In a comment to the 2008 White Paper on antitrust damages actions[83] the Max Planck Institute for Intellectual Property, Competition and Tax Law distinguished two options on how the two should be interrelated:

9.051

> If private enforcement is primarily seen as an annex or a supplement to public enforcement, the thrust will be to facilitate follow-on actions and to limit claims to strict compensation. If, however, private enforcement was to be seen as a tool to contribute to the enforcement of competition law in the public interest, one would have to promote the deterrent effect of private enforcement even beyond mere compensation.[84]

---

82 Suffice it therefore to give some suggestions for further reading: Thomas Eilmansberger, 'The Green paper on Damages Actions for Breach of the EC Antitrust Rules and Beyond: Reflections on the Utility and Feasibility of Stimulating Private Enforcement Through Legislative Action' (2007) 44 *Common Market Law Review* 431; Veljko Milutinovic, *The 'Right to Damages' under EU Competition Law: From* Courage v. Crehan *to the White Paper and Beyond* (Wolters Kluwer 2010) section 1.2; Luís Silva Morais, 'Integrating Public and Private Enforcement of Competition Law in Europe – Legal Issues' in Philip Lowe and Mel Marquis (eds), *European Competition Law Annual 2011: Integrating Public and Private Enforcement of Competition Law – Implications for Courts and Agencies* (Hart Publishing 2014); Assimakis P Komninos, 'The Relationship between Public and Private Enforcement: *quod Dei Deo, quod Caesaris Caesari*' in Lowe and Marquis, ibid.; Ioannis Lianos, Peter Davis and Paolisa Nebbia, *Damages Claims for the Infringement of EU Competition Law* (Oxford University Press 2015) Ch. 7; and Vladimir Bastidas Venegas, 'The Damages Directive and Other Enforcement Measures in EU Competition Law' in Maria Bergström, Marios C Iacovides and Magnus Strand (eds), *Harmonising EU Competition Litigation: The New Directive and Beyond* (Swedish Studies in European Law vol. 8, Hart Publishing 2016).

83 Commission, 'White Paper on Damages actions for breach of the EC antitrust rules' COM(2008) 165 final.

84 Max Planck Institute, 'Comments of the Max Planck Institute for Intellectual Property, Competition and Tax Law on the White Paper by the Directorate-General for Competition of April 2008 on Damages for Breach of the EC Antitrust Rules' 15 July 2008, <http://ec.europa.eu/competition/antitrust/actionsdamages/white_paper_comments.html> (last accessed 31 May 2016) 3.

In Directive 2014/104/EU focus is on reparation. Deterrent damages awards (e.g., multiple or punitive damages) are banned.[85] It would therefore seem that the EU legislature has opted for the first of the two options identified by the Max Planck Institute, confining competition law damages to providing redress to harmed individuals as a supplement to public enforcement by the Commission and national competition authorities. This suggests heavy reliance on the capacity of public enforcement to pursue the public interest of deterrence. **9.052**

Although public enforcement of EU competition law has been called aggressive,[86] it is evident that competition law infringements persist. A 2007 Impact Study drafted for the European Commission estimated the detection rate for cartels to be in the range of 10–30 per cent.[87] The Impact Study further anticipated that private enforcement could make a significant contribution to the deterrent effect of EU competition law, for example by increasing the detection rate.[88] An increase in the detection rate might hopefully be accomplished through the harmonized reparatory damages regime of Directive 2014/104/EU, as it will bring new legal certainty on crucial aspects of competition law damages actions. Still, in an analysis by Simonsson with regard to actions for competition law damages before Swedish courts, the rules of the Directive were not expected significantly to increase the incentives for claimants to bring an action.[89] Therefore it is respectfully submitted that neither the existence of aggressive public enforcement of competition law nor the new private enforcement regime in the EU exhaust the need for consideration of the interest of deterrence from anti-competitive behaviour. Private enforcement can accordingly still contribute further to deterrence if allowed to do so. **9.053**

One might therefore regret the approach chosen in Directive 2014/104/EU with regard to the defence of passing-on. As argued in sub-section 7.E.II.c this choice of approach is a missed opportunity to enhance the deterrent effect **9.054**

85 Directive 2014/104/EU (n 4) Art. 3(3).

86 Alison Jones and Brenda Sufrin, *EU Competition Law: Text, Cases and Materials* (5th edn, Oxford University Press 2014) 1078.

87 Centre for European Policy Studies, Erasmus University Rotterdam and Luiss Guido Carli, 'Making antitrust damages actions more effective in the EU: welfare impact and potential scenarios' Final Report 21 December 2007 <http://ec.europa.eu/competition/antitrust/actionsdamages/files_white_paper/impact_study.pdf> (last accessed 31 May 2016) 95.

88 Impact Study (n 87) 103, but notice also the refinements in the following sections of the Impact Study.

89 This analysis of whether the rules of the Directive will increase incentives claimants to bring an action for competition law damages before Swedish courts is available in Ingeborg Simonsson, 'Challenges for Swedish Courts: Will the New Directive on Antitrust Damages Actions Help?' in Maria Bergström, Marios C Iacovides and Magnus Strand (eds), *Harmonising EU Competition Litigation: The New Directive and Beyond* (Swedish Studies in European Law vol. 8, Hart Publishing 2016).

of private enforcement of EU competition law, as the pulverization of harm makes it less likely that all potential claimants will bring an action and as Gamma claimants may face difficulties with regard to proving a causal link between the infringement and the harm incurred by them. If, therefore, fewer than all claimants bring a successful action, Alpha will retain some of the fruits of its infringement unless successfully disgorged through public enforcement proceedings. It was further submitted in paragraph 7.254 that if the deterrent effect of the combined public and private enforcement systems should prove insufficient, the risk of multiple liability for Alpha and the risk of damages awards in excess of harm absorbed should not discourage the EU legislature from discarding the defence of passing-on for the purposes of EU competition law damages in future reconsiderations of the Directive.

9.055 It may however be unrealistic to hope for a recast of the rules of Directive 2014/104/EU. An alternative way of enhancing the deterrent effect of private enforcement of competition law is to encourage restitutionary actions brought by Beta in situations where such an action is a viable option to damages. In light of the European private law materials reviewed in sub-section 8.C.II.c it seems most Member States would reject the defence of passing-on in the context of horizontal restitution. Under such circumstances the combined force of Beta claims for restitution paired with multi-level claims for damages in respect of reduced sales might add to the deterrent effect of private enforcement. Restitutionary actions brought by Beta would also be compatible with the Rush/Berlin model for subsequent redistribution of the award, as described in sub-section 9.E.I.b. In that way, the interests of both deterrence and reparation could both be served. The elements of this suggestion will be outlined further in the next section. Another way of boosting deterrence, which is not related to the passing-on problem, would be to ensure that liability in damages arises automatically in the event of a breach of competition law, without being subject to any additional requirement of fault.[90]

9.056 In horizontal actions related to infringements of other provisions of EU law there is no mechanism of public enforcement. The arguments submitted in favour of finding ways to increase the deterrent effect of damages and/or restitution would therefore seem to apply *a fortiori* in respect to such actions. It may be counterargued, however, that the greater losses suffered by the citizens and institutions of the EU and its Member States by reason of infringements of competition law give rise to a special interest of ensuring deterrence from such infringements which is not present in respect of other infringements of EU law by private individuals. On balance this author is inclined to agree with

90 See the discussion in paras 7.045–7.048.

the latter argument, but would first and foremost wish for the solutions chosen to be as congruent as possible.

F. CONCLUSIONS AND SUGGESTIONS

In this inquiry it has been endeavoured to find solutions that serve consistency in EU law, but it is apparent that the conclusions drawn in Section 9.E rather suggest differentiation based on the character of defendants, the private law distinction between restitution and damages, and the strength of public enforcement of EU law. It has moreover been noted that factual circumstances such as the possibility of tracing a certain charge along the supply chain should be crucial to the choice of approach in the individual case. In order to reconcile these seemingly contradictory tendencies in the text, consistency must be distinguished from uniformity. Striving for consistency in law is good for foreseeability and therefore for legal management, but we must not lose the relevant distinctions established in law that help us to treat like cases alike and different cases differently.[91] Consistency must accordingly be specific to the relevant context as defined in law: i.e., the relevant legal context as defined by the relevant legal materials. A strive for consistency must likewise be open to the ever-shifting facts particular to the case at hand.[92] It is therefore hoped that this inquiry has sufficiently highlighted the differences between the legal contexts examined in Chapters 3–8 for the reader to be willing to accept that consistency must be pursued within the boundaries of each context[93] and with close attention to particular circumstances. As a consequence the general approach of EU law to the passing-on problem should not be rigid. In finding the proper approach the court seized with a dispute in which the passing-problem arises will need to take into account a number of factors. The most important ones identified in this inquiry are probably the following. **9.057**

First, there is the issue of jurisdiction. One must take into account whether the choice of approach falls within the exclusive jurisdiction of the EU, or whether it falls within the procedural autonomy of the Member States – circumscribed as it is by the various requirements of EU law designed to safeguard effective **9.058**

91 On this principle of formal justice see e.g., Herbert L A Hart, *The Concept of Law* (2nd edn, Clarendon Law Series, Oxford University Press 1994) 159–67.

92 Cf. the so-called cost-plus exception to the Gamma bar in US federal antitrust law; Herbert Hovenkamp, *Federal Antitrust Policy: The Law of Competition and Its Practice* (4th edn, West Publishing Co 2011) 677.

93 Although cross-references occur they will not necessarily be intended as a transplantation of case law from one context to the next. And where an element of law is transplanted between contexts, it must always be actively integrated into the context to which it is transplanted. Cf. sub-section 7.E.II.a on cross-references in *Courage* (n 20) and *Manfredi* (n 20).

judicial protection of EU law rights described in Chapter 2. Actions for damages and restitutionary actions brought against the EU itself will thus fall within the exclusive jurisdiction of EU law, and the EU therefore has full jurisdiction (and responsibility) for the development of an approach to the passing-on problem. In the absence of EU law harmonization the other actions, i.e., those against Member States and against private individuals, fall within the circumscribed procedural autonomy of the Member States. Such harmonization is now in place, however, in respect of competition law damages. For the purposes of that action the approach to the passing-on problem has accordingly been defined in Directive 2014/104/EU. Outside that action Member States are still free to choose their own approach, subject to the requirements of EU law and the interpretations of those requirements that the European Court of Justice delivers from time to time.

9.059 Second, there is the issue of the legal character of the action. It has been submitted that it is of essence whether the action brought is a damages action or a restitutionary action. The passing-on problem will prompt parties to adopt different legal strategies. Beta claimants might prefer to bring an action for restitution, if possible, as Beta will not need to prove causation but only the existence of an unlawful transaction and its amount. Furthermore, as indicated by the European Court of Justice itself, the defence of passing-on seems to be derived from a damages approach rather than a restitution approach.[94] Work on this inquiry has indeed led this author to take the view that much of the confusion vexing the passing-on problem is attributable to difficulties in upholding the distinction between damages and other actions, in particular restitution. As seen in sub-section 8.C.II.c especially, it follows from European private law materials that the defence of passing-on is less commonly accepted in restitution law. Indeed the only instance in which a defence of passing-on has been accepted – or perhaps it is better to say, tolerated – by the Court of Justice for the purposes of restitution is where it is available under national law concerning the repayment of charges levied in breach of law.[95] It must be remembered that the reason behind this view is not essentially an endorsement of the defence in restitution law, but deference to the division of powers between the Member States and the EU. The real power to decide on the defence in this context therefore rests with the Member States. In restitution

94 *Ireks-Arkady* (n 19) para. 14; *Interquell Stärke-Chemie* (n 19) para. 17; and *Dumortier frères* (n 19) para. 15.

95 But see Karen Dykjær-Hansen, 'Restitution af beløb opkrævet med urette' (1994) *Ugeskrift for Retsvæsen* B 407, 408, who observed that the notorious U.1952.974:H was the only Danish Supreme Court judgment in the twentieth century in which the defence of passing-on had been explicitly embraced in order to rule out liability to repay an amount levied in breach of law, and that the legal reasoning of the Supreme Court in that judgment was not easily compatible with traditional views on such repayment in Danish law. Such were the circumstances when Pandora's box was opened in *Just* (n 33)!

from the EU there is no case law on the defence and, as noticed in Section 4.D.III, the Court would arguably be wise to reject the defence of passing-on in that context. All in all a restitutionary action is usually the better option for Beta, if the circumstances are such that restitution is a viable option. By contrast, if Gamma claimants wish to bring an action against Alpha, they will most likely prefer to bring an action for damages. Circumstances would need to be quite particular for an action for restitution brought by Gamma against Alpha, leapfrogging Beta, to be successful.

Third, there is the issue of legal purpose. The question is, in other words, if there are other interests to take into account, such as the interest of deterrence from a breach of the relevant EU law provisions? It was demonstrated in Section 9.E.II that the need to take such considerations will vary between contexts, as the availability and capacity of public enforcement to satisfy those other interests varies. **9.060**

Finally, the factual circumstances are of the essence. Is the relevant market, and circumstances at large, such that it would be very easy to trace a charge down the supply chain? Or is it difficult even to detect causation between the original unlawful transaction and the prices set by Beta? **9.061**

The plea for consistency is consequently also a plea for making relevant distinctions and paying attention to different circumstances. The passing-on problem is by no means a single and coherent legal problem which it is possible to discuss or to 'solve' in an either-or fashion. Rather, as demonstrated in Section 1.A, passing-on is a specific set of factual circumstances that triggers a number of distinct legal problems. This inquiry has shown that those legal problems take different shapes depending on factors such as those just outlined. Accordingly a balanced legal response to the passing-on problem must be specific to the legal and factual context at hand. **9.062**

The many different solutions and suggestions discussed have nevertheless made it possible to submit a modest proposal. The competent courts and legislatures might thus consider the following mixed approach to the passing-on problem: **9.063**

1. Where possible, permit Beta to claim restitution of the entire amount of the original unlawful charge or overcharge paid to Alpha (or, in circumstances such as those in the gritz and quellmehl cases, to claim retroactive payment of the entire amount due but not paid).
2. If the claim is successful, make Beta subsequently liable to distribute portions of the award to Gamma claimants at the next level of the supply

chain to the extent that the original unlawful charge or overcharge has been passed on to them. Successful Gamma claimants should then in turn be liable to distribute to the next level of Gamma claimants, and so on.

3. Where an action for restitution is not a viable option for Beta, permit Beta and Gamma claimants alike to bring damages actions in respect of the amount of the original unlawful charge, overcharge, or amount due but not paid that has been borne by them respectively but encourage Beta and Gamma claimants downstream from the Beta claimant at issue to bring their actions jointly.
4. Irrespective of whether Beta brings an action for restitution under (1) or for damages under (3), permit Beta and Gamma claimants alike to claim damages from Alpha in respect of harm incurred in the form of reduced sales caused by the original unlawful charge, overcharge, or non-payment.
5. Place the onus of proving the relevant facts, e.g., the existence and extent of passing-on, on the party relying on those facts.

9.064 This suggestion is incentive-driven. Only claimants who have sound prospects of successfully recovering a substantial amount would be likely to enter into litigation. Nonetheless, in restitution, the comparative ease for Beta claimants to prove the amount of the overcharge should suffice to achieve the 'watchdog' effect advocated by Rudden and Bishop.[96] Therefore this suggestion should serve to boost the deterrent effect of private enforcement where restitution is a viable option for Beta.

9.065 This suggestion avoids multiple liability for Alpha with regard to the initial overcharge, at least if Beta and Gamma bring an action for damages jointly, but does not avoid liability for harm caused by reduced sales even though the combined burden of restitutionary and damages liability may exceed the amount of the overcharge. It is submitted that liability for both the amount of the overcharge (*damnum emergens*) and for reduced sales (*lucrum cessans*) fits the general approach of EU law well. The effect of distinguishing restitution and damages but combining them where possible may thus increase the deterrent effect of private enforcement without giving rise to excessive liability for Alpha.

9.066 This suggestion would respect the traditional differences between restitutionary awards and damages awards. The concept of restitution would not need to be strained by Gamma actions brought against Alpha directly, leapfrogging

96 Rudden and Bishop (n 70) 256.

Beta. The concept of damages would not be artificially extended to encompass the recovery of sums exacted unlawfully, but Beta could focus on the reversal of the transaction (or, where applicable, retroactive payment of sums due but not paid). The estimation of restitutionary awards would not need to encompass losses better covered by damages for *lucrum cessans*. In sum this suggestion fits the traditional distinctions of private law well.

This suggestion is without prejudice to the availability of complementary actions that can co-exist with it. For instance it does not follow from this approach that Gamma claimants must be barred from bringing an action of restitution against Alpha. In specific circumstances, such as those in *Danfoss*,[97] Article 47 of the EU Charter and/or the EU law principle of effectiveness might even require for Gamma claimants to have access to such an action. Therefore, where circumstances are such that a damages or restitutionary action brought by Gamma against Alpha is a sound option in the view of the Gamma claimant (e.g., where Beta has omitted to bring an action against Alpha), the competent court should usually allow such an action and consider it on its merits. **9.067**

Importantly, if the suggested distinction between restitution from a Member State and horizontal restitution from private individuals is upheld, this suggestion would be perfectly available to EU law. In restitutionary actions brought against the EU pursuant to Article 340(2) TFEU the lack of case law leaves it open to the Court of Justice to adopt the restitution elements in the approach above. The damages elements are fully compatible with case law on Article 340(2) TFEU. With regard to actions brought against a Member State it is still the Member States that have jurisdiction to adopt or to reject the defence of passing-on for the purposes of actions for repayment of charges levied in breach of EU law. It would not in any way be contrary to EU case law for a Member State to adopt the restitution elements of the suggested approach. The damages elements are also fully compatible with EU law. Finally the Member States still have jurisdiction to adopt or to reject the defence of passing-on for the purposes of actions for horizontal restitution without prejudice to Directive 2014/104/EU. **9.068**

The author will thereby conclude this inquiry, in the hope of having contributed to continuing discussions on the passing-on problem in private enforcement of EU law. **9.069**

97 *Danfoss* (n 2).

INDEX